Sociolinguistics and Language Education

NEW PERSPECTIVES ON LANGUAGE AND EDUCATION
Series Editor: Professor Viv Edwards, *University of Reading, Reading, Great Britain*
Series Advisor: Professor Allan Luke, *Queensland University of Technology, Brisbane, Australia*

Two decades of research and development in language and literacy education have yielded a broad, multidisciplinary focus. Yet education systems face constant economic and technological change, with attendant issues of identity and power, community and culture. This series will feature critical and interpretive, disciplinary and multidisciplinary perspectives on teaching and learning, language and literacy in new times.

Full details of all the books in this series and of all our other publications can be found on http://www.multilingual-matters.com, or by writing to Multilingual Matters, St Nicholas House, 31–34 High Street, Bristol BS1 2AW, UK.

NEW PERSPECTIVES ON LANGUAGE AND EDUCATION
Series Editor: Professor Viv Edwards

Sociolinguistics and Language Education

Edited by
Nancy H. Hornberger and
Sandra Lee McKay

MULTILINGUAL MATTERS
Bristol • Buffalo • Toronto

Library of Congress Cataloging in Publication Data
A catalog record for this book is available from the Library of Congress.
Sociolinguistics and Language Education/Edited by Nancy H. Hornberger and Sandra Lee McKay.
New Perspectives on Language and Education: 18
Includes bibliographical references and index.
1. Sociolinguistics. 2. Language and education. 3. Language and culture.
I. Hornberger, Nancy H. II. McKay, Sandra.
P40.S784 2010
306.44–dc22 2010018315

British Library Cataloguing in Publication Data
A catalogue entry for this book is available from the British Library.

ISBN-13: 978-1-84769-283-2 (hbk)
ISBN-13: 978-1-84769-282-5 (pbk)

Multilingual Matters
UK: St Nicholas House, 31–34 High Street, Bristol BS1 2AW, UK.
USA: UTP, 2250 Military Road, Tonawanda, NY 14150, USA.
Canada: UTP, 5201 Dufferin Street, North York, Ontario M3H 5T8, Canada.

The policy of Multilingual Matters/Channel View Publications is to use papers that are natural, renewable and recyclable products, made from wood grown in sustainable forests. In the manufacturing process of our books, and to further support our policy, preference is given to printers that have FSC and PEFC Chain of Custody certification. The FSC and/or PEFC logos will appear on those books where full certification has been granted to the printer concerned.

Typeset by Techset Composition Ltd., Salisbury, UK.
Printed and bound in Great Britain by Short Run Press Ltd.

Contents

Part 4: Language and Literacy

Part 5: Language and Identity

Part 6: Language and Interaction

Part 7: Language and Education

Contributors

H. Samy Alim is Assistant Professor of Anthropology at the University of California, Los Angeles. Author of *Roc the Mic Right: The Language of Hip Hop Culture* (Routledge, 2006) and *You Know My Steez* (Duke, 2004), he also has recent coedited volumes on *Global Linguistic Flows: Hip Hop Cultures, Youth Identities, and the Politics of Language*, with A. Ibrahim and A. Pennycook (Routledge, 2008); and *Talkin Black Talk: Language, Education, and Social Change*, with J. Baugh (Teachers College Press, 2007). His research interests include style theory and methodology, Global Hip Hop Culture(s), language and race(ism), and the language and literacy development of linguistically profiled and marginalized populations.

Patricia Duff is Professor of Language and Literacy Education and Director of the Centre for Research in Chinese Language and Literacy Education at the University of British Columbia. Her research, teaching, and publications, including three books and many book chapters and articles, deal primarily with language socialization across bilingual and multilingual settings; qualitative research methods (especially case study and ethnography) and generalizability in applied linguistics; issues in the teaching and learning of English, Mandarin, and other international languages; the integration of second-language learners in high schools, universities, and society; multilingualism and work; and sociocultural, sociolinguistic, and sociopolitical aspects of language(s) in education.

Christina Higgins is an assistant professor in the Department of Second Language Studies at the University of Hawai'i at Mānoa, where she specializes in sociolinguistics, discourse analysis, and intercultural communication. Her research focuses on East Africa, where she has analyzed linguistic and cultural hybridity in a range of contexts. She has investigated the discursive construction of gendered responsibility in NGO-sponsored HIV/AIDS prevention and the role of language in the realm of beauty pageants in Tanzania. She is the author of *English as a local language: Post-colonial identities and multilingual practices* (Multilingual Matters) and the co-editor of *Language and HIV/AIDS* (with Bonny Norton).

Nancy H. Hornberger is Professor of Education and Director of Educational Linguistics at the University of Pennsylvania, USA. Her research interests include sociolinguistics in education, ethnography in education, language policy, bilingualism and biliteracy, Indigenous language revitalization and heritage language education. Recent three-time Fulbright Senior Specialist, to Paraguay, New Zealand, and South Africa respectively, Hornberger teaches, lectures, and advises on multilingualism and education throughout the world and has authored or edited over two dozen books and more than 100 articles and chapters, including most recently *Can Schools Save Indigenous Languages? Policy and Practice on Four Continents* (Palgrave Macmillan 2008), and the ten-volume *Encyclopedia of Language and Education* (Springer 2008).

Hilary Janks is a Professor in the School of Education at the University of the Witwatersrand, Johannesburg, South Africa. She is the editor and an author of the *Critical Language Awareness Series* of workbooks and the author of *Literacy and Power* (2009). Her teaching and research are in the areas of language and education in multilingual classrooms, language policy and critical literacy. Her work is committed to a search for equity and social justice in contexts of poverty.

Jürgen Jaspers holds a Postdoctoral Fellowship from the Flemish Research Foundation and lectures at the University of Antwerp, Belgium. His research involves ethnographic and interactional discourse analysis and his main research interests cover the areas of sociolinguistics, education, urban multilingualism and language policy. He is co-editor of *Society and language use* (2010), and co-editor of a special issue on *Journal of Pragmatics* (forthcoming). His current research investigates how substandard language forms in the classroom interact or compete with pedagogical goals and the teacher's voice. Recent publications include articles in *Language and Communication*, *Linguistics and Education* and *International Journal of Bilingualism*.

Nkonko M Kamwangamalu is professor of linguistics at Howard University, Washington, DC. He has also taught linguistics at the National University of Singapore, University of Swaziland, and the University of Natal in Durban, South Africa. His research interests include language policy and planning, codeswitching, World Englishes, language and identity, and African linguistics. He is the author of the monograph *The Language planning situation in South Africa* (Multilingual Matters, 2001), and editor of special issues for the following journals all on language in South Africa: *Multilingua* 17 (1998), *International Journal of the Sociology of*

Language 144 (2000), *World Englishes* 21 (2002), and *Language Problems and Language Planning* 28 (2004).

Gabriele Kasper is Professor at the University of Hawai'i at Manoa, where she teaches in the graduate programs in Second Language Studies. Her teaching and research focus on language and social interaction, in particular on applying conversation analysis to second language interaction and learning and on qualitative research methodology.

Ryuko Kubota is a professor in the Department of Language and Literacy Education in the Faculty of Education at the University of British Columbia, Canada. She has worked as a second/foreign language teacher and teacher educator in Japan, U.S.A., and Canada. Her research intersects culture, politics, second language writing, and critical pedagogies. Her articles appeared in such journals as *Canadian Modern Language Review, Critical Inquiry in Language Studies, English Journal, Journal of Second Language Writing, TESOL Quarterly, Written Communication*, and *World Englishes*. She is a co-editor of *Race, culture, and identities in second language: Exploring critically engaged practice* (2009, Routledge).

Joseph Lo Bianco is professor of language and literacy education at the University of Melbourne. He was author of Australia's first language policy, the National Policy on Languages (1987), and director between 1989 and 2002 of the National Languages and Literacy Institute of Australia. His recent books include *China and English: Globalisation and Dilemmas of Identity* (2009) and *Second Languages and Australian Schooling* (2009). At present he has under preparation a volume on learner subjectivity in second languages and an international research project on intercultural approaches to teaching Chinese. His areas of interest include language planning, language rights, English in Asia, Sri Lankan education, Italian studies and bilingual education.

Constant Leung is Professor of Educational Linguistics at King's College London. He is currently serving as Deputy Head of the Department of Education and Professional Studies. He is Chair of the MA English Language Teaching and Applied Linguistics programme, and Director of MA Assessment in Education programme. His research interests include education in ethnically and linguistically diverse societies, second/additional language curriculum development, language assessment, language policy and teacher professional development. He has written and published widely on issues related to ethnic minority education, additional/second language curriculum, and language assessment nationally and internationally.

Mary McGroarty is professor in the applied linguistics program of the English Department at Northern Arizona University, Flagstaff, Arizona. She has served on editorial boards for professional journals in the United States, United Kingdom, and Canada and is a former president of the American Association for Applied Linguistics and editor of the *Annual Review of Applied Linguistics*. Research and teaching interests include second language pedagogy, language policies; bilingualism; and assessment. Related articles have appeared in *Annals of the American Academy of Political and Social Science, Applied Linguistics, Canadian Modern Language Review, Language Learning, Language Policy, Language Testing, TESOL Quarterly*, and in other handbooks and edited collections.

Sandra McKay is Professor Emeritus of English at San Francisco State University. Her books include *Teaching English as an International Language: Rethinking Goals and Approaches* (2002, Oxford University Press) and *Sociolinguistics and Language Teaching* (edited with Nancy Hornberger, 1996, Cambridge University Press). Her newest book is *International English in its Sociolinguistic Contexts: Towards a Socially Sensitive Pedagogy* (with Wendy Bokhorst-Heng, 2008, Frances Taylor). She has also published widely in international journals. Her research interest in language and society and English as an international language developed from her Fulbright Grants, academic specialists awards and her extensive work in international teacher education in countries such as Chile, Hong Kong, Hungary, Latvia, Morocco, Japan, Singapore, South Africa, South Korea and Thailand.

Bonny Norton is Professor and Distinguished University Scholar in the Department of Language and Literacy Education, University of British Columbia, Canada. Her award-winning research addresses identity and language learning, education and international development, and critical literacy. Recent publications include *Identity and Language Learning* (Longman/Pearson, 2000); *Critical Pedagogies and Language Learning* (Cambridge University Press, 2004, w. K. Toohey); *Gender and English Language Learners* (TESOL, 2004, w. A. Pavlenko); and *Language and HIV/AIDS* (Multilingual Matters, 2010, w. C. Higgins).

Makoto Omori is a Ph.D. candidate at the University of Hawai'i at Manoa, where he teaches in the undergraduate programs in Second Language

Studies. His research focuses on language and social interaction, in particular on applying ethnomethodology, conversation analysis, membership categorization analysis and discursive psychology to the study of second language interaction and learning.

Alastair Pennycook, Professor of Language Studies at the University of Technology Sydney, is interested in how we understand language in relation to globalization, colonial history, identity, popular culture, politics and pedagogy. Recent publications include *Global Englishes and transcultural flows* (Routledge, 2007; winner of the BAAL Book Award in 2008) and two edited books, *Disinventing and reconstituting languages* (with Sinfree Makoni; Multilingual Matters, 2007) and *Global Linguistic Flows: Hip Hop Cultures, Youth Identities, and the Politics of Language* (with Samy Alim and Awad Ibrahim; Routledge 2009). His latest book is *Language as a Local Practice* (Routledge, 2010).

Angela Reyes is Associate Professor of Linguistics in the Department of English at Hunter College, City University of New York. She received her Ph.D. in Educational Linguistics from the University of Pennsylvania in 2003. Her books include *Beyond Yellow English: Toward a Linguistic Anthropology of Asian Pacific America* (Oxford University Press, 2009) and *Language, Identity, and Stereotype Among Southeast Asian American Youth: The Other Asian* (Lawrence Erlbaum, 2007). Her work examines discursive constructions of ethnic and racial boundaries in interactional contexts, particularly in informal educational sites. She is currently carrying out a study on Asian American cram schools in New York City.

Betsy R. Rymes is Associate Professor of Educational Linguistics in the Graduate School of Education, University of Pennsylvania. Her linguistic anthropologically informed educational research appears in numerous articles and in two books, *Conversational Borderlands* (Teachers College Press, 2001), and *Classroom Discourse Analysis* (Hampton Press, 2009).

Jack Sidnell (PhD Toronto, 1997) is an associate professor of Anthropology and Linguistics at the University of Toronto. His research focuses on the structures and practices of social interaction in a range of contexts. In addition to research on English conversation, he has studied talk in legal settings and among young children. His current research focuses on conversation in Vietnamese. His publications include: *Conversation Analysis: An Introduction* (Blackwell, 2010), *Conversation Analysis: Comparative Perspectives* (edited, Cambridge University Press, 2009), *Conversational Repair* *and Human Understanding* (edited with Makoto Hayashi and Geoffrey Raymond, Cambridge University Press, frth) and the *Handbook of Conversation Analysis* (edited with Tanya Stivers, Blackwell, frth).

Jeff Siegel is Adjunct Professor of Linguistics at the University of New England in Australia. He has conducted research in the Pacific region (mainly Fiji, Papua New Guinea, and Hawai'i), focusing on the origins of contact languages, such as pidgins and creoles, and the use of these varieties and unstandardised dialects in formal education. His most recent books are *The Emergence of Pidgin and Creole Languages* (Oxford University Press, 2008) and *Second Dialect Acquisition* (Cambridge University Press, 2010).

Brian Street is Professor of Language in Education at King's College, London University and Visiting Professor of Education in the Graduate School of Education, University of Pennsylvania. Over the past 25 years he has undertaken anthropological field research and been consultant to projects in these fields in countries of both the North and South (e.g. Nepal, S. Africa, India, USA, UK). He is also involved in research projects on academic literacies and in a Widening Participation Programme for EAL students in the London area as they make the transition from school to university. In 2008 he was awarded the National Reading Council Distinguished Scholar Lifetime Achievement Award. He has published 18 books and 120 scholarly papers.

Phillip A. Towndrow is an English language teacher, teacher educator and educational researcher at the National Institute of Education, Nanyang Technological University, Singapore. His research and writing interests include: Computer Assisted Language Learning (CALL), pedagogy and practices in using Information and Communication Technology (ICT) and new media in teaching and learning. Phillip has developed, implemented and evaluated courses in the use of ICT in education at pre-service, in-service and advanced levels. He has also designed, developed and managed computer resources including learning environments, networks and e-learning tools. Personal Web: http://web.mac.com/philliptowndrow/e-Portfolio_Web/Introduction.html

Viniti Vaish is Assistant Professor at Singapore's Nanyang Technological University, National Institute of Education. She has a Ph.D. from the University of Pennsylvania's Graduate School of Education in Educational Linguistics. Her areas of interest are bilingualism, language problems of disadvantaged children and comparative education. She has published in

Applied Linguistics and *World Englishes*, amongst other journals. Her research sites are India and Singapore. Currently she has a grant to explore the Learning Support Program in Singapore, which is a special class for primary school children with reading problems. Regarding data from India she is working on 'Culture and Code-switching on Indian TV'.

Introduction

Two terms commonly heard today in language educators' public and professional lives are *globalization* and *the social turn*. Both of these phenomena have had a significant impact on the field of sociolinguistics. The first has resulted in greater movement of individuals within countries and across borders motivating some to acquire new languages and identities, and leading many sociolinguists to investigate the hybridity of current language use. Globalization has also resulted in more attention being devoted to the relationship between language and power and critical approaches to language use and language learning. The second, the social turn in the field of applied linguistics, has resulted in far more attention being given to the social aspect of language use, so that today there are a growing number of studies on the relationship between such things as language and identity, style and styling, and language and gender. One of the major purposes of this book is to provide an up-to-date overview of the effect of these two phenomena on language use and the development of the field of sociolinguistics.

We believe that this text, addressed to experienced and novice language educators, is necessary today given changes in the global situation and continuing evolution in the field of sociolinguistics. The following factors of the political, social and academic world today are contributing to the need for a sociolinguistic text addressed to language educators. First, throughout the world, multicultural and multilingual classrooms are becoming the rule rather than the exception. Hence, on a daily basis, language professionals are witnessing the results of languages in contact where codeswitching and codemixing are common and where students bring to the classroom various ways of using language. Second, growing research in the field of sociolinguistics has led to new areas of specialization, for example critical language awareness, multimodality literacies and language socialization, along with more long-standing areas such as language planning, multilingualism and cross-cultural variation in language use, each with its own view of how language and society interact. Finally, recently there has been a growing recognition of the ideological basis of language use, with a focus on the need to promote a critical approach to language teaching. Because of the central importance of ideology in making educational decisions, this book begins with attention to ideologies.

The first section of this book, *Language and Ideology*, explains how ideologies can inform specific lines of research and pedagogies. In the opening chapter, 'Language and Ideologies', Mary McGroarty begins by discussing various meanings of the term *ideology* and the conceptual foundations of work in linguistic ideologies. Next she summarizes seminal quantitative studies on language attitudes, corpus-based research on language ideologies and qualitative studies on classroom interaction, interaction around norms for literacy, language choice in bilingual classrooms and ideologies underlying teaching tasks and materials. In the next chapter, 'Language, Power and Pedagogies', Hilary Janks explores the different theoretical underpinnings of critical literacy and how these have been translated into different classroom practices in a range of contexts. The different theories and their associated practices constitute an open set of approaches that teachers can adapt to their own contexts. In the final chapter of this section, 'Nationalism, Identity and Popular Culture', Alastair Pennycook challenges the notion that the nation state is the most productive way to understand the relationship between language and culture. In order to suggest an alternative approach to language and culture, one that recognizes that new identities may have little to do with nationhood, he analyzes the global spread of hip hop music as a way of exemplifying new languages, new cultures and new identities brought about by globalization. In closing, he explains the challenges that exist in researching language and pop culture and considers the pedagogical implications of the recent global flow of people and languages.

The chapters in the second section of the text, *Language and Society*, address the manner in which the larger social and political context affects language use at a macro level. In the first chapter, 'English as an International Language', Sandra McKay differentiates various paradigms used to describe the current spread and use of English including World Englishes, English as a Lingua Franca and English as an International Language. She then summarizes central research on the spread of English related to imagined communities, identity and technology. In closing, she describes major challenges faced by the field of English pedagogy in terms of equality of access to language learning, othering in English pedagogy and standards in English teaching and learning. In the next chapter, 'Multilingualism and Codeswitching in Education', Nkonko Kamwangamalu focuses on codeswitching practices in language classrooms as he examines the central question of why bilingual teachers and students codeswitch and whether or not this is a productive pedagogical strategy. He then distinguishes codeswitching from other phenomena such as borrowing, language shift, diglossia and codecrossing. Next he discusses common approaches to codeswitching research including the interactional, markedness and political–ideological approaches. In closing, he argues that codeswitching is indeed a resource for second-language learning and he identifies common research methods employed in codeswitching research. In the final chapter, 'Language Policy and Planning', Joseph Lo Bianco begins by defining key terms in the field; he then describes major approaches to language planning including language policy as a science, language policy as problem solving, and language policy as an interactive democratic practice. It is the latter approach that he considers most promising. In closing, he elaborates on the pedagogical implications of language planning emphasizing how the norms and standards that language teachers promote in their discourse and classrooms are powerful examples of language planning.

The chapters in Section 3, *Language and Variation*, move to a more micro level of linguistic analysis and examine how the larger social context interacts with the particular linguistic forms that an individual uses. In the opening chapter, 'Style and Styling', Jürgen Jaspers notes that while early studies on style were concerned with identifying discrete linguistic features of styles, more recent approaches to styling investigate how styling is related to identity and to community participation. In the next part of the paper, he examines the development of variationist sociolinguistics and the challenges that existed in this approach. He closes by arguing that future research in styling should focus on the process rather than the product of linguistic variation and seek to reconcile the regularity of linguistic behavior with individual creativity. In the next chapter, 'Critical Language Awareness', Samy Alim opens with an analysis of the political and media discourse surrounding Barack Obama's language as a way of illustrating what is meant by critical language awareness. He then examines the discourse of well-meaning teachers to demonstrate the ideologies that inform their language use. In closing, he argues for the need for language teachers to examine their own discourse in order to determine what ideologies they are promoting. In the final chapter, 'Pidgins and Creoles', Jeff Siegel starts by defining pidgins and creoles. He then summarizes research in the field that focuses on the development of pidgins and creoles, their role in the society where they are spoken, their linguistic features and their educational implications. He closes by discussing the advantages of using pidgins and creoles in educational programs, especially for initial literacy, and he highlights the awareness approach – with sociolinguistic, contrastive, and accommodation components – as the most promising of the ways pidgins and creoles have been incorporated into schooling, where P/C vernaculars are seen as a resource for learning the standard, rather than as an impediment.

Section 4, *Language and Literacy*, has a specific educational focus in its attention to literacy as an expression of sociocultural factors, as well as its examination of how various modalities of communication influence current language use. Ryuko Kubota's chapter, 'Cross-cultural Perspectives on Writing: Contrastive Rhetoric', opens the section with an informative and critical review of contrastive rhetoric, the cross-cultural analysis of the ways written texts are organized. She summarizes the assumptions, methods and background of this controversial field, as well as criticisms of its tendency toward fixed and essentialist characterizations of culture, language and English as a second language (ESL) writers, and above all its prescriptive ideologies. She closes with classroom implications, calling on educators to be reflective about how we approach cultural and linguistic differences. In their chapter on 'Sociolinguistics, Language Teaching and New Literacy Studies', Brian Street and Constant Leung review first the contributions of sociolinguistics to language teaching since the 1960s in the areas of communicative language teaching, classroom ethnography and functional linguistics, and then the contributions of the New Literacy Studies, with its ideological model and social practices view, toward furthering a social perspective on language and literacy learning and teaching. Bringing these two strands together, they close with the example of an academic literacies/English as additional language course they and their colleagues offer at their own institution. The last chapter in this section, by Viniti Vaish and Phillip A. Towndrow, takes up the topic of Multimodal Literacy in Language Classrooms, defining key terms and goals for work in this area, including the need for rich descriptions of actual sites of multimodal learning, analysis of multimodal design work, theories of multimodal meaning-making and new multimodal pedagogical approaches. They go on to review research on multimodal literacy practices in and out of schools and in teacher education, closing with their own recent study of a new one-to-one laptop program in a Singapore secondary school.

Section 5, *Language and Identity*, reflects the current interest in how identity and sociocultural context mutually influence one another and language use. Bonny Norton's chapter, 'Language and Identity', highlights poststructuralist conceptual foundations and qualitative research methods in language and identity research. She discusses language and identity in relation to the constructs of investment and imagined communities, as well as the ways learners' identities may impact their learning processes, their engagements with literacy and their resistance to undesirable or uncomfortable positionings in educational settings. She concludes with recent research on language and identity in classroom teaching and points to language teacher education and the decolonization of English language teaching as areas for future research in this field. In the next chapter, 'Gender Identities in Language Education', Christina Higgins continues these themes with a specific focus on how gendered social relations and ideologies of gender mediate people's experiences in learning and using additional languages. She exhorts teachers to engage with structural constraints that learners face when negotiating access to their desired communities of practice and presents suggestions for pedagogical practices that incorporate gendered experiences into learning opportunities, including intercultural pedagogy and critical pedagogy.

Angela Reyes continues the focus on identity with a chapter on 'Language and Ethnicity', beginning with an overview of key concepts and research methods, outlining both distinctiveness-centered and performance-based approaches. She provides brief overviews of language and ethnicity research on African Americans, Latinos, Native Americans, Asian Americans and European Americans in the United States. She points to promising recent studies embracing an emergent account of language and ethnicity and to future avenues of research on language crossing in language learning contexts, ethnic target varieties for language learners, and media and popular culture in classrooms. She closes with a reminder to teachers that ethnicity is a social and political construct, bearing no one-to-one relation with language. In 'Language Socialization', the final chapter of this section and a transition to the next, Patricia Duff highlights the field's fundamental focus on acquisition of linguistic, pragmatic and other cultural knowledge through social experience and on how individuals become socialized into particular identities, worldviews or values, and ideologies as they learn language, whether it is their first language or an additional language. In her review of classroom research on explicit and implicit language socialization in both formal and informal educational contexts, she points out that language socialization involves the negotiation and internalization of norms and practices by novices, but may also lead to the creation of new or hybrid norms, failure to learn expected norms, or conscious rejection or transgression of existing norms. She concludes with consideration of methods, challenges and practical implications of language socialization research, emphasizing that, especially in diaspora and postcolonial contexts, language socialization is a complicated multilingual, multimodal process and that teachers and policy makers must remember that what may be very obvious to them after a lifetime of language and literacy socialization and professional education into the dominant discourses of society may not at all be obvious or even comprehensible to newcomers.

Section 6, *Language and Interaction*, examines the ways in which specific social interactions and identities lend themselves to particular types of language use. In 'Language and Culture', Gabriele Kasper and Makoto Omori start by discussing various concepts of culture and approaches to intercultural communication. They go on to review interdisciplinary research traditions in intercultural interaction, including communication accommodation theory, cross-cultural speech act pragmatics, interactional sociolinguistics, and conversation analysis and membership categorization analysis. Throughout, they highlight that rather than seeing cultural diversity as fraught with problems as in sociostructural/rationalist approaches, discursive/constructionist approaches treat cultural diversity as a resource that participants can exploit to construct social solidarity or antagonism. They conclude with a caution that teaching to students' assumed cultural identities, as sometimes happens even in well-intentioned multicultural education and culturally responsive teaching, is a risky undertaking; and they call for continued research that puts the construction of cultural identities in educational settings under the microscope. Jack Sidnell's chapter on 'Conversation Analysis' offers a methodology for just such a microscope, as he probes the key concepts, methodological principles and insights of conversation analysis work with its focus on conversation as a system. After tracing the emergence of Conversation Analysis and of its crucial insight that analysts can use the same methods in studying conversation as those conversationalists use in producing and understanding it, he turns to the use of collections (in this case a collection of 'next turn repeats') to uncover participants' normative practices and orientations. He closes with examples of recent conversation analysis research findings on interactional organization in language classrooms, including insights into normatively organized activities participants orient to, as well as on distinctive features and practices around 'correctness' in second-language classrooms. The last chapter in this section, 'Classroom Discourse Analysis: A Focus on Communicative Repertoires', takes us even more directly into classrooms as Betsy Rymes shows how teachers may use the concept of communicative repertoire to understand and analyze interaction in classrooms. After briefly defining the concept of communicative repertoire, she organizes her chapter around five critical issues: rethinking correctness, emerging and receding repertoires, accommodating repertoires different from our own, analyzing communicative repertoires, and gaining metalinguistic awareness. She closes the chapter with a look at methods of classroom discourse analysis and some how-to advice to teachers.

The final section, *Language and Education*, draws all of the foregoing chapters together around themes of power, fluidity of languages, identity and critical language awareness, framed in relation to the continua of biliteracy and illustrated in the experience of an innovative bilingual undergraduate program in Limpopo, South Africa, taught through the medium of English and an Indigenous African language. In all, we hope the chapters in the volume open up a myriad of approaches to language education to meet the complex and diverse social and linguistic contexts of today.

Part 1

Language and Ideology

Chapter 1
Language and Ideologies

MARY E. McGROARTY

Definitions

This chapter defines and describes language ideologies, the abstract (and often implicit) belief systems related to language and linguistic behavior that affect speakers' choices and interpretations of communicative interaction (Silverstein, 1998). Language ideologies frame and influence most aspects of language use, but their influence is not always directly observable. Often their scope and constraints must be inferred from the nature of individual and group actions, expectations and decisions occurring in pertinent social realms (Lippi-Green, 1997; McGroarty, 2008). In describing language policy, Shohamy (2006) and Spolsky (2004, 2009) use a tripartite distinction, noting that language policy, the sum of decisions about and practices related to language, is shaped by three main factors: language practices, the actual language-related behavior of individuals and institutions; language management, the official and unofficial rules regarding the choice and nature of language codes; and language ideologies, the most abstract of these dimensions, the understandings, beliefs and expectations that influence all choices made by language users even when implicit. Whether explicit or implicit, language ideologies inevitably incorporate, often unconsciously, speakers' sometimes-idealized evaluations and judgments of appropriate language forms and functions along with opinions about individuals and groups that follow or flout conventional expectations.

Actual language behavior may not always be consistent with explicitly proclaimed language ideologies, for many reasons. One is that ideologies can include elements that are internally contradictory. Another is that ideologies related to language and language use do not exist in a vacuum, conceptually or temporally; they overlap and continually share social and conceptual territory with other core beliefs and related agendas that influence decisions regarding appropriate alternatives in education, work, government policies and so on in an ever-dynamic policy stream (Kingdon, 1995). The study of language ideologies pertains to all languages and

3

language users. As May (2001) explains, it is not the sole province of those attentive principally to minority languages, but rather an approach to investigation that can illuminate analysis of all languages, all communicative interactions and all circumstances of formal and informal language learning and teaching.

Blommaert (1999) makes the case for the urgency of linguistic research informed by an ideological perspective because of the three distinctive contributions it can make. These contributions, he argues, expand the possible impact of much conventional linguistic and applied linguistic research, which, in his view, has traditionally focused solely or mainly on language forms or functions without appropriate attention to the essential dimensions of the following: (1) historical context, or historicity, in relation to analyses of human interpretations and interactions within and across institutions; (2) materialism, which he defines as 'an ethnographic eye for the real historical actors, their interests, their alliances, their practices, and where they come from, in relation to the discourses they produce' (Blommaert, 1999: 7), a dimension that includes considerations of social and political power; and (3) verifiable reproducibility, the extent to which linguistic ideologies are absorbed into and transmitted by all sorts of institutions, including schools, administrative agencies, military and religious organizations, publications, advertisements and other media. He explains that the more a linguistic ideology is taken up in any setting, the more likely it is to undergo normalization, a 'hegemonic pattern in which the ideological claims are perceived as "normal" ways of thinking and acting' (1999: 10–11). Linguistic ideologies thus influence our understanding of what is usual; they shape a constellation of 'common sense' beliefs about language and language use. As these beliefs continue to hold sway, they assume ever-greater force, regardless of their accuracy or correspondence to present realities. Blommaert's dimensions of attention to the historicity of language practices, the details of their material context and their social reproducibility underscore the concern for power relationships of all types that informs language ideological research. Increased attention to the roles of power relationships within and across all institutions has characterized many applied linguistic investigations in the last 20 years, especially those done with an explicitly critical orientation (Pennycook, 1994, 2001) and scholarly areas such as language policy (Ricento & Hornberger, 1996).

Power relationships, of course, emerge in all human endeavors, for individuals and all the institutions that they create, maintain, challenge, and continually alter and reconstruct through their patterns of transaction and interaction. However, concerns about the relative power of individuals and groups have become particularly crucial and contentious at this moment because of the forces of globalization. Globalization is a multifaceted phenomenon with a tremendous variety of causes and manifestations, only some of which encompass language. As McKay and

Bokhorst-Heng note, globalization has been defined in many ways, including internationalization, liberalization, universalization, Westernization, modernization and, most recently, deterritorialization, meaning an alteration of social space 'so that space is no longer mapped in terms of territorial places, distances, or borders' (McKay & Bokhorst-Heng, 2008: 2). They observe that many of these definitions have been recognized for decades, and remark that the last definition, which foregrounds the roles of mass communication, has been most prominent in recent theoretical work, although the conditions reflecting other definitions are still relevant. In this chapter, we will use their definition of globalization: 'a reformulation of social space in which the global and local are constantly interacting with one another' (2008: 2; also see the McKay chapter, this volume). Whether, overall, it might qualify as beneficial (Bhagwati, 2004; de la Dehesa, 2007), deleterious (Rupp, 2006) or rather as problematic and uneven in its effects as a function of several geographic and demographic factors (Sassen, 1998) depends on many criteria and is beyond the scope of this chapter. Nevertheless, all educators everywhere must attend to Luke's call to work out what the pressures and possibilities of globalization might mean for them. For language educators in particular, the facts of globalization at play in their spheres of action raise questions about both the material conditions affecting their work and 'which languages, whose languages, which texts and discourses' will be privileged and promoted to 'forge new critical and contingent relationships with globalizing economies and mass cultures' (Luke, 2005: xviii). In Luke's view, the appropriate project for related language policy and practices demands both interpretive and empirical study of what goes on in language classrooms and all their surrounding and supporting institutional actors. In its explicit invocation of language ideologies and identification of relevant data, research on language ideologies responds to his mandate. This chapter examines several types of ideologically oriented research in language education. The intent is to demonstrate the robustness of language ideology as an area of inquiry, summarize some of its diverse applications to analysis of language learning and consideration of appropriate pedagogy and provide a foundation for other chapters in this volume. A fuller grasp of this research can sharpen our appreciation of the many influences affecting language learning and teaching and assist educators in elaborating pedagogical practices informed by heightened social awareness and sensitivity (Luke, 2005; McKay and Hornberger chapters, this volume; McKay & Bockhorst-Heng, 2008).[1]

Conceptual Foundations

Before turning to current research that describes and addresses various manifestations of language ideologies in language education, it is worthwhile to summarize the principal conceptual themes and foci of related scholarship. This précis draws heavily on two influential reviews on the topic by linguistic anthropologists who have conducted foundational research. Readers wishing more detail on the diverse genesis and present scope of this academic area are encouraged to read the original reviews in full. Fifteen years ago, Woolard and Schieffelin noted that their discussion of 'ideologies *of* language [was] an area of scholarly inquiry just beginning to coalesce' (Woolard & Schieffelin, 1994: 55), emphasizing that such ideologies deserved scholarly scrutiny because they simultaneously reflect and constitute 'links of language to group and personal identity, to aesthetics, to morality, and to epistemology' (1994: 56). Thus language ideologies serve to differentiate individuals and groups, provide speakers with a sense of what is admirable and appropriate and shape speakers' understandings of the nature of knowledge that language encodes. Woolard and Schieffelin remarked that previous social scientists had resisted research into language ideology because it was too diffuse and unbounded as a focus for investigation, but these authors further observed that such intellectual resistance had begun to recede by the early 1990s.[2] They identify a continuing major difficulty for the study of language ideologies in that no single core literature exists to guide researchers. Hence decisions about which topics are appropriate for study, what counts as data, which investigative methods should be used and what constitutes criteria for academic quality are left to individual investigators to work out following their particular disciplinary predilections. This theoretical and methodological diversity observed by Woolard and Schieffelin continues very much in force, as will be evident from the variety of research described in this chapter.

In particular, two crucial distinctions used by these authors to characterize work in linguistic ideology can assist language educators in understanding the scope and potential of related scholarship. The first is the authors' differentiation of 'neutral' and 'critical' uses of the term 'language ideology' (1994: 57). Neutral uses include investigations of all systems of cultural representation described in an objective manner, while critical uses of the term extend only to certain linguistic phenomena that emphasize the social–cognitive function of ideologies and concomitant possibilities for bias and distortion based on speakers' social and political interests. The consequent distortion, they note, may help to legitimize mechanisms of social domination, and is often foregrounded in research on language politics and on language, literacy and social class (see also Auerbach, 1992; Pennycook, 2001, this volume; Street and Leung, this volume).

The second essential distinction in their review is that of the various possible sites, and thus nature of data, appropriate for the study of language ideologies. They observe that 'some researchers may read linguistic ideology from linguistic usage, but others insist that the two must be carefully differentiated' (1994: 57). They further point out that some theorists have taken metalinguistic discourse about language (i.e. explicit discussions of language forms and uses) as the most accurate instantiation of linguistic ideologies, while others, in contrast, have seen ideologies as necessarily 'behavioral, pre-reflective, or structural' so that ideologies must be discerned 'not in consciousness but in lived relations' (1994: 58). Such fundamental differences in assumptions about data appropriate for the study of language ideologies affect choices of research methods and interpretive frameworks. Regardless of these differences in assumptions, however, they concur that researchers concerned with language ideology organize their investigations around the experience of and response to a particular social position. By doing so, their analyses will then reflect 'a commitment to address the relevance of power relations to the nature of cultural forms and to ask how essential meanings about language are socially produced as effective and powerful' (1994: 58). They celebrate research on language ideology as a vital link between linguistic and social theory; they also caution observers to be aware of the ironic contrasts between the casual generalizations about language found in the popular press (and elsewhere), which treat language attitudes and ideologies as uniform, invariant properties of individuals or groups, and the related scholarship demonstrating that, in contrast, ideologies are fluid, contested and situationally variable.

Ten years later, Kroskrity (2004) amplified several of the themes found in the 1994 article and also proposed five axioms characterizing related scholarship at the beginning of the 21st century. The first is that, while the perceptions of language and discourse implicated in language ideologies have been constructed in the interest of a specific group, current scholarship highlights the diversity of language behaviors and judgments that exist even in seemingly homogeneous social groups. These indicate that 'even shared cultural practices can represent the constructions of particular elites who obtain the required complicity' of others (Kroskrity, 2004: 501), as shown in his documentation of development of appropriate speech in the kivas (ceremonial chambers) of the Arizona Tewa. (Only men of a certain age can enter these, but their language use then becomes a norm to be recognized by the whole community.) This crucial insight then suggests that the distinction between *neutral ideological analysis* and *critical ideological analysis* is more a continuum than a clear dichotomy, a point particularly relevant for the present chapter.

The second axiom is that language ideologies are not unitary but internally diversified. They are 'multiple because of the plurality of meaningful social divisions (class, gender, clan, elites, generations, and so on) ... that have the potential to produce divergent perspectives expressed as indices of group membership' (Kroskrity, 2004: 503). A pertinent example is Hill's (1998) work on Mexicano (Nahuatl) communities showing that older speakers who may make comments like 'Today there is no respect' because of what they perceive as decreased use of honorific terms in conversation tend to be men, while women, whose social position has changed for the better, show more ambivalence in their attitudes toward this leveling of linguistic usage.

Third, also consequential for this chapter, Kroskrity reminds us that, within all speech communities (also an idealized notion), it cannot be assumed that members share similar consciousness of their own or others' language-related beliefs. Such variation in awareness arises in part from differences in life experience; language awareness is shaped, articulated and consolidated in a variety of settings, what Silverstein (1998) calls *ideological sites*, and might include religious institutions or ceremonies, courtrooms or classrooms, among others. Not all these sites are uniformly accessible to all members of any group. Relatedly, the salience of linguistic awareness differs substantially across as well as within communities. Some communities are marked by a considerable concern for and active contestation of language ideologies, whereas others show what Kroskrity calls 'practical consciousness with relatively unchallenged, highly naturalized, and definitively dominant ideologies' (2004: 505). In these latter communities, language ideologies go largely unrecognized because of their correspondence to common-sense assumptions. (Such assumptions may not be accurate. Indeed, work by Preston [see Niedzielski & Preston, 1999; Preston, 2004a] and others suggests that they are often erroneous or incomplete.) Still, such assumptions are enormously powerful in shaping speakers' views of variations within their native language (Lippi-Green, 2004; Preston, 2004b).

His fourth axiom is that language ideologies mediate between the social structures that channel the experience of language users and forms of talk practiced therein. In other words, speakers' involvement in and perceptions of the life activities that occur within all the social units in which they participate, be they families, neighborhoods, villages, work groups, schools and classrooms, clubs, or religious and occupational institutions, shape their construction of linguistic ideologies. Hence, in the course of time, speakers associate the experience of using certain patterns of language and discourse regularly during activities in various social settings with those settings, such that these linguistic and discoursal patterns then come to index or denote a necessary contextual relationship, for speakers' experiences there.

The fifth axiom, one familiar to sociolinguists and cultural theorists, is that language ideologies are major determinants of social and cultural identities. Like Gal and Irvine (1995), he refers to the core notion so characteristic of 'classical' linguistics in the 18th and 19th centuries, namely that shared language forms and discursive genres constitute an essential feature of a modern nation, with acknowledgment and awareness of their

use contributing to the 'imagined communities' (Anderson, 1991) of contemporary statehood. Simultaneously, however, the imputation of nationhood to relatively homogeneous linguistic groups overlooks another key
property of language, its socially conditioned variability: 'when a language is used in the making of national or ethnic identities, the unity
achieved is underlain by patterns of linguistic stratification which subor-
dinates the groups who do not command the standard' (Kroskrity, 2004:
509). Tensions between standard forms and other variants of language are
very much a part of current research directions in language ideologies (see
Pennycook, this volume).

For educators, an analytical focus on language ideologies thus helps to
promote recognition that existence of a national or regional 'standard' language advantages some speakers who share it and simultaneously disadvantages those who do not, whether the issues are related to varieties of
English in the United States (Lippi-Green, 1997), Quechua in the Andean
Highlands (Hornberger, 1995), kiva speech of the Arizona Tewa (Kroskrity,
1998) or alternation between English and local vernaculars in India
(Ramanathan, 2005). Moreover, because speakers can, and do, use various
combinations of the languages and varieties they know, the study of language ideologies helps to refine the understanding of the boundary- and
identity-marking functions within a community. Concurrently, it illuminates the fluidity of boundaries, as speakers 'exploit or celebrate their
hybridity through mixing' (Kroskrity, 2004: 510), demonstrating multiple
identities and affiliations through language. Additionally, there is considerable attention to forms of language mixture and hybridity (see the chapters by Pennycook, Kamwangamalu, and others in this volume) that attest
to the creativity of contemporary language users in creating or displaying
new identities.

At present, identification and exploration of language ideologies represent a lively arena for research. Among recent studies are documentation
of Paraguayan educators' views on two varieties of the Guaraní language,
one viewed as more 'academic' and one as more colloquial (and also
mainly oral), each of which may have a role in early language instruction
(Mortimer, 2006); explication of the rise of pan-ethnic vernaculars comprising aspects of several different languages systematically and widely
used by many speakers to express not ethnic affiliation but degree of
urbanization in Zimbabwe (Makoni *et al.*, 2007); identification of the pedagogical ideologies shaping English instruction in Japan (Seargeant, 2008)
and internal contradictions in the ideologies related to Singapore's literacy
policies (Chua, 2004); a survey of the language attitudes of the first postcolonial generation in Hong Kong high schools (Lai, 2005); exposition of
the sometimes hostile or ambivalent attitudes toward English in Quebec
that affect both popular sentiment and language education, particularly
but not only teacher training (Winer, 2007); and comparative accounts of

the ways in which particular educational institutions mediate the influence of language-related beliefs and practices on local educational policies in Philadelphia and the Andean region (Hornberger & Johnson, 2007). The varied linguistic, geographic, social and educational foci of this research represent a rich resource for language researchers and teachers desirous of expanding their grasp of the nature, power, and influence of language ideologies in education.

Research on language ideologies is interdisciplinary as well as both diachronic and synchronic. Beliefs about language have been investigated by scholars from many disciplines using research methods that correspond to their training, disciplinary traditions and access to sources of information. In what follows, I present a brief survey of research approaches used to investigate language-related beliefs and interpretations over the past five decades, along with some examples of current investigations. The 'quantitative/qualitative' distinction provides a convenient organizational strategy, with one proviso: this dichotomy implies far too simple a contrast to capture the nuances of both data and argument in many recent and some earlier studies, which often combine research methods and data sources in the interest of more comprehensive and enlightening treatment of a particular topic. For example, Zhou and Bankston's (1998) account of Vietnamese adaptation to life in a minority community in New Orleans is an extended case study that used participant observation, intensive interviews and direct surveys of high schools students, along with analysis of numerous secondary sources such as archival records, related opinion polls, data from the US census and other government agencies, and results of Louisiana's high school graduation tests. Each research approach and all studies summarized illuminate aspects of beliefs about language, provide valuable descriptive insights on the nature of 'situated policy enactments' (Ramanathan & Morgan, 2007), and raise further questions about the complexity of social forces driving individual and institutional language choices and optimal instructional practices that promote effective language learning, all areas of major import to educators.

Quantitative Research on Language Attitudes

Social psychological studies and some current examples

Certain themes in current scholarship on language ideologies overlap to an often-overlooked degree with social–psychological research on language attitudes conducted since the 1960s. While it may seem odd to include 'classic' attitudinal research when considering work on language ideologies, inclusion is justified for this volume because both streams of investigation help to identify the many influences on language use and language learning, core concerns for teachers. Furthermore, attitudes, such as ideologies, are very often latent; that is, they are not always stated directly, but must be inferred from various forms of observable behavior. Following the then-dominant research methods used in North American social psychology, research on language attitudes has used surveys and questionnaires administered to large groups of learners to identify patterns of individual opinions and attributes correlated with success in language learning, with success often measured by indicators such as course grades. Dörnyei (2005) notes that initial work with the Attitude and Motivation Test Battery (AMTB) developed by Gardner and subsequently used by him and other collaborators around the world fell squarely within the individual-difference paradigm of psychology. Indeed, in a recent meta-analysis (Masgoret & Gardner, 2003), Gardner observes that, for the first two decades of its use, the AMTB was concerned principally with individual differences, then the dominant concern of educational psychology, and has been extended to include broader concerns. The survey methodology elaborated by Gardner and colleagues has been refined in subsequent studies and remains a useful source of insight into language attitudes, which are both input to and reflections of broader language ideologies.

Standard survey methods continue to provide useful information about speakers' evaluations of the varieties of language to which they may be exposed in the community, in schools or in both venues. The tradition of accent evaluation within English-speaking communities goes back nearly 80 years in Great Britain and remains vital, attracting investigation by scholars from several disciplines (Giles & Billings, 2004). A recent example is the study by Coupland and Bishop (2007) investigating the attitudes of informants around the United Kingdom to more than 30 accents in the English they were likely to hear, including regional variants and varieties influenced by other world languages. Findings indicated several intriguing trends, among them a tendency for women to admire accents more than men, for men to rate accents like their own relatively higher, for younger respondents to be more tolerant of diverse varieties and for all respondents to be less favorably disposed toward innovative urban vernaculars.

Students' attitudes toward their own languages as well as languages encountered in the course of schooling have also stimulated research. Lai's (2005) timely study of Hong Kong secondary students' attitudes toward English, Cantonese (the local vernacular) and Putonghua (the newly important, more standard form of Chinese that rose greatly in importance after the 1997 handover of Hong Kong to China) documents some of the complexities of this contemporary multilingual context. Lai surveyed more than 1000 students representing the first group of secondary pupils subject to the changed educational policies following political union of Hong Kong with China. These policies had downplayed the importance of English in favor of the use of Cantonese, the students' mother tongue, in primary education, and added Putonghua as a core subject. The results of an attitude questionnaire showed that the students were very favorably oriented to Cantonese and English, in that order, with both of these showing high integrative values; respondents were relatively neutral, although not negative, regarding the integrative value of Putonghua. Interestingly, responses to items rating perceived instrumental values of these varieties showed that English rated highest, then Cantonese, with Putonghua also perceived as relatively neutral, although with positive tendencies in its relationship to goals such as occupational success and future prosperity. The investigator interprets these findings to mean that students have a clearer sense of the value of both Cantonese and English in contemporary Hong Kong, while for them the sociolinguistic role of Putonghua is still being consolidated. To validate these results, a matched-guise measure was also administered. (The matched guise is another assessment of evaluative reactions to language varieties, in which listeners hear and rate language samples produced, unbeknownst to them, by the same multilingual speaker; see Lambert's original explanation [1972], the discussion in Gardner and Lambert (1972), the useful summary of this technique provided in Jenkins (2007, Chapter 3), and an account of a related technique used to detect discrimination toward callers seeking rental housing in Baugh (2003)). Results of the matched-guise test showed that Cantonese received the highest ratings for attributes connected with social solidarity, such as friendliness and trustworthiness. English received the highest ratings for connections with wealth, modernity and higher education; and Putonghua was rated lower than the other varieties, in a pattern that corroborated the survey findings.

Another recent framework deriving in part from earlier AMTB work and adding to it some important constructs, such as the nature of an individual's identification with the first and second language community, actual contact with the L2 community and use of L2 media, is the expanded sociocontextual model (Rubenfeld *et al.*, 2006). This approach also employs survey methodology to determine how cultural representations of the 'other' community are perceived, in this case by university-level learners in the Francophone/Anglophone context of Ontario, Canada. It combines measures of individuals' confidence in and frequency of L2 use, and exposure to L2 oral and print media, to predict outcomes such as feelings of L2 identity and positive attitudes, termed 'positive cultural representations' of the L2 community. This research demonstrates innovation in both conceptual design and analysis. Regarding design, data were collected and analyzed separately for French and English speakers because the researchers wished to incorporate differences in the ethnolinguistic vitality of these two communities, with Francophones representing a minority and Anglophones representing a majority perspective. Based on initial work by Giles *et al.* (1977), ethnolinguistic vitality was defined in this recent project as the collective feature of any social group such as 'demographic representation [size], social status, and institutional support' (2006: 613). For analysis, the investigators developed a set of hypothesized relationships amenable to testing through path analysis. This technique builds on regression analysis, which seeks mathematically optimal combinations of variables influencing an outcome, and makes the model more precise by specifying the sequence, or order, in which these variables operate. While results cannot be interpreted as causative, they at least suggest processes at play in the particular research setting.

Findings were explained according to the 'additive versus subtractive' forms of bilingualism, distinguishing educational approaches that enable learners to add a second language to their native language skills (hence, additive) from those requiring that learners actually lose or forget skills in their initial language as they learn a second (thus, subtractive; see Gardner & Lambert, 1972; and Lambert, 1980).[3] Intriguingly, the results did not demonstrate the subtractive (for Francophones) or additive (for Anglophones) stances expected of these highly educated bilinguals. Instead, and crucial for language educators, findings indicated that the amount of experience using the L2 produced positive cultural representations of the respective L2 communities for both groups of participants, although the developmental path leading to the confidence resulting from frequency of L2 use differed for French and English speakers. (Confidence in one's ability to use a second language has also been identified as important in qualitative work; see Nikolov, 2000.) For Francophones, there was a link between L1 and L2 identity, whereas no such path existed for Anglophones. The investigators interpreted this finding to mean that the lower ethnolinguistic vitality of French in Ontario meant that French speakers needed to establish their L2 identity securely before acquiring stronger L2 skills. Such research shows that investigations of language-related attitudes in bi- or multi-lingual communities must examine the relative status, or vitality, of each community involved to be maximally informative.

Social psychologists interested in language pedagogy have begun to build on these advances and extend them explicitly to second-language classrooms. Much of the 'classic' work conducted by Lambert and Gardner and colleagues was mainly descriptive of various student profiles derived through correlation and factor analysis and did not generally address instructional practices. However, more current formulations include closer attention to pedagogy. Dörnyei (2001) extends the model explicitly to language instruction and notes that, to improve the odds of success, instructors need to promote and enhance attitudes related to L2 speakers as well as attitudes that reflect a realistic notion of the effort required to learn, that is, to achieve an 'ideal L2 self' (2001: 102–105). He has also spearheaded a considerable amount of related research to help elucidate the factors responsible for success in a variety of instructional settings. In this model, positive attitudes, including, notably, positive attitudes toward what happens in L2 classrooms, are theorized as influential factors contributing to effort, which can produce success in L2 learning; such success can, in turn, increase positive attitudes, including favorable attitudes toward the L2 classroom, suggesting a reciprocal relationship between these two classes of variables.

Contemporary attitude researchers, including Dörnyei, have noted the importance not only of attitudes toward the L2 community and its speakers but also attitudes toward the language course itself, noting that it takes a long period of time to acquire a new language and that students' attitudes toward the instruction they receive affect willingness to persist in the sometimes tedious efforts needed to do so. Such investigators are often explicitly committed to identifying the nature and degree of the relationship between language attitudes and another construct crucial to learning, motivation. Attention to student motivation could perhaps be viewed as extraneous to consideration of language ideologies; however, the practical pressures of most educational settings demand that educators recognize factors affecting learners' dispositions toward language learning and take action to create and sustain positive instructional experiences. Seen in this light, a clearer understanding of the potential motivational effects resulting from the language ideologies of students, and teachers, and other important educational agents is directly germane to this discussion.

The importance of relationships between conditions surrounding instruction and students' motivation to learn language has been confirmed in several recent large-scale studies conducted with L2 students at different levels. One documented an association between Hungarian university students' positive disposition toward English and dissatisfaction with traditional teacher-centered instruction; this disjunction was interpreted to produce demotivation contributing to student ambivalence (Kormos *et al.*, 2008). A second, done with secondary, tertiary and adult language students in Hungary, showed that high school students were attracted to English by the access to English cultural products that they perceived, whereas the older groups' interest was predicted only by potential instrumental uses of the L2 (Kormos & Czisér, 2008). A third recent study in this general paradigm examined multiple classrooms using a highly standardized curriculum for English instruction in South Korean junior high schools and was designed with more explicit attention to the effect of classroom experiences on students' attitudes. Researchers (Guilloteaux & Dörnyei, 2008) included systematic classroom observation as well as assessment of students' attitudes and reactions to teachers' various motivational practices during classroom instruction. These included using tangible tasks, giving neutral feedback, using creativity and fantasy in lessons and personalizing instruction, among others. Findings showed that teachers using explicitly motivational methods of instruction increased student motivation decisively. It is then assumed that this increase would, in turn, improve attitudes toward language instruction, an improvement that would presumably contribute to better outcomes for L2 study. Hence, this contemporary work on language attitudes suggests that positive attitudes can both contribute to and result from good and varied L2 instruction. In so doing, it highlights the dynamic and reciprocal relationships between learners' and teachers' individual attributes and experiences and language learning success. Such studies illustrate the complex interplay between learners' attitudes, learning environments and processes, and positive learning outcomes, an interplay also at issue in the more qualitative approaches to research to be discussed shortly. First, however, let us turn to another quantitative method of investigating language ideologies.

Corpus-based research on language ideologies

Another quantitative technique relevant to the study of language ideologies is corpus linguistics, which takes frequency of language forms rather than opinions of language users or learners as its source of data. Corpus linguistics (Biber *et al.*, 1998), the use of quantitative techniques to identify patterns of use in large samples of texts, either oral or written, provides a new and rather different quantitative method for research on language ideologies. It is based on statistical analyses of very large samples of different types of texts or corpora (a Latin plural) rather than on respondents' levels of positive or negative evaluation or strength of their agreement/disagreement with survey or questionnaire statements related to languages and language study. Corpus research begins by systematic identification of extremely large (with size defined by number of words of running text, typically in hundreds of thousands or even millions) samples of naturally occurring texts (e.g. written texts might comprise novels, textbooks, newspapers, students' essays or advertisements; oral texts might consist of speeches, conversations, television or radio programs) and assigning codes to the grammatical, lexical and discourse features chosen. Corpus techniques can be used diachronically, to investigate language change over time, or synchronically, to better describe similarities and differences of text types from the same time period. The data of interest for analysis then arise from the relative frequencies of particular linguistic forms and patterns of co-occurrence and association (or lack thereof) between some forms and terms and others, patterns typically identified through correlation and factor analysis. Thus, unlike the deductive research on attitudes, which uses individuals' responses to predetermined survey items as the source of data for analysis, corpus research takes a more inductive stance; it uses patterns of linguistic co-occurrence to generate quantitatively based factors that are then interpreted in accordance with functional attributes of interest. Developed as a method for characterizing the linguistic features of texts serving various communicative purposes, it can also then be used to determine degrees of linguistic similarities and differences between types of texts. These similarities and differences can, in turn, be interpreted as an indicator of content or topic similarities, where similar topics are denoted by the same or different patterns of lexical and grammatical choice.

Key word analysis (Baker, 2006; Johnson & Ensslin, 2006) represents a subtype of corpus-based approaches that pursues analysis of frequency of thematically relevant content words (words referring to a specific semantic field; for example in a text on water-related topics, relevant content words might be *boat*, *ocean* or *rain*; these are contrasted with words such as *of*, *and* and *it*, which are function words). This is the approach taken by Fitzsimmons-Doolan (2009) in a corpus-based study of the degree of relationship, or co-referentiality, between streams of discussion in the state of Arizona related to two topics relevant to language ideologies, (1) immigration and (2) language minority education, including three related subtopics: (a) Official English legislation and practices, including a 2000 ballot proposition that mandated English as medium of instruction for K-12 learners, (b) developments in a court case, *Flores v. Arizona*, that had been prosecuted in the federal courts since 1992 and at the time of the research was under appeal and (c) English immersion. The two corpora for investigation, one for immigration and one for language minority education, were constructed by collecting articles related to all the above topics appearing in three newspapers published in the two largest cities in the state, one from Phoenix, generally characterized as a conservative political environment, and two from Tucson, usually described as politically liberal, between 1999 and 2007. These corpora were then searched to identify the 100 most frequent key terms in each one, with an expectation that similarity of lexical choice would mean that newspaper discourse on these two topics was related. Counter to predictions based on the pluralist position often proposed by applied linguists and others interested in matters of language rights, there was almost no overlap in key terms between these two streams of discourse; only six words (including e.g. *Arizona*, *federal* and *law/s*) overlapped, and those words had to do with comments on jurisdictional concerns and policy in general rather than any specific aspect of either immigration or language education. The researcher concludes that this analysis refutes the notion that coverage of language minority issues and matters related to immigration represent in any way the same stream of discourse; rather, findings are consonant with prior empirical research documenting diverse rationales underlying singular policy directions, a reality demanding revision of some of the more sweeping pluralist theoretical narratives and requiring further research.

Quantitative research on belief structures as related to language and language learning thus uses the study of relatively large groups of individuals, whose responses are then analyzed to yield interpretable patterns consistent with theoretical models that include other constructs. Sometimes these constructs, like ethnolinguistic vitality, are drawn from the realm of social relations as well as the earlier focus on individual differences; sometimes this research includes constructs related specifically to education such as motivation or responses to particular aspects of the language class experienced by learners. Hence the disciplinary models that inspire the design of any questionnaires or surveys used require careful elucidation, for it is their various components (often formalized into subscales) that signal the vision guiding the research. In contrast, corpus linguistics is more inductive. Results from the detailed tallies of linguistic features (i.e. various types of nouns, verbs and qualifiers; pronouns; invariant word sequences [sometimes called 'strings' or 'bundles']; etc.) in large corpora provide numeric measures of similarity and dissimilarity and relative co-occurrence of particular lexical and grammatical structures. These patterns are then interpreted in light of what is known about the functions of various text types in general and, more particularly, about the communicative functions realized in certain genres such as situation comedies on television, academic lectures, textbooks or, as in the research summarized above, newspaper articles. In each type of research, quantitative information serves to identify and define phenomena of interest. The results of both social–psychological and corpus analyses offer information about the way the world works. Both analytical approaches seek to better describe the world and, with reference to the theme of this chapter, the ways in which groups of individual human respondents perceive or large samples of text reflect attitudinal and ideological positions. Each is, thus, broadly descriptive in a 'product-oriented' sense, and offers a portrait of 'things as they are' at a particular point in history.

However, neither approach captures the texture of interactions between individual language users and speakers, between individuals in different social positions, or between language users and texts. Much, although not all, of the qualitative research to which we now turn, particularly that done in the ethnographic and interpretive traditions, uses an examination of interactional processes as a principal site for identification of language ideologies. Let us next situate the pertinent research traditions and then examine some recent studies.

Qualitative Research on Language Ideologies

Research on classroom interaction

As with social–psychological research discussed earlier, research into classroom interaction has grown and changed since the pioneering work

of the 1960s and 1970s. Just as the growing capabilities of computers facilitated the large-scale analyses required for attitudinal research and corpus
linguistics, the wider availability of audio and, later, video recording technology gave investigators unprecedented access to enormous amounts of
talk in many settings, classrooms included. Classroom discourse has been
and remains a major focus for scholars from many academic traditions
and fields (see Rymes, this volume). In the United States, some of this earlier work took a more quantitative approach in which utterances of teachers (and, to a smaller extent, students) were tallied, and the tallies then
interpreted to identify principal types of linguistic actions, or moves (see
Bellack *et al.*, 1966). Other North American work had a more qualitative
character, in which excerpts from ongoing teacher–student interactions
were selected to illustrate some aspect of interest such as teachers'
approaches to promoting students' responses or labeling alternatives
during questioning (e.g. Cazden *et al.* 1972). Similarly, research in the
United Kingdom was from these early days focused on identifying the
superordinate patterns of discourse functions that related to pedagogical
aims and activities (Edwards & Furlong, 1978; Sinclair & Coulthard, 1975).
In the intervening decades, qualitative work on classroom discourse has
been further enriched by ethnographic research that has included long-
term involvement in and analysis of classroom experiences (e.g. Heath,
1983), often conducted through participant observation. All such research
was, thus, descriptive in orientation, although it was often carried out to
serve the goal, sometimes implicit, of identifying classroom processes in
order to improve learning and instruction.

The descriptive goal of research into classroom interaction remains
robust, with investigators examining classroom discourse to identify questions of perennial relevance, for example, patterns of teacher correction
(Santagata, 2004), teacher ability to build on student comments for effective impromptu content-area instruction (Jurow & Creighton, 2005) and a
host of other pedagogical concerns. Some current research on classroom
interaction, often but not only the work done within a critical discourse
analysis framework (see the contributions of Alim, Janks, Pennycook and
Rymes, this volume), explicitly addresses various aspects of language ideologies, generally by examining the interaction patterns and/or related
linguistic and lexical choices and inferring ideological stances from these.
In many such studies, language ideologies are foregrounded through
the interpretive lenses applied as well as the choice of classroom types,
episodes and artifacts analyzed.

Interactions around norms for literacy

Classroom instruction and interaction related to the nature and choice of
language norms have proven to be productive sites for ideologically

oriented work, as shown in three recent studies, two conducted in the United States and one in South Africa. It is no accident that these studies all deal with secondary education, the level at which control of standard forms in written language assumes ever-greater importance as an educational gatekeeper. All these studies revolve around identification of putative errors, but the analysts show that, in fact, concepts of what counts as 'error' in any setting are not given, but rather a product of local sociolinguistic realities and student and teacher aspirations, which, in many school systems, require high levels of mastery of the academically acceptable code.

The contrasts between pressures affecting the choice of language varieties, specifically the contrasts between African-American vernacular versus standard English, serve as the focus for one recent study that examined interactions observed during 'Daily Language Practice' (in some US school districts, it is also often called 'Daily Oral Language', a misnomer, for it consists of efforts to engage students in daily practice of the rules of prescriptive grammar through correction of errors in single sentences that students see on the blackboard) in 10th grade English classes that served mainly African-American pupils in an urban US school district (Godley *et al.*, 2007). Observational evidence indicated that all students spoke both standard and African-American English (a not uncommon situation; see Baugh (2004) and Rickford (1999) on the degree of bidialectalism across African-American users of English and also Rampton (2009) on the ability of British adolescents to shift across local dialects of English for stylistic purposes). In these classes, the daily language practice activity was used as a class opener, intended to take about 10 minutes. It had been adopted, in part, because of concern about student performance on the federally-mandated standardized tests involving both multiple choice exams and free writing. The investigators (who included the teacher) audio- and videotaped these activities regularly over the course of a school year, and later selected episodes for analysis. Using inductive methods characteristic of the ethnography of communication, they studied transcripts and viewed and reviewed tapes to identify recurring themes.

The themes were collaboratively coded (a high-inference procedure) for the source and content of language ideologies. Sources of language ideologies included external requirements (state and district standards, the mandated standardized tests), curriculum materials, the activity structure, and teacher and student talk observed during its unfolding, all influences that shape most classrooms. Regarding content, findings showed a predominance of unifying, monolithic beliefs about a single, correct, authoritative standard form for written English (a perennially powerful ideology in education; Siegel, 2006); a disconnect between form and function; a belief that there was one 'proper' dialect, while others were 'slang'; and the pervasive equation of grammar instruction with editing. At the same time, other themes less frequently articulated but still present indicated awareness that there were several dialects of English, each appropriate for a specific context, and that optimal grammar instruction and practice should be dialogic, positioning learners as skilled language users. Hence, importantly, the ideological content animating these activities, when considered holistically, showed some internal tensions and contradictions. While the 'prescriptive' thrust was stronger, there was nonetheless an undercurrent that acknowledged the contextually and situationally bound nature of the choice of appropriate language forms and student capabilities to recognize and display such knowledge.

Another project highlighting ideological influences on demonstration of student knowledge about language is reported by Razfar (2005), who studied the repair practices observed in two classes serving English language learning (ELL) students in a Midwestern high school in the United States. This year-long case study combined participant observation, video recordings, teacher interviews and student surveys. In analysis of the video data, the researcher paid special attention to the evidence for language ideologies, or orientations toward authoritative language use, revealed by either the explicit articulations regarding language use or the language practices of teachers and students reflecting their co-constructed judgments about the accuracy and correctness of one form versus another. Interestingly, the majority of repairs related to pronunciation. The nature of the exchanges showed that the teachers in general viewed themselves, and were viewed by the students, as arbiters of acceptable pronunciation in English. However, when words of non-English origin were encountered, a regular but not frequent event, teachers were receptive to public input from students who spoke the indicated language. In these classrooms, teachers were highly likely to repair public use of non-standard forms such as *ain't*, and might do so in a mocking manner, evidence that they realized students were, in fact, well aware that this form was considered inappropriate but apparently believing that it should not go uncorrected. Analysis of peer-editing activities showed that students engaged in other correction (pointing out, e.g. that *childrens* was not a standard plural without giving a reason), also demonstrating an orientation to preference for a single standard form in language. Hence, both comments and classroom processes, taken together, reinforced the notion that a unitary standard for English existed, that the teacher was legitimately positioned to monitor it and students were to follow that model, except in the rare cases where their own language capabilities might confer linguistic authority on them.

A third related investigation was done in a settlement near Cape Town, South Africa, in an extremely diverse school community struggling to help students make progress in a fast-changing context where knowledge of English was becoming ever more vital to hopes of educational progress, although it was the mother tongue for a very small number (Blommaert *et al.*, 2005). Researchers used a variety of ethnographic and qualitative methods in their four months of fieldwork in the 8th, 9th and 10th grade classrooms, which were taught either through English, the medium in which most black learners studied, or through Afrikaans, used in the classrooms enrolling mostly colored students (in the South African system, 'colored' was the designation for students who were not white, not black and not Indian, and so considered mixed race). Modes of data gathering included being present at the school daily, taking extensive field notes, holding extended interviews with teachers and the principals, and analyzing two writing assignments done by all students, one the construction of a 'language map' and the other an account of personal educational history. Evidence showed overwhelming enthusiasm for acquisition of what teachers and students saw as the kind of English linked with social and economic mobility, but extremely limited opportunities to acquire and practice this aspirational target. While there was considerable English used, it reflected the local norms and varieties created through the contact and intermingling of English with the other languages. Most relevant for this chapter is the researchers' conclusion that, in such a setting, it makes little sense to speak of 'errors' in standard academic English when there is so little access to the standard. Rather, in this extraordinarily heteroglossic and dynamic environment, different but related norms emerge. While these may well serve local pedgagogical goals appropriately, they can simultaneously prevent learner progress in higher levels of education. They conclude that emergence of such local norms 'reproduces systemic inequalities' and thus exacerbates the gap between educational centers and peripheries (2005: 399).[4] Relatedly, Hill (2001) points out that some attempts by English speakers in the United States to use a few words of Spanish reflect not an acceptance of the language and its speakers but a covert form of racism, which could work to limit rather than expand educational equity. In considering the hybrid forms of communication now emerging in many similar settings, Lam (2006) reminds us that linguistic identities are now often dispersed across time and space, and calls for educators to use the images and codes emerging in popular cultures to heighten engagement of otherwise marginalized learners rather than further alienating them (see Alim, Pennycook and Rymes, this volume).

Language choice in bilingual classrooms

Ideological influences on the choice between two different languages in bilingual classrooms where either could plausibly be used have been favorite sites for research. In the United States, most such work has examined occasions of and motivations for language choices and alternation in Spanish–English classrooms. Many of the findings of this work are also potentially relevant to other bilingual settings, although the languages at issue, education systems and community and national contexts determine the extent of comparability.

The effect of contending language ideologies and their influences on the language choices made by children are outlined in Volk and Angelova's (2007) study of first-graders' peer interactions in a dual-language program. It is worth remarking that the school where the study was conducted was in only its second year of implementation of the first dual language program in the state, and that this program was designed to create an environment where the use of Spanish had a central and crucial academic role. The design reflected this, for students spent part of each day in two classrooms, one taught in English and the other in Spanish, and were expected to participate in whole-class and small-group activities in both. These researchers investigated the peer interactions of four girls, two English dominant and two Spanish dominant on school entry.

Their findings showed that even these comparatively young children could articulate their (occasionally contradictory) beliefs about language, that they reported liking both languages, and that they were extremely sensitive to both the overall dominance of English and the school's efforts to imbue Spanish with cultural capital as a medium of instruction. Still, choice of language for peer activities appeared to be done almost automatically when students were in the English classroom, while in the Spanish classroom (where use of Spanish should, similarly, have been the automatic default because of the program's design and philosophy), children often tried to negotiate language choice. Doing so had two effects: it soon became apparent that students needed overt reminders to use Spanish, so the teacher appointed one child to be the 'Spanish police' during small group work; and it sometimes sidetracked coverage of academic content as the English speakers tried to get their peers to use English despite being in the classroom meant to develop Spanish as an academic language.

Furthermore, the children's own comments along with the classroom observations revealed that the students' ideological constructions of the two languages were very much emergent phenomena, changing with their developing language abilities and situational constraints and in response to their ongoing involvement in the dual-language program. This insight provides a critical caution to educators interested in language ideologies as determinants of behavior: ideologies of students (and, we might surmise, teachers also), although unquestionably affected by the status of languages in the society at large, are malleable to some degree, so that the types of interactions and the communicative successes and failures experienced in school settings can and will contribute to revisions in an individual's (and, in this case, to an entire educational program's) commitment to using and mastering the languages of import in the environment. Moreover, it must be remembered that the children showed heterogeneity in attitudes and behaviors (as was also true with the Turkish–German children and young adults studied by Queen (2003) and the Luxembourgish children observed by Weber (2008)). This too is a key insight, not to be undervalued: in bilingual, as in monolingual, communities, members are not uniform in their ideologies of language.

Another project that identifies the ideological influences, along with the interactional and contextual cues, that affect language choices made even by very young children is Relaño Pastor's (2008) investigation of interactions in a special program aimed at educational enrichment of three- to five-year olds in San Diego, California, close to the Mexican border. This program, sited at an elementary school, took place twice a week, immediately after the regular morning session. It followed what the researcher calls a laissez-faire language policy; that is children were encouraged to use whatever form of whichever language, standard or non-standard English or Spanish, they might wish to use during problem-solving activities in order to maximize opportunities for involvement. (Most but not all the participating children spoke Spanish at home.) This policy reflected a deliberate programmatic choice instituted to prioritize children's ability to make meaning through any language. Some activities were computer-based, done individually with the assistance of undergraduate tutors from a nearby university, who tended to be English dominant; others were collaborative, carried out in small groups under the supervision of Spanish-dominant volunteer mothers. The researcher set out to investigate the socialization of young bilingual children in this enrichment setting, and thus followed a research protocol that included the multiple sources of evidence specified for such work (see also Duff, this volume). Over the 2003–2004 academic year, she conducted classroom visits, observations, interviews with the program coordinators, adult volunteers and tutors. Findings indicated that the children were constantly 'processing competing language frameworks and revealing emergent language ideologies in their daily interactions with peers and adults' (2008: 5).

The behavior of both child and adult participants reflected a variety of language ideologies, ranging from implicit endorsement of English as the main vehicle of academic progress, a position exemplified by some teachers and generally by the undergraduate tutors, not all of whom could speak Spanish, to explicit accounts of the value of bilingualism and biculturalism revealed through the stories shared by volunteer mothers and regularly overheard by children. Despite the program's commitment to equal status and development of both English and Spanish, the researcher concludes that the laissez-faire language policy made it difficult to achieve this goal because of the competing ideologies related to the hegemony of English and the frequently subordinate role of Spanish that all participants experienced, some in their families and all in the broader community setting of an increasingly polarized southern California city and a country with a strongly monolingual orientation (Lippi-Green, 1997, 2004; Wiley, 2004; Wiley & Lukes, 1996) despite its many areas of vibrant bilingualism.

Teacher language choice is the focus of Shannon's (1999) discussion. Based on ethnographic data gathered in a large southwestern school district that had been legally enjoined to provide bilingual instruction, most parents tolerated a situation in which little or no Spanish was actually used in classrooms. This circumstance affected teacher selection – teachers with minimal Spanish proficiency were assigned to bilingual classrooms – and to instructional processes, which gravitated heavily toward English. Additionally, she describes a sample practicum lesson in which a bilingual teacher trainee in a 5th grade classroom conducted a Spanish-only small group activity somewhat by accident. The trainee subsequently realized that it had been more effective than the dual-language delivery she had previously attempted but would, at the same time, require far more deliberate concentration on use of Spanish for academic purposes than the master teacher ever modeled. Shannon analyzes this situation as a reflection of the societal hegemony of English, a far more pervasive influence than the district's official ostensibly bilingual language policy in setting socially constructed parameters for teacher language choices.

Ideologies underlying teaching tasks and materials

Curricular materials, as evidence and models of certain language ideologies, have also been the focus of recent ideologically informed studies. These projects may address curricular content, language used in curricular documents or both. One example of change in curricular content is the report of an elective class in Chicana literature at a university in a small city on the Texas–Mexico border in an area where even the local high school curriculum included few Hispanic authors (Mermann-Joswiak & Sullivan, 2005). Among other goals, the course instructors (who were also the researchers) planned the class to expose enrolled students, mostly Mexican-American but including Euro-Americans, to works of contemporary authors not typically found in the local secondary school curricula. In their course projects, students selected poems, participated and analyzed a local community event and developed a brief survey about language-related opinions. They were then required to share the works with community members outside the course and bring community responses back to the course for discussion.

Relevant for this chapter is the finding that engagement with these multiple forms of content and analysis had two effects: it elicited individual reactions that were personal, often stronger, more expressive and opinionated than what might be found in more traditional classes; and importantly, it demonstrated that neither the enrolled students nor the community members shared a uniform ideological approach to the activities and their interpretation. Notably, the more numerous Mexican-American students were not unanimous in their reactions or analyses, but internally diversified; further, some students of all backgrounds indicated that the experience of studying communication in this way had changed their awareness of the history and power of linguistic and social hierarchies in their community.

Textbooks for language study invite examination of the ideological framing of both content and the language forms used as targets and media of instruction. Leeman and Martínez (2007) investigated the ways in which Spanish has been positioned in textbooks for heritage language users (i.e. those who have learned the language, often informally, through exposure and use in family or other community settings, although the definition of heritage language learners is, in fact, contentious; see Hornberger & Wang, 2008) over a 30-year period from the 1970s to 2000. Through analysis of the titles and prefaces of a dozen Spanish as a Heritage Language (SHL) textbooks, they trace several intriguing developments and interpret them through reference to evolving themes in university mission statements, public discourse about language and the tides of change in the politics of knowledge considered more broadly. Two of their findings are directly relevant to this discussion.

First, the ideological framing of Spanish has changed from an emphasis on ethnically marked to global perspectives. Textbooks of the 1970s highlighted efforts to validate local varieties, while at the same time refining them, and to honor connections between students' ethnic identities and the Spanish language, emphasizing 'localized knowledge, inheritance, and student ownership of language' (2007: 48). By the later 1990s, textbooks appealed not to the value of local forms of Spanish but to the potential that language mastery offered students and their eventual employers, reflecting commodification of language knowledge and justifying its study as a passport to participation in a globalized marketplace (a trend also identified, as they note, in Heller's work on French in Canada, although Heller's work focuses on the rationale for official government policies rather than pedagogical materials; see da Silva and Heller (2009) and Heller (2003)). Such a construction in heritage language textbooks decenters the language norm from local varieties to some putative global standard, often implicitly drawn from national standards outside the United States. This trend was confirmed in another study of the discourse related to norms for academic Spanish in a large university Spanish department analyzed by Valdés *et al.* (2008). Such practices, ostensibly aimed at promoting the ability of the learner to use forms of language appropriate for public discourse in Spanish in globalized domains, provide an intriguing parallel to the potentially harmful effect of a generalized global orientation in English teaching discussed by McKay and Bockhorst-Heng (2008: Chapter 7). In countries where English is regularly used as a second language so that it has become nativized, they note, 'the nativized variety [is] often marginalized in favor of exonormative standards and pedagogy'

(2008: 182). It thus appears that commodification of language, whatever be the language, has the dual potential to devalue local varieties even when educators and others might want to promote them, an ironic development similar to what Dorian (1998) has observed with respect to language maintenance efforts for some small languages.

Leeman and Martinez's second major conclusion is that while such commodification of language is legitimately viewed as problematic given that the justification for linguistic knowledge is almost entirely based on presumed economic consequences, it nonetheless demonstrates the possibility of a continuing public role for Spanish in US contexts. This in itself might create opportunities for use that would, in turn, motivate Spanish speakers (and others) to forge new communicative practices (as well as products) attesting to the normality and legitimacy of its presence. Hence, in this study, once again, we observe that ideologies related to language respond to other ideologies of diversity and the nature of appropriate social futures. The researchers, too, conclude that the ideologies they have outlined contain elements that, while seemingly contradictory, may in fact simply reflect that language ideologies, like other beliefs, are multifaceted and regularly reflect and contribute to discourse in other social domains. Achugar (2008) also found a multiplicity of positions articulated by individuals with varied professional and personal affiliations and a variety of ideologies conveyed in articles in the local newspaper in her descriptive portrait of the roles of and attitudes toward Spanish in the border city of El Paso, Texas, reminding us that neither local (Canagarajah, 2005) nor national perspectives on languages and language uses are monolithic. Both the textbook analysis and the account of opinion leaders in a major bilingual city reveal the intertextuality across time and the interpenetration of language ideologies by other social beliefs. Ideologies of language continually interact with other ideologies in the ever-dynamic marketplace of ideas.

The ideological content of English language lessons themselves has also been analyzed by several investigators over the last four decades. Typically, researchers conduct such content analyses to investigate the social roles stated and implied by textbook activities, in addition to other themes of possible interest for the settings and presumed users, students and teachers, of the texts. One recent example is Taki's (2008) comparison of the ideological positions represented and implied by activities found in the government-approved English textbooks required in all public secondary schools in Iran and those depicted by a selection of widely sold international English textbooks, often used in Iran's private language centers. Taki investigated the social relationships and subject positions of textbook characters and other forms of content in the texts. Findings showed a propensity for the local textbooks to leave participants' social roles in dialogues only vaguely specified, often simply as 'A' and 'B', and to omit cultural contrasts, festivals and customs, creating the impression of English as a relatively 'culture-free' language. The internationally published texts, in contrast, tended to cast characters in teaching dialogues as friends, customers and servers, or workmates, emphasizing egalitarian occupational and social relationships often framed within a market economy where even forms of entertainment require commercial transactions. The researcher concludes that such a portrayal aligns with a neo-liberal position emphasizing the 'internationalization of capitalism' (Taki, 2008: 139, following Holborow, 1999). This situation is not surprising; prior research on textbooks used for adult second-language literacy in the United States (Auerbach, 1995; McGroarty & Scott, 1993) has also documented the pervasive attention to individual economic survival and concurrent absence of much social and any political rationale for second-language mastery.[5]

Ideologies in institutions beyond the classroom

Qualitative research driven by concerns for and about language ideologies has also been conducted to highlight educational processes beyond single classrooms and schools and explore the experience of learners and educators embedded within larger social agencies, such as entire school districts, special teacher training programs, university departments (Valdés et al., 2008) and national educational programs. As Shannon's (1999) investigation suggests, official designation as 'bilingual', by itself, is not sufficient to guarantee effective instruction in two languages. Furthermore, school promotion of multiculturalism may actually devalue the specific linguistic and cultural strengths of particular student groups, creating, paradoxically, a de facto subtractive environment that favors assimilationist pedagogies and outcomes (Garza & Crawford, 2005). Full curricular integration of a commitment to genuine bilingualism, along with a supportive educational philosophy, is crucial to creating instructional opportunities to develop two languages.

Besides program design, curricular integration of languages and language varieties also reflects local conditions and language ecologies (Dutcher, 2004; Hornberger & Hult, 2008); this means that educators must recognize and reckon with linguistic environments external to schools as they strive to plan and implement efficacious language pedagogies. Moreover, contact situations that include the same languages even in close geographic proximity do not share similar linguistic ideologies, as shown by the heterogeneity documented for Spanish and English in southern California (Reese & Goldenberg, 2006), Navajo in the southwest (Romero-Little, 2006; Romero-Little & McCarty, 2006; Smallwood et al., 2009), Hawai'ian in charter schools dedicated to native culture on the big island of Hawai'i (Buchanan & Fox, 2003) and Quechua in southern Ecuador

(King, 2004), among other studies. Variations in individual, family and group experience, along with changes over time, continually alter linguistic ideologies.

A growing body of research shows that sustained efforts to create environments that include activities, artifacts and practices that constantly and explicitly valorize the first languages of learners in multilingual settings outside as well as inside schools are key to learner and program success (Suárez-Orozco *et al.*, 2008). All such efforts include an ideological component that acts to promote the value of the language used in home and community settings and, simultaneously, to counteract the ambivalent or negative messages of the larger, dominant culture (see also Duff, this volume; Bayley & Schecter, 2003; Freeman, 1998; and Potowski, 2007). These efforts take place within homes, as parents strive to assist children with acquisition of language and literacy in first, second and sometimes even third languages. Zentella's (2005) collection includes attention to some forms of family assistance provided to their children by Hispanic families in California (also documented in Chavez, 2007, and Delgado-Gaitán, 2001) and New York; some are similar to those noted by Dagenais and Moore (2008), who report on the support for development of Chinese offered by Chinese parents with children in early French–English immersion programs. Importantly, such family support is not confined to the home, but extends to community settings such as play groups, public celebrations, religious services and other venues where use of non-majority languages could and would be natural. Concerned parents not only help with homework and practice reading in more than one language, but they also ensure that their children participate, to the extent possible, in social activities, informal and formal, with other speakers of their own languages. As family circumstances allow, they ensure that learners see and use audio and print materials in their native languages and even enroll them in supplementary schools using these languages (Peterson & Heywood, 2007).

Following Fishman's (1991) dictum that school instruction alone cannot effect full language proficiency or inspire interest in genuine language use, educational agencies concerned with language development and revitalization have increased their impact through creation of attractive, age-appropriate materials that have a life beyond the classroom. One example is the English–Navajo bilingual newspaper published by high school students at the Rock Point Community School (McLaughlin, 1992); another is the development of a CD-ROM related to hockey, a sport popular with many Ojibwe youth (Williams, 2002); another comes from a program to revive and promote Welsh for use by families with infants and very young children, which provided parents with a CD and bilingual Welsh–English coloring and activity book, both of which could be used repeatedly, whenever they might fit into a family's routine (Edwards & Newcombe, 2005). All these innovative materials give children, young people and families opportunities to participate in events structured in and through native languages and literacies, a condition for successful literacy acquisition noted by Heath (1986). For the older learners in a model program for Spanish-speaking high schoolers described by Abi-Nader (1990), proactive program philosophies emphasizing ongoing relevance of the native language, its role as path to educational opportunities and continued link to their own communities proved essential. Furthermore, the curriculum included regular chances to hear and interact with successful program graduates who returned to the school to share accounts of the successes and difficulties they continued to face, helping younger participants realize that demands for persistence and hard work were as relevant for bilingual as for monolingual students.

Ideological currents in the larger sociocultural context affect teacher training, and innovative programs have found ways to address their impacts directly. Winer (2007) describes the concerns of undergraduate teacher candidates in a TESL degree program in Québec, a city and province marked by various degrees of hostility and ambivalence toward, but also consistent governmental support for, English and the teaching of English. For the student teachers completing the required practicum, working in such a milieu raised numerous issues, among them heightened trainee anxiety about their own language proficiency (which had been certified as acceptable on the required test); acceptance by Francophone professional colleagues at the schools to which they were assigned; dealing with student demotivation in a setting where parents were often more uniformly supportive of English study, which they saw as connected to the future educational or occupational possibilities, than were the students in elementary or secondary schools; and the nature of appropriate cultural content for English instruction in an environment where English may be resented despite the avowedly 'intercultural' orientation of the school system. By enabling all trainees to contribute their experiences, maintaining an ongoing record of these concerns, and altering some policies and practices, Winer outlines some of the options and constraints that shape programmatic responses to teacher training in an ideologically charged environment.

Hornberger and Johnson (2007) report on two focal participants in an innovative program based in Bolivia designed to provide master's degrees for speakers of Andean-region Indigenous languages who will be better prepared to return to their home areas ready to be agents of transformative educational practices. To participate in this intensive program, candidates had to self-identify as Indigenous; the researchers note that their informants' most prominent responses mentioned 'living close to the land, speaking their native language, and experiencing discrimination by others' (2007: 522). Part of their core professional identity as language educators thus consisted not only of well-developed proficiency in their two languages (Quechua and Spanish for one; Aymara and Spanish for the other), but also, notably, of their life-long awareness of the discrimination experienced by them and others who spoke the minority languages, paralleling McCarty's (2002) accounts of the Navajo educators who founded a pioneering bilingual community school. Through participation in the special master's degree program, these two participants and others went through a process of re-evaluation of the value of their Indigenous languages and growing recognition that they were becoming far better able to articulate the local and national value of their bilingualism, important for external audiences, as well as create curricular opportunities and a favorable educational environment in which fellow teachers and younger learners could learn in and through Indigenous languages. As the researchers observe, the master's degree program helped these educators identify and expand 'layered transnational ideological and implementational spaces' (2007: 525) necessary to realize the goals of genuine personal and societal bilingual education.

Educational Language Ideologies in An Era of Global Communication

Investigations such as those included here reflect the dimensions of historicity, materiality and evidence of reproducibility in actions and artifacts that Blommaert specified for ideologically driven research. Nevertheless, it would be too simple to say that educators must attend to sociocultural context and leave it at that, for all such contexts include considerable internal variability and particularity even when they seem similar to outsiders (or unreflective insiders). Just as language attitudes differ within speech communities and change over time, so do the ideologies latent and explicit in sociocultural contexts. Community language ecologies generate, direct and constrain language and literacy acquisition, maintenance and ongoing support. Contact situations even within relatively circumscribed geographic locations reveal a range of language ideologies that correspond to other social divisions and reflect variations in individual, family and other group experiences. Ideological variation and contestation is the norm, whether we consider varieties of English, Chinese, Navajo or Spanish, or the full panoply of contact situations around the world. Furthermore, the continuing pressures and processes of communication in a globalized era create access to multiple forms of language inside and outside school settings. These new forms of communication can reflect and convey ideologies with the potential to inspire or alienate learners and teachers. Educators who appreciate the power, scope and latent contradictions elucidated here and in other chapters of this book can, as committed individuals and colleagues, take up the challenge of deconstructing and reconstructing the linguistic ideologies that surround their efforts. Such knowledge can help them to create and implement the proactive class-room and school climates and varied instructional activities needed to provide the engaging and varied language and literacy learning experiences that they and their learners deserve.

Notes

1. My deepest thanks to the editors of this volume for the opportunity to consider this topic, for their own substantial research in this area, and for their patience and perspicacity in providing useful comments and suggesting necessary clarifications during the preparation of the chapter.
2. While the study of linguistic ideology as a distinct area dates from, approximately, the early 1990s, it should also be noted that some of the ideological aspects of language and its use had been discussed at least a decade earlier, often within the framework of critical discourse analysis (e.g. Kress & Hodge, 1979, revised 1993). In addition, scholarship analyzing the ideological component of education generally without specific reference to language issues has also had a long and distinguished history (see e.g. Apple, 1979; Apple & Weis, 1983; Dreeben, 1968).
3. The 'additive–subtractive' contrast in types of bilingualism is one of the oldest and best established distinctions in the social psychological literature on bilingualism. While still relevant, recent commentators have suggested that this distinction may reflect a latent monolingual bias because speakers are implicitly categorized according to monolingual norms in each language. They suggest that contemporary social and educational conditions may require other terms, such as *recursive* to describe efforts to add or revive languages once used but abandoned for a time and *dynamic* to denote the highly situation-specific forms of bilingual language use evoked by novel communication demands managed by speakers of two or more languages in interaction with multilingual others (see e.g. Clyne, 2003; García, 2009: chap. 3).
4. Such a development, in which pressures to conform to a world standard coexist with social forces favoring the expansion of local varieties, is not limited to English. Niño-Murcia *et al.* (2008) trace similar progression in which Spanish as used in Spain, the United States and areas of Latin America is concurrently undergoing 'globalized localization and localized globalization', with results varying by context. Although their analysis is oriented to linguistics rather than language pedagogy, it establishes the ubiquity of these simultaneous effects on language change, effects that could well affect educational standards and processes in the focal areas.
5. Of additional interest in Taki's analysis is that, in the locally produced textbooks, participants' gender is unspecified 85% of the time, so that texts can be used in schools for either young men or young women. In these texts, then, vagueness regarding gender reflects salient social facts about the instructional environment. Although exploration of ideologies related to gender portrayal is beyond the scope of the present discussion (but see the chapters of Higgins and Norton, this volume), it is nonetheless intriguing to note that explicit, even extreme, detail related to appropriate gender roles was characteristic of texts used for adult instruction in the United States during the 'classic' Americanization period of 1900–1924 (Pavlenko, 2005). Elision (or unusually specific emphasis) on gender roles can thus function as an indicator of the social ideals reflected in textbooks.

Suggestions for further reading

Blommaert, J. (ed.) (1999) *Language Ideological Debates*. Berlin: Mouton de Gruyter.
A multivalent resource for much current scholarship, this collection elaborates on the academic foundations for the study of language ideologies across a broad array of intellectual and geographic contexts. It includes contributions that illuminate beliefs and perceptions related to many languages, including Catalan, Corsican, Flemish, French, German, Hebrew, Mandarin, Portuguese and Spanish; varieties within some of these codes; and, for some, consideration of the lengthy historic connections and educational issues arising from the coexistence of certain of these languages and English in divergent contact situations. Thus, it demonstrates that many concerns felt keenly by contemporary English language educators are not exclusive to the learning and teaching of English, but have historic and contemporary parallels for other languages too.

McKay, S. and Bokhorst-Heng, W. (2008) *International English in its Sociolinguistic Contexts: Towards a Socially Sensitive EIL Pedagogy*. New York: Routledge.
Written specifically for English language educators seeking to offer appropriate language instruction for learners of different ages and different aims studying in very different educational systems embedded in multiple international contexts, this book deals with ideological components as well as instructional questions related to the teaching of English. The first three chapters offer a timely and well-grounded discussion of the varieties of language contact settings including English around the globe; the latter four chapters identify pedagogical issues related to local and national language policies, the nature and extent of variation, relevant standards, interactional concerns when English is used as a lingua franca and matters of authentic representation in language teaching materials.

Ricento, T. (ed.) (2000) *Ideology, Politics, and Language Policies: Focus on English*. Amsterdam: John Benjamins.
This collection offers several careful accounts of the intersection of ideologies (both linguistic ideologies and those relevant to other social domains), politics and language policies affecting education. The discussions are valuable for their historical perspectives, levels of insight and comprehensive geographic coverage, with chapters explicating related issues in Australia, India, South Africa and the United States and settings reflecting specific national, postcolonial and international pressures affecting public perceptions and demands shaping the use of and requirements to learn English.

Suárez-Orozco, C., Suárez-Orozco, M. and Todorova, I. (2008) *Learning a New Land: Immigrant Students in American Society*. Cambridge, MA: Harvard University Press.
This volume presents eloquent accounts of the tremendous diversity of experiences of immigrant students in US schools based on the authors' five-year study of over 400 students enrolled in school districts in the greater Boston and San Francisco Bay areas. The authors document the multiplicity of interacting factors, including the types of social networks and quality of schools, that affect the likelihood that these young people, most highly optimistic on school entry, will improve or decline in achievement and attitudes toward education as they continue through the grades. Chapter 4, on students' perceptions of learning English and learning through English, offers a comprehensive yet concise summary of difficulties related to mastery of academic English and notes the challenges for instruction and assessment raised by this process. Although focused entirely on

student experiences in the United States, the underlying concepts, research methods and individual trajectories outlined merit comparison with other national settings where newcomers must master a new language in order to have access to education.

References

Abi-Nader, J. (1990) "A house for my mother": Motivating Hispanic high school students. *Anthropology and Education Quarterly* 21, 41–58.

Achugar, M. (2008) Counter-hegemonic language practices and ideologies: Creating a new space and value for Spanish in southwest Texas. *Spanish in Context* 5 (1), 1–19.

Apple, M. (1979) *Ideology and Curriculum.* Boston: Routledge.

Apple, M. and Weis, L. (eds) (1983) *Ideology and Practice in Schooling.* Philadelphia: Temple University Press.

Anderson, B. (1991) *Imagined Communities: Reflections on the Origins and Spread of Nationalism.* London: Verso.

Auerbach, E. (1992) Literacy and ideology. *Annual Review of Applied Linguistics* 12, 71–85.

Auerbach, E. (1995) The politics of the ESL classroom: Issues of power in pedagogical choices. In J. Tollefson (ed.) *Power and Inequality in Language Education* (pp. 9–33). Cambridge: Cambridge University Press.

Baker, P. (2006) *Using Corpora in Discourse Analysis.* London: Continuum.

Baugh, J. (2003) Linguistic profiling. In S. Makoni, G. Smitherman, A. Ball and A. Spears (eds) *Black Linguistics: Language, Society, and Politics in Africa and the Americas* (pp. 155–168). London: Routledge.

Baugh, J. (2004) Ebonics and its controversy. In E. Finegan and J. Rickford (eds) *Language in the USA: Themes for the 21st Century* (pp. 305–318). Cambridge: Cambridge University Press.

Bayley, R. and Schecter, S. (eds) (2003) *Language Socialization in Bilingual and Multilingual Societies.* Clevedon: Multilingual Matters.

Bellack, A., Kliebard, H., Hyman, R. and Smith, F.L. Jr (1966) *The Language of the Classroom.* New York: Teachers College Press.

Bhagwati, J. (2004) *In Defense of Globalization.* Oxford: Oxford University Press.

Biber, D., Conrad, S. and Reppen, R. (1998) *Corpus Linguistics: Investigating Language Structure and Use.* Cambridge: Cambridge University Press.

Blommaert, J. (1999) The debate is open. In J. Blommaert (ed.) *Language Ideological Debates* (pp. 1–38). Berlin: Mouton de Gruyter.

Blommaert, J., Muyllaert, N., Huysmans, M. and Dyers, C. (2005) Peripheral normativity: Literacy and the production of locality in a South African township school. *Linguistics and Education* 16 (4), 378–403.

Buchanan, N. and Fox, R. (2003) To learn and to belong: Case studies of emerging ethnocentric charter schools in Hawai'i. *Education Policy Analysis Archives* 11 (8). Retrieved July 27, 2009 from http://epaa.asu.edu/epaa/v11n8/.

Canagarajah, S. (2005) *Reclaiming the Local in Language Policy and Practice.* Mahwah, NJ: Erlbaum.

Cazden, C., John, V. and Hymes, D. (eds) (1972) *Functions of Language in the Classroom.* New York: Teachers College Press.

Chavez, C. (2007) *Five Generations of a Mexican-American Family in Los Angeles: The Fuentes Story.* Lanham, MD: Rowman and Littlefield.

Chua, C.S.K. (2004) Singapore's literacy policy and its conflicting ideologies. *Current Issues in Language Planning* 5 (1), 64–76.

Clyne, M. (2003) *Dynamics of Language Contact: English and Immigrant Languages.* Cambridge: Cambridge University Press.

Coupland, N. and Bishop, H. (2007) Ideologised values for British accents. *Journal of Sociolinguistics* 11 (1), 74–93.

Dagenais, D. and Moore, D. (2008) Représentations des littératies plurilingues, de l'immersion en français et des dynamiques identitaires chez des parents chinois. *Canadian Modern Language Review* 65 (1), 11–31.

da Silva, E. and Heller, M. (2009) From protector to producer: The role of the State in the discursive shift from minority rights to economic development. *Language Policy* 8, 95–116.

de la Dehesa, G. (2007) *What Do We Know About Globalization? Issues of Poverty and Income Distribution.* Malden, MA: Blackwell.

Delgado-Gaitán, C. (2001) *The Power of Community: Mobilizing for Family and Schooling.* Lanham, MD: Rowman & Littlefield.

Dorian, N. (1998) Western language ideologies and small-language prospects. In L. Grenoble and L. Whaley (eds) *Endangered Languages: Language Loss and Community Response* (pp. 3–21). Cambridge: Cambridge University Press.

Dörnyei, Z. (2001) *Motivational Strategies in the Language Classroom.* Cambridge: Cambridge University Press.

Dörnyei, Z. (2005) *The Psychology of the Language Learner: Individual Differences in Second Language Acquisition.* Mahwah, NJ: Erlbaum.

Dreeben, R. (1968) *On What is Learned in School.* Reading, MA: Addison-Wesley.

Dutcher, N. (2004) *Expanding Educational Opportunity in Linguistically Diverse Societies* (2nd edn). Washington, DC: Center for Applied Linguistics. On WWW at http:// www.cal.org/resources/pubs/fordreport_040501.pdf. Accessed 1.8.09.

Edwards, A.D. and Furlong, V. (1978) *The Language of Teaching: Meaning in Classroom Interaction.* London: Heinemann.

Edwards, V. and Newcombe, L.P. (2005) When school is not enough: New initiatives in intergenerational language transmission in Wales. *International Journal of Bilingual Education and Bilingualism* 8 (4), 298–312.

Fishman, J. (1991) *Reversing Language Shift.* Clevedon: Multilingual Matters.

Fitzsimmons-Doolan, S. (2009) Is public discourse about language policy really public discourse about immigration? A corpus-based study. *Language Policy* 8 (4), 377–402.

Freeman, R.D. (1998) *Bilingual Education and Social Change.* Clevedon: Multilingual Matters.

Gal, S. and Irvine, J. (1995) The boundaries of languages and disciplines: How ideologies construct difference. *Social Research* 62 (4), 967–1001.

García, O. (2009) *Bilingual Education in the 21st Century: A Global Perspective.* Malden, MA: Wiley-Blackwell.

Gardner, R. and Lambert, W. (1972) *Attitudes and Motivation in Second Language Learning.* Rowley, MA: Newbury House.

Garza, A. and Crawford, L. (2005) Hegemonic multiculturalism: English immersion, ideology, and subtractive schooling. *Bilingual Research Journal* 29 (3), 599–619.

Giles, H. and Billings, A. (2004) Assessing language attitudes: Speaker evaluation studies. In A. Davies and C. Elder (eds) *The Handbook of Applied Linguistics* (pp. 187–209). Malden, MA: Blackwell.

Giles, H., Bourhis, R. and Taylor, D. (1977) Towards a theory of language in ethnic group relations. In H. Giles (ed.) *Language, Ethnicity, and Intergroup Relations* (pp. 307–348). New York: Academic Press.

Godley, A., Carpenter, B. and Werner, C. (2007) "I'll speak in proper slang": Language ideologies in a daily editing activity. *Reading Research Quarterly* 42 (1), 100–131.

Guilloteaux, M. and Dörnyei, Z. (2008) Motivating language learners: A classroom-oriented investigation of the effects of motivational strategies on student motivation. *TESOL Quarterly* 42 (1), 55–77.

Heath, S.B. (1983) *Ways With Words: Language, Life, and Work in Communities and Classrooms.* Cambridge: Cambridge University Press.

Heath, S.B. (1986) Critical factors in literacy development. In S. deCastell, A. Luke and K. Egan (eds) *Literacy, Society, and Schooling: A Reader* (pp. 209–229). Cambridge: Cambridge University Press.

Heller, M. (2003) Globalization, the new economy, and the commodification of language and identity. *Journal of Sociolinguistics* 4, 473–493.

Hill, J. (1998) "Today there is no respect": Nostalgia, "respect," and oppositional discourse in Mexicano (Nahuatl) language ideology. In B. Shiefflelin, K. Woolard and P. Kroskrity (eds) *Language Ideologies: Practice and Theory* (pp. 68–86). Oxford: Oxford University Press.

Hill, J. (2001) Mock Spanish, covert racism, and the (leaky) boundary between public and private spheres. In S. Gal and K. Woolard (eds) *Languages and Publics: The Making of Authority* (pp. 83–102). Manchester: St. Jerome Publishing.

Holborow, M. (1999) *The Politics of English: A Marxist View of Language.* London: Sage.

Hornberger, N. (1995) Five vowels or three? Linguistics and politics in Quechua language planning in Peru. In J.W. Tollefson (ed.) *Power and Inequality in Language Education* (pp. 187–205). Cambridge: Cambridge University Press.

Hornberger, N. and Hult, F. (2008) Ecological language education policy. In B. Spolsky and F. Hult (eds) *The Handbook of Educational Linguistics* (pp. 280–296). Malden, MA: Blackwell.

Hornberger, N. and Johnson, D.C. (2007) Slicing the onion ethnographically: Layers and spaces in multilingual educational policy and practice. *TESOL Quarterly* 41 (3), 509–532.

Hornberger, N. and Wang, S. (2008) Who are our heritage language learners? Identity and biliteracy in heritage language education in the United States. In D. Brinton, O. Kagan and S. Bauckus (eds) *Heritage Language Education: A New Field Emerging* (pp. 3–35). New York: Routledge.

Jenkins, J. (2007) *English as a Lingua Franca: Attitude and Identity.* Oxford: Oxford University Press.

Johnson, S. and Ensslin, A. (2006) Language in the news: Some reflections on keyword analysis using *Wordsmith Tools* and the BNC. *Leeds Working Papers in Linguistics and Phonetics* 11. On WWW at http://www.leeds.ac.uk/linguistics/WPL/WP2006/5.pdf. Accessed August, 2009.

Jurow, A.S. and Creighton, L. (2005) Improvisational science discourse: Teaching science in two K-1 classrooms. *Linguistics and Education* 16 (3), 275–297.

King, K. (2004) Language policy and local planning in South America: New directions for enrichment bilingual education in the Andes. *International Journal of Bilingual Education and Bilingualism* 7 (5), 334–347.

Kingdon, J. (1995) *Agendas, Alternatives, and Public Policies* (2nd edn). New York: Addison Wesley Longman.

Kormos, J. and Csizér, K. (2008) Age-related differences in the motivation of learning English as a foreign language: Attitudes, selves, and motivated learning behavior. *Language Learning* 58 (2), 327–355.

Kormos, J., Csizér, K., Menyhárt, A. and Török, D. (2008) 'Great expectations': The motivational profile of Hungarian English language students. *Arts & Humanities in Higher Education* 7 (1), 65–82.

Kress, G. and Hodge, R. (1979) *Language as Ideology.* London: Routledge and Kegan Paul. (Second edition published as Hodge and Kress, same title, 1993.)

Kroskrity, P. (1998) Arizona Tewa kiva speech as a manifestation of a dominant language ideology. In B. Schieffelin, K. Woolard and P. Kroskrity (eds) *Language Ideologies: Practice and Theory* (pp. 103–122). Oxford: Oxford University Press.

Kroskrity, P. (2004) Language ideologies. In A. Duranti (ed.) *A Companion to Linguistic Anthropology* (pp. 496–517). Malden, MA: Blackwell.

Lai, M-L. (2005) Language attitudes of the first post-colonial generation in Hong Kong secondary schools. *Language in Society* 34 (3), 363–388.

Lam, W.S.E. (2006) Culture and learning in the context of globalization: Research directions. *Review of Research in Education* 30, 213–237.

Lambert, W. (1972) A social psychology of bilingualism. In A.S. Dil (ed.) *Language, Psychology, and Culture: Essays by Wallace E. Lambert* (pp. 212–235). Stanford, CA: Stanford University Press.

Lambert, W. (1980) An overview of issues in immersion education. In *Studies on Immersion Education: A Collection for United States Educators* (pp. 8–30). Sacramento, CA: California State Department of Education.

Leeman, J. and Martinez, G. (2007) From identity to commodity: Ideologies of Spanish in heritage language textbooks. *Critical Inquiry in Language Studies* 4, 35–65.

Lippi-Green, R. (1997) *English With An Accent: Language, Ideology and Discrimination in the United States.* Routledge: London.

Lippi-Green, R. (2004) Language ideology and language prejudice. In E. Finegan and J. Rickford (eds) *Language in the USA: Themes for the 21st Century* (pp. 289–304). Cambridge: Cambridge University Press.

Luke, A. (2005) Foreword: On the possibilities of a post-colonial language education. In A.M.Y. Lin and P.W. Martin (eds) *Decolonisation, Globalisation: Language-in-Education Policy and Practice* (pp. xiv–xix). Clevedon: Multilingual Matters.

Makoni, S., Brutt-Griffler, J. and Mashiri, P. (2007) The use of "indigenous" and urban vernaculars in Zimbabwe. *Language in Society* 36 (1), 25–49.

Masgoret, A-M. and Gardner, R. (2003) Attitudes, motivation, and second language learning: A meta-analysis of studies conducted by Gardner and associates. *Language Learning* 51 (3), 123–163.

May, S. (2001) *Language and Minority Rights: Ethnicity, Nationalism, and the Politics of Language.* Harlow, Essex: Pearson Education.

McCarty, T. (2002) *A Place to be Navajo: Rough Rock and the Struggle for Self-Determination in Indigenous Schooling.* Mahwah, NJ: Erlbaum.

McGroarty, M. (2008) The political matrix of language ideologies. In B. Spolsky and F. Hult (eds) *The Handbook of Educational Linguistics* (pp. 98–112). Malden, MA: Blackwell.

McGroarty, M. and Scott, S. (1993) Reading, writing, and roles in U.S. adult literacy textbooks. *TESOL Quarterly* 27 (3) 563–573.

McKay, S. and Bokhorst-Heng, W. (2008) *International English in its Sociolinguistic Contexts: Towards a Socially Sensitive EIL Pedagogy.* New York: Routledge.

McLaughlin, D. (1992) *When Literacy Empowers: Navajo Language in Print.* Albuquerque, NM: University of New Mexico Press.

Mermann-Jozwiak, E. and Sullivan, N. (2005) Local knowledge and global citizenship: Languages and literatures of the United States–Mexico borderlands. In S. Canagarajah (ed.) *Reclaiming the Local in Language Policy and Practice* (pp. 269–286). Mahwah, NJ: Erlbaum.

Mortimer, K. (2006) Guaraní académico or Jopará? Educator perspectives and ideological debate in Paraguayan bilingual education. *Working Papers in Educational Linguistics* 21 (2), 45–71.

Niedzielski, N. and Preston, P. (1999) *Folk Linguistics.* Berlin: Mouton de Gruyter.

Nikolov, M. (2000) A study of unsuccessful language learners. In Z. Dörnyei and R. Schmidt (eds) *Motivation and Second Language Acquisition* (pp. 149–169). Honolulu, HI: Second Language Teaching and Curriculum Center, University of Hawai'i at Mañoa.

Niño-Murcia, M., Godenzzi, J.C. and Rothman, J. (2008) Spanish as a world language: The interplay of globalized localization and localized globalization. *International Multilingual Research Journal* 2, 48–66.

Pavlenko, A. (2005) "Ask each pupil about her methods of cleaning": Ideologies of language and gender in Americanisation instruction (1900–1924). *International Journal of Bilingual Education and Bilingualism* 8 (4), 275–297.

Pennycook, A. (1994) *The Cultural Politics of English as an International Language.* London: Longman.

Pennycook, A. (2001) *Critical Applied Linguistics: A Critical Introduction.* Mahwah, NJ: Erlbaum.

Peterson, S.S. and Heywood, D. (2007) Contributions of families' linguistic, social, and cultural capital to minority-language children's literacy: Parents', teachers' and principals' perspectives. *Canadian Modern Language Review* 63 (4), 517–538.

Potowski, K. (2007) *Language and Identity in a Dual Immersion School.* Clevedon: Multilingual Matters.

Preston, D. (2004a) Folk metalanguage. In A. Jaworski, N. Coupland and D. Galasinski (eds) *Metalanguage: Social and Ideological Perspectives* (pp. 75–101). Berlin: Mouton de Gruyter.

Preston, D. (2004b) Language attitudes to speech. In E. Finegan and J. Rickford (eds) *Language in the USA: Themes for the 21st Century* (pp. 480–492). Cambridge: Cambridge University Press.

Queen, R. (2003) Language ideology and political economy among Turkish–German bilinguals in Germany. In B. Joseph, J. De Stefano, N. Jacobs and I. Lehiste (eds) *When Languages Collide* (pp. 201–234). Columbus: The Ohio State University Press.

Ramanathan, V. (2005) *The English–Vernacular Divide: Postcolonial Language Politics and Practice.* Clevedon: Multilingual Matters.

Ramanathan, V. and Morgan, B. (2007) TESOL and policy enactments: Perspectives from practice. *TESOL Quarterly* 41 (3), 447–463.

Rampton, B. (2009) Interaction ritual and not just artful performance in crossing and stylization. *Language in Society* 38 (2), 149–176.

Razfar, A. (2005) Language ideologies in practice: Repair in classroom discourse. *Linguistics and Education* 16, 404–424.

Reese, L. and Goldenberg. C. (2006) Community contexts for literacy development of Latino/a children: Contrasting case studies. *Anthropology and Education Quarterly* 37 (1), 42–61.

Relaño Pastor, A.M. (2008) Competing language ideologies in a bilingual/bicultural after-school program in southern California. *Journal of Latinos in Education* 7, 4–24.

Ricento, T. and Hornberger, N. (1996) Unpeeling the onion: Language planning and policy and the ELT professional. *TESOL Quarterly* 30 (3), 401–427.

Rickford, J. (1999) *African American Vernacular English: Features, Evolution, Educational Implications.* Oxford: Blackwell.

Romero-Little, M.E. (2006) Honoring our own: Rethinking Indigenous languages and literacy. *Anthropology and Education Quarterly* 37 (4), 399–402.

Romero-Little, M.E. and McCarty, T. (2006) Language planning challenges and prospects in Native American communities and schools [EPSL-0602-105-LPRU]. Tempe, AZ: Education Policy Studies Laboratory. On WWW at http://www.

asu.edu/educ/epsl/EPRU/documents/EPSL-0602-105-LPRU.pdf. Accessed 28.7.09.

Rubenfeld, S., Clément, R., Lussier, D., Lebrun, M. and Auger, R. (2006) Second language learning and cultural representations: Beyond competence and identity. *Language Learning* 56 (4), 609–632.

Rupp, G. (2006) *Globalization Challenged: Conviction, Conflict, Community.* New York: Columbia University Press.

Santagata, R. (2004) "Are you joking or are you sleeping?" Cultural beliefs and practices in Italian and U.S. teachers' mistake-handling strategies. *Linguistics and Education* 15 (1–2), 141–164.

Sassen, S. (1998) *Globalization and its Discontents.* New York: The New Press.

Seargeant, P. (2008) Ideologies of English in Japan: The perspective of policy and pedagogy. *Language Policy* 7 (2), 121–142.

Shannon, S.M. (1999) The debate on bilingual education in the U.S.: Language ideology as reflected in the practice of bilingual teachers. In J. Blommaert (ed.) *Language Ideological Debates* (pp. 171–199). Berlin: Mouton de Gruyter.

Shohamy, E. (2006) *Language Policy: Hidden Agendas and New Approaches.* New York: Routledge.

Siegel, J. (2006) Language ideologies and the education of speakers of marginalized language varieties: Adopting a critical awareness approach. *Linguistics and Education* 17, 157–174.

Silverstein, M. (1998) The uses and utility of ideology. In B. Shiefflelin, K. Woolard and P. Kroskrity (eds) *Language Ideologies: Practice and Theory* (pp. 123–145). Oxford: Oxford University Press.

Sinclair, J.M. and Coulthard, R. (1975) *Towards an Analysis of Discourse: The English Used by Teachers and Pupils.* Oxford: Oxford University Press.

Smallwood, B., Haynes, E. and James, K. (2009) *English Language Acquisition and Navajo Achievement in Magdalena, New Mexico.* Washington, DC: Center for Applied Linguistics. On WWW at http://www.cal.org/projects/magdalena_report.pdf. Accessed 5.8.09).

Spolsky, B. (2004) *Language Policy.* Cambridge: Cambridge University Press.

Spolsky, B. (2009) *Language Management.* Cambridge: Cambridge University Press.

Suárez-Orozco, C., Suárez-Orozco, M. and Todorova, I. (2008) *Learning a New Land: Immigrant Students in American Society.* Cambridge, MA: Harvard University Press.

Taki, S. (2008) International and local curricula: The question of ideology. *Language Teaching Research* 12 (1), 127–142.

Valdés, G., González, S., López García, D. and Márquez, P. (2008) Heritage languages and ideologies of language: Unexamined challenges. In D. Brinton, O. Kagan and S. Bauckus (eds) *Heritage Language Education: A New Field Emerging* (pp. 107–130). New York: Routledge.

Volk, D. and Angelova, M. (2007) Language ideology and the mediation of language choice in peer interactions in a dual-language first grade. *Journal of Language, Identity, and Education* 6 (3), 177–199.

Weber, J.J. (2008) Safetalk revisited, or: Language and ideology in Luxembourgish educational policy. *Language and Education* 22 (2), 155–169.

Wiley, T. (2004) Language planning, language policy, and the English-Only Movement. In E. Finegan and J. Rickford (eds) *Language in the USA: Themes for the 21st Century* (pp. 319–338). Cambridge: Cambridge University Press.

Wiley, T. and Lukes, M. (1996) English-only and standard English ideologies in the US. *TESOL Quarterly* 30 (3), 511–535.

Williams, S.I. (2002) Ojibway hockey CD-ROM in the making. In B. Burnaby and J. Reyhner (eds) *Indigenous Languages Across the Community* (pp. 219–224). Flagstaff, AZ: Center for Excellence in Education, Northern Arizona University.

Winer, L. (2007) No ESL in English schools: Language policy in Quebec and implications for TESL teacher education. *TESOL Quarterly* 41 (3), 489–508.

Woolard, K. and Schieffelin, B. (1994) Language ideology. *Annual Review of Anthropology* 23, 55–82.

Zentella, A.C. (ed.) (2005) *Building on Strength: Language and Literacy in Latino Families and Communities.* New York: Teachers College Press.

Zhou, M. and Bankston, C. (1998) *Growing up American: How Vietnamese Children Adapt to Life in the United States.* New York: Russell Sage Foundation.

Chapter 2

Language, Power and Pedagogies

HILARY JANKS

Overview

In one classroom concerned with language and power, you might see students redesigning a sexist advertisement, and in another one, constructing a linguistic profile of the class or figuring out how the word *perhaps* changes the meaning of a statement. Students might be calculating their own ecological footprints after watching Gore's *An Inconvenient Truth* or discussing how to address the problem of bullying in their grade. Underpinning the work in these different classrooms are different approaches towards teaching students the relationship between language and power; language, identity and difference; language and the differential access to social goods. This sociocultural approach to language education is referred to by different names: critical literacy (Freire, 1972a, 1972b), critical linguistics (Fowler & Kress, 1979), critical language awareness (Clark *et al.*, 1987; Fairclough, 1992), and critical applied linguistics (Pennycook, 2001), New Literacy Studies (Barton & Hamilton, 1998; Barton *et al.*, 2000; Street, 1984), multiliteracies (Cope & Kalantzis, 2000), or multimodal literacies (Kress, 2003). These moments embody the history of the field, with critical literacy being the most generic of the terms to describe it. Critical literacy resists definition because power manifests itself differently in different contexts and at different historical moments; it is affected by changing technologies and different conditions of possibility. What remain constant, however, is its social justice agenda and its commitment to social action, however small it be, that makes a difference.

Many teachers fear critical literacy because they think of it as too political. In thinking about power and politics, it is important to draw a distinction between *Politics* with a big *P* and *politics* with a small *p*.[1] Politics with a capital *P* is the big stuff, worldly concerns. It is about government and world trade agreements and the United Nations peace-keeping forces; it is about ethnic or religious genocide and world tribunals; it is about apartheid and global capitalism, money laundering and linguistic imperialism.

It is about the inequities between the political North and the political South. (I use these terms to contest the terminology of 'first world' and 'third world', which ignores the colonial politics that produced disparities between countries in the northern and southern hemispheres). It is about oil, the ozone layer, genetic engineering and cloning. It is about the danger of global warming. It is about globalisation, the new work order (Gee *et al.*, 1996) and sweatshops in Asia (Klein, 1999).

Little-*p* politics, on the other hand, is about the micro-politics of everyday life. It is about the minute-by-minute choices and decisions that make us who we are. It is about desire and fear; how we construct them and how they construct us. It is about the politics of identity and place; it is about small triumphs and defeats; it is about winners and losers, haves and have-nots, homophobes and their victims; it is about how we treat other people day by day; it is about whether or not we learn someone else's language or act to save the planet by recycling our garbage. Little-*p* politics is about taking seriously the feminist perspective that the personal *is* the political. This is not to suggest that *politics* has nothing to do with *Politics*. On the contrary, the sociohistorical and economic contexts in which we live produce different conditions of possibility and constraints that we all have to negotiate as meaningfully as we can. While the social constructs who we are, so do we construct the social. This reciprocal relationship is fluid and dynamic, creating possibilities for social action and change. Working with the politics of the local enables us to effect small changes that make a difference in our everyday lives and those of the people around us.

Because it is tied to the politics of the local, critical literacy has to remain fluid, dynamic, responsive to change. This does not mean that the field is not constructed by its history. What this chapter will show is how the history of the field has created a 'repertoire' of practices (Comber, 2006: 54) that teachers can adapt to the ever changing circumstances in which they work. The next section considers the theoretical formation of critical literacy over time and the kinds of classroom work that the shifts in theory have made possible.

Research: A History of Theorised Practice

Critical literacy is more a set of theorised practices that constitute a pedagogy than an approach to research or a set of research methods. The theories that inform this approach see language and literacy as social practices that produce effects. This section will look at the theoretical work in the field as well as selected examples from research in classrooms that show the enactment of these theories. Most of this research is school- or classroom-based and uses qualitative research methods from ethnography, action research, case-study research and classroom observation. For ease of discussion, I have divided the development of the field into four moments: critical literacy, critical linguistics, multiliteracies, literacy and space.

A History of Theory and Practice

Critical literacy: Reading the word and the world

Paulo Freire was the first to challenge our assumptions about literacy as simply teaching students the skills necessary for reading and he helps us to understand that reading the word cannot be separated from reading the world. His two seminal books, *Cultural Action for Freedom* (1972a) and *Pedagogy of the Oppressed* (1972b), show how in the process of learning how to read both the *word* and the *world* critically, adult literacy learners regain their sense of themselves as agents who can act to transform the social situations in which they find themselves. He used literacy as a means of breaking the 'culture of silence' of the poor and dispossessed. For Freire

> To exist, humanly, is to *name* the world, to change it. Once named, the world in its turn reappears to its namers as a problem and requires of them a new *naming*. Men are not built in silence, but in word, in work, in action-reflection. ... It is in speaking their word that men transform the world by naming it, dialogue imposes itself as the way in which men achieve significance as men. (Freire, 1972b: 61, italics in the original)

Recognising that a situation is less than ideal and naming what is wrong as a problem are the first step in transformative social action. Freire's approach to literacy as social action is based on neo-marxist views of power as relations of domination and oppression that are maintained by either coercion or consent (Gramsci, 1971).

Many teachers in North America such as Elsa Auerbach, Linda Christenson, Carole Edelsky, Brian Morgan and Jerome Harste have built their critical literacy practices on the work of Freire. Vivian Vasquez shows with great clarity how it is possible to create a critical literacy curriculum out of the issues and problems that emerge spontaneously in classrooms (Vasquez, 2004). Vasquez's skill is in taking her students' everyday concerns seriously and helping them to 'name' them as problems in order to imagine possible courses of enquiry and action. She also has the ability to stay with a topic and to explore it from a number of different angles, following the suggestions made by the students. For example, when her students expressed concern that Anthony, one of their classmates, was unable to eat the hot dogs and burgers at the school barbecue because he is a vegetarian, Vasquez used this as an opportunity to problematise exclusionary practices. They began by reading the flyer announcing the barbecue with a critical eye. 'Join us for our Annual School Barbeque' is the first line of the flyer. Melanie, one of the students, says:

> The invitation says *our* but doesn't really mean Anthony so it's yours and mine (pointing to the other children who are not vegetarian and herself) but not his (pointing to Anthony) and that's not fair. (Vasquez, 2004: 104)

She was able to do this because Vasquez had spent time in previous lessons discussing with the students how pronouns can work to include and exclude people. The students agreed that one of the girls would write a letter to the chair of the barbecue committee, which she did after consulting with other children on the wording. They chose to use the pronoun 'we' and imperatives like 'have to' to state their case strongly: that in future there should be food that vegetarians can eat. When they received no reply, they re-read their letter to see if they should change the wording in a more polite follow-up letter. This time the chair replied and invited them to come and talk to her about the matter.

The students decided to read up about vegetarianism in order to prepare for the meeting, only to discover that there were no books about vegetarians in the library. Undaunted they wrote to the librarian to say that all children should be able to find books about people like them in the library. By allowing the problem to run its course, Vasquez teaches her students to follow an issue to its resolution. When they finally received assurances that their school would cater to the dietary needs of vegetarians at future functions, one child wondered if other schools could benefit from their experience. This led the students to conduct a survey to see if neighbouring schools catered to the needs of *their* vegetarian students.

Notice how much purposeful reading and writing, initiated by the students themselves, are taking place. Notice how students learn to pay attention to words and to deal with setbacks. Notice how Vasquez constructs her students as agents of change on a bigger platform than the specific needs of Anthony. This is not difficult for teachers to do. After all, Vasquez did it with a class of 4-year-olds and she is not alone.

This kind of close attention to language is also evident when Helen Grant (1999) works with students who are newly arrived immigrants in Australia, learning English for the first time. She teaches English as an additional language to Grades 1 through 7 at an elementary school and also withdraws groups for more focused interventions. Her success in using critical language awareness with these students shows that children whose main language is not English can work with and question the use of language and the concepts language signifies. One telling example is the students' response to working with Janks' notion of 'top dogs' and 'underdogs' in the *Critical Language Awareness Series* (Janks, 1993a).

In Janks' workbook activity (Janks, 1993b: 12) children are asked the following questions.

(1) Given that you have many different identities, in which of your identities do you feel like a top dog?
(2) In which identities do you feel like an underdog?
(3) Who is top dog in your family in most situations?
(4) Name a situation in which someone else is top dog?
(5) Among your friends, is there competition to be top dog?
(6) In your school, how do students become top dogs?
(7) In your school, how do teachers become top dogs?
(8) How do the top dogs you know treat the underdogs?
(9) How do the top dogs you know talk to the underdogs?

Grant found that this activity helped students to think about power relations in their own lives but was particularly taken by some of the children's arguments that they were neither top dogs nor underdogs. Together the class developed the notion of 'middle dogs'. What these young children are successfully able to do is challenge the false binary set up in this activity and to question the authority of both the teacher and the classroom materials.

Another example of Freirean social action can be seen in the classroom of Marg Wells, also a teacher in Australia. Wells encouraged her students to do a survey of the trees in the neighbourhood of the school, after they noticed that poorer suburbs seemed to have fewer parks and trees. Recognising trees as a marker of social class is perhaps not remarkable, except when the researchers are in Grade 2/3 (Comber *et al.*, 2001). Wells' students reported their findings to the local authorities, who agreed to plant more trees in these suburbs. She and her students later went on to make suggestions as to what kind of park the local developers should build, contributing design ideas and their own art works.

In all these examples of literacy as social action, we see students reading texts to see how they are positioned and positioning, naming their world, writing letters, taking care to establish their authority and to use words so as to position the reader to respond favourably, conducting surveys, and working with developers to put their own stamp on a local park. All these literacy practices contribute to solving a problem that the students identified and preparing them for socially responsible active citizenship.

Linguistic approaches to critical literacy: Critical linguistics, critical discourse analysis, critical language awareness and critical applied linguistics

What the approaches to the field discussed in this section share is a profound understanding of and respect for the power of words. 'Power' is signalled by the use of the word *critical*. *Critical linguistics* focuses on linguistic choices in speech and writing and their effects; *critical discourse analysis* focuses on how these choices are affected by the processes and the social conditions in which texts are received and produced; *critical language awareness* is a classroom application of these theories to teaching and *critical applied linguistics* questions the normative assumptions of the whole applied field of linguistics as well as the consequences of these assumptions. Each of these approaches is discussed in more detail in what follows.

Rooted in an understanding of grammar and lexis, these approaches have been developed by linguists. The old adage that 'sticks and stones may break our bones, but words can never harm us' is simply not true. Halliday (1985) sees grammar and words as 'meaning potential'. In selecting from the range of possible options when we speak or write, we realise that potential for good or ill. Although Saussure argues that the (linguistic) sign is arbitrary (Saussure, 1972: 67), which sign we select is always motivated. According to the *Truth and Reconciliation Commission of South Africa Report*, which investigated crimes against humanity during the time of apartheid and the liberation struggle,

> Language ... does things: it constructs social categories, it gives orders, it persuades us, it justifies, explains, gives reasons, excuses. It constructs reality. It moves people against other people. (TRC, 1998: 7, 124, 294)

This is another way of describing the power of naming. In calling themselves *pro-life*, the anti-abortion lobby constructs people who support abortion as pro-death; in naming our enemies as *the axis of evil*, we assume the moral high ground; in calling foreign Africans *Makwerekwere*,[2] as is the case in South Africa, we foment xenophobia; in calling genocide, *ethnic cleansing*, we name killing as hygiene. In all these cases language is being used to create divisive social categories by naming them in particular ways.

When people use language to speak or write, they constantly have to make choices. Not only do they have to decide what words to use, they have to decide whether to be definite or tentative, approving or disapproving, inclusive or exclusive. They have to choose between the present, the past and the future tense; between quoted and reported speech; between active or passive voice. Multilingual speakers have to decide which of their languages to use, when and with whom. For example, the choice of the present continuous tense in 'Rising temperatures *are causing* climate change' is more authoritative than 'Temperatures *may be rising* and *may be causing* climate change' because the modals 'can' and 'may' introduce uncertainty. In addition, the choice of the continuous tense suggests that the process is ongoing. The choice of active voice requires that we show who is doing the action as in 'Soldiers *tortured* prisoners'. The passive voice allows us to hide who is responsible for the action as in 'Prisoners *were tortured'*.

All spoken and written texts are assembled by an ongoing process of selection from a range of lexical, grammatical and sequencing options. Because texts are put together, they can be taken apart. This unmaking of the text increases our awareness of the choices that the writer or speaker has made. Every choice foregrounds what was selected and hides or backgrounds what was not selected. Awareness of these choices enables us to ask critical questions: Why did the writer or speaker make these choices? How do these choices work to position the readers or listeners? Whose interests do they serve? Who benefits? Who is disadvantaged? Critical linguists pay attention to the way in which reality is mediated by language; to the ways in which speakers and writers use language to construct the texts that represent their versions of reality. Choices do not, however, produce meaning divorced from context and our choices are shaped by the ways of speaking, writing, believing, doing and valuing of the communities we live in (Gee, 1990: 142). These ways with language are called discourses and critical discourse analysis requires that we analyse texts in relation to their processes and conditions of production and reception (Fairclough, 1989). In other words, critical discourse analysts are interested in how texts are affected by what meanings are possible for their writers and readers, in particular places, at particular times.

The writers of the *Critical Language Awareness Series* (Janks, 1993a) use a critical linguistic approach for reading against texts. Their use of call-outs, otherwise known as speech bubbles, helps to zoom in on particular linguistic choices. This can be illustrated with questions on an article taken from *SL* magazine's tongue-in-cheek guide to cars for students (see Figure 2.1). *SL* stands for student life, and it is important that this refers to student life in South Africa. The ability to answer the questions on this text depends on cultural knowledge that learners in other contexts may not have.

Why, one might ask, should one spend time with students looking at this text critically? It is after all an informative, playful, everyday text. It is precisely because seemingly innocuous, every-day texts work to produce us as particular kinds of human subjects, that we need to examine their underlying values and assumptions. Claiming that we are what we drive is itself a questionable assumption. Moreover, the Palio text naturalises consumerism, materialism and ostentation. In conjunction, the description of the Tazz undermines 'being sensible' by portraying it as boring. By suggesting that long-term relationships, which one can expect with a reliable Tazz, are 'not such a bad thing', it damns them with faint praise.

Writers of the Chalkface Press workbooks (Mellor & Patterson, 1996; Mellor *et al.*, 1991) use a feminist post-structuralist approach to critical analysis and they work mainly with literary texts. They also hone in on the

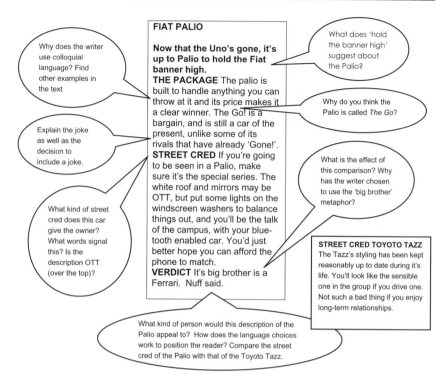

The palio is built to handle anything you can throw at it and its price makes it a clear winner. The Go! is a bargain, and is still a car of the present, unlike some of its rivals that have already 'Gone!'.
STREET CRED If you're going to be seen in a Palio, make sure it's the special series. The white roof and mirrors may be OTT, but put some lights on the windscreen washers to balance things out, and you'll be the talk of the campus, with your blue-tooth enabled car. You'd just better hope you can afford the phone to match.
VERDICT It's big brother is a Ferrari. Nuff said.

Figure 2.1 Asking critical questions using call-outs

ways in which verbal meaning is communicated. The activities help students to unpack the social construction of difference in relation to race, gender and class. Teachers in the United States working with Vivian Vasquez have developed strategies for reading children's literature critically (Vasquez *et al.*, 2003). Martino (1997) and Kenworthy and Kenworthy (1997) have used post-colonial theory to deconstruct the construction of aboriginal Australians and 'white fella' new Australians. Particularly important is Wallace's (2003) account of teaching critical reading, which addresses the question of what it means to be a critical reader in an additional language.

Pennycook's (2001) work, *Critical Applied Linguistics*, problematises the field of Applied Linguistics itself by examining its truth effects. In doing so, he reminds us that the global spread of English began as an imposition on local populations through the political and military dominance of Britain and the United States. He sees it historically as a colonising language that diminishes the power of national and local languages and others their speakers. Focusing on the cultural politics of English as an international language, Pennycook invites us to think of how this might translate into different approaches to teaching English as an additional language. In South Africa, we use the terminology of 'additional language' precisely to refuse the othering discourse implied in TESOL, teaching English to speakers of *othered* languages. His work demonstrates Foucault's contention that

> 'Truth' is to be understood as a system of ordered procedures for the production, regulation, distribution, circulation and operation of statements. [It] is linked in a circular relation with systems of power which produce and sustain it, and to effects of power which it induces and which extend it. (Foucault, 1980: 133)

According to Bourdieu (1991), the education system is the key means for the privileging of a particular language (or variety) and for legitimating its dominance. He draws attention to the fact that while the education system fails to provide students from subordinated classes with *knowledge of* and *access to* the legitimate language, it succeeds in teaching them *recognition of* (misrecognition of) its legitimacy (Bourdieu, 1991: 62, my emphasis). What is needed, in the teaching of a powerful language like English, is classroom pedagogy that reverses this – that gives mastery of English, together with a critical view of its status. Education needs to produce students who understand why linguistic diversity is a resource for creativity and cognition, who value all the languages that they speak and who recognise the paucity of English only. In addition, 'ESL' teachers have to take the identity issues that inform decisions about the teaching of pronunciation and appropriateness seriously. Is it our job as English teachers to turn learners into cultural clones, or should we encourage them to use their own cultural norms for turn-taking, politeness, formality? Whose norms should prevail in cross-cultural communication? These questions ask us to rethink communicative competence and the communicative approach to language teaching.

Janet Orlek put the question of the unequal status of different languages and different varieties of the same language at the heart of her workbook in the *Critical Language Awareness Series* (Orlek, 1993). She begins with activities that establish multilingualism as the norm followed by an exploration of the relationship between language and identity. She goes on to explore the spread of English in the world and the relationship between English and languages in the learners' own country, in this instance South Africa. Her activity on world Englishes works to de-stabilise both a unitary and a normative view of English. Finally, she invites students to find out about their country's language policy and language-in-education policy and to interrogate them.

The first activity on multilingualism asks students to talk to one another about their own names. Immediately, this surfaces cross-cultural naming practices and shows students how their names relate to their family's history and values. Having names in more than one language speaks of communities that have been dispossessed or displaced and of parents who have therefore given their children names to remind them of who they are and where they come from as well as a name in whatever happens to be the language of power at the time. This multilingual naming practice literally entitles these children to hybrid identities. The relationship between naming practices and power has been evident in South Africa in the decade since the advent of democracy. In the past, many African parents gave their children English and African names. Most of my university students chose to use their English names. Now, after liberation, the students use their African names and place the onus on English speakers to pronounce them correctly. Another example can be found in the poignant poem, *School Visit*, by Michael Rosen (1992). He tells the story of a young student named Patricia Kaufpisch (Sellpiss) and his own distress at the names given to Jews in Nazi Germany. Jews who could not afford to buy a pretty name like Rosenthal (Valley-of-the-roses) were given names such as 'Ochsenschwantz, Eselkkopf, Saumagen and Hinkedigger: Oxprick, Asshead, Pigbelly and Cripple' (p. 21). He wonders whether or not Patricia Kaufpisch knows what her name means and he concludes the poem by saying

... if I could talk to her on her own, I could tell her

But she is saying, Goodbye thank you for talking to us,

Mr Rosen.

Rosen? It means roses.

So? I was one of the lucky ones.

(Rosen, 1992: 21)

Another activity requires students to work out the linguistic repertoire of their class and to discuss the relative positions of the class' languages in hierarchies of power. Orlek's activities on English in the world contest the notion of a pure language and argue that the spread of English has led to the growth of many Englishes, which compete for power with standard British or American English in different contexts. Students are given guidance on how to investigate the history of English in their own country and how to interrogate existing language policies and the practices that arise from them.

Multimodal critical literacy

While a critical applied linguistics approach to critical literacy questions the discursive practices of applied linguistics itself, the multiliteracies

(Cope & Kalantzis, 2000) approach to literacy asks us to re-examine mean-ing-making in an age of the visual sign. Kress' work on multimodality (Kress, 2003) argues that the verbal is just one of many modalities for making meaning and that it has been privileged in the teaching of literacy. New digital technologies have changed the processes of text production; desktop computers have made it easy to include images, movement, sound, spatiality, gesture. To be literate now requires us to read across a range of modes and to understand the effects of their interplay when they work in concert. Multimodality presents a difficult challenge for critical work as different modes have different ways of naturalising their representations. Photography, for example, is a realistic medium and we have to remind ourselves that cameras do lie, particularly in an age of digital morphing. The work of Kress and van Leeuwen (1990, 2001) has led the way in pro-viding strategies for reading images critically.

One's ability to read texts produced with new digital technologies is easier if one has hands-on experience with these technologies. In Australia, Helen Grant uses film-making as a means of teaching English and multimodal literacies to recently arrived immigrant and refugee children (Comber, 2006). Decisions about what stories to tell in their films, and how to construct these stories semiotically, led students to explore the politics of representation. Like Moll (1992), Grant encourages her students to draw on their linguistic and cultural funds of knowledge. Her aim is to counteract negative representations of immigrants in the media; in the process her students acquire the kind of critical multimodal literacy that enables them to read against media texts and to construct alternative discourses.

Not all teachers have the know-how or the equipment to make videos with students. Fortunately, a great deal can be done just with printed images and they can be found everywhere. Students can bring images from newspapers and magazines to class. They can use disposable cam-eras and photograph visual texts on the street. They can collect and anal-yse food packaging. There are many activities that help students to de-construct visual texts. One can literally cut them up to show the effects of cropping (see Figure 2.2); one can juxtapose them to see how their meaning changes when they are placed alongside other texts; one can remove either the background or the foreground to see the effect this has on meaning (see Figure 2.2); one can compare visuals for the identical product marketed to different audiences; one can ask students to compare their own homes or bedrooms with those depicted in décor magazines; one can study the images in advertisements to pinpoint how they create desire in readers; one can compare images of sportsmen and sports women; one can compare representations historically by looking at repre-sentations of a single product, for example Coca Cola, over time.

Figure 2.2 The effects of cropping. *The Star*, 15 July 2008, front page

In Figure 2.2, the effect of cropping is startling. Figure 2.2a was what I saw first because Oscar Pistorius' legs were hidden by the fold in the newspaper that can be seen in Figure 2.2b. In Figure 2.3, the unexpected context is key to the message. Figure 2.3b is an image used to advertise Cell C, a mobile phone service provider. The accompanying text, 'Surprise someone with a song (but make sure you send it to the right address)' makes it clear that this image is a visual metaphor for what happens if you send the song to the wrong address.

In using these examples with a class, one would present Figure 2.3a for discussion before Figure 2.3b. A more complex example of staging the presentation of a single text is given in Figure 2.4. Here you literally take the image apart and feed it bit by bit to the students so that they come to understand how the bits mean something different from the whole.

One's reading of the meaning changes as one sees more and more of the text. Initially one interprets the word 'nigger' in isolation as signalling a

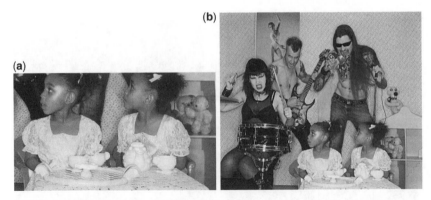

Figure 2.3 (a) Where are these girls? What's happening? What could be being advertised? (b) How does the context change the meaning? What could be being advertised? *SL*[3] November 2004, back cover

racist text. Only later is one able to understand that the word has been chosen to oppose racist assumptions. The journalists are deliberately writing back to old discourses and giving them new meaning. In this context 'trouble' for the insurance industry is good for 'the economy, policyholders and companies' according to the subheading of the article, which welcomes the shake-up instigated by Vuyani Ngalwana (*Financial Mail*, 5 August 2005, Johannesburg).

Pippa Stein's (2008) *Multimodal Pedagogies in Diverse Classrooms* provides countless examples of classroom practice. In her story-telling project in Spruitview with students aged 12–16, Stein demonstrates the power of harnessing students' semiotic resources across a range of languages and a range of modalities. Students tell their stories to the class in their home language, they write them and translate them into English, and they draw them. Stein's presentation of the stories and her analysis of them give her readers a clear understanding of the power of this approach to teaching

Figure 2.4 The staging of text[4]

literacy. Lungile is a 13-year-old girl from a Zulu-speaking family in a Spruitview primary school, which draws children from nearby African townships. In her analysis of Lungile's performance of her story, Stein demonstrates how Lungile draws on 'resources of spoken language, space, gesture, narrative and vocalization ... ways of saying, doing and being that she has learnt in her community' (Stein, 2008: 58). Stein's analysis constantly returns to the question of power and how identities are constituted in these practices. She shows how Lungile is 'doing gender in her performance as she behaves in accordance with cultural norms of femaleness' (Stein, 2008: 60). Stein's account of the Olifantsvlei *Fresh Stories Project* in which she explores the practices of eight children in making fertility dolls, playing with them and writing about them, is no less compelling.

Pahl and Rowsell's (2006) *Travel Notes from the New Literacy Studies* sits at the interface between New Literacy Studies (Barton *et al.*, 2000; Gee, 1990; Street, 1984) and multimodality. It includes studies of young children's digital literacy practices at home, an adolescent's email correspondence on the subject of rap, Wiccan websites, weblogs, alphabet books produced by children in different contexts, de Bono's 'thinking hats' as represented on the internet and in classrooms. Here we see the importance of and the challenge for critical literacy in a digital world, where students who are connected can enter new spaces and use their literacies to communicate with real audiences in an entirely new landscape of local, global and virtual communities.

Space and place in critical literacy

The content of *Travel Notes in the New Literacy Studies* resulted in the inclusion of 10 references to space in the previous paragraph, not least of which is the travel metaphor in the title of the book:

> ... literacy practices *at home* ... Wiccan *websites* ... produced by children in different contexts ... on the internet ... and *in classrooms. Here* ... in a *digital world, where* students ... can *enter new spaces* ... in an entirely *new landscape* ... of *local, global and virtual* communities.

Lefebvre (1991a, 1991b) asks us to recognise that just as everything occurs in time, everything also occurs in space and that this is a vital part of our lived experience. Sociality occurs in space (Lefebvre, 1991a). Where many cultural geographers use the word 'place', Lefebvre captures the concreteness, the immediacy and the cultural attachments to place in his combined use of 'everyday life' and 'lived space' (Soja, 1996: 40). Views of literacy as a social practice have to pay attention to both time and space.

This is exemplified in Dixon's (2007) examination of the relationship between literacy, power and the embodied learner in early schooling. Dixon's focus on the body led to a careful examination of how children's bodies are managed by literacy routines and their organisation in time and space. The study, which builds on the work of Leander and Sheehy (2004) on literacy and space, is situated in five literacy classrooms: Grade 00 and Grades 1–3. It tracks the way learners' bodies are increasingly regulated as they move into and through the early years of schooling. In the pre-school (Grade 00), children have greater freedom to choose the activities they wish to engage in and to move across the spaces of the classroom – shared work tables, the book corner and the carpet. Opportunities are created for exploratory and pleasurable reading and writing, both communal and individual. This shifts in the early years of a typical South African elementary school (Grades 1–3) where young learners are expected to be individual, silent, on-task readers, confined to their desks and regulated by the bells that control school time. As Dixon's analysis shows, the classroom is only one kind of confining space within schools where space and time are deployed as disciplinary technologies for the containment and regulation of children and their bodies.

An outstanding example of classroom practice that works critically with spatial literacies, 'ways of thinking about and representing the production of space' (Comber *et al.*, 2006: 228), is the collaborative project *Urban renewal from the inside out*. Staff and students in the fields of literacy education, architecture, communication and journalism at the University of South Australia worked with Marg Wells, a Grade 3/4 teacher, and a Grade 5/6 teacher, Ruth Trimboli, to provide students with the conceptual resources and skills needed to redesign an unused, uncared for, and unnamed space in the school grounds. Building on Wells' work on neighbourhood action, discussed earlier, this project asked students to create 'a belonging space' based on their own re-visioning of lived school space.

In their discussion of this dynamic and multi-layered school project, Comber *et al.* locate their work in all of the approaches to critical literacy discussed: Freirean reading of the world; access to new discourses; the acquisition of the linguistic vocabularies and design discourses necessary for the critical analysis of designs and for participation in design decisions; an ability to work with a wide range of semiotic resources for designing and redesigning space. The students needed to assemble a range of resources in order to participate in the production, not just the consumption, of their lived space.

Research Findings

This survey of both the theoretical literature that underpins critical approaches to literacy and the research on critical literacy as practised in classrooms shows that the history of the field provides an ever-growing repertoire for practice. Although theory is a contested site, and new theories challenge and even displace earlier ones, yet the ongoing addition of new dimensions to literacy, new understandings of power, new semiotic grammars, and new forms of analysis serve to increase the possibilities for critical literacy work. In relation to pedagogy, the history of ideas continues into the present, offering a number of ways of enabling students to become critically literate.

In developing her notion of a critical repertoire for teachers, Comber documents the work of practising teachers, including Helen Grant, who she argues have a 'critical habitus' (2006: 51). According to Bourdieu, habitus is our ingrained, unconscious, embodied ways of being. This concept was popularised by Gee (1990: 142) in his definition of discourse as 'speaking(writing)–doing–being–valuing–believing combinations'. The discourses we inhabit produce us as particular kinds of human subjects and they are profoundly tied up with our identities. This is as true for students as it is for teachers. Taking on new literacies, new ways of doing, valuing and believing, in essence new ways of naming the world, often threatens our identity investments. It also constitutes a challenge to taken-for-granted social relations, practices and institutions that work to maintain existing relations of power. In this way, education can work to disrupt the micro politics of everyday life that serve the interests of those who are powerful.

Janks (2000) has argued that a critical literacy education has to take seriously the ways in which meaning systems are implicated in reproducing relations of power and it has to provide access to dominant languages and literacies while simultaneously using diversity as a productive resource for redesigning social futures and for changing the 'horizon of possibility' (Simon, 1992). This includes both changing dominant discourses as well as changing which discourses are dominant. Any one of power, diversity, access or design/redesign without the others creates a problematic imbalance. Views of language acquisition that negate creativity work to bolster the variety of native speakers; deconstruction without reconstruction or redesign reduces human agency; diversity without access ghettoises students. Without difference and diversity we lose the alternative points of view that rupture the taken-for-granted and enable us to challenge the status quo. The need for change motivates redesign. Each redesign is a renaming of the world and this brings us back full circle to the work of Paulo Freire (see Figure 2.5).

Relevance for Classroom Practice

In describing the critical literacy teachers whose work in classrooms she admires, Comber (2006) suggests that they have both a 'critical habitus' and a 'critical repertoire'. The repertoire is given its critical edge when it is put to work to produce a more just society. Critical literacy educators teach their students both how to engage with the ways in which meaning is produced and how to resist meanings that benefit some at the expense

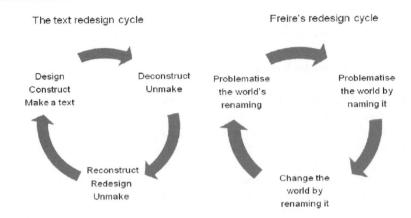

Figure 2.5 The redesign cycle

of others. In their classrooms, reading, writing and designing are put to work to make a difference by being linked to ways of being, doing and valuing that serve the interests of all.

Conclusion

This chapter has suggested ways of working critically with both the consumption and the production of meaning by tracing the evolution of pedagogies that enable students to understand the little-p, big-P, politics of meaning. As an example of little-p politics, Figure 2.6 provides some of the linguistic options from which we can choose when asking someone to do the household chores. Differences in power, between a speaker and the person spoken to, affect decisions on how direct or indirect to be. When we speak to people with more power, we tend to be more hesitant, more indirect, less sure.

1. You don't seem to have cleaned the kitchen yet.
2. When do you plan to clean the kitchen?
3. You must clean the kitchen.
4. This place is really dirty.
5. Why haven't you cleaned the kitchen?
6. How many times must I remind you to clean the kitchen?
7. Can you grab a dust rag and just clean around?
8. You should have time to clean before you go.
9. I'm sure you wouldn't mind cleaning around the kitchen.
10. Please will you clean the kitchen.
11. Isn't it your turn to clean?
12. Is it your turn to clean?
13. Didn't you ask me to remind you to clean the kitchen?
14. You're supposed to help me to keep this place clean.
15. It's your turn to clean.

Figure 2.6 Indirect requests (adapted from Janks, 1993a: 14)

The choice of mode (statement, question or command), the choice of speech act (suggestion, request, hint, instruction), the choice of tense or modality (*seemed, supposed, I'm sure*), as well as the choice of positive and negative constructions (*Is it your turn? Isn't it your turn?*), are all tied to the amount of authority one can command in any situation. What is interesting is that we make all these choices in the blink of an eye without even consciously thinking about them based on our reading of the social situation. Often our choices are based on our raced, classed or gendered positions and they naturalise normative expectations for behaviour in the communities we inhabit. By becoming aware of the positions we take up unconsciously, we can choose to construct more empowered positions from which to speak in order to challenge these norms. In everyday life, in the realm of little-*p* politics, the language choices we make matter. They matter practically in that strategic choices can help us to get things done (like getting the kitchen cleaned); they matter psychologically in that the positions we do and do not take up ultimately construct our sense of self and of others. The same principle is at work in the larger realm of big-*P* Politics.

Lakoff (2004), a politically progressive linguist and cognitive scientist, shows how the way we frame our world affects our ways of doing, believing and valuing. For example, George W. Bush's White House chose to frame 'tax cuts' as 'tax relief'.

> Think of the framing for *relief*. For there to be relief there must be an affliction, an afflicted party, and a reliever who removes the affliction and is therefore a hero. And if people try to stop the hero, those people are villains for trying to prevent relief. (Lakoff, 2004: 3)

Lakoff explains that

> Frames are mental structures that shape the way we see the world. As a result they shape the goals we seek, the plans we make, the way we act, and what counts as good or bad outcomes of our actions. In politics our frames shape our social policies. To change our frames is to change all of this. ... Reframing is changing the way the public sees the world. It is changing what counts as common sense. Because language activates frames, new language is required for new frames. Thinking differently requires speaking differently. (xv)

In his book, *The Audacity of Hope*, this is exactly what Barack Obama (2006) did. He provided a new frame of 'hope' that invited his fellow Americans into a different worldview: one of cooperation rather than competition; a view of the United States as not red or blue, but as united; a world in which one can disagree without being disagreeable; of a country where ordinary people, not just wealthy people, can make change happen; a world in which diplomacy, rather than war, is the preferred solution to conflict. This new framing is tied, as Lakoff suggests, to new social policies and to a different way of doing Politics, with a capital *P*.

In a globally connected world, frames travel. Adegoke's (1999) research demonstrates how negative ways of talking about Africa in the world media become the norm. In so doing, they provide journalists with unconscious resources to draw on when they write about Africa, so that even the South Africa press reproduces these frames. This is the way in which discourses shape what and how we think. We pick them up unconsciously and they speak through us. Bigelow and Peterson (2002) raise many of the issues for teaching justice in an unjust (globalised) world as does Klein (1999, 2007).

Underlying all of this work is the need to produce fully literate human subjects who can manipulate symbols, read critically and think for themselves. The new brain research makes it clear that reading is not innate.

> Reading can only be learned because of the brain's plastic design, and when reading takes place, that individual brain is changed forever, both physiologically and intellectually. (Wolf, 2007: 5)

In learning to read, the brain's plasticity enables new neural pathways to establish themselves. These pathways have to be developed to the point where processing text is so fast that readers have enough time to reflect on what they are reading while they are reading. The sustained reading of a book is different from the ways in which readers scroll through and read digital texts. Because, as yet, we do not know what new pathways for reading these new practices will develop, Wolf (2007) argues that we should not allow the new reading pathways to replace the existing pathways for reading; rather they need to be established *in addition* to the old pathways. Her book, subtitled *The Story and Science of the Reading Brain*, helps us to understand that in teaching our brains to read we changed the intellectual evolution of our species. New developments in cognitive neuro-science should not be ignored by social practice theories of literacy. Similarly, reading occurs in social contexts and has social effects. Science alone is not enough.

Notes

1. I am indebted to Barbara Kamler for this distinction, which emerged in a conversation in which we were playfully applying Gee's (1990: 142) notion of little *d* discourse and big *D* discourse to the ways in which critical literacy works with the politics of the everyday.
2. *Makwerekwere* is an insulting word for foreign Africans. It is derived from the unfamiliar sounds of their languages; *kwerekwere* refers to the sounds that people, who do not speak these languages, hear.
3. *SL* is short for student life.
4. I am grateful to my colleague Ana Ferreira for her permission to use this example of teaching students to read verbal–visual texts critically.

Suggestions for further reading

Negotiating Critical Literacies with Young Children by Vivian Vasquez is an award-winning account of building a critical curriculum around young children's concerns.

Multimodal Pedagogies in Diverse Classrooms by Pippa Stein is a moving account of how harnessing multiple literacies can give marginalised children the resources to claim their place in a democratic society.

Critical Reading in Language Education by Catherine Wallace explores different strategies for teaching critical reading to learners for whom English is an additional language.

Travel Notes from the New Literacy Studies edited by Kate Pahl and Jennifer Rowsell combines work in New Literacy Studies and multimodality with examples of practice from around the world.

Negotiating Critical Literacies in Classrooms edited by Barbara Comber and Anne Simpson includes articles by critical literacy teachers working at all levels of education in a range of different contexts each of which has different conditions of possibility.

References

Adegoke, R. (1999) Media discourse on foreign Africans and the implications for education. Unpublished Master's research report, University of the Witwatersrand.

Barton, D. and Hamilton, M. (1998) *Local Literacies*. London and New York: Routledge.

Barton, D., Hamilton, M. and Ivanič, R. (eds) (2000) *Situated Literacies: Reading and Writing in Context*. London and New York: Routledge.

Bigelow, B. and Peterson, B. (2002) *Rethinking Globalization. Teaching for Justice in an Unjust World*. Milwaukee: Rethinking Schools.

Bourdieu, P. (1991) *Language and Symbolic Power* (J.B. Thompson, trans.). Cambridge: Polity Press.

Clark, R., Fairclough, N., Ivanic, R. and Martin-Jones, M. (1987) Critical language awareness. Unpublished manuscript.

Comber, B. (2006) Critical literacy educators at work. In K. Cooper and R. White (eds) *The Practical Critical Educator*. Dordrecht: Springer.

Comber, B., Nixon, H., Ashmore, L., Loo, S. and Cook, J. (2006) Urban renewal from the inside out: Spatial and critical literacies in a low socioeconomic school community. *Mind, Culture and Activity* 13 (3), 228–246.

Comber, B. and Simpson, A. (2001) *Negotiating Critical Literacies in Classrooms*. Mahwah, NJ: Lawrence Erlbaum and Associates.

Comber, B., Thomson, P. and Wells, M. (2001) Critical literacy finds a "place": Writing and social action in a neighborhood school. *Elementary School Journal* 101 (4), 451–464.

Cope, B. and Kalantzis, M. (eds) (2000) *Multiliteracies*. London: Routledge.

Dixon, K. (2007) Literacy, power and the embodied subject: Literacy learning and teaching in the foundation phase of a Gauteng Primary School situated in the southern suburbs of Johannesburg. Doctoral thesis, University of the Witwatersrand.

Fairclough, N. (1989) *Language and Power*. London: Longman.

Fairclough, N. (ed.) (1992) *Critical Language Awareness*. London: Longman.

Foucault, M. (1980) *Power/Knowledge: Selected Interviews and Other Writings 1972–1977*. New York: Pantheon Books.

Fowler, R. and Kress, G. (1979) Critical linguistics. In *Language and Control*. London: Routledge and Kegan Paul.

Freire, P. (1972a) *Cultural Action for Freedom*. Harmondsworth: Penguin.

Freire, P. (1972b) *Pedagogy of the Oppressed*. Harmondsworth: Penguin.

Gee, J.P. (1990) *Sociolinguistics and Literacies. Ideology in Discourse*. London: Falmer Press.

Gee, J., Hull, G. and Lankshear, C. (1996) *The New Work Order*. Sydney: Allen and Unwin.

Gramsci, A. (1971) *Selections From the Prison Notebooks*. London: Lawrence and Wishart.

Grant, H. (1999) Topdogs and underdogs. *Practically Primary* 4 (3), 40–42.

Halliday, M.A.K. (1985) *An Introduction to Functional Grammar* (1st edn). London: Arnold.

Janks, H. (ed.) (1993a) *Critical Language Awareness Series*. Johannesburg: Hodder and Stoughton and Wits University Press.

Janks, H. (1993b) *Language Identity and Power*. Johannesburg: Wits University Press and Hodder and Stoughton.

Janks, H. (2000) 'Domination, access, diversity and design: A synthesis model for critical literacy. *Educational Review* 58 (2), 175–186.

Kenworthy, C. and Kenworthy, S. (1997) *New Australians Old Australians. Part 2 Changing Places*. Fremantle, Australia: Fremantle Arts Press.

Klein, N. (1999) *No Logo*. New York: Picador.

Klein, N. (2007) *The Shock Doctrine. The Rise of Disaster Capitalism*. New York: Metropolitan.

Kress, G. (2003) *Literacy in the New Media Age*. London: Routledge.

Kress, G. and van Leeuwen, T. (1990) *Reading Images*. Geelong: Deakin University Press.

Kress, G. and van Leeuwen, T. (2001) *Multimodal Discourse*. London: Arnold.

Lakoff, G. (2004) *Don't Think of an Elephant*. White River Junction, VT: Chelsea Green.

Leander, K. and Sheehy, M. (2004) *Spatializing Literacy Research*. New York: Peter Lang.

Lefebvre, H. (1991a) *The Production of Space*. Oxford: Blackwell.

Lefebvre, H. (1991b) *Critique of Everyday Life, Volume 1: Introduction* (J. Moore, trans.). London: Verso.

Martino, W. (1997) *New Australians Old Australians. Part 1: From the Margins*. Freemantle Arts Centre Press.

Mellor, B. and Patterson, A. (1996) *Investigating Texts*. Scarborough: Chalkface Press.

Mellor, B., Patterson, A. and O'Neill, M. (1991) *Reading Stories*. Scarborough: Chalkface Press.

Moll, L. (1992) Literacy research in community and classroom. A sociocultural approach. In J.G.R. Beach, M. Kamil and T. Shanahan (eds) *Mulitdisciplinary Perspectives on Literacy Research*. Urbana, IL: National Council of Teachers of English.

Morgan, B. (1998) *The ESL Classroom*. Toronto: University of Toronto Press.

Obama, B. (2006) *The Audacity of Hope*. New York: Crown Publishers.

Orlek, J. (1993) *Languages in South Africa*. Johannesburg: Hodder and Witwatersrand University Press.

Pahl, K. and Rowsell, J. (eds) (2006) *Travel Notes from the New Literacy Studies. Instances of Practice*. Clevedon: Multilingual Matters.

Pennycook, A. (2001) *Critical Applied Linguistics*. UK: Lawrence Erlbaum Associates Publishers.

Rosen, M. (1992) *Mind the Gap*. London: Scholastic.

Saussure, F. (1972) Harris, R. (1990) (ed.) *Course in General Linguistics*. London: Duckworth.

Simon, R. (1992) *Teaching against the Grain. Texts for a Pedagogy of Possibility*. Toronto: OISE Press.

Soja, E. (1996) *Thirdspace: Journeys to Los Angeles and Other Real-and-Imagined Places*. Cambridge: Blackwell.

Stein, P. (2008) *Multimodal Pedagogies in Diverse Classrooms: Representation, Rights and Resources*. London and New York: Routledge.

Street, B. (1984) *Literacy in Theory and Practice*. Cambridge: Cambridge University Press.

TRC. (1998) *Truth and Reconciliation Commission of South Africa report* (Vol. 5). Cape Town: Juta and Co.

Vasquez, V. with Muisem, M., Adamson, S., Hefferman, L., Chiola-Nakai, D. and Shear, J. (2003) *Getting Beyond 'I like the book'*. Newark, DE: International Reading Association.

Vasquez, V. (2004) *Negotiating Critical Literacies with Young Children*. Mahwah, NJ: Lawrence Erlbaum and Associates. ◆

Wallace, C. (2003) *Critical Reading in Language Education*. Houndmills: Palgrave Macmillan.

Wolf, M. (2007) *Proust and the Squid. The Story and Science of the Reading Brain*. New York: Harper Collins.

Chapter 3

Nationalism, Identity and Popular Culture

ALASTAIR PENNYCOOK

Introduction: Beyond Language and Nation

A central problem for sociolinguistic approaches to language is nation-hood. Being the defining framework for much discussion of both language and culture in popular and academic domains, the concept of nation has had a huge influence on the ways in which languages and cultures have been defined. From language policies based around national languages to plans to save endangered languages, the relation between nation, on the one hand, and language and culture, on the other, has remained central to many discussions of these themes. In response to the perceived threat of English in Europe, namely the concern that unless English is opposed, we may, as Phillipson (2003: 192) warns, 'be heading for an American-English only Europe', one strategy is to argue for the need to safeguard diversity through the support of other European languages. As Hagège (2006: 37) argues in *Combat pour le Français*, for example, greater support for French is a crucial part of support for cultural and linguistic diversity more broadly: 'défendre une culture, c'est aussi défendre la langue dans laquelle elle s'exprime' (to defend a culture is also to defend the language in which it is expressed). Discourses of endangerment and language rights all too often fall back onto such a position, arguing that in order to maintain diversity in the face of languages such as English, we need to prop up a relationship between languages, cultures and nations. Missing from such a view is the understanding that linguistic and cultural diversity is far more complex; a much greater variety of influences needs to be considered here.

This connection between language and nation has a long history; indeed it was at the very heart of the development of linguistics. Linguists, as Errington (2008: 4) explains, 'can be regarded as a small, rather special group of colonial agents who adapted European letters to alien ways of talking and, by that means, devised necessary conduits for communication across lines of colonial power'. As a result, the description of languages was intimately linked to the wider colonial emphasis on human hierarchies, so that 'the intellectual work of writing speech was never entirely distinct from the "ideological" work of devising images of people in zones of colonial contact' (2008: 5). This also entailed the use of language difference 'in the creation of human hierarchies, such that colonial subjects could be recognized as human, yet deficiently so' (2008: 5). Language descriptions cannot be abstracted from the colonial imperatives to control, subdue and order. The description of languages, therefore, has to be seen not so much as a scientific division of a language spectrum along natural lines but rather a colonial project in the defining and dividing of colonized people. As Irvine and Gal (2000: 47) describe the process of 'linguistic description' of Senegalese languages by 19th century European linguists, 'The ways these languages were identified, delimited, and mapped, the ways their relationships were interpreted, and even the ways they were described in grammars and dictionaries were all heavily influenced by an ideology of racial and national essences'.

In his discussion of the imposition of Bahasa Indonesia, Heryanto (2007: 43) argues that it was through the introduction via European colonialism of 'the idea of "language"' that 'the old word *bahasa* came to articulate this newly acquired concept. The adoption of a pre-existing word in East Asia to articulate a new concept from modern Western Europe helped make the concept appear universal'. Since language was taken to be a universal human property, it was also assumed that the word 'language', or the local words, such as *bahasa*, that came to be used as translations of this concept, likewise referred to a shared linguistic property tied to nation and culture in similar ways. This introduced concept, Heryanto suggests, did not accord with local understandings of language. In Malay and Javanese, the two most widely spoken and influential languages in Indonesia, 'there was no word for "language". More importantly, there was neither a way nor a need to express its idea until the latter part of the 19th century' (2007: 43). This newly introduced concept of language entered 'a world with no language', in the process replacing vernacular views of language and how it worked. In speaking of 'a world with no language', the point, to be sure, is not that these contexts involved any less language use, but rather that these language users did not speak 'languages'.

This history of linguistic invention and its connection to nationhood has by now been widely discussed. As Sinfree Makoni and I (Makoni & Pennycook, 2007) have argued, current approaches to diversity, multilingualism and so forth all too often start with the enumerative strategy of counting languages and romanticizing a plurality based on these putative language counts. While opening up questions of diversity from one perspective, at the same time such strategies also reproduce the tropes of colonial invention, overlooking the contested history of language inventions, and ignoring the collateral damage that their embedded notions of language may be perpetrating. By rendering diversity a quantitative question of language enumeration, such approaches continue to employ the census strategies of colonialism while missing the qualitative question of where diversity lies. They continue to use the underlying ideology of countability and singularity, where language objects are physically located in concepts of space founded on a notion of territorialization. Heller and Duchêne (2007: 11) remark that we need to 'rethink the reasons why we hold onto the ideas about language and identity which emerged from modernity'. Addressing the question of language preservation, they suggest that rather than assuming we must save languages, 'we should be asking instead who benefits and who loses from understanding languages the way we do, what is at stake for whom, and how and why language serves as a terrain for competition'.

Although the control that nation states have taken over the regulation and construction of languages and cultures has had a great influence over them, especially in the ways in which standard languages and national cultures have been produced, it has never been the case that nations have been good ways of thinking about language and diversity. This relationship is being challenged in two distinct ways. First, from a theoretical point of view, the tendency to assume relations between language and nation has been questioned on the basis that linguistics has profoundly misconstrued language through its myths about autonomy, systematicity and the rule-bound nature of language, privileging supposedly expert, scientific linguistic knowledge over everyday understandings of language. Harris (1990: 45) asks whether 'the concept of a language, as defined by orthodox modern linguistics, corresponds to any determinate or determinable object of analysis at all, whether social or individual, whether institutional or psychological'.

'If there is no such object', he goes on to argue, 'it would be difficult to evade the conclusion that modern linguistics has been based upon a myth'. Worth questioning, then, is this very focus on separate and distinguishable languages: 'linguistics does not need to postulate the existence of languages as part of its theoretical apparatus' (Harris, 1990: 45). It is therefore important to grasp the extent to which languages are inventions of the discipline that makes them. How, we might ask, can we go about exploring language diversity without positing the existence of languages? The historical and contemporary interests behind the long construction of things called languages oblige us to ask in whose interests we continue to divide language into these named entities.

The second challenge to assumed relations between language and nation derives from studies of language and globalization, and in particular of the influence of new media and flows of people, language and culture. This is not to suggest that the nation state has withered away – they still play a major role in the regulation of much social, political and economic activity – but rather that it has become increasingly clear that it is not a very useful construct for thinking about language and culture. Nowhere is this more evident than in the domain of popular culture. While studies of language and globalization often take economic or various utilitarian goals as primary driving forces behind both the spread and takeup of different languages, it is also important to understand the roles of pleasure and desire, and the possibilities that popular culture may hold out for new cultural and linguistic relations, and for new possible modes of identity. This chapter addresses questions raised by globalization and popular culture, suggesting that the ways in which languages are being mixed and changed present new possibilities for identities that have little to do with national identifications. Using the global spread of hip hop as a particular example, this chapter discusses new languages, new cultures and new identities made possible by global flows of language and culture. Such changes have major implications for language education, since the languages and boundaries we have assumed as our educational goals may no longer be what learners and users are tuning in to.

Globalization and Cultural Flows

We need first of all to understand how languages operate in an uneven world (Radhakrishnan, 2003) and how languages relate to the deep global inequalities of poverty, health and education. Rather than viewing global-ization merely as synonymous with economic disparity, however, it is more useful to explore the complexities of global flows of culture and knowledge within this uneven world. Unlike those who insist that global-ization implies '*the homogenization of world culture* ... spearheaded by films, pop culture, CNN and fast-food chains' (Phillipson & Skutnabb-Kangas, 1996: 439; italics in original), the argument in this chapter is that we need to deal with globalization beyond this dystopic, neo-Marxist, critique based only on political economy, and to engage with 'pop culture' in terms beyond the gloomy Frankfurt School image of the duping of the global masses. To suggest that globalization is only a process of US or Western domination of the world is to take a narrow and ultimately unproductive view of global relations. Likewise, to view culture and language in terms only of reflections of the economic – as with views that relate language and culture too intimately with nationhood – is to miss the point that new technologies and communications are enabling immense and complex flows of people, signs, sounds, and images across multiple borders in multiple directions. If we accept a view of popular culture as a crucial site of identity and desire, it is hard to see how we can proceed with any study of language and globalization without dealing comprehensively with popular culture. The 'real question before us', argues Scott (1999: 215), 'is whether or not we take the vernacular voices of the popular and their modes of self-fashioning seriously, and if we do, how we think through their implications'.

It is indisputable that flows of popular culture are dominated at one level by a weight and directionality that are part of the unevenness of global relations. Thus, Pennay (2001: 128) comments in his discussion of rap in Germany that 'the flow of new ideas and stylistic innovations in popular music is nearly always from the English-speaking market, and not to it'. Similarly, in her discussion of the Basque rap group Negu Gorriak (featuring the Mugurza brothers), Urla points out that 'unequal relations between the United States record industry and Basque radical music mean that Public Enemy's message reaches the Mugurza brothers in Irun, and not vice versa' (Urla, 2001: 189). Perry (2004: 17) meanwhile critiques what she calls the 'romantic Afro-Atlanticism' of Gilroy's (1993) notion of the *Black Atlantic*, with its view of multiple influences across communities of African origin around the Atlantic. 'Black Americans as a community', she insists, 'do not consume imported music from other cultures in large numbers' and thus ultimately the 'postcolonial Afro-Atlantic hip hop community is . . . a fantastic aspiration rather than a reality' (2004: 19).

While it may be the case that there is little takeup of imported music in US communities, however, there is also a strong case to be made that the circles of flow of popular culture are far more complex than a process of undirectional spread. Mitchell (2001) points out that as hip hop has spread, it has become a vehicle through which local identity is reworked. Indeed, if we want to find 'innovation, surprise, and musical substance in hip-hop culture and rap music' he argues (2001: 3), it is increasingly necessary 'to look outside the USA to countries such as France, England, Germany, Italy, and Japan, where strong local currents of hip-hop indigenization have taken place'. Androutsopoulos (2003: 11) suggests that since 'hip-hop is a globally dispersed network of everyday cultural practices which are productively appropriated in very different local contexts, it can be seen as paradigmatic of the dialectic of cultural globalization and localization' (my translation). Within these relations of cultural globalization and localization, furthermore, there are numerous significant sites of cultural production outside the United States. While the United States may be less influenced by external changes in global hip hop, countries such as France, with a very different postcolonial history, are far more influenced by the diverse Francophone world, which inhabits its urban environments.

Elsewhere in the world, there are diverse linguistic/cultural circuits of flow. In the relations between Samoan, Hawaiian, Maori and other Pacific Islander communities, we can see a 'pan-Pacific hip-hop network that has bypassed the borders and restrictions of the popular music distribution industry' (Mitchell, 2001: 31). These circles of hip-hop flow are at times overlapping: Hawaii, for example, where Sudden Rush have developed 'ne mele paleoleo, Hawaiian hip hop, a cut n' mix of African and Jamaican reggae rhythms, Hawaiian chanting, and subversive rapping in the English and Hawaiian languages' (Akindes, 2001: 91), links the Pacific to the United States, while French-influenced parts of the Pacific, such as French Polynesia (Tahiti) and New Caledonia link the Pacific to the French circuit. Certainly, there is now 'scarcely a country in the world that does not feature some form of mutation or rap music, from the venerable and sophisticated hip-hop and rap scenes of France, to the "swa-rap" of Tanzania and Surinamese rap of Holland' (Krims, 2000: 5).

Les patnais vont chiller ce soir. Urban Codes in the Francophone World

The French language hip-hop scene has been one of the most significant for the past 20 years, a complex interlocked circle of flow that links the vibrant music scenes in Paris and Marseille in France; Dakar, Abidjan and Libreville in West Africa; and Montreal in Quebec. Hip hop in France developed in the *banlieues* – the suburban housing projects where many poor, and first and second generation immigrant populations live. Here, in multiethnic mixes of people of Maghreb (Algeria, Tunisia, Morocco), French African (Mali, Senegal, Gabon), French Antilles (La Martinique, Guadeloupe) and other European (Portugal, Romania, Italy) backgrounds, hip hop emerged as a potent force of new French expression. Rap in France 'uses a streetspeak version of French that includes African, Arab, gypsy and American roots and is viewed with disapproval by traditionalists for its disregard for traditional rules of grammar and liberal use of neologisms' (Huq, 2001: 74). While Paris became a centre for many movements and crossings of French language musicians, dancers and artists, the southern port city of Marseille looked more resolutely southwards. Typical of the movement was the popular Marseille group IAM, who developed an ideology that Prévos (2001: 48) calls 'pharaoism', thus both linking to the Arabic background of many French immigrants and, as Swedenburg (2001: 69) argues, giving 'Egyptianist Afrocentricity a Mediterranean inflection, asserting a kind of "black Mediterranean"'.

The rap scene in France, as Huq (2001: 81) describes it, 'stands out as the ideal soundtrack to accompany the post-industrial, post-colonial times ushered in by the new millennium, in which the new tricolore (the French national flag), is black, blanc, beur'.[1] While the many flows of immigrant influence into France have thus greatly affected French hip hop, the 'diasporic flows' (Prévos, 2001: 53) of hip hop back into the wider Francophone circle of influence have in turn changed the music and linguascapes of other regions of the world. In Libreville, Gabon, rappers mix English, French and local languages such as Fang and Téké. English, as Auzanneau (2002) explains, is never used on its own, but always in conjunction with French, while vernacular languages may be used on their own, with each other, or with French, but never with English. The use of vernacular languages signals a clear identity with the Gabonese community while keeping a distance from France which 'is perceived as economically exploitative, culturally assimilating, and a former colonizer' (2002: 114). The rap movement in Gabon, therefore, which puts Gabonese languages and cultures on a public stage both within and beyond the country, has become part of a process of revalorization of vernacular languages: 'Formerly associated with out-of-date and archaic values (and thus with "backwardness"), these languages are now becoming languages of "authenticity" and "roots" and thus claim for themselves an identiary role both in rap and in the city' (2002: 114). A modern cultural formation such as hip hop may not necessarily therefore be tied indelibly to those languages and cultures perceived to be inherently modern. Once it becomes localized, rap can become a vehicle for the mobilization of vernacular languages, cultures and values.

The French that is used in Gabon, meanwhile, is pulled in several different directions: 'departures from standard French' serve as 'factors of social differentiation and thus identification' (Auzanneau, 2002: 108). Libreville rap uses a mix of standard and non-standard French, including various created forms, neologisms and *verlan*, borrowings from Gabonese languages, languages of migration, and standard and non-standard English. Not only is *verlan* a form of French slang that reverses standard French (hence the term 'beur', used to refer to people of Arabic descent, is derived from 'Arabe' and the term 'verlan' itself derives from the French term 'l'envers' meaning the other way round) but also, as Doran (2004: 94) explains, it is 'a kind of linguistic *bricolage*' formed from the multilingual and multicultural mixes of immigrants from North Africa, West Africa, Asia and the Caribbean. When such codes are imported (or to some extent reimported) to the Libreville rap scene, there is a vast array of language and cultural influences at work. The choices local performers make between languages is crucial: 'the place given to English or to French *verlan* can diminish in favor of terms taken from Libreville French or local languages' depending on the different ways in which the songwriter wishes to negotiate his or her Gabonese identity in the song (Auzanneau, 2002: 117). By using a local, Gabonese form of French, for example, performers 'mark their attachment to Gabonese culture at the same time as they make their break with the values of both their own traditional society and the dominant Western society' (2002: 118). Gabonese hip hop artists can thus perform 'their *métissée* (mixed) identity as young urbanites' (2002: 118).

Another node on this global circuit is Montreal, where the languages of popular culture reflect the city's location in North America (rendering African–American English both easily available and significantly rejectable), the locality within Quebec (making Quebec French a badge of

difference from other parts of the French circuit), and the immigrant pop-
ulations with their various connections to French. While immigrants from
Mali, Senegal and Gabon may find a space for their French, Africans from
non-Francophone nations, as Ibrahim (1999, 2008) points out in the Franco-
Ontarian context, may often identify with Black English as their African
identities are stripped away in favor of an identification as *Black*. The large
Haitian population, meanwhile, forges a new relationship between
Haitian Creole and the other languages of Montreal. Sarkar and Allen
(2007: 122) cite an interview with Montreal's Impossible: 'Le style montré-
alais ... c'est la seule place où t'as un mélange culturel comme ça, que t'as
un mélange des langues comme ça, que ça soit l'anglais, créole, pis le français, mais un français quand même québécois' (Impossible, 2004/06/04)
('Montreal style ... is the only place where you have a cultural mix like
that, where you have a mixture of languages like that, whether it's English,
[Haitian] Creole, then French, but all the same a Quebec French'. Sarkar
and Allen's translation). This reported mix of Quebec French, English and
Creole is unique in certain ways; it does not seem to be the case, however,
that Montreal is so distinctive in supporting this level of diversity.

While at one level this mixing of language is a reflection of the codemixing on Montreal streets, in other ways it is more than this. According
to J. Kyll of Muzion 'en général, on chante, on rap comme on parle' ('in
general, we sing, we rap the way we speak') (Sarkar & Allen, 2007: 122),
and yet we also need to see such language use as productive as well as
reflective of local realities. As Rampton (1995, 2006) has observed in urban
contexts in the United Kingdom, such language use often involves 'crossing' or the use of languages in which the speakers are not fluent. As
another of Sarkar and Allen's participants explained, although he was not
himself Haitian, he was often identified as such and felt free to speak and
use Creole. Rappers in this study claim that rather than such language
mixes alienating listeners, they enable listeners to relate to diversity in
new ways. Thus, a line like 'Où est-ce que les patnais vont chiller ce soir?'
('Where is the gang going to chill [hang out] tonight?' which contains the
Haitian Creole term *patnai* for 'good friend') might now be heard from
young Montrealers of many backgrounds. According to Sarkar (2009: 147),
this new generation of urban Quebecers has integrated words from both
Haitian (*popo* 'police', *kob* 'cash', *ti-moun* 'kid', and *kget* 'a swearword')
and Jamaican Creole (*ganja* 'marijuana', *spliff* 'joint', *skettel* 'girl, loose
woman', and *rude bwoy* 'aggressive youth') into their everyday language
and rap, whatever their ethnic background.

Given these mixes, labels such as 'Francophone' need to be applied
with caution to such circles of flow. While on one level these music scenes
are connected by their postcolonial use of French, this French is also widely
divergent and, as with English, cannot be easily assumed to be one entity.
According to Glissant (1997: 119) 'there are several French languages

today, and languages allow us to conceive of their unicity according to a new mode, in which French can no longer be monolingual'. Unlike the vision of Hagège (2006), cited above, where 'French' needs to be defended in order to defend diversity against the onslaught of English and Anglo-Saxon culture, here Glissant argues that such monolingual conceptualizations of French miss the point: 'If language is given in advance, if it claims to have a mission, it misses out on the adventure and does not catch on in the world' (1997: 119). The languages and cultures that circulate within these flows are constantly mixed with other languages and cultures, so that new mixtures arrive in new places and remix once again as they become relocalized. As Auzanneau puts it, rappers in Libreville, Gabon, 'are inserted into large networks of communication that confer on them a plurality of identities', using a wide 'diversity of languages with their variants, along with their functioning as markers of identity (of being Gabonese, African, or an urbanite)' (2002: 120). In this circuit of hip hop, then, being 'Francophone' does lead to certain commonalities of influence, and yet these are infused by radical variations from the mixed codes of urban identity formation.

Three-Sixty Degrees: Imagining New Worlds

There are many such circles of flow, including the Spanish, which connects the hip-hop scenes in Cuba, Spain, Mexico and South America (and which, due to the large Hispanic communities in the United Sates, does have some effect on that market) (Cepeda, 2003; Fernandes, 2003), the Lusophone (Roth-Gordon, 2009), the Chinese (Ho, 2003; Lin, 2009) and so on. These different circles also intersect in many places, above all in Africa, where as N'Dongo D from Senegalese group Daara J explains, 'In Africa you will find Portuguese, Spanish, French, English all mixed together in the culture in the same continent' (Interview 05/03/05, my translation).[2] For Daara J, furthermore, hip hop is an African art form that has returned home: 'Born in Africa, brought up in America, hip hop has come full circle' (Boomerang). According to Faada Freddy, 'this music is ours! It is a part of our culture!' Somali-Canadian artist K'Naan similarly argues that while West Africa has its *griots* and Somalia has a long tradition of oral language use, in 'any given country in Africa, you will find an ancient form of hip hop'. It is natural, he suggests, 'for someone from Africa to recite something over a drum and to recite it in a talking blues fashion, and then it becomes this thing called hip hop' (K'Naan, Interview, 25/04/06).

Elsewhere in Africa, we find similar patterns of localization. Higgins' (2009: 96) analysis of Tanzanian hip-hop culture, for example, suggests that there is far more going on than a unidirectional influence from the centre to the periphery: Rather there is a 'two-way cultural flow' as 'Tanzanian youths perform a range of identities' drawing on different local and global resources. As she points out, for example, the development of new 'street Swahili' terms such as *"bomba"* ('awesome'; originally from Portuguese *bomba*, 'pump') is likely affected by the African–American term common in hip-hop circles *da bomb* (the best). Similarly in the Nigerian context, Omoniyi (2009) discusses the various discursive strategies that Nigerian hip-hop artists use to construct local identities within the global hip-hop movement. Codeswitching (which, Omoniyi argues, needs to include not just language but modes of dressing, walking and other patterns of social behavior), in particular, marks forms of local Nigerian identity, with artists using mixes of Yoruba, English, Pidgin and Igbo. In Weird MC's 'Ijoya' (Yoruba: Time to dance), for example, we find in one stanza English juxtaposed with Yoruba: 'We own the dance/Awa la ni ijo [Yoruba: we own the dance]/*Ah trust us, we OWN dis dance*/-Awa la ni ijo [Yoruba: we own the dance]'; and Pidgin with both Yoruba and Igbo: 'Na we getam [Pidgin: We own it]/Awa la ni *gini* [Yoruba/*Igbo*: We own *what*?]/Awa la ni ijo ijo [Yoruba: we own the dance]' (Omoniyi, 2009: 130; Omoniyi's language identifications and translations in brackets).

Linguistic and cultural flows can also intersect with domains such as religion. Looking at rap by British and French musicians of Islamic background, for example, Swedenburg (2001: 76) argues for 'the importance of paying close attention to popular cultural manifestations of "Islam" in Europe'. British band Fun-Da-Mental's engagement with Islam is 'central to its multipronged intervention: Islam instills religioethnic pride among Asian youth, serves as an image of antiracist mobilization, creates links between Asians and Afro-Caribbeans, and shocks and educates white leftists and alternative youth' (Swedenburg, 2001: 62). Similarly, Swedenburg argues that the French group IAM's Islamic engagement is part of their 'effort to widen the space of tolerance for Arabo-Islamic culture in France, through its lyrical subject matter, its deployment of Arabic words and expressions, and its musical mixes, splattered with Middle Eastern rhythms and samples of Arabic songs' (2001: 71).

In a rather different context, Malay rappers Too Phat saw both a spiritual and commercial opportunity in developing rap with lyrics from the Koran in Arabic. 'Alhamdulillah' (from the CD 360°), as producer Pietro Felix (interview 12/12/03) explains, was originally conceived as 'an R&B "thankyou, praise Allah" kind of thing', which, they felt, 'sounded very Arabic, it sounded very Malay, more prayer, religious kind of sound' so they got Yasin, an Arabic singer, to do the lyrics. The song is largely a critique of materialist values with thanks to Allah for the gifts they have received – 'I thank Allah for blessing me to be creative/So here's a diss for me for bein' unappreciative/Wanted a perfect life, yeah smile then die old/Fame, money, women, phat cribos and white gold/' – and a warning for not saying 'alhamdulillah'. As Felix Pietro goes on, 'suddenly we thought "this is great marketing". A lot of Malay kids will love this, plus we can check this out to ... all the way East kind of thing' (Interview 12/12/03). This plan to gain sales in Middle Eastern countries such as Saudi Arabia, however, was not so successful: 'they didn't want to play it because it seems their censorship board does not allow songs that have anything to do with praise Allah'. Meanwhile, with less strict rules of what can and cannot be done in popular music, the song 'gets great airplay' in Malaysia. 'People were blown away with the song. They never thought a rap song would have Koran lyrics, Arabic lyrics' (Interview 12/12/03). From rappers of Turkish background in Germany, such as Islamic Force (see Kaya, 2001) to Malaysian Too Phat, from French bands such as IAM to the verbal intifada of Palestinian rappers (Sling Shot Hip Hop, 2008), it is possible to talk in terms of what Alim (2006) has called a *transglobal hiphop ummah* (a global community of Islamic hip hop).

Lin (2009) suggests that the language of hip hop also makes possible connections along class lines. MC Yan from Hong Kong uses predominantly colloquial Cantonese (rather than common mixed Cantonese/English code), especially the vulgar and largely taboo *chou-hau*. By defying the linguistic taboos of mainstream middle-class society, Lin suggests, MC Yan communicates his political message by linking Hong Kong slang and working class defiance with a broader translocally defiant underclass through hip hop. Meanwhile, MC Yan becomes part of other circuits of flow: Hong Kong DJ Tommy's compilation, 'Respect for Da Chopstick Hip Hop' – the title itself a play on global (Respect/Da) and local (Chopstick Hip Hop) elements – features MC Yan from Hong Kong, K-One, MC Ill and Jaguar all from Japan, and Meta and Joosuc from Korea, with tracks sung in English, Cantonese, Japanese and Korean. Such collaborations are common. Too Phat's 360°, for example, contains a track '6MC's', featuring Promoe of Loop Troop (Sweden), Vandal of SMC (Canada), Freestyle (Brooklyn, New York) and Weapon X (Melbourne, Australia): 'From sea to sea, country to country/6 MC's bring the delicacies/It's a meeting of the minds to ease the turmoil/360 degrees around the earth's soil'. Weapon X turns up again on Korean MC Joosuc's track Universal Language, in which Weapon X uses English and Joosuc Korean (with some English). As DJ Jun explains, this track 'is about different languages but we are in the same culture which is hip hop. So language difference doesn't really matter. So hip hop is one language. That is why it is called universal language' (Interview, 02/11/03). From this perspective, hip hop as a culture rises above different languages: The universal language is not English; it is hip hop.

Languages Remixed

There is, then, a constant mixing, borrowing, shifting and sampling of music, languages, lyrics and ideas. This can include borrowings and imitations of African–American English, as in the Japanese group Rip

Slyme's use of 'Yo Bringing that, Yo Bring your style' (see Pennycook, 2003, 2007) or Malaysian Too Phat's 'Hip hop be connectin' Kuala Lumpur with LB/Hip hop be rockin' up towns laced wit' LV/Ain't necessary to roll in ice rimmed M3's and be blingin'/Hip hop be bringin' together emcees'. It is already worth observing, however, that while Too Phat here use African-American-styled lyrics (be connectin' and so forth) and lace their lyrics with references to consumerist cultural products (LV/M3s), they are at the same time distancing themselves from this world through their insistence that hip hop is about connecting MCs across time and space rather than the accoutrements of bling culture (ostentatious consumerism and display of wealth, especially large jewelry). Meanwhile, more complex mixes of English with local languages can be found in Rip Slyme's lyrics when they describe themselves as '錦糸町出 Freaky ダブル の Japanese' 'Freaky mixed Japanese from Kinshichoo', literally: 'from Kinshichoo' (a suburb of Tokyo, written in Japanese *kanji*) 'Freaky' (in English), 'double' (the word 'double' written in katakana, used to refer to people of ethnically mixed background) and Japanese (using the English word, written in Roman script). Korean singer Tasha meanwhile uses codemixed lyrics: 'Yo if I fall two times I come back on my third 절대로포 기않지 and that's my word'. The lyrics in Korean, meaning 'I never give up', complement the English meaning, but what Tasha achieves here is not just to move between languages, creating a set of new meanings by doing so, but also she moves in and out of different flows. By artfully integrating the flows of English and Korean rap styles in a bilingual performance, she presents English and Korean in new relationships.

'Now lisnen up por pabor makinig 2004 rap sa Pinas yumayanig lalong lumalakas never madadaig', rap GHOST 13 (Guys Have Own Style to Talk – 1 group, 3 rappers) from Zamboanga in western Mindanao in the Philippines. GHOST 13 use what they call 'halo-halong lenguaje' (mixed language), which may include Tagalog, Visaya, Cebuano, Chavacano and Tausug, as well as English. In these lines, for example, they mix English (Now lisnen up/never), Chavacano (por pabor) and Tagalog (makinig ... rap sa Pinas yumayanig lalong lumalakas ... madadaig): 'Please listen to 2004 Philippines rap getting stronger and never beaten'. And they are insistent that, in global hip hop style, they 'represent' Zamboanga, and at the same time are not imitative: 'Listen everyone we are the only one rap group in the land who represent zamboanga man!/Guyz have own style, style to talk a while di kami mga wanna [we are not imitators] because we have own identity'.

Zamboanga, known as the City of Flowers, is home to Zamboangueño, one of several Spanish-based creole languages in the Philippines, usually grouped together under the general term Chavacano (from the Spanish *chabacano* 'vulgar'): 'Chavacano de Zamboanga siento porsiento ... kami magdidilig sa city of flower' – in Chavacano, Tagalog and English: 'One hundred per cent Chavacano from Zamboanga ... we water the city of flowers'. As can be seen from these examples, Zamboangueño, the most widely spoken creole in the region, has predominantly Spanish vocabulary, with Cebuano as the substrate language. And like all creoles, it never exists on its own; it is always in relation with other languages. GHOST 13 also clearly take great pride in their version of Chavacano, which, like many creole languages, is often derided (with terms such as 'Filo-Spanish'). For them it is a central means for the expression of a Zamboangan hip-hop identity, to be held up to display, paraded as a language to be respected. To announce this identity, to place it centrally in their rap lyrics, is a significant act of language politics. Not only are GHOST 13 on stage, but so is Chavacano.

The use of creoles in rap can be a sign of street credibility, of local authenticity. Since creole languages are often viewed as non-standard, local languages, their very use also provides an avenue for an oppositional stance in terms of language politics. While much is made of rap lyrics as the central means by which we can interpret the cultural and political stance of hip-hop artists, it is equally important to look sociolinguistically at the linguistic varieties and mixes artists use. Most creole languages are tied to slavery, colonialism, migration and the African diaspora. From Jamaican *patwa* in the United Kingdom, to Haitian creole in Montreal, or to Cabo Verde (Cape Verde) rappers such as The Real Vibe and Black Side in Holland, and, arguably, from African–American English to Aboriginal Australian English, to use creole is to invoke a certain cultural politics and to take up a space within this historical and contemporary circle of flow. As with the hip-hop crews in Libreville, whose mixing and use of languages were clearly overt, the use of creole and other languages by groups such as GHOST 13 is part of an explicit challenge to forms of identity. It is a reclamation of a non-institutionalized language world that has often been hidden beneath the patina of nationalist language policy, a world where language mixing and immanent variety are the historical and geographical norm.

Such a view ties in with the position on *créolité* argued by Glissant (1997) and Chamoiseau and Confiant (1999), who suggest that not only are creoles a crucial form of expression for local, Caribbean and other populations, but also they are a model for understanding language diversity in the world. This view on *créolité* takes *métissage*, mixing, and multiple origins of language as the norm, rather than focusing on diversity in terms of the countability of formalized language systems. Using the term 'creole' more loosely, Kaya (2001: 147) argues that Turkish rappers in Berlin use a form of creole based on a mixture of Turkish, German and American English: 'This new form of city speech in the migrants' suburbs is a verbal celebration of ghetto multiculturalism, twisting German, Turkish and American slang in resistance to the official language'. Creole linguists may object here and point out that this is not a 'true creole', and given the long battle to establish the legitimacy of creoles, there may be good reason not to open the doors to all comers. Nevertheless, if we follow Mufwene's (2001: 10) lead 'to identify primarily those varieties that have been identified as "creole" or "patois" by nonlinguists', we may be able to take seriously the notion that the transgressive language uses of rap – mixing and borrowing, using language from wherever, deliberately changing the possibilities of language use and language combinations – may be seen as creolizing practices.

In other words, the hip-hop practices of créolité may be a force in the production of linguistic diversity both in terms of diversity within languages and in terms of the creation of new languages. While Chavacano in the Philippines or the creoles of the Caribbean may be older and different in a number of ways, to reject the Turkish-German-English creole of Berlin hip hop would be to overlook the ways in which languages are created. If, as many people rightly are, we are concerned about the decline of languages in the world (Skutnabb-Kangas, 2000), we might then see hip hop not, as conservative critics would suggest, as an engine of linguistic degeneration, but rather as a potential driver towards diversity. This may be both in terms of what Halliday (2002; and see Pennycook, 2007) has termed semiodiversity – the diversity of meaning within languages – and in terms of glossodiversity – the diversity of languages themselves. And if, as Mufwene (2001) argues, there is no reason to discount creoles from the purview of world Englishes, then a Turkish-based creole, with German and English relexification, might just have to be considered as one of those Other Englishes, as one of the many global Englishes.

Challenging Language Realities

The mixed codes of the street, and the hypermixes of hip hop, pose a threat to the linguistic, cultural and political stability urged by national language policies and wished into place by frameworks of linguistic analysis that posit separate and enumerable languages (Makoni & Pennycook, 2007). As Jacquemet (2005: 274) puts it, we need to not only understand contact linguistics but to 'examine communicative practices based on disorderly recombinations and language mixings occurring simultaneously in local and distant environments. In other words, it is time to conceptualize a linguistics of xenoglossic becoming, transidiomatic mixing, and communicative recombinations'. Hip-hop language use can therefore be read as resistant or oppositional not merely in terms of the lyrics but also in terms of language choice. Keeping it linguistically real is often a threat to those who would prefer to keep it linguistically pure. For many communities, using a variety of languages, mixing languages together, is the norm. The notion that people use separate and discrete languages is a very strange language ideology that has arisen at a particular cultural and historical moment (Makoni & Pennycook, 2007). Furthermore, to the extent that many hip hoppers come from marginalized communities where the straightjackets of linguistic normativity have had less effect, their mixed-code language will likely reflect local language use. It would be strange for someone from Zamboanga not to use at least Chavacano, Tagalog, Cebuano, Tausug and English in different daily interactions. This is not only a question, however, of reflecting local language use.

Choices in language use are deeply embedded in local conditions, from the economy and the local music industry infrastructure (limited recording facilities may militate against local practices and languages, for example) to the historical background, language policies, language ideologies, aesthetics, and other local and regional concerns. Berger (2003: xiv–xv) points out that while, on the one hand, language choice in music reflects local or dominant language ideologies, the effects of particular language use in music provide a context for listeners to reflect on those language practices: 'rather than merely reproducing existing ideologies, singers, culture workers, and listeners may use music to actively think about, debate, or resist the ideologies at play in the social world around them'. Language choice and use, particularly in domains of public performance, need to be seen as far more than reflective of local circumstances since 'an appropriation of own or other cultures is an active and intellectually intensive and demanding exercise which mobilizes rational and sensual faculties, always' (Gurnah, 1997: 126). With respect to language performances in general, Bauman (2004) argues that when language is publicly put on display, made available for scrutiny, rendered an object of conscious consideration, it takes on different transformative possibilities.

Following Bauman, it is also of course important to take questions of genre and style into account here. A focus on genres ('the integrated, multi-level analyses that participants themselves implicitly formulate for their own practical activity'), Rampton (2006: 128) suggests, can provide the key for understanding the relationship between popular culture and linguistic practice. Drawing on the work of Bakhtin (1986), Rampton argues that these temporary stabilizations of form provide insights into the ways in which styles may transfer from the realm of popular culture to domains of everyday language use. Likewise focusing on the active use of style, Coupland (2007: 3) points to the importance of understanding 'how people *use* or *enact* or *perform* social styles for a range of symbolic purposes'. This enables us to see that 'style (like language) is not a *thing* but a *practice*' (Eckert, 2004: 43; see also Jaspers, this volume). A focus on style can thus shed light on several aspects of the role of hip hop in relation to everyday language practices: People engage in particular language practices because they are seen as having a certain style. Once a group of rappers put a creole language such as Chavacano on stage as part of both a profoundly local linguistic performance and a global cultural performance, they give it a style that changes its status. And particular language styles, particular language varieties, are taken up in order to perform certain effects. Language styles are practices that are performed as part of larger social and cultural styles. Language styles within hip hop are therefore precisely part of the process of change, making new language and new language mixes available to others, as well as taking up those styles that are deemed to have a particular street resonance.

Auzanneau (2002) argues that the language choices that the rappers in Libreville made were clearly intentional. Although at one level these language choices may therefore be viewed as reflecting local diversity, at another level they are also intentionally producing local diversity. Rather than merely reproducing local language practices, language use in hip hop may consequently have as much to do with change, resistance and opposition as do lyrics that overtly challenge the status quo. This is particularly true of musicians such as rap artists, whose focus on verbal skills performed in the public domain renders their language use a site of constant potential challenge. The importance of this observation in terms of understanding popular cultures, languages and identities is that it gives us an insight into the ways in which languages are used to perform, invent and (re)fashion identities across borders. Thus, in performing their acts of semiotic reconstruction, it is no longer useful to ask if Rip Slyme are using Japanese English to express Japanese culture and identity as if these neatly preexisted the performance, or whether Too Phat are native speakers of a nativized variety of English, as if such nationally constructed codes predefine their use, or whether Tasha's bilinguality is unrepresentative of language use in Korea, as if national language policy precludes alternative possibilities, or whether GHOST 13's lyrics reflect local language mixing in Zamboanga, as if language use was so easily captured and represented.

When we talk of such popular language use, we are talking of the performance of new identities. To be *authentic* in such contexts is a discursive accomplishment, rather than an adherence to a pregiven set of characteristics (Coupland, 2003; Pennycook, 2007). And, like popular culture, these new identities are performances that are always changing, always in flux.

Once we understand languages from a local perspective – once we see language ideologies as contextual sets of beliefs about languages, as cultural and political systems of ideas about social and linguistic relationships – we will realize that the ways in which languages are used and thought about are never just about language but also about community and society. Language ideologies are about what it means to be a person in a particular context (Woolard, 2004). The performative nature of hip-hop lyrics, therefore, may not only reflect local language conditions but may both actively resist current ways of thinking and produce new ways of thinking about languages and their meaning. Rap, Auzanneau

(2002: 120) suggests, 'is a space for the expression of cultures and identities under construction'. And not only is it a place for presenting identities under construction but it is also a site of identity construction, as well as language use and cultural practices which may then circulate beyond the music in wider social spheres. 'Rap thus reveals and participates in the unifying gregarity of the city's activities, and works with the city on the form, functions, and values of its languages' (Auzanneau, 2002: 120). By working on the languages of the city, while simultaneously being part of a larger global circuit of language and music, rap takes up and 'spits out' new cultural and linguistic possibilities that are then made available again for recycling.

Mixing and sampling is a significant element of hip-hop culture, extending not only to the use of sound samples, different backing tracks, and different instruments, but also to the mixing and sampling of languages. Just as lyrics may oppose social orthodoxies, the use of multiple languages may be purposive acts in opposition to ortholinguistic practices, performatively enacting new possibilities for language use and identity. The use of popular languages and styles within popular cultures questions commonly held notions of language origins (Pennycook & Mitchell, 2009), of language purities, of possible codemixes, and puts on stage new possibilities for identifications across borders. The unortholinguistic practices of popular culture display new and fluid linguistic, cultural and identificatory possibilities that may then be taken up, reworked, and reprocessed back through the global circuits of cultural and linguistic flow. Once we take seriously the vernacular voices of the popular and their modes of self-fashioning (Scott, 1999), we are obliged to rethink the ways that languages and cultures work in relation to nation, culture and society.

Researching Language and Popular Culture

Researching popular culture presents numerous challenges – as well as a lot of pleasure. One concern has to do with face, or the perception that popular culture is not a proper focus for serious study. Although applied linguists may eschew a high/low cultural divide, many tend nevertheless to be happier, on the one hand, making reference to canonical rather than popular texts (*King Lear* rather than *Harry Potter*), while, on the other, favoring a view of culture as the naturally occurring unconscious background to how we think and behave. Popular culture is deemed to be artificial, commercialized, manipulated, inauthentic, or just downright bad. All of this, of course, misses the point that most studies of popular culture may be more interested in the sociology of cultural movements than in the cultural products themselves. But it also misses the point that under this clumsy label of the 'popular', there is a very wide range of different creative work. Despite all the work in cultural studies that looks at film, popular music, street art and so on, it is still hard to gain legitimacy within applied linguistics for studies involving popular cultural forms.

Popular culture is also not an easy object of study in itself. Unlike less popular forms of culture, it does not stay still for very long. This is an issue both for research and for a pedagogical engagement with popular culture, since what is popular today may not be so tomorrow. There is also the question of research sites. Colleagues who do the hard work of classroom ethnographies, or gather linguistic data from remote communities, or collect vast sets of recorded data for transcription, have been known to mutter deprecating comments about those of us who apparently do our research by hanging out in nightclubs. Now there is certainly something to be said here about the choices we make for our research and the sites we end up researching. Choosing a particular research domain is in some ways a lifestyle choice as well as an intellectual interest. Studying the global spread of English has given me good cause to visit many interesting parts of the world, and working on popular culture has likewise given me access to some fascinating venues – backstage interviews, late night gigs, impromptu interviews in bars. And yet, to be good research, you still have to put in the long hours of thought, analysis and writing. Good research in popular culture may look to some like 'hanging out' in interesting places, but at some point the hard work on texts, interactions, lyrics, images, and languages has to be done.

Another question that may be asked is whether analysis of CD lyrics or performances is representative of more general language use. The answer to this is a complex one. First, we need to consider the question of whether performance should be considered as data, since in a number of ways it may not be considered to be 'natural'. A great deal can be learned, however, by looking at the language that is put on display in performance (Bauman, 2004) both as linguistic and cultural artifact and as language made available for others. Hip-hop artists, furthermore, typically draw from the local linguistic environment and thus may give us access to varieties and styles that are not easily accessed elsewhere. As suggested above, they are also active in deliberately changing language, and at this point the question of whether this represents authentic language use misses the point: Authenticity is an active accomplishment rather than a reflection of a presumed reality (Pennycook, 2007). As long as we are careful, therefore, about the nature of the claims we are making, the study of language in performance can tell us a great deal.

Like Alim (2009) and Rampton (2006), I am interested in the mutual contributions that sociolinguistics and cultural studies can make to each other. On the one hand, cultural studies can open up sociolinguistics to a broader set of concerns than is often the case: Language use in popular culture, performance as language use, and so on. On the other hand, good sociolinguistic analysis can help anchor the often wayward analyses of cultural studies by bringing more rigorous forms of discourse analysis, study of language variety and so on. It may surprise some readers to see 'rigor' (such an old-fashioned sounding term) used in such contexts, but just as cultural performers – from jugglers to graffiti artists, from break dancers to rappers – bring rigor to their performances, so researchers need to bring rigor to their work. Alim (2006), for example, does a close socio-linguistic analysis of copula use in what he calls Hip Hop Nation Language (HHNL), showing how 'street conscious copula variation' (conscious vari-ation of copula absence by artists) is used to maintain a sense of staying 'street' (connected to the linguistic and cultural world of Hip Hop). Omoniyi (2009), Higgins (2009), Lin (2009) and others likewise engage in close sociolinguistic analysis of rap lyrics.

Like all research around texts and language, furthermore, it is impor-tant that we bring a wide range of analytic tools. 'Mainstream discourse analysis', observes Blommaert (2007: 115), 'often starts from a socio-linguistically and culturally unproblematised object': Texts, documents, lyrics are often assumed to be in a certain language without exploring in far greater complexity the more complex sociolinguistics of language use. As we have seen from many of the examples above, to start with the prop-osition that certain lyrics are in certain languages is to operate from a soci-olinguistically inadequate starting point. It is also important, as Blommaert (2005: 233) elsewhere remarks, 'to develop a broadly based approach to language in society, in which the contextualisation of discourse is a central element'. Above all, this means not relying on forms of textual analysis alone, but instead making ethnography central, as a 'perspective on lan-guage as intrinsically tied to context and to human activity' (2005: 233). Alim (2006) uses the term *hiphopography* to describe an approach to study-ing hip-hop language on the streets through a mixture of sociolinguistics, ethnography and oral history, demanding a direct engagement with the artists in the contexts of their work. Let us by all means question language, nationality, culture and identity, but let us also bring close, careful and thoughtful analysis to such contexts.

Educational Implications: Teaching with the Flow

There are many educational implications of the picture I have been outlining here. According to McCarthy *et al.* (2003: 462), we are con-fronted as educators by the challenge to 'address the radical reconfigura-tion and cultural rearticulation now taking place in educational and social life'. The changing dynamics of globalization, increased migration and digital media, are shifting 'the commonly taken-for-granted stabili-ties of social constructs such as "culture", "identity", "nation", "state" and so forth'. This chapter has suggested that the ways in which language may be used in popular cultural forms such as hip hop makes new forms of identification possible. New language use presents us not only with basic pedagogical questions of form and access – what should be taught to whom – but also with questions of how cultural forms are interrelated with language use, and how the appropriation of language and culture presents different possibilities for imagined identities, imagined traditions and imagined languages.

Opening educational doors to popular culture does not mean, as Willis reminds us, 'a lazy throwing open of the school doors to the latest fad, but rather committing to a principled understanding of the complexity of contemporary cultural experience' (Willis, 2003: 411). The location of classrooms within global transcultural flows, however, implies that they can no longer be considered as bounded sites, with students entering from fixed locations, with identities drawing on local traditions, with curricula as static bodies of knowledge. Popular music, as Connell and Gibson (2003) argue, unsettles common distinctions between the local and global, the traditional and contemporary, and reflects the flows, fluxes and fluidity of life in an era of globalization. Students refuse attempts to be pinned down, despite the array of educational technologies (tests, uniforms, architecture, psychological theories of identity) designed to do so. Popular music 'remains an important cultural sphere in which identities are affirmed, challenged, taken apart and reconstructed' (Connell & Gibson, 2003: 117). If we believe that education needs to proceed by taking student knowledge, identity and desire into account, we need to engage with multiple ways of speaking, being, and learning, with multilayered modes of identity at global, regional, national and local levels.

Such a view has numerous repercussions for language education. First, we need to question the ways in which we teach languages as bounded entities. From both theoretical and practical stances, it is becoming increasingly clear that to talk of 'French', 'English', 'Japanese', 'Chinese' and so on – as if these were discrete languages that existed in isolation – is to overlook the ways in which languages are always interrelated. The mixed codes of the hip-hop world resist the monolingual obsessions of nations and their educational institutions, opposing, for example, the many interests and complicities that have supported the use of English and only English in classrooms, where English has been seen as a language that operates only in its own presence. As Huq (2001: 75) notes in the context of using French rap in French classes, the messages, languages and ethnicities of French rap are 'redefining what it is to be French'. The lessons we draw from the multilingualism of hip hop demand that we reintroduce translation in all its complexity into English language teaching, that we open up and explore the many possible meanings that can start to flow in and out of languages in relation to English, and that we stop treating languages as objects in isolation (Pennycook, 2008).

Second, the role that popular culture plays across classroom boundaries suggests the need for a better understanding of informal education and affective engagement (see also Duff, Jaspers, Rymes, this volume). Pardue points out that in the Brazilian context, 'Hip-hoppers have become increasingly persuasive that their work is educational because they reach large populations of urban youth that previously were isolated from public education' (Pardue, 2004: 412). As educators we need to grasp the different digital worlds of identification that our students inhabit as well as this interplay between the flow, fixity and fluidity of culture, language and identity (Pennycook, 2005). Popular culture not only raises the question of the permeability of classroom walls (discourses and identities are constructed across the educational boundaries of walls, desks, tests and texts) but also links students across time and space. Popular music forms 'transnational networks of affiliation, and of material and symbolic interdependence ... Music nourishes imagined communities, traces links to distant and past places' (Connell & Gibson, 2003: 271). The fluidity and (downloadable) availability of music, its link to place and imagined community, and the possibilities it presents for diverse identifications render popular culture an important site of affective engagement, informal education and cultural learning.

Finally, we can look to sociolinguistic analyses of language to inform our pedagogical approaches to language awareness. Alim (2009, this volume) argues for the need for a variety of forms of critical language awareness – for both teachers and students – as part of an education about how language is used in different communities. These critical hip hop language pedagogies (CHHLPs), which include ethnographies of local language use, are an important first step towards 'challenging a given social order (including the structure of the dominant linguistic market)'. Assisting students to become aware of the ways in which language works locally can be a significant '"wake-up call" that encourages students and teachers to interrogate received discourses on language, which are always connected to issues of race, class, gender, sexuality, and power' (2009: 228). Alim (2009: 228) concludes that 'as sociolinguists, we must do more than study the relationships between language, society and power – we must do what we can to alter those relationships. That's real talk'. This is where sociolinguistics, research and pedagogy come together, a crucial relationship that is about teaching towards a better world based on significant sociolinguistic insights into the workings of language and society.

Discography

Daara J. (2004) *Boomerang*. UK: Wrasse Records.
DJ Tommy (2001) *Respect for da Chopstick Hip Hop*. Hong Kong: Warner Music.
GHOST 13 (2004) *GHOST 13*. Philippines: GMA Records.
Rip Slyme (2002) *Tokyo Classic*. Japan: Warner Music.

Tasha (no date) *Hiphop Album*. Korea: Gemini Bobos Entertainment.
Too Phat (2002) *360°*. Malaysia: EMI.

Notes

1. This phrase, meaning Black, White, Arab (Beur derives from the common *verlan*, inversion of the word 'Arabe'), is a reference to the opposition that emerged to the French hyper-nationalism of the red, white and blue of the tricolor. Black, Blanc, Beur presents an alternative, multiracial, multilingual, multicultural vision to the monolingual – cultural – racial view ascribed to by French nationalists who cling to the traditions of the red, white and blue.
2. These interviews were part of two research projects on global and local hip hop between 2003 and 2008. For further details, see Pennycook (2007).

Suggestions for further reading

Alim, H.S. (2006) *Roc the Mic Right: The Language of Hip Hop Culture*. London & New York: Routledge.
Alim's work brings together a close sociolinguistic analysis of language in Hip Hop in the United States with an interest in language and education.

Alim, H.S., Ibrahim, A. and Pennycook, A. (eds) (2009) *Global Linguistic Flows: Hip Hop Cultures, Youth Identities, and the Politics of Language*. New York: Routledge, 213–230.
This book has a wide range of contemporary work looking at hip hop (as well as education) from sociolinguistic perspectives. Contexts range from Hong Kong to Brazil, from Germany to Montreal.

Blommaert, J. (2008) *Grassroots Literacy: Writing, Identity and Voice in Central Africa*. London: Routledge.
Jan Blommaert is another scholar who combines ethnography, text analysis, popular culture and politics. In this book he looks at the relationship between globalization and the writing of ordinary people.

Pennycook, A. (2007) *Global Englishes and Transcultural Flows*. London: Routledge.
My own book on this topic covers a lot of the ground discussed in this chapter, and like Alim's work, attempts to bring together sociolinguistics, cultural studies and pedagogy. It takes a broad focus on the global spread of hip hop and the global spread of English, and tries to show the complex interrelations between the two.

Rampton, B. (2006) *Language in Late Modernity: Interaction in an Urban School*. Cambridge: Cambridge University Press.
Ben Rampton's work, looking in close detail at the language of kids in an urban school, has been a cornerstone for fastidious research methodology as well as innovative thinking about language use beyond narrow ascriptions of identity.

References

Akindes, F.Y. (2001) Sudden rush: *Na Mele Paleoleo* (Hawaiian Rap) as liberatory discourse. *Discourse* 23 (1), 82–98.
Alim, H.S. (2006) *Roc the Mic Right: The Language of Hip Hop Culture*. London & New York: Routledge.
Alim, H.S. (2009) Creating 'An empire within an empire': Critical hip hop language pedagogies and the role of sociolinguistics. In H.S. Alim, A. Ibrahim and

A. Pennycook (eds) *Global Linguistic Flows: Hip Hop Cultures, Youth Identities, and the Politics of Language* (pp. 213–230). New York: Routledge.

Androutsopoulos, J. (2003) Einleitung. In J. Androutsopoulos (Hg/ed.) *HipHop: Globale Kultur – Lokale Praktiken* (pp. 9–23). Bielefeld: Transcript Verlag.

Auzanneau, M. (2002) Rap in Libreville, Gabon: An urban sociolinguistic space. In A-P. Durand (ed.) *Black, Blanc, Beur: Rap Music and Hip-Hop Culture in the Francophone World* (pp. 106–123). Lanham, Maryland: The Scarecrow Press.

Bakhtin, M. (1986) *Speech Genres and Other Late Essays.* Austin, TX: University of Texas Press.

Bauman, R. (2004) *A World of Others' Words: Cross-Cultural Perspectives on Intertextuality.* Oxford: Blackwell.

Berger, H. (2003) Introduction: The politics and aesthetics of language choice and dialect in popular music. In H. Berger and M. Carroll (eds) *Global Pop, Local Language* (pp. ix–xxvi). Jackson: University Press of Mississippi.

Blommaert, J. (2005) *Discourse: A Critical Introduction.* Cambridge: Cambridge University Press.

Blommaert, J. (2007) Sociolinguistics and discourse analysis: Orders of indexicality and polycentricity. *Journal of Multicultural Discourses* 2 (2), 115–130.

Cepeda, M.E. (2003) *Mucho Loco* for Ricky Martin: Or the politics chronology, crossover, and language within the Latin(o) music 'boom'. In H. Berger and M. Carroll (eds) *Global Pop, Local Language* (pp. 113–129). Jackson: University Press of Mississippi.

Chamoiseau, P. and Confiant, R. (1999) *Lettres Créoles.* Paris: Gallimard.

Connell, J. and Gibson, C. (2003) *Sound Tracks: Popular Music, Identity and Place.* London: Routledge.

Coupland, N. (2003) Sociolinguistic authenticities. *Journal of Sociolinguistics* 7, 417–431.

Coupland, N. (2007) *Style: Language Variation and Identity.* Cambridge: Cambridge University Press.

Doran, M. (2004) Negotiating between *Bourge* and *Racaille:* Verlan as youth identity practice in suburban Paris. In A. Pavlenko and A. Blackledge (eds) *Negotiation of Identities in Multilingual Contexts* (pp. 93–124). Clevedon: Multilingual Matters.

Eckert, P. (2004) The meaning of style. *Texas Linguistic Forum* 47, 41–53.

Errington, J. (2008) *Linguistics in a Colonial World: A Story of Language, Meaning and Power.* Oxford: Blackwell.

Fernandes, S. (2003) Fear of a black nation: Local rappers, transnational crossings, and state power in contemporary Cuba. *Anthropological Quarterly* 76 (4), 575–608.

Gilroy, P. (1993) *The Black Atlantic: Modernity and Double Consciousness.* London: Verso.

Glissant, E. (1997) *Poetics of Relation* (B. Wing, trans.). Ann Arbor: University of Michigan Press.

Gurnah, A. (1997) Elvis in Zanzibar. In A. Scott (ed.) *The Limits of Globalization* (pp. 116–142). London: Routledge.

Hagège, C. (2006) *Combat pour le Français: Au nom de la diversité des langues et des cultures.* Paris: Odile Jacob.

Halliday, M.A.K. (2002) *Applied Linguistics as an Evolving Theme.* Plenary address to the Association Internationale de Linguistique Appliqué, Singapore, December, 2002.

Harris, R. (1990) On redefining linguistics. In H. Davis and T. Taylor (eds) *Redefining Linguistics* (pp. 18–52). London: Routledge.

Heller, M. and Duchêne, A. (2007) Discourses of endangerment: Sociolinguistics, globalization and social order. In A. Duchêne and M. Heller (eds) *Discourses of*

Endangerment: Ideology and Interest in the Defence of Languages (pp. 1–13). London: Continuum.

Heryanto, A. (2007) Then there were languages: Bahasa Indonesia was one among many. In S. Makoni and A. Pennycook (eds) *Disinventing and Reconstituting Languages* (pp. 42–61). Clevedon: Multilingual Matters.

Higgins, C. (2009) From Da Bomb to *Bomba*: Global hip hop nation language in Tanzania. In H.S. Alim, A. Ibrahim and A. Pennycook (eds) *Global Linguistic Flows: Hip Hop Cultures, Youth Identities, and the Politics of Language* (pp. 95–112). New York: Routledge.

Ho, W.C. (2003) Between globalisation and localisation: A study of Hong Kong popular music. *Popular Music* 22 (2), 143–157.

Huq, R. (2001) The French connection: Francophone hip hop as an institution in contemporary postcolonial France. *Taboo: Journal of Education and Culture* 5 (2), 69–84.

Ibrahim, A. (1999) Becoming black: Rap and hip-hop, race, gender, identity and the politics of ESL learning. *TESOL Quarterly* 33 (3), 349–370.

Ibrahim, A. (2008) The new flaneur: Subaltern cultural studies, African youth in Canada and the semiology of in-betweenness. *Cultural Studies* 22 (2), 234–253.

Irvine, J. and Gal, S. (2000) Language ideology and linguistic differentiation. In P.V. Kroskrity (ed.) *Regimes of Language: Ideologies, Politics and Identities* (pp. 35–85). Santa Fe, NM: School of American Research Press.

Jacquemet, M. (2005) Transidiomatic practices, language and power in the age of globalization. *Language & Communication* 25, 257–277.

Kaya, A. (2001) *'Sicher in Kreuzberg' Constructing Diasporas: Turkish Hip-Hop Youth in Berlin*. Bielefeld: Transcript Verlag.

Krims, A. (2000) *Rap Music and the Poetics of Identity*. Cambridge: Cambridge University Press.

Lin, A. (2009) "Respect for Da Chopstick Hip Hop": The politics, poetics, and pedagogy of cantonese verbal art in Hong Kong. In H.S. Alim, A. Ibrahim and A. Pennycook (eds) *Global Linguistic Flows: Hip Hop Cultures, Youth Identities, and the Politics of Language* (pp. 159–177). New York: Routledge.

Makoni, S. and Pennycook, A. (2007) Disinventing and reconstituting languages. In S. Makoni and A. Pennycook (eds) *Disinventing and Reconstituting Languages* (pp. 1–41). Clevedon: Multilingual Matters.

McCarthy, C., Giardina, M., Harewood, S. and Park, J.K. (2003) Contesting culture: Identity and curriculum dilemmas in the age of globalization, postcolonialism, and multiplicity. *Harvard Educational Review* 73 (3), 449–465.

Mitchell, T. (2001) Introduction: another root – Hip-Hop outside the USA. In T. Mitchell (ed.) *Global Noise: Rap and Hip-Hop Outside the USA* (pp. 1–38). Middletown, CT: Wesleyan University Press.

Mufwene, S. (2001) *The Ecology of Language Evolution*. Cambridge: Cambridge University Press.

Omoniyi, T. (2009) "So I choose to Do Am Naija style": Hip Hop, language, and postcolonial identities. In H.S. Alim, A. Ibrahim and A. Pennycook (eds) *Global Linguistic Flows: Hip Hop Cultures, Youth Identities, and the Politics of Language* (pp. 113–135). New York: Routledge.

Pardue, D. (2004) "Writing in the margins": Brazilian hip-hop as an educational project. *Anthropology and Education* 35 (4), 411–432.

Pennay, M. (2001) Rap in Germany: The birth of a genre. In T. Mitchell (ed.) *Global Noise: Rap and Hip-Hop Outside the USA* (pp. 111–133). Middletown, CT: Wesleyan University Press.

Pennycook, A. (2003) Global Englishes, Rip Slyme and performativity. *Journal of Sociolinguistics* 7 (4), 513–533.

Pennycook, A. (2005) Teaching with the flow: Fixity and fluidity in education. *Asia Pacific Journal of Education* 25 (1), 29–43.

Pennycook, A. (2007) *Global Englishes and Transcultural Flows*. London: Routledge.

Pennycook, A. (2008) English as a language always in translation. *European Journal of English Studies* 12 (1), 33–47.

Pennycook, A. and Mitchell, T. (2009) Hip Hop as dusty foot philosophy: Engaging locality. In H.S. Alim, A. Ibrahim and A. Pennycook (eds) *Global Linguistic Flows: Hip Hop Cultures, Youth Identities, and the Politics of Language* (pp. 25–42). New York: Routledge.

Perry, I. (2004) *Prophets of the Hood: Politics and Poetics in Hip Hop*. Durham, NC: Duke University Press.

Phillipson, R. (2003) *English Only Europe? Challenging Language Policy*. London: Routledge.

Phillipson, R. and Skutnabb-Kangas, T. (1996) English only worldwide or language ecology? *TESOL Quarterly* 30 (3), 429–452.

Prévos, A.J.M. (2001) Postcolonial popular music in France: Rap music and hip-hop culture in the 1980s and 1990s. In T. Mitchell (ed.) *Global Noise: Rap and Hip-Hop Outside the USA* (pp. 39–56). Middletown, CT: Wesleyan University Press.

Radhakrishnan, R. (2003) *Theory in an Uneven World*. Oxford: Blackwell.

Rampton, B. (1995) *Crossing: Language and Ethnicity among Adolescents*. London: Longman.

Rampton, B. (2006) *Language in Late Modernity: Interaction in an Urban School*. Cambridge: Cambridge University Press.

Roth-Gordon, J. (2009) Conversational sampling, race trafficking, and the invocation of the *gueto* in Brazilian Hip hop. In H.S. Alim, A. Ibrahim and A. Pennycook (eds) *Global Linguistic Flows: Hip Hop Cultures, Youth Identities, and the Politics of Language* (pp. 63–78). New York: Routledge.

Sarkar, M. (2009) "Still Reppin' Por Mi Gente" The transformative power of language mixing in Quebec hip hop. In H.S. Alim, A. Ibrahim and A. Pennycook (eds) *Global Linguistic Flows: Hip Hop Cultures, Youth Identities, and the Politics of Language* (pp. 139–157). New York: Routledge.

Sarkar, M. and Allen, D. (2007) Hybrid identities in Quebec hip-hop: Language, territory, and ethnicity in the mix. *Journal of Language, Identity, and Education* 6 (2), 117–130.

Scott, D. (1999) *Refashioning Futures: Criticism after Postcoloniality*. Princeton, NJ: Princeton University Press.

Skutnabb-Kangas, T. (2000) *Linguistic Genocide in Education – or Worldwide Diversity and Human Rights?* Mahwah, NJ: Lawrence Erlbaum.

Sling Shot Hip Hop. (2008) The Palestinian Lyrical front. On WWW at http://slingshothiphop.com/. Accessed 30.10.08.

Swedenburg, T. (2001) Islamic hip-hop vs Islamophobia. In T. Mitchell (ed.) *Global Noise: Rap and Hip-Hop Outside the USA* (pp. 57–85). Middletown, CT: Wesleyan University Press.

Urla, J. (2001) 'We are all Malcolm X!' Negu Gorriak, Hip-Hop, and the Basque political imaginary. In T. Mitchell (ed.) *Global Noise: Rap and Hip-Hop Outside the USA*. (pp. 171–193). Middletown, CT: Wesleyan University Press.

Willis, P. (2003) Foot soldiers of modernity: The dialectics of cultural consumption and the 21st-century school. *Harvard Educational Review* 73 (3), 390–415.

Woolard, K. (2004) Is the past a foreign country?: Time, language origins, and the nation in early modern Spain. *Journal of Linguistic Anthropology* 14 (1), 57–58.

Part 2

Language and Society

Chapter 4

English as an International Language

SANDRA LEE McKAY

This chapter begins by examining the various ways in which present-day English use has been characterized. I argue in the first section that although existing definitions and approaches provide insight into the role of English today, what is needed is a comprehensive view of English use that takes into account the local linguistic ecology and recognizes the hybridity of current English use. The next section of the chapter summarizes key research findings regarding English language learning and how it is related to imagined communities, identity and technology. This is followed by a discussion of challenges facing the field in terms of inequality of access to English language learning, othering in English pedagogy and standards in English teaching and learning. In closing, I set forth principles that I believe should inform a socially sensitive English pedagogy.

Defining Present-day English Use

World Englishes

The terminology used to describe present-day English reflects the different approaches to English use offered by professionals in the field. One of the most prevalent perspectives aims to describe the phonological, grammatical, lexical and pragmatic features of the current use of English as a factor of geographical region. This perspective is typically referred to as *World Englishes*. The term *World Englishes* is based on Kachru's (1986) early description of institutionalized varieties of English. Kachru distinguishes three major types of users of English: (1) native users of English for whom English is the first language in almost all functions, (2) nonnative users of English who use an institutionalized second-language variety of English, and (3) non-native users of English who consider English as a foreign language and use it in highly restricted domains. Kachru refers to speakers in the first group as members of the Inner Circle (e.g. speakers from the United States, United Kingdom and Australia), the second group as members of the Outer Circle (e.g. speakers from the Philippines and South Africa) and the last group as members of the Expanding Circle (e.g. speakers from China and Hungary). Kachru argues that speakers in the Outer Circle have an institutionalized variety of English, which he describes in the following manner:

> The institutionalized second-language varieties have a long history of acculturation in new cultural and geographical contexts; they have a large range of functions in the local educational, administrative, and legal system. The result of such uses is that such varieties have developed nativized discourse and style types and functionally determined sublanguages (registers) and are used as a linguistic vehicle for creative writing. (Kachru, 1986: 19)

According to Kachru, World Englishes have developed largely in former British colonies where English is used in many domains on a daily basis and has been influenced by local languages and cultures. While Kachru's model was instrumental in initially recognizing the validity of varieties of English, the spread of English has brought with it far more complexity in use than can be captured by the model.

At present, there are a growing number of standardized varieties of English – not just in Kachru's Outer Circle countries, but also as Lowenberg (2002) documents, in many Expanding Circle nations as well. According to Lowenberg (2002: 431), in certain intranational and regional domains of language use (e.g. across Europe), English actually functions as a second language, and often develops nativized norms. In addition, these processes of nativization have resulted in not just the development of different varieties of Standard English between countries, but also varieties of English within countries (see, e.g. Bamgbose, 1998). In addition there exists a variety of English proficiency levels within a specific social context.

This situation has led Pakir (1991), drawing on the varieties of English spoken in Singapore, to depict the use of English within Singapore and other countries as a factor of the formality of the context and the speakers' level of proficiency (see Figure 4.1). She places variation in Singapore English along two clines (influenced by Kachru's (1983) 'cline of English bilingualism'): the *proficiency* cline and the *formality* cline, reflecting the *users* and *uses* of English. Pakir's model is represented through a series of expanding triangles, which represent the differing ranges of styles of English-speaking Singaporeans, with education and English proficiency offering an increasing range of choice. Those users of English with higher education are located at the top ends of both the formality and proficiency clines. They often are capable of the whole range of English expressions, and able to move along the whole length of the formality cline. Those at the base of the

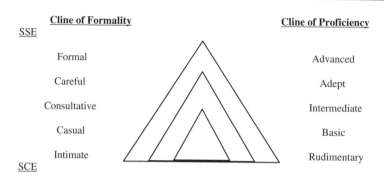

Figure 4.1 Pakir's expanding triangles of Singapore English (SSE, Singapore Standard English; SCE, Singapore Colloquial English) (*Source:* Pakir, 1991: 174)

triangle have lower levels of proficiency, typically have lower levels of education, and tend to come from a lower socio-economic background. They are more restricted in their movement along the formality cline, and can usually speak only the colloquial forms of Singapore English.

What World Englishes interpretations attempt to do is to develop a model that describes and legitimizes a pluricentric view of English, and one that moves away from a view of there being just one standard form against which all others are measured. As argued by Kachru (1983, 1992), English has 'blended itself with the cultural and social complex' (1983: 139) of the country and has thereby become 'culture-bound' (1983: 140) in it. Therefore, he argues, new Englishes cannot be characterized in terms of acquisitional inadequacy, or be judged by the norms of English in Inner Circle countries. The World Englishes paradigm attempts to place all varieties of English on par with each other without any one being a reference point. Although the paradigm has made a significant contribution to our understanding of international English in its recognition of the pluricentric nature of current English use, what it fails to do is to recognize the localized nature of English language use in which bilingual/multilingual individuals draw on their full linguistic repertoire to signal their local and global identity.

English as a Lingua Franca

Recently, a good deal of attention has been focused on an analysis of interactions between L2 speakers of English, termed *English as a Lingua Franca (ELF)* talk. Firth (1996) provided one of the earliest definitions of ELF stating that ELF interactions are those in which English is used as 'a "contact language" between persons who share neither a common native tongue nor a common (national) culture, and for whom English is the chosen *foreign* language of communication' [emphasis in original] (p. 240). Such interactions occur frequently in Expanding Circle countries where English is used for business, political, academic and travel purposes.

Pragmatic features

Some of the current research on ELF has focused on identifying the pragmatic features of ELF interactions, as was done in Firth's (1996) seminal article on ELF. Firth's data involved a collection of telephone calls from two Danish international trading companies involving Danish export managers and their international clients. As Firth points out, one of the major advantages of analyzing such discourse from a conversational analysis perspective rather than as 'foreigner talk', 'interlanguage talk' or 'learner interaction' perspective is that the participant is viewed as 'a *language user* whose real-world interactions are deserving of unprejudiced *description* rather ... than as a person conceived *a priori* to be the possessor of incomplete or deficient communicative competence, putatively striving for the "target" competence of an idealized "native speaker"' [emphasis in original] (p. 241). Firth contends that an unprejudiced description of ELF interactions clearly demonstrates that 'lingua franca talk is not only meaningful, it is also "*normal*" and, indeed, "*ordinary*"' [emphasis in original] (p. 242).

Summarizing the findings of existing data on the pragmatic aspect of ELF interactions, Seidlhofer (2004) provides the following generalizations regarding the pragmatics of ELF:

- Misunderstandings are not frequent in ELF interactions; when they do occur, they tend to be resolved either by topic change, or less often, by overt negotiation using communication strategies such as rephrasing and repetition.
- Interference from L1 interactional norms is very rare – a kind of suspension of expectations regarding norms seems to be in operation.
- As long as a certain threshold of understanding is obtained, interlocutors seem to adopt what Firth (1996) has termed the 'let-it-pass principle', which gives the impression of ELF talk being overtly consensus-oriented, cooperative and mutually supportive, and thus fairly robust. (Seidlhofer, 2004: 218)

Grammatical features

Current work in ELF research is also investigating the grammatical and phonological features of ELF interactions. Significant contributions to identifying the grammatical features of ELF are under way through the compilation of the Vienna-Oxford International Corpus of English (VOICE) now in progress at the University of Vienna under the supervision of Siedlhofer. The corpus includes face-to-face interactions among fairly fluent speakers of English from a wide range of first-language backgrounds in a variety of settings in which participants have various roles and relationships. At this point, an initial data analysis has highlighted the use of several grammatical forms that, although often emphasized in language classrooms as being in need of corrections, do not appear to cause problems in communicative success. These include:

- Dropping the third person present tense *–s*.
- Confusing the relative pronouns *who* and *which*.
- Omitting the definite and indefinite articles where they are obligatory in ENL [English as a native language], and inserting them where they do not occur in ENL.
- Failing to use correct tag questions (e.g. *isn't it?* or *no?* instead of *shouldn't they?*).
- Inserting redundant prepositions, as in *We have to study about ...*
- Overusing certain verbs of high semantic generality, such as *do, have, make, put, take.*
- Replacing infinitive-constructions with *that*- clauses, as in *I want that*
- Overdoing explicitness (e.g. *black color* rather than just *black*).

(Seidlhofer, 2004: 220)

Phonological features

Finally, research on ELF interactions has led to the identification of the phonological features of ELF interactions. Jenkins (2000), in her work on the phonology of English as an International Language (EIL), analyzed the interactions of six learners of English – two Japanese, three Swiss-German and one Swiss-French – all at the upper-intermediate to low-advanced level, who were recorded as they practiced for the Cambridge Certificate in Advanced English speaking examinations. Some of these interactions were between interlocutors with the same L1, others were between speakers of different L1s. Using this data, Jenkins identified 40 occasions where there was a breakdown in communication due to pronunciation, lexis, grammar, world knowledge or ambiguity. All of the breakdowns in the data occurred between speakers of different L1 backgrounds. In addition, the vast majority of breakdowns (27) were due to pronunciation problems, with another eight due to lexis.

On the basis of her investigation, Jenkins (2000) delineates what she terms a phonological Lingua Franca Core, that is, phonological features that appear to be most crucial for intelligibility among L2 speakers of English. Based on her data, the central features of this core appear to be the following (Jenkins, 2000: 132):

(1) Most consonant sounds.
(2) Appropriate consonant cluster simplification.
(3) Vowel length distinction.
(4) Nuclear stress.

She argues that since these features have the greatest potential for causing breakdowns in communication between speakers of different L1 backgrounds, the pedagogical focus in ELT classrooms should be on the production of most consonant sounds, initial consonant clusters, vowel length and nuclear stress. Less attention needs to be given to word stress, rhythm, and features of connected speech. While the World Englishes paradigm has highlighted the pluricentric nature of English standards, the ELF perspective has contributed to our understanding of some of the pragmatic, grammatical and phonological features of L2 speakers of English in contact with other L2 speakers.

English as an international language

In sorting through various perspectives on present-day English use, it is helpful to consider Pennycook's (2003) categorization of current views toward the spread of English. The first is what he calls the *homogeny position*, which views the spread of English as leading to a homogenization of world culture. For some, this homogenization is viewed favorably and almost triumphantly. Crystal (2003), for example, cites various statistics to document the pervasiveness of English today and tends to view this pervasiveness as a positive characteristic of globalization. Others, however, see homogenization as essentially a negative feature of globalization, reflecting imperialism and colonization (Phillipson, 1992), and leading to the loss of other languages (Nettle & Romaine, 2000). What is lacking in this perspective is an account of the agency of individuals to react to imperialism and language loss, a point raised by Brutt-Griffler (2002), Canagarajah (2005) and Pennycook (1998, 2007).

The second position delineated by Pennycook (2003) is the *heterogeny position* in which individuals like Braj Kachru describe the features of World Englishes as a sign of the pluricentricism that has been brought about by globalization. The goal of the World Englishes paradigm has been to describe the manner in which English has become localized, creating different varieties of English around the world. The ELF perspective, by and large, shares the same goal. For Pennycook (2003), there is a major shortcoming with these perspectives. As he puts it,

> While the homogeny argument tends to ignore all these local appropriations and adaptations, this heterogeny argument tends to ignore the broader political context of the spread of English. Indeed there is a constant insistence on the neutrality of English, a position that avoids all the crucial concerns around both the global and local politics of the language. Furthermore, by focusing on the standardization of local versions of English, the world Englishes paradigm shifts the locus of

control but not its nature, and by so doing ignores power and struggle in language. (Pennycook, 2003: 8)

In the end, Pennycook (2003) argues that the ultimate effect of globalization on the use of English is neither homogenization nor heterogenization; rather it is 'a fluid mixture of cultural heritage ... and popular culture ..., of change and tradition, of border crossing and ethnic affiliation, of global appropriation and local contextualization' (Pennycook, 2003: 10). This, he contends, is what the new global order is about.

Sharing Pennycook's belief that more attention needs to be given to the 'power and struggle in language', I will use the term *English as an international language* as an umbrella term to characterize the use of English between any two L2 speakers of English, whether sharing the same culture or not, as well as between L2 and L1 speakers of English. I will argue that any examination of EIL must include attention to the global and local aspect of English and explore the way in which a specific use of English is impacted by issues of power and struggle. A specific example of English use will help to clarify my perspective.

In our recent research (Kubota & McKay, 2009), we examined the role of EIL in the linguistic landscape of a rural community in Japan where there is a growing number of language minority migrant workers, mainly from Brazil, China, Thailand and Vietnam. The local lingua franca is, of course, Japanese. However, the current emphasis on EIL in Japan has resulted in all children learning English rather than any of the minority languages spoken in the local area. It has also resulted in a commonly accepted assumption that the way to communicate with these migrants is through Japanese or English rather than other languages. In fact, when one of the middle school teachers found that a recent immigrant in her classroom did not understand Japanese, she resorted to English, assuming that these young immigrants should understand an 'international language'.

While on the local level, bilingual speakers of Portuguese, Chinese, Thai and Vietnam are sorely needed, the second language that almost everyone is engaged in learning is English because as one teacher put it, 'you can't soar into the world with Portuguese.... Improving Japan with Portuguese won't let the country soar into the world'. It is situations such as this that demonstrate the need to examine the power and struggles that inform local uses of English. While in this particular local context Japanese, not English, is serving as a lingua franca, still the global role of English is exerting invisible symbolic power. My approach to current English use then emphasizes the localized nature of interactions and the power and struggle that informs these interactions. Often in the local linguistic ecology, English plays more of a symbolic role than an actual medium of communication.

Recent Findings

With English being considered by many as a global language, individuals around the world are striving to learn English, leading to a large English teaching/learning industry. In summarizing current research on EIL, there are three areas in which I believe we have gained important insights into the teaching and learning of English. These have to do with:

- imagined communities as incentives for English learning;
- the role of identity in English language learning; and
- the value of technology as a learning tool.

Imagined communities as incentives for English learning

Back in 1986, in a book titled *The Alchemy of English*, Kachru (1986: 1) argued that 'knowing English is like possessing the fabled Aladdin's lamp, which permits one to open, as it were, the linguistic gates to international business, technology, science and travel. In short, English provides linguistic power'. This belief in the power of English has resulted in many language learners imagining the various benefits that can develop if they learn English. Often these 'imagined communities' (Anderson, 1983) are depicted in the narratives of language learners. Such narratives reinforce the belief of many English learners that if they invest in English learning, they will reap the benefits of social and intellectual mobility.

Recent research on English learning has documented some of these narratives of imagined communities. Norton and Kamal (2003), for example, report on a study they conducted with middle-school children in Karachi, Pakistan, in which young learners of English were asked to reflect on what they would like to do to help Afghan refugee children in Pakistan thrive. Many of the young Pakistani children believed that it was important for the Afghan refugees to develop literacy and to learn some English. The reasons they gave for wanting the Afghan refugee children to learn English illustrate the kind of narrations that can idealize the benefits of joining an imagined community of English speakers. The following statements, written by young Pakistani students, are representative of such narrations.

> English is the language spoken commonly. This language is understood throughout the world. If the Afghan children learn English, know English, speak English they will be able to discuss their problems with the people of the world.

> The English language is an international language spoken all over the world and it is the language of science. Therefore to promote their education and awareness with modern technologies, it is important to teach them English. (Norton & Kamal, 2003: 309)

Niño-Murcia (2003) cites Peruvian narratives that recount other benefits of joining an imagined community of English speakers. Niño-Murcia examined the beliefs of English learners in Tupichocha, an agro-pastoral village of 1543 inhabitants that is losing its population from emigration. While people over 40 generally do not express an interest in learning English, this is not true for the younger generation. Many of these young people want to learn English so that they can take distance-learning courses on the internet; others want to learn English so that they can go to an English-speaking country and earn more money. For example, one respondent, Luz (aged 25), when asked why she was studying English, responded that she wanted to learn English so she could go to the United States and earn a good salary. In her mind, English proficiency was the key to both immigration and making money. Yet as Niño-Murcia points out,

> For the participants, the United States is not only an imagined geographical site, but also the land where their needs will be fulfilled. The irony is that the rhetoric of free trade, global market and capital flow comes together with tightening frontiers to prevent human flow. Luz's illusions aside, English is in reality a very minimal factor in whether people are able to surmount the barrier. While the popular media contain vast amounts of false information about both English and the countries where it prevails, they give little or no accurate information about how in fact the immigration/illegal migration system works. It is the financial requirements of the embassy, not the language factor at all, which actually sets limits on legal access to the USA. While capital and goods can 'freely' move, the human element should stay where they 'belong'. (Niño-Murcia, 2003: 132)

Park and Abelmann (2004) offer a poignant account of the imagined communities Korean mothers want their children to belong to. Arguing that at present in South Korea there is 'a veritable English language mania' (Park & Abelmann, 2004: 646) brought on largely by the implementation of English learning in the elementary school in South Korea, Park and Ableman investigated the aspirations of English learning of South Korean women of various economic classes. Regardless of economic class, all of the mothers yearned for their children to acquire English so that they would become cosmopolitan, living at home yet part of the world. While many of the upper class women could afford to help their children become part of this world by giving them private English lessons or sending them abroad for their elementary education, this was not the case for less affluent families. The authors describe how less affluent mothers still imagine their children as part of this cosmopolitan world. As one less affluent mother put it, she 'still dreams that her children might someday live abroad in a "bigger world" – "even if they have to live abroad as beggars *(koij)*"' (Park & Abelmann, 2004: 654). Like many less affluent mothers around the world, this mother imagines 'her children on a broader stage, despite their likely lower status abroad' (Park & Abelmann 2004: 654).

The concept of an imagined community is one that has not gone unnoticed by ELT private schools. Evidence of this is the establishment of theme villages that depict an imagined environment. Seargeant (2005), for example, describes British Hills in Japan, a leisure language-learning complex that seeks to simulate an 'authentic' English-speaking environment. In fact, the sales slogan 'boasts that the complex is "More English than England itself"' (Seargeant, 2005: 327). The village is staffed by native speakers recruited from Britain, Canada, Australia and New Zealand. In their job description, they describe some of the duties of the staff as follows:

- Meeting buses arriving at British Hills with a friendly hello and lots of waving.
- Being on the steps to wave goodbye to groups leaving British Hills.
- Taking the time to stop in the passages/in your department to CHAT to the guests.
- Being sociable and friendly to all guests: whether on or off duty.
- Offering to take and star in hundreds of photographs.
- Basically just going the extra mile to make that personal connection with as many guests as possible. (Seargeant, 2005: 340)

By hiring only native speakers and promoting native speaker competency, the village promotes a reality that is far different from the multilingual/multicultural Britain of today. In doing so,

> The overall effect is to create an environment which is not necessarily truthful to the original upon which it is purportedly based but is instead an imagined idea with its own logic and reality. The authenticity upon which British Hills prides itself is not a representation of Britishness as it is currently constructed and enacted in mainstream British society. Instead, it is an image drawn from aspects of the popular imagination in Japan, from a tourist industry template . . . and also from local protocol for foreign language education. (Seargeant, 2005: 341)

In this context, authenticity becomes not the genuine item but a fake representation of a different reality. As Seargent (2005: 341) puts it, 'simulation replaces reality, becomes its own reality. A place like British Hills is not merely representing Britishness but reconstructing it, thus presenting itself as a detailed realistic image of something that actually exists only within its own depiction. The use of the concept of authenticity is almost an irony of the process . . .'. The theory underlying such villages is that learning can be enhanced by students actually imagining themselves in the role of a fluent speaker in an 'authentic' environment.

We have then learned much about how imagined communities can further reinforce Kachru's idea of English competency as a kind of Aladdin's

lamp. We have also seen how these imagined communities can be a powerful force in commercial aspects of language learning. Linked closely to
language learners' imagined community of English speakers is the new
identity that may potentially come from belonging to this community,
either as an aspiration or as a reality. Indeed another area in which we
have learned a great deal is the role of identity in language learning.

The role of identity in language learning

Examining the identity of second-language learners is a relatively recent
interest in second-language acquisition research. In the past, major attention was devoted to interlanguage analysis, with little recognition given to
learning processes, individual variables, or the social context in which a
second language is learned. However, recent work, informed by poststructuralist approaches and critical theory (e.g. McKay & Wong, 1996;
Peirce, 1995; Rampton, 1995), has begun to examine how educational
institutions can position students in particular ways. Work that is especially relevant to our discussion examines how school discourses can position English language learners within the educational context and, hence,
give them a particular identity.

Harklau's (2000) ethnographic study of three English learners (ELs)
transitioning from a US high school to a community college is particularly
insightful on the relationship between educational institutions and learner
identity. Within the high school context investigated by Harklau, the
three target students tended to be 'affiliated with and the responsibility of
the ESOL program and teacher' (Harklau, 2000: 45). Harklau found that
in the high school, the students and teachers 'collaboratively regenerated
and perpetuated' (Harklau, 2000: 46) a representation of ELs as highly
motivated students who provide an inspiration for everyone by their
heroic struggles during their immigration to the United States and their
acquisition of a second language.

At the same time, the teachers in the school often expressed doubts
about the students' academic and cognitive ability. Given prevalent negative social attitudes in the United States toward bilingualism and an educational context in which English is the exclusive medium of instruction,
Harklau did not find it surprising that teachers cast these students' ability
to communicate in two languages not as a special talent or strength but
rather as a disability, emphasizing what immigrant students could not do
relative to monolingual, standard English speakers. One teacher, for example, commented, 'It must be like somebody who's very bright and has a
stroke. And can't express themselves' (Harklau, 2000: 50). In our study of
Chinese junior high school students (McKay & Wong, 1996), we too found
that in general teachers, by refusing to recognize any knowledge that students might have brought with them (including native-language literacy

and school experiences), tended to see the ELs as linguistically and cognitively deficient. In this way, the social and educational context often positions English learners in particular ways, frequently as deficient learners.

Duff's (2002) study is helpful in examining the manner in which peer dynamics is influential in matters of identity. Duff's study focuses on language use and socialization in a Canadian Social Studies class composed of Canadian students of various ethnic backgrounds and immigrant English as a Second Language speakers, many of whom were Mandarin and Cantonese speakers. Class discussions were quite common, as were topics dealing with Chinese culture. In examining several class discussion excerpts, Duff found that the contributions of ELs tended to be 'short, muted, tentative, and inaccessible to others. As a result, they forfeited – or resisted – opportunities to convey aspects of themselves, their knowledge, interests, and opinions to others, or to make the personal connections for others' (Duff, 2002: 305). When asked in an interview context about their participation, nonlocal students said that they were afraid of being laughed at or criticized by their peers for their comments. This presented them with a significant dilemma.

> Silence protected them from humiliation. However, interactional withdrawal attracted disdain from local students (who confirmed this), for whom silence represented a lack of initiative, agency, or desire to improve one's English or to offer interesting material for the sake of the class. The NNES students were therefore caught between what appeared to be two unfavorable options: silence or mockery and hostility. (Duff, 2002: 312)

Gee (2004) argues that teaching and learning English language and literacy is not just about teaching and learning English but also about teaching and learning specific social languages. He maintains that what students need to get right is not just the language but what he calls Discourse, that is, 'multiple ways of acting-interacting-speaking-writing-listening-reading-thinking-believing-valuing-feeling with others at the "right" times and in the "right" places so as to be recognized as enacting an "appropriate socially-situated identity"' (Gee, 2004: 25). Although there is little doubt that the nonlocal students referred to in Duff's (2002) study needed to adopt the 'right' way of acting in order to be accepted members of the social studies class, the question is whether or not the nonlocal students had the desire or language ability to do this. As Duff (2002) points out, what is clearly needed is more investigation of

> the extent to which students actually *want* to display their identities and personal knowledge in class or to conform to the dominant, normative local sociolinguistic behaviors – that is, whether they consider those behaviors and disclosures as signs of competence or incompetence, of

strength or weakness – a community standard and ideology toward which they *choose* to become socialized, or rather something they just endure, resist, or circumvent by demonstrating their capabilities in other ways. [emphasis in the original] (Duff, 2002: 313)

One area that allows English learners to assume a new identity, challenging the identity often given to them as 'deficient' learners, is cyber space. In fact, recent research is documenting the many ways in which the internet opens new opportunities for English learners.

Technology and language learning

Lam's (2000) study documents how computer-mediated communication (CMC) allows language learners to assume a new identity, one that can enhance literacy skills. Lam's was a case study of a Chinese immigrant teenager to the United States, named Almon. When Lam first began studying Almon, he had little confidence in writing in English, which he contended was always his worst subject. However, after designing his own home page and joining an electronic community interested in Japanese pop culture, he gained confidence in his literacy through his on-line exchanges with pen pals. Lam contends that the community Almon joined on the web allowed him to develop a new identity, one that gave him self-confidence. She concludes that:

> Whereas classroom English appeared to contribute to Almon's sense of exclusion or marginalization (his inability to speak like a native), which paradoxically contradicts the school's mandate to prepare students for the workplace and civic involvement, the English he controlled on the Internet enabled him to develop a sense of belongingness and connectedness to a global English-speaking community. Almon was learning not only more English but also more relevant and appropriate English for the World Wide Web community he sought to become a part of. (Lam, 2000: 476)

Whereas before Almon joined the electronic community on Japanese pop culture he viewed English as his biggest problem believing that even in 10 years his English wouldn't be that good, his experience in the chat room and the friends he made changed his outlook. As he puts it,

> I've changed a lot in the last 2 months, actually. I have kind of changed my determination. I'm not as fearful, or afraid of the future, that I won't have a future. I'm not as afraid now … When I was feeling *negative*, I felt the world doesn't belong to me, and it's hard to survive here. And I felt not many people understand me, or would. I didn't feel like I belong to this world … But now I feel there's nothing much to be afraid of. It really depends on how you go about it. It's not like the world always has power over you. It was [names of a few chat

mates and e-mail pen pals] who helped me to change and encouraged me. If I hadn't known them, perhaps I wouldn't have changed so much … Yes maybe the *Internet* has changed me. (interview, October 5, 1997) (p. 468)

Black (2006) finds similar benefits with the use of fanfiction by L2 learners. Fanfiction 'is writing in which fans use media narratives and pop cultural icons as inspiration for creating their own texts' (Black, 2006: 172). While the majority of the fiction is in English there is a good deal of incorporation of other languages and culture. Based on a year of focused participant observation of one fanfiction website, Black (2005) found that many fan authors created linguistically hybrid texts in which they would ask other participants to help them incorporate aspects of the other participants' cultures into their texts. In so doing they often constructed a hybridized identity in their texts. Black also found that there was a great deal of peer review and proofreading that went on through the participants' interaction with one another. This occurred because frequently participants included an author's note in which they identified themselves as an English language learner who was trying to improve their composition skills. In light of the positive effect that pop culture and the world wide web can engender in learners' identity, confidence and literacy skills, one cannot help but agree with Lam (2000: 478) that 'TESOL in today's global, multicultural world needs a broad and critical conception of language and literacy that is responsive to students' relations to multiple target languages and cultural communities'.

One obstacle to the use of technology and pop culture in the classroom may be teachers themselves. Rymes (2004), for example, argues that pop culture can make teachers very uncomfortable since its use can displace teachers from a position of expertise. In her study of a second-grade phonics class, Rymes cites an example when recognizing Chansey as a Pokemon was key to understanding what was happening in an ESOL peer group. In this case, in a phonics game, one of the students, Rene, had pulled a card with the word *chancy* written on it and the teacher is helping him sound it out (Rymes, 2004: 209).

CHANCY/CHANSEY

Teacher:	-c-h[- says.
Student:	[(caːn)
Rene:	aːn (.) (chaːn)
Teacher:	Chaːn (.) –c—y-.
	(2.0)
Rene:	Chances
Teacher:	Chaːnːːcːy
Rene:	Chancy

Rene:	Ohp! ((looking at Dante and smiling)) [Pokemon.
Teacher:	And you have to tell me {why the –a- is sho:rt.
David:	[Chancy. (.) I got it
Teacher:	You need to li:sten. ((looking at David))
Rene:	Cause the –c-
	(1.0)
Rene:	The –y-

(Rymes, 2004: 209)

As Rymes points out, while the teacher is comfortable carrying out the routine of 'little known-answers initiation questions' (Rymes, 2004: 330), she ignores the reference to the popular game, scolding David for his recognition and reminding him he needs to listen. In the end, Rymes concedes that it can be disconcerting for anyone to forego their expertise status, but much could be gained if teachers would let learners be the experts in areas of popular culture that the teachers are unfamiliar with.

A second obstacle to the use of technology in the L2 classroom is documented by Turbill (2001) who began his research by trying to investigate how teachers of young children are incorporating technology into their early literacy classes. However, after finding very little use of technology in early literacy classes, he changed his focus to studying why teachers find it difficult to incorporate technology into their literacy classrooms. Working with one kindergarten classroom in Sydney, he and the classroom teacher tried to incorporate the use of technology into the students' two-hour Literacy Block. In the process Turbill encountered a variety of obstacles including long wait periods for web pages to download into the computer, old computers needing to be rebooted to work properly, about half of the children not having computers at home and, hence, being unfamiliar with how to operate a computer, insufficient number of computers, and a large number of students in the classes.

While such practical concerns are disconcerting, when Turbill and the classroom teacher did finally manage to get children to use the computer for the reading programs, he found some significant advantages in the use of technology. For example, he regularly saw how as children become more familiar with the storyline and visual texts of stories they were reading, they begin 'talking more about the characters, predicting what is going to happen in the storyline and in the animations' (Turbill, 2001: 269). Turbill also found that as the children gain familiarity with the text and the format of the activities, the teacher could leave them alone to work in groups reading their favorite books. In the end, Turbill concludes that for technology to be effectively used in the classroom, certain factors have to exist. Teachers need the time and training to consider how to incorporate technology into their language-learning activities. Teachers need to reconceptualize their view of literacy and move beyond a 'focus on learning to "break-the-code" of print' (Turbill, 2001: 274) and to see literacy in a broader framework. Finally, up-to-date hardware is needed along with more innovative software. While it is clear we have gained a lot of insights into the role of imagined communities, identity and technology in language learning, it is important to consider some of the challenges that current research is posing to the profession.

Challenges Ahead

Inequality of access in English learning

An economic divide in the teaching of English is evident in South Korea where, Park and Ableman (2004) argue, 'English has long been a class marker in South Korea: namely knowledge of and comfort with English has been a sign of educational opportunity, and for some of the experience of travel or study abroad and contact with foreigners in South Korea' (p. 646). The size of the English language market in South Korea is estimated to be about $3333 million dollars a year with another $833 million spent on study abroad programs. The private after-school education market is also booming, particularly after it was announced in 1995 that English would become an elementary school subject. Many Korean parents are sending their children to English-language kindergartens, even though such schools are typically three times more expensive than ordinary kindergartens (Park, 2006).

Unfortunately, this economic divide in access to English is often reinforced by Ministries of Education themselves. China is a case in point. In 1976, Deng Xiaoping launched a national modernization program in which English education was seen as a key component: 'English was recognized as an important tool for engaging in economic, commercial, technological and cultural exchange with the rest of the world and hence for facilitating the modernization process' (Hu, 2005: 8).

In 1978, the Ministry of Education issued the first unified primary and secondary curriculum for the era of modernization. This curriculum introduced foreign language learning at Primary 3. The directive also mandated that efforts in promoting English language proficiency were to be aimed at strengthening English language teaching in elite schools, which were expected to produce the English-proficient personnel needed to successfully undertake national modernization. In fact, in 1985 the Ministry of Education exempted poorly resourced schools from providing English instruction. In addition, the Ministry of Education gave several economically developed provinces and municipalities the autonomy to develop their own English curricula, syllabi and textbooks for primary and secondary education (Hu, 2005). These materials tended to be more innovative, learner-centered and communicative than earlier classroom texts and materials.

The directives summarized above illustrate the dangers that can arise from state mandated guidelines for language teaching. First, such mandates can determine when foreign language learning begins in the public school system. The Chinese Ministry of Education, like many other Asian countries, is formally promoting the early learning of English, even though the issue of early exposure to foreign language learning is still being debated. Second, state mandates can determine who has access to English language learning. In China, recent policies have tended to support English learning among Chinese elite, in this way exacerbating educational inequality.

An economic divide in English learning is also evident in the current English education policies in Hong Kong where, in 1997, the Department of Education announced a sweeping change in the medium of instruction in schools so that most schools were asked to adopt Chinese as the medium of instruction. At the same time, the government made an exemption for a minority of schools that had been operating successfully in English to continue using English as the medium of instruction (Choi, 2003). According to Choi (2003), the policy, 'which provided for the selection of the best primary school graduates for monolingual education, was designed to be a cost-effective way of training in English skills for those who had the economic and cultural capital to benefit from it. Meanwhile, the majority of students were barred from sufficient exposure to English, the language of power and wealth' (Choi, 2003: 673). Choi contends that the policy was basically engineered by business interests right before the changeover in 1997 and that its ultimate effect was to 'perpetuate a form of linguistic imperialism' (Choi, 2003: 673).

In order to justify the policy, the government extolled the benefits of mother-tongue education; however, many parents believed that what would be best for their children was for them to go to English-medium schools and potentially gain the economic capital that they believed, rightly or wrongly, would come from proficiency in English. Many parents strove to get their children into the small number of English-medium schools or enroll them in expensive international schools and even send their children overseas to Anglophone countries to study, options that were available only to a small proportion of economically elite families. The Hong Kong language policy then had several negative effects brought on by globalization and the spread of English: first, it encouraged an economic divide in the learning of English; second, it minimized the value of using the mother tongue in education with its implicit suggestion that this option was in some ways less desirable; and finally, it promoted the idea of the desirability of an English-only classroom in the acquisition of English.

Leibowitz's (2005) case study of black students at the University of Western Cape in South Africa, an institution that caters to predominately black students, demonstrates how English in higher education is a key to academic success. However, young people from less affluent backgrounds often face special obstacles in partaking in this success. In the 1990s, the language of instruction at the University of the Western Cape shifted mainly from Afrikaans to English. Many of the black students attending Western Cape went to township schools under apartheid where little English was heard with a reliance on mother-tongue instruction and where the content emphasis was on domestic and agricultural work rather than intellectual or professional work.

In her case study, Leibowitz (2005) documents the disadvantages that students face coming to the University with less developed English skills. Students reported that their lack of proficiency in English affected their ability to follow lectures, their interpersonal communication with teachers and classmates and their essay writing. Reading in English was also a far more time-consuming task than reading in the students' first language. But perhaps most importantly Leibowitz found that many of the black students had not been exposed to the kind of academic discourse that was necessary to succeed in a university setting. Several students reported that in their previous education, they had not been asked to employ the kind of critical evaluation that was asked for at the University. All of these factors made it far more difficult for these students to succeed in a university setting than for students from a middle-class background with high levels of English proficiency.

Leibowitz (2005) concludes that access to English in South Africa is a necessary but not sufficient condition for academic success. Students need exposure to both English and to the discourse of schools in order to succeed, both of which are far more likely to occur in the more privileged schools in South Africa. The situation in South Africa is far from unique. Ramanathan (1999), for example, reports on the difficulties that the lower caste groups in India have in succeeding in India's institutions of higher education.

The current state of English education raises several critical issues of access. The first is how to convince parents and students of the value of supporting bilingual/biliterate education. At the present time in many countries, parents, school administrators and teachers support an English-only agenda in the schools in the belief that this is best for their children. Often, a child's first language is viewed as a problem rather than as a resource. The second issue is how to provide less advantaged children in the society with equal access to English so they can succeed in institutions of higher education.

A tendency of othering in EIL pedagogy

A second area that presents a challenge for the ELT profession is the tendency toward Othering in EIL pedagogy. *Othering* refers to the ways in which the 'discourse of a particular group defines other groups in opposition to itself; an Us and Them view that constructs an identity for the

Other and, implicitly for the Self' (Palfreyman, 2005: 213–214). In EIL pedagogy this discourse often positions English learners and bilingual teachers
as deficient in comparison to native speakers. This discourse also idealizes
the so-called native speaker and negates the right of English speakers outside Inner Circle countries to nativize the language for the local cultural
context. Finally, the Self–Other discourse has at times positioned certain
groups as incapable of participating in 'modern' methods of language
learning that typically involve group participation and 'critical thinking'.

Often in discussions of the implementation of communicative language
teaching (CLT) in Outer and Expanding Circle countries, there is a suggestion that the culture of learning in these countries is not conducive to CLT.
In the early 1990s, educators like Ballard and Clanchy (1991) began to
argue that different cultures have different attitudes regarding the nature
of knowledge and its function in society. They contend that there is a continuum of attitudes toward knowledge ranging from what they term a
conserving attitude toward knowledge to an *extending* attitude toward
knowledge. In the case of the former, the learning approach is highly
reproductive and learning strategies involve memorization and imitation.
Activities often involve summarizing and applying formulae and information in order to achieve correctness. On the other hand, as the continuum moves to an extending attitude, the learning approach is analytic and
speculative, involving critical thinking and a search for new possibilities.
Activities entail questioning, judging, speculating and hypothesizing with
the aim of creativity and originality. Ballard and Clancy go on to argue
that although there are individual differences within a culture, a conserving attitude toward knowledge is prevalent in many Asian societies.

> ... it remains true that the reproductive approach to learning, favor-
> ing strategies of memorization and rote learning and positively dis-
> couraging critical questioning of either the teacher or the text, is the
> dominant tendency in formal education in much of Southeast Asia
> and other Asian countries. And it is the case that in the Australian
> system, even at the primary level, the dominant tendency is to urge
> students toward an ultimately speculative approach to learning, to
> encourage them to question, to search for new ways of looking at the
> world around them. (Ballard & Clancy, 1991: 23)

Such Othering discourse regarding approaches to knowledge and
learning styles is evident in a good deal of the discourse surrounding the
implementation of CLT. Flowerdew (1998), for example, discusses the use
of group work and students' oral participation, central components of
CLT, in reference to Chinese learners. She begins by asking,

> Why is it that when one poses a question to a group of Arab students
> the whole class is clamouring to answer, while a question addressed

to a class of Chinese learners may elicit no response, followed by a
stony silence or, as the Chinese say, 'dead air'? Even if one nominates
a particular student to reply in a class of Chinese learners, the question may still be met with a muffled reply and averted eyes. The
answer lies, to some extent, in certain cultural and psychological
factors deriving from Confucian philosophy. (Flowerdew, 1998: 323)

Flowerdew goes on to discuss the use of group work with Chinese
learners and argues that group work can be implemented with Chinese
students if the group is viewed as a collective body that offers suggestions
to one another not as individuals but as a group. Underlying her argument are the assumptions that group work in a classroom is admirable
and conducive to language learning and that a particular group of learners,
in this case Chinese students, are not open to group work and oral
participation.

An Othering discourse is also evident in some discussions of critical
thinking, a key component of an extending view of knowledge that is promoted in CLT. Atkinson (1997), for example, argues that critical thinking,
while extremely difficult to define, is clearly a social practice and that
some cultures promote such learning while others do not. He then goes on
to compare 'critical thinking and nonnative thinkers' (a powerful Othering
discourse) arguing that 'cross-cultural research into the early socialization
and educational practices of non-European peoples' suggests that there
are 'three areas of potential discontinuity between cultural assumptions
that may underlie critical thinking and modes of thought and expression
prevalent among non-Western cultural groups' (Atkinson, 1997: 79). These
involve notions of relations between individuals and society, differing
norms of self-expression, and different perspectives on the use of language
as a means for learning. Underlying the discussion is a clear Othering
between Westerners who engage in critical thinking and non-Westerners
or 'nonnative thinkers' whose social practice may not encourage critical
thinking. At issue is exactly what is meant by critical thinking and if it is
necessary for 'nonnative thinkers' to engage in Western concepts of critical
thinking in order to learn English.

Othering is not limited to depiction by Western scholars of Asian cultures of learning. Such rhetoric is evident in the discourse of some Asian
scholars themselves who characterize an entire culture of learning with
broad generalizations. Le (2004), for example, in discussing how to mediate what he refers to as Asian and Western values in ELT practice, makes
the following generalization regarding learning in the West and East:

The most outstanding differences between Western classical human-
ism and Asian educational philosophy is that the former places
greater emphasis on the cultivation of intellectual skills to foster the
next generations' leaders while the latter is primarily concerned with

the development of moral virtue to promote a static social order. (Le, 2004: 169)

In his rhetoric then the West is linked with 'the cultivation of intellectual skills' while the East is linked with a 'static social order'. He continues this Othering in his characterization of the role of teachers in the two cultures when he states:

The confrontation between Asian and western educational ideologies lies in opposing views of the teacher's role. If Asian teachers are expected to be transmitters of culture who are to maintain the status quo in schools and transmit prevailing culture, western teachers are considered to be the transformers of culture. (Le, 2004: 171)

Once again, the West is depicted in positive terms as 'transformers of culture' while the East 'maintains the status quo in schools' and transmits 'prevailing culture'.

The question of standards

A final concern that needs more attention is the notion of standards in reference to an international language. The spread of English has brought with it the development of many new varieties of English, which has led to much discussion regarding what standards should be promoted in the teaching of English. Implicit in discussions of variation are the notion of standards, a standard language, and issues of power and identity that are built into such concepts. *Standard language* is the term generally used to refer to that variety of a language that is considered the norm. It is the variety regarded as the ideal for educational purposes, and usually used as a yardstick by which to measure other varieties and implement standard-based assessment. The related notion of *language standards* has to do with the language rules that inform the standard and that are then taught in the schools.

The challenge that World Englishes present to the Standard English ideology is one of plurality – that there should be different standards for different contexts of use and that the definition of each Standard English should be endonormative (determined locally) rather than exonormative (determined outside of its context of use). However, if there are different forms of Standard English, the concern of mutual intelligibility emerges. The fact that some speakers of English use a variety of English that is quite different from a standard variety of English has led some to argue that the use of these varieties of English will lead to a lack of intelligibility among speakers of English. It is this fear that has led to a widespread debate over standards in the use of English.

One of the early debates over standards occurred at a 1984 conference to celebrate the 50th anniversary of the British Council. At this conference, Randolph Quirk and Braj Kachru, two key figures in the growing debate over standards in international English, expressed conflicting views on the issue of standards in relation to international English. Quirk argued for the need to uphold standards in the use of English in both countries where English is spoken as a native language and in countries where English is used as a second or foreign language. He maintained that tolerance for variation in language use was educationally damaging in Anglophone countries and that 'the relatively narrow range of purposes for which the nonnative needs to use English ... is arguably well catered for by a single monochrome standard form that looks as good on paper as it sounds in speech' (Quirk, 1985: 6). For Quirk, a common standard of use was warranted in all contexts of English language use.

Kachru (1985), on the other hand, argued that the spread of English had brought with it a need to re-examine traditional notions of codification and standardization. As he put it,

> In my view, the global diffusion of English has taken an interesting turn: the native speakers of this language seem to have lost the exclusive prerogative to control its standardization; in fact, if current statistics are any indication, they have become a minority. This sociolinguistic fact must be accepted and its implication recognized. What we need now are new paradigms and perspective for linguistic and pedagogical research and for understanding the linguistic creativity in multilingual situations across cultures. (Kachru, 1985: 30)

Kachru maintained that allowing for a variety of linguistic norms would not lead to a lack of intelligibility among varieties of English; rather what would emerge from this situation would be an educated variety of English that would be intelligible across the many varieties of English.

The debate regarding the teaching of standards continues today with some arguing for the promotion of a monolithic model of English, while others support a pluricenter model. Those like Quirk who argue for a monolithic model contend that native-speaker models should be promoted because they have been codified and have a degree of historical authority. The monolithic model is in keeping with one of the central tenets that Phillipson (1992) argues has traditionally informed English language teaching, namely, that the ideal teacher of English is a native speaker. This perspective also lends support to the notion of the insider and outsider, the Self and the Other, since it is native speakers who are seen as the guardians of standard English. On the other hand, those like Kachru who support a pluricentric model of English contend that language contact necessarily leads to language change. They argue that the development of new varieties of English is a natural result of the spread of English. In many ways, the debate reflects a tension between the global and the local brought about by the new social space of globalization. Whereas global space has brought exposure to English, local space has taken the language and modified it for the local context. What is important to add to the pluricentric perspective is that today language use is often not just English but a mix of a variety of languages that highlights the speaker's identity and proficiency. In such encounters, the question of standards needs to be highly contextualized.

It is perhaps in the question of standards that many of the issues we have discussed here come together. The fact that new varieties of English have developed is closely associated with issues of identity. These new varieties are a factor of cultural and linguistic contact; they reflect individuals' desire to signal their unique identity while speaking a global language. The new varieties also become a basis for Othering in which those with more power assert that their variety is in fact the 'standard'. Finally, what is considered by many to be the standard is the variety promoted in educational institutions, places to which those with less affluence often have limited access.

Implications for Pedagogy

In view of the many diverse social and sociolinguistic contexts of EIL use, what principles should inform a socially sensitive EIL pedagogy? The following are what we believe to be key principles.

Foreign- and second-language curricula should be relevant to the local linguistic ecology

Earlier in the chapter it was noted that in many countries such as Japan, the local linguistic ecology calls into question the value of English learning. What is needed in these contexts is a knowledge of the local lingua franca, as well as a valuing of other local languages. In situations where English has little relevancy and there is another local lingua franca, students' time might be better served in a language awareness class than in a traditional English classroom. In such classes, students of all backgrounds could learn about the diversity of languages spoken today, the attitudes and values associated with them, and the variety of language use that exists in all languages.

EIL professionals should strive to alter language policies that serve to promote English learning only among the elite of the country

In many countries we have seen how those with privilege are most likely to have access to English learning. It is often those who have both the economic resources and time for language learning who gain proficiency in English. To avoid English fluency contributing to a greater economic divide, educational leaders and planners need to establish policies that afford English access to learners of all economic backgrounds. This may well mean establishing more government-funded opportunities for English learning for all citizens. In contexts in which gaining proficiency in English may threaten mother-tongue use and development, English programs should be established in such a way that the local language is fully supported.

EIL curricula should include examples of the diversity of English varieties used today

Recent research has documented the diversity of English use today, illustrating both the regularity of these varieties and the manner in which they are a source of personal and social identity. In light of this diversity, a socially sensitive EIL pedagogy needs to first of all afford equal status to all varieties of English and, second, promote an awareness of variation in English use. Which particular varieties are dealt with will depend on the local context. Promoting an awareness of the varieties of English spoken today may enhance learners' receptive skills in processing different varieties of English and promote an awareness that English, as an international language, no longer belongs solely to speakers of the Inner Circle. Recognition of the hybridity and fluidity of modern day English use will afford full status to second-language speakers of the language.

EIL curricula need to exemplify L2–L2 interactions

Given that the majority of English interactions today are among L2 speakers, EIL curricula need to include far more examples of L2–L2 English interactions. Including examples of actual L2–L2 interactions will be beneficial in two ways. First, it will create an awareness that one important value of English is that it allows individuals to communicate across a great variety of geographical and cultural boundaries and not merely with speakers from Inner Circle countries. Second, including actual examples of L2–L2 interactions can provide a context for discussing various means by which individuals can seek clarification and establish relationships when they may have gaps in their knowledge of English.

Full recognition needs to be given to the other languages spoken by English speakers

For too long, a good deal of ELT pedagogy has been informed by an English-only discourse. Yet, often bilingual speakers of English have a rich linguistic repertoire, which they use to signal their personal identity and social relationships. Codeswitching is an important means by which they do this. Encouraging codeswitching in EIL classrooms is beneficial in that it will provide equal status to all of the languages learners speak and provide a context for students to investigate reasons for codeswitching. And most importantly it allows for a discretionary use of the first language as a means of developing proficiency in English.

EIL should be taught in a way that respects the local culture of learning

In many instances, globalization has led to the introduction of materials and methods that are not in keeping with the local culture of learning. When this occurs, local teachers may be placed in a situation in which their credibility as competent teachers is challenged because they do not know about some aspect of Western culture that appears in a textbook or they are encouraged to use group work when this is not in keeping with typical student roles. Local teachers are the ones most familiar with local expectations regarding the roles of teachers and learners. They are also familiar with the manner in which English is used in the local context. Because of this, they are in a strong position to design a pedagogy that respects the local culture of learning.

In summary, it is clear that present-day globalization, migration and the spread of English have resulted in a great diversity of social and educational contexts in which English learning is taking place. Because English is an international language, effective pedagogical decisions and practices cannot be made without giving special attention to the many varied social contexts in which English is taught and learned. An appropriate EIL pedagogy is one that promotes English bilingualism for learners of all backgrounds, recognizes and validates the variety of Englishes that exists today and teaches English in a manner that meets local language needs and respects the local culture of learning.

Suggestions for further reading

Jenkins, J. (2005) *World Englishes: A Resource Book for Students*. London: Routledge. This book provides a readable introduction to the World Englishes paradigm. It defines key topics in World Englishes and discusses central issues and debates in the field.

McKay, S.L. (2002) *Teaching English as an International Language: Rethinking Goals and Approaches*. Oxford: Oxford University Press. This book provides an introduction to English as an international language. It discusses reasons for the spread of English, the question of standards in relation to the teaching of English, and the role of culture in ELT materials and methods.

McKay, S.L. and Bokhorst-Heng, W. (2008) *International English in its Sociolinguistic Contexts: Towards a Socially Sensitive Pedagogy*. New York: Frances Taylor. This book examines the social and sociolinguistic contexts of present-day English education. It also provides an introduction to key constructs in sociolinguistics including multilingualism, language planning and policy and interactional sociolinguistics.

Rubdy, R. and Saraceni, M. (eds) (2006) *English in the World: Global Rules, Global Roles*. London: Continuum. This collection of readings focuses on two major topics: conceptualizing English as an international language (EIL) and the pedagogical implications of EIL. The first section addresses the topic of World Englishes, ELF and standards, while the second deals with pedagogical goals and curricula.

References

Anderson, B. (1983) *Imagined Communities.* New York: Verso.

Atkinson, D. (1997) A critical approach to critical thinking in TESOL. *TESOL Quarterly* 31 (1), 71–95.

Ballard, B. and Clanchy, J. (1991) Assessment by misconception. Cultural influences and intellectual traditions. In L. Hamp-Lyons (ed.) *Assessing Second Language Writing in Academic Contexts* (pp. 19–36). Norwood, NJ: Ablex Publishing Corporation.

Bamgbose, A. (1998) Torn between the norms: Innovations in World Englishes. *World Englishes* 17 (1), 1–14.

Black, R. (2005) Access and affiliation: The literacy and composition practices of English-language learners in an online fanfiction community. *Journal of Adolescent and Adult Literacy* 49, 118–128.

Black, R. (2006) Language, culture and identity in online fiction. *E-Learning* 3 (2), 170–184.

Brutt-Griffler, J. (2002) *World Englishes: A Study of its Development.* Clevedon: Multilingual Matters.

Canagarajah, S.A. (ed.) (2005) *Reclaiming the Local in Language Policy and Practice.* Mahwah, NJ: Lawrence Erlbaum Associates.

Choi, P.K. (2003) 'The best students will learn English': Ultra-utilitarianism and linguistic imperialism in post-1997 Hong Kong. *Journal of Education Policy* 28 (6), 673–694.

Crystal, D. (2003) *English as a Global Language.* Cambridge: Cambridge University Press.

Duff, P. (2002) The discursive co-construction of knowledge, identity and difference: An ethnography of communication in high school mainstream. *Applied Linguistics* 23 (3), 289–322.

Firth, A. (1996) The discursive accomplishment of normality. On 'lingua franca' English and conversation analysis. *Journal of Pragmatics* 26, 237–259.

Flowerdew, L. (1998) A cultural perspective on group work. *ELT Journal* 52 (4), 323–329.

Gee, J.P. (2004) Learning language as a matter of learning social languages within discourses. In M. Hawkins (ed.) *Language Learning and Teacher Education: A Sociocultural Approach* (pp. 13–31). Clevedon: Multilingual Matters.

Harklau, L. (2000) From the "good kids" to the "worst": Representations of English language learners across educational settings. *TESOL Quarterly* 34 (1), 35–67.

Hu, G. (2005) English language education in China: Policies, progress, and problems. *Language Policy* 4, 5–24.

Jenkins, J. (2000) *The Phonology of English as an International Language.* Oxford: Oxford University Press.

Kachru, B.B. (1983) *The Indianization of English: The English Language in India.* New York: Oxford University Press.

Kachru, B.B. (1985) Standards, codification and sociolinguistic realism: The English language in the outer circle. In R. Quirk and H. Widdowson (eds) *English in the World: Teaching and Learning the Language and Literatures* (pp. 11–30). Cambridge: Cambridge University Press.

Kachru, B.B. (1986) *The Alchemy of English.* Oxford: Pergamon Press.

Kachru, B.B. (1992) Models for non-native Englishes. In B.B. Kachru (ed.) *The Other Tongue: English Across Cultures* (2nd edn) (pp. 48–74). Urbana and Chicago: University of Illinois Press.

Kubota, R. and McKay, S.L. (2009) Globalization and language learning in rural Japan: The role of English in the local linguistic ecology. *TESOL Quarterly* 43 (4), 593–619.

Lam, W.S. (2000) L2 literacy and the design of the self: A case study of a teenager writing on the Internet. *TESOL Quarterly* 34 (3), 457–482.

Le, V.C. (2004) From ideology to inquiry: Mediating Asian and Western values in ELT practice. *The Journal of Asian TEFL* 1 (1), 167–183.

Leibowitz, B. (2005) Learning in an additional language in a multilingual society: A South African case study on university-level writing. *TESOL Quarterly* 39 (4), 661–681.

Lowenberg, P. (2002) Assessing English proficiency in the Expanding Circle. *World Englishes* 21 (3), 431–435.

McKay, S.L. and Wong, S.C. (1996) Multiple discourses, multiple identities: Investment and agency in second-language learning among Chinese adolescent immigrant students. *Harvard Educational Review* 66, 577–608.

Nettle, D. and Romaine, S. (2000) *Vanishing Voices: The Extinction of the World's Languages*. Oxford: Oxford University Press.

Niño-Murcia, M. (2003) English is like the dollar: Hard currency ideology and the status of English in Peru. *World Englishes* 22 (2), 121–142.

Norton, B. and Kamal, F. (2003) The imagined communities of English: Language learners in Pakistani school. *Journal of Language, Identity and Education* 2 (4), 301–317.

Pakir, A. (1991) The range and depth of English-knowing bilinguals in Singapore. *World Englishes* 10 (2), 167–179.

Palfreyman, D. (2005) Othering in an English language program. *TESOL Quarterly.* 39 (2), 211–233.

Park, C. (2006) Parents push early English learning. *The Korea Times.* On WWW at http://www.search.hankooki.com/times/times. Accessed 20.11.06.

Park, S.J. and Abelmann, N. (2004) Class and cosmopolitan striving: Mother's management of English education in South Korea. *Anthropological Quarterly* 77 (4), 645–672.

Peirce, B. (1995) Social identity, investment, and language learning. *TESOL Quarterly* 29, 9–31.

Pennycook, A. (1998) *English and the Discourses of Colonialism*. London: Routledge.

Pennycook, A. (2003) Beyond homogeny and heterogeny: English as a global and worldly language. In C. Mair (ed.) *The Politics of English as a World Language*. (pp. 3–17). Amsterdam: Rodopi.

Pennycook, A. (2007) *Global Englishes and Transcultural Flows*. London: Routledge.

Phillipson, R. (1992) *Linguistic Imperialism*. Oxford: Oxford University Press.

Quirk, R. (1985) The English language in a global context. In R. Quirk and H. Widdowson (eds) *English in the World: Teaching and Learning the Language and Literatures* (pp. 1–6). Cambridge: Cambridge University Press.

Ramanathan, V. (1999) "English is here to stay": A critical look at institutional and educational practices in India. *TESOL Quarterly* 33 (2), 211–233.

Rampton, B. (1995) *Crossing: Language and Ethnicity among Adolescents*. New York: Longman.

Rymes, B. (2004) Contrasting zones of comfortable competence: Popular culture in a phonics lesson. *Linguistics and Education* 14, 321–335.

Seargeant, P. (2005) 'More English than England itself': The simulation of authenticity in foreign language practice in Japan. *International Journal of Applied Linguistics* 15, 326–345.

Seidlhofer, B. (2004) Research perspectives on teaching English as a lingua franca. *Annual Review of Applied Linguistics* 24, 209–239.

Turbill, J. (2001) A researcher goes to school: Using technology in the kindergarten literacy curriculum. *Journal of Early Childhood Literacy* 1 (3), 255–279.

Chapter 5

Multilingualism and Codeswitching in Education

NKONKO M. KAMWANGAMALU

Introduction

This chapter reviews research findings on one of the key issues to which language contact in an educational setting has given rise, namely, the rationale for codeswitching practices in the classroom. In particular, the chapter reports on why bilingual teachers and students sometimes resort to codeswitching, and whether classroom codeswitching is an impediment or a resource to learning. *Codeswitching*, the *intersentential* alternating use of two or more languages or varieties of a language in the same speech situation, has been one of the most researched topics in sociolinguistics over the past 30 years (Blom & Gumperz, 1972; Ferguson, 2003; Heller, 1988; Jacobson, 1990; Kachru, 1978; Kamwangamalu & Lee, 1991; Myers-Scotton, 1993; Rubdy, 2007). A related term, *codemixing*, refers to the *intrasentential* alternating use of two or more languages or varieties of a language and is often used in studies of grammatical aspects of bilingual speech (Muysken, 2000; Poplack & Meechan, 1995). Grammatical studies of codemixing are concerned with, among other things, determining the types (e.g. nouns, verbs, etc.) of codemixing patterns that occur often in bilingual speech and why; investigating whether codemixing is syntactically random or rule-governed; and exploring whether the rules or constraints that govern codemixing are universal or language-specific.

Although traditionally a distinction is made between codemixing and codeswitching, current literature generally uses the term *codeswitching*, and this will be the case in the rest of this chapter, as a cover term for all instances of bilingual language alternation, whether intra- or intersentential. Auer (1995) refers to the alternating use of two or more languages as *code alternation*. He uses the term *code alternation* to cover 'all cases in which semiotic systems are put in a relationship of contiguous juxtaposition, such that the appropriate recipients of the resulting complex sign are in a position to interpret this juxtaposition as such' (1995: 116).

Code alternation, remarks Gumperz (1982), is one kind of 'contextualization *cue*'. Contextualization cues are 'constellations of surface features of message form ... by which speakers signal and listeners interpret what the activity is, how semantic content is to be understood and how each sentence relates to what precedes or follows' (Gumperz, 1982: 131). As a contextualization cue, codeswitching 'signals contextual information equivalent to what in monolingual settings is conveyed through prosody or other syntactic or lexical processes. It generates the presuppositions in terms of which the context of what is said is decoded' (Gumperz, 1982: 98; see also Kasper & Omori, this volume).

Codeswitching, henceforth CS, is a by-product of language contact. As Haugen (1972) observes, when two or more languages come into contact, as is the case in multilingual communities around the world, they tend to color one another. This coloring, or what Haugen (1972) has termed *interlingual contagion*, manifests itself in language contact phenomena such as CS, borrowing, code-crossing, diglossia, language shift, to name but a few. CS differs from the other language contact phenomena in many respects, as will be explained in the next three sections. The chapter then goes on to review some of the perspectives from which CS has been investigated to provide the reader with a broader view of CS, namely the interactional, markedness and political–ideological approaches. Following that, I highlight key findings on the central question of this chapter: Why do bilingual teachers and students sometime use CS in the classroom? This will be followed by a discussion of the implications of classroom CS for the English-only argument in the United States, as well as in English-medium or ESL/ EFL classrooms worldwide. The last section describes common research methods in CS studies, and is followed by a conclusion including a note on directions for further research into CS.

Codeswitching, Borrowing and Language Shift

Borrowing across languages is defined with reference to the 'end product' rather than the process (Kamwangamalu, 1996: 296). Gumperz (1982: 66) defines borrowing as the introduction of single words or short, frozen, idiomatic phrases from one language into another. The lexical items in columns A and B below, for instance, are examples of borrowings from English into two African languages, IsiZulu and Ciluba, respectively. Ciluba is one of the four national languages (including KiSwahili, Lingala and Kikongo) in the Democratic Republic of Congo, formerly Zaire, and is spoken as first language by about 10 million people. IsiZulu is one of the 11 official languages (including Afrikaans, English, IsiNdebele, IsiXhosa, Sepedi, Sesotho, SiSwati, Setswana, Tshivenda and Xitsonga) in South Africa, and is spoken by about 9.5 million people as first language.

A. isiZulu   B. Ciluba
ibhola 'ball'   *mbulanketa* 'blanket'
isikholo 'school'   *mbekeci* 'bucket'
isiphuni 'spoon'   *kanife* 'knife'
iayani 'iron'   *kandeya* 'candle'

These items provide support for the view that when a linguistic item is borrowed it is integrated, phonologically, morphologically and syntactically, into the grammatical system of the borrowing language (Poplack, 1981[1980]). In some cases, however, the borrowed items may resist integration. Poplack (1978) calls such items *'nonce borrowings'*, and defines them as linguistic items from one language (e.g. French) used in discourse in the other language (e.g. English) which do not show any adaptation, at least in their written form, to the linguistic system of the borrowing language. Examples of nonce borrowings include English phrases such as *'charge d'affaires, déjà vu, comme ci, comme ça'* and lexical items such as *chauffeur, coiffeur*, etc., all of which are borrowings from French. It is worth noting that despite their lack of adaptation, in terms of social integration (Hasselmo, 1972: 180), nonce borrowings are a part and parcel of the linguistic system of the borrowing language. Hasselmo uses the term *social integration* to refer to the degrees of consistency, regularity, and frequency with which linguistic items from one language are used in discourse in the other language.

Borrowing, whether nonce or integrated, does not require or presuppose any degree of competence in two languages, but CS does. Put differently, borrowing can occur in the speech of both monolingual and bilingual speakers alike; however, CS is strictly speaking a characteristic feature of the linguistic behavior of bilingual speakers. Also, in terms of function, generally speakers use borrowing to fill lexical gaps in their languages. However, they engage in CS for a variety of reasons, such as the following: to express in-group solidarity, to exclude someone from a conversation by switching to a language the person does not understand, to emphasize a point by repeating it in two languages, etc. (Finlayson & Slabbert, 1997; Myers-Scotton, 1993). (I will return to the motivations for CS later, with a focus on its occurrence in the classroom.) Further, unlike borrowing, CS can lead to the formation of mixed language varieties including pidgins (e.g. *fanagalo* and *Tsotsitaal* in South Africa, *pidgin English* in Nigeria) and creoles (e.g. *Franglais* in Mauritius, Haitian *creole*) or to language *shift* (see Siegel, this volume).

Concerning language shift, Fasold (1984) explains that it is a gradual process in which a speech community, for one reason or another, gives up its language and adopts a new one. The process of language shift, as Joshua Fishman puts it, refers particularly to 'speech communities whose native languages are threatened because their intergenerational continuity is proceeding negatively, with fewer and fewer users or uses every generation' (Fishman, 1991: 1). Over the past few years, I have informally observed language shift as it happens in immigrant African families in the Washington DC area. It seems that soon after they arrive in the United States younger African children in particular become bilingual in English and their original African language. However, it does not take long before they start speaking English only, especially when interacting with peers or with siblings. As Romaine (1994) notes, the starting point of language shift is bilingualism – often accompanied by *diglossia* (see the following section) – as a stage on the way to monolingualism in a new language, in this case English. Romaine explains that 'typically, a community which was once monolingual becomes bilingual as a result of contact with another (usually socially and economically more powerful) group and becomes transitionally bilingual in the new language until their own language is given up altogether' (Romaine, 1994: 50).

Codeswitching and Diglossia

The concept of diglossia has received considerable attention in the literature over the years (Ferguson, 1972[1959]; Fishman, 1967, 1971; Schiffman, 1997). Ferguson (1972[1959]) uses the term *diglossia* to refer to a situation where two genetically related varieties of a language, one identified as the *H(igh)* (or standard) variety and the other as the *L(ow)* (i.e. nonstandard) variety, have clearly distinct functions in the community. Ferguson (1972: 236) notes that the H variety is used in formal settings, whereas the L variety is used in informal interactions. More specifically, the H variety is used, for instance, for giving sermons in churches or mosques, speeches in the parliament, formal lectures at universities, broadcasting the news on radio and television and for writing editorials in newspapers. In contrast, it is observed that the L variety is used for giving instructions to servants, waiters, workers and clerks; in conversations with family, friends and colleagues; and in folk literature and soap operas on the radio. According to Ferguson (1972[1959]), anyone who uses H while engaged in an informal activity like shopping, or who uses L during a formal activity like a parliamentary debate, runs the risk of ridicule. Generally, H is learnt at school, while L is more spontaneously acquired in informal settings. H is generally perceived as more aesthetically pleasing and beautiful, and has more prestige than L. H has a literary tradition, whereas L does not. And if there does exist a body of literature in L, it is usually written by foreigners rather than by native speakers. Taking the above characteristic features of diglossia into account, Ferguson defines diglossia as

> a relatively stable language situation in which, in addition to the primary dialects of the language (which may include a standard or regional standards), there is a very divergent, highly codified (often

grammatically more complex) superposed variety, the vehicle of a large and respected body of written literature, either of an earlier period or in another speech community, which is learned largely by formal education and is used for most written and formal spoken purposes but is not used by any sector of the community for ordinary conversation. (Ferguson, 1972: 245)

Although Ferguson's definition of diglossia is concerned specifically with two varieties (H and L) of the same language, Fishman (1971: 75) has extended the definition to include situations where two genetically unrelated languages are used in the community, one in formal settings and the other in informal settings. This extended or *broad diglossia* as it has come to be known, best describes the relationship that holds among languages, especially in multilingual post-colonial settings (Kamwangamalu, 2000a: 103). In such settings, former colonial languages, for instance French, Portuguese, Spanish and English in Africa; English in parts of Asia (e.g. the Philippines, India, Pakistan, etc.) and Spanish and Portuguese in Latin America, coexist with local languages in a diglossic relationship, where the ex-colonial language is the H language and the local languages are the L languages.

Most studies of diglossia have, expectedly, focused on the functional dependency or complementarity between the participating languages, arguing that where one language is used the other is not and vice versa. For instance, in his study of vernacular–Swahili–English triglossia in Tanzania, Mkilifi (1978) describes the functional distribution of the three languages, pointing out that each of the languages is assigned to certain domains in the community: the vernacular is used as an intra-group language and is associated with rural African culture-related activities; Kiswahili is associated with pre-industrial, nontechnological urban type of African culture; English is associated with technology and official business. Wald (1986) makes a similar point about Yakoma and Sango in the Central African Republic, noting that the former is the L language and the latter is the H language. However, in spite of the strict compartmentalization of languages that is at the heart of the concept of diglossia, research shows that CS involving H and L is widespread in multilingual communities around the world (Auer, 1998; Blom & Gumperz, 1972; Heller, 1988; Jacobson, 1990; Kachru, 1978; MacSwan, 2000; Proshina & Ettkin, 2005; Watkhaolarm, 2005). Also, there is evidence that CS can and does occur in any domain of language use, formal (including the classroom) or informal; its occurrence in either domain is determined by variables of the context of situation, especially the topic and the interlocutors (Bamiro, 2006; Gafaranga & Torras, 2002; Li, 1998; Martin-Jones, 1995; Slotte-Luttge, 2007). And yet, it seems that the relationship between CS and diglossia in a formal context such as the classroom has hardly been explored. This constitutes a fertile area for further research into CS. Also, the very fact that CS can occur in a formal domain such as the classroom calls for a redefinition of diglossia, for modern language practices in multilingual communities around the world are at odds with the premise on which diglossia is based, namely, strict functional compartmentalization of languages (see also Pennycook, this volume).

Codeswitching and Code-crossing

Earlier it was pointed out that CS is a contextualization cue in the sense Gumperz (1982) defines. Related to CS as a contextualization cue is what Ben Rampton (1995) has termed *code-crossing*, a concept that is central to Rampton's (1995) book titled *Crossing*. Rampton describes *code-crossing* as 'code alternation by people who are not accepted members of the group associated with the second language they employ. It is concerned with switching into languages that are not generally thought to belong to you' (Rampton, 1995: 280). An example of this phenomenon would be, in the case of the United States, a non-African American rapper using African American Vernacular English, a variety with which the artist may not be associated in the wider American society.

CS differs from *code-crossing* in many respects. First, *code-crossing* is an out-group phenomenon; but '[CS] is an in-group phenomenon, restricted to those who share the same expectations and rules of interpretation for the use of the two languages. [It] is thus usually seen as a device used to affirm participants' claims to membership and the solidarity of the group in contrast to outsiders' (Woolard, 1988: 69–70). Second, the difference between in-group CS and out-group *code-crossing*, argues Rampton (1995: 282), resides in the fact that in *in-group* practice, both languages can also be used in the unexceptional conduct of everyday life. *Code-crossing*, however, does not have this flexibility: 'the code-alternation it entails is much more likely to be "flagged" (e.g. "marked by pauses, hesitation phenomena, repetition and metalinguistic commentary")' (Rampton, 1995: 282). Third, unlike CS, '*code-crossing* involves a disjunction between speaker and code that cannot be readily accommodated as a normal part of ordinary social reality' (Rampton, 1995: 283). However, whatever code or language is selected not only carries social meaning (Rampton, 1995: 284), but it is also prestigious and powerful (Rampton, 1995: 286). Fourth, unlike CS, *code-crossing* bears the distinctive characteristic of being always marked in the sense Myers-Scotton (1993) defines, that is, it always entails use of the least expected language or language variety in a given linguistic interaction. Finally, the occurrence of CS in bilinguals' interactions presupposes no violation of the norms that govern language use in the community of which the participants are members. In *code-crossing*, however, the speaker may choose to challenge these norms by diverging from what Bell (1984) calls the *referee* and converging toward the audience, namely the addressee. In this regard, Bell observes that the 'audience' may have more than one circle. He explains that while in every interaction there is a second person whom the speaker directly addresses – the addressee – in some instances, there may also be third parties who, though not physically present, are actually ratified participants of the interaction. As noted elsewhere (Kamwangamalu, 2001: 90), these third parties or the *referee* as Bell calls them, sometimes possess such salience for a speaker that they influence his/her speech even in their absence. This influence can be so great that the speaker diverges from the addressee and converges toward the 'referee'.

Despite the differences outlined above between CS and *code-crossing*, both phenomena are, again, contextualization cues as defined in Gumperz (1982). As such, they can serve as acts of identity: through them the speaker may 'project his [her] inner universe, implicitly with the invitation to others to share it, at least insofar as they recognize his [her] language as an accurate symbolization of the world, and to share his [her] attitudes towards it' (Le Page & Tabouret Keller, 1985: 181). Having discussed the difference between CS and related language contact phenomena such as borrowing, language shift, diglossia and code-crossing, I shall now discuss briefly some of the approaches from which CS has been studied. The aim here is to underscore the fact that classroom language practices are a microcosm of language practices in the wider bilingual/multilingual society.

Approaches to Codeswitching

CS has been investigated from a number of approaches, among them grammatical, psycholinguistic and sociolinguistic approaches. The goal of grammatical approaches to CS has already been described (see Introduction). Psycholinguistic approaches to CS explore, among other issues, how CS sentences are processed, whether CS sentences take longer to process than monolingual sentences, whether CS derives from the interaction of monolingual grammars or from a separate grammar, the so-called third or CS grammar (Costa, 2004; Ewing, 1984; Lederberg & Morales, 1985). Sociolinguistic approaches to CS seek to determine why bilingual speakers sometime engage in CS. In this section, I shall concentrate on the latter approaches, for they provide the background against which classroom CS can be understood better. Some of the approaches to be discussed below include the interactional approach (Gumperz, 1982), the markedness approach (Myers-Scotton, 1993) and the political–ideological approach (Heller, 1988). [For additional sociolinguistic approaches to CS, see Auer, 1995; Kamwangamalu, 1998; Milroy & Muysken, 1995.]

The interactional approach to codeswitching

The interactional approach is at the heart of John Gumperz's research into CS. Its focus is not so much on details of constituent structure but rather on the social meaning of CS and, as Milroy and Muysken (1995: 9) note, on the discourse and interactional functions that CS performs for speakers. In this approach, CS is viewed as a contextualization cue, as Gumperz (1982) defines. Myers-Scotton (1993: 57) comments that within the interactional approach, speakers are understood to use language in the way they do not simply because of their social identities or because of other factors. Rather, they exploit the possibility of linguistic choices in order to convey intentional meaning of a socio-pragmatic nature. Code choices then, including CS, are not just choices of content, but are *discourse strategies*.

Gumperz's interactional approach to CS is mostly known for the distinction it makes between *situational codeswitching* and *metaphorical codeswitching*. A parallel distinction can be found in Oksaar (1972: 492), who uses the terms *external codeswitching* and *internal codeswitching*, or in Jacobson (1978), who distinguishes between *sociologically conditioned codeswitching* and *psychologically conditioned codeswitching*. *Situational CS* (i.e. external or sociologically conditioned CS) has to do with the social factors that trigger CS, such as the participants, the topic, and the setting. The bilingual's code choice is partly dependent on them. *Metaphorical CS* (i.e. internal or psychologically conditioned CS) concerns language factors, especially the speaker's fluency and his/her ability to use various emotive devices.

The Gumperz approach has been criticized for its taxonomic view of CS (Myers-Scotton, 1993: 52–55), which consists in listing the functions of CS in a particular speech situation. The criticism stems from the fact that language is dynamic. Not a single individual speaks the same way all the time, nor does anyone, including monolinguals, use a single register or style in every speech situation. Also, there are a variety of domains, topics and situations in which bilingual speakers may use CS. Therefore, listing the functions of CS, as the Gumperz approach does, distracts from the search for generalizations on the functions of CS in multilingual societies.

Notwithstanding these criticisms, Gumperz' approach supports the idea, documented by many scholars including Gumperz himself, that CS is not meaningless or a deficit to be stigmatized. Rather, it can and does indeed serve a wide range of functions in bilingual interactions, such as to express modernization, confidentiality, solidarity or in-groupness identity, sympathy and intimacy, to list a few (Gumperz, 1982; Kachru, 1978; see also chapters on Language and Interaction and on Language and Identity, this volume).

The markedness approach to codeswitching

The markedness approach has evolved from Myers-Scotton's research into CS in East Africa, especially in Kenya. The main claim of this approach is that all linguistic choices, including CS, are indices of social negotiations of rights and obligations existing between participants in a conversational exchange (Myers-Scotton, 1993: 152–153). These rights and obligations are said to derive from whatever situational features are salient to the exchange, such as the status of the participants, the topic and the setting. It is the interplay between these features and more dynamic, individual considerations that determines the linguistic choices that individuals make about media for conversational exchanges.

The markedness approach predicts (Myers-Scotton, 1993: 156) CS as a realization of one of the following three types of negotiations. First, in conventionalized exchanges, CS may be an unmarked choice between peers, unmarked in the sense that it is the expected choice for the exchange in question and its use signals solidarity and in-groupness identity amongst the participants. Second, with any participants in such exchanges CS may be a marked choice, that is, it is the unexpected choice in that exchange and therefore signals social distance amongst the participants. And, third, in nonconventionalized exchanges or uncertain situations, CS is an exploratory choice presenting multiple identities. It is explained that in these situations, since there is no apparent unmarked choice, speakers nominate an exploratory choice as the basis for the exchange. In other words, speakers 'negotiate' one code first as a medium for the exchange and, depending upon the outcome of the negotiation, they may negotiate another code until they are satisfied that they have reached the balance of rights and obligations required for that particular conversational exchange.

The markedness approach has indeed contributed significantly to our understanding of why bilingual speakers use their languages the way they do in their communities. However, it has been criticized for being too static to account for the social motivations for CS across languages and cultures (Kamwangamalu, 1996; Meeuwis & Blommaert, 1994). Consider, for instance, the following conversation between a lecturer and his students in a lecture room at the University of Swaziland in Southern Africa. The lecturer (the author) negotiates an early date for a test with his students, but the students would prefer to write the test later because they have already committed to writing tests for other courses. Not to challenge the lecturer openly, one student switches to siSwati in appealing to fellow students for support against writing the test sooner. The student uses siSwati so that the lecturer, not a siSwati speaker himself, would not understand what the student is saying.

Following the markedness approach, the switch from English to siSwati is clearly a marked choice intended to create distance between the lecturer and the students, for siSwati is the least expected medium of communication in a University lecture room, especially if the parties involved all do not share this language (siSwati). Note, however, that from the speaker's perspective, CS to siSwati also qualifies as an unmarked choice, for it is intended to create solidarity between the speaker and his fellow students. What this means is that CS as a marked choice can be a double-edged sword: it can simultaneously exclude and include; it can create rapprochement and distance, much as it can reinforce the we-ness versus the other-ness among the participants in a conversational exchange.

siSwati-English CS (Kamwangamalu, 1996: 299)

Lecturer: What if I gave you a short test tomorrow.
Students: No, sir, tomorrow we are writing a test for another course.
Lecturer: When do you think we can write it? We should definitely have one this week.

One student (turning to his fellow students):

Yeyi nine ningadli nivune kutsi siyibuale le-TEST. Onkhe maviki sibhala iTEST yakhe ingatsi ngiyo yodwa iCOURSE lesiyentakiko (Translation: Hey, you! Never agree to write the test! Every week we write his tests as if his is the only course we are taking this term)

Lecturer (to the student who was addressing his classmates):
        What are you saying?
The Student: I'm saying, Sir, what if we write it next week.

[The rest of the class laughs.]

This example of siSwati-English classroom CS shows clearly that CS as a marked choice does not necessarily or always entail social distance among the participants. This point holds also for CS as a marked choice in other formal settings, such as political rallies, church services, etc. For instance, when politicians use CS at public rallies or in formal meetings, their aim is not so much to distance themselves from their audiences or addressees. Rather, they use CS to create an opposite, no matter how symbolic, effect: rapprochement, oneness and solidarity with their audiences. Other examples of CS as a marked choice include cases discussed in Kamwangamalu (1998: 291–292): Koffi Annan's use of French-English CS in his 1997 maiden speech at the UN to seek rapprochement with the French, who had reportedly opposed his candidacy as UN Secretary General; Nelson Mandela's use of Afrikaans-English CS at meetings with the Afrikaners while negotiating the end of apartheid in South Africa; a Zimbabwe mayor's use of Ndebele-English CS in the legislature. Contrary to the predictions of the markedness approach to CS, the unexpected (i.e. marked) use of French, Afrikaans and Ndebele, respectively in these cases is clearly intended to create rapprochement rather than distance between the speakers and their audiences.

A similar criticism of the staticness of the markedness approach to CS can be found in Meeuwis and Blommaert (1994). In particular, Meeuwis and

Blommaert call into question the key claim of the markedness approach that the negotiation of identities, rights and obligations is the explanation for all the uses, functions and meanings of CS in every CS society. More specifically, Meeuwis and Blommaert are very critical of what they call 'the disappearance of ethnographic specificity' in Myers-Scotton's approach to CS. In their view, Myers-Scotton (1994: 412) neglects ethnographic description because of 'her ambitions to postulate innateness and universality as the level at which CS should be explained'. In making a 'quantum leap over and beyond ethnography', Meeuwis and Blommaert (1994: 397) argue further, the markedness approach is '"a-social" and fails to account for the community-specific "empirical facts" that account for most of the "social" in communication'.

Indeed, one cannot explain the function of CS in bilingual/multilingual societies solely in terms of the negotiation of identities in interpersonal communication, for, as we will see below in the discussion of the ideological–political approach, CS is sometimes used for political gains (Heller, 1992). Nevertheless, there seems to be no justification in Meeuwis and Blommaert's describing as a-social a theory, the markedness theory, which attempts to account for the social motivations for CS.

The political–ideological approach to codeswitching

While Myers-Scotton maintains that all linguistic choices including CS are indexical of social negotiations of rights and obligations, there are studies of code choice in which the political and language–ideological dimensions of CS are stressed (Bamiro, 2006; Heller, 1992; Kamwangamalu, 2000b; Lin, 1996; Meeuwis & Blommaert, 1994). In these studies, CS is seen as a point of entry into the exploration of processes whereby dominant groups use conventions of language choice to maintain relations of power, while subordinate groups may (at times simultaneously) acquiesce to, resist or even exploit conventions of language choice to redefine them (Heller, 1992). Accordingly, CS is seen as *linguistic capital* and one of the powerful and potentially effective strategies that people have at their disposal and that they use to achieve pre-determined social goals, such as exercise power over others or identify with certain groups for political gains (e.g. votes). The distribution of this capital in the community is related in specific ways to the distribution of other forms of capital (e.g. economic capital, cultural capital, etc.) that define the location of an individual within the social space (Bourdieu, 1991).

In some communities the linguistic capital itself may, as Meeuwis and Blommaert (1994) note with regard to Fabian's (1982) study of French-Swahili CS in former Zaire, now the Democratic Republic of Congo, be the locus *par excellence* of conflict and contest in language. In his study, Fabian documents resistance against 'standard' norms of communication, noting that neither the 'standard' nor the 'heretic' is neutral: both are political instruments either at the service of hegemony or at the service of resistance to this hegemony. Similarly, Heller's (1992) study of language choice and French-English CS in Quebec, Canada, reveals that like Fabian's study, CS is not arbitrary but concerns relations of power – different ways of seeing the world in struggle with each other. The individuals who participate in this struggle are said to have different aims – some will seek to preserve the status quo, others to change it – and differing chances of winning or losing, depending upon where they are located in the structured space of their respective positions in society (Bourdieu, 1991). Heller concludes in her study that 'in order to understand the role and significance of CS [as political choice], it is essential to understand not only its distribution in the community, but, more importantly, how that distribution is tied to the way groups control both the distribution of access to valued resources and the way in which that value is assigned' (1992: 139–140). In this regard, Bourdieu (1991) theorizes that people make choices about what languages to use in particular kinds of *markets*, which he defines as places where different kinds of resources or capital are distributed. Multilingual classrooms represent one such market where decisions about language choice are made. In the section that follows I highlight key findings on why bilingual teachers and students sometime choose to use CS in this particular market, the classroom.

Pedagogical Motivations for Codeswitching

Classroom CS entails simultaneous use of two languages including a target language (L2) such as English and students' first language (L1), or of two varieties of the target language, one standard and one nonstandard, for classroom interaction and instructional exchanges. The use of both African American Vernacular English or Ebonics and Standard American English in the classroom, for instance, constitutes an example of CS involving two varieties of the same language, English (see Alim, this volume). The literature indicates that some scholars support the promotion of Ebonics as a variety of English in its own right; but others oppose it in favor of Standard American English (Rickford, 2006). I shall return to this issue later when I discuss the implications of classroom CS for the (Standard) English-only argument in the United States, as well as in English-medium or ESL/EFL classrooms worldwide.

CS involving L1 and L2 in education has been documented in many countries around the world, for example Edstrom (2006), Franquiz and del Carmen (2004) and Flowers (2000) in the United States; Arthur (2001) in Botswana and Tanzania; Merritt *et al.* (1992) and Bunyi (1998) in Kenya; Peires (1994) in South Africa; Canagarajah (1995) in Sri Lanka; Rubdy (2007) in Singapore; Lin (1996) in Hong Kong; Liu *et al.* (2004) in Korea;

Slotte-Luttge (2007) in Finland; etc. The central quest of this research has been to explain why bilingual teachers and students use CS in the classroom and especially whether classroom CS is an impediment or a resource to learning.

The literature including that listed above has shown that classroom CS is not detrimental to the acquisition of the target language or variety. Rubdy (2007: 320) notes that on the contrary and far from being a dysfunctional form of speech behavior, as some educational authorities have implied, classroom CS can be an important, even necessary, communicative resource for the management of learning. As such, classroom CS is a teaching/learning aid that can be used to meet a wide range of classroom needs: it can be used to build rapport and provide a sense of inclusiveness (Peires, 1994; Rubdy, 2007), to compensate for a lack of comprehension (Edstrom, 2006), to manage the classroom and transmit content (Butzkamm, 1998), to express solidarity with the students (Camilleri, 1996; Elridge, 1996), to praise or scorn (Moodley, 2003), and so on.

For instance, in an investigation into the use of Singlish (Singapore Colloquial English) in education in Singapore, Rubdy (2007) reports that despite the stigma with which it is associated, Singlish is more often than not used in the classroom. Indeed, the official mandate stipulates that only Singapore Standard English should be used in the classroom. However, it seems that teachers switch to Singlish because it best serves their teaching needs: it empowers them to explain difficult points or concepts, to inject humor, to establish a warmer, friendlier atmosphere in the classroom, to encourage greater student involvement, etc. (Rubdy, 2007: 314, 322).

In a similar but practitioner research study, Edstrom (2006) documents her own teaching practices using English in an otherwise Spanish classroom in the United States. In particular, the author sought to discover how much English she used in a first-semester Spanish course, to identify the functions or purposes for which she used it, to compare her perceptions, and those of her students, with her actual practices, and to critique her L1/L2 use in light of her own pedagogical belief system. Edstrom reports that she found Spanish/English classroom CS useful. She used it, for instance, for grammar instruction, classroom management, and for compensating for a lack of comprehension (Edstrom, 2006: 283). Edstrom cautions teachers not to adhere blindly to a professional guideline, but rather to identify, and perhaps re-evaluate their moral obligations to their students and their objectives for the language learning process (Edstrom, 2006; 289). Likewise, Hadjioannou (2009: 287) remarks that instead of alienating or disenfranchising dialect speaking students by rejecting their mother tongue and stigmatizing its use in school, teachers should develop a healthier attitude toward diglossia to foster student academic success. Ferguson (2003) anticipated this point, in noting that as both members of a profession and members of the local community, teachers may wish from time to time to step out of their teachers' persona and stress co-membership of the local vernacular community with their students. They can do so, for instance, by switching to the vernacular when they scold or praise the students. In this regard, Liu *et al.* (2005, cited in Rubdy, 2007: 322) argue that in an increasingly globalized world, CS may need to be added as curriculum objective, a required life skill.

Other scholars, such as Franquiz and del Carmen (2004), make an even stronger argument in their study of language practices in the education of Mexican–American students. In particular, the authors argue that teachers should practice a humanizing pedagogy to foster healthy educational orientations for their students. A humanizing pedagogy entails '... valuing the students' background knowledge, culture, and life experiences, and creating learning contexts where power is shared by students and teachers' (Bartolome, 1996: 176). Teachers who practice a humanizing pedagogy make use of what Moll and Greenberg (1992) have termed 'the funds of cultural knowledge' of their students' heritage community; that is, in their literary practices such teachers focus on what students can do and achieve with the linguistic and cultural resources they bring to the classroom from outside of school (Franquiz & del Carmen, 2004: 49). In this regard, I concur with Delpit (1995) when she remarks that 'acquiring the ability to function in a dominant discourse need not mean that one must reject one's home identity and values, for discourses are not static, but are shaped, however reluctantly, by those who participate within them and the form of their participation' (Delpit, 1995, cited in Filmer, 2003: 267).

It is crucial, then, that teachers reflect seriously on how they respond to the linguistic resources that their students bring to learning. As McKay (2008: 23) observes, in classrooms in multilingual contexts where the teacher shares a first language with the students, teachers need to carefully consider how they can best make use of their students' first language to enhance their competence in a target language. The literature suggests that where teachers do not share a first language with the students, other teaching strategies, such as peer-teaching or peer-tutoring, should be employed (Finnochiaro, 1988; Sionis, 1990). Peer-teaching, or what Finnochiaro (1988) has termed the 'buddy system', refers to any activity involving students helping one another to understand, review, practice and remember (Bassano & Christison, 1988: 8). It entails switching to the language that the learners know best, their L1 or what Butzkamm (1998: 1) has termed 'a conversational lubricant', and use it as a springboard for acquiring a target language. More specifically, peer-teaching involves using learners as models, sources of information, and interactants for each other in such a way that learners assume roles and responsibilities normally taken by a formally trained teacher (Gaies, 1985: 131). By using peer-teaching the teacher sub-contracts, as it were, some of his prerogatives to pairs or small groups of students headed by what Sionis (1990: 9) has termed 'surrogate teachers'. Instructional exchanges between teachers and students or between students and students provide opportunities for learners to practice L2 skills, to test out their hypotheses about how the language works, to get useful feedback (Ernst, 1994: 294) and, in short, to make what Allwright (1980: 185) calls 'real attempts at communication'.

Peer-teaching, a much publicized practice in contemporary education, has emerged as a response to the challenges and changes in the language teaching profession and to the need to make language instruction as effective and meaningful as possible. This method of teaching attained great popularity in Britain during the early 20th century. The appeal of using children to teach other children was due to the very promising reports about the academic and social effects of tutoring programs (Gartner *et al.*, 1971, quoted in Allen, 1976: 10). The reports showed that the tutor (the pupil teacher) and the tutee (the pupil learner) did not only gain in academic achievement, but there was also improvement in social behavior, attitudes and self-esteem as well. Also, in entrusting the tutors with the task of tutoring their less proficient classmates, the teacher acknowledges that these aides are good at what they are doing. In doing so, the teacher instills confidence in the tutors and stimulates them to work even harder in their studies. On the other hand, as Sionis (1990: 5) notes, the tutees are constantly stimulated and perceive the level of their tutors as more easily attainable than that of native speakers, their teacher or other language models.

The English-only Argument

The research reviewed in the foregoing sections indicates that classroom CS is a resource rather than an impediment to learning. Very often, however, the question whether a native language or language variety should be used in the classroom has been a source of controversy and debate among applied linguists and policy makers of all persuasion, as pointed out earlier with respect to the Ebonics controversy in the United States.

The debate, which has come to be known as the English-only argument in the United States or Teach-English-Through-English (TETE) in Asia and in many English-medium or ESL/EFL countries worldwide, seems to be far from over (Auerbach, 1993; Kim, 2003; Lucas & Katz, 1994). As Auerbach (1993: 14) notes, the proponents of the English-only argument in the United States, just like the proponents of what may be called the 'TETE' argument in Asia and elsewhere, claim that English is best taught monolingually, that the more English is taught, the better the results, that using students' L1 or variety will impede the development of thinking in English, and that if other languages are used too much, standards of English will drop (Auerbach, 1993; Lucas & Katz, 1994). Contrary to these claims, several studies including those cited above have shown that students' L1 has an important role to play in an English-only classroom, especially for learners who are less proficient in the target language, English (Cook, 2001; Hemmindinger, 1987; Kim, 2003; Shamash, 1990).

For example, in a study comparing academic oral interaction in TETE (i.e. English-medium) lectures and Korean-medium lectures, Kim (2003: 15) reports that, due to their limited proficiency in English, students encountered more difficulty expressing themselves in TETE lectures than in Korean-medium lectures. It is observed that not only did the students have more difficulty with lecture comprehension and note-taking in TETE lectures than in Korean-medium lectures, but they also had difficulty participating in small group discussions, oral presentations, and whole class discussions in English-medium lectures (Kim, 2003: 13, 14). In a similar study investigating South Korean teachers' attitude toward TETE, Kim (2008: 68) notes that teachers experience a high degree of anxiety associated with TETE, for they themselves, like their students, have limited proficiency in English. It seems that using students' and teachers' L1 (i.e. Korean) in the classroom would help both teachers and students develop proficiency in the target language, English.

As already pointed out, research shows that L1 plays a positive role in L2 learning. For instance, Shamash (1990) provides an account of the use of learners' L1 in ESL classes at the Invergarry Learning Center in Vancouver, Canada. At the Center, students are allowed to start writing about their lives in their L1. With the assistance of more proficient learners or bilingual tutors, the texts produced by the learners are translated into English, the target language. The outcome of this exercise is that it validates the learners' lived experience, provides the learners with opportunities to experiment and take risks with English, and constitutes a natural bridge for overcoming problems of vocabulary, sentence structure and language confidence (Shamash, 1990: 72, 75). Like Shamash (1990), Cleghorn and Rollnick (2002) provide several examples of classroom CS in science lessons in Southern and East Africa, noting that the switch to the learners' home language serves to render the culturally unfamiliar familiar, make the implicit explicit, provide contextualization cues, and raise learners' metalinguistic awarness (2002: 360).

Another benefit of using students' L1 in an (Standard) English-only classroom is that L1 reduces affective barriers to the acquisition of English and allows for more rapid progress in the language. Referring to a study by Hemmindinger (1987) on ESL teaching to Hmong refugees, Auerbach (1993: 19) notes that the refugees made greater progress in class in learning English when they were allowed to use their L1 as well. Hemmindinger attributes the learners' success in part to the fact that the combined use of L1 and English (L2) allows for language and culture shock to be reduced. Likewise, Lucas and Katz's (1994) study of Special Alternative Instructional Programs (SAIPS) in the United States provides further support for the usefulness of students' L1, in this case Spanish, in ESL learning. In particular, Lucas and Katz note that 'when students see that their languages are valued for their communicative power and when they have the opportunity to develop their native language abilities, their self-esteem and identity are strengthened' (1994: 559). A similar study by Kamwangamalu and Virasamy (1999) of peer-tutoring at a Durban City secondary school in South Africa shows that students' L1, in this case Zulu, can be put to many uses in the classroom: it can be used for eliciting the subject content, for asking questions or for triggering cooperation among students. Interviews with Zulu-speaking pupils indicated an overwhelming support for using Zulu in the classroom, for the language provided the learners with opportunities to '... participate in the lesson and ... feel encouraged to do things' (Kamwangamalu & Virasamy, 1999: 67; see also McKay & Chick, 2001).

Requiring the students not to use their L1 in the classroom, as is customary in ESL teaching both locally and globally as well as in many EFL countries, can have a detrimental effect on the learners' academic development. Consider, for instance, the case of Mexican–American ESL students. Research shows that a school's attempt to assimilate young Mexican–American students into the dominant society by subtracting their language and culture has a damaging effect on the students' academic performance. Goldstein (2003) notes that *subtractive schooling*, a concept that she borrows from Valenzuela (1999) and that demands that students invest only in the dominant (Euro-American middle class) school culture and divests them of important social and cultural resources, leaves the Mexican–American youths vulnerable to academic failure (2003: 248). Along these lines, Ribadeneira (1992) points out that Spanish-speaking pupils tend to drop out of school when they are forced not to speak Spanish in the classroom because they feel that

> [they] are treated like garbage. I kept getting suspended because when I spoke Spanish with my homeboys, the teachers thought I was disrespecting them. They kept telling me to speak in English because I was in America. I wasn't going to take that ... So I left and never went back. Some of those teachers don't want us. That hurts, that really hurts. (Ribadeneira, 1992, quoted in Auerbach, 1993: 9)

A similar situation exists in most post-colonial settings around the world as well. In South Africa, for instance, formerly 'Indian' and 'white' schools have admitted large numbers of African pupils who learn English as L2. Since in many of these schools English is the sole medium of instruction, students are sometimes punished or fined when they use their L1 within the school compound. Press reports indicate that 'some school principals speak with pride about beating children to stop them speaking their native tongue' at school (*Mail & Guardian*, July 5, 1997). Raising educators' awareness about the resourcefulness of classroom CS should help them re-assess their attitude toward L1 and its role in L2 learning.

Research Methods in CS

This section offers a brief description of common research methods used in CS studies. These methods, which are discussed in detail elsewhere (e.g. Kamwangamalu, 1989: 176–210), include written texts, tape recording, interviews, and language survey questionnaires. In addition, I will discuss ethnographic observations, for they also serve as a productive source of data for research into various aspects of CS, including classroom CS.

Written texts

Written texts in which CS is commonly found include, for instance, scripts of bilingual TV and radio programs, bilingual newspaper articles, published literature by bilingual writers and so on. CS is used in written texts for diverse reasons. Depending on the context of situation, CS may provide clues about the education, socio-economic status, regional provenance, register, religion, etc. of a particular participant or a character in a novel, for instance. For example, Dabke (1983: 370, 372) discusses the fictional use of standard German and Swabian (dialect of German) CS in novel, *Familienfest*. He points out that the characters in this novel codeswitch Standard German and Swabian to demonstrate their social or regional provenance. Also, Dabke observes that in this novel CS is used to structure a scene and serves as the reader's guide in that it marks pause and climax, beginning and closure of narrative summary and speech event. Characters in a novel may also use CS to express emotion, anger, disgust and so on, just as bilingual speakers would express similar feelings in everyday interaction with members of their community.

Tape recording and interviews

Tape recording and interviews have served as another good source of data for CS studies. Tape recordings are often used in contexts such as the family for recording conversations between friends or family members on certain occasions, for example, parties, ceremonies and the like. Some scholars have used tape recording to record doctor–patient interactions, customer–salesperson interactions, courtroom or classroom interactions and so on (Gardner-Chloros, 1985). Others have used tape recording to record interviews with bilingual speakers (Jacobson, 1978). Tape recording and recorded interviews allow the investigator to gather a larger body of data than do, for instance, rapid notes of spontaneous CS in bilingual interactions. The challenge facing tape recording and interviews with bilingual speakers lies, however, in what Labov (1978) has termed the 'observer's paradox': to obtain the data most important for linguistic analysis, we have to observe how people speak when they are not being observed (Labov, 1978: 354, 6). On the other hand, however, the observer cannot make secret recordings of people's speech because such practice is unethical and often difficult. Also, in interviews the participants may not feel comfortable expressing themselves freely especially if they are aware that their speech is being recorded.

Some investigators (e.g. Poplack, 1981[1980]) have suggested that the observer's paradox can be avoided by having an in-group member interview or record the speech of his/her peers in natural settings. The observer, who in this case is an in-group member, can collect reliable CS data due to his/her familiarity with the peers that are being recorded (Poplack, 1981 [1980]: 595). However, anticipating Poplack's study, other investigators (e.g. Jacobson, 1978) showed that whether the observer is an in-group or an out-group member, the bilinguals who are engaged in CS would refrain from it when they realize that they are being observed or tape recorded. For instance, a Mexican–American fieldworker in Jacobson's CS project reports that it was easy for her as an in-group member and peer of her informants to witness CS practices but extremely difficult to record these on tape. The fieldworker observes further that her informants were codeswitching continuously when the tape recorder was turned off but when it was on, they would speak a single language (Jacobson, 1978: 234).

Language surveys

In addition to written texts, interviews and tape recording, CS scholars have also made use of language surveys to explore various aspects of CS. Generally, language-use surveys consist of lengthy questionnaires intended to determine, among other things, the speakers' attitudes toward the languages available to them, and to determine the language the speaker uses when, where, with whom and for what purpose (Fishman, 1972). Some scholars have been very skeptical about the adequacy of language surveys to account for language use. Labov (1978), for instance, observes that language surveys generally represent the investigator's, rather than the bilingual's, theory of speaking. In Labov's (1978: 354) view, any theory of language must be consistent with the language used by ordinary people in the course of their daily business. That is, a valid theory of language should fit the characteristics of the language that speakers actually use when the linguist is not present (Labov, 1978: 353).

Ethnographic observations

Besides the methods discussed above, researchers interested in investigating classroom CS have also made use of ethnographic observations including participant observations and audio and/or video recording of language use in bilingual classrooms (Hadjioannou, 2009; Lin, 1990; Martin-Jones, 1995; Zentella, 1981). For instance, Hadjioannou (2009) reports on an ethnographic study of Standard Greek–Greek Cypriot dialect CS she conducted in bilingual classrooms in Cyprus, noting that teachers engaged in CS for classroom management, for elaboration or clarification, or for joking. Similarly, Martin-Jones (1995) describes two ethnographic studies of CS, one by Zentella (1981) based on observations of Spanish-English bilingual classes in New York and the second by Lin (1990) on English–Cantonese bilingual classrooms in Hong Kong. The results of these studies reveal that teachers engaged in CS to mitigate the effect of admonition, to make asides, to make metalinguistic commentaries (Zentella, 1981), or to ensure thorough understanding of the teaching points by reiterating and elaborating them in L1 (Lin, 1990). It must be said, however, that the very presence of the investigator–participant observer in the classroom, together with the recording instruments, makes ethnographic observations somewhat intrusive. As such, ethnographic observations run into the same problem of the observer's paradox that Labov (1978) has raised. Nevertheless, data from ethnographic observations not only provide insights into the ways in which teachers and learners get things done bilingually in the classroom (Martin-Jones, 1995), but also indicate, as observed earlier, that classroom CS is a mirror image of language practice in the wider bilingual society. As Joshua Fishman would put it, 'societal factors dictate much of *what* is taught and *to whom*; as well as *how* it is taught and by whom; and finally how all of those involved in the teaching-learning process interact with each other' (Fishman, 1977: 32).

To summarize, the methods described above, namely, written texts, interviews, tape recording, language surveys, and ethnographic observations, have generated a significant body of data for CS analysis. They do, however, each have their limitations and challenges, as already noted with respect to the observer's paradox (Labov, 1978). An eclectic approach, one that uses a combination of some of these methods for data collection, might help counter the challenges and allow the investigator to gain more insights into CS, especially its use in the educational context.

Conclusion and Directions for Further Research

This chapter has highlighted research findings on why bilingual teachers and students sometime use CS in the classroom. Research shows that classroom CS, just like CS in the wider multilingual society, is not random.

Rather, teachers and students have recourse to CS to meet delineable class-room needs, such as to compensate for a lack of comprehension, encourage greater student participation, build rapport and express solidarity with the students, and so on.

The chapter has also briefly discussed the relationship between class-room CS and other language contact phenomena such as diglossia. I have argued that by the very definition of diglossia, CS involving an H language and an L language or variety should not occur at all in the class-room or in any other formal context, since diglossia is premised on a strict functional compartmentalization of languages. And yet, as research has shown, CS can and does occur in any domains of language use, formal or informal; its occurrence in either domain is governed by the context of situation and the communication needs of the participants. Accordingly, the concept of diglossia needs redefining to reflect not only general language practices but also classroom language practices in multilingual communities around the world.

Finally, the chapter has discussed the implications of classroom CS for the English-only argument in the United States, as well as in English-medium or ESL/EFL classrooms worldwide. It was noted that using L1 in an L2 classroom validates learners' lived experience, provides the learners with opportunities to experiment and take risks with English, and consti-tutes a natural bridge for overcoming problems of vocabulary, sentence structure and language confidence. In spite of its significance for class-room management and interaction, L1–L2 classroom CS has been viewed by some as an impediment rather than a resource to learning, and as a mark of linguistic deficiency (Auerbach, 1993; Elridge, 1996; Martin-Jones, 1995; Peires, 1994; Rubdy, 2007). Research is needed to educate teachers and language policy makers about the benefit of classroom CS, to change their attitudes toward classroom CS, to raise their awareness about the significance of CS for classroom interaction, and to underscore the impor-tance of L1 in L2 learning (Cleghorn & Rollnick, 2002; Cook, 2001). Until that research is done, educators need to heed to Elridge's admonition that '... we understand precisely the causes, motivations, and effects of CS, and ... avoid making rash, censorial judgements on its classroom mani-festations' (1996: 303). The more we know about the social motivations for CS, the greater will be our appreciation of its manifestations in bilingual classrooms around the world.

Suggestions for further reading

Those interested in learning more about CS will find the following sources very useful. The sources provide further insights not only into classroom CS, but also into various aspects of CS not covered in the present chapter, such as grammatical, psycholinguistic, pragmatic and neurolinguistic aspects of CS.

Bhatia, T.K. and Ritchie, W.C. (2007) *The Handbook of Bilingualism*. Malden, MA: Blackwell Publishing.
This book reviews the foundations of bilingualism and offers an in-depth discussion of its various aspects including CS. In particular, the reader will find a wealth of information about CS in the section 'The Bilingual Repertoire: Code Mixing and Code Switching and Speech Accommodation' (pp. 282–378), and in the section 'Bilingualism: The Media, Education, and Literacy' (pp. 512–601).

Jones, G.M. (ed.) (1996) Bilingualism through the classroom: Strategies and practices. *Journal of Multilingual and Multicultural Development*. Special Issue 17 (2–4). Clevedon: Multilingual Matters.
The articles in this volume explore topics in language practices in bilingual classrooms and how bilingual education policies are realized by teachers, with a focus on Asia. Language teachers will find the following articles of particular interest, for they all deal with classroom CS: 'Using two/Three Languages in Philippine Classrooms' by Andrew Gonzales; 'Mother Tongue Use in Bilingual/Bidialectal Education' by Carl James; and 'Codeswitching in the Primary Classroom: One Response to the Planned and the Unplanned Language Environment in Brunei' by Peter W. Martin.

Milroy, L. and Muysken, P. (eds) (1995) *One Speaker, Two Languages: Cross-Disciplinary Perspectives on Code-Switching*. Cambridge: Cambridge University Press.
This collection offers a number of cross-disciplinary perspectives on codeswitching, including grammatical, sociolinguistic, and psycholinguistic perspectives. The reader will find the first two parts of the book very informative, for they provide insights into CS in institutional and community settings, as well as into its occurrence in everyday bilingual encounters.

Paradis, M. (ed.) (1978) *Aspects of Bilingualism*. Columbia, SC: Hornbean Press.
Published about 30 years ago, this volume remains a valuable resource, for it offers the reader the background knowledge against which current developments in CS research can be better understood. In particular, the volume provides insights into various aspects of CS, ranging from developmental aspects, linguistic aspects, pedagogical aspects, and neurolinguistic aspects, to sociolinguistic aspects of CS.

Slotte-Luttge, A. (2007) Making use of bilingualism – construction of a monolingual classroom and consequences. *International Journal of the Sociology of Language* 187/188, 103–128.
This article is an empirical study of Swedish-Finnish codeswitching in Finland. More specifically, the article examines classroom discourse in a Swedish-speaking school in a Finnish-dominated area. Its aim is to show how linguistic norms are maintained, and what the implications of these norms are for participating pupils in classroom interaction.

Yeh, Christine J., Jennifer Chen, Agnes Kwong, Lilian Chiang, Yu-Wei Wand and Florence Pu-Folkes (2002) Educators of Asian bilingual students: Pedagogical techniques, strategies and challenges. *Journal of Multilingual and Multicultural Development* 23 (4), 296–315.
As the title indicates, this paper explores pedagogical strategies and challenges in the education of Asian bilingual students in the United States. This it does by examining the strengths and weaknesses of educators teaching Asian bilingual students, and discussing the activities, training and resources that Asian bilingual educators believe would help them improve their teaching. The paper lists the following as pedagogical challenges facing Asian bilingual teachers: lack of culturally relevant teaching materials, varying language proficiencies, and overcrowded

classes. Some pedagogical strategies (e.g. organization of lessons around themes, small group activities, conference with individual students, etc.) are suggested to overcome the identified challenges. It is concluded that teachers should involve parents in the children's learning, familiarize themselves with the students' cultural background and immigration history, and demonstrate respect for cultural differences.

References

Allen, V.L. (1976) *Children as Teachers: Theory and Research on Tutoring*. New York: Academic Press.

Allwright, R. (1980) Turns, topics, and tasks: Patterns of participation in language learning and teaching. In D. Larsen-Freeman (ed.) *Discourse Analysis in Second Language Research* (pp. 165–187). Rowley, MA: Newbury House.

Arthur, J. (2001) Perspectives on educational language policy and its implementation in African classrooms: A comparative study of Botswana and Tanzania. *Compare* 31 (3), 347–376.

Auer, P. (1995) The pragmatics of codeswitching: A sequential approach. In L. Milroy and P. Muysken (eds) *One Speaker, Two Languages: Cross-disciplinary Perspectives on Codeswitching* (pp. 115–135). Cambridge: Cambridge University Press.

Auer, P. (1998) Introduction: Bilingual conversation revisited. In P. Auer (ed.) *Codeswitching in Conversation: Language, Interaction and Identity* (pp. 1–24). London: Routledge.

Auerbach, E.R. (1993) Re-examining English only in the ESL classroom. *TESOL Quarterly* 27 (1), 9–32.

Bamiro, E.O. (2006) The politics of codeswitching: English vs. Nigerian languages. *World Englishes* 25 (1), 23–35.

Bartolome, L. (1996) Beyond the methods fetish: Toward a humanizing pedagogy. *Harvard Educational Review* 64, 173–194.

Bassano, S. and Christison, M.A. (1988) Cooperative learning in the ESL classroom. *TESOL Newsletter* 22 (2), 1–8.

Bell, A. (1984) Language style as audience design. *Language in Society* 13 (2), 145–204.

Blom, J.P. and Gumperz, J. (1972) Social meaning in linguistic structure: Codeswitching in Norway. In J. Gumperz and D. Hymes (eds) *Directions in Sociolinguistics* (pp. 307–434). New York: Holt, Rinehard and Winston.

Bourdieu, P. (1991) *Language and Symbolic Power*. Cambridge: Polity Press.

Bunyi, G. (1998) Teaching/learning bilingually in post-colonial African classrooms: Ethnographic evidence and analysis from Kenya. Paper presented at Sociolinguistics Symposium 12, University of London Institute of Education, 26–28 March 1998.

Butzkamm, W. (1998) Codeswitching in a bilingual history lesson: The mother tongue as a conversational lubricant. *International Journal of Bilingual Education and Bilingualism* 1 (2), 81–99.

Camilleri, A. (1996) Language values and identities: Codeswitching in secondary classrooms in Malta. *Linguistics and Education* 8, 85–103.

Canagarajah, S. (1995) Functions of codeswitching in ESL classroom: Socializing bilingualism in Jaffna (Sri Lanka). *Journal of Multilingual and Multicultural Development* 6 (3), 173–195.

Cleghorn, A. and Rollnick, M. (2002) The role of English in individual and societal development: A view from African classrooms. *TESOL Quarterly* 36 (3), 347–372.

Cook, V. (2001) Using the first language in the classroom. *The Canadian Modern Language Review* 57, 402–423.

Costa, A. (2004) Speech production in bilinguals. In T. Bhatia and W. Ritchie (eds) *The Handbook of Bilingualism* (pp. 201–223). Malden, MA: Blackwell Publishing.

Dabke, R. (1983) Codeswitching and segmentation in Hartling's Familienfest. *Language and Style* 16 (3), 361–373.

Delpit, L. (1995) *Other People's Children: Cultural Conflict in the Classroom*. New York: New Press.

Edstrom, A. (2006) L1 use in the L2 classroom: One teacher's self-evaluation. *The Canadian Modern Language Review* 62 (2), 275–292.

Elridge, J. (1996) Codeswitching in Turkish secondary school. *English Language Teaching (ELT) Journal* 50 (4), 303–311.

Ernst, G. (1994) "Talking circle": Conversation and negotiation in the ESL classroom. *TESOL Quarterly* 28 (2), 293–322.

Ewing, A. (1984) Polish-English codeswitching: A clue to constituent structure and processing mechanisms. *Chicago Linguistic Society* 20, 52–64.

Fabian, J. (1982) Scratching the surface: Observations on the poetics of lexical borrowing in Shaba Swahili. *Anthropological Linguistics* 24, 14–50.

Fasold, R. (1984) *The Sociolinguistics of Society*. Oxford: Blackwell.

Ferguson, C.A. (1972 [1959]) Diglossia. *Word* 15, 325–340.

Ferguson, G. (2003) Classroom codeswitching in post-colonial contexts: Functions, attitudes and policies. *IRAL Review* 16, 38–51.

Filmer, A.A. (2003) African–American Vernacular English: Ethics, ideology, and pedagogy in the conflict between identity and power. *World Englishes* 22 (3), 253–270.

Finlayson, R. and Slabbert, S. (1997) I'll meet you halfway with language – codeswitching within a South African urban context: In M. Putz (ed.) *Language Choices: Conditions, Constraints, and Consequences* (pp. 381–422). Amsterdam: John Benjamins.

Finnochiaro, M. (1988) Teacher development: A continuing process. *English Teaching Forum* 26 (3), 2–5.

Fishman, J.A. (1967) Bilingualism with and without diglossia; Diglossia with and without bilingualism. *The Journal of Social Issues* 23 (2), 29–39.

Fishman, J.A. (1971) *Bilingualism in the Barrio*. The Hague: Mouton.

Fishman, J.A. (1972) Language maintenance in a supra-ethnic age. In A. Dil (ed.) *Language in Socio-cultural Change* (pp. 48–75). Stanford: Stanford University Press.

Fishman, J.A. (1977) The social science perspective. In *Bilingual Education: Current Perspectives: Social Science* (pp. 1–49). Arlington, VA: Center for Applied Linguistics.

Fishman, J.A. (1991) *Reversing Language Shift*. Clevedon: Multilingual Matters.

Flowers, D.A. (2000) Codeswitching and ebonics in urban adult basic education. *Education and Urbana Society* 32, 221–236.

Franquiz, M.E. and del Carmen Salazar, M. (2004) The transformative potential of humanizing pedagogy: Addressing the diverse needs of Chicano/Mexicano students. *High School Journal* 87 (4), 36–53.

Gafaranga, J. and Torra, M.C. (2002) Interactional otherness: Towards a redefinition of codeswitching. *International Journal of Bilingualism* 6 (1), 1–22.

Gaies, S.J. (1985) *Peer Involvement in Language Learning. Language in Education: Theory and Practice 60*. Orlando: Harcourt Brace Jovanovich.

Gardner-Chloros, P. (1985) Language selection and switching among Strasbourg shoppers. *International Journal of the Sociology of Language* 54, 117–135.

Gartner, A., Kohler, M. and Reissman, F. (1971) *Children Teach Children*. New York: Harper & Row.

Goldstein, T. (2003) Contemporary bilingual life at a Canadian high school: Choices, risks, tensions, and dilemmas. *Sociology of Education* 76, 247–264.

Gumperz, J. (1982) *Discourse Strategies*. London: Cambridge University Press.

Hadjioannou, X. (2009) Possibilities for non-standard dialects in American classrooms: Lessons from a Greek Cypriot class. In J.C. Scott, D.Y. Straker and L. Katz (eds) *Affirming Students' Right to Their Own Language: Bridging Language Policies and Pedagogical Practices* (pp. 275–290). New York and London: Routledge.

Hasselmo, N. (1972) Codeswitching as ordered selection. In E.S. Firchow (ed.) *Studies for Einar Haugen* (pp. 261–280). The Hague: Mouton.

Haugen, E. (1972) The stigmata of bilingualism. In A. Dil (ed.) *The Ecology of Language* (pp. 307–324). Stanford: Stanford University Press.

Heller, M. (1988) *Codeswitching: Anthropological and Sociolinguistic Perspectives*. Berlin: Mouton de Gruyter.

Heller, M. (1992) The politics of codeswitching and language choice. *Journal of Multilingual and Multicultural Development* 13, 123–142.

Hemmindinger, A. (1987) Two models for using problem-posing and cultural sharing in teaching the Hmong English as a second language and first language literacy. Unpublished master's thesis, St Francis Xavier University, Antigonish, Canada.

Jacobson, R. (1978) The social implications of intrasentential codeswitching. In R. Romo and R. Paredes (eds) *New Directions in Chicano Scholarship* (pp. 227–256). La Jolla, CA: Chicano Studies Monograph Series.

Jacobson, R. (ed.) (1990) *Codeswitching as a Worldwide Phenomenon*. New York: Peter Lang.

Kachru, B.B. (1978) Toward structuring codemixing: An Indian perspective. *Studies in the Linguistic Sciences* 5 (1), 73–92.

Kamwangamalu, N.M. (1989) Codemixing across languages: Structure, functions, and constraints. PhD thesis, University of Illinois.

Kamwangamalu, N.M. (1996) Sociolinguistic aspects of siSwati-English bilingualism. *World Englishes* 15 (3), 295–305.

Kamwangamalu, N.M. (1998) We-codes, they-codes, and the codes-in-between: Identities of English and codeswitching in post-apartheid South Africa. In N.M. Kamwangamalu (ed.) *Aspects of Multilingualism in Post-apartheid South Africa: A Special Issue of Multilingua* (Vol. 17; 2–3) (pp. 277–296). Berlin & New York: Mouton.

Kamwangamalu, N.M. (2000a) Languages in contact. In V. Webb and K. Sure (eds) *African Voices: An Introduction to the Languages and Linguistics of Africa* (pp. 88–108). Cape Town: Oxford University Press.

Kamwangamalu, N.M. (2000b) The state of codeswitching research at the dawn of the new millennium (2): Focus on Africa. *Southern African Linguistics and Applied Language Studies* 18, 59–71.

Kamwangamalu, N.M. (2001) Ethnicity and language crossing in post-apartheid South Africa. *International Journal of the Sociology of Language* 152, 75–95.

Kamwangamalu, N.M. and Lee, C.L. (1991) Chinese-English codemixing: A case of matrix language assignment. *World Englishes* 10 (3), 247–261.

Kamwangamalu, N.M. and Virasamy, C. (1999) Zulu peer-tutoring in a multiethnic English-only classroom. *South African Journal for Language Teaching* 33 (1), 60–71.

Kim, E-J. (2003) A comparative study of academic oral interaction in English-medium lectures and Korean-medium lectures. *English Teaching* 58 (3), 3–20.

Kim, S-Y. (2008) Five years of teaching English through English: Responses from teachers and prospects for learners. *English Teaching* 63 (1), 51–70.

Labov, W. (1978) Sociolinguistics. In W.O. Dingwall (ed.) *A Survey of Linguistic Science* (pp. 339–376). Stamford, CT: Greylock, Inc.

Lederberg, A. and Morales, C. (1985) Code-switching by bilinguals: Evidence against a third grammar. *Journal of Psycholinguistic Research* 14 (2), 113–136.

Le Page, R.B. and Tabouret-Keller, A. (1985) *Acts of Identity: Creole-Based Approaches to Ethnicity and Language.* Cambridge: Cambridge University Press.

Li, W. (1998) The "why" and "how" questions in the analysis of conversational codeswitching. In P. Auer (ed.) *From Codeswitching via Language Mixing to Fused Lects: Toward a Dynamic Typology of Bilingual Speech* (pp. 156–176). London: Routledge.

Lin, A.M.Y. (1990) *Teaching in Two Tongues: Language Alternation in Foreign Language Classrooms. Research Report, 3.* Hong Kong: City Polytechnic of Hong Kong.

Lin, A.M.Y. (1996) Bilingualism or linguistic segregation? Symbolic domination, resistance and codeswitching in Hong Kong schools. *Linguistics and Education* 8 (1), 49–84.

Liu, D., Ahn, G., Baek, K. and Han, N. (2004) South Korean high school English teachers' codeswitching: Questions and challenges in the drive for maximal use of English in teaching. *TESOL Quarterly* 38 (4), 605–638.

Lucas, T. and Katz, A. (1994) Reframing the debate: The roles of native languages in English-only programs for language minority students. *TESOL Quarterly* 28 (3), 537–562.

MacSwan, J. (2000) The architecture of the bilingual language faculty: Evidence from intrasentential code switching. *Bilingualism: Language & Cognition* 3 (1), 37–54.

Martin-Jones, M. (1995) Codeswitching in the classroom: Two decades of research. In L. Milroy and P. Muysken (eds) *One Speaker, Two Languages: Cross-disciplinary Perspectives on Codeswitching* (pp. 90–111). Cambridge: Cambridge University Press.

McKay, S.L. (2008) Sociolinguistics and language variation. In N. van Deusen-Scholl and N. Hornberger (eds) *Encyclopedia of Language and Education* (2nd edn) (Vol. 4) (pp. 17–27). New York, NY: Springer.

McKay, S. and Chick, K. (2001) Positioning learners in post apartheid South African schools: A case study of selected multicultural Durban schools. *Linguistics and Education* 12 (4), 393–408.

Meeuwis, M. and Blommaert, J. (1994) The 'Markedness Model' and the absence of society: Remarks on codeswitching (a review article). *Multilingua* 13 (4), 387–423.

Merritt, M., Cleghorn, A., Abagi, J.O. and Bunyi, G. (1992) Socializing multilingualism: Determinants of codeswitching in Kenyan primary classroom. In C. Eastman (ed.) *Journal of Multilingual and Multicultural Development. Special Issue on Codeswitching* 13 (1–2), 103–121.

Milroy, L. and Muysken, P. (eds) (1995) *One Speaker, Two Languages: Cross-disciplinary Perspectives on Codeswitching.* Cambridge: Cambridge University Press.

Mkilifi, A.M. (1978) Triglossia and Swahili-English bilingualism in Tanzania. In J. Fishman (ed.) *Advances in the Study of Societal Multilingualism* (pp. 129–149). The Hague: Mouton.

Moll, K.C. and Greenberg, J. (1990) Creating zones of possibilities: Combining social contexts for instruction. In L.C. Moll (ed.) *Vygotsky and Education* (pp. 319–348). NY: Cambridge University Press.

Moodley, V. (2003) Language attitudes and codeswitching behaviour of facilitators and learners in language, literacy and communication senior phase outcomes-based education classrooms. Unpublished PhD thesis, University of Natal.

Muysken, P. (2000) *Bilingual Speech: A Typology of Codemixing.* Cambridge: Cambridge University Press.

Myers-Scotton, C. (1993) *Social Motivations for Code-Switching: Evidence from Africa.* Oxford: Clarendon Press.

Oksaar, E. (1972) On codeswitching: An analysis of bilingual norm. In J. Qvistgaard, H. Schwarz and H.H. Spang-Hanssen (eds) *The Proceedings of the Third Congress of the International Association for Applied Linguistics* (pp. 491–500). Heidelberg: Julius Groos Verlag.

Peires, M. (1994) Codeswitching as an aid to L2 learning. *Southern African Journal of Applied Language Studies* 3 (1), 14–22.

Poplack, S. (1978) Syntactic structure and the social function of codeswitching. In R. Duran (ed.) *Latino Language and Communicative Behavior* (pp. 169–184). Norwood, NJ: Ablex Publishing Corporation.

Poplack, S. (1981 [1980]) Sometimes I'll start a sentence in Spanish y termino en Espanol: Toward a typology of code-switching. *Linguistics* 18, 581–618.

Poplack, S. and Meechan, M. (1995) Patterns of language mixture: Nominal structure in Wolof-French and Fongbe-French bilingual discourse. In L. Milroy and P. Muysken (eds) *One Speaker, Two Languages: Cross-disciplinary Perspectives on Codeswitching* (pp. 199–232). Cambridge: Cambridge University Press.

Proshina, Z.G. and Ettkin, B.P. (2005) English-Russian language contacts. *World Englishes* 24 (4), 439–444.

Rampton, B. (1995) *Crossing: Language and Ethnicity among Adolescents.* London/New York: Longman.

Ribadeneira, D. (1992) Hispanics say plight ignored in crisis. *Boston Globe*, May 7, pp. 1, 7.

Rickford, J.R. (2006) Using the vernacular to teach the standard: A revised version of the paper delivered at the Conference on Ebonics at California State University on March 29, 1997. On WWW at http://www.stanford.edu/~rickford/papers/vernacularToTeachStandard.html. Accessed May 2008.

Romaine, S. (1994) *Language in Society: An Introduction to Sociolinguistics.* New York: Oxford University Press.

Rubdy, R. (2007) Singlish in the school: An impediment or a resource? *Journal of Multilingual and Multicultural Development* 28 (4), 308–317.

Schiffman, H. (1997) Diglossia as a sociolinguistic situation. In F. Coulmas (ed.) *The Handbook of Sociolinguistics* (pp. 205–216). New York: Blackwell.

Shamash, Y. (1990) Learning in translation: Beyond language experience in ESL. *Voices* 2 (2), 71–75.

Sionis, C. (1990) Let them do our job! Towards autonomy via peer-teaching and task-based exercises. *English Teaching Forum* 28 (1), 5–9.

Slotte-Luttge, A. (2007) Making use of bilingualism – construction of a monolingual classroom, and its consequences. *International Journal of the Sociology of Language* 187/188, 103–128.

Valenzuela, A. (1999) *Subtractive Schooling: U.S.-Mexican Youth and the Politics of Caring.* Albany, NY: SUNY Press.

Wald, P. (1986) Diglossia applied: Vernacular mixing and functional switching with Bangui Yakomas. In J.A. Fishman (ed.) *The Fergusonian Impact* (Vol. 2) (pp. 417–430). New York: Mouton de Gruyter.

Watkhaolarm, P. (2005) Think in Thai, write in English: Thinness in Thai English literature. *World Englishes* 24 (2), 145–158.

Woolard, K.A. (1988) Codeswitching and comedy in Catalonia. In M. Heller (ed.) *Codeswitching: Anthropological and Sociolinguistic Perspectives* (pp. 53–76). The Hague: Mouton. [Also available in *International Pragmatic Association Papers on Pragmatics* 1, 106–122 (1987)].

Zentella, A.C. (1981) 'Ta bien, you could answer me en cualquier idioma': Puerto Rican codeswitching in bilingual classrooms. In R. Duran (ed.) *Latino Language and Communicative Behavior* (pp. 109–132). Norwood, NJ: Ablex Publishing.

Chapter 6

Language Policy and Planning

JOSEPH LO BIANCO

Introduction

This section contains a brief overview of the field of language planning (LP). It begins by describing the origins of the term LP and some of the goals of the activity. There is also a brief discussion of the relevance of LP to teachers.

The term LP was probably first invoked by the linguist Uriel Weinreich in the early 1950s in New York. Weinreich was working in the context of immigrant languages and dialects, in interaction with each other and with English. His famous work, *Languages in Contact* (Weinreich, 1953), discussed bilingual communication, including the mixing of a fading first language with a replacing second language. Linking anthropology and theoretical linguistics sharpened Weinreich's observations of ties between social phenomena and aspects of language and communication. He noted that speakers in bilingual communities do not keep their languages and dialects separate, but instead produce a hybrid 'interlanguage' as a composite single proficiency that blends features of the available communication forms.

Another sociolinguistics pioneer was the Norwegian American Einar Haugen, who expanded the meaning of the term LP. He studied language change in Norway and the use of Norwegian in America. He produced an influential account of the Norwegian policy to eradicate the influence of Danish on Norwegian. Norway had been united with Denmark and was effectively under Danish control for centuries until 1814, when it was transferred to Swedish control, eventually gaining independence in 1905. As a result, both written and spoken Norwegian borrowed pronunciation and spelling norms from Danish sources. Individual writers and nationalists wanted to develop an indigenous variety modelled on rural Norwegian dialects, which they regarded as 'uncontaminated'. In the course of time, this popular movement became a national policy to produce a distinctive and locally sourced Norwegian mode of expression. Haugen's account (1966) used the term LP for processes of selecting new norms and for cultivating and spreading language change throughout society, from radio weather announcers to elementary school teachers.

Haugen's other major works described Norwegian as an immigrant language and gradually developed the idea that communication was like a natural ecology (Haugen, 1953, 1972). In this he helped pioneer an 'ecological approach' to the general study of language in society. In recent years, a new version of 'eco-linguistics' has become popular. Today eco-linguistics is also a political project, arguing that healthy multilingual and multidialectal ecologies must be preserved to support natural biological diversity among plants and animals (http://www.terralingua.org/). Haugen expanded the understanding of LP to encompass all intervention by a society to influence language.

The main categories of LP were consolidated with the addition of the term *'status planning'* in the work of the German linguist Heinz Kloss (1969). Status planning describes how societies allocate roles and functions (e.g. medium of instruction and official language) to languages through laws and regulations. Kloss distinguished this from corpus planning, in which the focus is directed away from social phenomena towards the internal features of languages, reflecting also the internal standpoint of linguistics at the expense of the practices and procedures of communication. A focus on corpus planning only has become problematical for approaches to LP more interested in social context than linguistic code. In addition, new theories of communication (Hanks, 1996; Mühlhäusler, 1995) challenge the very existence of 'language' as an autonomous entity (see Pennycook, this volume). Some deny the possibility that language can ever be separated from social context (LePage & Tabouret-Keller, 1985) and pose a radical challenge to the possibility of LP.

The combined ideas of Haugen and Kloss remain important for many professional language planners today. In essence this is a typology for classifying the choices government authorities make regarding language and social life. Classically these choices involve identification of a language or communication problem, the formulation of alternative ways of resolving this problem, deciding the norm to be promoted, and implementing it via the education system: a language problem leads to a language policy, which leads to LP.

LP and sociolinguistics expanded rapidly over the following decades absorbing influences from individuals and institutions from across the world. Two institutions in particular made notable contributions: The East West Center at the University of Hawaii at Honolulu, tasked with fostering dialogue and a role for American interests across the Asia-Pacific, and the Central Indian Institute of Languages in Mysore, set up to facilitate internal communication and cohesion after national independence. Individuals such as Joshua A. Fishman, Charles A. Ferguson, Bjorn H. Jernudd, Joan M. Rubin and J.V. Neustupny were particularly important in setting new directions and professionalising the study of LP, and Indian, Indonesian and Filipino scholars such as Jyotirindra Das Gupta, Takdir S. Alisjahbana and Bonifacio Sibayan devised new and original LP frameworks applicable to multilingual nation building in post-colonial Asia. The main technique of LP, the sociolinguistic survey, was devised originally for use in the Horn of Africa, to find out, as Fishman famously later put it, 'who speaks what language to whom and when' (Fishman, 2000/1965: 89).

One of the main areas of discussion in LP theories has been education but for most of its life as an academic discipline LP has tended to see education as a field in which policy on language is applied or implemented. The present chapter discusses LP and education in a more comprehensive way seeing teachers, teaching and classroom interaction as activities of language change as much as delivering or implementing language decisions taken by policy makers.

Key Terms

Definitions

There is no generally accepted or standard definition of LP. A frequently quoted but controversial definition is Cooper's: 'Language planning refers to deliberate efforts to influence the behavior of others with respect to the acquisition, structure, or functional allocation of their language codes' (1989: 45). However, other definitions include existing practices and attitudes alongside policies: 'Language policy can be defined as the combination of official decisions and prevailing public practices related to language education and use' (McGroarty, 1997: 1); while others restrict the scope of LP to procedural calculations: 'The match of national language capacity to need' (Brecht & Walton, 1993: 3).

Many definitions try to reconcile the decision making power of officials with the expertise of sociolinguists. In a seminal text, Rubin and Jernudd (1971) call LP 'normative intervention' by those empowered to decide, guided by specialist sociolinguists whose research provides alternative courses of action. This approach reflects modernist political thinking with clear divisions between the realms of knowledge, power and action. Troubling attempts to devise stable definitions of LP is the tendency of language questions to tap into conflicting interests (ethnic, national, cultural and ideological) and power (hard and soft). Rubin and Jernudd's volume acknowledged that interests do represent obstacles to a 'science' of LP, but not all language planners have been so flexible. Tauli (1984), for example, asserted that the planner is a scientist who produces technically valid conclusions about language problems. In this view, the recommendations of language planners should always prevail over the preferences of language users, insisting that scientific criteria of efficiency, modernity and instrumentalism should prevail over 'nostalgia and sentiment'.

In reality there are few occasions when LP is unproblematic. Perhaps one example is the Swedish Academy, many of whose rulings on terminology or spelling change have been readily adopted by teachers, publishers, editors and the general public. Dahlstedt (1976) attributes this professional credibility to a pervasive national ideology, which accepts that language change should be rational, efficient and expert-driven. There is often consultation with ordinary language users but rarely overt government involvement. The critical factor here is the decisive role of language attitudes, but these are subject to change, with research showing that mass migration and globalisation are destabilising aspects of the Swedish approach (Boyd, 2007).

Some proposals about the scope of LP (Neustupny, 1983) go much further and include individual language behaviours in models of LP. The inclusion of an individual's language choices and behaviour, such as self-correction, personal verbal monitoring and management of one's expressive alternatives takes LP into radically new territory with links to human consciousness and social psychology. If we see even mundane personal language, and people adjusting speech as they talk with others, as instances of LP this would bring into question a key assumption of many definitions that LP involves only deliberate or intended change to language from public authorities. It would also have major implications for teaching and ordinary classroom language, especially language used by teachers to model correct language for students. In some LP today (Kaplan & Baldauf, 1997), researchers use an ecological model of communication. Building on insights from Haugen and more recent eco-linguistics, this approach also challenges the classic assumption of LP that policy needs to be intended or deliberate to count as LP. Restrictive early definitions have been challenged so that today there is a wider array of understandings of what counts as LP: ranging from LP as a sub-set of rational and technical public policy to a view of language change happening through speaker attitudes to language in ordinary communication. This range becomes apparent if we look at the activity of LP.

The activity

A recent systematisation by Hornberger (2006) brings together various definitions into an 'integrative framework' for LP. This specifies three categories of activity that count as LP: status, acquisition and corpus; and two approaches: *policy planning* (when the focus of activity is on the form of language) and *cultivation planning* (when the focus shifts to language function). *Status planning* is 'about uses of language', *acquisition planning* about 'users of language' and *corpus planning* 'about language'.

In practice these activities and approaches are often inseparable. Formal status planning is as diverse as the myriad legal contexts in which it occurs, dependent on sovereignty (exclusive legal power) and jurisdiction (delegated legal power). Ultimately, the status of a language refers to its legal standing and public functions and is typically ascribed via public texts, such as constitutional provisions of sovereign nations. Status planning is mostly done by people with formal power who produce public texts such as regulations, laws, constitutional provisions and authoritative reports. The goals of status planning are often dictated by interests of nations, as perceived by elites, and stress national cohesion and cultural continuity over a given sovereign territory.

Sub-national groups, such as regions or provinces operating under autonomy statutes, can also modify or even contradict laws and statutes when there is overlapping sovereignty. An example is the special status accorded to Hong Kong and Macau in the Constitution of the People's Republic of China (Lo Bianco, 2007). Supra-national groupings, such as the European Union and the Council of Europe, can also attribute status, as occurred in 1992 with the European Charter for Regional and Minority Languages (Beacco, 2007; ECRML, 1992).

Corpus planning, which deals with what is internal to a language, is as widespread as status planning but is often in the hands of professional linguists in collaboration with 'ordinary' speakers. The work involves proposing modifications to the internal resources of a language, which can include devising a new, or modifying an existing, writing system, or linking an existing writing system with an external one. Chinese, for example, is written in both traditional (full-form) and simplified characters, and has several forms of 'romanisation'. The Latin script serves for computers and is learned by students who need a clear pronunciation guide. These writing systems co-exist in different Chinese-speaking polities (Gottlieb & Chen, 2001), depending on sovereignty and jurisdiction, and perform different functions. All were 'planned' even if not deliberately or consciously by professional linguists.

Vietnamese was initially written using traditional characters when it was a Chinese colony in ancient times. Then a modified system of characters was devised by nationalists to distinguish written Vietnamese from Chinese, and centuries later, French missionaries and colonists devised a romanised system to represent the tones and sounds of Vietnamese. In its anti-colonial struggle and civil war of the 20th century, Vietnamese leaders adopted romanised writing, Quoc Ngu, as the official script (Lo Bianco, 2001). We can see the Vietnamese struggle over script as an extended LP exercise, with moments of status, corpus and acquisition planning, using both policy and cultivation approaches, under legal remits ranging from colonial dependency (resistance), to independent nationhood (sovereignty) to devolution (jurisdiction).

Corpus work often involves expanding vocabulary to introduce scientific or technical terms, or standardising existing spelling in alphabet systems to make them more phonetic, or codifying expressions to reduce variation. All languages change to absorb new information and changed meanings, making corpus change, planned and unplanned, universal and constant. Governments drive corpus change to pursue goals of national re-construction or reclamation for endangered languages but so do social movements with political ambitions who want to change the world through words, what is said as well as how it is said. English examples include University campus speech codes to promote anti-racism and counter-sexism, making corpus planning a tool of ideology to change political belief via discourse. This kind of activity is motivated by a performative view of language; the principle that language as discourse enacts social identities and helps to form our subjective idea of ourselves and the groups we belong to (Butler, 1997). Neustupny's idea that personal language use can be seen as LP, combined with performative views of discourse, takes LP activity well beyond status and corpus planning. This is discussed below as discourse planning, after a brief review of three other common LP activities.

Acquisition planning typically describes language teaching policies (Cooper, 1989). Foreign/second-language instruction can be motivated by humanistic rationales, responses to the needs and rights of minorities, calculations about economic interest, or assessments about security and geopolitical anxieties (Lo Bianco, 2008a). International comparisons of literacy standards have also influenced literacy teaching policies in many countries.

Usage planning involves increasing the domains in which a language is used. Usage planning occurs mostly in opposition to a dominant language after political change or is done to regenerate dying languages. Ireland is engaged in usage planning to expand the domains of Irish beyond school and university classrooms into all workplaces, digital media, government administration and sports and recreation (Ó Flatharta *et al.*, 2008).

Prestige planning (Haarmann, 1990) focuses on aesthetic or intellectual regard of a linguistic code. Many of today's major languages have benefited from prestige planning by poets, philosophers and religious figures. Esteem is conferred on a language in proportion to the quality and extent of its important works of literature. Italy's national poet, Dante Alighieri, combined corpus and status planning, in a cultivation approach to prestige planning. Between 1303 and 1305 he wrote the Latin text *De Vulgari Eloquentia*, putting forward a theory about how to invent a new language and arguing that an independent nation needs a distinctive vernacular for political unity. He interrupted this theorising and wrote his great epic poem, the Divine Comedy in Italian, helping to produce both the vernacular and the nation he had advocated (Lo Bianco, 2005).

Many dialects of standardised languages have benefited by a change in esteem (informal status) because of authoritative works by poets, novelists or scientists. Noted works help standardise the language (corpus) and gain admiration for it (status). This isolated work of individuals is sometimes organised within official academies created to support literature production for individual languages.

However, literature is not the only source of prestige. What is admired and emulated in speech can be what disrupts and undermines traditional notions of correctness or formal rules of appropriateness. These transgressive kinds of prestige confer cultural capital, the material and symbolic resources valued by particular communities. Subversive modes of talk, music and performance create images and behaviours that produce community and identity for particular groups rather than any intrinsic or objective value.

A distinctive, and controversial, category of LP relates to the links between discourse and ideology. Some LP scholars dispute whether attitude and ideology formation through discourse can be included under LP at all. *Discourse planning* has a range of meanings. The most straightforward refers to education to develop persuasive or assertive ways of expression, such as to help young people participate in society and accomplish personal goals through effective communication. In ancient Rome and Greece rhetoric was essential preparation for lawyers, politicians, generals and even poets and 'expression' has remained a central goal of schooling.

Participation in public life relies on language abilities to express opinion, progress economically, prevent exploitation or abuse, explore identity and make connections. Discourse planning, in its worst sense, however, means propaganda or brain washing rather than persuasion or self-expression. Both extremes refer to how individuals deploy persuasive talk or writing to modify or reinforce worldview and attitudes. Advertising aims to persuade customers to purchase or recognise and recall products, political movements and parties engage in persuasion on policy and political philosophy. 'Spin' is the angle attached to information by politicians' media staffers; it is exemplary discourse planning because it involves a slant, or perspective attached to events and incidents to favour particular interpretations of the those events and incidents. Spin often aims to change conventional or expected word meanings. We recognise a version of discourse planning as thought-control, or brainwashing in the writings of George Orwell: *1984* and *Animal Farm*. But thought control is only the most extreme end of a continuum of persuasive language, increasingly studied by cognitive linguists. A well-known example is George Lakoff's analysis of swing voters during the 2004 US presidential election, in the best-seller *Don't Think of An Elephant* (Lakoff, 2005). Adding (1) *discourse planning* to (2) *status*, (3) *corpus*, (4) *acquisition*, (5) *usage* and (6) *prestige planning* aims to produce a comprehensive but non-mechanistic picture of the six kinds of activity that generate language change. These are more or less conscious, more or less deliberate, and are rarely pursued in isolation.

Development of the Field

Reviewing the intellectual history of LP, Ricento (2000) suggested three phases of post-war LP. An initial technocratic and confident period with modernist assumptions was followed by criticism and re-appraisal following failure of LP to produce economic 'take-off' in developing countries. The third phase, he argues, features 'alarm' about issues such as linguistic imperialism and language extinction and is accompanied by transformed ideas about what language, literacy and culture actually are; instead of bounded categories these are now seen as variable, hybrid and contested social practices. There is value in this analysis, but the picture of LP today, both the practice 'on the ground' and the theory and analysis, is highly diverse. Some is unchanged from the earliest thinking and practice but there are also instances of critical, innovative and experimental practices. If the initial decades of LP (1950s–1960s) were characterised by field definition and concept building and the middle decades (1970s–1980s) by professionalisation, technical skills and managerial procedures, the 1990s saw a highly critical reaction against claims that an autonomous, politically neutral, ethical and technically grounded LP had emerged.

Policy as a 'science'

During the same years in which LP was an emerging academic discipline, political scientists were engaged in a process of attempting to professionalise government in Western industrialised democracies. The main way this was done was to link economics with politics and the result was the new discipline of policy analysis. Some language planners incorporated ideas from the emergent 'policy sciences', which promised to make public policy more technical and systematic, beginning a move away from strictly sociolinguistic approaches to LP. LP began to resemble the 'rational choice matrix' of public policy analysis, in which a specialist applies techniques of cost–benefit calculations, to generate compared alternatives for action to recommend to decision makers.

Discussing such links from several angles, Rubin (1977, 1986) defined the emerging LP science either as solutions to language problems that are obtained through discussion about various alternative goals and means or as how alternatives are formulated and evaluated in considering how to solve language problems. In this work, Rubin distinguished between 'tame' problems, which are relatively amenable to policy attention and 'wicked' problems, which defy easy solution, with most language problems being seen as 'wicked'. Overall, Rubin's approach was to describe LP as a normative practice and to work towards a theory of LP as public intervention. Perhaps the most ambitious version of the scientific aspiration was by Fishman, while introducing the field of sociolinguistics to new readers: 'Language planning as a rational and technical process informed by actuarial data and by ongoing feedback is still a dream, but it is by no means so farfetched a dream as it seemed to be merely a decade ago' (Fishman, 1971: 111). This early period saw many scholars specify orderly and systematic requirements for LP such as the establishment of goals, selection of means and prediction of outcomes.

Commenting on this energetic period of LP theory building, Rubin (1985: 137) reported that the '... field of language planning has grown both in theoretical base and in adherents over the years ...' citing a sequence of 10 summer institutes, a quarterly journal (*Language Problems and Language Planning*), a regular newsletter (*Language Planning Newsletter*) and 'a developing paradigm' as evidence of vitality. In several parts of the world, professional training was instituted, signalling a move from the academic world to the world of application, and several notable socio-linguists were commissioned by governments, mostly in developing countries, to support literacy and language standardisation for national modernisation (Fishman, 1973). A high point in the professionalisation of LP was the 1977 Summer Linguistic Institute at the University of Hawaii with over 40 countries sending visiting scholars, LP agency directors and staff and students (NLP, 1979–1983).

A growing optimism led to perhaps the maximal claim that LP was a unitary field with a shared moral purpose: '... a field that seeks to foster ethnic interaction, world communication, and national identity' (Eastman, 1983: 126). Despite considerable progress towards creating a specialised profession and despite the over-reach suggested by Eastman's optimism, the problems that LP dealt with meant that it would fall far short of the planning models used in general public policy and that practitioner aims should be more modest and look instead for a regular, consistent and coor-dinated practice aware of the inherent difficulties of planning languages.

LP as 'problem solving'

A central feature of LP analysis has been the notion of 'language prob-lems', seen largely as pre-existing and relatively objective. This is well expressed by Dua (1985), who argued that a '... systematic account of lan-guage problems of a speech community is a prerequisite to an adequate theory of policy formulation, LP and language treatment' (Dua, 1985: 3). This was a popular view for much of the history of LP, stimulating research into the nature of language problems. This research led to classification systems, of which one impressive example is by Nahir (1984), who sepa-rates language problems according to 11 LP treatments such problems are given, such as *purification, lexical modernisation* and *auxiliary-code stan-dardisation*. These treatments are all code-focused. Dua (1985) offers a typology based on who defines language problems and what needs dif-ferent language problems reflect, for example, *normative needs* (experts' definitions); *felt needs* (affected groups' definitions); *expressed needs* (actioned felt needs) and *comparative needs* (requiring contrasting processes).

These schemes are impressive but they mostly support research and ultimately face the same limitations as all taxonomies: they tend towards mechanistic accounts of what in reality are fluid and dynamic realities. No overarching classification can reflect the localised reality of most language problems and debates and the fact that problems, as Dua notes, meet different needs according to who is doing the defining. Ultimately LP is a situated activity, whose specific history and local circumstances influence what is regarded as a language problem, and whose political dynamics determine which language problems are given policy treatment. An identical language issue in one setting might not be regarded as a problem in another. The effects of lobbying, mobilisation and political will might succeed in converting language issues in one political system to policy attention while failing to do so in another. The Swedish example indicates that some language problems lend themselves to being tractable in policy (tame problems), while others are wicked and lead to politicisation or dispute. Language problems are not neutral of interests. Bilingualism resulting from immigrant communities retaining their languages in host societies is often more controversial than bilingualism resulting from mainstream learners acquiring foreign languages. It is also clear that many societies with indigenous minorities are more disposed to grant these minorities language rights if there are no territorial or separatist connotations attached to their claims. Language problems merge readily with socio-political realities.

Critical reactions to LP as an objective science

Writing about nationalism in the Middle East, historian Elie Kedourie anticipated both the optimism of the policy sciences and the sharp reactions of the 1990s, in a scathing 1961 assessment of LP: 'It is absurd to think that professors of linguistics ... can do the work of statesmen and soldiers ... academic enquiries are used by conflicting interests to bolster up their claims, and their results prevail only to the extent that somebody has the power to make them prevail .... Academic research does not add a jot or a tittle to the capacity for ruling ...' (Kedourie, 1961: 125).

This assessment is dismissive but also restrictive. While it is ultimately true that LP is part of 'ruling', LP has never only been in the hands of soldiers and statesmen. Poets, musicians, and teachers, as well as professional sociolinguists, have a hand in directing the fortunes of language change and evolution.

The archetypal 'rational' method of LP is the sociolinguistic survey informing a sequence of steps: (1) Problem Identification (fact-finding); (2) Goal Specification (policy); (3) Cost–Benefit Analysis (costed demonstration of alternatives); (4) Implementation; (5) Evaluation (comparing predicted to actual outcomes). The harshest critics of LP have argued that such a scheme aims to transfer formal managerial public policy methods to the messy, un-ordered ideology-based world of ever-changing communication. Extending this criticism from the process of LP to its practitioners, some critics have alleged that LP specialists 'masquerade' as neutral information-collecting scholars who use 'scientific' instruments all the while concealing or misunderstanding the essentially political manoeuvres underlying government interest in LP in the first place. Some critics accuse LP professionals of being complicit in technocratic management of the lives of vulnerable minority communities, such as when they gather data about Indigenous peoples (Sommer, 1991) that really only serve the interests of government bureaucracies.

The methods of LP were called a 'pretence to science' by Luke *et al.* (1990), who argued that LP is 'complicit' with social repression in the interests of state and class, and criticised LP for 'professionalising' decision making. Professionalisation raises barriers to involvement of speaker communities in making decisions about their own languages. The tension between 'ordinary language users' and professional specialists is a recurring theme in criticisms of LP. Alleging undemocratic practices, Moore (1996) claims that LP specialists are not sufficiently critical or even aware of troubling issues regarding LP.

Mühlhäusler (1995) exposes how developed-country LP experts have transferred assumptions of modernity and monolingual 'efficiency' in education, public administration and the economy to vastly different Pacific island contexts. Taking for granted ideas about a single standardised language and universal literacy can become a judgment against multilingualism as inefficient rather than a natural feature of human existence, and lead to moves towards uni-lingualism in intergenerationally stable multilingual communities. This kind of LP leads to hierarchical diglossia (one language reserved for *high functions* and others for *low functions*) and eventual erosion or extinction of languages occupied mostly with *low function* activities.

Some critics associate LP with the spread of English, Westernising modernity and political ideologies of neo-liberal capitalism. Some critics of LP draw on eco-linguistics to argue against language assimilation, in defence of distinctive life-worlds and against depletion of minority world-views (Nettle & Romaine, 2000; Phillipson & Skutnabb-Kangas, 1996). Another allegation has been that LP entrenches economic inequalities for immigrants in first world societies through language education schemes tracking new arrivals into low-paid, marginal jobs (Tollefson, 1991).

In response, Fishman (1994) accepts some but rejects many of these criticisms, and calls on LP scholars to adopt stances, conceding that LP is neither ideology-free nor does it have an inbuilt moral code. It is a tool used by 'ethnicisers, nativisers and traditionalisers' who 'engage in language planning for their own purposes' (Fishman, 1994: 96). This response acknowledges some of the impossible and reductionist ideals that had come into LP during its 'scientific' period. After all some of the most repugnant regimes in history have been active language planners, the most extreme being the 'mother-tongue fascism' of the Nazi Third-Reich and its 'science of language' (Hutton, 1999).

Critics of LP make valid points regarding negative consequences and poor theorisation, but go too far. Few offer alternatives and most fail to acknowledge that LP is rapidly expanding across the world, in response to growing real-world communication problems in the wake of economic globalisation, mass migration and communication technologies. LP is associated with both democratic enfranchisement and with institutionalised discrimination. LP was a key feature of Apartheid's practices of domination, and in the early 1990s, the unjust LP of apartheid was replaced with official recognition of 11 national languages and rights to universal literacy (Webb, 2002). In this new policy dispensation, new and more participatory practices of LP were also explored. Reform to LP as an applied method of sociolinguistics and as a field of research is warranted, and criticism of shortcomings can be helpful to encourage reflection and improvements, but are unlikely to produce professional and disciplinary renewal. Fishman's (1994: 97) sobering observation that '... very little language planning practice has actually been informed by language planning theory' shows that neither LP theory, nor criticism of LP theory, has much traction in real-world language policy making. Most actual LP work continues to be done by non-specialists, language policies rarely draw on academic theory or concepts and most assume that planning language is merely an unproblematic subset of general public policy. The insistence by classical LP scholars that LP must be deliberate and conscious, and undertaken by authoritative bodies and that it is then implemented by teachers, among others, has blinded observers to the dynamic, daily practice of LP that resides in concrete activities, especially teaching.

A key argument of this chapter is for an expanded understanding of what counts as LP, and to see all teaching, and especially language and literacy teaching, as intimately involved in LP. The past tendency of LP scholars and practitioners to rigidly separate 'planning' from 'implementation' hinders appreciation of what is an essentially continuous sequence of actions of 'acting on' language. While it is unlikely that there will ever be full agreement about the entire field of LP, a coherent account depicting the distinctive roles of policy makers, academic specialists and teachers of language and literacy would be valuable. The following anecdote, from a 2004 conference convened by Defense and Education agencies of the US Federal Government to write a joint policy on the foreign language needs of Defense personnel, underscores this point. Late in the conference a senior Defense official became frustrated by the educators and language planners responding to Defense calls for action with calls for more research, more exploration and more debate before formulating policy. Interpreting this as stalling she declared: 'We can do this NOW! We just say what languages we need, get the money, train the teachers, and they do it. It isn't rocket science!' (Lo Bianco, 2008a: 172).

Sources of LP Data and Moves Towards An Interactive, Democratic Practice

LP might not be rocket science, but it is a complex and elusive activity. We both change and confirm language as we use it. The discussion below proposes an interactive democratic LP based on dialogue accompanying technical expertise, and explores the unique role of teaching, and teachers, in LP.

We can compare two classic and popular definitions of LP to begin exploration of new directions. These definitions are Cooper's (1989: 45), quoted above, '... deliberate efforts to influence the behavior of others with respect to the acquisition, structure, or functional allocation of their language codes'; and Fishman's (1994: 92) '... authoritative allocation of resources to language'. These definitions capture features of past approaches to LP reflecting code-focus and expert-centred activity.

In Cooper's definition, the key idea is conscious influence brought to bear on the linguistic behaviour of others in three domains: learning, linguistic structure and functional use of languages. In this uni-directional approach through research, knowledge influence is exercised on the languages of other people. Fishman's definition identifies the role of authorities and resources and ties LP to official decision making and power. Both imply division between experts who gather knowledge, authorities who make decisions, and language users, teachers, or societies who take direction.

Both definitions have the advantage of clarity and accurately depict a dominant academic view of what counts as LP and a component of the practice of LP. However, they unduly limit the scope of LP activity as it is, and more importantly what it could be; restricting the participants to non-elected experts recommending courses of action to non-expert officials. While allowing that officials change or reject recommendations, possibly influenced by their constituents, the models imply that this is rare. There are both obvious and obscure problems with such assumptions, because when we look very closely at how language change actually happens, we can see that even quite routine and ordinary social processes shape how language works, how it is used and how aspects of language are changed. Overly formal and deliberate requirements obscure the micro-dynamics of language change. Another unfortunate result of these definitions is that teachers and teaching are construed as mere implementers of plans and policies devised by others, conduits of pre-existing plans rather than actors. Mechanistic depictions of the activity of LP fail to incorporate the critical role of interaction between users of language and agencies and individuals who try to influence language, including experts.

More dynamic and multidimensional understandings of language change can account for how features of language and their use have been changed in the past and for processes of change underway today. Language change arises by informal processes, sometimes without or against authorities and their policy intentions, and by private action, professional practice, citizenship agitation and transgressive practices of artists, political radicals and celebrities.

Some researchers view language change using ethnographic perspectives and tend to see the language behaviours, identities, social status and struggle for power of individuals as factors influencing how language usage evolves. In a similar way, we can see daily activity of teachers as LP due to the impact of teacher language use on communication practices and language attitudes (see Ricento & Hornberger, 1996).

Understood this way, language teaching becomes more than simply teachers enacting or implementing in a functional way decisions taken by curriculum authorities or education ministries. Classroom language use becomes a site, not completely autonomous and divorced from ministry or official requirements, but sufficiently separated and distinctive to count as a factor in shaping how language develops and changes. Official allocation of resources and pursuit of solutions to language problems, as noted by Fishman, and deliberate influence on the linguistic behaviour of others, as Cooper describes, are undeniably common dimensions of LP, but so too are the professional activities of teachers.

The general policy sciences have also undergone challenge in recent decades especially regarding their relationship to objective science and objective methods of data gathering and adjudication of alternative courses of action. As a result, schools of thought in the policy sciences increasingly explore the role of insider experience of diverse policy actors and the relation of their subjective experience with outsider experience, the 'objectivity' of policy professionals and their methods of work. These developments point towards new ways to do policy based on combinations of data and conversation. Persuasion, and therefore language, is critical. Persuasion relies on a mixture of evidence and argument, occasionally supported by facilitated debates (Majone, 1989). The critical role of rhetoric, persuasion through evidence and the role and value of narrative (experience as a form of credibility) become key areas of research to understand how to account for what becomes policy and how to build more democratic models for doing policy. In the policy sciences, research is shifting from efficiency, towards conviction and credibility and to how 'problems' are framed and understood (Turnbull, 2005). These developments have direct bearing on LP since policy as argument is ultimately an issue of language, and the object of LP is language itself.

The next section describes a wider approach to LP that moves towards a non-mechanistic understanding supported by these developments in the policy sciences. It will serve as a preamble to an account of how the regular work of language teachers forms a crucial component of an overall approach to LP.

Armed with these indications of a more comprehensive approach, where do we look to find language policy? Where is LP located? People usually look to two main sources, implied in the cited definitions, to identify language policies. These are *public texts* and *public discourse (or debate)*. Observing how LP and how language changes come about however, requires the addition of a third rich source of LP activity. This refers to the modelling of language behaviours by key individuals, referred to here as *performance*. The three sources of LP activity in this view are texts, argument-discourse and performance, or performative action.

Public texts

The term public texts refers to the official documentation issued by a state or its agencies. A national constitution is the most obvious and highest example of a public or official state text. Many countries have constitutional clauses devoted to language, sometimes simply acknowledging a widely spoken national language as official (prevailing practice becoming formal policy), sometimes declaring official a language which is not widely spoken (New Zealand and Ireland are examples), sometimes declaring equal status for more than one language. Most name a single language as official, but the South African Constitution designates 11 languages official while India schedules national and regional official languages. Formal declarations about the role and standing of languages seem straightforward, but because constitutional declarations can be symbolic as well as practical and can enshrine or seek to change an existing state of affairs, constitutional language clauses carry meaning beyond their declarative intent. While constitutions are slow-acting and long-lasting, they are often present in debates about what is intended, permitted, or desired, as suggested in the expression 'the spirit of the constitution'. Collective engagement with the meanings of the constitution is 'constitutionalism' (Tully, 1997) suggesting a political community's relationship with its founding or key documents. Beyond the political accommodations they contain, public texts symbolise nationality and give direction and order to the expressive and collective life of the political community.

LP has serious practical consequences and constitutions as public texts are the ultimate expression of the resolution of LP disputes and struggle between interests among society's component groups. For example,

Bangladesh exists due to LP-based war. The Partition of British India in 1947 divided Hindu-majority India from Muslim-majority Pakistan, the latter comprising the non-contiguous West Pakistan and East Pakistan separated by vast territories of sovereign India. In 1948, Governor-General Mohammad Ali Jinnah made a language policy declaration that *'Urdu, and only Urdu'* would be the national language of all Pakistan. At the time, Urdu was mostly spoken by elites in West Pakistan while East Pakistan, although Muslim by religious affiliation, was a cultural extension of the Indian state of West Bengal, forming a broad ethno-linguistic unity. The declaration provoked protests from Bengali students, suppressed on 21 February 1952 with many deaths. The tragedy is commemorated annually as Language Martyr's Day (in 1999 UNESCO declared it *International Mother Language Day*) and a unique monument, the *Shaheed Minar*, was erected in Dhaka, capital of Bangladesh, to recognise the Language Martyrs. Despite some amelioration to linguistic assimilation, resistance spread from elites to masses, culminating in the ferocious 1971 civil war, and, with Indian support, the emergence of independent Bangladesh.

Urdu remains the official language of Pakistan today while article 23 of the Constitution of Bangladesh makes Bangla the official and national language and creates the Bangla Academy. The Constitution requires the state to '... adopt measures to conserve the cultural traditions and heritage of the people, and so to foster and improve the national language, literature and the arts ...'. The Bangla Academy is designated within the national academy of arts and letters as a language cultivation agency (Mohsin, 2003; Moniruzzaman, 1979) and is charged with continual elaboration of Bangla, its terminology, literature, and expressiveness, with general promotion and specifically with dissemination of new grammatical and phonological norms. The Bengali Academy Ordinance of 1978 guarantees autonomy, designates the President of the Republic as Patron-in-Chief and specifies that funding is provided by the Ministry of Culture. An eminent educationist, appointed Academy president for two-year terms by the Patron-in-Chief, convenes an annual meeting but lacks executive responsibilities. Membership is open to distinguished persons or scholars of 'prestigious scientific merit or literary accomplishments', with the bulk of the membership, and its work, entrusted to linguistic experts.

This example reveals that constitutions are critical language policy texts, the fundamental statements of national existence, but both the symbolic and practical messages require continual interpretation. Constitutions also make available the procedures for modification. The constitution is therefore the most public and declared mode of LP, the ultimate public text, and involves laws, regulations, and formal operations of planning and implementation. Even when constitutions are clear and unambiguous, the circumstances in which they arose change, interpretations are needed, new or changed values and political arrangements emerge. The original authors are generals, lawyers and politicians; 'downstream' changes are in the hands of teachers, literary figures and celebrities.

Constitutions fit Cooper's test for LP of deliberate efforts to influence functional roles and acquisition of language codes of a society and match Fishman's test that LP involves authorities pursuing organised solutions to language problems and allocating resources to implement solutions. Neither definition captures the dynamic interaction of agitation, political demands and popular legitimacy. Although participation in constitutional formation is legalistic and authorship resides with powerful individuals and groups, constitutionalism involves interaction across the whole society, what Tully (1997) has called a 'multi-logue'. In this way, a constitution can be imagined as a conversational practice. Constitutionalism refers to this process of ongoing deliberation about the ultimate political text of a nation, embedding language policy in ongoing LP.

Even so, not all nations have declared official, or national, languages, indeed, not all states have full or comparable constitutions, and the standing and public use of languages is often determined according to other procedures.

Public discourse

Official documentation such as constitutions, laws, regulations and procedures reflect the intentions of powerful groups and individuals towards language. However, these intentions are framed in public debate/discourse or argument, and, in most political systems, require popular legitimacy. The need for legitimation connects public texts to popular discourse permitting wider social groups participation in discussion and argument on language issues as public texts are promulgated, interpreted or challenged.

Argument is a key mechanism of LP, consisting of a collection of statements, discussion and public attitudes that accompany, respond to or precede public texts. This is an essential component of LP because formal declarations are rarely unambiguous, and even when clear and specific, they are often not implemented. Sometimes public texts are deliberately ambiguous, essentially political rhetoric to placate lobby groups without really endorsing their claims, or they can be genuine statements at the declarative level but their enactment is hindered by rival interests. For these reasons, even policy statements which are clear and sincerely intended can still be contested by groups disadvantaged or aggrieved by the policy, or who desire different policy content.

Policy discourse is also important for more mundane reasons such as the contrast between the generality of constitutional provisions and the specificity required in implementation, or because public attitudes change, or new possibilities emerge that had not been anticipated. In 1918, education laws in several Australian states banned instruction in and through languages other than English (Clyne, 2005; Ozolins, 1993). At the time there was little overt opposition to these bans because the affected minorities were small, dispersed and relatively powerless. In the course of time, these provisions became redundant and ignored. For decades, schools set up instruction in languages other than English which was technically illegal. Innovation and change in language pedagogy stimulated local experimentation in methods of teaching and few people made a connection between actual practice and the rather distant intentions of the law. Curriculum decision making had changed radically. In 1918, curriculum was a central responsibility policed by inspectors; by the 1970s, local decision making was common and teaching choices were influenced by local needs.

The 1970s saw a great deal of experimentation and innovation in community languages in Australia. Many schools replaced traditional foreign languages with the languages of minority populations, both immigrant and indigenous, in programmes intended to produce bilingual competence, intergenerational retention of locally spoken languages and improvements to the educational attainments of minority children, specifically their acquisition of English. This embrace of multilingualism clashed with the 'spirit' of the 1918 legislation, drawn up in the context of war and official anxiety about the citizenship loyalties of minorities, leading to a stark contrast between a public text banning what public discourse supported. The same government authorities providing large public funding and lauding multiculturalism in public reports, press statements, ministerial announcements, radio and television interviews and political campaigning, operated under the jurisdiction of legal instruments that technically proscribed these measures.

This example points to a deficiency with formal and legalistic definitions which would consider the ignored law, rather than the actual programmes, to be the LP. Eventually, the law caught up with the reality and the 'prohibiting' clauses were removed. This example also points to the situated nature of LP, meaning that national styles of governance produce radically different ways of doing LP. Under a more explicitly literal and law-based policy style this circumstance would have been impossible. The 1918 measures were the outcome of prevailing public debate, reflecting concerns of dominant groups and the circumstances, problems and ideologies of the time. In this way public texts distil the political arrangements that apply at a given point in time and enshrine political solutions current to the prevailing configurations of power. Similarly, LP texts evolve and change as attitudes and ideologies alter in the course of time and new circumstances arise that displace previous understandings of issues, or alter the ways in which political interests align and compromise.

However, not all societies make laws on language, and many do not debate language issues and even in societies that do, political, cultural and personal interests diverge markedly. The dynamic time-based relationship between discourse and text needs to be taken one step further to reflect dynamic local language change, stratifications of power and influence, and diverse voices within a given society. This is the third mode in which LP occurs, *performative action*, which describes instances of language used both to convey messages in regular communication and at the same time to represent models for emulation of language forms.

Performative action

For present purposes, regular use of language, both professional and personal, can be divided into two broad kinds: *mundane* (e.g. *transactional*) and *ideological* (i.e. *performativity*). This simplification of the broader intentions of communication is to focus attention on those occasions, purposes and kinds of regular use of language, which in addition to their message-conveying function also model intended language changes, and therefore operate as discursive LP.

Ordinary use of language, whether personal or professional, always reflects standards, norms and communicative rules taken for granted by a speech community. Much of it is transactional and hence aimed at unproblematic message sending. Some philosophers have thought of all language in this way, as 'telementation', in which one mind passes messages directly to another mind (see Harris, 1988). In the present discussion, ideological use of language is purposive, containing a range of other functions in addition to message transfer, and among these ideological uses some are focused on effecting language change (others might be ideological but not interested in language change). People whose use of regular language is intended to display and model ideological messages are not necessarily consistent in their usage of these intended forms. In general, however, there are frequent instances of performativity in regular language use, investing ordinary communication with layers of noticeable features of intonation, lexical choice, syntax variations which model, indicate or promote language designed to produce ideological/attitudinal outcomes beyond message content. These performances display a speaker's adherence to a speech ideology community and model its use for emulation.

In conventional sociolinguistics, *mundane use of language* is correlative; it varies according to relatively stable (1) social categories (e.g. regional dialects, social dialects, ethno-lects correlate with place of origin, or social class or ethnic background) or (2) professional roles (e.g. medical or management jargon) or (3) communicative purposes (e.g. soothing or comfort talk, or aggressive harangues, or dispassionate information delivery). However, variation for performative display of LP differs from these conventional three kinds of variation. Although (1)–(3) represent ways in which ordinary communication is inflected and therefore not 'telementation', the variation is primarily due to socialisation in regional, class or ethnic group, professional role or communicative purpose. We learn to speak these ways because the communication environments to which we are exposed model these language varieties. These varieties help to constitute identity and are performative of identifications.

However, *ideological use of language* as described here is heavily laden with performativity and profoundly constitutive of its message; that is its use helps form and influence patterns of language, social relationships and meanings. This kind of variation in language is intended to bring about language change (but it often also signals identity and belonging as well). Commonly recognised forms of performance language are feminist rejection of male bias in language, or anti-racist speech. Negatively racist and sexist speech and all forms of hate speech are ideological and purposive language, aiming to both deliver messages of hate or ideology and to defy political correctness by insisting on the use of pejorative ways to describe the groups against whom hatred is directed. When the intended ideology relates to language itself, such as active preference for Latinate expression in English, or active modelling of plain English expression, or active use of blasphemy in contexts where this would have been forbidden previously, these are examples of ideological language policy, displayed as it is performed.

Although powerful and significant individuals, celebrities, charismatic leaders, and dominant institutions provide the communicative models, it is the effect of such modelling on 'ordinary users' that determines the success or failure of performative LP. Even mundane ordinary language, but certainly ideological use of ordinary language, operates as a series of 'acts of identity' (LePage & Tabouret-Keller, 1985) available for emulation as listeners and speakers modify speech to align with the displayed models. In this way, regular communication becomes part of ongoing processes of LP.

Performative action interacts with public debate focused on LP decisions, and with public texts, which distil agreements or compromises about language problems at a given point in time and in a given place and social setting. Public texts are therefore decided instances of LP, public discourses are ongoing debates about language problems, and performances are the ongoing modelling of language forms desired and valued by speakers or writers. Performative action can reinforce or violate LP distilled in public texts or LP as suggested in prevailing discourses. Ideological LP performance is what an English-fluent French delegate at a conference in Austria was engaged in when he refused to comply with a decision to conduct the seminar in English. In private or professional uses, in classrooms or courtrooms, language performances can extend, play with and elaborate existing LP, or modify, contest, destabilise, contradict and subvert LP.

Pedagogical Implications

In the dynamic relationship between actual language use and LP described above, a chain of actions and interactions arises between the conscious activity of planning language as required in formal LP theory, and instances of communication that 'comment on' the planned language, that is in actual usage rather than as a topic of discussion (Hanks, 1996). This means that LP is spread over a continuum involving public texts, public discourses and performative action. Laws (public texts), debates (public discourse) and communication (performative action) are all linked to LP and ultimately become examples of LP. What are the educational implications of this way of thinking about LP?

The role of schooling, and of schools, of teaching and of teachers, around language has ancient precedents. To cite one example, recruiting teachers to the job of producing the language futures of society was one of the highest objectives of the French revolution, concerned to 'do away' with what its ideologues considered 'vestiges of feudalism' represented by regional and social dialects. In 1791 the nobleman and diplomat, Talleyrand, made a decisive announcement at the French Convention that aimed to invent a new political entity conceived as radically different from all preceding forms of state. The revolutionary obligation was to replace tradition with modernity and this overturning of the past was a task vested in primary schools. Talleyrand noted that the standard form of French was spreading abroad through colonial expansion while in regional areas and among the urban poor, non-standard varieties of the language continued: 'Elementary education will put an end to this strange inequality. In school all will be taught in the language of the Constitution and the Law and this mass of corrupt dialects, these last vestiges of feudalism will be forced to disappear' (cited in Wright, 2004: 62).

Brunot (1927) has documented the process by which Parisian French, sometimes called *le français neutre*, passed itself off as neutral, when, like all standard varieties it was the dialect of dominant groups. In this process of 'linguistic consolidation', the highest ideals of republican citizenship were seen to depend on equal access to standard French for all, and the critical moment according to Brunot was when the state decided that families would no longer have exclusive rights over the linguistic socialisation of their children. This was a job for the state, in the hands, or the mouth, of the elementary school teacher.

In sovereign political systems, LP is undertaken by education systems, which are intimately connected to the goals and aspirations of the state, even when devolved to regional, parental, and sometimes to religious communities. In recent years, mass migration (Castles & Miller, 2003), and spreading multiculturalism across the globe (García *et al.*, 2006), have made multilingualism a potent 'language problem' alongside the multidialectalism, which was Brunot's concern. Dialects of course remain critically important in today's LP, such as in Ebonics debates and disputes in the United States, Aboriginal Englishes in Australia and indeed in all language communities in which regional and social differences are reflected in variations within language (see Alim, Reyes, Siegel, this volume). These intra-language questions combine with inter-language questions through multilingualism. Multilingualism is the cutting edge issue of school LP in many societies today (Suarez-Orozco & Qin-Hilliard, 2004). Similarly, digital communications have made multimodal texts the literacy equivalent of the multilingual challenge. Both make the sociolinguistic environments of today's schools diverse and pluralistic in unprecedented ways. English as international *lingua franca* (Graddol, 2006) or First Foreign Language (Cha & Ham, 2008) is practically a mirror of major global events over the past 155 years and this ties practically all language teaching, including the choice of foreign languages, to large-scale, real-world, political events, and the world's traffic in goods, services, science and communication.

Societal multilingualism and dominant English require schools and education systems to make choices, and these choices are invested with significance related to the wider social and political forces which have produced the context in which these choices are made. The earliest language socialisation is in the home, where language is acquired and proto-literacy emerges. School teachers are *in loco parentis* not only for legal reasons; they occupy the place of parents as socialisers and educators, and as remunerated professionals engaged by society, replacing care-giving intimates. Even if the politics of dialect and language today are more sophisticated than the blunt choices of 18th century revolutionaries, the essential relationship between schools, teachers and schooling on the one hand, and homes, parents and care-giving on the other, remains similar. In the transfer from home to school, the language of learning is decided, and the messages, overt and covert, which this transfer signifies, are conveyed. Teachers and teaching cannot therefore be just implementers of status planning or acquisition planning choices delivered to them from outside. Multilingual homes mean multilingual learning. Schools aggregate students mostly on the basis of residential geography, bringing children together across differences of background, ability, interests and preparation. In this transfer of socialisation, profound LP activity occurs and individual teachers enact communicative, pedagogic and ideological decisions which can entrench lifelong patterns of communication skill, identity and ability.

Teachers as language planners

Teachers can choose to participate in formal processes of LP in their private roles of citizens or activists, but in their professional lives they are inescapably engaged in LP activity. This involvement is deeper than simply acting as implementers of language changes willed by others. Even straightforward implementation of LP as determined by curriculum bodies or ministries of education involves teachers in LP activity. However, the relationship between teaching and LP runs deeper. The pervasiveness of communication in human social relations (e.g. commerce and public life) means that teachers are invested with LP obligations and involvements endemic to their professional practice.

Restrictive definitions of LP limited to formal decision making and resource allocation miss how apparently routine practices of classroom interaction can serve as models of language use for learners. As citizens, teachers may or may not engage in responses to language influences originating outside of education institutions, but as to their professional endeavours, all teaching indirectly, and language and literacy teaching directly, are acts of implementation of existing LP and, more deeply, acts of LP in an ongoing dynamic and dialogical way (Bakhtin, 1981; Dentith, 1995). In reflections on literature and communication, Bakhtin proposed a view of conversation and its central role in recalling past things said, and anticipating reply, which is critical to this way of seeing LP. Linked to Neustupny's insight that ordinary language use, self-monitoring and correction involve micro-LP, we can see the classroom as a process of conversational interaction in which forms of language are the focus of intense engagement (see Jaspers, this volume).

Personal language expression, how we speak and perceive ourselves to speak, is monitored, and as we notice what we say, we may correct, adjust and modulate our expression to enhance meaning or to project intended identities. We are all engaged in continual LP as we converse, and this personal programme of planning our subjective self is located on a continuum with the collective, public action of institutions. A literacy teacher constructs the capabilities of learners in the codes, modes and meanings of the various literacy resources which society, the education system, school and parental expectations require of learners (Lo Bianco & Freebody, 2001). In stratified multilingual and multiliterate contexts, school practices give effect to decisions that must be made about what to teach and how to teach. Some of these choices confirm existing practice of the wider society, some resist and some produce change. Curriculum content and pedagogy are the result of choices; that is selections made from what curriculum content and pedagogical practices are available and possible. The totality of curriculum content and pedagogy choices ultimately constitute an enacted language and literacy policy.

Classroom language as LP

In addition to curriculum and pedagogy choices, a dialogical approach to language suggests that classroom language functions as LP, in at least four ways, focusing here mostly on teacher talk.

First, teacher classroom language implements norm choices, of code and register, made from those available to the participants in that setting, that is the learner and the teacher. Teachers' authoritative position as regulators and controllers of permitted language (topics and arguments, what can be said), and their role in 'policing' how things are said, constitutes the teacher as a LP authority. Teacher-enacted choices may confirm, modify or subvert what is required by the curriculum.

Second, teacher classroom language reflects subject or disciplinary codes, that is specialised terminologies, discourses and vocabularies. These structure and organise the content which is conveyed in classroom interactions.

Third, teacher classroom language contains moments of metalinguistic reflection, observation and analysis. These are occasions during which teachers might attach connotative meaning, that is value, emotion or ideology, to linguistic form.

Fourth, the literacy and literate practices of the teacher and what the teacher promotes and validates as acceptable literacy practice from the students, involve teachers implementing written language norms and standards in a similar way to those teachers implement for spoken language.

However, teacher classroom language necessarily interacts with students' communication and in this dialogic relation with student talk, teachers cannot simply impose norms and expectations of how communication itself should be conducted. Instead, teacher talk contains persuasion and rhetoric as well as making and limiting choices in what students are encouraged to say and write. Student talk and writing is responded to, promoting and discouraging, in subtle and overt ways, modes of politeness, permitted topics for discussion or personal disclosure, how questions are asked of others, word choices, taboo subjects etc. In this way teachers attempt to socialise learners into conversational competence, concerning entire behaviours regarding the conduct of conversations (see Rymes, this volume).

Perhaps the greatest effort of classroom teacher language is directed towards mastery of the required register of school education for example 'educated school English'. Essentially, teachers enact the past language policy; what it has been agreed constitutes educated speech and writing and how this agreed form will be assessed. This is rarely set down explicitly as required norms but is known through the kind of language found in textbooks, examinations and other procedures for public display of knowledge. By contrast, multimodal texts and the literacy demands of multimodal texts are more recent and teachers and schools are required to make overt efforts to introduce, extend or defend multimodal texts in curricula. As a result, the language surrounding multimodal literacy is more promotional and defending, and more obviously counts as LP activity. In addition, when computer technicians and teachers negotiate around technical terms and ways to talk and write about moving image, still images, graphs and charts and their role in teaching and learning, and how to assess and judge quality work that uses multimodal texts, they are also 'planning' the language that surrounds this area of learning. This activity is largely taken for granted in teaching speech or print literacy.

Language teaching as LP

Similarly, the LP function of teachers who teach language subjects is more easily perceived. Specialist language teachers (e.g. ESL support staff, or Reading Recovery tutors), foreign language teachers and general literacy teachers, but also primary/elementary classroom teachers, are directly concerned with language and therefore with metalinguistics. The object and focus of instructional activity centre around aspects of language and its use. Such teachers forge the lingual capabilities of learners for the various roles the now-young will come to play as future citizens and workers, and in their professional, personal or recreational and intellectual pursuits. This LP is not in the hands of remote policy makers in the broad and distant realms of national capitals, testing agencies, curriculum bodies or grammar and dictionary textbook writers. Instead, this LP is located in the activity of performing language for instruction, in which the focus of talk is the forms of talk and writing. As a reflexive kind of LP, language teaching involves iterative processes, that is to-and-fro communication between teachers and learners. This 'surrounds' the language used to deliver information and impart skills, that is the message-conveying language. As a result, the entire process of dialogical exchange of information, routine interaction and classroom tasks between teachers and students, or students and other students, constitutes dynamic micro-LP.

It might be objected that neither the four classroom language functions nor the specifically language focused work of specialist language teachers counts as an example of LP, seeing them instead as the elaborated implementation of broad goals for schooling established by others. This would be an unacceptably reductive understanding of both policy and teaching. Teachers, both language/literacy specialists and non-language specialists, *develop* learners' language skills and attitudes, norms and expressive practices. Mandated curricula, syllabus, textbook activities and assessment expectations establish only generic policies but teaching exceeds the intention and aspirations contained in curriculum statements or textbooks. Both pedagogy and the needs and circumstances of learners in their immediate network of communication peers require of teachers active, personalised and class-specific LP in a myriad of micro-interactions governed by explanation, abstraction, generalisation and application of knowledge.

This pedagogy-based LP occurs because local contexts and personal needs of learners, and the cultural, technological and economic changes that characterise communities, cannot be anticipated in formal policy documents, textbooks and examination procedures. The immediately focused communication required by teachers' routine work of imparting knowledge and skill involves regular micro-LP as learners are assisted to master educated speech and both print and multimodal literacies. At this level, LP activity in education shares features of educational linguistics (Spolsky, 1978). Educational linguistics came into being around questions such as: *How can language be defined for teaching? How can language learning be sequenced for teaching? How does learner processing of linguistic input influence teaching and curriculum design? How can language learning be assessed; how does literacy relate to spoken language?* These questions are readily reformulated in LP terms. Whether in the primary linguistic socialisation described by Watson-Gegeo (2004) or in secondary linguistic socialisation (Lo Bianco, 2008b), educational linguistics focuses attention on teachers' most direct enactment of LP activity. Instructional language integrates content and language by (1) extending home registers of language knowledge for 'majority' children to include educated school registers; (2) extending non-standard language competence of minority communities towards educated school registers; (3) modelling elevated linguistic registers and styles; (4) teaching the national standard language to non-speakers; (5) teaching subject literacy in print and multimedia forms; (6) teaching standard language and literacy for children with language-connected special needs; (7) mother-tongue teaching for minority speakers; and (8) teaching prestige foreign languages (Lo Bianco, 2008b: 113–114).

Schooling often validates middle class and educated modes of linguistic expression, imposing these as the required register of exchange in classrooms, and as the modelled norm for what is sociolinguistically appropriate for educated circles generally. This is reinforced by the literacy demands particular to different subjects. Multilingual/multiliterate settings offer a greater repertoire of languages, expressive styles and literacies aligned along a multifaceted continuum (Hornberger, 2002) but the choices validated by schooling are typically narrow and often perform the assimilationist policy demanded by dominant interests (Corson, 1999). This policy is reflected in the series of language and literacy selections that are made and by the omission of those languages and literacies deselected.

Responses to language diversity and the multilingual consequences of globalisation and mass migration convert schools and teachers into actors in elaborated LP activity. LPs often reflect an underlying 'orientation' to this reality (Ruiz, 1984, 2010). Multilingual homes make available to education systems, schools and individual teachers both pedagogical choices and ideological possibilities. We can see these as gradations along a continuum combining pedagogy and ideology. Three are identified here as orientations. *Assimilationist LP* combines a pedagogy of strictly monolingual and monoliterate dominant language instruction with ideological messages of equality tied to cultural sameness. *Diglossic LP* combines a pedagogy of language transfer and hierarchy, with ideologically positive messages about bilingualism and multiculturalism confined to private domains. *Pluralist LP* combines a pedagogy of active multilanguage and multiliterate communication with ideologically affirmative messages of linguistic human rights and social justice.

LP fuses with linguistic socialisation and educational linguistics (see Duff, this volume). Conventional ways to see LP would fail to recognise many of the language education activities of schools and classroom teachers as LP because these fail the tests of being overt, conscious or deliberate, thereby reducing school and teacher LP to simply giving effect to mandates from outside, or reflections of existing social practices. This is an unduly restrictive notion of what counts as LP and more dynamic understandings suggested above are warranted in the light of the deep consequences that flow from teaching. In a study on US Spanish-English programmes, Shannon (1999) shows how in the absence of explicit policy, teachers and schools revert to a default position, the position of current attitudes, rather than researched or reflected or studied alternatives. Past practice is default policy in the absence of explicit current policy.

Teacher voice

The absence of formal policy merely obscures operational or enacted language policy. The present argument is premised on this understanding of LP as embedded in the routine and dynamic activities of teaching, including in conversations that surround the practice of imparting knowledge and skill. In this way, conversations that are pedagogically oriented bring about specific micro kinds of language change. Teaching involves expanding the semiotic potential of learners' communication abilities, and a dynamic, fluid, and participatory approach to LP opens this to an expanded view of how LP is done, when and by whom. Expanding LP to include how language change can be effected in pedagogical activity and conversation has the added advantage of identifying the influence teaching can bring to public debates about language issues and problems. Classical definitions restrict LP to overt, deliberate or conscious managerial decisions, the 'tips of icebergs', with the effect of restricting the roles and influence of teacher voices. The less mechanistic approach proposed here grants teachers conversational credibility in formal LP formulation based on a more accurate appreciation of their role as active language planners.

Even formal analytical approaches to policy require citizenship validation and public legitimacy through the political process. This legitimation and validation is sought in debate and voting, voice and vote democracy.

In electorally open societies, both voice and vote procedures grant citizens influence over the direction of most kinds of public policy, despite the excessive power of some interests, unequal access to and influence in various mass media and prospects of manipulation and misrepresentation.

A more open understanding of LP opens space for practitioner reflection and teacher voices, invited into policy conversations. This will demand recognition of the experiential immediacy and knowledge produced by the acts of negotiating languages/literacies in the course of teaching. Teacher narratives and accounts of language development and socialisation expose the role of teaching as *latent policy making*. In many settings today, there is a notable absence of the voice of the authentic experience of LP in action, and this constitutes a *de facto* withdrawal of legitimacy from public policy. However, the teacher voice as the prime example of enacted LP must be joined to the voice and interests of researchers, policy experts and communities as the main collection of interests involved. The pooled perspectives of these categories of policy interest would produce more democratic practices of LP formulation. Teachers' unique proximity to language development and language problems should considerably increase their credibility and prominence in debates about language as a public resource. Teacher perspectives can lend authenticity, experience, immediacy and validated encounter, the flavour of *enacted* LP. Teachers can enter LP conversations as practitioners and performers of ongoing language socialisation and policy, rather than recipients of mandates from outside.

Public texts of policy are the solidified and already decided form of LP. Public debate is the ongoing, discursive consideration of future LP. In their performance role, teachers enact past policy and make continuing LP in activities of language development and socialisation. An activity-centred approach to LP allows analysts to conceptualise the processes of planned language change in a richer depiction of how language use intersects with teaching and how these shape the directions of the code and content of language. In turn this will allow practitioners greater points of intervention in public debates about language rights and opportunities, implications of multilingualism and the communication effects of new technologies. All these acknowledge the wider range of roles teachers and teaching play and contribute towards a more just and democratic kind of LP. The new kind of LP imagined here also expands the number of agents involved and the modes of participation various players can have in LP. These should not obscure the reality that organised interests constrain more democratic language futures as the forces against language rights in times of anxiety are many and powerful. These forces often seek to convert teachers, and teaching, simply into instruments of policy implementation, constrained by assessment regimes, tight syllabus designs, and employment practices that limit teachers' autonomy and professional responsiveness.

All voices in policy debates are differentiated by their unique experiences and perspectives. Differentiated discussion allows for participation in public framing of language problems according to multiple angles of understanding and representation. The organised and targeted interventions of language teachers are a remit, or a kind of enfranchisement, for engaging in discussions of policy. Certainly such discussions should be granted more attention and credibility, especially in today's times of economic difficulty and public anxiety due to globalisation and mass mobility of populations.

Suggestions for further reading

Ager, D. (2001) *Motivation in Language Planning and Language Policy*. Clevedon: Multilingual Matters.
Focuses on what stimulates the activity of language policy making, and deals with LP needs, goals and strategies, emphasizing the 'real world' character of LP and applied linguistics.

Baker, S. (ed.) (2002) *Language Policy: Lessons from Global Models*. Monterey, CA: Monterey Institute for International Studies.
Contains expert reflections on the practice of LP making in the late 1990s in a range of national (African, Asian, American, and European) and other settings.

Corson, D. (1999) *Language Policy in Schools*. London: Lawrence Erlbaum.
One of the few works to apply the notion of LP directly to the concerns of individual schools in their regular teaching and learning practices.

Crawford, J. (1999) *Bilingual Education, History, Politics, Theory and Practice* (4th edn). Los Angeles, CA: Bilingual Education Services.
A comprehensive treatment of the policy politics surrounding bilingual education in the United States.

Davis, K. A. (1994) *Language Planning in Multilingual Contexts. Policies, Communities and Schools in Luxembourg*. Amsterdam/Philadelphia: Benjamins Publishing Company.
Analyses LP with close attention to multiple factors that impact choices that people make in various institutional settings, and especially the interaction between individual and governmental domains.

Jaffe, A. (1999) *Ideologies in Action. Language Politics on Corsica*. Berlin and New York: Mouton de Gruyter.
An ethnographic examination of language use and planning on Corsica in the context of the steady erosion of the social domains of Corsican towards domination by French.

References

Bakhtin, M. (1981) *The Dialogic Imagination*. Austin: University of Texas Press.
Beacco, J-C. (2007) From Linguistic Diversity to Plurilingual Education. Council of Europe, Strasbourg. On WWW at http://www.coe.int/t/dg4/linguistic/Guide_niveau3_EN.asp#TopofPage/. Accessed 1.3.2010.
Boyd, S. (2007) Communication and community. In A. Pauwels, J. Winter and J. Lo Bianco (eds) *Maintaining Minority Languages in Transnational Contexts* (pp. 201–223). London: Palgrave.

Brecht, R. and Walton, R. (1993) *National Strategic Planning in Languages*. Baltimore, MD: Johns Hopkins.

Brunot, F. (1927) Histoire de la langue française des origins à 1900, t. IX, 1ère partie (pp. 3–14). Paris: Armand Colin.

Butler, J. (1997) *Excitable Speech: A Politics of the Performative*. London: Routledge.

Castles, S. and Miller, M. (2003) *The Age of Migration* (3rd edn). Basingstoke: Palgrave Macmillan.

Cha, Y-K. and Ham, S-H. (2008) The impact of English on the school curriculum. In B. Spolsky and F. Hult (eds) *Handbook of Educational Linguistics* (pp. 313–328). London: Blackwell.

Clyne, M. (2005) *Australia's Language Potential*. Sydney: University of New South Wales Press.

Cooper, R.L. (1989) *Language Planning and Social Change*. Cambridge: Cambridge University Press.

Corson, D. (1999) *Language Policy in Schools*. London: Lawrence Erlbaum.

Dahlstedt, K-H. (1976) Societal ideology and language cultivation. *International Journal of the Sociology of Language* 10, 17–50.

Dentith, S. (1995) *Bakhtinian Thought*. London: Routledge.

Dua, H. (1985) *Language Planning in India*. New Delhi: Harnam.

ECRML (1992) European Charter for Regional and Minority Languages. Strasbourg: France. 5.XI. On WWW at http://www.interculturaldialogue.eu/web/files/33/en/CECRML-T.pdf. Accessed 1.3.2010.

Eastman, C. (1983) *Language Planning*. Novato, CA: Chandler and Sharp.

Fishman, J.A. (1971) *Sociolinguistics*. Rowley, MA: Newbury House.

Fishman, J.A. (1973) Language modernization and planning. *Language in Society* 2 (1), 23–44.

Fishman, J.A. (1994) Critiques of language planning. *Journal of Multilingual and Multicultural Development* 15 (2 & 3), 91–99.

Fishman, J.A. (2000/1965) Who speaks what language to whom and when. In L. Wei (ed.) *The Bilingualism Reader* (pp. 89–106). London: Routledge.

García, O., Skutnabb-Kangas, T. and Torres Guzmán, M. (eds) (2006) *Imagining Multilingual Schools: Language in Education and Glocalization*. Clevedon: Multilingual Matters.

Gottlieb, N. and Chen, P. (2001) *Language Planning and Language Policy: East Asian Perspectives*. Richmond: Curzon.

Graddol, D. (2006) *English Next*. London: The British Council.

Haarmann, H. (1990) Language planning in the light of a general theory of language: A methodological framework. *International Journal of the Sociology of Language* 86, 103–126.

Hanks, W.F. (1996) *Language and Communicative Practices*. Boulder, CO: Westview Press.

Harris, R. (1988) *Language, Saussure and Wittgenstein*. London: Routledge.

Haugen, E. (1953) *The Norwegian Language in America: A Study in Bilingual Behavior*. Philadelphia: University of Pennsylvania Press.

Haugen, E. (1966) *Language Conflict & Language Planning*. Cambridge, MA: Harvard University Press.

Haugen, E. (1972) *The Ecology of Language*. Stanford, CA: Stanford University Press.

Hornberger, N.H. (2002) Multilingual language policies and the continua of biliteracy: An ecological approach. *Language Policy* 1, 27–51.

Hornberger, N.H. (2006) Frameworks and models in language policy and planning. In T. Ricento (ed.) *An Introduction to Language Policy* (pp. 24–41). Malden, MA: Blackwell Publishing.

Hutton, C. (1999) *Linguistics & the 3rd Reich: Mother-Tongue Fascism, Race & the Science of Language*. London: Routledge.

Kaplan, R. and Baldauf, R. (1997) *Language Planning from Practice to Theory*. Clevedon: Multilingual Matters.

Kedourie, E. (1961) *Nationalism*. London: Hutchinson.

Kloss, H. (1969) *Research Possibilities on Group Bilingualism*. Quebec: Center for Research on Bilingualism.

Lakoff, G. (2005) *Don't Think of an Elephant!* Carlton North, Vic: Scribe.

LePage, R.B. and Tabouret-Keller, A. (1985) *Acts of Identity*. Cambridge: Cambridge University Press.

Lo Bianco, J. (2001) Vietnam: Quoc Ngu, colonialism and language policy. In N. Gottlieb and P. Chen (eds) *Language Policy in East Asia* (pp. 159–207). London: Curzon Press.

Lo Bianco, J. (2005) Globalisation & national communities of communication. *Language Problems & Language Planning* 29 (2), 109–135.

Lo Bianco, J. (2007) Emergent China and Chinese. In J. Lo Bianco (ed.) *The Emergence of Chinese, Language Policy* (pp. 3–26) (Vol. 6, Issue 1). Dordrecht: Springer.

Lo Bianco, J. (2008a) Tense times and language policy. *Current Issues in Language Planning* 9 (2), 155–178.

Lo Bianco, J. (2008b) Educational linguistics and education systems. In B. Spolsky and F.M. Hult (eds) *Handbook of Educational Linguistics* (pp. 113–126). London: Blackwell.

Lo Bianco, J. and Freebody, P. (2001) *Australian Literacies*. Melbourne: Language Australia.

Luke, A., McHoul, A.W. and Mey, J.L. (1990) On the limits of language planning. In R.B. Baldauf and A. Luke (eds) *Language Planning and Education in Australasia and the South Pacific* (pp. 25–44). Clevedon: Multilingual Matters.

Majone, G. (1989) *Evidence, Argument, and Persuasion in the Policy Process*. New Haven, CT: Yale University Press.

McGroarty, M. (1997) Language policy in the USA. In W. Eggington and H. Wren (eds) *Language Policy* (pp. 1–29). Amsterdam: Benjamins.

Mohsin, A. (2003) Language, identity and the state in Bangladesh. In M.E. Brown and S. Ganguly (eds) *Fighting Words* (pp. 81–104). Cambridge: MIT Press.

Moore, H. (1996) Language policies as virtual realities. *TESOL Quarterly* 30 (1), 473–497.

Moniruzzaman, M. (1979) Language planning in Bangladesh. *Language Planning Newsletter (East-West Center, Honolulu)* 5 (3), 1, 3.

Mühlhäusler, P. (1995) *Linguistic Ecology*. London: Routledge.

Nahir, M. (1984) Language planning goals. *Language Problems & Planning* 8 (3), 294–327.

Nettle, D. and Romaine, S. (2000) *Vanishing Voices*. Oxford: Oxford University Press.

Neustupny, J. (1983) Towards a paradigm for LP. *Language Planning Newsletter* 9 (4), 1, passim.

NLP (1979–1983) *Language Planning Newsletter (East-West Center, Honolulu)* 4 (4)–5 (1), 1, passim.

Ó Flatharta, P., NicPháidín, C., Williams, C., Grin, F. and Lo Bianco, J. (2008) *20-year Strategy for Irish*. Fiontar: Dublin City University.

Ozolins, U. (1993) *The Politics of Language in Australia*. Cambridge: Cambridge University Press.

Phillipson, R. and Skutnabb-Kangas, T. (1996) English-only worldwide or language ecology? *TESOL Quarterly* 30, 429–452.

Ricento, T. (2000) Historical and theoretical perspectives in language policy and planning. In T. Ricento (ed.) *Ideology, Politics and Language Policies* (pp. 9–25). Amsterdam: Benjamins.

Ricento, T.K. and Hornberger, N.H. (1996) Unpeeling the onion: Language planning and policy and the ELT professional. *TESOL Quarterly* 30 (3), 401–428.

Rubin, J. (1977) Language standardization in Indonesia. In J. Rubin, B. Jernudd, J. Das Gupta, J.A. Fishman and C.A. Ferguson (eds) *Language Planning Processes* (pp. 157–180). Mouton: The Hague.

Rubin, J. (1985) Review of Carol M. Eastman. Language planning: An introduction. *Language in Society* 14 (1), 137–141.

Rubin, J. (1986) City planning and language planning. In E. Annamalai, B. Jernudd and J. Rubin (eds) *Language Planning* (pp. 105–123). Honolulu: Central Institute of Indian Studies and East-West Center.

Rubin, J. and Jernudd, B. (1971) *Can Language be Planned?* Honolulu: University of Hawaii Press.

Ruiz, R. (1984) Orientations in language planning. *NABE Journal* 8, 15–34.

Ruiz, R. (2010) Reorienting language-as-resource. In J. Petrovic (ed.) *International Perspectives on Bilingual Education: Policy, Practice, and Controversy* (pp. 155–172). Charlotte, NC: Information Age Publishing.

Shannon, S.M. (1999) The debate on bilingual education in the US. In J. Blommaert (ed.) *Language Ideological Debates* (pp. 171–201). Berlin: de Gruyter.

Sommer, B.A. (1991) Yesterday's experts: The bureaucratic impact on language planning for aboriginal bilingual education. *Australian Review of Applied Linguistics*, Series S 8, 109–135.

Spolsky, B. (1978) *Educational Linguistics*. Rowley, MA: Newbury House.

Suarez-Orozco, M.M. and Qin-Hilliard, D.B. (2004) *Globalization*, culture and education in the new millennium. Berkeley: University of California Press.

Tauli, V. (1984) The failure of LP research. In A. Gonzalez (ed.) *Panagani: Language Planning, Implementation and Evaluation* (pp. 85–93). Manila: Linguistic Society of the Philippines.

Tollefson, J.W. (1991) *Planning Language, Planning Inequality*. New York: Longman Cheshire.

Tully, J. (1997) *Strange Multiplicities: Constitutionalism in an age of Diversity.* Cambridge: Cambridge University Press.

Turnbull, N. (2005) Rhetoric, questioning and policy theory. *Melbourne Journal of Politics* 30 (1), 39–58.

Watson-Gegeo, K.A. (2004) Mind, language, and epistemology: Toward a language socialization paradigm for SLA. *The Modern Language Journal* 88 (iii), 331–350.

Webb, V. (2002) *Language in South Africa*. Amsterdam: Benjamins.

Weinreich, U. (1953) *Languages in Contact, Findings and Problems*. New York: Linguistic Circle of New York.

Wright, S. (2004) *Language Policy and Language Planning: From Nationalism to Globalisation*. Basingstoke: Palgrave.

Part 3

Language and Variation

Chapter 7
Style and Styling

JÜRGEN JASPERS

Introduction

Unlike what fashion magazines often imply, this chapter is about how, on a linguistic level at least, everybody has style. In fact, there is no escaping from style. In every word we say we creatively select linguistic, as well as other resources, that have social meaning and thus make ourselves available for others to see us as styling this way or that.

The fact that people engage in different ways of speaking has attracted much attention from sociolinguists in the past decades. Initially, quantitatively oriented sociolinguists tried to map with what frequency speakers conventionally shifted styles in different social contexts, and consequently showed how social hierarchies are inscribed on routine speech patterns. But this approach only paid scant attention to exceptional and self-conscious speech.

More recently therefore, interaction-oriented scholars have tried to reconcile both conventional styles as well as contrived fragments of speech as two manifestations of the same process: language users continually employ familiar and less familiar linguistic and other meaningful tools to (re)build their social surroundings as well as the self and other identities that are part of it. This has brought about a significant shift in interest in the principles of styling rather than the resulting styles.

Since learning is increasingly viewed as identifying oneself with new social practices and promises – indeed, a kind of styling – teachers and policy makers may need to take into account that not only instructed styles (such as standard varieties) can be a daunting social hurdle, but also styles of instruction may become a stake in local social struggle.

The Linguistic and the Social

During my ethnographic fieldwork in a secondary school in Antwerp, Belgium, I once asked Mourad, one of the students I was following, how the weather had been in Belgium, since I had just been on a brief holiday abroad. Mourad immediately replied, but I failed to understand, no doubt partly because we were walking among dozens of others in a noisy school hall. As soon as I asked him to repeat, though, I suddenly realised I had heard 'shit weather' (in Antwerp dialect). Yet, Mourad repeated his answer and said: 'bad weather, in your language', in a less dialectal voice. On another occasion, in an interview with Mourad and two of his classmates, I had just asked in which cases they thought they would be needing Standard Dutch, when Mourad suddenly switched into an exaggerated Standard Dutch voice to say 'so you are a repeater' to Moumir, in order to highlight the fact that the latter had just inadvertently, and to the amusement of his classmates, given himself away as a grade repeater (see Jaspers, 2006 – I will come back to this example at the end of the chapter).

Both examples draw attention to distinctive ways of speaking. In the first, Mourad seems to have thought I did not immediately catch what he said because of the dialectal quality of his utterance, which he seemed to perceive as different from my own regular Dutch. Also, in addressing Moumir in an educated, Standard Dutch voice in the second example, he not only managed to poke fun at his classmate and friend, but also implicitly suggested that educational success and failure often entail different ways of speaking. But while addressee-designed vernacular-to-standard shifts such as Mourad performs in the first example have been intensely studied as 'style shifts' (though admittedly, studies of style shifting have traditionally discussed phonological and/or morphological shifts rather than lexical ones), much sociolinguistic work has tended to ignore what Mourad does in the second. It has, moreover, tended to avoid forging links between styles in speaking and more popular notions of style in the social world. Naturally, the term 'style' in the social world is generally related to fashion, as in expressions such as 'she is really stylish' and implicitly in pejorative utterances like 'he wears white socks!' and 'that is so last season!'. But although this popular conception of style is different from the sociolinguist's definition of it, it may be unwise to see them as unrelated (cf. Irvine, 2001): in both cases, style is used to talk about distinctiveness appreciated in an evaluative framework which contains other styles (e.g. wearing other kinds of socks). An approach that attends to both the linguistic and the social thus needs to develop a framework that can account for popular talk about style as well as phonological differences.

Definition and Primary Goals of Study

If style shifts and popular talk about style are not unrelated, how can we define style? A good starting point is to say that 'style refers to a way of doing something' (Coupland, 2007: 1). And since humans do a lot of things, this can apply to practically anything, going from how we walk, the ways we do our make-up and build houses, to the way we dress, sing, act and indeed, the ways in which some of us teach. Usually though, when we use the term 'style', the idea is to capture *how* one does all of these things, that is an aesthetic dimension is evoked: someone sings 'beautifully', someone's handwriting 'has style'.

It is important to realise, however, that styles never come alone. They are always part of a system where several other styles exist and in which it makes sense to see one style as different from another: we would not be talking about a certain hair 'style' if we all did our hair in exactly the same way (if that was at all possible). Consequently, style refers to a distinctive way of doing something as compared to others, a reason why it is 'seldom useful to examine a single style in isolation' (Irvine, 2001: 22), since each style partly shapes itself in relation to neighbouring others. Moreover, this system of distinction implies that there are witnesses paying attention to what makes a certain style different from another. So, style is, next to a way of doing something, inextricably bound up with perceiving and evaluating others as doing something in relation to a meaningful system. Distinctiveness, and aesthetics, are indeed in the 'eye of the beholder'. This beholder is furthermore part of a social world where particular ways of doing and habits have come to obtain the social colour of the communities in which they are seen to frequently occur – to the extent that an accent, a particular expression, a typical piece of clothing or a certain type of music may become recognisable as, or stand for, a community: (listening to) classical music is often seen as 'elitist', for example, and local accents often stand for conviviality. Thus, ways of doing are inseparably bound up with a meaningful social world that provides an arsenal of different 'socially coloured' resources for its inhabitants.

Therefore all ways of doing, regardless of their intended aesthetic quality, may in principle be evaluated as aesthetic and stylish, or not. But of course, things are not as arbitrary as that, as is also illustrated by the classical music example above: all 'beholders' of meaningful variation live in a hierarchically organised world where elites are distinguished from the working class. This hierarchy is commonly supported and legitimised by widespread and ideologised views of appropriateness, articulateness, educatedness and beauty (Irvine, 2001; McGroarty, this volume). It is significant to see that people's personal aesthetic preferences are channelled by these dominant preferences. For example being a tough leader, with all the styling that it implies in terms of dress, language or interaction patterns, is often found to 'defemininise' women as it jars with dominant heteronormative views of women as submissive and insecure (*cf.* Cameron & Kulick, 2003; Higgins, this volume). 'Doing femininity' interacts with its ideologised representation, and so not all doings may be found stylish in the world governed by this representation – though all such doings will count as styling acts underneath.

In addition, ways of doing that are recognised as ways of doing point at a certain routine or convention (*cf.* Coupland, 2007). Because of this convention or habit, we often cease to perceive the distinctive quality of our own ways of doing, only to be startled when something or someone confronts us with our own style and shocks us out of our perceptual habit, as also Mourad did in his recast above, or as might befall a tough female CEO when confronted with gossip among her male staff about her 'unsexy' behaviour.

Clearly, given all this, it is fair to say we are surrounded by an immense variety of ways of doing and thus live in a thoroughly styled world. An important consequence of living in such a world is that one cannot 'not style': everything we do will unequivocally be interpreted and evaluated by others as a certain way of doing things as compared to other ways of doing. In everything we do we make ourselves available for others to see us as styling this way or that: there is no 'unstyled' hair, 'unstyled' clothing, and indeed there is no such thing as 'unstyled' language or 'non-social' language (*cf.* Blommaert, 2005: 10). Every speaking act can be seen as a pulling together of different meaningful linguistic resources, making a temporary edifice, so to say, of different linguistic bricks. This is always done in combination with selecting other meaningful, but non-linguistic elements. Although this chapter will mainly focus on linguistic styling, it will emphasise that linguistic features are only some of the meaningful resources we have at our disposal in daily life for styling, and are usually combined with and influenced by non-linguistic resources (producing certain vowels differently may combine with long hair, smoking and hanging out at specific places at school, *cf.* Eckert, 2000). As we will see at the end of this chapter, styles are also part of our learning process: an indispensable part of our social competence is to learn about the value of linguistic elements and to recognise, act upon and use several linguistic styles. Which styles speakers learn, however, depends in some measure on their interest and on the social position (and the related access to particular styles) they occupy.

Finally, 'styling' may be said to relate to 'style' as speaking does to speech. Speech and style are then the products, or the sediment, of the preceding interaction; the interaction itself, in turn, may be seen as 'styling/speaking-in-action'. A number of current authors have also identified 'stylisations', which have come to be viewed as exceptional, unexpected and spectacular acts of styling designed to attract attention and invite others to decipher the special effect they create in the situation-on-hand (Coupland, 2001; Rampton, 2001a, 2006).

In view of the above, the primary goals of the study of style and styling may up to this point be summarisd as follows:

(1) What linguistic and non-linguistic ways of doing exist in specific communities, and how are they related to the available battery of resources?
(2) How are these ways of doing related to the meaningful system that participants in these communities orient to, reproduce or deviate from?

(3) How does this meaningful system organise and structure the community, what images and understandings legitimise it, and what benefits and disadvantages does it have in store for different participants?

These goals, and the definition of style given above, differ somewhat from how style has traditionally been approached in (socio)linguistics. So, in what follows, I will first look into the development of the linguistic study of style and styling, at one of the main approaches that emerged for the linguistic study of style (namely 'variationism'), and at the different challenges this approach has been facing. Consequently, I will explain a theoretical reorientation that I think helps address most of the limitations of this traditional perspective. After that, I will outline the main principles for the future study of style and styling and finally, I will present data from an educational context to illustrate some of the points I make in this chapter.

The Linguistic Study of Style and Styling

The fact that people engage in different ways of speaking has attracted copious attention from sociolinguists in the past decades. It is important to realise that this attention has not at all been evident, or that, at least up until the 1960s, describing and analysing different ways of speaking was not really an acceptable thing for a linguist to do. Of course, dialectologists in the 19th century described the different distribution of linguistic variants, but mainly as a way to document the speech of older versions of the national language, which then subsequently provided 'objective' historical proof for nation-building projects (see also Bucholtz, 2003; Gal & Irvine, 1995). At the same time, philologists such as Franz Bopp, Jacob Grimm, Rasmus Rask and Karl Verner attempted to design universal and exceptionless sound laws that determined how particular sounds from a particular language or language family changed through time. These same laws were then relied on to reconstruct a common ancestral, but lost, European Ur-language. In this frame, contemporary language use could only illustrate fragmentation. Thus, linguistics in the 19th century was mostly concerned with looking back, and it approached linguistic variation mainly in historical terms.

But at the end of the 19th century, structuralist linguists such as de Saussure disagreed with this rearward focus and argued for a linguistics that would observe contemporary language use. De Saussure was, among other things, fascinated by the intriguing fact that linguistic variability is almost endless but can still guarantee stable meaning in human communication. He presumed that underneath this amazing variability one would be able to find a deeper, stable structure that kept everything in place (de Saussure, 1972). For this reason, he objected to what he saw as the naked comparison of isolated linguistic elements that was the goal of mainstream linguistics at his time, and he insisted that language is in fact a system where everything hangs together. A sound from one (historical) variety cannot, therefore, be compared with a sound from another variety, since the function of both sounds in the linguistic system they belong to is not necessarily the same. As a result, de Saussure said, it is not individual sound changes that need to be studied but the change from one linguistic system to another. In doing so, de Saussure made a crucial distinction between language use (or *parole*) and the linguistic system (the *langue*): it was the latter that was to be worthy of attention from linguists. So by the 1960s, the view was firmly established that 'real' linguists devoted all their time and energy to describing the (grammatical) structures of (a) language and that in order to do so, it was necessary to take language use out of its social surroundings and study it in isolation. It was the implicit knowledge of this system that Chomsky saw as speakers' actual linguistic *competence*. In his view, moreover, an efficient description of the linguistic system was only possible without the noise and the other limitations of 'real-life' language use by specific speakers in specific sociocultural contexts (such as interruptions, hesitations, lapses, muttering, etc.). The linguistic products of these imperfect, constraining or noisy circumstances were viewed as only the momentary and arbitrary realisations, that is the mere *performance* of a primary, and possibly universal, systematic cognitive structure. For this reason, Chomsky famously based his analysis on 'ideal speakers and hearers in a completely homogeneous linguistic community' (Chomsky, 1965: 3). In doing this, it was not as much his intention to deny heterogeneity and variation, than to see these as surface features that were irrelevant for the explanation of deeper lying linguistic systematicity. In the same way as his structuralist predecessors, Chomsky and his followers only perceived systematicity and norm-following within language (and its cognitive foundation) rather than in actual language use itself. Hence, where in the 19th century linguistic variation was mostly seen in historical terms, it had now become an irrelevant and impure surface feature of a deeper-lying linguistic system.

Variationist sociolinguistics

In the 1960s and 1970s, however, the sociolinguist William Labov as well as scholars from other disciplines such as Joshua Fishman (sociology of language) and Dell Hymes (linguistic anthropology) were among the first to take up the gauntlet against the postulation of homogeneity and the apparent irrelevance of linguistic variation. They pointed out, among other things, that linguistic homogeneity does not exist, neither at the level of linguistic communities nor at the level of individual grammars. Moreover, Hymes maintained that language use is permeated by the sociocultural context in which it occurs; so, in order to communicate competently, one must have both a linguistic as well as a sociocultural competence (Hymes, 1972). Most significantly, in terms of its effect on the linguistic discipline, Labov drew attention to the fact that the assumption of linguistic homogeneity obfuscates the systematics of language change. After all, structuralists were aware they were studying a constantly evolving object, so in their wish to study the systematicity of language they temporarily froze their object of study in time, at the cost of making abstraction from real time altogether and creating a static linguistic object. Consequently, they could not explain linguistic evolution, or did so only by jumping discontinuously from one internally structured system to another (*cf.* Meeuwis & Brisard, 1993: 15ff.). It is one of Labov's great achievements that he was able to demonstrate that all language use is characterised by structured rather than random variability, and furthermore, that these structured linguistic differences could be seen as evidence of linguistic change in progress (*cf.* Coupland, 2007).

More particularly, Labov managed to show how language use in New York City was socially distributed (*cf.* also Coupland, 2007: 33–37; Hudson, 1996: 155–159; Labov, 1966). He was aware that New Yorkers sometimes used a postvocalic [r] in words such as 'far' or 'fourth', but at other moments refrained from this. The choice, furthermore, appeared to stand for a change taking place: New Yorkers were gradually moving away from a 'British' norm (with no [r] produced in a word like 'farm') to a more general American trend where [r] in postvocalic position is always pronounced. As the newer trend was associated with the high-status community outside New York, Labov predicted that the 'zero'-form (with no or very few [r]s) would still be used by lower-status speakers, and that higher-status speakers would generally adopt the 'innovative' pronunciation. He collected his data by asking shop-assistants where certain articles were that Labov knew were on the fourth floor: 'Excuse me, where are the women's shoes?', to which most shop-assistants unsurprisingly replied 'fourth floor' or 'on the fourth floor'. He would then lean forward, pretending not to have understood, to allow himself a second opportunity to listen to the directions given and observe whether a second, more careful utterance would make any difference. It turned out that shop-assistants in high-status shops produced a higher frequency of postvocalic [r], and that this frequency was systematically lower or very low in shops visited by middle- and low-status clienteles. Labov furthermore noticed that those who did not usually use a postvocalic [r], precisely did so on occasions where speakers paid more attention to their speech, and in this way symbolically dressed themselves with prestige or social status.

In so doing, Labov did not only manage to point out that very small linguistic differences laid bare a thoroughly hierarchised social context, but also that language users were somehow aware of these differences. Most importantly, with regard to structural linguistics, Labov managed to show that correlations between social variables (such as purchasing power) and 'superficial' linguistic variables (the realisation of a certain sound) delivered dynamic sociolinguistic patterns: the use of postvocalic [r] by financially disadvantaged groups proliferated, influencing other vowel and consonant combinations. In this way, Labov afforded researchers a means to observe linguistic change in progress: linguistic habits were changing under the influence of social processes that were leading speakers to adopt certain linguistic forms and refrain from using others. In other words, Labov found systematicity where none of it was expected, and proved that it seriously affected the structure of language. Accepting the idea of homogeneity was then not just screening out some surface features, but missing out on a general property of language (*cf.* Cameron, 1990: 56; Coupland, 2007: 26, 32–33). Additionally, there was a serious political effect: by showing orderliness in so-called 'non-standard' speech, sociolinguists made clear it was necessary to look beyond 'elite' speech and in this way dignified non-elite speakers.

These groundbreaking findings, and the almost mathematical quality of the data analysis, gave rise to a whole new discipline Labov hoped would replace structural linguistics. But eventually it was named variationist, Labovian (or 'quantitative' after its main methodological approach) sociolinguistics.

Style shifting in variationist sociolinguistics

With regard to style, Labov's work was important because he established that speakers' capacity to change something about their way of speaking was related to social parameters (class, in the case above) and to situations where these parameters mattered. In other words, he proved that intra-speaker variation (in the speech of individual speakers) was related to inter-speaker variation (in speech across groups of speakers). Our linguistic styles are, in other words, bound up with social trends and with our competent use of those linguistic features that have come to be valued by these trends. The name traditionally given to this practice of adapting our speech is 'style shifting', and the sociolinguistic study of style shifting from then on usually involved (1) identifying phonological and morphosyntactic features (typically a standard and vernacular form) that are routinely produced differently according to the formality of the context (or the composition of the speaker's audience, see below) and (2) quantifying the extent to which this is done (*cf.* Hudson, 1996; Schilling-Estes, 2002).

Initially, the main theory for intra-speaker variation was 'differential degrees of attention paid to speech' (Eckert, 2000: 18; Hudson, 1996: 199; Labov, 1994: 157; Rickford & Eckert, 2001: 2–3). That is, the extent to which you pay attention to your speech determines how much you move away from your ordinary or 'natural' way of speaking, and this generally meant moving to a more prestigious or higher status form. The 'most natural', uncorrected speech was then the 'older' form, which differed from the 'newer' form, spoken by those who have prestige. This is how the presence of postvocalic [r] in New York meant high prestige but was fairly new and on the increase, whereas the absence of it signified low prestige and symbolised a declining tradition. Thus, in a situation where high social prestige matters, people will often change to the prestigious form. So clearly, next to 'attention paid to speech', another principle was that speakers displayed an upwardly mobile tendency, meaning that all speakers gradually adapt to high social status forms, or that the standard language is the stylistic target for all speakers (Eckert, 2000: 18): speakers of low social prestige are seen to have a 'natural' way of speaking, but to move from their 'unstyled' speech to a 'styled' version of it when they adapt to higher social status conditions.

Consequently, sociolinguists shared an immense methodological concern on how to reach these older vernacular forms that speakers of lower prestige use in their 'true' linguistic habitats, which were considered authentic, uncorrected, unmonitored, or in short, 'real' speech (*cf.* Bucholtz, 2003). This was a major concern, since Labov and others usually noted that such speakers did in fact *not* produce such unmonitored or 'unstyled' speech when they were being interviewed by sociolinguists. Interviewees often felt that the research situation itself was of high social prestige, and they produced the forms they had learnt to produce in similar high prestige circumstances. Labov termed this problem the 'observer's paradox' (Labov, 1975), and variationists worked hard on their empirical discovery procedures to avoid it and be able to reach the linguistic forms it was seen to stand in the way of. One of the procedures was to manipulate the topics in the interview from casual (talking about childhood customs or dangerous situations) to formal or careful (reading passages, word lists) and in this way talk interviewees into producing highly formal as well as 'normal' or 'authentic' speech.

This approach received a fair amount of criticism, however. It was pointed out, for example, that casual and careful might not be as easily distinguishable in practice as Labov suggested, since speaking carefully does not always imply using standard linguistic features – one can carefully and consciously shift into the vernacular; similarly, speaking in dialect does not always point to casualness (Coupland, 2007: 6–7, 38–39; Schilling-Estes, 2002: 382–383). More or less at the same time, Labov and other researchers furthermore noticed that speakers did not always adopt prestigious forms (Labov, 1972a; Trudgill, 1983). 'Why do not all people speak in the way that they obviously believe they should?', Hudson quotes Labov asking, since some groups prefer using their own, less prestigious, variants instead (1996: 210). This suggested the existence of alternative markets where older linguistic forms retained currency and survived, or where other stylistic targets prevailed than the standard language in the attention paid to speech framework. In order to explain this, a distinction was made between forms that have an 'overt' prestige (acknowledged by everyone as forms with a high status because of the high prestige of their speakers), and forms with a 'covert' prestige in a specific, local non-prestige group (Hudson, 1996: 211, 240; Trudgill, 1983: 89ff.). Consequently, to explain variation (both intra- and inter-speaker) one started to appeal to the concept of the social norm or the group norm that was seen to pressure speakers to adapt their speech in conformity to their local networks. But in the next section I will explain that (1) this use of norms was also fraught with problems, as was (2) the idea of 'authentic' language use.

Challenges for variationist sociolinguistics

Explaining norms and variation

Mostly, in variationist sociolinguistics (but also in older forms of linguistic anthropology and sociology of language) norms are considered as the consensus or the shared perspective present in a speech community on what counts as normal, attractive or desirable language use, and they are usually seen as implanted during early socialisation. Moreover, it is often suggested that the more closely knit the network members live in, the more the group members will show a high degree of conformity to these norms, and the higher the possibility that particular forms will obtain covert prestige. Looser networks, on the other hand, much more permit external forms to get distributed and adopted by their members (*cf.* Hudson, 1996: 190–192; *cf.* Milroy, 1980).

However, some researchers have indicated that tightly knit communities and linguistic conformity might not as easily go hand in hand as is often thought (Dorian, 1994). But more problematic than the empirical counterevidence is the assumption that speakers can be assigned membership of empirically identifiable communities. In effect, as the concept was used, speech communities were seen to contain speakers who were more or less alike, or who shared a certain linguistic (or other) essence. In this way however, community and the individual speaker become almost interchangeable, at the cost of destroying individuality or internal diversity within the community. In relation to this, the main view of normativity in variationism was severely deterministic. Much of variationist sociolinguistics shies away from making explicit the sociological premises that underlie its appeal to social norms, and even consequently avoids an open interaction with sociological theory formation (*cf.* Cameron, 1990; Hudson, 1996: 4; Trudgill, 1983; Williams, 1992). But many of their premises are at least partly informed by Parsons' (1937) structural-functionalism that sees social norms as internalised socialisation processes. In this perspective, social practices and psychological profiles are largely isomorphic. A number of authors have insisted that these premises reduce people to judgmental dopes or pre-programmed clones that are merely responsive to changes in a pre-existing external world (*cf.* Duff, this volume; Eckert, 2000; Eckert & Rickford, 2001; Garfinkel, 1967; Heritage, 1984; Schilling-Estes, 2002). It is difficult to see how such clones would be able to engage in self-conscious variation or resistance, since the self-consciousness needed for this is deleted to account for normative behaviour. Hence, in the same way as structuralist linguists could not explain the change between static linguistic systems, variationists' construction of a static community precludes an explanation of how communities can change (*cf.* also Eckert, 2000: 34).

In truth, much of this is due to variationists' focus on ordered rather than unprincipled linguistic heterogeneity, and their resultant search for 'a unit of analysis at a level of social aggregation at which it can be said that the heterogeneity is organized' (Eckert, 2000: 30). This may also explain the tendency for looking at variation and deviance as only temporary: after the introduction of an innovation (such as a postvocalic [r] or a new meaning of an older word), variationists assume there is a certain period of relative uncertainty which, though, eventually leads to a new consensus and general acceptance of the innovation (*cf.* Milroy, 1992). Alternatively, new elements or variations are described as symptomatic of another, thus far hidden subgroup in the speech community. Nevertheless, variationist sociolinguists in this way reintroduced the homogeneity they criticised in structuralist accounts of language: speech communities are seen as heterogeneous but in an orderly way, that is, with their separate parts as homogeneous(ly acting) communities that either share a consensus or are on the way back to one. In this view, variation and (political) conflict are mainly perceived between homogeneous groups, but are abstracted away or ignored within those groups (Rampton, 1998: 18; *cf.* also Ortner, 1995; Pratt, 1987).

Finding the 'authentic' speaker

These difficulties also impact on variationist methodology. As stated above, the primary interest in variationist work is to explain how linguistic systems evolve. This led to a focus on retrieving linguistic data that were as close as possible to people's everyday 'authentic' speech forms. But this search consequently weeded out most interest for exceptional and self-conscious speech forms as well as for speech from 'inauthentic' speakers such as recent outsiders or second language users. Given the ubiquity of such 'inauthentic' speakers and forms in contemporary societies, the consistent disregard of them not only illuminates the blood, sweat and tears variationist sociolinguists shed to carve out 'good data', but also that their data-construction ironically enough re-installed a homogeneous, monolingual, but now called authentic, speech community, where self-conscious and exceptional uses seemed to be viewed as noisy and irrelevant performance features one needed to ignore to hear the deeper, systematic, authentic language user (*cf.* Coupland, 2007: 25).

In addition, the search for the authentic speaker portrayed style-shifting as an inauthentic social action, and suggested that speakers at their most casual self are *not* paying attention to their speech. Both ideas are problematic, and seem to be based on the underlying idea of an isolated place where speakers are free from any exterior linguistic influences that would necessitate paying attention to speech. Obviously, it is hard to imagine that such homogeneous and a-political safe havens exist, and if they did, it remains unclear how any linguistic change can take place within them. Arguably, too, authenticity cannot be considered the intrinsic quality of anyone or any object, but needs to be viewed as a social meaning, namely as something that depends on people's judgement of a particular person, situation or object. According to Goffman, for example, it is participants' 'framing' of the situation that decides whether they see speech as 'owned' by the one who produced it, or as modulated and 'put on' (Goffman, 1971, 1974, 1981). Authenticity should not, therefore, be a condition of the research design, but is a concept that should be used in the analysis itself for speakers' judgements of each other's ways of speaking (Coupland, 2007: 25; Jaspers, 2006: 135). Clearly in that case, sociolinguists' decisions on linguistic authenticity can become the object of critical concern (Bucholtz, 2003).

Of course, this does not mean that it is useless to appeal to social norms for the explanation of language use. But I hope the above has made clear that we cannot simply import norms into sociolinguistic analysis as ready-made explanatory tools, since they stand in need of explanation themselves. Relevant questions are then: how does normativity come into being, and how does it relate to our linguistic behaviour? How do individuals relate to 'groups'? (Cameron, 1990). Up to now, Cameron points out, variationist sociolinguistics has mainly tended to endorse the principle that your language use merely 'reflects' the group or network you belong to. Alternatively, she says, some authors argue that you use your language to mark your social (group) identity. Yet, in both cases it is problematic that language use is viewed as a mere 'performance' product or the output of a primary and deeper lying, this time social structure (Cameron, 1995: 15). If we think this is undesirable, we need to focus on how the social world gets constructed in practice rather than merely acted out, and on how the social and the linguistic interact with each other.

For describing social practice, we can hardly rely on the quantitative methods in the variationist's toolkit. Although these methods help to make a probabilistic measure of the distribution of certain linguistic variables and are very useful for obtaining a general appreciation of widespread tendencies, they necessarily abstract away from particular contexts and particular interactions (Coupland, 2007). If we want to gain insight into specific social interactions and the meaning of linguistic products-in-context, context-sensitive and interpretive methods are needed, and in the following paragraph, I will briefly describe some of these. After that I will explain an important theoretical framework that I think provides interesting answers to the questions I raised above.

Social practice rather than mere variation

Since Labov's 'attention paid to speech' principle at least in its first formulations did not include the context people found themselves in, or only an extremely limited version of it (being in a formal versus a less formal context), the 1960s and 1970s already saw a number of sociolinguistic approaches, both variationist as well as otherwise, that proposed a more relational/interactional perspective on style: 'audience design' within variationist sociolinguistics, which was mainly related to the work of Allan Bell (1984), and communication accommodation theory, which was originally based in social psychology (Giles & Powesland, 1975). Both approaches addressed some of the limitations in an attention paid to speech model: they argued that people style shift in response to their audiences or co-members rather than in response to shifts in the amount of attention they pay to their speech, and they also included more naturalistic speech events besides the sociolinguistic interview (Coupland, 2007; Schilling-Estes, 2002). For example, Bell described how the same radio announcer catered for different audiences and adapted his speech style to achieve this. Yet, this approach tended to see style shifting essentially as a responsive happening, although it has become clear that many shifts are made creatively by speakers precisely to alter, strategically intervene or comment on the situation in which they participate (but see Bell, 1999). And crucially, these approaches kept leaning on quantifications that correlate linguistic choices with abstract situations, which, as we have seen, do not help describe particular speaker strategies with regard to style shifts (for a thorough discussion of these approaches, see Coupland, 2007: 54–81).

At that time, sociology saw the emergence of several interesting new perspectives such as ethnomethodology (Garfinkel, 1967), and Goffman's micro-sociology (Goffman, 1967, 1971). Without doing enough justice to them here, these authors were fundamental to several new approaches to language, such as conversation analysis (Sidnell, this volume), politeness theory (Brown & Levinson, 1987) and interactional sociolinguistics (Gumperz, 1982). A lot of research of this kind, however, refrained from making clear how local interactions link up with wider social patterns: there was an intense focus on the moment-to-moment unfolding of the interaction, but less on how the identity constructions in these interactions affected wider social patterns and conventions; as a result there was a danger of trivialising these conventions as mere resources in the interaction, or exaggerating the power of individual agents (Rampton, 2003: 53). One serious attempt at overcoming these difficulties and reconciling social conventions as well as individual agency has been offered by social constructionist theory (Giddens, 1976, 1984).

In general, social constructionism holds that people in their daily lives are neither the victims of powers they do not comprehend or understand, nor omnipotent creators of their own circumstances (cf. Varenne & McDermott, 1999). Principally, people are seen to at least partly create their (unequal, socially stratified) societies anew in their daily interactions. Hence, social constructionists suggest that how we speak is more than the mere reflection of or response to pre-existing social structures. Rather, language is one of the primary resources for social actors to actively and creatively shape and reshape their social surroundings. A crucial point is that these interactions do not take place in a vacuum: they are curbed and streamlined because social life tends to congeal and produces routines and habits that consequently constrain the range of possible new actions. Although social actors are constantly recreating the social world, they are mostly encouraged to reproduce the existing social structures. Still, these habits do not totally determine what social actors can do, and allow for actions that resist, question or negotiate with current routines. In this way, social constructionism reconciles the stability and continuity of social systems with their susceptibility to change.

A potent motive for people's tendency to reproduce social routines is that they generally trust each other to reproduce the world as they know it, since the routines in that world provide recognisable frames, identities and relations (Giddens, 1984: 60ff). Conversely, deviating from routine behaviour causes confusion and indignation: it displays a different interpretation of the interaction, and indicates that existing identities and relations cannot be taken for granted anymore. Sociologists such as Garfinkel and Goffman have described how those who (potentially) deviate or offend are therefore persistently held accountable or held in check with a variety of delicate reproaches but also less subtle social penalties (Garfinkel, 1967; Goffman, 1967, 1971). Indeed, since each person is fundamentally on his or her own, non-routine behaviour ultimately threatens the idea of an intersubjectively shared world (Giddens, 1984: xxiii). Deviations from the routine will therefore often be avoided, minimised or presented as exceptional and temporary. Of course, those in power will agree that this is necessary, whereas those with less influence will often feel ill at ease or apprehensive about deviating from the routines in which they have learned to think, feel and act.

Taken together, the concepts of routine, trust and accountability force all social actors to take into account existing habits up to the point where they nearly always reproduce them; and while they are doing that, they are always unavoidably visible for others as (dis)affiliating with these habits, and subsequently as producing an appropriate or inappropriate identity. Every local happening is thus unavoidably related to, and is seen as informed by an awareness of, established and widespread social patterns and traditions (*cf.* Rampton, 1995a: 304ff.). From a social constructionist point of view then, social norms are neither a set of predefined rules anymore nor an internalised socialisation programme, but the daily products of face-to-face interaction that also depend on this face-to-face interaction for their reproduction. Note that in this perspective normative behaviour is still creative, since it is seen as involving the construction of normative behaviour.

Although social constructionism does not really theorise beyond the idea that people use language to construct identities and relations, it may be assumed that it also applies to the form of language, namely that all language use can similarly be viewed as a question of (dis)affiliating oneself, or, as a matter of styling in relation to established linguistic routines. These routines may concern the use of the voice (pitch, tone, articulation), and lexical, grammatical and interactional choice trends, 'the repetition of which contributes to the construction of a "congealed" social and personal identity for the speaker' (Cameron, 1995: 17). Speaking is not merely acting out a linguistic programme or following rules, but at every moment actively and creatively selecting from a range of available linguistic resources that have social meanings to re-build one's social world and all the relations it contains – a creative process for which one is subsequently held accountable as to how and if one has done that. In this way, '[s]tyle is at the same time an individual and communal endeavour' (Eckert, 2000: 41; Schilling-Estes, 2002: 376). Additionally, if people are seen constantly to recreate their social and linguistic environment, this puts into perspective the 'authentic' quality of speech. Its routine production may make it seem as if it is a fixed part of our nature, but all speech is constructed, styled to the occasion. And if this is the case, Coupland indicates, also well-known concepts such as a 'dialect' have to be looked at with different eyes, rather than mere variation, dialect styles have to be seen as a form of social action, that is as instances of 'styling place' or constructing a local identity (2007: 121–125).

As already indicated, even if routines pull most actors back into line, it is possible to deviate, and people also do. Certain (linguistic and other) deviations can even come to be cherished, recognised and named (talking like a Valley girl or a hip-hopper, being a burnout at school). But they may also fade away ('Mods', 'Teddy boys', 'punks') when the actions that constitute them are not repeated anymore. In sum, whereas variationist sociolinguistics 'says that how you act depends on who you are; [social constructionism] says that who you are (and are taken to be) depends on how you act' (Cameron, 1995: 15; see also Norton, this volume).

Principles of Styling

This change in perspective has led to a number of significant changes in sociolinguistics and related fields – though many older approaches are still in place – and has piloted the idea that students of linguistic style should be concerned with the principles and processes of styling more than with the style itself (Irvine, 2001). Without claiming full comprehensiveness, I think that four key concepts in this search for principles and processes may be as follows: communities of practice, politics, perceptions and ideologies and (exceptional) performances.

Although anthropologists and ethnographers have been attending to face-to-face interaction since the 1970s (see Erickson; 1975; Gumperz, 1982; Hymes, 1972), and though also variationists have taken on ethnographic projects (Labov, 1972b; Milroy, 1980, 1992), it is fair to say that, rather than working with abstract and pre-defined communities, more and more sociolinguists are now focusing on interaction in what are called 'communities of practice' (Lave & Wenger, 1991; Wenger, 1998; see Rampton (1998) for an overview of this evolution). Communities of practice can be described as 'loosely identifiable socio-cultural collectivit[ies], with a shared set of orientations, practices and standards of competent conduct' (Eckert, 2000: 35; Ochs, 1988: 6; Rampton, 1995b: 494; see also Duff, this volume), and which are situated at a mid-level unit between individual action and large-scale social practices. Common examples of them are, among others, reading clubs, families, churches, garage bands and classrooms. The focus is thus on local meaning making and local categorisations (e.g. between appropriate and inappropriate music for the band, between 'having a laugh' in class and 'being a nerd'); and while investigating this, the attention is not so much on language only, but on all the resources that are recruited to reproduce, negotiate or resist local meanings and categorisations. It is argued, too, that the relevance and impact of pre-defined categories (such as 'ethnicity', 'race', 'social class') on local interaction cannot be presupposed, and that emphasis should be on how people make sense of and respond to such categories in their daily activity (*cf.* Rampton, 2001b: 261–262; 2006: 14ff).

These practice communities are not held to be necessarily harmonious, since, and this is the second key-concept, there has come a heightened awareness that the often-used concept of the 'consensus' or 'norm' is really the product of interaction between unequally positioned participants. This has *brought politics, hierarchy and the mechanisms of inclusion and exclusion* in the spotlight: if social conventions are the product of a struggle between unequals, this may lead to marginalisation, a denial of access and disablement for those whose behaviour is seen as deviant, unintelligible or undesirable (*cf.* Varenne & McDermott, 1999). These political relations are seen to exist not only between members of the same practice community, but also between different communities and aggregates of communities. So, communities of practice do not stand in isolation, but need to be viewed as part of a wider framework where they stand in a hierarchical relation and are evaluated in terms of that hierarchy. In this framework, certain communities may wish to pursue their difference from (what they see as) other communities, a reason why it is not very helpful to study style in isolation: without a 'standard' variety, there is no 'vernacular', and vice versa (Coupland, 2007: 21).

Third, *not only practices but also perceptions* have become an indispensable object of study. More in particular, practices and perceptions are regarded as inextricably bound up with each other. This means that social actors are viewed as the owners of images and understandings regarding the quality, function, status or 'taste' of particular forms and linguistic varieties, as well as of their relation to specific social groups and communities (*cf.* Blommaert, 2005; Duranti, 1999). A certain way of doing something may, for example, be evaluated as aloof, female, chic or tough. These images and understandings subsequently guide people in their communicative behaviour and lead to practices that mostly reproduce these images and understandings, which then again channel subsequent action (Calvet, 2006). Indeed, if sounding 'posh' (more precisely, what you understand as being 'posh') is something you wish to avoid, this will often make you want to draw on linguistic resources that steer clear of a possible interpretation by others that you speak 'posh'; you may even mock some of your friends if you find their speech verges on 'posh'. In contrast, speakers may know of regular stylings (hip hop, gothic) that they find appealing for several reasons (because they evoke images of masculinity, rebelliousness, etc.). Consequently, they might adorn themselves with some of the sartorial building blocks the style is regularly constructed with as well as appropriate its 'voice' and accompanying linguistic resources (verb inflections, specific words, pronunciation). In this frame, many researchers from a variety of linguistic subdisciplines have elucidated different kinds of such self- and other-styling (see, among others, Bucholtz, 1999; Cameron, 2000; Cameron & Kulick, 2003; Coupland, 2007; Cutler, 1999, 2008; Eckert, 2000, 2008; Pennycook, this volume; Pujolar, 2001; Rampton, 1995a, 1999, 2006; and see Section 5 in this volume).

As said above, these images and understandings depend in some measure on one's own social position, interest and access to practices (Irvine, 2001: 23–24), and they are shaped by and interact with ideologised representations of language and society that legitimise the existing social order. In the same way as norms therefore, also images of language (such as 'dialect is beautiful/ugly') can be the sites of conflict. But the insight that practices and socially positioned perceptions mutually inform each other has also had its effect on sociolinguistics as a scientific discipline. If everything must go through the filter of human perception, there is no ideology-free platform from which we can observe linguistic phenomena. This has given the impetus for much language-ideological research and critical reflection on, among others, linguists' neglect of the social world, their involvement in the construction and naming of (static) languages, varieties and speech communities, as well as the impact of these constructions on everyday language use (Calvet, 2006; Harris, 1998; Pratt, 1987; Rampton, 1998; Schieffelin *et al.*, 1998; see also McGroarty *et al.*, in this volume).

Fourth and finally, a principles and processes approach invites attention for *exceptional linguistic performances*, such as 'stylisations' (as in the second example in the introduction: 'so you are a repeater'). These were mainly ignored in traditional variationist sociolinguistics because they were considered inauthentic, caused by the observer's paradox, or unsystematic and thus irrelevant for the explanation of language change. But if even the most routine language use is essentially constructed, there is no reason why exceptional constructions should be kept out of the analysis. All the more so, given that stylisations can be extremely informative of local perceptions and routine talk. Stylisations are defined as the intensification and exaggeration of a particular, but mostly culturally familiar, way of speaking that deviates from the style that is usually expected in the current situation (Coupland, 2001; Rampton, 2001a: 85, 2006: 224–225). They are mostly produced by highly self-conscious and creative speakers, who are often emphatically artificial and invite others to interpret how their spectacular linguistic product comments on the business-on-hand and evaluate how well it does that. Both their production and reception, therefore, can give off information on local perceptions of what is routine and artificial, acceptable and strange, and of what it is that language users think they, or others, are doing as well as the (linguistic) building blocks they have available.

In addition, as a kind of social action, it is argued that stylisations are symptomatic of and therefore particularly apt for capturing some of the complexities of 'late-modern' and the so-called globalised societies (*cf.* Coupland, 2007: 30). More and more, contemporary western societies are seen as featuring a social climate characterised by high levels of geographical and also social mobility, a transnational consumer culture and techno-popular industry, and omnipresent media. As a result of this, authors have shown how attractive lifestyles are increasingly commodified and sold/bought (*cf.* Heller, 2003), while a wide variety of (linguistic) identities intensely circulate, create new opportunities and get introduced in new contexts and at other levels than where they are usually seen to operate (Blommaert, 2003). If future sociolinguistic work wants to address some of these processes, stylisation can provide a useful entry point for this.

Clearly, in order to tap into these, and to discover their effect in local communities, a much more ethnographic rather than a quantitative approach is needed. Anthropology and micro-sociology have, for this reason, gained a great deal in importance in the recent study of style and styling; and a lot of data that used to be mistrusted by variationists as caused by the observer have now come to the forefront as offering an interesting window on local perceptions of socially positioned academics/ethnographers (e.g. see the first example in the introduction).

Summary of research results and future research lines

Summing up, we have seen that:

(1) before the 1960s, linguistic variation was either discussed in historical terms, or seen as the arbitrary realisation of an underlying linguistic system; but at that time,

(2) Labov managed to show how individual style shifting echoes the different social styles in society, and that evolving patterns of linguistic variation can change the language system; however,

(3) the variationist sociolinguistics that developed from this was much more interested in linguistic rather than social change, and tended to treat social structures and norms as independent variables, although they stand in need of explanation themselves as relatively unstable social constructs;

(4) its main methodology, moreover, abstracted away from social interactions and ignored most of language users' purposeful style-shifting; but,

(5) the social-constructionist turn in the social sciences smoothed the way for a perspective on language that reconciled the regularity of linguistic behaviour with individual creativity, and suggests that all social (not just linguistic) action is inescapably (seen as) styled in relation to constraining conventions; and that therefore,

(6) future students of style should be concerned with the principles of styling more than with the style itself, or with the process rather than with the product, and redirect their focus on communities of practice, politics, perceptions and ideologies in relation to practices, and exceptional performances; finally, we saw that

(7) insight into styling processes requires close-up or ethnographic attention to speaker strategies in situations speakers themselves understand and contribute to, rather than quantification of linguistic variation over abstract situations, even if quantification may help to situate local interaction in broader social tendencies.

I have not yet looked very much at styling in relation to learning and the school. I will do so now in the next paragraphs.

Learning to Style

In contrast with widespread notions (e.g. among policy makers) that learning takes place within the individual mind, anthropologists such as Lave and Wenger see learning as social activity and so 'locat[e] learning squarely in the processes of coparticipation, not in the heads of individuals' (Hanks, 1991: 13). In truth, also Parsons' (1937) structural-functionalist theory saw learning as a social activity, but while he presumed that a process of punishment and rewards led to an internalisation of normative values, newer perspectives see socialisation as the process in which individuals are progressively treated as conscious of – and thus accountable in terms of – the normative organisation of their social surroundings (Garfinkel, 1967; Heritage, 1984: 120). Lave and Wenger's ideas echo this when they view learning as a process of negotiating meaning with other people, and as something which 'involves the construction of identities' in a broader system of relations (1991: 53). Eckert argues along the same lines when she posits that childhood is about continuously learning to be the next step older, 'a continual move beyond the childish, a need to be age-appropriate' (2000: 8). Crucially, this implies becoming more and more sensitive to the purchase of different linguistic resources on the linguistic market (*cf.* Bourdieu, 1991). When children move from childhood to adolescence and enter secondary school, they become aware of the social significance of standard speech, and learn about its value on the general linguistic market of the school in comparison to its value on the increasing amount of other markets students suddenly find themselves to be buyers on (such as the heterosexual market, the popularity market, the market of their educational trajectory and their future potential, and so on). In addition, as they become older, students view each other's behaviour increasingly as the product of a personal choice: that is as produced while being 'conscious of the normative organisation of their world' and its rewards and penalties. In other words, they locate each other's behaviour – or find themselves located – in an unequally rewarding system of meaning, and learn what the effects are of styling this way or that in terms of their clothing, language use, musical preferences, hobbies, and so on.

Learning to style can also apply to ways of teaching. Teaching involves the organisation of (power) relations between teacher and students, and these relations can be styled in different ways. Classically, the standard view of teaching consists of whole-class teacher-led instruction with, conventionally, the use of the IRE-sequence (Initiation, Response, Evaluation) as a structuring device (see Rymes, this volume); however, there are other, more student-centred styles that, for example, invite students to challenge their teachers' statements and provide convincing counter-arguments. In the same way as linguistic styles, teaching styles stand in relation to, and are regimented by, ideological representations of them and the teaching routines shaped in response to these, and both have been the object of much debate: routine 'conservative' teaching styles have been critically reviewed as to their (in)efficiency, and in the domain of language teaching alone this has given rise to significant new pedagogies (communicative language teaching, task-based learning) that urge language teachers to style their teaching accordingly; in addition, teaching styles, the communicative organisation they imply in the classroom and the learning output they are thought to generate are frequently seen as symbolic for the organisation of social conduct in society at large; they can therefore become important political emblems and nourish moral or grammar panics, which, for example, push policy makers to re-install 'old school' pedagogies and yearn for teacher-fronted rows-of-desks classes (*cf.* Cameron, 1995; Rampton, 2006: 3–12).

Notwithstanding political preferences, some teaching styles may considerably rub against pupil preferences. That is, teachers may have to learn that certain styles that work well with middle-class and high-aspiring students may be hard to sustain in schools populated by low-income, inner-city students who, given their current curriculum track, are permitted few hopes of gaining access to interesting or rewarding jobs. In schools such as the latter, students often find it difficult to produce the patient deference and passivity that is required by whole-class teacher-centred instruction and its strict regimentation of turns-at-talk. Students may, in addition, deplore their teachers' lack of mediating between knowledge of popular culture and the official curriculum (Rymes, 2003). Consequently, such students find themselves disengaging, taking issue with or disrupting classroom organisation, or parodying the lesson (see e.g. Heller, 1995). Alternatively, as some researchers have shown, students may negotiate new interactional arrangements with (some of) their teacher(s) and develop a working consensus in which at least some 'challenges to authority could be accepted as a legitimate part' of life at school (Rampton, 2006: 88). For example, in ethnographic research I have done in a working class secondary school in Antwerp (Belgium) (see Jaspers, 2005, 2006, 2008 for more details), several students engaged in a practice they themselves called 'doing ridiculous', which could involve faking co-operative enthusiasm or giving confusing or inappropriate answers that sometimes considerably delayed the rhythm and fluent organisation of what in their eyes were the 'boring' or too 'serious' situations represented by such activities as lessons or research interviews. In this way, students deviated from the traditional participation framework, but were not entirely unruly. Rather, they were dragging their feet without openly confronting, or they were stretching the rules of classroom participation while avoiding any decisive interruption and the possible consequences this could entail (*cf.* Foley, 1990; Grahame & Jardine, 1990). Interestingly, with those teachers who managed to play along, this stretching could be mutually enjoyable and lead to high amounts of on-task activity (see also Dubberley, 1993; Woods, 1976) – though it must be added that students who did not manage to 'do ridiculous' could be effectively marginalised by their peers into the wings of the classroom stage.

One of the tools with which 'doing ridiculous' was done, moreover, was by playing with language and linguistic varieties, and this brings us back to the second example I mentioned in the introduction of this chapter ('so you are a repeater'), which can inform us about the relevant symbolic markets for the students in my research. Significantly simplified and trans-lated from Dutch, the interview extract this stylisation comes from is as follows (see Jaspers (2006) for a detailed transcript and discussion):

JJ:	when do you think you will be needing Standard Dutch?
Adnan:	well, you learn to talk better, so that when you go apply for a job or something, at least you won't be making a fool of yourself
Moumir:	that was last year, uh, I could write a letter like that, I've done such – such an application letter
JJ:	yeah
Moumir:	and uh, and this year we're also going to be writing one, isn't it? isn't guys? And uhm, so uhm, yeah ...
Adnan and Mourad:	[laughing]
Mourad: [very close to the microphone:]	so you are a repeater [laughter]
Mourad:	Moumir Talhaoui, 22 years old! [laughter]
JJ:	but, but, right, when you uh, when you take a look at [etc.]

Mourad comments on Moumir's contribution to make fun of him: the latter has unexpectedly and to the amusement of his mates exposed him-self as a grade repeater (and as someone who's ashamed of it) by talking about 'last year', which Adnan and Mourad cannot of course confirm. Mourad does this in a stylised Standard Dutch, using careful pronuncia-tion, and also making sure that it will certainly be recorded by speaking directly into the table-top microphone. Interestingly, Mourad self-selects here, which is usually only the prerogative of turn-allocating authorities such as teachers and interviewers, and this naturally adds to the evalua-tive and authoritative quality of his comment. Mourad thus very aptly and humorously highlights a stigmatised school identity in a teacher-like voice. But clearly, that it was also understood in this way by the other interview participants and that it caused some appreciative laughter is only possible if Standard Dutch is conventionally associated with high-status, teachers' voices and a certain standoffishness (participants would have had to look for quite different, and much more opaque, meaning if Mourad had stylised Antwerp dialect).

No doubt one of the reasons for this conventional association is that the school these ethnic minority students (most of the ones I followed were of Moroccan descent) attended is part of a wider community called Flanders, the Dutch-speaking northern part of Belgium. Linguistically, widespread images and understandings of what Flanders should look like put a premium on Standard Dutch, and on speaking Dutch rather than ethnic minority languages. This was echoed in the school language rules ('When at school, speak Standard Dutch'), and a small variationist analysis I did bore out that these understandings had also inscribed themselves on speakers' daily speech routines: students used more standard features in formal situations, and more vernacular features on less formal occasions. Moreover, in the interviews I organised with them, students largely seemed to agree with official language policies, since they explicitly and repeatedly supported Standard Dutch as a very useful, prestigious and necessary variety, for example in potential future jobs. Yet, in daily interactions they mostly refrained from speaking Standard Dutch and dearly avoided getting identified as speaking it by their friends, and by looking at the example above, it may be possible to see why. Both this apposite stylisation as well as the interview reports suggest that these ethnic minority and working-class students have learned very well what the value is of Standard Dutch on the official market, but also what its consequent low(er) value or unappealing character is for them in non-official personal territories, given their own current educational track and related future job careers, where academic or Standard Dutch does not play a major role (cf. Bezemer & Kroon (2008) for an overview of studies focusing on standard language in multicultural classrooms).

The posh quality of Standard Dutch did not mean however, that students such as Mourad and his friends embraced the local vernacular (namely Antwerp dialect) on the rebound. Quite the opposite, since especially for ethnic minority students, Antwerp dialect generally evoked images of racism and stereotyping, which was undeniably nourished by the fact that up to a third of the Antwerp population voted for the anti-foreigner extreme right at the time of my data collection. Consequently, minority students tried to steer clear of getting identified as speaking Antwerp dialect in a non-ironical way – as if it was (to be seen as) their authentic voice – and they ridiculed those classmates who verged on doing so. Because of this, their linguistic styling often contained a mixture of dialectal and less dialectal features and so situated itself out of the reach of common identifications as 'Standard Dutch' or 'dialect': teachers tended to perceive their speech as 'better Dutch' than the dialect styling that many white students produced, whereas it was not called Standard Dutch either.

Of course, minority students found it very amusing to be called better speakers of Dutch than their white classmates, and they also capitalised on this by openly stigmatising these white classmates' 'broad' dialect, which has low value in the standard language-dominated symbolic hierarchy (*cf.* Jaspers, 2005: 289–291). In other words, Standard Dutch and Antwerp dialect, and their stereotypical speakers, served as points of negative reference (or were considered spoken by those who were 'higher' and 'lower' on the symbolic ladder, respectively) that helped define, and thus style, 'ordinary' linguistic behaviour for these minority speakers (cf. Rampton, 1995b: 499). Paradoxically, on other occasions Antwerp dialect features could serve to construct a tough or assertive masculine identity on the heterosexual market, while the same dialect features could also be used to style speech in such a way that it suggested a born-and-bred Antwerp identity in contrast with a possible identification as 'immigrant'.

Thus, rather than producing one variety on account of their belonging to an ethnic minority group, these students can be described as trying to come to grips with several conflicting linguistic market principles, where they, through being held accountable by others and learning about their own possibilities and limitations, learn how to style competently in different ways.

Conclusion

In this chapter, I have tried to explain that using linguistic features and varieties, as well as wearing pieces of clothing or having specific haircuts, are a form of social practice rather than mere variation. These social practices, moreover, never stand on their own, but are always part of a hierarchical web of meanings where using a linguistic feature or wearing a specific sweater inevitably has social effects. These effects may range from being barely noticed (when actions are designed not to stand out from the ordinary) to being applauded or booed (when actions are thought to stand out), and being ostracised or declared (learning) disabled (when actions are thought inarticulate or dangerous). Given the social hierarchy they come to learn their own position in, social actors may feel drawn to (the promises and identities couched in) certain styles rather than others, up to the point that for a fair number of people, learning the standard language style, or a dominant language, may be a daunting social hurdle. Likewise, teacher-centred instructional styles may become a stake in local social struggle if they marginalise student voices in those classrooms where the products of less successful action-and-social effect chains wash up.

If styling, and evaluating each other as styling, is what we all do in multidimensional ways everyday, more emphasis should probably go to the principles of styling, their dynamic 'contrasts and relationships' (Irvine, 2001: 42), rather than on trying to determine the specific characteristics of a (i.e. one) resultant style. An awareness of these principles may help to develop a sensitivity for how classroom interaction engages with and responds to the world beyond school walls, and may invite (language) teachers to help their students become critical observers of the rewards and penalties that are attributed to ways of doing in the different social contexts and communities they are seen to belong to or hope to become a part of.

Suggestions for further reading

Coupland, N. (2007) *Style. Language Variation and Identity*. Cambridge: Cambridge University Press.
In this recent and very readable analysis of style and styling, Coupland draws on both classic sociolinguistic and newer anthropological approaches of style in language, not to mention his own decades-long work, to situate regular and exceptional linguistic variation firmly into social practice.

Eckert, P. and Rickford, J.R. (eds) (2001) *Style and Sociolinguistic Variation*. Cambridge: Cambridge University Press.
This collection gives the floor to a lively debate between anthropological approaches to style and all sorts of variationist treatments (Labovian, audience design, functionalism). Papers are also followed by commentaries from other style experts, contributing to a stimulating and wide-ranging cross-displicinary exchange of ideas.

Labov, W. (1972a) *Sociolinguistic Patterns*. Philadelphia: University of Philadelphia Press.
This book remains a landmark for sociolinguistics. It contains Labov's major findings, hypotheses, definitions and methodology. A must-read and eloquent example for any student of sociolinguistics.

Rampton, B. (ed.) (1999) *Styling the Other*. Special issue of *Journal of Sociolinguistics*, 3 (4).
Authors in this collection discuss linguistic styling based on a variety of empirical data across the globe, extending the support for Rampton's work on 'crossing', namely the practice of using voices or varieties that are not usually seen to belong to you. Readers will find insightful treatments of how speakers aspire to, appropriate or challenge others' voices and cross traditional linguistic boundaries.

Rampton, B. (2006) *Language in Late Modernity. Interaction in an Urban School*. Cambridge: Cambridge University Press.
This book provides a unique combination of empirical depth and theoretical width in describing adolescent linguistic practices in relation to popular culture, changing communicative trends, foreign language teaching and the construction of social class through playful and less playful linguistic styling of Cockney and 'posh' English.

References

Bell, A. (1984) Language style as audience design. *Language in Society* 13, 145–204.
Bell, A. (1999) Styling the other to define the self: A study in New Zealand identity making. *Journal of Sociolinguistics* 3 (4), 523–541.
Bezemer, J. and Kroon S. (2008) Teachers' practical knowledge, standard language and multicultural classrooms. In M. Martin-Jones, A.M. de Mejia and

N.H. Hornberger (eds) *Encyclopedia of Language and Education* (2nd edn), *Volume 3: Discourse and Education* (pp. 225–236). New York: Springer Science + Business Media LLC.

Blommaert, J. (2003) Commentary: A sociolinguistics of globalization. *Journal of Sociolinguistics* 7 (4), 607–623.

Blommaert, J. (2005) *Discourse. A Critical Introduction.* Cambridge: Cambridge University Press.

Bourdieu, P. (1991) *Language and Symbolic Power.* Cambridge: Polity Press.

Brown, P. and Levinson S. (1987) *Politeness.* Cambridge: Cambridge University Press.

Bucholtz, M. (1999) You da man. Narrating the racial other in the production of white masculinity. *Journal of Sociolinguistics* 3 (4), 443–460.

Bucholtz, M. (2003) Sociolinguistic nostalgia and the authentication of identity. *Journal of Sociolinguistics* 7 (3), 398–416.

Calvet, L-J. (2006) *Towards an Ecology of World Languages.* Cambridge: Polity Press.

Cameron, D. (1990) Demythologizing sociolinguistics: Why language does not reflect society. In J.E. Joseph and T.J. Taylor (eds) *Ideologies of Language* (pp. 79–93). London: Routledge.

Cameron, D. (1995) *Verbal Hygiene.* London: Routledge.

Cameron, D. (2000) *Good to Talk? Living and Working in a Communication Culture.* London: Sage.

Cameron, D. and Kulick, D. (2003) *Language and Sexuality.* Cambridge: Cambridge University Press.

Chomsky, N. (1965) *Aspects of the Theory of Syntax.* Cambridge, MA: MIT.

Coupland, N. (2001) Dialect stylization in radio talk. *Language in Society* 30 (3), 345–375.

Coupland, N. (2007) *Style. Language Variation and Identity.* Cambridge: Cambridge University Press.

Cutler, C. (1999) Yorkville crossing. White teens, hip hop and African American English. *Journal of Sociolinguistics* 3 (4), 428–442.

Cutler, C. (2008) Brooklyn style: Hip-hop markers and racial affiliation among European immigrants in New York City. *International Journal of Bilingualism* 12 (1/2), 7–24.

de Saussure, F. (1972) *Cours de Linguistique Générale.* Paris: Payot.

Dorian, N. (1994) Varieties of variation in a very small place: Social homogeneity, prestige norms, and linguistic variation. *Language* 70, 631–696.

Dubberley, W.S. (1993) Humor as resistance. In P. Woods and M. Hammersley (eds) *Gender and Ethnicity in School. Ethnographic Accounts* (pp. 75–94). London: Routledge.

Duranti, A. (1999) *Anthropological Linguistics.* Cambridge: Cambridge University Press.

Eckert, P. (2000) *Linguistic Variation as Social Practice.* Oxford: Blackwell.

Eckert, P. (2008) Where do ethnolects stop? *International Journal of Bilingualism* 12 (1/2), 25–42.

Eckert, P. and Rickford, J.R. (eds) (2001) *Style and Sociolinguistic Variation.* Cambridge: Cambridge University Press.

Erickson, F. (1975) Gatekeeping and the melting pot: Interaction in counselling encounters. *Harvard Educational Review* 45, 44–70.

Foley, D. (1990) *Learning Capitalist Culture. Deep in the Heart of Tejas.* Philadelphia: University of Pennsylvania Press.

Gal, S. and Irvine, J. (1995) The boundaries of languages and disciplines: How ideologies construct difference. *Social Research* 62 (4), 967–1002.

Garfinkel, H. (1967) *Studies in Ethnomethodology*. Englewood Cliffs, NJ: Prentice-Hall.

Giddens, A. (1976) *New Rules of Sociological Method. A Positive Critique of Interpretative Sociologies*. London: Hutchinson.

Giddens, A. (1984) *The Constitution of Society. Outline of the Theory of Structuration*. Cambridge: Polity Press.

Giles, H. and Powesland, P. (1975) *Speech Style and Social Evaluation*. London: Academic Press.

Goffman, E. (1967) *Interaction Ritual. Essays on Face-to-Face Behaviour*. London: Penguin.

Goffman, E. (1971) *Relations in Public. Microstudies of the Public Order*. New York: Basic Books.

Goffman, E. (1974) *Frame Analysis. An Essay on the Organization of Experience*. Boston: Northeastern University Press.

Goffman, E. (1981) *Forms of Talk*. Philadelphia: University of Pennsylvania Press.

Grahame, P.R. and Jardine, D.W. (1990) Deviance, resistance and play. A study in the communicative organization of trouble in class. *Curriculum Inquiry* 20 (3), 283–304.

Gumperz, J. (1982) *Discourse Strategies*. Cambridge: Cambridge University Press.

Hanks, W.F. (1991) Foreword. In J. Lave and E. Wenger (eds) *Situated Learning. Legitimate Peripheral Participation* (pp. 13–24). Cambridge: Cambridge University Press.

Harris, R. (1998) *Introduction to Integrational Linguistics*. Oxford: Pergamon.

Heller, M. (1995) Language choice, social institutions and symbolic domination. *Language in Society* 24 (3), 373–405.

Heller, M. (2003) Globalisation, the new economy and the commodification of language and identity. *Journal of Sociolinguistics* 7 (4), 473–492.

Heritage, J. (1984) *Garfinkel and Ethnomethodology*. Oxford: Blackwell.

Hudson, R.A. (1996) *Sociolinguistics*. Cambridge: Cambridge University Press.

Hymes, D. (1972) On communicative competence. In J. Pride and J. Holmes (eds) *Sociolinguistics* (pp. 269–293). London: Penguin.

Irvine, J. (2001) 'Style' as distinctiveness. The culture and ideology of linguistic differentiation. In P. Eckert and J.R. Rickford (eds) *Style and Sociolinguistic Variation* (pp. 21–43). Cambridge: Cambridge University Press.

Jaspers, J. (2005) Linguistic sabotage in a context of monolingualism and standardization. *Language and Communication* 25 (3), 279–297.

Jaspers, J. (2006) Stylising Standard Dutch by Moroccan boys in Antwerp. *Linguistics and Education* 17 (2), 131–156.

Jaspers, J. (2008) Problematizing ethnolects. Naming linguistic practices in an Antwerp secondary school. *International Journal of Bilingualism* 12 (1/2), 85–103.

Labov, W. (1966) *The Social Stratification of English in New York City*. Washington, DC: Center for Applied Linguistics.

Labov, W. (1972a) *Sociolinguistic Patterns*. Philadelphia: University of Philadelphia Press.

Labov, W. (1972b) *Language in the Inner City*. Oxford: Blackwell.

Labov, W. (1975) *What is a Linguistic Fact*. Lisse: The Peter De Ridder Press.

Labov, W. (1994) *Principles of Linguistic Change. Volume 1: Internal Factors*. Oxford: Blackwell.

Lave, J. and Wenger, E. (1991) *Situated Learning. Legitimate Peripheral Participation*. Cambridge: Cambridge University Press.

Meeuwis, M. and Brisard, F. (1993) *Time and the Diagnosis of Language Change*. Antwerp Papers in Linguistics, 72, Antwerp.

Milroy, L. (1980) *Language and Social Networks*. Oxford: Blackwell.

Milroy, J. (1992) *Linguistic Variation and Change. On the Sociolinguistics of English*. Oxford and Cambridge, MA: Blackwell.

Ochs, E. (1988) *Culture and Language Development*. Cambridge: Cambridge University Press.

Ortner, S.B. (1995) Resistance and the problem of ethnographic refusal. *Comparative Studies in Society and History*, 37 (1), 173–193.

Parsons, T. (1937) *The Structure of Social Action*. New York: McGraw-Hill.

Pratt, M.L. (1987) Linguistic utopias. In N. Fabb, D. Attridge, A. Durant and C. MacCabe (eds) *The Linguistics of Writing* (pp. 48–66). Manchester: Manchester University Press.

Pujolar, J. (2001) *Gender, Heteroglossia and Power. A Sociolinguistic Study of Youth Culture*. Berlin and New York: Mouton de Gruyter.

Rampton, B. (1995a) *Crossing. Language and Ethnicity among Adolescents*. London: Longman.

Rampton, B. (1995b) Language crossing and the problematisation of ethnicity and socialisation. *Pragmatics* 5 (4), 485–513.

Rampton, B. (1998) Speech community. In J. Verschueren, J.-Ö. Ostman, J. Blommaert and C. Bulcaen (eds) *Handbook of Pragmatics*. Amsterdam/Philadelphia: John Benjamins.

Rampton, B. (1999) Styling the other. Introduction. *Journal of Sociolinguistics* 3 (4), 421–427.

Rampton, B. (2001a) Critique in interaction. *Critique of Anthropology* 21 (1), 83–107.

Rampton, B. (2001b) Language crossing, cross-talk and cross-disciplinarity in socio-linguistics. In N. Coupland, S. Sarangi and C. Candlin (eds) *Sociolinguistics and Social Theory* (pp. 261–296). London: Longman.

Rampton, B. (2003) Hegemony, social class, and stylisation. *Pragmatics* 13 (1), 49–83.

Rampton, B. (2006) *Language in Late Modernity. Interaction in an Urban School*. Cambridge: Cambridge University Press.

Rickford, J.R. and Eckert, P. (2001) Introduction. In P. Eckert and J.R. Rickford (eds) *Style and Sociolinguistic Variation* (pp. 1–18). Cambridge: Cambridge University Press.

Rymes, B. (2003) Contrasting zones of comfortable competence: popular culture in a phonics lesson. *Linguistics and Education* 14, 321–335.

Schieffelin, B., Woolard, K. and P. Kroskrity (eds) (1998) *Language Ideologies. Practice and Theory*. New York: Oxford University Press.

Schilling-Estes, N. (2002) Investigating stylistic variation. In J.K. Chambers, P. Trudgill and N. Schilling-Estes (eds) *The Handbook of Language Variation and Change* (pp. 375–401). Oxford: Blackwell.

Trudgill, P. (1983) *Sociolinguistics. An Introduction to Language and Society*. Harmondsworth: Penguin.

Varenne, H. and McDermott, R. (1999) *Successful Failure. The School America Builds*. Boulder: Westview Press.

Wenger, E. (1998) *Communities of Practice. Learning, Meaning and Identity*. Cambridge: Cambridge University Press.

Williams, G. (1992) *Sociolinguistics. A Sociological Critique*. London: Routledge.

Woods, P. (1976) Having a laugh, an antidote to schooling. In M. Hammersley and P. Woods (eds) *The Process of Schooling* (pp. 178–187). London: Routledge.

Chapter 8
Critical Language Awareness

H. SAMY ALIM

This chapter focuses on *critical language awareness* (CLA), a growing area of specialization in sociolinguistics with direct implications for language education. In this chapter, I briefly outline the theoretical underpinnings of CLA and focus more concretely on the educational applications of the field. I begin with a commentary about the political and media discourse around Barack Obama's language as a means to illustrate the perspective of CLA, or what it means to be 'critical'. I will further illustrate the critical approach with an in-depth examination of a dialogue with a well-meaning teacher in an effort to highlight the centrality of ideology in CLA. I will then focus my attention on some classroom applications of CLA as well as the implications for sociolinguists and educators. Finally, we will revisit the conversation with the well-meaning teacher in order to take a critical, reflexive look at sociolinguistics by making connections between race, gender, sexuality and language use. The chapter concludes by envisioning a new approach to language education and social transformation.

'I Love Barack Obama – He's Just So Articulate!': What It Means to be 'Critical'

Critical language study, according to Fairclough (1992: 7), 'highlights how language conventions and language practices are invested with power relations and ideological processes which people are often unaware of'. Throughout the chapter, this central point will be highlighted, as it is a core component of CLA. This section illustrates what it means to adopt a 'critical' view, or as Freire (1985) once put it, the perspective of someone 'who questions, who doubts, who investigates, and who wants to illuminate the very life we live', by examining some widely taken-for-granted linguistic conventions and beliefs in the discourse about the US President Barack Obama.

The historic 2008 US presidential election generated and continues to generate an incredible amount of discourse on race and race relations in the United States. The majority of this discourse has focused on Barack Obama, the nation's first African–American president, and his incredibly 'gifted' speaking abilities. Recently, I received a phone call from a journalist writing for one of the more progressive internet news websites, asking if I would comment on the 'growing trend' of Black parents and educators wanting their children, not to 'be like Mike', but rather to 'talk like Barack', that is 'to speak standard English'. After speaking with the journalist for only a few minutes, she demonstrated a clear awareness that Barack Obama was a skilled speaker and it was very clear that she was well-intentioned and genuinely concerned about the educational plight of African–American students.

However, the journalist was unaware of several things. One, it is questionable whether or not this was even a 'growing trend'. In fact, in my own work I have found that most parents want their children to be fluent in multiple language varieties, including 'Black Language' *and* 'standard English' [see also Smitherman (1990) for multilingualism in Black American communities]. Two, she must have been unaware that she used the word 'articulate' to describe Barack Obama about a dozen times in the half-hour interview, and that it was often accompanied by other adjectives such as 'good' and 'upstanding'. Three, she finally recognized that she held a strong desire and hope that 'Barack Obama's public speaking abilities [would] influence African Americans to move away from African American English' (personal communication, 9 April 2009). Rather than seeking a linguist to endorse her own views, I suggested to her that she might consider that members of the Black community that I study certainly do respect President Obama for his mastery of 'standard English', but he is more often admired as a linguistic role model for his ability to seamlessly shift in and out of different ways of speaking, rather than for abandoning a language variety used in many Black American communities as an identity resource and a symbol of solidarity. Needless to say, *that* story never made it to print.

Other well-intentioned observers might ask the following set of questions: So, what's wrong with all of this? What's wrong with calling someone 'articulate'? What's wrong with wanting Black children to move away from 'African American English' when their language is socially and economically handicapping them? A critical linguist might ask a different set of questions: Why is it that the adjective 'articulate' is used to most often to refer to Black speakers? By the same token, how come skilled White speakers are not as frequently referred to as 'articulate'? What does this pattern of usage reveal about our underlying beliefs as a society about the way Black Americans speak? Why did Vice President Biden's comments about Barack Obama ('He's the first mainstream African American who is articulate and bright and clean and a nice-looking guy', http://www.

cnn.com/2007/POLITICS/01/31/biden.obama/) and former President George Bush's comments ('He's an attractive guy. He's articulate', http:// www.freerepublic.com/focus/f-bloggers/1781517/posts) incite uproar from members of the Black community?

The frequent juxtaposition of 'articulate' with other adjectives such as 'clean', 'bright', 'attractive' and 'good' suggests that, within a worldview that (un)consciously privileges Whiteness, Blackness is expected to be 'unclean', 'dull', 'unattractive', 'bad', and yes, 'inarticulate' (or as Black comedian Chris Rock succinctly put it, 'You only ever call somebody "articulate" when you expect them to be stupid!'). From this worldview, it is rare when you find 'one of them' that is clean, nice-looking, attractive and articulate, and thus, it is something to remark upon; otherwise, it would be taken-for-granted as the norm.

Another question that might arise is: 'Well, doesn't the media refer to White candidates as "articulate" as well?' Yes, in fact, they do. But interestingly enough, they tend to do so when the candidate is from the South or represents a combination of other marginalized social identities such as being 'working-class' and/or 'a woman'. This adjective was applied generously to John Edwards with the implicit meaning that 'He's not like those *other* Southerners who can't talk right', revealing ideologies of language that are loaded with regional stereotypes that depict Southerners as stupid, lazy and slow (just like Obama's not like those *other* Blacks who can't speak English correctly). The critical linguist might also go beyond racially differentiated patterns of use to ask about factors such as age. Do we use 'articulate' more often to describe children than adults? If so, what does that mean? The critical linguist would then also ask about the immediate interactional context of the comments, the broader social and political contexts, including US racial politics, the historical relations that position Blacks as ignorant, lazy speakers of English, along with the historical use of 'articulate' to describe 'gifted' Black speakers, as well as the position of 'Black Language' *vis-à-vis* 'standard English' in relation to and within institutions such as schools. And the list of questions is endless.[1]

Many observers were surprised that seemingly harmless statements like, 'I love Barack Obama – he's just *so* articulate!' would send some Black folks into a furor over the implicit and patronizing racist assumptions of the speaker, and have White folks 'walking-on-eggshells' when giving their Black friends and colleagues what they believe to be compliments? To think like a critical linguist is to assume, from the start, that language is never neutral, never simply a 'means of communication'. It is to take for granted that language use is always loaded with issues of power, hierarchy and dominance, as well as contestation, resistance and transformation. It is to seek to uncover society's contradictions and to reveal the many taken-for-granted assumptions and ideologies of race, class, gender, sexuality, nationality, etc., that undergird our actions, as well as how these ideologies intersect and are related to language. It is to draw unexpected connections between seemingly different topics, situations, groups, histories or identities. It is to recognize that these unexpected connections cannot be fully understood without considering multiple layers of context, such as the immediate sociolinguistic context, the broader sociopolitical context and the historical context, all in terms of relations to power. Finally, and perhaps most importantly, it is not only *to think* about these issues of power, but it is also *to do* something about them.

'But Here That's Never Acceptable': Uncovering the Language Ideologies of Well-meaning Teachers

In this section, I relate the concept of critical language study directly to its educational applications. This dialogue with a well-meaning teacher describes a difficult educational situation that many teachers are faced with on a regular basis. While this teacher is well-intentioned, we will see how a close examination of her speech reveals her beliefs about her students' language (her language ideologies, see McGroarty, this volume) and other assumptions. The main point to keep in mind throughout this section, and it is one of the primary reasons why CLA approaches are needed, is best stated by Corson (1999: 140–141): 'If schools uncritically present the standard variety of English as more appropriate and correct than other varieties of English, and better than other languages, then this devalues the other languages and varieties because inevitably students begin to see them [and I would add, *themselves*] as having a lesser role in places like schools where prestige really matters'.

Before the dialogue, it is necessary to provide a brief description of the background and context. This research was conducted as part of an ongoing ethnographic and sociolinguistic study of the language and linguistic practices of students at Haven High, an ethnically, racially and linguistically diverse high school located in a working-class 2.5 square-mile suburb in the San Francisco Bay Area of about 33,000 people (see full study in Alim, 2004a). At the time of the study, the high school was approximately 70% Black, 25% Latino and 5% Indian American and Pacific Islander. The study is based on approximately two years of fieldwork as a teacher-researcher (teaching my own courses on language and communication) and an additional year and a half beyond the teaching experience as a regular participant in the community's most (in)famous barbershop. I continue to work in this same community today.

While it is impossible to do justice to the community context in this chapter, it is helpful to note that this suburb is one of the California's growing number of minority–majority 'cities of color' (Camarillo, 2007). The community was once a thriving Black community that led the nation in

Black consciousness and nationalism, establishing the nation's only independent Black pre-school through college educational system in the 1960s and 1970s. Since the government's forced closure of the city's only high school in the 1970s, the Black community has experienced an increasing sense of displacement in what was once known as 'a Black city', as the Latino population rises and Whites begin to move in slowly. For two decades, the community did not have a high school and Black students experienced a 65% drop-out rate in the schools of the neighboring suburbs, all of which were predominantly White and upper-middle class. The gentrification of the community by White real estate developers is directly linked to educational concerns, since the city's relatively new 28-acre shopping plaza (and expensive hotels) stands on the grounds of the former high school (similar situations are occurring nationwide, of course).

For the purposes of this chapter, I will not spend time legitimizing the value of Black language. There are plenty of works that clearly demonstrate the systematic and rule-governed nature of Black language (Alim, 2004a; Baugh, 1983; Green, 2001; Rickford, 1999), so I will not repeat that information here. What will be important for our analysis below is recognizing that it is the language and communicative norms of those in power, in any society, that tend to be labeled as 'standard', 'official', 'appropriate', 'normal', 'respectful', and so on. This fact often goes unrecognized, particularly by members of the dominant group. This dialogue with a teacher from Haven High serves as an entry point to our discussion of how Black Language (and its speakers) are viewed in American educational institutions. We enter this conversation as the teacher is describing the 'communication' goals of the school, and the language and communicative behavior of her Black students:

Teacher: They [Haven High] have a lot of presentation standards, so like this list of, you know, what you *should* be doing when you're having like an oral presentation – like you should speak slowly, speak loudly, speak clearly, make eye contact, use body language, those kinds of things, and it's all written out into a rubric, so when the kids have a presentation, you grade on each element. And so, I mean, in that sense, they've worked with developing communication. I mean, I think the thing that teachers work with, or combat the most at Haven High, is definitely like issues with standard English versus vernacular English. Um, like, if there was like one of the *few* goals I had this year was to get kids to stop sayin, um, 'he was, she was ...'

Alim: They was?

T: 'They was. We be'. Like, those kinds of things and so we spent a lot of time working with that and like recognizing,

'Okay, when you're with your friends you can say *whatever you want* but ... this is the way it is. I'm sorry, but that's just the way'. And they're like, 'Well, you know, it doesn't make sense to me. This sounds right'. 'She was'. Like, and that's just what they've been used to and it's just ...

A: Well, 'she was' is right, right? You mean, like, 'They was'?

T: 'They was'.

A: And 'we was' and that kinda thing ...

T: Yeah, 'we was'. Everything is just 'was'.

A: [Laughter] ...

T: And like, just trying to help them to be able to differentiate between what's acceptable ... There's a lot of 'ain't', 'they was', 'we ain't not ...'

A: [Laughter] ...

T: And they can't codeswitch that well ...

A: Uh-huh ...

T: Um, and I have to say it's kind of disheartening because like despite *all* that time that's been spent focusing on grammar, like, I don't really see it having helped enormously. Like, if I stop them in class and they're like, you know, 'The Europeans, they was really blah-de-blah ...' and I'd be like, 'Oh, they *was*?' And they'd be like, 'they were', like they'll correct themselves, but it's not to the point where it's natural ... They're like, 'Why does it matter?'

A: 'You knew what I said, right?'

T: Yeah ... I'm not sure they understand *why* it's necessary ...

A: Do you have any other ideas about language at the school, like maybe the way the kids speak to themselves versus the way they speak in class, or do you notice ...

T: Well, I mean, of course, they're not gonna be as free as when they're speaking to each other when they're speaking to me. I mean, I guess the only thing is not so much spoken language as it's like unspoken language, like tone, like a lot of attention is paid to like tone and body language, in terms of respectful attitudes ... For a lot of kids, they don't see the difference. They're like [loud voice and direct speech] 'Yeah, I just asked you to give me my grade. Like, what's the big deal?' And I'm like, 'You just ordered me. I mean, you talked to me like that'. Like, it's like, [loud again] 'You didn't give me a grade!' like that, it's very abrasive, but they don't realize that it's abrasive. And so, I mean, it's just like, I guess, teaching them like the nuances of like when you're talking with people, what's appropriate? Should you be sitting up, or should you be kinda be leaning over [and she leans in her chair] ...

A: [Laughter] ...

T: Like that your body language and your facial features like speak just as loudly if not *more* loudly than what you *actually* say ... I mean, just even bringing awareness to that, like, it's upsetting to them and it's like shocking to them that we'll comment on that, like, maybe their parents let them get away with that and speak to them that way and having to be like, 'Hey, you know what, like, maybe your parents let you, but here that's never acceptable'. Like, there's just so many – I mean, thinking about it, it's just, it's asking a lot of them to do, not only to speak standard English but to know all these other like smaller nuances that they've never experienced before and never had to think about. Like, it's probably on some level pretty overwhelming to them to have to deal with all of these things at once. Because, I mean, their parents say 'they was ...'

A: Yeah, is there any talk about what they're being expected to do, and what they do ordinarily, in the community, in the home, or anything?

T: Um, I mean, not officially or regularly, but I'll always be like, 'I know you might speak this way at home, but in an academic setting, or if you're interviewing for a job, or if you're applying to college, and you talk to someone like that, they will like not even give you the time of day ...'

A: Do they ever ask why?

T: Yeah, they're just like, you know, 'Why?' and I'm like, 'I don't know!' [Laughter!] 'You know, that's just the way that it is! You have to learn how to play the game guys! I'm sorry'.

A: Right, and I can see that being such an inadequate answer for a student who doesn't care about 'they was' or 'they were', being like, 'What's the difference? What's the big deal? Like what's the overall picture?'

T: Right, and I don't know how to provide that ...

A: Yeah ...

After years of working as a teacher-researcher in Philadelphia and San Francisco Bay Area schools, I am often struck by how remarkably consistent teachers' language ideologies are, particularly regarding the language of their Black students. Much like the journalist at the start of this chapter, many teachers consistently see the language of their Black students as something to eradicate, even the most well-meaning of us. In fact, this particular teacher is wholeheartedly committed to seeing as many of her students attend college as possible. And when she states, 'I have to say it's kind of disheartening because like despite *all* the time that's been spent focusing on grammar, like, I don't really see it as having helped enormously', one gets the impression that she is actually disheartened and saddened by her lack of success.

What many teachers are probably not aware of is how their genuine concern can be interpreted as enacting Whiteness and subscribing to an ideology of linguistic supremacy (elevating one particular language variety over all others) within a system of daily cultural combat. It is revealing that the teacher describes the language of her Black students as the thing that teachers at Haven High '*combat* the most'. In fact, her attempt to eradicate the language pattern of her Black students has been 'one of the *few* goals' she has had all years. The teacher not only works to stamp out her students' language, but she also responds negatively to what she calls 'unspoken language', or the students' 'tone'. Black students and their ways of speaking are described with adjectives like 'abrasive' and not 'respectful'. This attribution of negative characteristics due to cultural differences has been well documented in studies of intercultural communication (Gumperz, 1982a, 1982b).

In the conversation, the teacher notes her students' failure to speak 'standard English', while her own speech is only marginally 'standard'. As many readers have probably already noted to themselves, the teacher's speech might be classified as 'Valley Girl Talk' (Fought, 2006), notable for, among other features, 'like' multiple instances of 'like' using the word 'like' in the same sentence! ('And so, I mean, it's just *like*, I guess, teaching them *like* the nuances of *like* when you're talking with people, what's appropriate?'). Further, when the teacher illustrates her students' inability to speak 'standard English' by emphasizing what linguists refer to as *the generalization of* was *to use with plural and second person subjects* (Wolfram, 1993), not only does she erroneously point out 'he was' and 'she was' as cases of Black Language (this is actually found in all varieties of English) and imply that the variety has a random system of negation ('we ain't not', on the other hand, *ain't* found in Black Language or any other variety), but she is clearly unaware of the stylistic sensitivity in the use of *was* and *were*. When the teacher says, rather exasperatedly, 'Everything is just "was"', she is not recognizing the subtle alternation of *was* and *were* that Black speakers employ across various contextual and situational factors, including the race and age of the person with whom they are speaking. In fact, the teacher goes as far as to say that her Black students can't 'codeswitch', something that is clearly refuted in the larger study (Alim, 2004a).

Toward the end of the conversation, the teacher says that she explains to her students that she knows they might 'talk this way at home, but in an academic setting, or if you're interviewing for a job, or if you're applying to college, and you talk to someone like that, they will like not even give you the time of day'. Sensing that this might be an inadequate answer for her more critical students, I probe further and ask if her students ever ask *why* particular varieties are associated with power, prestige and upward mobility while *their* variety is not. The teacher's answer to them is a frustrated and apologetic: 'I don't know! You know, that's just the way it is! You have to learn how to play the game guys! I'm sorry'. The students, as all speakers do, see their language as intimately connected to who they are. If their language is not good enough for society, then the logical connection to be drawn is that neither are they. Students continue to resist the imposition of what are essentially White ways of speaking while the teacher's traditional focus on grammar (without a critical examination of the social, cultural, and political forces at play in language use) continues to fall short of the mark. In terms of helping her students think more critically about language, she concludes by admitting that she honestly does not know 'how to provide that'.

This well-meaning teacher is indeed in a tough situation. Despite loving her students and genuinely wanting the best for them, and 'despite *all* that time that's been spent focusing on grammar', she, like many of her colleagues, continues to feel as if she has failed her Black students. Or as one teacher put it, capturing the frustration that many teachers feel at not being able to resolve the tensions that accompany the politics of language teaching, 'I feel like I'm banging my head against the wall with this standard English thing'. As social demographics continue to shift and classrooms become more ethnically and linguistically complex (Ball, 2009), what is needed is a revisioning of language education, one that radically departs from the traditional approaches which teachers often find limiting.

The rest of this chapter focuses heavily on pedagogical approaches that might help teachers provide answers to their students' critical questions about language and to work through the tensions around language teaching by confronting them head on with a CLA approach. Working as a teacher-researcher in Haven High, and as a critical linguist, it was not enough for me to uncover teacher's ideologies about the language of their students. CLA, at least as I have fashioned it here, requires the analyst to engage the community in search of solutions to their expressed concerns. Working with the school, I was given the opportunity to design my own pedagogy, some of which I share below, and most of which is constantly shifting and evolving. I want to emphasize that this is not a 'one size fits all' curriculum; if critical pedagogies are to be relevant and effective, they must be locally situated and constantly negotiated.

Applying CLA

In many respects, the specific critical pedagogy presented below draws from the work of Norman Fairclough and colleagues (1995) and Alastair Pennycook's writings on *critical applied linguistics* (2001). Although these approaches differ in some important ways, both critically view educational institutions as designed to teach citizens about the current sociolinguistic order of things without challenging that order. This view of education interrogates the dominating discourse on language and literacy and foregrounds the examination and interconnectedness of identities, ideologies, histories/herstories and the hierarchical nature of power relations between groups. Importantly, as the Obama example and the conversation with the well-meaning teacher have demonstrated, this approach is not concerned with the study of decontextualized language but rather with the analysis of 'opaque and transparent structural relationships of dominance, discrimination, power and control as manifested in language' (Wodak, 1995) and how these relationships are performed and contested (Pennycook, 2004).

This approach also draws on a Freireian critical pedagogy (Freire, 1970) of language that educates linguistically profiled and marginalized students about how language is used and, importantly, how language can be used against them. Questions central to the overall project are: 'How can language be used to maintain, reinforce, and perpetuate existing power relations?' And, conversely, 'How can language be used to resist, redefine and possibly reverse these relations?' This approach engages youth in the process of consciousness-raising, that is the process of actively becoming aware of one's own position in the world and what to do about it (as in the Black, Chicana/o, Women's and LGBT Liberation movements). By learning about the full scope of their language use and how language can actually be used against them (Baugh, 2003; Bertrand & Mullainathan, 2003), students become more conscious of their communicative behavior and the ways by which they can transform the conditions under which they live.

As Reagan (2006) and others have critiqued CLA for being in danger of becoming an overly theorized and under-applied enterprise, the remainder of this chapter will focus specifically on pedagogical approaches that empower diverse students. Although each unit can be described at much greater length, the following sections introduce the main pedagogical initiatives and provide sample exercises. This pedagogical framework furthers what Gutierrez (2005) refers to as 'sociocritical literacy' by providing a progression of language learning experiences that illustrate a developmental approach, one that brings a theoretically grounded and socioculturally rich pedagogy alive. Moreover, as Morrell (2004) has shown, engaging students in critical research relating to popular culture can be particularly effective, especially when deep and meaningful learning is too often preserved for more privileged others. CLA approaches connect meaningfully with local contexts by viewing local cultures and language practices as powerful resources for learning. In the case of Haven High, the dominant youth culture was heavily influenced by Hip Hop Culture, music and language, as seen in the next several subsections.

'That's Real Talk': Developing an awareness of sociolinguistic variation

'Real Talk', in the language of the Hip Hop nation, is an idiomatic expression that builds upon what generations of Black Americans have referred to as 'straight talk'. Real Talk is the Hip Hop generation's version of an evolving discourse on language and authenticity in the Black community. This approach borrows the phrase 'Real Talk' to create an alternative metalinguistic discourse on language in educational contexts. The project utilizes 'real talk' (naturally occurring conversations) to socialize students into an awareness of sociolinguistic variation. This project builds upon the 'dialect awareness' programs spear-headed by Walt Wolfram and his colleagues at North Carolina State University and supported by Carolyn Adger and Donna Christian of the Center for Applied Linguistics (Wolfram *et al.*, 1999).

Importantly, as pointed out in Alim (2005) and Siegel (2006), a cognitive 'awareness' of language is the foundation for CLA approaches, but CLA developed as a means to go beyond cognitive awareness and move toward social and political consciousness-raising and action, thus radically transforming most 'language and dialect awareness' approaches. By uncritically presenting language varieties as 'equal' but differing in levels of 'appropriateness', language and dialect awareness programs run the risk of silently legitimizing 'standard English', or what Fairclough (1992: 15) refers to as 'dressing up inequality as diversity'.

The attractiveness of these programs, however, is that they infuse the fundamental principles of sociolinguistic variation into school curricula. The programs get students excited about the inherent variability of language and meet standards proposed by the International Reading Association and the National Council of Teachers of English that students should 'develop an understanding of and respect for diversity in language use, patterns, and dialects across cultures, ethnic groups, geographic regions, and social roles' (NCTE/IRA, 1996: 3). One of the most exciting aspects of the programs is that they encourage students to become ethnographers and collect their own speech data from their local communities.

The 'Real Talk' project begins with the sociolinguistic analysis of a conversation with one of the local area's most well-known street Hip Hop artists, JT the Bigga Figga. The class exercise begins by listening to an audio-taped interview, and copies of the tape are then distributed to the students, each of whom has their own tape recorder. Each student is instructed to transcribe the first small portion of the tape *exactly as they hear it*. What we then find out as a class is that we have each produced a unique transcript of the same speech sample. Invariably, some students will 'standardize' the speech samples, and others will 'vernacularize' them. As we search for differences between our transcriptions, students begin to notice sociolinguistic patterns in the rapper's speech (e.g. In the first sentence he said, 'He run everything', and then later he said, 'He runs everything'). We take this one feature of the rapper's spoken speech (third person singular –s variability) and conduct a sociolinguistic analysis of his speech, which leads to a larger understanding of the structure and systematicity of spoken speech. Students are not only learning about the sociolinguistic variation of spoken language, but they are also being introduced to a curriculum that introduces it as a viable modality for learning.

Studying what gets 'checked at the door': Language learning through reflexive, ethnographic analyses

After learning about the systematicity of spoken speech, and that sociolinguistic variation refers to the variable frequencies of certain features within a linguistic system, we introduce the concept of variation in terms of language use, or 'ways of speaking'. The 'Language in my life' project begins by introducing students to Dell Hymes' (1964, 1972) theory of the 'Ethnography of Speaking' and ends with student-conducted, reflexive, ethnographic analyses of their own speech behavior. The goal is for students to answer the question: How do I use language in my life? They are given an 'Ethnography of Speaking' reference sheet that they keep in their binders throughout the unit. The sheet reviews basic concepts in this area, such as *speech situation*, *speech event* and *speech act*, as levels of analysis in a communicative encounter. (In this case, the speech situation is a Hip Hop concert in Oakland, CA; the speech event is an interview with Juvenile; and speech acts include greetings, jokes, etc.).

Students are presented with another sample of 'Real Talk' – this time with New Orleans rapper Juvenile (in order to use a speaker who is *not* from their local community) – and are guided through an 'ethnography of speaking' analysis of an interview, which they learn is a 'speech event'. A small sample from the interview is used to create a worksheet (full interview appears in Spady *et al.*, 2006):

Interview with Juvenile
J = Juvenile
A = Alim

A: Wassup, Juve?
J: Wassup, woadie?
A: What's goin on?
J: Chillin, you know me. I'm chillin.
A: How would you describe the last year/year and half for you?
J: Spectacular, man! I've been blessed, you know.
A: It's a blessing, ha?

J: Workin real hard, you know. Just a lot of things. A lot of things have been goin on and so far everything's been goin right. I've been makin the right moves ...

Students are encouraged to notate the transcript in detail. They are usually adept at identifying a certain level of informality (through the use of 'slang' such as 'wassup', 'chillin', 'you know what I'm saying?') as well as regionalisms in the New Orleans based-rapper's speech (such as 'woadie', which can mean, 'man, homie', etc.; 'It's all gravy!' for the commonly used 'It's all good'.), and my use of 'ha?' as an attempt to build rapport with (or 'be cool with') the rapper by using one of his most famous expressions.

But, of course, the students are told, you can only gather so much information by reading a transcript – you have to 'go out into the field'. After introducing the theory and doing a hands-on ethnography of speaking analysis, I wanted the students to be able to analyze their own communication behavior in their everyday environments, from their actual lived experiences. After challenging students and asking them if they thought that *they* could do an ethnography of speaking with their own language data, I introduced the 'Language In My Life' project. The students were instructed to analyze their own communication behavior as it shifted across contexts and situations. As ethnographers, they were charged with carrying an ethnography notebook and documenting their communicative encounters. The notebook consisted of grids that were to be filled in throughout the day. An example from an eighth grader is as follows:

Language in my life

Date: **Time:**
November 22nd   Early in the morning, like, 7am

Mode of Language (reading, speaking, writing, listening, etc.):
Speaking, listening, rappin

Name of Language:
Mostly in slang, or Ebonics, but sometimes in standard English because my aunt was there and she talks like that.

Context (who's involved, where is it happening, what's happening):
I was sitting in the kitchen with my dad, eating cereal before I had to go to school. Before that, I was reading this rap I had wrote over and over again in my room, so I wanted to rap it for my dad. I did, and he was feelin it! He said the he could do a better one, so he tried, but it wasn't better. He called my mom and aunt over from the other room and told me to rap for them and I did. My mom was like, "Wow, Lamar! You bad!" I said, "I know." (Being cocky, as I am!) And my aunt said, "What a talented young man." My dad said he was gonna battle me after school.

Comments on the style(s) of language used:
The language with me and my dad was mostly in slang, or Ebonics, as I like to call it. Nah, I mostly say slang. And my mom, too. But my aunt, she talks standard English. I don't know, maybe because she's older.

Immediately, this project validates the language practices that students engage in outside of the classroom – for example *rappin* or *battlin* – by allowing the students to see their speech behavior taken as a subject of analysis. Further, after collecting data on their own speech, students gain a much higher level of metalinguistic awareness (speaking of themselves as styleshifters possessing multiple languages and a range of speech styles) that allows them to not only better understand the abstract theory of 'speaking', but also to better understand the linguistic landscape of their social worlds. These worlds are not marginalized in the classroom, or 'checked at the door', but they are viewed as valuable cultural and linguistic spaces for learning.

Hiphopography: The ethnography of culture and communication

After the students have learned about and conducted sociolinguistic and ethnographic analyses of their own speech behavior, we expand the scope of the pedagogy and encourage students to 'go back into the field' to study their social worlds through an analysis of their peer group and peer culture. As seen in this example below, one of the primary ways to accomplish this is through the study of localized lexical usage. We begin by raising students' awareness to the variety of lexical innovations within Hip Hop culture (of course, most students are already aware of this, since they actively participate in these innovations). To pique their interest, as well as to localize the dialogue by focusing on the Bay Area, we provide a specific example of a research interview about the language of Hip Hop culture with JT the Bigga Figga. In the short excerpt below, JT provides an 'emic' view of Hip Hop's evolving lexicon (full interview appears in Spady *et al.*, 2006).

J = JT the Bigga Figga
A = Alim

A: What does it mean to be certified with game?
J: **Certified** mean you official . . . How it got incorporated into our language in the streets, from my first experience with the word in the streets, was from **mobb** cars. And the mobb cars is Caprice Classics or Chevy Impalas '87 to '90. Them three years right there. And if you get a mobb car and it don't have a certain seal on it, it's not certified. So when dudes buy the car, it have to have that seal. You want yo car to be certified, you know what I'm saying? And that's just like if you into the collector's cars and if it don't have the same steering wheel or if you change something it's not certified no more. So it's original, you know what I'm saying? *And* another

meaning for certified meaning that you *official* ... If I say, 'Man, Alim's gon handle it. If he said he gon handle it, he certified, man. He gon handle it'. So somebody who word is good.

Upon reading the transcript aloud as a class, students immediately respond by critiquing phrases, calling some out-of-date, providing new or similar phrases, comparing with other regional phrases, etc. This excitement is channeled into further training in ethnographic methods. For this particular case, we borrow from the introduction to linguist Geneva Smitherman's *Black TAlk: Words and Phrases from the Hood to the Amen Corner* (1994 [2000]). The following worksheet translates academic language into a familiar Hip Hop-stylized way of writing (again, validating both academic language and the language of Hip Hop Culture).

> **Ethnographic Methods** used by Geneva Smitherman to write *Black Talk: Words and Phrases from the Hood to the Amen Corner*. We should use all of these methods in writing our own book (by the way, we need a title – what's up?)

(1) *Written language surveys and word lists* completed by Black people. She made up surveys and gave them to some folks that she knew, and many that she didn't, and asked them to fill out the surveys. What would a survey look like?

(2) *Songs and hit recordings.* Basically, she blocked out 30 min or so in her daily schedule to play some of her CD's and tapes. As the songs played, she listened really closely for any unique words and phrases. Most of us listen to music way more than 30 min a day, right? I know I do.

(3) *Radio shows.* My radio stay *locked* on KMEL, so this one should be easy. Whether you listen to Chuy in the morning or Big Von in the evening for the 7 O'clock Drop, you'll hear tons of slang words and phrases.

(4) *Movies and television.* You can block out 30 min to watch your favorite TV show (106th and Park, Rap City, BET, whatever) and catch all the slang that's being used. If you happen to be watching a movie that day, or that week, pay extra attention to the slang. You can probably get *hecka* words from one movie.

(5) *Collecting words* from community bulletins, leaflets, magazines, announcements or other written material. Can you think of any that you might use?

(6) *Face-to-face interviews.* You can literally ask people if they know any slang words or phrases that you can include for your slang dictionary. Sometimes we can't think of all of these terms by ourselves, right, so we need some help from our people. How would you ask somebody to help you? Who would you ask?

(7) *Eavesdropping.* I ain't gotta tell y'all about that one. Mmm-hmmmm ...

(8) *Participant observation.* Participant observation means that you are not only *observing* the event or the scene, but you are also *actively participating* in it. In what events or scenes do you hear lots of slang talk? I bet you the talk at lunch time is full of slang words and phrases, huh? This is your first official ethnographic assignment. You are to be a participant observer at lunch tomorrow (Thursday) and at least one other day before we meet again next Wednesday. Keep your lil notebooks handy so you can jot words down as you hear them. I know some of you are dying to ask, so yeah, you can combine this with *eavesdropping*, but if you get popped in the eye, I'ma be like Silkk the Shokker and say, 'OOOOOH, it ain't my fault!'

Students are given further training in these methods as we move through the unit. This type of assignment generates intense interest in ethnographic fieldwork and some students go above and beyond expectations by interviewing peers, family members, neighbors and others until they completely run out of tape! One thing that needs to be emphasized is that this is not just a way to 'get students excited' about language, but rather, students are told that they are contributing to the body of scholarly literature on their own speech variety. They are charged with the historical responsibility of archiving Black culture – in this case, Hip Hop culture – through words. In my experience, students have contributed much to the literature. One example is the term *rogue*, a localized example of semantic inversion that highlights a very specific regionality, as it is used *only* within the 2.5 square miles of Sunnyside (Alim, 2004a). The term is used to refer to youth in Sunnyside who possesses a non-conformist, street ethic, but also more broadly by young people to refer to their friends and associates.

'When they saw I was a Black person': From language discrimination to social transformation

Thus far, I have outlined projects that develop students' metalinguistic awareness, particularly in the area of language use. As I stated earlier, our goal is to develop an approach that does more than provide students with the tools to analyze language and to theorize its use in their local, social worlds (which is a substantial development in its own right). But beyond this, we are also obligated to expose the nature of power relations *vis-à-vis* language that exist within and beyond our students' social worlds. Many of our students, particularly those who speak marginalized language varieties, are already acutely aware of the fact that people can use language to discriminate against 'others'; they and their families are often those 'others'. Other students, those for whom a more 'standard' variety of English is native, may not have had similar experiences, yet as Baugh (1998) has already argued, those students also need an education that makes explicit linguistic discrimination, one that recognizes the privileged status of native 'standard' English speakers in relation to linguistically profiled and marginalized groups.

In an effort to incorporate the full range of what linguists know about language and its use in society, we begin this lesson by drawing from sociolinguistic research conducted on *linguistic profiling*. Baugh's research (2003) describes linguistic profiling as the auditory equivalent of racial profiling. This type of profiling (usually occurring over the phone), for example, can prevent potential homeowners from moving into certain neighborhoods. Linguistic profiling covers the full range of discriminatory practices based on racial, geographic, gender, class, sexuality inferences made from speech alone.

Students are introduced to this compelling research by watching a video of recent cable news coverage of the linguistic profiling project (LPP in Alim, 2005). The LPP research findings (Purnell *et al.*, 1999), which show that the overwhelming majority of us can make correct racial inferences based on the pronunciation of the single word 'Hello', inspire a whole unit of activities designed to investigate this phenomenon. After introducing *linguistic profiling* research as 'applied linguistics', the students collect data from the community about similar experiences. The following worksheet is given to students as they watch the video and includes various short assignments:

Linguistic Profiling Worksheet

What is *linguistic profiling*? What is the relationship between linguistic profiling and racial profiling? Do you think you can tell whether somebody 'sounds White' or 'sounds Mexican' or 'sounds Black' or 'sounds Indian' or 'sounds Arab' or any other race or ethnic group? Today we are going to talk about the relationship between race, language, profiling and discrimination. We are about to watch a news story that ran on ABC News with Peter Jennings. This news segment is a case of what we call, 'Applied Linguistics' – that is an area of research where linguists apply their scientific knowledge about language to real-life situations that affect everyday people – like you and me.

FREEWRITE: First impressions. What do *you* think?

OUTLINE OF NEWS STORY:

8:52 – Language as a criterion for discrimination. Linguistic profiling → racial profiling.

9:32 – James Johnson's housing application, his experience and his experiment. Fair housing agency experiment.

10:32 – John Baugh, Stanford University professor – one simple word, "Hello." Linguistics and the law.

11:24 – Linguistic profiling experiment at Stanford in Alim's hip hop class. Percentages of correct answers. Is this reality?

SUMMARY PARAGRAPH

[Open space for students' summary of the research presented in the news story]

ASSIGNMENT

Let's design a series of interview questions. In the coming week, interview 3 or 4 people (or more, if you choose) – they can be family or friends – about linguistic profiling and record or take notes about their responses. Compile your responses and submit for next week.

It is at this point in the developmental progression of the unit that students begin to explore the relationships between language and discrimination, as well as the connective marginalities across linguistically profiled and marginalized populations. One brief example illustrates this point. While one Black American student interviewed his aunt and discovered that she had a very painful experience of discrimination in the housing market (i.e. she would often be told that units were 'still open' only to be turned away upon arrival), a Latina student shared a narrative from her father in which he was fired from his truck-driving job because of 'phony' charges of tardiness. In the first case, the Black American aunt spoke 'proper' on the phone, but she was still often denied access to housing based on the visual representation of her race ('when they saw I was a Black person'). And in the second case, the Latino father spoke English as a second language and believed that he was fired *not* because of his job performance (or his race) but his 'problem with English', as he put it.

These narratives are sites of exploration and critical interrogation of the links between language, discrimination and power. Further, students are often animated through these explorations of linguistic profiling in their communities and they are motivated to engage in community activism around issues of linguistic discrimination. Students are not only thinking critically about language, but they are also putting their knowledge to work for their communities by developing consciousness-raising campaigns and helping provide resources for community members to engage in the transformation of their neighborhoods. To paraphrase Janks and Ivanic (1992: 305), 'awareness' is only helpful if it leads to 'action'.

Conclusion

Moving from 'That's just the way it is' toward a new vision of the way it can *be*

In conclusion, CLA approaches can arm teachers with the knowledge that is needed to radically change our conventional approaches to language teaching. As a community of concerned educators, we need to seriously consider the language ideological combat that is being waged inside and outside of our classroom walls. Otherwise, we will continue to produce language pedagogies that fail our students. Explanations of academic failure as the result of students' ideological opposition to formal schooling and 'acting White' often miss the complexity and multidirectionality of ideological combat. More directly, ethnographic studies (Alim, 2004a; Carter, 2005) reveal that teachers can spend as much time devaluing students' language and culture as students spend rejecting that devaluation (which is not the same as rejecting 'acting White'). Further, while Bourdieu (1977[1993]: 63–64) insists that students will continue to maintain the laws of the dominant linguistic market despite the intentions of 'radical' and 'populist' teachers, actual teaching experience suggests otherwise.

In order to address our students' needs, we need to recognize that the full body of available research on language, its structure, its use and its role in constructing identities and mediating intergroup relations is not produced solely for the consumption of scholars. Rather, this knowledge can be used to develop pedagogies that create high levels of metalinguistic awareness through reflexive ethnographic and sociolinguistic analyses of speech. Further, this approach operationalizes the vast body of research on language for the purposes of raising the linguistic and social consciousness of all students with the goal of social transformation.

Recalling the conversation with the well-meaning teacher, students are not the only ones who are frustrated. Teachers of linguistically profiled and marginalized youth often struggle with the contradictions emerging from their own ideological positions, training, lived experiences and sometimes overwhelmingly antidemocratic school cultures and practices. This approach aims to engage teachers in the same type of critical language pedagogies outlined for students in this chapter. Teachers, too, can benefit greatly from reflexive analyses of their own language behaviors and ideologies. In fact, it is only once teachers develop a meta-ideological awareness that they can begin to work to change them – and be more fully prepared to teach all students more effectively. This is the final reason to revisit the Obama example and the conversation with the well-meaning teacher above.

Although the discourse on race and race relations in the United States has expanded (at least quantitatively if not qualitatively) since the election of the nation's first Black president, discussions about race are often highly emotional and politically charged, filled with feelings of guilt, fear, distrust, anger and anxiety. If my teacher workshops are a good indication, I am certain that some readers of this chapter are still not sure how to make sense of the conversation with the well-meaning teacher. While this particular teacher is obviously not dressed in all white sheets, foaming at the mouth and shouting out racial slurs (a limited depiction of 'racists'), what I want to present next is an exercise that gets at the subtle workings of racism evident in our examination of her language ideologies. At the same time, this is also a reflexive exercise and an opportunity to turn this critical examination inward upon sociolinguistics to figure out how we may be complicit in this type of covert racism.

The first step here is to ask the question: How did the teacher arrive at the belief that her students absolutely needed to learn 'standard English' in order to succeed in society? First, while teachers are some of the most hard-working members of society, and often seem to have supernatural stores of energy, they do not have superhuman abilities. Teachers, like any other members of society, are not immune to the language ideologies that are part and parcel of our language socialization as Americans (we all harbor discriminatory language ideologies unless we are explicitly reso-cialized out of them). Still, it is interesting to ask how she might have arrived at the following conclusion:

> I know you might speak this way at home, but in an academic setting, or if you're interviewing for a job, or if you're applying to college, and you talk to someone like that, they will like not even give you the time of day ... that's just the way that it is! You have to learn how to play the game guys! I'm sorry.

Rather than agreeing for one reason or another, that we 'absolutely have' to provide 'these students' with 'standard English', we might ask: By what processes are we all involved in the construction and mainte-nance of the notion of a 'standard dialect', and further, that the 'standard' is somehow better, more intelligent, more appropriate, more important, etc., than other varieties? In other words, how, when, and why are we all implicated in the elevation of one particular variety over all others, even when all of our linguistic knowledge and theories tell us that 'all languages are equal in linguistic terms'? Why does this continue when linguists know that 'standard' simply means that this is the language variety that those in authority have constructed as the variety needed to gain access to resources? Further, why does the 'standard' continue to be imposed despite the fact that linguists can agree that what we have for a 'standard English' in the United States is nothing short of the imposition of White linguistic norms and ways of speaking in the service of granting access to resources to Whites and denying those same resources to as many others as possible, including poor, marginal Whites?

These are very complex questions. We can begin by taking a closer look at the teacher's training. This teacher was actually a student in one of my teacher education courses in an elite, private university located within a few miles of Haven High. In that three-week course, I taught preservice teachers about Black language, linguistic diversity, language ideologies and pedagogical strategies for linguistically and culturally diverse students. Not only did the course fail to have a lasting impact in this particular case, I believe the course may have been responsible for perpetuating the racist language ideologies it was meant to counter. I uncritically showed the film, *American Tongues*, during one of my sections. The film, although somewhat outdated, is ideal for exposing teachers to linguistic diversity in the United States. It not only is an excellent introduction to language variation but it also provides several examples of linguistic, racial and regional discrimination (see Ball & Alim, 2006).

After discussing Black language at length, the film cuts to an interview with one of the foremost sociolinguists in the field, who concludes, somewhat apologetically:

> Let's face it. There are certain consequences for not speaking a standard dialect. For example ... you may have certain limitations in terms of the job market. If you don't wanna deal with the negatives, it may be very helpful to learn a standard dialect for certain situations. It may not be fair, but that's the way it is. (Walt Wolfram)

It is clear from this example that the American sociolinguistic establishment, by and large, has been complicit in speaking from a position of privilege that depicts speaking a 'standard dialect' as a simple question of individual choice and not one that is inextricably linked to a whole complex array of social, cultural and political issues. Sociolinguists, like teachers, are also clearly not immune to the broader circulation of discriminatory language ideologies, nor do they always recognize their own racism and privilege.[2]

Another question arises: Given that this sociolinguist, like many others, has devoted his entire life to the study of marginalized language varieties and has worked tirelessly in disadvantaged communities, why would he refer to himself as a racist in his own work? Clearly, he was trying to call attention to the need for a kind of ethnosensitivity (Baugh, 1983) in sociolinguistics that would be needed in order to unpack the subtle nature of covert racist practices in our field (Morgan, 1994). Toward this end, it may be useful to consider the teacher's and sociolinguist's strikingly similar comments from the perspective of gender and sexuality.

To begin with, we can imagine a White teacher telling her Black students:

> Sorry, Black children, in order to succeed in this world, you must adopt a way of speaking that is modeled very closely upon White linguistic norms and ways of speaking, also known as 'standard English'. It may not be fair, but that's just the way it is.

Again, this might not seem 'racist' at all, but the problem with this statement – which I take to be the underlying guiding principle of most traditional approaches to language education of Black students, including 'dialect awareness' approaches – is that it does not challenge the current sociolinguistic and sociopolitical order. Rather, it perpetuates it by allowing the arbitrary elevation of 'standard dialects' to continue unquestioned. Another less obvious problem is that we know full-well that language fluency alone does not guarantee upward mobility, and that factors such as race, class, gender and sexual discrimination, etc. are equally as important. Further, statements such as these ignore the fact that 'racism' is not an individual problem, but that is a social and institutional process that impacts marginalized populations, regardless of whether or not any one individual engages in racist practices.

Let us paraphrase the teacher's comments above with the following exercise. Now, keeping race constant, imagine a male teacher telling all of his female students:

> Sorry, young ladies, in order to succeed in this world, you must adopt a way of speaking that is modeled very closely upon male linguistic norms and ways of speaking, also known as 'standard English'. It may not be fair, but that's just the way it is.

Certainly, a statement such as this would fly in the face of feminist attempts to rid society of patriarchy and ideologies and systems of repression against women. Why should women have to model their speech after *male* ways of speaking in order to have a chance at success or upward mobility? What is wrong with the way young girls speak that they should be denied access to resources if they cannot learn to talk like young boys? These are rhetorical questions, but they are stated here to point out the connections between race and gender, and to raise the possibility that, for whatever reason, we may be more willing to accept covert racism than covert sexism.

Given that the struggle for equal rights for the LGBT communities in the United States has gained significant ground, particularly with several states now allowing same-sex marriage, we can take this one step further. Again, keeping race constant, imagine a heterosexual teacher telling all of his homosexual students:

> Sorry, gay students, in order to succeed in this world, you must adopt a way of speaking that is modeled very closely upon heterosexual linguistic norms and ways of speaking, also known as 'standard English'. It may not be fair, but that's just the way it is.

Not much discussion is needed at this point, but clearly, something like this would not fly in most schools. In fact, while many Americans, like the journalist in the beginning of this chapter, uncritically agree that Black children need to speak a particular way in order to succeed in life, I wonder if many of those same people would also support the linguistic coercion of women and gays. Is the linguistic coercion of racial and ethnic 'minorities' somehow more acceptable?

Most readers would agree that gay and lesbian youth should not need to learn how to *not* 'sound gay' in order to have a chance in life. After all, it is it not true that, according to linguists, a particular language variety or way of speaking bears no relation to intelligence? The goal of CLA, and my research in this particular context, is 'to make the invisible visible' – or in the case of language, to make the inaudible audible (Bucholtz & Hall, 2004) – by examining the ways in which well-meaning people attempt to silence speakers of marginalized varieties by inculcating speakers into what are, at their core, White ways of speaking and seeing the word/world, that is, the norms of White, middle-class, heterosexist males. This approach helps us better understand why the well-meaning teacher's comments are problematic. It encourages us to think about difference and discrimination across race, gender, sexuality and all socially marginalized identities.

Arriving at this critical awareness is seen as the first step in challenging a given social order, a 'wake-up call' that encourages students and teachers to interrogate received discourses and ideologies of language, which are always connected to issues of race, class, gender, sexuality and power. As Fairclough (1989 in Reagan, 2006: 14) has pointed out, critical language pedagogies have a 'substantial "shock" potential' and 'can help people overcome their sense of impotence by showing them that existing orders of discourse are not immutable'. Training in critical language issues can help teachers be not only well-meaning but also well-informed enough to address student questions about the imposition of dominant language norms. With such an approach, teachers can stop apologizing for 'the way things are', and begin helping their students imagine the way things can *be*. As sociolinguists and scholars of language, we can help teachers become 'agents of change' (Ball, 2006; Smitherman, 1986), armed with a particular set of knowledges and pedagogies. Teachers can create a space where dominant ideologies are interrogated and, over time, dismantled with the goal of providing equal language rights for all.

Following Pennycook (2001: 176), we must recognize that language teaching and learning, as well as the study of these practices, is 'always already political and, moreover, an instrument and a resource for *change*, for challenging and changing the wor(l)d'. Change begins with one student, one teacher, one classroom, one school, one district, at a time, and this cannot be overemphasized. Countless social changes have been initiated and bolstered through the active work of educational institutions. Understandings of gender, racial and sexual identification and orientation, for example, have benefited greatly through changes in the official discourses of schools. CLA has the potential to help students and teachers abandon old, restrictive and repressive ways of thinking about language and to resocialize them into new, expansive and emancipatory ways of thinking about language and power. Change from the school outwards carries the potential of creating a deeper understanding of linguistic diversity (Alim & Baugh, 2007). As sociolinguists and educators, we must do more than study the relationships between language, society and power – we must do what we can to change them.

Notes

1. Among the most taken-for-granted practices is the labeling of Barack Obama as 'African American' without a careful consideration of the diversity of *Blacknesses* in the United States. A critical approach might recognize Barack Obama's self-identification as African American and in the same breath problematize the erasure of diversity that occurs under such a broad label. The same, of course, holds for other categories of ethnoracial identification such as 'Latino' or 'Asian American', etc. In this particular case, I can ask myself to what extent am I participating in this erasure by making a case for Black Language in the United States using Barack Obama as an example, given that he learned Black Language largely as part of his secondary socialization as a young adult? To what extent is strategic essentialism at play here? These points are not lost on me, but more evidence is needed for critical investigation. Like I said, the questions are endless.
2. Walt Wolfram has been on the cutting-edge of research on marginalized language varieties for the better part of five decades. It should be noted that his specific comments here were not at all controversial to the majority of sociolinguists when *American Tongues* was produced; in fact, with some notable exceptions, such as Geneva Smitherman, James Sledd and a few others, his comments were par for the sociolinguistics course. To the best of my knowledge, his more recent bold, reflexive efforts to unpack his own racism stand as the sole example in the field and only provide more evidence that he continues to be a pioneer in sociolinguistics. His paper was delivered on October 21, 2005 at NWAV 34 in NYU, officially titled, 'Sociolinguistic Myths in the Study of African American English', and unofficially subtitled, 'Confessions of a White Male Racist'. My own work is indebted to Walt and his colleagues at Duke-NC State where I spent a very productive postdoctoral year in 2003–2004.

Suggestions for further reading

As a field, CLA is very much associated with the work of Norman Fairclough. Of his many works, I would suggest his 1992 edited volume, *Critical language Awareness* and his 1995 work, *Critical Discourse Analysis: The Critical Study of Language* (see the reference list for both suggestions). The edited volume is important in that it brings together a group of scholars to reassess the 'language awareness' movement and presents various examples of what a CLA might look like. Specifically, the collective argues for a language education that pays greater attention to sociopolitical issues in language and society. The 1995 work provides some more theoretical and methodological insights into critical language study. Of particular interest is the final section of the book, which addresses CLA specifically by exploring the educational applications of the field.

For a broad breakdown of many of the CLA-related issues discussed in this chapter, I would recommend David Corson's 1999 textbook *Language Policy in Schools: A Resource for Teachers and Administrators* (see the reference list) and his

2001 textbook *Language Diversity in Education* (Lawrence Erlbaum Associates, Inc.). Both books are very clear and accessibly written and provide teachers and administrators with much of the information needed to create a more responsive and responsible language policy for linguistically and culturally diverse schools. Useful examples and applications permeate the texts as does Corson's goal of social justice through education.

Finally, for those interested in Black language specifically, and other marginalized varieties by extension, I would suggest H. Samy Alim and John Baugh's 2007 edited volume, *Talkin Black Talk: Language, Education, and Social Change* (Teachers College Press). This volume aims to revise our approaches to language and literacy learning in diverse classrooms. One of the book's strengths is that it presents creative, classroom-based, hands-on pedagogical approaches (from Hip Hop culture to the art of teaching reading comprehension) along with linguistic analyses by leading sociolinguists and educators.

On a final note, while this chapter has focused largely on 'Black language', it is less about Black language and more about teaching marginalized students, regardless of race or ethnicity, in a way that respects and take seriously the cultural and linguistic varieties that our youth bring to the classroom. Further, as with *Talkin Black Talk*, the issues here go beyond language teaching and into every aspect of society, aiming to transform our way of thinking about language and to resocialize students, teachers, sociolinguists – all of us – into a more critical view of language, identity and power.

References

Alim, H.S. (2004a) *You Know My Steez: An Ethnographic and Sociolinguistic Study of Styleshifting in a Black American Speech Community*. Publications of the American Dialect Society, No. 89. Durham, NC: Duke University Press.

Alim, H.S. (2004b) Hearing what's not said and missing what is: Black language in White public space. In C.B. Paulston and S. Keisling (eds) *Discourse and Intercultural Communication: The Essential Readings*. Malden, MA: Blackwell.

Alim, H.S. (2005) Critical language awareness in the United States: Revisiting issues and revising pedagogies in a resegregated society. *Educational Researcher* 34 (7), 24–31.

Alim, H.S. and Baugh, J. (eds) (2007) *Talkin Black Talk: Language, Education, and Social Change*. New York: Teachers College Press.

Ball, A.F. (2006) *Multicultural Strategies for Education and Social Change: Carriers of the Torch in the United States and South Africa*. New York: Teachers College Press.

Ball, A.F. (2009) Toward a theory of generative change in culturally and linguistically complex classrooms. *American Educational Research Journal* 46 (1), 45–72.

Ball, A.F. and Alim, H.S. (2006) Preparation, pedagogy, policy, and power: Brown, the King case, and the struggle for equal language rights. In A.F. Ball (ed.) *With More Deliberate Speed: Achieving Equity and Excellence in Education – Realizing the Full Potential of Brown v. Board of Education*. Malden, MA: Blackwell.

Baugh, J. (1983) *Black Street Speech: Its History, Structure, and Survival*. Austin: University of Texas Press.

Baugh, J. (1998) Linguistics, education, and the law: Educational reform for African American language minority students. In S. Mufwene, J. Rickford, G. Bailey and J. Baugh (eds) *African–American English: Structure, History and Use*. London and New York: Routledge.

Baugh, J. (2003) Linguistic profiling. In S. Makoni, G. Smitherman, A.F. Ball and A.K. Spears (eds) *Black Linguistics: Language, Politics and Society in Africa and the Americas*. London: Routledge.

Bertrand, M. and Mullainathan, S. (2003) Are Emily and Greg more employable than Lakisha and Jamal?: A field experiment on labor market discrimination. NBER Working Paper No. 9873.

Bourdieu, P. (1977[1993]) What talking means. Paper delivered to the Association Francaise des Enseignants de Francais, Limonges, 30 October 1977. Published in Pierre Bourdieu's (1993) *Sociology in Question*. London: Sage Publications.

Bucholtz, M. and Hall, K. (2004) Language and identity. In A. Duranti (ed.) *A Companion to Linguistic Anthropology* (pp. 268–294). Oxford: Basil Blackwell.

Camarillo, A. (2007) Cities of color: The new racial frontier in California's minority–majority cities. *Pacific Historical Review* 76, 1–28.

Carter, P. (2005) *Keepin' it Real: School Success Beyond Black and White*. New York: Oxford University Press.

Corson, D. (1999) *Language Policy in Schools: A Resource for Teachers and Administrators*. Mahwah, NJ and London: Lawrence Erlbaum Associates.

Fairclough, N. (1989) *Language and Power*. London: Longman.

Fairclough, N. (ed.) (1992) *Critical Language Awareness*. London and New York: Longman.

Fairclough, N. (1995) *Critical Discourse Analysis: The Critical Study of Language*. London: Longman.

Fought, C. (2006) *Language and Ethnicity*. New York: Routledge.

Freire, P. (1970) *Pedagogy of the Oppressed*. New York: Seabury Press.

Freire, P. (1985) *The Politics of Education*. New York: Macmillan.

Green, L. (2001) *An Introduction to African American English*. New York: Routledge.

Gumperz, J. (1982a) *Discourse Strategies*. Cambridge: Cambridge University Press.

Gumperz, J. (1982b) *Language and Social Identity*. Cambridge: Cambridge University Press.

Gutierrez, K. (2005) Building sociocritical literacies: A decolonizing tool for contemporary demographics of inequality. Paper presented at the American Educational Research Association.

Hymes, D. (1964) Introduction: Towards ethnographies of communication. In J. Gumperz and D. Hymes (eds) *The Ethnography of Communication. American Anthropologist* 66 (6), 1–34.

Hymes, D. (1972) Models of interaction of language and social life. In J. Gumperz and D. Hymes (eds) *Directions in Sociolinguistics* (pp. 35–71). New York: Holt, Rinehart and Winston.

Janks, H. and Ivanic, R. (1992) Critical language awareness and emancipatory discourse. In N. Fairclough (ed.) *Critical Language Awareness* (pp. 305–331). London: Longman.

Morgan, M. (1994) The African American speech community: Reality and sociolinguistics. In M. Morgan (ed.) *Language and the Social Construction of Identity in Creole Situations* (pp. 121–148). Los Angeles: CAAS Publications UCLA. Reprinted in A. Duranti (ed.) (2001) *Linguistic Anthropology: A Reader*. Malden, MA: Blackwell.

Morrell, E. (2004) *Becoming Critical Researchers: Literacy and Empowerment for Urban Youth*. New York: Peter Lang.

National Council of Teachers of English/International Reading Association (1996) *Standards for the English Language Arts*. Newark, DE: IRA/NCTE.

Pennycook, A. (2001) *Critical Applied Linguistics: A Critical Introduction*. Mahwah, NJ: Lawrence Erlbaum Associates.

Pennycook, A. (2004) Performativity and language studies. *Critical Inquiry in Language Studies* 1 (1), 1–19.

Purnell, T., Idsardi, W. and Baugh, J. (1999) Perceptual and phonetic experiments on American English dialect identification. *Journal of Language and Social Psychology* 18 (1), 10–30.

Reagan, T. (2006) The explanatory power of critical language studies: Linguistics with an attitude. *Critical Inquiry in Language Studies* 3 (1), 1–22.

Rickford, J. (1999) *African American Vernacular English*. Malden, MA: Blackwell.

Siegel, J. (2006) Language ideologies and the education of speakers of marginalized language varieties: Adopting a critical awareness approach. *Linguistics and Education* 17, 157–174.

Smitherman, G. (1986) *Talkin and testifyin: The language of Black America* (rev. ed.). Detroit: Wayne State University Press. (Original work published in 1977.)

Smitherman, G. (1990) The 'mis-education of the Negro' – and you too. In Harvey A. Daniels (ed.) *Not Only English: Affirming America's Multilingual Heritage* (pp. 109–120). Urbana, IL: NCTE.

Smitherman, G. (1994 [2000]) *Black Talk: Words and Phrases from the Hood to the Amen Corner*. Boston and New York: Houghton Mifflin.

Spady, J.G., Alim, H.S. and Meghelli, S. (2006) *The Global Cipha: Hip Hop Culture and Consciousness*. Philadelphia: Black History Museum Press.

Wodak, R. (1995) Critical linguistics and critical discourse. In J. Verschueren, J. Ostman and J. Blommaert (eds) *Handbook of Pragmatics* (pp. 204–210). Philadelphia: John Benjamins.

Wolfram, W. (1993) A proactive role for speech-language pathologists in sociolinguistic education. *Language, Speech and Hearing Service in Schools* 24, 181–185.

Wolfram, W., Adger, C.T. and Christian, D. (1999) *Dialects in Schools and Communities*. Mahwah, NJ: Lawrence Erlbaum Associates.

Chapter 9
Pidgins and Creoles

JEFF SIEGEL

Pidgins and creoles are new varieties of language that emerge when people speaking different languages come into contact with each other. The study of these 'contact languages' falls mainly under the heading of sociolinguistics, but also intersects with many other subdisciplines, such as contact linguistics and applied linguistics. This chapter begins by providing some background: definitions of key terms and information about the current status and use of these languages. Then it describes four areas of research in pidgin and creole studies (sometimes called 'creolistics'). The next section concentrates on educational policy and practice. It discusses the use of pidgins and creoles for classroom instruction and special programmes aimed at speakers of these languages.

Background
Definitions

Pidgins and creoles develop out of a need for communication among people who do not share a common language – for example, among plantation labourers from diverse geographic origins. Most of the words in the vocabulary of the new language come from one of the languages of the people in contact, called the 'lexifier' (or sometimes the 'superstrate') – usually the language of the group with the most power or prestige. However, the meanings and functions of the words, as well as the way they're pronounced and put together (i.e. the grammatical rules) of the pidgin or creole, are different to those of the lexifier. These rules may sometimes resemble those of the other languages in contact, usually referred to in pidgin and creole studies as the 'substrate languages'.

An example is the following sentence from Bislama, the dialect of Melanesian Pidgin spoken in Vanuatu. This language arose among Pacific Islanders working as plantation labourers in Queensland (Australia) in the late 1800s.

(1) | *Woman* | *ia* | *bae* | *i* | *kilim* | *ol* | *pig* | *long* | *garen* | *blong* | *hem.* |
|---|---|---|---|---|---|---|---|---|---|---|
| woman | this | FUT | SRP | hit | PL | pig | in | garden | POSS | 3SG. |

'This woman will attack the pigs in her garden'.

All the words in this sentence are derived from the lexifier, English, but most with different meanings or functions. For example *kilim* is based on *kill him*, but here it means 'hit' or 'strike'; *long* is a general preposition derived from *along*; and *hem*, from *him*, is used for *he, she, it, him* and *her*. The word *bae* (from *by and by*) indicates future, and *blong* (from *belong*) is used to show possession. The way the words are put together reflects the rules of the substrate languages, the Eastern Oceanic languages of the southwestern Pacific. For example the word *ia* (derived from *here*) means 'this', but it follows the noun *woman* rather than preceding it as *this* does in English. Also, the small particle *i* (from *he*) is required before the verb to indicate that the subject (*this woman*) is singular. And the word *ol* (derived from *all*) precedes the noun *pig* to indicate plural rather than a following *-s* as in English *pigs*.

Contact languages such as Melanesian Pidgin begin to emerge when people speaking different languages first develop their own individual ways of communicating, often by using words and phrases they have learned from other languages (most often from the lexifier) that they think others might be familiar with, but leaving out words such as prepositions. The combination of these individualized ways of communicating is called a 'jargon' or 'pre-pidgin'. Here are two examples from the early 'South Seas Jargon', which first emerged from contact between Pacific Islanders and Europeans in the early 1800s (from Clark, 1979: 30; Keesing, 1988: 43):

(2) a. *Go my house; me got plenty fruit my house.* (Rarotonga – 1860)
    b. *He too much bad man.* (Kosrae – 1860)

If the different language groups remain in contact, or if several groups start to use the pre-pidgin as a lingua franca (i.e. a common language), certain communicative conventions may develop, resulting in a new language, called a pidgin. In the Pacific, this occurred after 1863 when islanders from diverse regions were recruited to work on plantations in Queensland and other areas. A stable pidgin emerged, using some features from the pre-pidgin more consistently, while dropping others – for example (from Keesing, 1988: 42–43):

(3) a. *Me want to go along big fellow house* ... (Queensland – 1870s)
    b. *big wind broke ship belonga me.* (Efate [New Hebrides] – 1878)
    c. *man here no good* ... (Tanna [New Hebrides] – 1877)

These examples show the use of the preposition *along* for 'to, at', and *belonga* for possessives (*belonga me* replacing *my*). These became *long* and *blong* in modern Melanesian Pidgin. While *got* meaning 'have' in example (2a) remains in modern Melanesian Pidgin, *bad* was replaced by *no good* when the pidgin stabilized, as shown in (3c).

Once a stable pidgin has emerged, it generally continues to be learned as an auxiliary language and used only when necessary for intergroup communication. Its total vocabulary is small, and it has little, if any, grammatical words and endings – for example, to indicate tense or plural. This is called a 'restricted pidgin'. Here is an example from a restricted pidgin, Chinese Pidgin English, once an important trade language in southern China and Hong Kong (Li *et al.*, 2005):

(4)   *he more better takee two piecee coolie along he.*
      'He'd better take two coolies with him'.

In some cases, however, the use of a pidgin is extended into wider areas – for example, as the everyday lingua franca in a multilingual community, and even as a language used in religion and government. As a result, the language expands over time in its vocabulary and grammar, and becomes what is fittingly called an 'expanded pidgin'. This is what happened with Melanesian Pidgin, which expanded when it became an important lingua franca after returned plantation labourers brought it back to their multilingual home countries. Thus, the example of Bislama in (1) is that of an expanded pidgin. Bislama has its own writing system, and is used widely not only for communication between people who have different mother tongues (Vanuatu has over 100 indigenous languages) but also in radio broadcasting, parliamentary debates and religious contexts. Another expanded pidgin that serves this role is Nigerian Pidgin.

In another scenario, people in a mixed community use a pidgin on a daily basis, and some of them shift to it as their primary language, which they speak to their children. Because of this extended use, the pidgin would already be expanded or in the process of expanding. Thus, children growing up in this context acquire the expanded pidgin as their mother tongue (or first language), and it becomes their community language. At this stage, the language is then called a 'creole'. Like any other vernacular language, a creole has a large vocabulary and a complex set of grammatical rules, and is not at all restricted in use, having a complete range of informal functions. This scenario occurred frequently among plantation slaves in the Caribbean, resulting in the English-lexified and French-lexified creoles that are still spoken there. Another example is Kriol, spoken in the Northern Territory and Kimberley region of Australia. This creole is thought to have emerged when people speaking different Australian Aboriginal languages took refuge at a mission station to escape from settlers who were killing

Aboriginal people in order to set up cattle stations on their land (see Harris, 1986). Here is an example sentence (Munro, 2004: 190):

(5) *olda*   *ol-bibul*   *bin*   *oldei*   *lenim*   *melabat*
     PL   old-people   PAST   CONTINUOUS   teach   us (EXCLUSIVE)
     'The old people were always teaching us'.

In the field of pidgin and creole studies, there are disagreements about the precise definitions of 'pidgin' and 'creole', arising from researchers focusing on different aspects of these languages. The perfect example is Melanesian 'Pidgin'. Some linguists who emphasize sociolinguistic criteria call it a pidgin, because it is a second language rather than the mother tongue for the large majority of its speakers. Others call it a creole because it has some native speakers and it is used in a wide range of functions. Those who consider only linguistic criteria call it a creole because of the grammatical features which it has developed are just as complex as those of clearly recognized creoles – as seen in a comparison of examples (1) and (5). However, the traditional term 'expanded pidgin' is used here for Melanesian Pidgin, because the vast majority of its speakers still speak other languages as well, and it is not the vernacular language of any distinct, newly emerged community.

A great deal of controversy also exists about what kind of languages can be labelled creoles and whether or not creoles can be distinguished as a class of languages according to linguistic criteria (e.g. McWhorter, 1998, 2001; DeGraff, 2001a, 2001b). Nevertheless, most linguists do agree that they can be delimited by sociohistorical criteria – for example, that they are varieties of language that developed as a result of extensive language contact (Mufwene, 2001; DeGraff, 2003).

It should be pointed out that the use of 'pidgin' and 'creole' to refer to particular types of contact languages are technical terms used by linguists. The speakers of these languages often use other labels. For example speakers of Jamaican Creole most often call their language Patwa (from *patois*), and speakers of Hawai'i Creole call their language Pidgin.

Current status and use

Restricted pidgins have arisen in many areas of the world. But because these languages are often short lived and, as their label shows, restricted in use, it is difficult to determine their numbers. Some examples of now extinct restricted pidgins are Pidgin French of Vietnam and Pidgin Hawaiian. Currently used restricted pidgins include Pidgin Fijian and Pidgin Hindustani in Fiji (see Siegel, 2008: 26).

On the other hand, it is known that there are currently over 50 different expanded pidgins or creoles spoken by an estimated 123 million people (based primarily on figures in Gordon, 2005). More than 101 million people speak expanded pidgins, with Nigerian Pidgin being the largest (an estimated 80 million speakers). Nigerian Pidgin and the other widely spoken expanded pidgins, Cameroon Pidgin (16 million speakers) and Melanesian Pidgin (4 million), are all lexified by English.

More than 23.1 million people speak creoles, approximately 10 million lexified by French, 6.5 million by English, 4.7 million by African languages (especially Kongo and Ngbandi), 1.5 million by Portuguese or Spanish and 0.4 by other languages, including Malay, Hindi and Arabic. Haitian Creole (HC) (French-lexified) is the largest (approximately 7.4 million speakers), followed by Jamaican Creole (English-lexified, 3.2 million). Expanded pidgins or creoles are spoken in at least 50 countries or territories, most of these former European colonies in the Caribbean region, Africa, the southwestern Pacific and the western Indian Ocean. Millions of speakers of these languages have also migrated to the United States, Canada, Britain, France and the Netherlands. For example it is estimated that there are as many as one million speakers of HC in the United States (Joseph, 1997).

Immigrants speaking an expanded pidgin or creole (hereafter abbreviated as P/C) are of course minorities in their adopted countries. Some P/C-speaking communities are also a minority in the country where they originated – for example, those speaking Gullah and Louisiana Creole in the United States and Kriol in Australia. In other places, P/C speakers are the majority in a particular state or territory, but a minority in the country as a whole – for example, in Hawai'i in the United States. However, in most places where a P/C is spoken, its speakers make up a majority of the population as a whole – for example, in Papua New Guinea (PNG), Solomon Islands and Vanuatu in the Pacific; Mauritius, Réunion and the Seychelles in the Indian Ocean; Cape Verde, Guinea-Bissau, Sierra Leone, Nigeria and the Central African Republic in Africa; and Belize, Suriname, Guyana, Haiti, Jamaica, Trinidad and Tobago, St Lucia, Dominica, Guadeloupe, Netherlands Antilles and Aruba in the Caribbean region.

Nevertheless, in nearly all of these places, the P/C is spoken only in informal contexts – at the market or among family and friends – while a different language is used for formal contexts, such as government, education and the legal system. This language is most often the standard form of a European language – French, English, Portuguese or Dutch – usually the former colonial language that has been chosen as the official language even after independence. Some of the reasons for this state of affairs are discussed below.

Areas of Research in Pidgin and Creole Studies

Research in pidgin and creole studies can be divided into four areas: (1) description and development, (2) language in society, (3) variation, and (4) applied issues. Each of these is described in turn.

Description and development

For many years, P/Cs were thought to be marginal languages – that is simply corrupted versions of standard languages, spoken by uneducated people. In the 1960s, however, scholars began to examine P/Cs and write detailed linguistic descriptions. These showed that P/Cs are legitimate, rule-governed varieties of language, in some ways even more complex than their lexifiers.

For example in Bislama gender is not distinguished in the pronoun system, and the pronoun *hem* (or sometimes *em*) can mean 'she', 'he' or 'it'. So, the sentence *Hem i stap long haos* can have three different meanings, depending on the context 'He's in the house', 'She's in the house' or 'It's in the house'. Also, in the sentence *Mi givim buk long hem*, the same pronoun *hem* can also mean 'him' or 'her'. Thus, it seems that Bislama has a pronoun system that is 'simpler' than that of English. However, this is not the full story. The pronoun system of Bislama makes some other distinctions that are not made in English. For example while standard English has only one second-person pronoun, *you*, that can refer to either singular or plural, Bislama has four different second-person pronouns: *yu* (singular – 'you'), *yutufala* (dual – 'you two'), *yutrifala* (trial – 'you three') and *yufala* (plural – 'you all'). Thus, Bislama pronouns make a four-way distinction in number whereas English pronouns sometimes make no distinction, as with *you*, or at the most only a two-way singular–plural distinction, as with *I* versus *we*.

Over the last few decades, many PhD students have done grammatical descriptions of a P/C for their dissertations, and detailed grammars of P/Cs continue to be published – for example, on Cape Verdean Creole (Baptista, 2002), Hawai'i Creole (Sakoda and Siegel, 2003) and Bislama (Crowley, 2004). A book comparing the grammars of 18 P/Cs was also recently published (Holm & Patrick, 2007).

One reason for the interest in grammatical comparisons of creoles is that various studies have reported many apparent similarities among these languages even though they may be located in very distant parts of the world – for example, Hawai'i and Haiti. Considering these purported similarities, along with the supposed rapid emergence of creole languages, and the extremely simplified nature of their pidgin predecessors, Bickerton (1981, 1984) put forth his Language Bioprogram Hypothesis. This proposed that children growing up on plantations had only a restricted pidgin as their input for language acquisition. Since this was not a fully developed language, they had to fall back on their innate linguistic capacity to turn it into one. Thus, according to the hypothesis, creoles the world over are similar because they reflect the human biological endowment for language – often called Universal Grammar.

For more than 20 years, the field of pidgin and creole linguistics was dominated by this universalist hypothesis, and research attempting to either support or reject it. Some of those who opposed it argued that creoles may emerge gradually rather than as rapidly (in one generation) as Bickerton had claimed (e.g. Arends, 1993, 1995). Others argued that the features of creoles could be attributed to the influence of the substrate languages (e.g. Alleyne, 1986; Lefebvre, 1998). Those with this view were called the 'substratists' (also labelled 'substratomaniacs' by Bickerton). Still others, known as the 'superstratists', argued that the features of creoles could be traced back to both standard and non-standard varieties of the lexifier language (e.g. Chaudenson, 1992, 2001). This controversy led to a great deal of sociohistorical research being done on the origins and development of P/Cs. Such research included rigorous documentation of the different substrate populations of slaves or indentured labourers in the various locations where P/Cs emerged, and accounts of the languages they spoke. Drawing on historical sources – such as early texts, travellers' accounts, court records and government reports – scholars have also been able to paint a clear picture of the historical development of the linguistic features of many P/Cs – for example, Bislama (Crowley, 1990) and Korlai Portuguese Creole (Clements, 1996), and more recently, Hawai'i Creole (Roberts, 2005) and Mauritian Creole (Baker and Fong, 2007).

Findings from the descriptive and sociohistorical work over the past two decades have refuted the Language Bioprogram Hypothesis. For example comparative descriptive work in Singler (1990) and Winford (1993) demonstrated that the degree of similarities among grammatical features of creoles has been exaggerated. Later, in addition to the earlier sociohistorical research reported in Arends (1995), Roberts (1998, 2000, 2005) showed that Hawai'i Creole, pivotal to Bickerton's hypothesis, took at least two generations to develop, and that the first generation of children born on the plantations were actually bilingual in their parents' language and the developing pidgin. Furthermore, research demonstrated that substrate languages, rather than any innate language faculty, most probably provided models for features of creoles, such as Hawai'i Creole (Siegel, 2000) and Suriname creoles (Migge, 2003) (see also Migge, 2007).

However, controversies about creole genesis remain. On one side is the classic view that creoles are the result of the expansion of a restricted pidgin predecessor (e.g. McWhorter, 2005; Siegel, 2008). On the other side is the view that creoles result from gradual restructuring of the lexifier through the usual processes of language change (e.g. Mufwene, 2001; DeGraff, 2003). The pidgin predecessor view sees creoles as new languages while the gradual restructuring view sees them as versions of their lexifier. (It is interesting to note that the latter view is held mainly by scholars working on French-lexified creoles [see Alleyne, 2000].) Nevertheless, one point that both sides agree on is the role of processes of second language acquisition (SLA) in creole formation, and recently this has become an important area of research (see e.g. Siegel, 2003; Lefebvre *et al.*, 2006; Mather, 2006; Plag, 2008).

Language in society

The second area of research is clearly sociolinguistic. It is concerned with the role of P/Cs in societies where they are spoken, their relationship to social identity and attitudes towards these languages.

Many sociolinguistic studies have examined the role of P/Cs in the construction of social identities. The most well known and comprehensive is LePage and Tabouret-Keller's *Acts of Identity* (1985). In this book, the authors use data from Caribbean Creoles (mainly from Belize and St Lucia) to put forward a theory that individuals create their own systems of linguistic behaviour to resemble those of groups they wish to identify with. More recent studies have been done by Dubois and Melançon (2000) on Louisiana Creole and Eades *et al.* (2006) on Hawai'i Creole. These studies and others show that like other languages, speakers of P/Cs often have positive attitudes towards their language as a marker of solidarity and local social identity, and that these languages are valued in the private domains of family and friendship. Other works, such as that done by Schnepel (2004) on Guadeloupe, examine the role of creole languages in national identity.

But unlike other languages, P/Cs are rarely valued in public formal domains and as a result, they generally suffer from overall negative attitudes and low prestige (see e.g. Rickford & Traugott, 1985; Winford, 1994; Mühleisen, 2002). (For a summary of some of the studies of the ambivalent attitudes towards P/Cs, see Wassink, 1999).

There are several possible reasons for the low prestige of P/Cs. First, it may be attributed to their history. Each P/C-speaking country or territory was formerly the colony of a European power. Those in control and those with economic advantage spoke the European language. The P/C speakers who later became the educated and well-off elite were those who acquired this language. When they became leaders, they supported the European language remaining as the official language. Thus, as the language of the former colonial power and the current leaders, the European language is seen as the key to upward mobility and economic success. In contrast, the P/C, as a language of former slaves or indentured labourers, is often associated with repression and powerlessness.

In addition, as the new languages of relatively recently formed speech communities, P/Cs suffer from comparison to the official languages. European languages have long historical traditions and bodies of literature, whereas P/Cs do not (Alleyne, 1994). Also, European languages are clearly standardized in both writing system and grammar, and have many dictionaries and grammar books, whereas most P/Cs do not have a widely recognized standard grammar or writing system, although many dictionaries and grammatical descriptions have been written by linguists.

Most significantly, however, P/Cs are often not considered to be legitimate languages, but rather deviant and corrupt forms of their lexifiers. This is especially true in situations where a P/C coexists with the standard form of its lexifier as the official language. This view is reinforced by the fact that, at least superficially, the P/C and the standard share the same lexicon. It is thought that the P/C does not have its own grammatical rules, and consequently, the way it is spoken is considered to be the result of performance errors rather than language differences. This lack of autonomy is exacerbated in countries like Jamaica and Guyana, where a P/C and the standard form of its lexifier are both commonly used and there seems to be no clear dividing line between them.

Hawai'i Creole, for example, has had a history of denigration by teachers, administrators and community leaders. It is still commonly referred to as a corrupt form of English, as indicated by this extract from a letter to the editor of a local newspaper: 'It's broken English. And when something is broken, you fix it' (*Honolulu Star-Bulletin*, 12 October 1999). Another letter stated: 'For the benefit of Hawai'i children, pidgin should become a thing of the past .... There are some things that deserve to die' (*Honolulu Advertiser*, 4 September 2002). And some people still make statements such as the following: 'pidgin is not a language, it's a sign of a stupid [person] that is lazy, and it rubs off on others' (from a *Honolulu Advertiser* blog, 31 March 2008).

However, with more understanding that P/Cs are legitimate languages, with their increased use in literature and the media, and with more realization of their importance to local identity, attitudes have begun to become more positive in some places, such as Hawai'i, Jamaica and other Caribbean countries (see Romaine, 1999; Shields-Brodber, 1997; Mühleisen, 2002). In fact, a large-scale survey of attitudes in Jamaica in 2005, described by Devonish (2007: 219–224), showed a significant shift in attitudes, with a desire for Jamaican Creole to be used in more public formal contexts, such as speeches in Parliament and education.

Variation

Another clearly sociolinguistic area of research in P/C studies focuses on the variation found in what is known as the 'creole continuum' – a cline of speech varieties of the creole ranging from what is called the 'basilect' (furthest from the lexifier) to the 'acrolect' (closest to the lexifier), with intermediate varieties, the 'mesolects'. This is illustrated for Jamaican Creole in Figure 9.1 (adapted from Alleyne, 1980).

The social conditions for a creole continuum, first outlined by DeCamp (1971: 351), include a standard form of the lexifier language being the

acrolect:	*he is eating his dinner.*
mesolect 1:	*(h)im is eating (h)im dinner.*
mesolect 2:	*(h)im eating (h)im dinner.*
mesolect 3:	*im a eat im dinner.*
basilect:	*im a nyam im dinner.*

Figure 9.1 Range of speech in the Jamaican Creole continuum

dominant official language, the partial breakdown of formerly rigid social stratification so that some social mobility is possible, and access to education in the dominant language. Thus, this phenomenon is supposedly the result of the lexifier language becoming the target and the creole then becoming heavily influenced or restructured by it, a process called 'decreolization'. Decreolization is usually defined as the gradual modification of a creole in the direction of the lexifier. However, some creolists (e.g. Mufwene, 2001) believe that actually the reverse process led to the development of the continuum – that is that the lexifier was gradually modified to become more basilectal.

Creole speakers have proficiency over different ranges of the continuum: Those with more education or higher socio-economic status control varieties more towards the acrolectal end, and those with less education or lower socio-economic status, towards the basilectal end. Speakers also shift their speech along the continuum depending on whom they are talking to and the context – more acrolectal in formal contexts and basilectal in informal contexts. For example an educated speaker of Jamaican Creole might say *him eating him dinner* to his wife at home, but *he is eating his dinner* to his boss at work. In contrast, an uneducated speaker in similar contexts might say *im a nyam im dinner* and *im eating im dinner*.

Some well-known studies of the creole continnum include those done by Rickford (1987) on Guyanese Creole and Patrick (1999) on Jamaican Creole. These and many other studies use the quantitative methodology of variationist sociolinguistics, or what is sometimes called the 'quantitative paradigm' (see Bayley, 2002), to examine the use of particular variables – that is linguistic features that vary along the continuum. For example in Figure 9.1, there are at least two variables, each with three variants. One concerns the subject pronoun: the use of *he, him* or *im* and the other concerns present continuous marking: *is* VERB*ing*, as in English, VERB*ing* (without the auxiliary) and *a* VERB. In a variationist sociolinguistic study, the frequency of use of each variant would be calculated for various speakers and statistical analysis would be done to see whether particular frequencies correspond to social variables such as age, ethnicity, socio-economic status and gender. These studies have confirmed earlier observations about factors affecting variation along the continuum.

Many variationist studies also look at the relationship between variable use and linguistic variables, such as the nature of the preceding or following word. One variable that is often examined in this way is copula absence – the absence of a form of the verb *to be* in sentences such as *he my friend* 'he is my friend'. This variable usually includes auxiliary absence as well, for example, *him eating him dinner* 'he is eating his dinner' in Figure 9.1. This variable has been examined in several creoles, such as Jamaican Creole (Rickford, 1999), Gullah (Weldon, 2003), Bahamian Creole (Reaser, 2004) and Hawai'i Creole (Inoue, 2007). These studies and many others have found that the copula is absent less frequently before particular types of words and more frequently before others, and that for each creole, there is the same order of frequency depending on the following type of word. This order is shown in Figure 9.2 (from least to most frequent copula absence) with examples from Hawai'i Creole:

Research in this area has been relevant to long-running debates about whether African American Vernacular English (AAVE) originates from dialects of English or from a creole. The findings that the order of frequency of copula absence in creoles is the same as that found in AAVE have been used to support the view that AAVE has creole origins (see Rickford, 1998).

type of following word	example
noun phrase	*Mai sista wan bas jraiva. (My sista one bus driver.)*
adjective	*Mai sista skini. (My sister skinny.)*
location	*Ken insaid da haus. (Ken inside the house.)*
VERB-*ing*	*Hi haelpin mi. (He helping me.)*
gonna, goin, gon	*Shi gon mis yu. (She gonna miss you.)*

Figure 9.2 Order of frequency of copula/auxiliary deletion depending on following word type

Applied issues

Applied research on P/Cs, sometimes called 'applied creolistics', is mainly in the areas of language planning and language in education.

Language planning

In some countries and territories where P/Cs are spoken by the majority, language planning efforts have been carried out to expand the use of these varieties into more formal domains. Two types of planning are involved: 'status planning' – dealing with the role of the language in society – and 'corpus planning' – dealing with the language itself. With regard to status planning, the aim has been to increase both the status and functions of the P/C so that it is used in official contexts alongside the existing official language. (This is called 'instrumentalization'.) Many of the arguments for such expansion are socio-political, pointing out that a large proportion of the population is disenfranchized by not knowing the established official language. The use of the P/C in formal education, government and other official domains would give people greater access and allow them to participate in decision-making processes, thus counteracting neo-colonialism and elitism (see e.g. Devonish, 2007). At present, P/Cs are accorded official status in the constitutions of less than a handful of countries, including Haiti, Vanuatu and PNG.

With regard to corpus planning, the major efforts have been in codification: choosing a 'standard' variety of the P/C to be used for these wider functions and developing a writing system for it (graphization). But because of the socio-political underpinnings of language planning efforts, and the lack of perceived legitimacy of P/Cs, as described above, the codification of a P/C has two goals not usually found in other contexts: (1) choosing a variety of the P/C that would be accessible to the majority of speakers of the language and (2) making the P/C autonomous from its lexifier so that it is perceived as a separate, legitimate language. In other language contexts, the standard is based on a prestige variety used by the social elite and found in an established literary tradition. In many cases, it is modelled on an already established standard used in the community (such as Latin in Europe in ancient times). In contrast, a P/C normally does not have an established literary tradition. Furthermore, the prestige variety of the P/C is the form closest to the lexifier and the established standard is often the lexifier itself – both generally spoken by only a small elite class (see Sebba, 1997). Obviously, the goals of accessibility and autonomy would not be accomplished by developing a standard form of the P/C on the basis of the lexifier.

This is most relevant to the choice of orthography (i.e. writing system). There are basically two types of orthographies used for P/Cs: etymological and phonemic. An etymological orthography is based on the conventional spelling of the lexifier language – for example in Hawai'i Creole: *They stay coming for talk with that old bugger.* 'They're coming to talk with that old guy'. A modified etymological orthography distinguishes some of the salient linguistic features of the P/C, especially in pronunciation (Winer, 1990). So the same example from Hawai'i Creole with modified etymological orthography would be: *Dey stay coming fo talk wit dat ol buggah.* In contrast, a phonemic orthography is based on the sounds that actually occur in the P/C without any reference to the lexifier, ideally with one letter for each phoneme (a sound that is used to distinguish meaning), or sometimes a digraph (a combination of two letters for one sound, such as *sh* in English). So the Hawai'i Creole example would be: *Dei ste kaming fo tawk wit daet ol baga*. An intermediate phonemic orthography basically has one letter for one phoneme, but in some cases it uses the spelling conventions of the lexifier – for example: <ou> for /u/ in French-lexified creoles (Schieffelin & Doucet, 1994) and <oa> for /oʊ/ as in boat in the English-lexified Belize Kriol (Decker, 1995).

It is the phonemic orthography that appears to meet the language planning goals of accessibility and autonomy for P/Cs. First of all, it is well known that a phonemic writing system is easier to learn when acquiring literacy because of its consistency and because new readers tend to decode sound by sound. In contrast, the etymological orthography preserves the inconsistencies and historical forms unrelated to pronunciation that are found in the lexifier language. Thus the phonemic system is more suitable if the P/C is to be used for teaching initial literacy, which is a goal of language planning efforts in some P/C contexts. Second, with regard to the goal of autonomy, the phonemic orthography (including the intermediate type) clearly makes the written form of the P/C look distinct from that of the lexifier. In contrast, the etymological orthography (including the modified type) reinforces the view that the P/C is a deviant variety of the lexifier. However, the reality of many P/C contexts is that speakers learn initial literacy in a standard European language (see below), and only later learn literacy in the P/C. This is the situation in Hawai'i and one reason that a modified etymological orthography based on English was chosen for the recent translation of the New Testament (*Da Jesus Book*, 2000). (For a more detailed discussion of orthographic issues, see Schieffelin and Doucet, 1994; Sebba, 2000; Mühleisen, 2002.)

Language in education

Because of some of the language attitudes discussed above and the lack of awareness of the descriptive research on pidgin and creole languages, educators and administrators in most P/C contexts believe that their own language is a deviant form of the standard and therefore not suitable for education (see e.g. Kephart (1992) regarding Carriacou; Mann (1996) regarding Nigeria; Rajah-Carrim (2007) regarding Mauritius). But even when P/Cs are recognized as legitimate languages, some educators, administrators and even linguists still argue that using them in education would be both impractical and detrimental to students. These arguments have to do with issues such as lack of standardization and fear of interference with acquisition of the standard form of the European official language, since learning of this standard is the ultimate goal of the education system everywhere P/Cs are spoken.

These attitudes and arguments have had a profound effect on educational policy and practice in P/C contexts, covered in detail in the following section.

Pidgins and Creoles in Educational Policy and Practice

Initial literacy acquisition in a P/C

P/Cs as official languages of education

There are only four countries or territories where the P/C has been officially designated as the medium of instruction for the early years of primary school, and is therefore the medium for acquiring initial literacy. These are the Seychelles with Seselwa (Seychelles Creole) (Mahoune, 2000); Haiti with HC (Howe, 1993); and Curaçao and Bonaire in the Netherlands Antilles as well as nearby Aruba (which has separate political status) with Papiamentu (Appel & Verhoeven, 1994; Dijkhoff, 1993; Ferrier, n.d.). The other official languages are both English and French in the Seychelles, French in Haiti, and Dutch in the Netherlands Antilles and Aruba.

These four places may seem like the success stories of status planning in P/C contexts, but the full story is something else. First of all, in all four situations, the programmes are transitional – meaning that literacy in the P/C is not seen as an end in itself but rather a means of acquiring literacy in the European official language(s), which are used for higher education and government. Second, in each location, there is still a good deal of resistance to the use of the local P/C as the language of literacy. In the Seychelles, Mahoune (2000) reports that people 'subconsciously associate development with French and English', that there is a growing tendency to use these languages rather than Seselwa, in public functions, and that people who actually write the standardized creole are very few. The following observations have been made on the situation in Haiti (Center for Applied Linguistics, 1994):

> Many sectors of the population do not see the value of becoming literate in Creole. This attitude is even found among the poor, who tend to view education as a means of escaping poverty rather than as a means of learning; as a result, they are especially concerned that their children learn French.

In the Netherlands Antilles, after the implementation of the education plan making Papiamentu the language of instruction, there was a dispute about freedom of choice that went to the courts. Since then, schools can be either bilingual (Papiamentu and either English or Dutch) or all Dutch (Christie, 2003: 57). Nevertheless, the official policy is still to strongly support Papiamentu as the language of education.

The only other country where the local P/C is widely used in formal education to teach literacy is PNG. A total reform of the nation-wide education system in the early 1990s instituted three years of Elementary School in which the language of instruction and initial literacy is chosen by the community. English is introduced in the second or third year of Elementary School and becomes the medium of instruction in the following six years of Primary School. Although exact figures are not available, many communities, especially in urban areas, have chosen Tok Pisin (the PNG dialect of Melanesian Pidgin) for their schools (Ray, 1996). Also, at least in one rural area, in the Sepik Province, there are at least 26 Elementary Schools using Tok Pisin (Wiruk, 2000).

P/Cs in bilingual (and trilingual) programmes

There are some other, less widespread, examples of the use of P/Cs to teach initial literacy in formal education – again, transitional programmes in the first few years of primary school.

In Australia, a bilingual programme with Northern Territory Kriol and English began at Barunga School in 1977. It was among other bilingual programmes run by the Northern Territory Department of Education, involving Aboriginal languages. Unfortunately, however, this bilingual programme, along with others, was terminated by the Territory government at the end of 1998. Also in Australia, the Home Languages Project began in 1995 at Injinoo School in north Queensland with a variety of Torres Strait Creole (Turner, 1997).

In the Caribbean, an experimental 'trilingual' programme using Islander English (or Creole), English and Spanish was started on San Andres Island, Colombia, in 1999 (Morren, 2001). On the island of Guadeloupe, there is an experimental (non-governmental) elementary school using the local French-lexified creole, Gwadloupéan (Faure, 2000). There are also other experiments involving teaching Gwadloupéan as a subject to older students in junior and senior high schools. (For a history of other educational efforts using Gwadloupéan, see Schnepel, 2004.)

In Jamaica, a Bilingual Education Project was approved by the government and implemented in 2004 in two pilot schools (Devonish & Carpenter, 2007). This was a consequence of the recent changes in attitudes towards the use of Jamaican Creole in formal domains, as mentioned above.

Finally, in the United States there have been bilingual programmes in Massachusetts, New York and Florida for immigrants speaking HC (Zéphir, 1997) and Cape Verde Creole (Gonsalves, 1996). In Massachusetts, however, the bilingual education law was overturned by voters and scrapped by the state government in 2003 (de Jong-Lambert, 2003).

Evaluative research

Only a few studies have been done to evaluate the use of P/Cs to teach literacy. One of the earliest and most thorough was done in Australia by Murtagh (1982) on the use of Kriol in the bilingual programme at Barunga, mentioned above. Murtagh compared several measures of oral language proficiency in Kriol and English of students in the first three grades at two different schools: the Kriol/English bilingual school at Barunga and an English-only school at Beswick Reserve, where the children are also Kriol speakers. The overall results were that students at the bilingual school scored significantly better than those at the monolingual school, especially in Grade 3. Murtagh concludes:

> The results of the study indicate very definite trends towards the superiority of bilingual schooling over monolingual schooling for Creole-speaking students with regard to oral language proficiency in both the mother tongue, Creole, and the second language, English. (Murtagh, 1982: 30)

In a study in the Seychelles, Ravel and Thomas (1985) examined the educational reform, which led to the use of Seselwa as the medium of instruction in primary education. They compared Grade 3 students in 1983, the last Grade 3 to be taught in English, the language of education, with Grade 3 students in 1984, the first to be taught in Seselwa. The findings were that the creole-educated students performed better than the English-educated students, not only on standardized tests but also in school subjects, namely English and mathematics. Bickerton (1988) reports the results of a similar study done two years later, which showed the creole-educated students achieving higher scores in French, mathematics, science and social studies. He concludes (1988: 3): 'The prediction by the enemies of creole, that education in creole would lower scores in English and French, has failed to be borne out'.

Burtoff (1985) conducted a study in New York City involving illiterate HC-speaking immigrants. Two groups were compared: the control group, who received instruction only in English as a second language (ESL) for 24 weeks, and the experimental group, who received instruction in ESL for 12 weeks and in HC literacy for 12 weeks. There were some problems with the research design and the low number of subjects, but the statistical results revealed that the HC literacy group developed ESL literacy skills greater than those of the ESL-only group, despite having half the amount of instruction.

Research in PNG (Siegel, 1997) examined the performance of three cohorts of primary school students on school term tests in English, mathematics and general subjects over a six-year period. The results of students who learned initial literacy and numeracy in Tok Pisin were compared to those of students who had learned only in English. The students who had learned in Tok Pisin scored significantly higher in all subjects, including English.

Two experimental studies in the Caribbean region have dealt with older creole-speaking children (Grade 5–6 and junior high school) who had reading problems in the educational language, English. In each study, a small group of children were taught literacy for the first time in their own vernacular – Carriacou Creole English (Kephart, 1992) and St Lucian French Creole (Kwéyòl) (Simmons-McDonald, 2004). In both cases, this led to marked improvement in the children's literacy skills in English.

There are also some reports that give an indication of the success of programmes using P/Cs to teach initial literacy – for example, in the Netherlands Antilles with Papiamentu (Arion, 2003) and on San Andres with Islander English (Morren, 2004).

Initial literacy acquisition in the standard language

Other than the few exceptions described above, P/C-speaking children generally have to acquire literacy not in their own language but in the standard European language that is officially used in the formal education system. Thus in their first few years of school, they have to acquire both a second language (L2) and literacy. Here we look at some teaching approaches and programmes that have been used for these children.

P/Cs as poor versions of the lexifier

As described above, except for a few countries such as St Lucia and Suriname, the official educational language is also the lexifier of the P/C. This is called the 'lexifier L2' situation by Craig (1998). As also described above, both educators and the general population in such situations often consider the P/C to be a substandard form of the lexifier/official language – for example, in creole-speaking countries in the Caribbean region where English is the official language. In such situations, students who speak the creole are sometimes considered to be poor speakers of the standard language rather than L2 learners, and the teaching of literacy is done as if their vernacular does not exist – what Craig (2001: 66) refers to as the 'English-as-the-mother-tongue tradition'. The linguistic features of the students' creole vernaculars are seen as 'bad habits' that must be replaced with the 'good habits' of the standard.

Such an approach is getting rarer in places where P/Cs speakers are the majority, but English-lexifier creole-speaking immigrants in the United States are still often treated as poor speakers of English and are put into special education classes (Devonish, 2007: 215).

P/Cs as non-standard varieties

P/Cs are also sometimes considered to be non-standard dialects of the lexifier. In the 1960s, when social dialects such as AAVE became recognized as legitimate, rule-governed varieties, methods from foreign language teaching (FLT) and teaching English to speakers of other languages (TESOL) began to be employed to teach standard English to speakers of these dialects. This became known as teaching standard English as a second dialect (SESD). Following the audiolingual approach popular in the late 1960s and 1970s, the emphasis was on habit formation and oral fluency, with teaching focused on particular grammatical structures. Contrastive analysis of the first dialect (D1) and standard English (D2) was done to determine which structures should be taught, and pattern practice and drills were used to teach them. Similar methods were used to teach standard English to speakers of English-lexified creoles in the Caribbean and Hawai'i (Craig, 1966, 1967; Crowley, 1968).

On the other hand, other researchers, such as Torrey (1972), reported only very limited positive results, and the problems of the uncritical use of FLT and TESOL methods became apparent (Politzer, 1973). These had to do with both the ineffectiveness of the teaching methods themselves and the special characteristics of contexts where the standard language is being taught to speakers of lexically related vernaculars such as P/Cs. (For more recent criticisms, see Malcolm, 1992.) The biggest factor goes back to the problem of autonomy. As pointed out long ago by Stewart (1964), in FLT and TESOL, two different autonomous linguistic systems are easily recognized. The learners' L1 often has its own dictionaries and grammars, just like the L2. But in SESD, because of similarities with the standard, the learners' vernacular is most often not recognized as a separate variety of language. This leads to both teachers and students thinking that there is only one legitimate language involved, and that the learners' vernacular is just 'sloppy speech'. For this reason, the dialect (or the P/C) is not even allowed in the classroom. Thus, students are clearly disadvantaged by not being allowed to express themselves in their own variety of language, a factor which has a negative effect on cognitive development and school achievement (see below).

Another popular FLT/TESOL methodology used in P/C contexts was the Communicative Language Teaching approach of the 1980s and 1990s, which emphasizes language function and use in real-life situations. This approach has been used in the Caribbean, but with little success (Craig, 1998, 2001). Again, some problems exist with the methods themselves, but in this case problems are also caused by linguistic factors. As Craig (1966, 1988) has observed, in most foreign or second language learning situations, learners have little if any familiarity with the target language. But in P/C situations where the standard variety is the target, learners already recognize and produce some aspects of it as part of their linguistic repertoires. Also, unlike learners of a separate language, P/C speakers learning the standard variety often have no communicative reason to keep using the target (i.e. the standard) in the classroom. As Craig (1998: 12) points out, in such situations 'learners can all retain their normal language usage for performing communicative tasks, and there is no need to learn anything new'. In addition, because of the similarity between the P/C and the lexifier, the learner might not be aware of some of the differences that do exist, and as Craig (1966: 58) notes, 'the learner fails to perceive the new target element in the teaching situation'.

More successful approaches

One educational programme aimed at P/C speakers that had more success is the Kamehameha Early Education Program (KEEP), which was started in the 1970s for ethnic Hawaiian children, mostly speakers of varieties of Hawai'i Creole. The programme took a conversational approach in teaching reading, making use of discourse strategies and participation structures similar to those in a speech event found in Hawai'i Creole called 'talk-story'. It was found that this approach facilitated learning to read in standard English (Speidel, 1987).

The Hawai'i English Program, which ran through the 1970s to the early 1980s, was a more far-reaching programme that also respected the students' home language, which at that time was mainly Hawai'i Creole. This programme, as described by Rogers (1996), was different from others in that it made specific use of the creole in several ways. First, it looked at particular features of the language in comparison to standard English. Second, some stories written in Hawai'i Creole were included and children were sometimes given the choice to read either these or others in standard English. Third, there was a unit on dialects that looked at dialect diversity outside Hawai'i, as well as containing activities, described by Rogers (1996: 233) as follows:

> These activities encourage elementary school students to view HCE [Hawai'i Creole English] as a complete and legitimate language form, to undertake some simplified linguistic analyses of HCE, and to witness dialectal flexibility in local role models.

The awareness approach

The Hawai'i English Program was a forerunner to later programmes using what has become known as the 'awareness approach'. In this approach, students' P/C vernaculars are seen as a resource to be used for learning the standard, rather than an impediment. This approach has two or three of the following components. In the sociolinguistic component, students learn about different varieties of language – such as regional dialects, pidgins and creoles – and explore the history and politics of language that led to one particular variety becoming accepted as the standard. This component helps both teachers and students to realize that all vernacular varieties of language are legitimate and that no variety is intrinsically better than another, even though some may have more practical benefits in some contexts. In the contrastive component, students examine the grammatical and pragmatic characteristics of their own vernaculars to see how they are rule-governed and how they differ systematically from the standard. Sometimes translation or role-playing activities are used. This component helps students to notice (and eventually learn) differences that they may not have realized to exist. In the accommodation component, teachers may make use of aspects of students' language and culture, as in the KEEP program or in having students study literature or song lyrics written in the P/C. Sometimes students may also be given the freedom to express themselves in their own varieties.

Two experimental programmes with components of the awareness approach were later carried out in Hawai'i in the 1980s and early 1990s. Project Holopono involved 300 students of limited English proficiency in Grades 4–6 in eight schools, of which half were Hawai'i Creole speakers (Actouka & Lai, 1989). Project Akamai was aimed at more than 600 Hawai'i Creole speakers in grades 9 and 10 in 11 schools (Afaga & Lai, 1994).

In Jamaica, the new CAPE high school syllabus 'Communication Studies' includes a 'Language and Society' module that focuses on the linguistic situations in Caribbean countries, as well as on aspects of the grammar of Creole vernaculars as compared to English (Kouwenberg, 2002). Furthermore, according to the recent Reform of Secondary Education in Jamaica, 'students should be allowed to express themselves freely, employing whatever variety makes them comfortable in the classroom and outside' (Christie, 2003: 46).

Many programmes using the awareness approach have been developed for P/C speakers in countries where they are a minority – for example, Kriol speakers in Western Australia (Berry & Hudson, 1997; Catholic Education Office, 1994) and English-lexified creole-speaking immigrants from the Caribbean in Canada (Coelho, 1988, 1991) and Britain (ILEA Afro-Caribbean Language and Literacy Project in Further and Adult Education, 1990). A good example in the United States is the Caribbean Academic Program at Evanston Township High School near Chicago (Fischer, 1992a; Menacker, 1998). Established in 1986, the programme aims to make Caribbean-born students aware that creoles and English are separate languages, and to make them aware of the linguistic differences between them. The ultimate goal is 'to develop bilingual students who have a good grasp of English and a high level of linguistic self-respect' (Fischer, 1991). In the programme, both English and various Caribbean English creoles are used in the classroom for speaking, reading and writing.

Some research has been done to evaluate the effects of the awareness approach on students' academic performance and to see whether the use of the P/C in the classroom does actually lead to interference in acquiring the standard.

With regard to Caribbean creoles, Elsasser and Irvine (1987) describe an experimental programme in the US Virgin Islands integrating the study of the local creole and English in a college writing programme. They report that the programme did not interfere with the learning of standard English. Rather, it led to increased interest in language in general, and to a greater 'understanding of the role of grammatical conventions, standardized spelling, and the rhetorical possibilities of both languages' (Elsasser & Irvine, 1987: 143). In another example, Decker (2000) reports on a study in a Grade 3 classroom in Belize. The use of a contrastive approach focussing on differences between Belize Kriol and English in four areas of grammar led to improvement in performance in these areas in standard English. A small-scale study of the Caribbean Academic Program in the United States, mentioned above, showed that after only one year in the programme, a large proportion of the students made significant academic advancements (Fischer, 1992b).

In Hawai'i, two programmes involving accommodation have been evaluated. Day (1989) describes the one in which kindergarten to Grade 4 teachers were first made aware of the history of creole languages and their rule-governed nature. Following this, they did not react negatively to students' using Hawai'i Creole in class (Day, 1989: 301–302). The study showed a significant increase over time in the scores of the students involved in the programme on standardized tests of abilities in standard English. Rynkofs (1993) presents an ethnographic study of one teacher's programme that accepted Hawai'i Creole features in early versions of students' writing. Through a process of modelling and recasting, rather than correction, the students became more proficient in written standard English.

Final year evaluations were also done of the two Hawai'i programmes with awareness components mentioned above. Project Holopono led to an increase in oral proficiency in standard English among 84% of the students (Actouka & Lai, 1989). Project Akamai resulted in increases of between 35% and 40% in tests of standard English use and oral language skills (Afaga & Lai, 1994).

Advantages of using P/Cs in educational programmes

Although the awareness programmes just described make use of students' P/C vernaculars in the classroom, evaluations do not show any evidence of interference retarding acquisition of the standard language of the education system. Rather, the evaluations, like those for programmes using P/Cs to teach initial literacy, demonstrate positive advantages: higher scores in tests measuring reading and writing skills in standard English and increases in overall academic achievement. The particular benefits of using P/Cs that account for these results appear to be related to three possible factors affecting students: greater cognitive development, increased motivation and self-esteem and ability to separate codes and notice differences.

First, it is well-known that children's self-expression is facilitated in a familiar language, especially without fear of correction (see e.g. UNESCO, 1968: 690), and that children are clearly disadvantaged when they are not allowed to express themselves in their own variety of language (Thomas & Collier, 2002). This is because self-expression may be a prerequisite for cognitive development (Feldman *et al.*, 1977). For example in a study of cognitive development and school achievement in a Hawai'i Creole-speaking community, Feldman *et al.* (1990) found that students who do not perform well in high school have not developed 'transfer ability'. This refers to the discovery or recognition by a learner that abstract reasoning processes learned with regard to materials in one context can be applied to different materials in a new context. For this to occur, new materials must be talked about, described and encoded propositionally. According to the authors, a problem exists in Hawai'i because the vernacular variety of many students (i.e. Hawai'i Creole) is conventionally not used in school and these students do not feel comfortable expressing themselves in the language of formal education, standard English. Thus, one possible benefit of the accommodation component in awareness programmes is that students are able to express themselves in their own varieties, thus better facilitating cognitive development.

Second, most theories of SLA agree that the affective variables of learner motivation, attitudes, self-confidence and anxiety have some effect on L2 attainment. These factors are especially important with regard to speakers of creoles, who often have a negative self-image because of the frequent correction of their language in the schools and sometimes the denigration of their speech and culture as well. It may be that the use of the creole in formal education results in positive values to these variables with regard to learning the standard. Certainly, many of the studies referred to above describe increased participation and enthusiasm in the educational process. As Skutnabb-Kangas (1988: 29) points out, when the child's mother tongue is valued in the educational setting, it leads to low anxiety, high motivation and high self-confidence, three factors that are closely related to successful educational programmes.

Another related factor is the P/C vernacular's importance as a marker of the socio-cultural group and a part of members' social identity (referred to above). As Tamura (1996: 439–440) points out for Hawai'i Creole speakers:

> [U]sing nonstandard English [i.e. Hawai'i Creole] symbolizes their solidarity within a social group. Such peer-group loyalty is especially strong among youths. As an intermediate school girl noted, 'If we speak good English, our friends usually say, "Oh you're trying to be hybolic (acting superior by using big words) yeah?!"'

The problem is that many educators believe that students must choose one variety or the other – ignoring the possibility of bilingualism in the P/C and the standard. For example in 1999 Mitsugi Nakashima, Chairman of the Hawai'i State Board of Education, made the following statement (*Honolulu Advertiser* 29 September 1999):

> If your thinking is not in standard English, it's hard for you to write in standard English. If you speak pidgin, you think pidgin, you write pidgin ... We ought to have classrooms where standard English is the norm.

This view is also reflected in one of the quotations given at the beginning of this chapter: 'For the benefit of Hawai'i children, pidgin should become a thing of the past ... There are some things that deserve to die'

(*Honolulu Advertiser*, 4 September 2002). Because of this view, many students feel they have to make a choice, and fear that learning and using the standard means abandoning their own language and thus risking being ostracized from their social group. As Delpit (1990: 251) observes, children often have the ability to speak standard English, but choose 'to identify with their community rather than with the school'.

The use of the P/C vernacular in the classroom would reduce some of this anxiety by demonstrating that both it and the standard have a role in society. Also, according to Clément's (1980) Social Context Model of SLA, such use of the L1 (here the P/C) would be expected to reduce fear of assimilation and thus increase motivation to learn the L2, here standard English. Again in Hawai'i, Reynolds observes:

> My own experience has revealed that when I am not trying to snatch away the language of my students, they do not feel that they have to hang onto it so tightly. Instead, the more we talk and plan and practice with both HCE [Hawai'i Creole English] and ASE [American Standard English], the more interested we all become in both languages .... (Reynolds, 1999: 310)

The third factor benefiting students' performance is the ability to separate codes and notice differences. We have seen that the similarities between a P/C and the standard form of its lexifier may make it difficult for learners to separate the two varieties. However, in the study of the Kriol/English bilingual programme in Australia described above, Murtagh (1982: 30) attributes the higher language proficiency of students in the programme to their 'progressively greater success at separating the two languages' as a consequence of 'the two languages being taught as separate entities in the classroom'. (For a psycho-linguistic discussion of the notion of separation, see Siegel, 1999: 711–716.)

Using a P/C in educational programmes may also make learners aware of differences between it and the standard that they may not otherwise notice. As referred to earlier, when speakers of P/Cs are being taught the standard, they often fail to perceive the new target element (Craig, 1966: 58). Cheshire (1982: 55) also observes that non-standard dialect-speaking children in British schools are unaware of specific differences between their speech and standard English: 'They may simply recognize that school teachers and newsreaders, for example, do not speak in quite the same way as their family and friends'. Again, SLA theory is relevant here. According to Schmidt's 'noticing hypothesis' (1990, 1993), attention to target language forms is necessary for acquisition; these forms will not be acquired unless they are noticed. It appears that in the contrastive component of awareness programmes, looking at features of their own varieties compared to the standard helps students to notice features of the standard that are different, which is the first step of acquisition.

Conclusion

Although some of the research on pidgin and creole languages is very technical and theoretical, there is much that is relevant for teachers – especially those who have students who do not always use standard English. First of all, their students' ways of speaking may reflect another legitimate, rule-governed variety of language, rather than laziness or lack of intelligence. Second, their students' language may vary significantly depending on the formality of the context and the interlocutors. Third, and most important, students learn best when their own way of speaking is valued and included in the educational process. Thus, although it may seem counter-intuitive to allow students to use or talk about a non-standard dialect or a P/C in the classroom, such practices have many educational benefits – including helping students to acquire the standard. And finally, classroom discussions of varieties or language, such as pidgins and creoles, and language diversity in general, will not only be interesting to students, but it will also help them to better understand themselves and the linguistic world we live in.

Suggestions for further reading

Craig, D.R. (1999) *Teaching Language and Literacy: Policies and Procedures for Vernacular Situations.* Georgetown, Guyana: Education and Development Services.
This book is aimed at teachers of students who speak creole languages or vernacular dialects such as AAVE. It reviews the educational problems found in such situations, and proposes some detailed practical solutions, including specific classroom activities.

Devonish, H.S. (2007) *Language and Liberation: Creole Language and Politics in the Caribbean* (new expanded ed.). Kingston: Arawak.
First published in 1986, this book contains a vivid socio-political discussion of the language policies and practices in the Creole-speaking Caribbean in the context of struggles against postcolonial control. More than 20 years later, the content is still relevant, and a new final chapter brings the reader up to date with recent developments.

Nero, S.J. (2001) *Englishes in Contact: Anglophone Caribbean Students in an Urban College.* Cresskill, NJ: Hampton Press.
This is a longitudinal study of college students who migrated to the United States from countries in the Caribbean where English-lexified creoles are spoken. It contains an in-depth examination of the students' written and spoken language, and deals with related issues such as language and identity and language attitudes.

Nero, S.J. (ed.) (2006) *Dialects, Englishes, Creoles, and Education.* Mahwah, NJ: Erlbaum.
The introduction and 12 chapters in this volume were written especially for teachers. They deal with educational issues concerning speakers of English-lexified pidgins and creoles from Hawai'i, Africa and Caribbean, as well as speakers of AAVE and other varieties of English. Each chapter has questions for discussion and reflective writing.

Sebba, M. (1997) *Contact Languages: Pidgins and Creoles*. New York: St Martin's Press.
This is a very accessible introduction to pidgin and creole languages, with good discussion of both theoretical and practical issues. It includes many illuminating case studies, as well as exercises.

References

Actouka, M. and Lai, M.K. (1989) *Project Holopono, Evaluation Report, 1987–1988*. Honolulu: Curriculum Research and Development Group, College of Education, University of Hawai'i.
Afaga, L.B. and Lai, M.K. (1994) *Project Akamai, Evaluation Report, 1992–93, Year Four*. Honolulu: Curriculum Research and Development Group, College of Education, University of Hawai'i.
Alleyne, M.C. (1980) *Comparative Afro-American: An Historical-Comparative Study of English-based Afro-American Dialects of the New World*. Ann Arbor: Karoma.
Alleyne, M.C. (1986) Substratum influences – Guilty until proven innocent. In P. Muysken and N. Smith (eds) *Substrata versus Universals in Creole Genesis* (pp. 301–315). Amsterdam: Benjamins.
Alleyne, M.C. (1994) Problems of standardization of creole languages. In M. Morgan (ed.) *The Social Construction of Identity in Creole Situations* (pp. 7–18). Los Angeles: Center for Afro-American Studies, UCLA.
Alleyne, M.C. (2000) Opposite processes in "creolization". In I. Neumann-Holzschuh and E.W. Schneider (eds) *Degrees of Restructuring in Creole Languages* (pp. 125–133). Amsterdam/Philadelphia: Benjamins.
Appel, R. and Verhoeven, L. (1994) Decolonization, language planning and education. In J. Arends, P. Muysken and N. Smith (eds) *Pidgins and Creoles: An Introduction* (pp. 65–74). Amsterdam: Benjamins.
Arends, J. (1993) Towards a gradualist model of creolization. In F. Byrne and J. Holm (eds) *The Atlantic Meets the Pacific: A Global View of Pidginization and Creolization*. Amsterdam: Benjamins.
Arends, J. (ed.) (1995) *The Early Stages of Creolization*. Amsterdam/Philadelphia: Benjamins.
Arion, F.M. (2003) Report: Skol Avansá Integrám, Kolegio Erasmo. *Pidgins and Creoles in Education (PACE) Newsletter* 14, 1.
Baker, P. and Fong, G. (eds) (2007) *The Making of Mauritian Creole*. London: Battlebridge.
Baptista, M. (2002) *The Syntax of Cape Verdean Creole: The Sotavento Varieties*. Amsterdam/Philadelphia: Benjamins.
Bayley, R. (2002) The quantitative paradigm. In J.K. Chambers, P. Trudgill and N. Schilling-Estes (eds) *The Handbook of Language Variation and Change* (pp. 117–141). Oxford: Blackwell.
Berry, R. and Hudson, J. (1997) *Making the Jump: A Resource Book for Teachers of Aboriginal Students*. Broome: Catholic Education Office, Kimberley Region.
Bickerton, D. (1981) *Roots of Language*. Ann Arbor: Karoma.
Bickerton, D. (1984) The Language Bioprogram Hypothesis. *Behavioral and Brain Sciences* 7, 173–221.
Bickerton, D. (1988) Instead of the cult of personality.... *The Carrier Pidgin* 16 (3), 2–3.
Burtoff, M. (1985) *Haitian Creole Literacy Evaluation Study: Final Report*. Washington, DC: Center for Applied Linguistics.
Catholic Education Office, Kimberley Region (1994) *FELIKS: Fostering English Language in Kimberley Schools*. Broome: Catholic Education Commission of Western Australia.

Center for Applied Linguistics (1994) *The Haitians: Their History and Culture.* Washington, DC: Center for Applied Linguistics, Cultural Orientation Resource Center. On WWW at http://www.cal.org/co/haiti/hlang.html. Accessed September 2008.

Chaudenson, R. (1992) *Des îles, des hommes, des langues.* Paris: L'Harmattan.

Chaudenson, R. (2001) *Creolization of Language and Culture (revised in collaboration with Salikoko S. Mufwene).* London: Routledge.

Cheshire, J. (1982) Dialect features and linguistic conflict in schools. *Educational Review* 14 (1), 53–67.

Christie, P. (2003) *Language in Jamaica.* Kingston: Arawak.

Clark, R. (1979) In search of Beach-la-mar: Towards a history of Pacific Pidgin English. *Te Reo* 22, 3–64.

Clément, R. (1980) Ethnicity, contact and communicative competence in a second language. In H. Giles, W.P. Robinson and P.M. Smith (eds) *Language: Social Psychological Perspectives* (pp. 147–154). Oxford: Pergamon.

Clements, J.C. (1996) *The Genesis of a Language: The Formation and Development of Korlai Portuguese.* Amsterdam/Philadelphia: Benjamins.

Coelho, E. (1988) *Caribbean Students in Canadian Schools, Book 1.* Toronto: Carib-Can Publishers.

Coelho, E. (1991) *Caribbean Students in Canadian Schools, Book 2.* Toronto: Pippin Publishing.

Craig, D.R. (1966) Teaching English to Jamaican Creole speakers: A model of a multi-dialect situation. *Language Learning* 16 (1&2), 49–61.

Craig, D.R. (1967) Some early indications of learning a second dialect. *Language Learning* 17 (3&4), 133–140.

Craig, D.R. (1988) Creole English and education in Jamaica. In C.B. Paulston (ed.) *International Handbook of Bilingualism and Bilingual Education* (pp. 297–312). New York: Greenwood.

Craig, D.R. (1998) *Afta yu laan dem fi riid an rait dem Kriiyol, den wa muo? Creole and the Teaching of the Lexifier Language.* Paper presented at the 3rd International Creole Workshop, Miami.

Craig, D.R. (2001) Language education revisited in the Commonwealth Caribbean. In P. Christie (ed.) *Due Respect: Papers on English and English-related Creoles in the Caribbean in Honour of Professor Robert Le Page* (pp. 61–76). Kingston: University of West Indies Press.

Crowley, D.P. (1968) The Keaukaha model for mainstream dialect instruction. *Language Learning* 18 (1&2), 125–138.

Crowley, T. (1990) *Beach-la-mar to Bislama: The Emergence of a National Language of Vanuatu.* Oxford: Clarendon Press.

Crowley, T. (2004) *Bislama Reference Grammar.* Honolulu: University of Hawai'i Press.

Da Jesus Book (2000) Orlando: Wycliffe Bible Translators.

Day, R.R. (1989) The acquisition and maintenance of language by minority children. *Language Learning* 29 (2), 295–303.

de Jong-Lambert, C. (2003) From the islands to the classroom and back. *The Christian Science Monitor*, 15 April. On WWW at http://www.edu-cyberpg.com/Linguistics/MassWriteCreole.html. Accessed September 2008.

DeCamp, D. (1971) Toward a generative analysis of a post-creole speech continuum. In D. Hymes (ed.) *Pidginization and Creolization of Languages* (pp. 349–370). Cambridge: Cambridge University Press.

Decker, K. (1995) *Orthography Development for Belize Creole.* Paper presented at the Society for Caribbean Linguisitics Conference, Georgetown, Guyana.

Decker, K. (2000) *The Use of Belize Kriol to Improve English Proficiency.* Paper presented at the 5th International Creole Workshop, Florida International University.

DeGraff, M. (2001a) On the origins of creoles: A Cartesian critique of Neo-Darwinian linguistics. *Linguistic Typology* 5 (2&3), 213–310.

DeGraff, M. (2001b) Morphology in creole genesis: Linguistics and ideology. In M. Kenstowicz (ed.) *Ken Hale: A Life in Language* (pp. 53–121). Cambridge, MA: MIT Press.

DeGraff, M. (2003) Against creole exceptionalism. *Language* 79 (2), 391–410.

Delpit, L.D. (1990) Language diversity and learning. In S. Hynds and D.L. Rubin (eds) *Perspectives and Talk and Learning* (pp. 247–266). Urbana, IL: National Council of Teachers of English.

Devonish, H.S. (2007) *Language and Liberation: Creole Language and Politics in the Caribbean* (new expanded ed.). Kingston: Arawak.

Devonish, H.S. and Carpenter, K. (2007) *Full Bilingual Education in a Creole Language Situation: The Jamaican Bilingual Primary Education Project*. St Augustine, Trinidad & Tobago: Society for Caribbean Linguistcs (Occasional Paper No. 35).

Dijkhoff, M. (1993) Report on the Netherlands Antilles. *Pidgins and Creoles in Education (PACE) Newsletter* 4, 1–2.

Dubois, S. and Melançon, M. (2000) Diachronic and synchronic attitudes toward Creole identity in southern Louisiana. *Language in Society* 29, 237–258.

Eades, D., Jacobs, S., Hargrove, E. and Menacker, T. (2006) Pidgin, local identity, and schooling in Hawai'i. In S.J. Nero (ed.) *Dialects, Englishes, Creoles, and Education* (pp. 149–163). Mahwah, NJ: Erlbaum.

Elsasser, N. and Irvine, P. (1987) English and Creole: The dialectics of choice in a college writing program. In I. Shor (ed.) *Freire for the Classroom: A Sourcebook for Literacy Teaching* (pp. 129–149). Portsmouth, MA: Boynton/Cook.

Faure, E. (2000) Report: Guadeloupe. *Pidgins and Creoles in Education (PACE) Newsletter* 11, 3–4.

Feldman, C.F., Stone, A. and Renderer, B. (1990) Stage, transfer, and academic achievement in dialect-speaking Hawaiian adolescents. *Child Development* 61, 472–484.

Feldman, C.F., Stone, C.A., Wertsch, J.V. and Strizich, M. (1977) Standard and non-standard dialect competencies of Hawaiian Creole English speakers. *TESOL Quarterly* 11, 41–50.

Ferrier, K. (n.d.). Educational system on the island of Aruba. On WWW at http://minority.homac.at/schoolsys/aruba.html. Accessed 25.2.2005.

Fischer, K. (1991) Report. *Pidgins and Creoles in Education (PACE) Newsletter* 2, 2.

Fischer, K. (1992a) Report. *Pidgins and Creoles in Education (PACE) Newsletter* 3, 1.

Fischer, K. (1992b) Educating speakers of Caribbean English in the United States. In J. Siegel (ed.) *Pidgins, Creoles and Nonstandard Dialects in Education* (pp. 99–123). Melbourne: Applied Linguistics Association of Australia (Occasional Paper no. 12).

Gonsalves, G.E. (1996) Language policy and education reform: The case of Cape Verdean. In C.E. Walsh (ed.) *Education Reform and Social Change: Multicultural Voices, Struggles and Visions* (pp. 31–36). Mahwah, NJ: Lawrence Erlbaum Associates.

Gordon, R.G. (2005) *Ethnologue: Languages of the World* (15th edn). Dallas: Summer Intstitute of Linguistics International.

Harris, J.W. (1986) *Northern Territory Pidgins and the Origin of Kriol*. Canberra: Australian National University (Pacific Linguistics C-89).

Holm, J. and Patrick, P.L. (eds) (2007) *Comparative Creole Syntax: Parallel Outlines of 18 Creole Grammars*. London: Battlebridge.

Howe, K. (1993) Haitian Creole as the official language in education and the media. In F. Byrne and J. Holm (eds) *Atlantic Meets Pacific: A Global View of Pidginization and Creolization* (pp. 291–298). Amsterdam: Benjamins.

ILEA Afro-Caribbean Language and Literacy Project in Further and Adult Education (1990) *Language and Power*. London: Harcourt Brace Jovanovich.

Inoue, A. (2007) Copula patterns in Hawai'i Creole: Creole origin and decreolization. In M. Huber and V. Velupillai (eds) *Synchronic and Diachronic Perspectives on Contact Languages* (pp. 199–212). Amsterdam/Philadelphia: Benjamins.

Joseph, C.M.B. (1997) Haitian Creole in New York. In O. García and J.A. Fishman (eds) *The Multilingual Apple: Language in New York City* (pp. 281–299). Berlin: Mouton de Gruyter.

Keesing, R.M. (1988) *Melanesian Pidgin and the Oceanic Substrate*. Stanford: Stanford University Press.

Kephart, R.F. (1992) Reading creole English does not destroy your brain cells! In J. Siegel (ed.) *Pidgins, Creoles and Nonstandard Dialects in Education* (pp. 67–86). Melbourne: Applied Linguistics Association of Australia (Occasional Paper no. 12).

Kouwenberg, S. (2002) *Bringing Language Awareness into the High School Curriculum: The Opportunities Offered by CAPE Communication Studies*. Paper presented at the 14th Biennial Conference of the Society for Caribbean Linguistics, University of the West Indies, St Augustine, Trinidad & Tobago.

Lefebvre, C. (1998) *Creole Genesis and the Acquisition of Grammar: The Case of Haitian Creole*. Cambridge: Cambridge University Press.

Lefebvre, C., White, L. and Jourdan, C. (eds) (2006) *L2 Acquisition and Creole Genesis*. Amsterdam/Philadelphia: Benjamins.

LePage, R.B. and Tabouret-Keller, A. (1985) *Acts of Identity: Creole-based Approaches to Language and Ethnicity*. Cambridge: Cambridge University Press.

Li, M., Matthews, S. and Smith, G.P. (2005) Pidgin English texts from the Chinese English instructor. In G.P. Smith and S. Matthews (eds) *Chinese Pidgin English: Texts and Contexts* (pp. 79–167). Hong Kong: The English Centre, University of Hong Kong (Special issue of the *Hong Kong Journal of Applied Linguistics* 10/1).

Mahoune, J-C.P. (2000) Seychellois Creole: Development and evolution. *IIAS Newsletter Online* 22. On WWW at http://iias.leidenuniv.nl/iiasn/22/regions/22ISA1.html. Accessed 25.2.2005.

Malcolm, I.G. (1992) English in the education of speakers of Aboriginal English. In J. Siegel (ed.) *Pidgins, Creoles and Nonstandard Dialects in Education* (pp. 14–41). Melbourne: Applied Linguistics Association of Australia (Occasional Paper no. 12).

Mann, C.C. (1996) Anglo-Nigerian Pidgin in Nigerian education: A survey of policy, practice and attitudes. In T. Hickey and J. Williams (eds) *Language, Education and Society in a Changing World* (pp. 93–106). Clevedon: Multilingual Matters.

Mather, P-A. (2006) Second language acquisition and creolization: Same (i-) processes, different (e-) results. *Journal of Pidgin and Creole Languages* 21 (2), 231–274.

McWhorter, J.H. (1998) Identifying the creole prototype: Vindicating a typological class. *Language* 74, 788–818.

McWhorter, J.H. (2001) The world's simplest grammars are creole grammars. *Linguistic Typology* 5 (2/3), 125–166.

McWhorter, J.H. (2005) *Defining Creole*. New York: Oxford University Press.

Menacker, T. (1998) A visit to CAP. *Pidgins and Creoles in Education (PACE) Newsletter* 9, 3–4.

Migge, B. (2003) *Creole Formation as Language Contact*. Amsterdam/Philadelphia: Benjamins.

Migge, B. (ed.) (2007) *Substrate Influence in Creole Formation*. Amsterdam/ Philadelphia: Benjamins (Special issue of *Journal of Pidgin and Creole Languages* 22/1).

Morren, R.C. (2001) Creole-based trilingual education in the Caribbean archipelago of San Andres, Providence and Santa Catalina. *Journal of Multilingual and Multicultural Development* 22 (3), 227–241.

Morren, R.C. (2004) *Linguistic Results of a Creole Reading Inventory*. Paper presented at the Conference of the Society for Caribbean Linguistics and the Society for Pidgin and Creole Linguistics, Curaçao.

Mufwene, S.S. (2001) *The Ecology of Language Evolution*. Cambridge: Cambridge University Press.

Mühleisen, S. (2002) *Creole Discourse: Exploring Prestige Formation and Change across Caribbean English-lexicon Creoles*. Amsterdam/Philadelphia: Benjamins.

Munro, J.M. (2004) Substrate language influence in Kriol: The application of transfer constraints to language contact in Northern Australia. Unpublished PhD thesis, University of New England, Australia.

Murtagh, E.J. (1982) Creole and English as languages of instruction in bilingual education with Aboriginal Australians: Some research findings. *International Journal of the Sociology of Language* 36, 15–33.

Patrick, P.L. (1999) *Urban Jamaican Creole: Variation in the Mesolect*. Amsterdam/ Philadelphia: Benjamins.

Plag, I. (2008) Creoles as interlanguages: Inflectional morphology. *Journal of Pidgin and Creole Languages* 23 (1), 114–135.

Politzer, R.L. (1973) Problems in applying foreign language teaching methods to the teaching of standard English as a second dialect. In J.S.D. Stefano (ed.) *Language, Society, and Education: A Profile of Black English* (pp. 238–250). Worthington, OH: Charles A. Jones.

Rajah-Carrim, A. (2007) Mauritian Creole and language attitudes in the education system of multiethnic and multilingual Mauritius. *Journal of Multilingual and Multicultural Development* 28 (1), 51–71.

Ravel, J.-L. and Thomas, P. (1985) *État de la réforme de l'enseignement aux Seychelles (1981–1985)*. Paris: Ministère des Relations Extérieures, Coopération et Développement.

Ray, C. (1996) Report: Papua New Guinea. *Pidgins and Creoles in Education (PACE) Newsletter* 7, 3.

Reaser, J. (2004) A quantitative sociolinguistic analysis of Bahamian copula absence: Morphosyntacitc evidence from Abaco Island, the Bahamas. *Journal of Pidgin and Creole Languages* 19 (1), 1–40.

Reynolds, S.B. (1999) Mutual intelligibility? Comprehension problems between American Standard English and Hawai'i Creole English in Hawai'i's public schools. In J.R. Rickford and S. Romaine (eds) *Creole Genesis, Attitudes and Discourse: Studies Celebrating Charlene J. Sato* (pp. 303–319). Amsterdam/ Philadelphia: Benjamins.

Rickford, J.R. (1987) *Dimensions of a Creole Continuum: History, Text, and Linguistic Analysis of Guyanese Creole*. Bloomington: Indiana University Press.

Rickford, J.R. (1998) The creole origins of African–American vernacular English: Evidence from copula absence. In S.S. Mufwene, J.R. Rickford, B. Guy and J. Baugh (eds) *African–American English: Structure, History and Use* (pp. 154–200). London/New York: Routledge.

Rickford, J.R. (1999) Variation in the Jamaican Creole copula and its relation to the genesis of AAVE. In J.R. Rickford and S. Romaine (eds) *Creole Genesis, Attitudes and Discourse: Studies Celebrating Charlene J. Sato* (pp. 143–156). Amsterdam/ Philadelphia: Benjamins.

Rickford, J.R. and Traugott, E.C. (1985) Symbol of powerlessness and degeneracy, or symbol of solidarity and truth? Paradoxical attitudes toward pidgins and creoles. In S. Greenbaum (ed.) *The English Language Today* (pp. 252–261). Oxford: Pergamon Institute of English.

Roberts, S.J. (1998) The role of diffusion in the genesis of Hawaiian Creole. *Language* 74, 1–39.

Roberts, S.J. (2000) Nativization and genesis of Hawaiian Creole. In J.H. McWhorter (ed.) *Language Change and Language Contact in Pidgins and Creoles* (pp. 257–300). Amsterdam/Philadelphia: Benjamins.

Roberts, S.J. (2005) The emergence of Hawai'i Creole English in the early 20th century: The sociohistorical context of creole genesis. Unpublished PhD dissertation, Stanford University.

Rogers, T.S. (1996) Poisoning pidgins in the park: The study and status of Hawaiian Creole. In J.E. Alatis, C.A. Straehle, M. Ronkin and B. Gallenberger (eds) *Georgetown University Roundtable on Languages and Linguistics, 1996: Linguistics, Language Acquisition and Language Variation: Current Trends and Future Prospects* (pp. 221–235). Washington, DC: Georgetown University Press.

Romaine, S. (1999) Changing attitudes to Hawai'i Creole English: Fo' find one good job, you gotta know how fo' talk like one haole. In J.R. Rickford and S. Romaine (eds) *Creole Genesis, Attitudes and Discourse: Studies Celebrating Charlene J. Sato* (pp. 287–301). Amsterdam/Philadelphia: Benjamins.

Rynkofs, J.T. (1993) Culturally responsive talk between a second grade teacher and Hawaiian children during writing workshop. Unpublished PhD dissertation, University of New Hampshire.

Sakoda, K. and Siegel, J. (2003) *Pidgin Grammar: An Introduction to the Creole Language of Hawai'i*. Honolulu: Bess Press.

Schieffelin, B.B. and Doucet, R.C. (1994) The "real" Haitian Creole: Ideology, metalinguistics, and orthographic choice. *American Ethnologist* 21, 176–200.

Schmidt, R. (1990) The role of consciousness in second language learning. *Applied Linguistics* 11, 129–158.

Schmidt, R. (1993) Awareness and second language acquisition. *Annual Review of Applied Linguistics* 13, 206–226.

Schnepel, E.M. (2004) *In Search of a National Identity: Creole and Politics in Guadeloupe*. Hamburg: Helmut Buske.

Sebba, M. (1997) *Contact Languages: Pidgins and Creoles*. New York: St Martin's Press.

Sebba, M. (2000) Orthography and ideology: Issues in Sranan spelling. *Linguistics* 38 (5), 925–948.

Shields-Brodber, K. (1997) Requiem for English in an "English-speaking" community: The case of Jamaica. In E.W. Schneider (ed.) *Englishes Around the World: Volume 2: Caribbean, Africa, Asia, Australasia: Studies in Honour of Manfred Görlach* (pp. 57–67). Amsterdam/Philadelphia: Benjamins.

Siegel, J. (1997) Using a pidgin language in formal education: help or hindrance? *Applied Linguistics* 18, 86–100.

Siegel, J. (1999) Stigmatized and standardized varieties in the classroom: Interference or separation? *TESOL Quarterly* 33, 701–728.

Siegel, J. (2000) Substrate influence in Hawai'i Creole English. *Language in Society* 29, 197–236.

Siegel, J. (2003) Substrate influence in creoles and the role of transfer in second language acquisition. *Studies in Second Language Acquisition* 25 (2), 185–209.

Siegel, J. (2008) *The Emergence of Pidgin and Creole Languages*. Oxford/New York: Oxford University Press.

Simmons-McDonald, H. (2004) Trends in teaching standard varieties to creole and vernacular speakers. *Annual Review of Applied Linguistics* 24, 187–208.

Singler, J.V. (ed.) (1990) *Pidgin and Creole Tense-Mood-Aspect Systems*. Amsterdam/ Philadelphia: Benjamins.

Skutnabb-Kangas, T. (1988) Multilingualism and the education of minority children. In T. Skutnabb-Kangas and J. Cummins (eds) *Minority Education: From Shame to Struggle* (pp. 9–44). Clevedon: Multilingual Matters.

Speidel, G. (1987) Conversation and language learning in the classroom. In K.E. Nelson and A. van Kleek (eds) *Children's Language* (Vol. 6) (pp. 99–135). Hillsdale, NJ: Erlbaum.

Stewart, W.A. (1964) Urban Negro speech: Sociolinguistic factors affecting English teaching. In R.W. Shuy, A.L. Davis and R.F. Hogan (eds) *Social Dialects and Language Learning* (pp. 10–18). Champaign, IL: National Council of Teachers of English.

Tamura, E.H. (1996) Power, status, and Hawaii Creole English: An example of linguistic intolerance in American history. *Pacific Historical Review* 65 (3), 431–454.

Thomas, W.P. and Collier, V.P. (2002) *A National Study of School Effectiveness for Language Minority Students' Long-term Academic Achievement*. Santa Cruz: Center for Research on Education, Diversity & Excellence.

Torrey, J. (1972) *The Language of Black Children in the Early Grades*. New London: Connecticut College.

Turner, C. (1997) The Injinoo Home Language Program: A positive community response to marginalisation and institutional racism. *Australian Journal of Indigenous Education* 25, 1–9.

UNESCO (1968) The use of vernacular languages in education: The report of the UNESCO meeting of specialists, 1951. In J.A. Fishman (ed.) *Readings in the Sociology of Language* (pp. 688–716). The Hague: Mouton.

Wassink, A.B. (1999) Historic low prestige and seeds of change: Attitudes toward Jamaican Creole. *Language in Society* 28, 57–92.

Weldon, T. (2003) Revisiting the creolist hypothesis: Copula variability in Gullah and southern rural AAVE. *American Speech* 78 (2), 359–397.

Winer, L. (1990) Orthographic standardization for Trinidad and Tobago: Linguistic and sociopolitical considerations. *Language Problems and Language Planning* 14 (3), 237–268.

Winford, D. (1993) *Predication in Caribbean English Creoles*. Amsterdam/Philadelphia: Benjamins.

Winford, D. (1994) Sociolinguistic approaches to language use in the Anglophone Caribbean. In M. Morgan (ed.) *The Social Construction of Identity in Creole Situations* (pp. 43–62). Los Angeles: Center for Afro-American Studies, UCLA.

Wiruk, E. (2000) Report: Papua New Guinea. *Pidgins and Creoles in Education (PACE) Newsletter* 11, 1.

Zéphir, F. (1997) Haitian Creole language and bilingual education in the United States: Problem, right, or resource? *Journal of Multilingual and Multicultural Development* 18 (3), 223–237.

Part 4
Language and Literacy

Chapter 10

Cross-cultural Perspectives on Writing: Contrastive Rhetoric

RYUKO KUBOTA

Introduction

Teachers who help second language (L2) learners develop academic writing skills often confront issues at the discourse level such as how to organize a paragraph or where to place a thesis statement. When they encounter nonnative features in discourse structure, they sometimes suspect a negative influence of the student's native language or culture on L2 writing. These teachers might be persuaded by the arguments offered by contrastive rhetoric research. Contrastive rhetoric, the cross-cultural analysis of the ways in which written texts are organized, also provides pedagogical implications for L2 writing. Its scope overlaps with broader fields such as intercultural communication, rhetoric and composition, applied linguistics, as well as more specific inquiry areas such as second language writing, text linguistics, and genre analysis (Connor, 1996). The field was developed in response to a pedagogical need to accommodate a rise of international students in US universities in the 1960s. It was initiated by Robert Kaplan (1966), who argued that specific cultural thought patterns associated with language influence the ways in which students write in their L1 and L2 and that cultural difference should be taken into account in teaching academic writing to international students. Since then, various researchers have investigated cultural differences in rhetorical organization manifested in written texts in many languages. Although many studies follow the conventional tenets of contrastive rhetoric, the recent *critical turn* of applied linguistics (Kumaravadivelu, 2006) has witnessed renewed understandings of culture, language and learner agency as well as the role these categories play in written communication. Contrastive rhetoric provides teachers and researchers with opportunities to become aware of not only the complexity of cross-cultural writing but also how inquiry approaches are influenced by historical shifts in academic discourse and at the same time influence linguistic and cultural shifts.

This chapter provides an overview of contrastive rhetoric research in terms of conceptual assumptions, historical background, multiple perspectives provided by criticisms, impact of the knowledge developed by the field on language shifts, and implications for practitioners who work with second language learners.

Assumptions and Findings of Contrastive Rhetoric Research

In his seminal article and subsequent publications, Robert Kaplan (1966, 1972, 1988) discussed how thought patterns differ according to language groups and how they are reflected in the discourse features of some essays written by international students in US universities in English as a second language (ESL). There are two major assumptions of contrastive rhetoric: (1) each language or culture has unique rhetorical conventions due to a culturally specific cultural thought pattern, and (2) the rhetorical conventions of students' first languages (L1) interfere with or negatively transfer to their ESL writing. These tenets were based on Kaplan's observation that academic essays written by ESL writers display features that are different from those in typical essays written in English as the first or native language (L1). The oft-cited figure that appeared in Kaplan (1966) offers graphic representations of cultural thought patterns, in which English is depicted with a linear line, Oriental languages with a centrifugal circle, Semitic languages with parallelism, Romance languages with digression and Russian with digression with a dotted line.

Many studies since then have investigated cultural difference in rhetoric and described the characteristics of written discourse in various languages. For instance, Ulla Connor (1996), a leading scholar of contrastive rhetoric, offers a summary of previous research on various languages: Arabic is characterized by a parallel construction with coordinate clauses, which can be traced back to classical texts such as the *Old Testament* and *Qur'an*. Chinese, Korean and Japanese are often lumped together and described as inductive and indirect, characterized by a four-unit organization called *qi-cheng-zhuan-he* in Chinese, *ki-sung-chong-kyul* in Korean or *ki-shô-ten-ketsu* in Japanese, which originates in Chinese classical poetry (see Hinds, 1983, 1987, 1990). Chinese rhetoric is also characterized by another model called the eight-legged essay, which was required for the civil service examination during the late Qing Dynasty (1644–1912) (e.g. Kaplan, 1972).

With regard to other languages, German is characterized as digressive and is focused more on content than form, Finnish as inductive and indirect, Spanish as elaborated and flowery with longer sentences and 'loose coordination' (Connor, 1996: 52–53), and Czech (as well as other Slavic languages such as Russian, Polish and Ukrainian – see Petrić, 2005) as less linear than English and with a delayed statement of purpose. One term that is often used to describe an inductive organization is *delayed introduction of purpose*, which was proposed by Hinds (1990) in describing Chinese, Korean, Japanese and Thai as opposed to a deductive structure with a thesis statement placed at the outset as in English. Another category is a distinction between reader responsibilities and writer responsibility (Hinds, 1987). According to Hinds, texts written in a reader-responsible language (e.g. Japanese) require readers to find a logical link between sentences or paragraphs due to a lack of explicit rhetorical devices, whereas texts written in a writer-responsible language (e.g. English) display a logical connection between arguments because the writer is responsible for making the connection explicit. Connor (2002) provides more updated summaries of previous studies on rhetoric in some languages in Europe (e.g. Finnish and Spanish), the Middle East (Arabic) and Asia (Chinese). While her review identifies some findings that are inconsistent with previous research (e.g. the study by Scollon and Scollon (1997), which found no evidence of the predominance of *qi-cheng-zhuan-he* or inductive pattern in Chinese; see also critiques below), her summary underscores L1–L2 transfer and cultural differences between English (which is seen as linear, direct and assertive) and various languages (which are not like English).

In terms of the second assumption of contrastive rhetoric – namely L1–L2 negative transfer of rhetoric – the identification of culturally specific rhetorical features in L2 texts led researchers to presume L1–L2 transfer (Kaplan, 1966, 1967, 1972; Ostler, 1987, 1990; Söter, 1988). Other studies that include actual analysis of students' L1 and L2 essays generally support L1–L2 transfer. Whereas earlier studies tend to confirm L1–L2 transfer of an inductive style as culturally specific and different from English (Indrasuta, 1988; Kobayashi, 1984; Oi, 1984), more recent studies found L1–L2 transfer of a deductive organization (Hirose, 2003; Kubota, 1998a; Wu & Rubin, 2000 – see more discussion later).

Overall, the mainstream contrastive rhetoric studies have depicted the characteristics of written discourse of English, especially standard American written English, as linear, deductive, logical and writer-responsible. These features of written English are manifested in the five-paragraph theme in school writing, which consists of 'one paragraph of introduction ("tell what you are going to say"), three of expansion and example ("say it"), and one of conclusion ("tell what you have said")' (Emig, 1971: 97). In contrast, languages other than English are usually depicted as what English is not. Contrastive rhetoric has actually constructed a peculiar kind of knowledge – a binary between English and non-English languages. Furthermore, this binary is not neutral; it implies superiority of English and inferiority of other languages. These issues, among others, make this field of study highly controversial (see criticisms below). In response to criticisms, Connor has proposed a new direction of contrastive rhetoric, which she calls *intercultural rhetoric* (Connor, 2004, 2008). As discussed in a later section, inquiry foci under the new name have become diversified, while the basic assumptions have remained unchanged in many studies.

With regard to pedagogical implications, contrastive rhetoric has proposed explicit teaching of the conventional rhetorical structure of English through mechanical means, such as rearranging scrambled paragraphs, writing according to an outline, developing an outline, imitating models, identifying topic structures and so on (Kaplan, 1966, 1967, 1972). Making students aware of cultural difference is another strategy (Kaplan, 1988; Reid, 1989; see Kubota & Lehner, 2004, for more details). Some recent studies have investigated the effects of the explicit teaching of English rhetoric on students' writing development (Kobayashi & Rinnert, 2007; Petrić, 2005). All in all, contrastive rhetoric tends to support explicit teaching of the rhetorical norm with a goal of integrating the students into the mainstream academic discourse community.

Methods of Investigation and Challenges

The above knowledge about cultural difference in rhetoric and L1–L2 rhetorical transfer has been developed through several methodological approaches, many of which contain limitations. It is important to keep in mind that the research impetus arose from pedagogical interest in helping ESL writers develop academic writing skills in English, and thus the research focus is on finding cultural differences between English and other languages. In general, carefully conducted studies that compare comparable texts illuminate a range of complexity of rhetorical features.

One method of investigating the culturally specific rhetorical structures of languages other than English is to analyze published texts in those languages. In oft-cited publications, Hinds (1983, 1987, 1990) mainly examined essays written for a Japanese newspaper column that appeared on the first page of the newspaper; he identified the unique four-unit organizational feature as the preferred style for expository writing in Japanese. Hinds argued that this culturally specific style makes the text difficult for native speakers of English to comprehend, because the third unit, *ten*, shifts the topic abruptly without any explicit transition from the previous content. However, McCagg (1996) and Donahue (1998) point out that Hinds' examples contain culturally loaded topics that reduce the level of perceived coherence and comprehensibility of the text. In other words, it is not the culturally specific rhetorical style but the audience's lack of prior knowledge of the topic that makes the texts difficult to comprehend. Moreover, this method of analyzing selective texts conflates journalist writing with academic writing, which have very different purposes, contexts and audiences (Kubota, 1997). As genre studies demonstrate (e.g. Johns, 2002), cross-cultural studies of texts need to take into account the compatibility of genre types and communicative purposes in analyzing textual structures. Moreover, rhetorical genre studies (e.g. Coe, 2002; Miller, 1984), which emphasize genre as social action rather than as a mere system of structures, shift our attention from static and neutral textual forms to a view of writing as social action through which writers conform, appropriate or bend textual expectations to express their meaning. As such, social, political and ideological contexts influence genre to be always (re)constructed and they make textual structures fluid and generative (see more discussion later). In this perspective, analyzing a text without taking into consideration the complexity and dynamics of genre produces limited insight.

Other studies conduct more careful comparisons of published texts within the same genre in two languages. They reveal some similarities as well as differences in cross-cultural rhetorical structures. For example, Taylor and Chen (1991) compared Chinese and English academic papers published in China in related fields of science to English papers in the same fields published in English-speaking countries; they found that the papers' introductions share similar rhetorical moves across cultures, although the Chinese-based papers tended to summarize the literature less frequently than did English papers, which the authors attributed to a reluctance to expose others' work as a source of shortcoming. Investigating the method of citation in Chinese and English academic papers, Bloch and Chi (1995) compared English articles published in *Science* magazine with Chinese articles published in equivalent journals. They found that Chinese authors use citations with varied functions, including critical ones, as English authors do, although they use them less frequently than English authors.

Partly because of the pedagogical focus and availability of data, other studies have examined students' ESL essays and made claims about culturally specific rhetorical structures and L1–L2 rhetorical transfer by implication (Kaplan, 1966, 1967, 1972; Ostler, 1987, 1990; Söter, 1988). For example, Kaplan (1966) supported cultural differences in thought patterns by comparing excerpts of L2 essays written by ESL students from different L1 backgrounds with a prototypical English essay. The identification of culturally specific rhetorical organizations leads to a claim for L1–L2 transfer of rhetoric. The underlying assumption is that ESL essays written by students from different L1 backgrounds exhibit unique group features because the students use L1 rhetoric in their L2 writing. However, this assumption is problematic; without knowledge about students' writing in their L1, L1–L2 transfer can only be speculated on. In addition, multiple factors besides L1 rhetorical features affect L2 writing process and products. These factors include L2 proficiency (lexical, syntactic and semantic competencies), L1 writing expertise (e.g. Cumming, 1989; Kubota, 1998a; Sasaki & Hirose, 1996), developmental issues including instructional focus (e.g. instructional tendency to focus on the sentence level rather than text organization in L2 classrooms – see Mohan & Lo, 1985), and individual writers' agency as reflected in their rhetorical intentions and preferences. L2 writing clearly involves multiple factors, of which L1–L2 transfer might only marginally impact L2 writing.

This problem is partly overcome by examining both L1 and L2 essays written by the same students. Some studies have confirmed transfer of prototypical L1 rhetorical features to ESL texts (e.g. Indrasuta, 1988; Kobayashi, 1984; Oi, 1984; Wu & Rubin, 2000), although Kobayashi (1984) and Oi (1984) examined L1 Japanese and L2 English essays written by different groups of Japanese students. More recently, Wu and Rubin (2000) compared L1 (Chinese) and L2 (English) essays written by the same Taiwanese college students with L1 (English) essays on the same topics written by American college students. They identified a relative degree of inductiveness and collective, rather than individualist, virtues among Taiwanese students' L1 essays as opposed to a prevalence of deductiveness with personal anecdotes among American students. However, the degree of directness was not statistically significant between L2 English and L1 English essays and the inductiveness found in L1 Chinese essays was in fact *relative* to L1 English essays (i.e. 47.5% of the L1 Chinese essays were wholly deductive as opposed to 90% in L1 English). In terms of L1–L2 transfer, Wu and Rubin (2000) found no difference in terms of thesis statement placement between L1 and L2 essays, thus confirming transfer. Yet, they did not identify transfer of certain aspects of rhetorical features, such as the use of first person singular and plural pronouns (the frequencies of these pronouns were higher in L2 essays).

Although these studies are carefully designed and conducted, from a perspective that views writing as an individual action for expressing the writer's self (Clark & Ivanič, 1997), the L1–L2 *between-group* comparison or comparing L1 and L2 texts in the aggregate may not reveal actual transfer at the individual level. A *within-subject* design would shed more light on whether individual writers actually use the same rhetorical patterns in L1 and L2 and what kind of individual perceptions and intentions influence the rhetorical decision (Hirose, 2003; Kubota, 1998a). These critiques assume that features of L2 writing are related to multiple factors and cannot be reduced solely to cultural influence.

As contrastive rhetoric is reconfigured and developed into intercultural rhetoric (Connor, 2004, 2008), the focus broadens from academic writing to journalistic writing, grant proposals, business writing, book reviews and so on. Choosing a specific genre as an inquiry focus reduces the problem of ignoring the genre factor in cross-linguistic text comparisons. Other more recent studies have examined the effects of instruction on students' L1 and/or L2 essay structures (Kobayashi & Rinnert, 2007; Petrić, 2005). Still other studies have investigated readers' evaluation of the quality of texts or their reading recall of texts with the assumption that expertise in a certain rhetorical structure would affect the ways readers comprehend and evaluate texts (Chu *et al.*, 2002; Kobayashi & Rinnert, 1996; Li, 1996; Rinnert & Kobayashi, 2001). A general finding is that readers with more experience with English discourse have a higher level of preference for and comprehension of English-type rhetoric than do less-experienced readers. In sum, contrastive rhetoric studies have mostly used published texts and texts written by student writers to investigate cultural patterns and L1–L2 transfer. However, earlier studies have been found to contain many methodological limitations.

Historical Background

In the 1960s, when contrastive rhetoric emerged, US universities witnessed a large influx of international students. Reviewing a history of second language writing instruction in the United States, Matsuda (2001) comments that between 1940 and 1950, there was a more than 450% increase in the number of international students. My review of the data compiled by the Institute of International Education indicates that between the academic years of 1951–52 and 1966–67 (a 15-year interval), the number of international students increased by more than 330% (Institute of International Education, 2005). This increase generated a need for instructional support to integrate these students into the academic community in English. Contrastive rhetoric was proposed in this historical context.

Contrastive analysis and error analysis

Another historical context that needs to be taken into account is the general trend of research inquiry into second language study at that time. In the 1950s and 1960s, contrastive analysis, as represented by the work of Lado (1957), emerged against the backdrop of behaviorism, which was at that time influential in the field of psychology (Gass & Selinker, 2001). In contrastive analysis, language learning was understood as habit formation involving sets of stimulus and response (e.g. hearing a word and pointing to the referent object or seeing an object and uttering the word). Learning a second language meant replacing a set of previous habits that the learners have developed in their L1 with a new set of habits. In this framework, comparing and contrasting the structures of L1 and L2 was considered to provide useful information for helping L2 learners establish new habits. Contrastive analysis emerged in this context with a strong pedagogical interest. Although contrastive analysis, as influenced by behaviorism and the field of linguistics at that time, was concerned with spoken language, contrastive rhetoric was clearly influenced by this conceptual and methodological framework. Assumptions behind contrastive analysis that are relevant to contrastive rhetoric can be summarized as below (see Gass & Selinker, 2001: 72–73):

(1) Contrastive analysis is based on a theory of language that claims that language is habit and that language learning involves a new set of habits.

(2) The major source of error in the production and/or reception of a second language is the native language.

(3) One can account for errors by considering differences between the L1 and the L2.

(4) A corollary to item 3 is that the greater the differences, the more errors will occur.

(5) What one has to do in learning a second language is learn the differences. Similarities can be safely ignored as no new learning is involved. In other words, what is dissimilar between two languages is what must be learned.

Different conceptualizations of the role of L1 in L2 learning divided contrastive analysis into two approaches: the strong form and the weak form. The strong form supported the predictability of learner output through comparing the learner's native language with the target language, whereas the weak form supported an explanatory view whereby the learner's output was analyzed and L1 influence was accounted for. Although the strong form of contrastive analysis provided a tool for hypothesizing the role of L1 in L2 learning, it lacked empirical analysis of the L2 learner's output data. This realization led to error analysis – an extension of the weak form of contrastive analysis – which collected, identified, classified and quantified linguistic errors made by L2 learners as well as analyzed the sources of errors including L1 linguistic features.

With regard to methodology, the strong version of contrastive analysis makes a comparison of linguistic structures between two languages in order to predict L1–L2 transfer, whereas the weak version predicts L1 influence from the L2 output of learners. Error analysis further compares errors made by L2 learners with the target language structures (Gass & Selinker, 2001). This is comparable to the methodology used by contrastive rhetoric research. The strong form of contrastive analysis is similar to contrastive rhetoric's text analysis in various languages, although the features of English rhetoric are often prescriptively assumed. The weak form of contrastive analysis and error analysis parallel the contrastive rhetoric approach to analyze ESL essays (plus sometimes L1 English essays) to predict L1–L2 transfer. Although contrastive rhetoric presented its unique focus on discourse, written language, and culture, it did not contradict the overall intellectual trend in the 1960s.

This brief overview of contrastive analysis and error analysis indicates that contrastive rhetoric at least initially followed the intellectual trend of the time, especially in terms of the second assumption of contrastive rhetoric (i.e. L1–L2 transfer). Methodological approaches of contrastive rhetoric can be compared to those of contrastive analysis and error analysis. Yet, as researchers such as Connor (2008) point out, the unique aspect of the initiation of contrastive rhetoric was its focus on discourse structures beyond the sentence level in written communication as opposed to sentence- or clause-level features of spoken language, which was the predominant focus of inquiry at that time. Another unique focus was cultural difference, to which I will now turn.

Whorfian linguistic relativity

The first assumption of contrastive rhetoric that focuses on cultural difference in thought patterns as reflected in written languages parallels the theory of Whorfian linguistic relativity proposed in the 1930s (or the Sapir–Whorf hypothesis, named after Benjamin Whorf and his mentor, Edward Sapir), which postulates that different language systems shape different thought patterns or worldviews. Whether this hypothesis influenced Kaplan's original idea about cultural thought patterns has been debated (Matsuda, 2001; Ying, 2000, 2001). However, Kaplan himself mentions the influence of the Sapir–Whorf hypothesis (Kaplan, 1972) and uses the term 'neo-Whorfian' to refer to the underlying assumption of contrastive rhetoric (Kaplan, 1988: 279; see also Kowal, 1998). Yet the fact that Whorfian linguistic relativity parallels the first assumption of contrastive rhetoric does not imply that both share an ideological stance in relation to a wider discourse of language and culture. In fact, they reflect quite different ideologies. To understand this difference, we need to historically and politically situate the conceptualization of cultural difference.

Benjamin Whorf was a linguist known for his work on Hopi, one of the Native American languages, in the 1930s and early 1940s. Although his idea that language shapes thought has often been criticized as promoting linguistic determinism, it was actually proposed in order to critique the narrow Eurocentric views of language and culture, which are based on what Whorf called 'Standard Average European (SAE)' languages and thought. While critiquing Western ethnocentrism, Whorf in turn celebrated the plurality of languages and multilingual consciousness (Kowal, 1998; Schultz, 1990). However, the subsequent popularity of Chomskyan generative linguistics undermined the Whorfian principle. Generative linguistics underscored linguistic universals and innateness, deemphasizing cultural aspects of language and thought and framing Whorf as a proponent of linguistic determinism. Whorf's political stance draws a sharp contrast with the conceptual underpinnings of contrastive rhetoric – that is, Anglocentric, assimilationist and essentialist. As discussed below, scholars have problematized this conceptual framework from various perspectives.

Criticisms of and Evidence against the Assumptions of Contrastive Rhetoric

As reviewed earlier, the dominant knowledge produced by contrastive rhetoric research since the 1960s has underscored cultural difference in rhetoric between English and other languages as well as L1–L2 negative transfer of rhetoric in academic ESL writing. The pedagogical proposals have been focused on explicit teaching of the prescriptive structure of English essays as well as raising awareness about cultural difference. However, such an approach has met many criticisms, especially with regard to the fixed and essentialist characterization of culture, language and ESL writers as well as the assimilationist, prescriptive and transmission-oriented pedagogy (see also Casanave, 2004 for a summary of criticisms).

Diverse, complex and nonessentialist view of language and culture

Scholars such as Matsuda (1997), Leki (1997), Spack (1997) and Zamel (1997) have criticized the reductionist, deterministic and essentialist orientation of contrastive rhetoric research, its prescriptive application to classroom teaching, and the parallel discourse in some related publications such as Fox (1994), Ramanathan and Kaplan (1996) and Carson (1992), which draw a rigid boundary between English (and academic culture represented by English) and ESL students' linguistic and cultural backgrounds. They critique the binary qualities created, such as linearity, individualism, critical thinking, clarity, reason and audience awareness for English writing versus opposing exotic and inferior qualities for writing in other languages. The critics advocate instead more attention to plurality, complexity, and hybridity of rhetorical patterns within one language as well as similarities among languages or cultures. They also propose to focus on the agency of students and view them as individuals with diverse educational experiences, subjectivities, and competencies. Leki (1997), for example argues that ignoring similarities leads to exoticizing the language and culture that ESL writers bring to ESL classrooms and dismissing the agency of writers as individuals.

Another critique has to do with diversity observed within a language. Kachru (1995, 1997, 1999) critiques traditional contrastive rhetoric as reducing English rhetoric to normative patterns and instructional models of American and British English. From a perspective of *world Englishes*, Kachru critiques contrastive rhetoric's sole focus on the Inner Circle varieties of English (i.e. English used in Anglophone countries) as a point of reference and its failure to validate Outer Circle rhetorical varieties of English (i.e. English used in former British and American colonies). Kachru (1997) points out the indirect style of an English essay written by a student writer of English in India and proposes to broaden the conceptualization of English rhetoric. Although the type of cultural difference that Kachru points out is consistent with the common assumption of contrastive rhetoric, which would be critiqued as essentialist based on a binary logic (see more discussion later), attention to the diversity of English problematizes the static and homogeneous view of English. An element of postcolonial critique is also evident in Kachru's proposal that Inner Circle readers (editors, professors, etc.) should raise awareness about different conventions of diverse varieties of English.

Focus on historical shifts

Kachru's perspective of the diversity within a language also raises a question of what ought to be compared or contrasted. As reviewed earlier, contrastive rhetoric research often compares an idealized contemporary English structure with essentialized classical styles of Arabic, Chinese, Korean, Japanese, and so on. This process exoticizes the images of these languages as the *Other*, while ignoring the shifting nature of language. Language indeed changes over time due to political and inter-linguistic/ cultural influence. In Chinese, critics argue that the *ba gu wen* (eight-legged essay), which has been claimed to affect Chinese students' writing in English (Kaplan, 1972), exerts little influence on contemporary writing in Chinese, particularly after the May 4th Movement of the Chinese Literary Revolution in 1919 (Kirkpatrick, 1997; Mohan & Lo, 1985). You (2008) provides a historical examination of Confucian influence on writing in China and demonstrates a historical shift from the use of the prescriptive eight-legged essay to its denunciation by emphasizing a clear theme and audience awareness during the Cultural Revolution, and to the subsequent depoliticization of themes, albeit some alignment with the dominant political ideology remains. Furthermore, Bloch and Chi (1995) argue that even classical Chinese rhetoric was never monolithic but invited varied views, some of which promoted logical argumentation and critical examination of the canon. Li (2002) argues that in high school writing in China, the eight-legged essay still exerts its influence, whereas university-level writing emphasizes logic, clarity, analysis, interpretation, and development of one's own ideas. Yet an analysis of junior high school language arts (L1 Chinese) textbooks in Mainland China identified some instructional emphases that are shared with English writing, including awareness of audience and purpose, clarity, good organization, effective supporting details and so on (Kubota & Shi, 2005).

Another classical style for East Asian languages is a four-unit pattern, *qi-cheng-zhuan-he* or *ki-shô-ten-ketsu*, which Hinds (1990) identifies as culturally specific. However, there is little evidence that this style influences contemporary expository writing in Chinese (Kirkpatrick, 1997) or

Japanese (Kubota, 1997) because there is no single definition of the form. Moreover, Cahill (2003) argues that Hinds's explanation that the third unit *zhuan* or *ten* prompts an abrupt turn of the topic and thus creates digression is untenable. Rather, the unit functions more loosely as a means to develop arguments in alternative ways.

The above observations indicate that essays written by Chinese- or Japanese-speaking students are unlikely to directly reflect classical rhetorical structures. In fact, contemporary academic writing across languages seems to be converging into the prescriptive style promoted in academic writing in English. In Arabic, Sa'adeddin (1989) distinguishes carefully planned *visual* texts used for scholarly writing from spontaneously developed *aural* texts marked by orality and argues that the former resembles English academic texts. The influence of Anglo-American conventions of academic writing on other languages is certainly related to the academic training in English that international students and scholars receive in Inner Circle countries. Research shows that professionals who were academically trained in Anglophone countries tend to use Inner Circle English conventions in publishing their papers in both their L1 (e.g. Chinese, Korean) and English (Eggington, 1987; Shi, 2002).

The influence of English on academic writing in other languages indicates historical shifts of rhetoric as You (2008) discusses in reference to Chinese. In Japanese, a historical overview reveals that the organization of contemporary academic texts is greatly influenced by Western rhetoric (Kubota, 1997). A series of recent education reforms since the late 1980s in Japan has revised the curriculum of L1 language arts including writing instruction. The trend has been an emphasis on a clear statement of purpose and the expression of the main idea at the outset (Kubota, 2002a, 2002b; Kubota & Shi, 2005). Thus, some of the more recent studies that examine L1 and L2 essays written by Japanese students, for instance, have found an increased use or preference of a deductive style (Hirose, 2003; Kobayashi & Rinnert, 2002, 2007; Kubota, 1998a, 1998b; Rinnert & Kobayashi, 2007).

Prescriptive versus descriptive gap

Another problem is a gap between prescriptive and descriptive forms of rhetoric. Contrastive rhetoric research often takes for granted prescriptive rhetorical conventions in English. This certainly has to do with its pedagogical focus – in order to integrate ESL students into academic discourse in English, an explicit presentation of the rhetorical form is pedagogically convenient. However, there is little evidence that the prototypical style, say the five-paragraph theme, is always preferred or even used in a majority of texts in English. In an analysis of junior high school English language arts textbooks published in Canada and the United States, Shi and Kubota (2007) found that the main idea in selected opinion essays is not necessarily presented in the introduction but rather in the middle or at the end of the essay. Thus, the fixed style in school writing (especially primary and secondary schools) is only one of many styles appreciated in English written discourse and elegantly written texts are not necessarily linear (Leki, 1997). In fact, the five-paragraph essay is not always preferred as an instructional goal; some teachers and researchers argue that it limits students' creativity and rhetorical choices (see Shi & Kubota, 2007). Likewise, although English-type rhetoric is promoted in China and Japan, the actual reading materials that appear in some textbooks do not always follow what is promoted (Kubota & Shi, 2005). The contextual specificities that texts and the act of writing are situated in pose the question of whether a universal concept of good writing exists (Coe & Freedman, 1998).

Critical contrastive rhetoric

The criticisms reviewed thus far reject ahistorical, fixed and simplistic definitions of cultural rhetoric and focus on human agency. These criticisms can be theorized in the framework of critical contrastive rhetoric, which draws on the so-called post-foundational (i.e. postmodern, post-structuralist and postcolonial) critiques that question normative and essentialist assumptions, illuminate the sociopolitical construction of our knowledge about language and culture, and offer possibilities for appropriating a linguistic form to express alternative meanings (Kubota & Lehner, 2004). As with critical applied linguistics and critical pedagogies (e.g. Pennycook, 2001), critical contrastive rhetoric problematizes and politicizes a common understanding of language, culture, teaching and learning to illuminate unequal relations of power involved in such knowledge and aims to transform oppressive discourse and social practice.

From a postmodern point of view, the modernist relativity that assumes fixed cultural and linguistic binaries are questioned. Instead, knowledge and practice are viewed as situated in sociopolitical arenas and historical trajectories, and are thus always in flux. Postmodernism focuses on the plurality of meaning and the hybrid, diasporic and dynamic nature of language and culture, while problematizing various forms of essentialism, including the static view of language and culture constructed by contrastive rhetoric research.

A poststructuralist approach to critical contrastive rhetoric views knowledge about language and culture of Self and Other as constructed by discourses rather than existing *a priori* divorced from politics and relations of power. This view allows us to explore how cultural difference in rhetoric and an implicit assumption of the superiority of English are discursively constructed in contrastive rhetoric research. In addition, student writers are viewed as agents with multiple subjectivities who act on

L1/L2 writing, rather than agent-less individuals who automatically transfer L1 rhetoric (whatever it is) to L2 writing.

Postcolonial perspectives critique the discourse of colonialism, which legitimates the unequal relation of power between the superior West (e.g. English rhetoric) and the inferior non-West (e.g. rhetoric of other languages) and perpetuates Othering. Such unequal relations of power and the concept of Self and Other are internalized by the marginalized (Fanon, 1967), creating symbolic violence (Bourdieu, 1991). It is important to note that this kind of worldview is constructed within our academic discourse rather than by individual researchers' personal bias. A postcolonial view of language and culture also situates rhetoric in a site of political struggle and allows a possibility of appropriating the language of power or using culturally specific rhetoric for the purpose of resistance.

Overall, critical contrastive rhetoric sheds light on political dimensions of rhetorical forms, practices and shifts through anti-essentialist and anti-Anglocentric explorations. It also views student writers as human agents who negotiate the rhetorical norms and their subjectivities in L1/L2 writing.

Recent Development of Contrastive Rhetoric into Intercultural Rhetoric

In response to many criticisms, Ulla Connor has made a series of proposals toward a renewed approach (Connor, 2002, 2004, 2008). With regard to the critique of the reductionist and essentialist tendency of contrastive rhetoric, Connor argues that the inquiry focus should move beyond cultural and linguistic binaries – such as deductive versus inductive pattern, linear versus nonlinear discourse, individualism versus collectivism and so on – and instead 'describe the vast complexities of cultural, social, and educational factors affecting a writing situation' (Connor, 2008: 304). As 'postmodern' maps, Connor proposes (1) Fairclough's (1992) approach to situate texts in sociopolitical contexts (although she does not mention the term critical discourse analysis, which Norman Fairclough is known for, nor does she refer to the role of language in relation to power, ideology and social change), (2) Holliday's (1999) idea of small versus large cultures, which moves beyond the essentialist notion of national culture and investigates practices in local institutions, and (3) a shift from cross-cultural investigation, which assumes communication across distinct cultures, to intercultural investigation, which focuses on interethnic communication (although the difference between 'cross-cultural' and 'interethnic' communication is not clearly made). Connor, thus, proposes a focus on complexity and dynamics in writing practices and a use of not only text analysis but also interviews with writers and readers as a research methodology.

Although the focus on local contexts and dynamics in written communication is consistent with the more recent trend within applied linguistics research in general, the new approach lacks in any significant way a critical edge or a perspective embraced by many critics of contrastive rhetoric – that is, a stance that problematizes the unequal relations of power observed in various categories such as language, culture and educational practice, as well as the discursive construction of cultural difference. Connor's endorsement of the latest writing of Kaplan (2005) as demonstrating an advancement of the field indicates that the fundamental assumptions are unchanged. The model proposed by Kaplan (2005) is certainly more complex than earlier conceptualizations in that it involves interactions among the writer, the reader and the text, mediated by genre, purpose, text conventions, shared experience and so on. However, it assumes incompatibility between language A and language B and consequently second language writers' *lack* of knowledge of the target language discourse conventions. This essentially reflects cultural/linguistic binaries and a deficit model that have been criticized for a long time, rather than an empowerment perspective, such as the concept of *funds of knowledge* or students' cultural resources that can be capitalized on in teaching (Moll *et al.*, 1992). Moreover, as globalization advances, international communication is increasingly converging into the Anglo-based communicative style (e.g. directness rather than indirectness) (Cameron, 2002), making an assertion of absolute incompatibility between two language systems questionable.

It is certainly the case that contrastive rhetoric research has become diversified, expanding its range of inquiry to include corpus analysis, a variety of genres, and social contexts investigated through interviews (Connor, 2004). The most recent volume edited by Connor *et al.* (2008) explores genres such as business letters, grant proposals, newspaper editorials and commentaries and academic book reviews. In addition, rhetorical diversity within a language (*cf.* Kachru, 1995, 1997, 1999) is incorporated, as in Ädel (2008) on difference between American and British students' writing in English and Pak and Acevedo (2008) on difference in Spanish newspaper editorials published in Mexico City, Madrid, New York and Los Angeles.

However, it is important to note that looking for differences within a narrower category or *small culture* (Holliday, 1999) still cannot escape essentialism, because small cultures or varieties of English, for instance, could be described with essentialist labels that are distinct from each other. Despite the range of diversity and some critical perspectives addressed (critical perspective of plagiarism by Bloch, 2008; a historical shift of Chinese rhetoric in relation to politics by You, 2008), the conclusions of many of the data-based studies still focus on cultural difference in written discourse. For instance, in investigating business writing in English and

Russian, Wolfe (2008) uses Hofstede's (1984) cultural dimensions that draw boundaries in terms of power distance, avoidance of uncertainty, individualism versus collectivism, and masculinity versus femininity. The cultural difference found in the analysis led to a conclusion that Russian speakers writing in English to American partners are likely to transfer their L1 conventions and cause miscommunication. One would wonder if this is a new approach to contrastive rhetoric when old cultural binaries are still used to explain rhetorical differences. Furthermore, why is miscommunication always attributed to the problem of Russian business people who do not use English conventions, and never vice versa? A question then is whether the focus on a dynamic and nonessentialist approach to rhetoric, as Connor proposes, is still within the modernist, rather than postmodernist, framework of seeking objective truths about differences between cultures (or small cultures) and whether renaming the field is merely a cosmetic, rather than paradigm, change.

Any field of inquiry should aim to contribute new knowledge. While contrastive rhetoric has certainly illuminated, albeit controversially, issues of culture in writing, one peculiar facet of contrastive rhetoric research is its impact on the rhetorical shift of languages other than English. This addresses the important social and ideological influences of the research, to which I will now turn.

Ideological Impact of Contrastive Rhetoric on Rhetorical Shift

As discussed earlier, the English-type mode of communication has recently been promoted in the Japanese language. I argue that this shift is influenced by the perceived linguistic and cultural differences between Japanese and English. Language educators in Japan have indeed drawn on assumptions of contrastive rhetoric, underscored cultural difference and argued for the need to improve communicative effectiveness in Japanese in the globalized world. Some have cited the graphic model offered by Kaplan (1966) to point out cultural difference in thought pattern, with the implication that the Japanese need to adopt English-type discourse in order to express their views and opinions clearly and convincingly in increasingly internationalized communicative settings (see Kubota, 2002b). The trend toward English-type rhetoric is reflected in L1 Japanese language textbooks. As Kubota and Shi (2005) indicate, these textbooks recommend that students use features similar to English conventions. In addition, the fact that recent studies have found in Japanese students a tendency to use a deductive style in their writing indicates that the knowledge created by contrastive rhetoric research has perhaps supported a discourse that the inductive and indirect style hinders international communication and that Japanese written (and spoken) discourse should become similar to the English counterpart. This implies that contrastive rhetoric research is never a neutral endeavor to discover cultural and linguistic patterns. Rather, the knowledge constructed by research can assign a range of positive to negative values to different languages and cultures, affect the ways people judge which language or culture is more superior or desirable than others, and prompt cultural and linguistic shifts.

The differing amounts of currency attached to languages are certainly related to the global hierarchy of power among languages. English is considered to be the most privileged international lingua franca and a 'marvelous tongue' (Pennycook, 1998: 133). Moreover, academic knowledge, such as contrastive rhetoric, created in the Anglophone world of the West has hegemonic power (Scheurich, 1997; Willinsky, 1998). Thus, for instance, when a researcher from the West conducts a contrastive rhetoric study funded by the Mexican government to investigate practices of teaching and learning writing in Mexico (LoCastro, 2008) and concludes that a lack of L1 and L2 writing instruction hinders EFL learners from acquiring international norms for academic writing, would the funding agency be compelled to preserve the perceived features of written Spanish (e.g. long sentences, loose coordination, or few cohesive markers) or would it try to introduce English-type writing in L1 and L2 writing instruction?

The above discussion, however, does not mean that all language groups in the world necessarily adopt Western knowledge or a preferred rhetorical style. In postcolonial societies, English has been appropriated to express religious and cultural identities for the political purpose of nation building, as seen in contemporary Pakistani English language textbooks, in which biographical texts (and other genres) prioritize a reference to Islamic faiths over factual information (Mahboob, 2009). Here, non-English-type rhetoric is purposely used in English to promote religious/cultural identity. From the mainstream contrastive rhetoric point of view, this would be viewed as a reflection of a unique *cultural* thought pattern. However, the definition of culture is contentious. Should culture be conceptualized as a primordial, objective and unchanging category or is it discursively constructed through political and ideological processes (Kubota, 1999)? Another related question is this: Is it the language or culture itself that decides what counts as a rhetorical norm or is it the educational institution, which is influenced by the politics and ideology of the nation state, that imposes the definition of what should be the norm (Kramsch, 2004)? If a Pakistani nationalist scholar promotes the uniqueness of the rhetoric of Pakistani English, should such an argument be interpreted as evidence of cultural uniqueness or as identity politics?

The problem of describing culturally specific rhetoric raises a question of the fundamental purpose of contrastive rhetoric research and its future. The field was originally developed in order to address pedagogical needs in the main. However, when the rhetorical features of languages other than English are implicitly depicted as inferior, a hidden message is created: change the habit of using those features. Studies that examine the impact of form-focused writing instruction (e.g. stating the thesis clearly and effectively in the introduction) on students' use of rhetorical organizations (e.g. Petrić, 2005) further confirm the effectiveness of such interventions and might reinforce the desirability of using English-type organization. While contrastive rhetoric researchers would argue that teaching rhetorical features of academic writing in English is not intended to encourage students to abandon their L1 writing style, members of non-Anglophone communities (e.g. students, teachers and education policy makers) might not be convinced by such an argument. If rhetorical structures for certain genres (academic writing, business writing, etc.) are indeed becoming homogenized worldwide, would contrastive rhetoric research lose its core impetus or will it continue to look for *exotic* rhetorical conventions in various linguistic niches? Will it explore more political dimensions of written discourse features? What is the social responsibility of contrastive rhetoric research?

Implications for Teachers, Students and Researchers

As evident from the above discussions, contrastive rhetoric is highly controversial. Yet, this controversial nature provides teachers with an opportunity to critically reflect on how to grapple with cultural and linguistic differences. It is quite easy for teachers in Anglophone societies to ignore cultural difference and impose the mainstream written English norm onto international or immigrant students who are L2 writers in English. It is equally easy for them to essentialize students' culture and language and create a rigid boundary between the dominant language/culture and that of the *Other*. Recognizing cultural difference is often well intended, as with the original pedagogical impetus of contrastive rhetoric. However, focusing on cultural difference has a hidden risk of *Othering* and patronizes L2 students, while viewing their language and culture as a deficit or an obstacle to learning to write in a second language. As many critics of contrastive rhetoric argue, it is important to both recognize and affirm L2 students' L1 background and understand that their writing does not directly reflect their exotic *culture* but is significantly shaped by educational practices, local politics and ideologies, as well as transnational discourses in the age of globalization. In encountering an essay organized in a way different from a typical English essay, teachers need to take into account multiple factors that could influence the text, such as L1 writing expertise, L2 proficiency, L1 and L2 writing experiences in a particular genre, the writer's intentions, and their own beliefs about cultural difference, instead of attributing the difference entirely to the student's culture.

The anti-essentialist approach to culture, language and students in second language writing can be extended to a critical understanding of culture in general in educational settings. For example, texts that describe cultural characteristics of ESL students (e.g. Ariza, 2006) underscore the importance of recognizing cultural implications for teaching and learning. Certainly not all students share the same kind of knowledge, skills, subjectivity or social conventions; nor should people who belong to an ethnic or linguistic group be lumped into a single cultural mold. An essentialist approach explains in a reductionist and fixed manner why people act in a certain way. It is important to critically reflect on a perceived cultural difference by situating individuals in complex power structures within political contexts, rather than accepting taken-for-granted categorization of people according to a static notion of culture.

One critical point here is that our understanding of the notion of cultural difference is often influenced by two liberal discourses that appear contradictory but coexisting: celebrations of cultural difference and color- or difference-blind views (Kubota, 2004; Larson & Ovando, 2001). On the one hand, many educational institutions celebrate cultural difference by holding international festivals, cultural events and so on. Yet, such celebrations are often focused on superficial elements such as food, fashion and folkdance. On the other hand, educators who celebrate cultural difference might simultaneously deemphasize racial, cultural and other individual differences in instructional settings based on the belief that culture or skin color does not matter, everyone is the same and therefore the same mainstream instruction can apply to all students. However, this approach supports assimilation and perpetuates the preexisting inequalities. A teacher who emphasizes cultural difference in writing might discuss differences in rhetorical conventions in positive terms in the classroom, while imposing the formulaic Anglo rhetoric on the students in teaching academic writing in English. While teaching the rhetoric of power is not in and of itself problematic since students need to function successfully in the dominant discourse community (Delpit, 1995), what needs to be reflected on are the political and ideological dimensions of the underlying beliefs about cultural difference and the purpose of learning the rhetoric of power, namely whether to assimilate into the dominant community both rhetorically and ideologically, or to appropriate the rhetoric of power to resist and critique the unequal cultural, linguistic and racial hierarchies of power while creating a new discursive space.

As a controversial field of inquiry, contrastive rhetoric offers many implications for cross-cultural teaching, especially questions with regard to how culture and language are conceptualized, how politics and ideologies are involved in writing instruction and what role research plays in relation to linguistic and cultural shifts. Inquiries into cultural and linguistic differences significantly influence our worldviews, which support or challenge the status quo of power relations among cultures and languages. It is important for teachers and administrators to engage in these inquiries through critical lenses and constant reflections.

Suggestions for further reading

Connor, U. (1996) *Contrastive Rhetoric: Cross-cultural Aspects of Second-language Writing*. Cambridge: Cambridge University Press.
This book synthesizes the findings of contrastive rhetoric research up to the mid-1990s and explores its relationship with other disciplines such as composition, text linguistics, translation studies, and genre studies. It offers implications for further research and pedagogy.

Connor, U., Nagelhout, E. and Rozycki, W.V. (eds) (2008) *Contrastive Rhetoric: Reaching to Intercultural Rhetoric*. Amsterdam: John Benjamins Publishing Company.
As the most updated edited volume, this book provides a range of foci, perspectives, and approaches to contrastive (intercultural) rhetoric studies. It contains data-based studies in specific genres, pedagogical issues and future directions of intercultural rhetoric.

Kubota, R. (2005) Unfinished knowledge: The story of Barbara. In H. Luria, D.M. Seymour and T. Smoke (eds) *Language and Linguistics in Context: Readings and Applications for Teachers* (pp. 107–113). Mahwah, NJ: Lawrence Erlbaum Associates.
This is a fictional narrative about a university-level writing teacher who experiences various conceptualizations of cultural difference in her private and professional life. It provides readers with some concrete examples of how these conceptualizations might be put into practice.

Kubota, R. and Lehner, A. (2004) Toward critical contrastive rhetoric. *Journal of Second Language Writing* 13, 7–27.
This article synthesizes criticisms of contrastive rhetoric research from theoretical and pedagogical points of view and offers postmodern, poststructuralist, and postcolonial approaches to contrastive rhetoric. Critical engaged practice in relation to cultural difference is proposed.

References

Ädel, A. (2008) Metadiscourse across three varieties of English: American, British, and advanced-learner English. In U. Connor, E. Nagelhout and W.V. Rozycki (eds) *Contrastive Rhetoric: Reaching to Intercultural Rhetoric* (pp. 45–62). Amsterdam: John Benjamins Publishing Company.

Ariza, E.N. (2006) *Not for ESOL Teachers: What Every Classroom Teacher Needs to Know About the Linguistically, Culturally, and Ethnically Diverse Student*. Boston, MA: Pearson Education, Inc.

Bloch, J. (2008) Plagiarism in an intercultural rhetoric context: What we can learn about one from the other. In U. Connor, E. Nagelhout and W.V. Rozycki (eds) *Contrastive Rhetoric: Reaching to Intercultural Rhetoric* (pp. 257–273). Amsterdam: John Benjamins Publishing Company.

Bloch. J. and Chi, L. (1995) A comparison of the use of citations in Chinese and English academic discourse. In D. Belcher and G. Braine (eds) *Academic Writing in a Second Language: Essays on Research and Pedagogy* (pp. 231–274). Norwood, NJ: Ablex.

Bourdieu, P. (1991) *Language and Symbolic Power*. Cambridge, MA: Harvard University Press.

Cahill, D. (2003) The myth of the "turn" in contrastive rhetoric. *Written Communication* 20, 170–194.

Cameron, D. (2002) Globalization and the teaching of 'communication skills.' In D. Block and D. Cameron (eds) *Globalization and Language Teaching* (pp. 67–82). London: Routledge.

Carson, J.G. (1992) Becoming biliterate: First language influences. *Journal of Second Language Writing* 1, 37–60.

Casanave, C. (2004) *Controversies in Second Language Writing: Dilemmas and Decisions in Research and Instruction*. Ann Arbor, MI: University of Michigan Press.

Chu, H-C.J., Swaffar, J. and Charney, D.H. (2002) Cultural representations of rhetorical conventions: The effects on reading recall. *TESOL Quarterly* 36, 511–541.

Clark, R. and Ivanič, R. (1997) *The Politics of Writing*. London: Routledge.

Coe, R.M. (2002) The new rhetoric of genre: Writing political beliefs. In A.M. Johns (ed.) *Genre in the Classroom; Multiple Perspectives* (pp. 197–207). Mahwah, NJ: Lawrence Erlbaum Associates.

Coe, R.M. and Freedman, A. (1998) Genre theory: Australian and North American approaches. In M.L. Kenney (ed.) *Theorizing Composition: A Critical Sourcebook of Theory and Scholarship in Contemporary Composition Studies* (pp. 136–147). Westport, CT: Greenwood Publishing.

Connor, U. (1996) *Contrastive Rhetoric: Cross-Cultural Aspects of Second-Language Writing*. Cambridge: Cambridge University Press.

Connor, U. (2002) New directions in contrastive rhetoric. *TESOL Quarterly* 36, 493–510.

Connor, U. (2004) Intercultural rhetoric research: Beyond texts. *Journal of English for Academic Purposes* 3, 291–304.

Connor, U. (2008) Mapping multidimensional aspects of research. In U. Connor, E. Nagelhout and W.V. Rozycki (eds) *Contrastive Rhetoric: Reaching to Intercultural Rhetoric* (pp. 299–315). Amsterdam: John Benjamins Publishing Company.

Connor, U., Nagelhout, E. and Rozycki, W.V. (eds) (2008) *Contrastive Rhetoric: Reaching to Intercultural Rhetoric*. Amsterdam: John Benjamins Publishing Company.

Cumming, A. (1989) Writing expertise and second language proficiency. *Language Learning* 39, 81–141.

Delpit, L. (1995) *Other People's Children: Cultural Conflict in the Classroom*. New York: The New Press.

Donahue, R.T. (1998) *Japanese Culture and Communication: Critical Cultural Analysis*. Lanham, MD: University Press of America.

Eggington, W.G. (1987) Written academic discourse in Korean: Implications for effective communication. In U. Connor and R.B. Kaplan (eds) *Writing Across Languages: Analysis of L2 Text* (pp. 153–168). Reading, MA: Addison-Wesley Publishing Company.

Emig, J. (1971) The composing process of twelfth graders (NCTE research report no. 13). Urbana, IL: National Council of Teachers of English.

Fairclough, N. (1992) *Discourse and Social Change*. Cambridge: Polity Press.

Fanon, F. (1967) *Black Skin, White Masks*. New York: Grove Weidenfeld.

Fox, H. (1994) *Listening to the World: Cultural Issues in Academic Writing*. Urbana, IL: National Council of Teachers of English.

Gass, S.M. and Selinker, L. (2001) *Second Language Acquisition: An Introductory Course* (2nd edn). Mahwah, NJ: Lawrence Erlbaum Associates.

Hinds, J. (1983) Contrastive rhetoric: Japanese and English. *Text* 3, 183–195.

Hinds, J. (1987) Reader versus writer responsibility: A new typology. In U. Connor and R.B. Kaplan (eds) *Writing Across Languages: Analysis of L2 Text* (pp. 141–152). Reading, MA: Addison-Wesley.

Hinds, J. (1990) Inductive, deductive, quasi-inductive: Expository writing in Japanese, Korean, Chinese, and Thai. In U. Connor and A.M. Johns (eds) *Coherence in Writing: Research and Pedagogical Perspectives* (pp. 87–109). Alexandria, VA: TESOL.

Hirose, K. (2003) Comparing L1 and L2 organizational patterns in the argumentative writing of Japanese and EFL students. *Journal of Second Language Writing* 12, 181–209.

Hofstede, G.H. (1984) *Culture's Consequences: International Differences in Work-Related Values* (abridged edn). Beverly Hill, CA: Sage Publications.

Holliday, A. (1999) Small cultures. *Applied Linguistics* 20, 237–264.

Indrasuta, C. (1988) Narrative styles in the writing of Thai and American students. In A.C. Purves (ed.) *Writing Across Languages and Cultures* (pp. 206–226). Newbury Park, CA: Sage Publications.

Institute of International Education (2005) *Open Doors: 1948–2004: Report on International Educational Exchange.* New York: Institute of International Education.

Johns, A.M. (ed.) (2002) *Genre in the Classroom; Multiple Perspectives.* Mahwah, NJ: Lawrence Erlbaum Associates.

Kachru, Y. (1995) Contrastive rhetoric in World Englishes. *English Today* 11, 21–31.

Kachru, Y. (1997) Cultural meaning and contrastive rhetoric in English education. *World Englishes* 16, 337–350.

Kachru, Y. (1999) Culture, context, and writing. In E. Hinkel (ed.) *Culture in Second Language Teaching and Learning* (pp. 75–89). Cambridge: Cambridge University Press.

Kaplan, R.B. (1966) Cultural thought patterns in inter-cultural education. *Language Learning* 16, 1–20.

Kaplan, R.B. (1967) Contrastive rhetoric and the teaching of composition. *TESOL Quarterly* 1, 10–16.

Kaplan, R.B. (1972) *The Anatomy of Rhetoric: Prolegomena to a Functional Theory of Rhetoric.* Philadelphia: Center for Curriculum Development.

Kaplan, R.B. (1988) Contrastive rhetoric and second language learning: Notes towards a theory of contrastive rhetoric. In A.C. Purves (ed.) *Writing across Languages and Cultures* (pp. 275–304). Newbury Park, CA: Sage Publications.

Kaplan, R.B. (2005) Contrastive rhetoric. In E. Hinkel (ed.) *Handbook of Research in Second Language Teaching and Learning* (pp. 375–392). Mahwah, NJ: Lawrence Erlbaum Associates.

Kirkpatrick, A. (1997) Traditional Chinese text structures and their influence on the writing in Chinese and English of contemporary mainland Chinese students. *Journal of Second Language Writing* 6, 223–244.

Kobayashi, H. (1984) Rhetorical patterns in English and Japanese. *TESOL Quarterly* 18, 737–738.

Kobayashi, H. and Rinnert, C (1996) Factors affecting composition evaluation in an EFL context: Cultural rhetorical pattern and readers' background. *Language Learning* 46, 397–437.

Kobayashi, H. and Rinnert, C. (2002) High school student perceptions of first language literacy instruction: Implications for second language writing. *Journal of Second Language Writing* 11, 91–116.

Kobayashi, H. and Rinnert, C. (2007) Task response and text construction across L1 and L2 writing. *Journal of Second Language Writing* 17, 7–29.

Kowal, K.H. (1998) *Rhetorical Implications of Linguistic Relativity: Theory and Application to Chinese and Taiwanese Interlanguage.* New York: Peter Lang.

Kramsch, C. (2004) Language, thought, and culture. In A. Davies and C. Elder (eds) *The Handbook of Applied Linguistics* (pp. 235–261). Malden, MA: Blackwell Publishing.

Kubota, R. (1997) Reevaluation of the uniqueness of Japanese written discourse: Implications for contrastive rhetoric. *Written Communication* 14, 460–480.

Kubota, R. (1998a) An investigation of L1–L2 transfer in writing among Japanese university students: Implications for contrastive rhetoric. *Journal of Second Language Writing* 7, 69–100.

Kubota, R. (1998b) An investigation of Japanese and English L1 essay organization: Differences and similarities. *The Canadian Modern Language Review* 54, 475–507.

Kubota, R. (1999) Japanese culture constructed by discourses: Implications for applied linguistic research and English language teaching. *TESOL Quarterly* 33, 9–35.

Kubota, R. (2002a) Japanese identities in written communication: Politics and discourses. In R.T. Donahue (ed.) *Exploring Japaneseness: On Japanese Enactments of Culture and Consciousness* (pp. 293–315). Westport, CT: Ablex.

Kubota, R. (2002b) Impact of globalization on language teaching in Japan. In D. Block and D. Cameron (eds) *Globalization and Language Teaching* (pp. 13–28). London: Routledge.

Kubota, R. (2004) Critical multiculturalism and second language education. In B. Norton and K. Toohey (eds) *Critical Pedagogies and Language Learning* (pp. 30–52). Cambridge: Cambridge University Press.

Kubota, R. and Lehner, A. (2004) Toward critical contrastive rhetoric. *Journal of Second Language Writing* 13, 7–27.

Kubota, R. and Shi, L. (2005) Instruction and reading samples for opinion and argumentative writing in L1 junior high school textbooks in China and Japan. *Journal of Asian Pacific Communication* 15, 97–127.

Kumaravadivelu, B. (2006) TESOL methods: Changing tracks, challenging trends. *TESOL Quarterly* 40, 59–81.

Lado, R. (1957) *Linguistics across Cultures.* Ann Arbor, MI: University of Michigan Press.

Larson, C.L. and Ovando, C.J. (2001) *The Color of Bureaucracy: The Politics of Equity in Multicultural School Communities.* Belmont, CA: Wadsworth/Thomson Learning.

Leki, I. (1997) Cross-talk: ESL issues and contrastive rhetoric. In C. Severino, J.C. Guerra and J.E. Butler (eds) *Writing in Multicultural Settings* (pp. 234–244). New York: The Modern Language Association of America.

Li, X. (1996) *"Good Writing" in Cross-Cultural Context.* Albany, NY: State University of New York Press.

Li, X. (2002) "Track (dis)connecting": Chinese high school and university writing in a time of change. In D. Foster and D.R. Russell (eds) *Writing and Learning in Cross-National Perspective; Transitions from Secondary to Higher Education* (pp. 49–87). Urbana, IL: NCTE and Mahwah, NJ: Lawrence Erlbaum Associates.

LoCastro, V. (2008) "Long sentences and floating commas" Mexican students' rhetorical practices and the sociocultural context. In U. Connor, E. Nagelhout and W.V. Rozycki (eds) *Contrastive Rhetoric: Reaching to Intercultural Rhetoric* (pp. 195–217). Amsterdam: John Benjamins Publishing Company.

Mahboob, A. (2009) English as an Islamic language: A case study of Pakistani English. *World Englishes* 28, 175–189.

Matsuda, P.K. (1997) Contrastive rhetoric in context: A dynamic model of L2 writing. *Journal of Second Language Writing* 6, 45–60.

Matsuda, P.K. (2001) On the origin of contrastive rhetoric: A response to H.G. Ying. *International Journal of Applied Linguistics* 11, 257–260.

McCagg, P. (1996) If you can lead a horse to water, you don't have to make it drink: Some comments on reader and writer responsibilities. *Multilingua* 15, 239–256.

Miller, C. (1984) Genre as social action. *Quarterly Journal of Speech* 70, 151–167.

Mohan, B. and Lo, W. (1985) Academic writing and Chinese students: Transfer and developmental factors. *TESOL Quarterly* 19, 515–534.

Moll, L., Amanti, C., Neff, D. and Gonzalez, N. (1992) Funds of knowledge for teaching: Using a qualitative approach to connect homes and classrooms. *Theory Into Practice* 31, 132–141.

Oi, M.K. (1984) Cross-cultural differences in rhetorical patterning: A study of Japanese and English. Unpublished doctoral dissertation, State University of New York at Stony Brook.

Ostler, S.E. (1987) English in parallels: A comparison of English and Arabic prose. In U. Connor and R.B. Kaplan (eds) *Writing across Languages: Analysis of L2 Text* (pp. 177–205). Reading, MA: Addison-Wesley Publishing Company.

Ostler, S.E. (1990) The contrastive rhetorics of Arabic, English, Japanese and Spanish. Paper presented at the *24th Annual TESOL Convention*, San Francisco.

Pak, C-S. and Acevedo, R. (2008) Spanish-language newspaper editorials from Mexico, Spain, and the U.S. In U. Connor, E. Nagelhout and W.V. Rozycki (eds) *Contrastive Rhetoric: Reaching to Intercultural Rhetoric* (pp. 123–145). Amsterdam: John Benjamins Publishing Company.

Pennycook, A. (1998) *English and the Discourses of Colonialism*. New York/London: Routledge.

Pennycook, A. (2001) *Critical Applied Linguistics: A Critical Introduction*. Mahwah, NJ: Lawrence Erlbaum Associates.

Petrić, B. (2005) Contrastive rhetoric in the writing classroom: A case study. *English for Specific Purposes* 24, 213–228.

Ramanathan, V. and Kaplan, R.B. (1996) Audience and voice in current L1 composition texts: Some implications for ESL writers. *Journal of Second Language Writing* 5, 21–34.

Reid, J. (1989) English as second language composition in higher education: The expectations of the academic audience. In D.M. Johnson and D.H. Roen (eds) *Richness in Writing: Empowering ESL Students* (pp. 220–234). New York & London: Longman.

Rinnert, C. and Kobayashi, H. (2001) Differing perceptions of EFL writing among readers in Japan. *The Modern Language Journal* 85, 189–209.

Rinnert, C. and Kobayashi, H. (2007) L1 and L2 pre-university writing experience: What effects on novice Japanese EFL writers? *Hiroshima Kokusai Kenkyû [Hiroshima Journal of International Studies]* 13, 65–92.

Sa'adeddin, M.A.M. (1989) Text development and Arabic-English negative interference. *Applied Linguistics* 10, 36–51.

Sasaki, M. and Hirose, K. (1996) Explanatory variables for EFL students' expository writing. *Language Learning* 46, 137–174.

Scheurich, J.J. (1997) *Research Method in the Postmodern*. London and Washington, DC: Falmer Press.

Schultz, E.A. (1990) *Dialogue at the Margins: Whorf, Bakhtin, and Linguistic Relativity*. Madison, WI: The University of Wisconsin Press.

Scollon, R. and Scollon, S. (1997) Point of view and citation: Fourteen Chinese and English versions of the "same" news story. *Text* 17, 83–125.

Shi, L. (2002) How Western-trained Chinese TESOL professionals publish in their home environment. *TESOL Quarterly* 36, 625–634.

Shi, L. and Kubota, R. (2007) Patterns of rhetorical organizations in Canadian and American language arts textbooks: An exploratory study. *English for Specific Purposes* 26, 180–202.

Söter, A.O. (1988) The second language learner and cultural transfer in narration. In A.C. Purves (ed.) *Writing Across Languages and Cultures* (pp. 177–205). Newbury Park, CA: Sage Publications.

Spack, R. (1997) The rhetorical construction of multilingual students. *TESOL Quarterly* 31, 765–774.

Taylor, G. and Chen, T. (1991) Linguistic, cultural, and subcultural issues in contrastive discourse analysis: Anglo-American and Chinese scientific texts. *Applied Linguistics* 12, 319–336.

Willinsky, J. (1998) *Learning to Divide the World: Education at Empire's End.* Minneapolis, MN: University of Minnesota Press.

Wolfe, M.L. (2008) Different cultures – different discourses? Rhetorical patterns of business letters by English and Russian speakers. In U. Connor, E. Nagelhout and W.V. Rozycki (eds) *Contrastive Rhetoric: Reaching to Intercultural Rhetoric* (pp. 87–121). Amsterdam: John Benjamins Publishing Company.

Wu, S-Y. and Rubin, D.L. (2000) Evaluating the impact of collectivism and individualism on argumentative writing by Chinese and North American college students. *Research in the Teaching of English* 35, 148–178.

Ying, H.G. (2000) The origin of contrastive rhetoric revisited. *International Journal of Applied Linguistics* 10, 259–268.

Ying, H.G. (2001) On the origins of contrastive rhetoric: A reply to Matsuda. *International Journal of Applied Linguistics* 11, 261–266.

You, X. (2008) From Confucianism to Marxism: A century of theme treatment in Chinese writing instruction. In U. Connor, E. Nagelhout and W.V. Rozycki (eds) *Contrastive Rhetoric: Reaching to Intercultural Rhetoric* (pp. 241–256). Amsterdam: John Benjamins Publishing Company.

Zamel, V. (1997) Toward a model of transculturation. *TESOL Quarterly* 31, 341–352.

Chapter 11

Sociolinguistics, Language Teaching and New Literacy Studies

BRIAN STREET and CONSTANT LEUNG

Introduction

In this chapter we will outline a social practices perspective on literacy, which we take following Street (1984: 1) to refer to 'the social uses of reading and/or writing'. Drawing in particular upon sources in what has come to be termed 'New Literacy Studies' (Gee, 1990; Street, 1995), we will explore the relationship between social practice views of literacy and contemporary notions of communicative language competence in the contexts of language learning. Literacy studies, we argue, can gain from the insights offered by recent work in sociolinguistics. At the same time, some popular and dominant pedagogic approaches that claim association with sociolinguistics have perhaps in the past treated literacy somewhat narrowly in terms of skills, structures, 'autonomous' meanings. The approach from New Literacy Studies that we outline here can help expand that sector of the field. The 'social' perspective being outlined challenges dominant models that assume literacy to be just a set of technical skills and language to be a set of cognitive properties residing within the individual. Critiques of the dominant position have referred to it as an 'autonomous' model; in other words, it has been assumed that literacy and language can be conceptualised and described as though they were autonomous of, or independent of, social context – a concept we will expand on below. We will explore these claims and arguments with particular reference to work in the field of language education, where the effect of these dominant models has been particularly strong. Our discussion will also pay attention to those situations where the impact of new, more socially based approaches is being felt.

Common research methods used by scholars in the social practice approach include an ethnographic perspective on literacy practices and language learning, and the application of discourse analysis. A reflexive approach to the description of actual uses of spoken and written language has been developed and in this chapter we will give examples of the strengths and weaknesses of the approach. Key research findings and directions for further research include the recognition that learning literacy, particularly academic literacy, in socially and linguistically diverse educational contexts involves more than learning language as structure and literacy as a set of generic skills and fixed genres. We will explore the relevance of these findings for teachers and students as they engage in classroom interaction. Classroom examples will be used to illustrate our arguments where appropriate. We will draw particular conclusions for additional/second language education and bilingual education as well as for mainstream classroom teachers.

Social Theories of Language

In the field of language studies and in particular of language education, and as we shall see below, with respect to literacy studies, there has recently been a shift away from dominant assumptions that language could be conceptualised and taught as though it were independent of social context. We will mainly draw upon two lines of developments in describing this shift. The first is the body of work broadly associated with ethnography of communication. In this respect, the work of Hymes and the Ethnography of Communication tradition has influenced not only how language is conceptualised for language education, but also how the social can be taken into account in complex linguistic and educational environments. The second is the development of systemic functional linguistics (SFL), with particular reference to the work of Halliday and his colleagues. The fundamental insight of SFL has been that the use of language is itself a constitutive part of social action and that linguistic resources, for example lexis and grammar, themselves embody social meaning.

We will briefly indicate where these currents in sociolinguistics have fed into language teaching and the role of literacies. In this discussion the term 'language teaching' is used broadly; examples will be drawn from the teaching of a language to students for whom it is not their mother tongue, for example English as a foreign language in Japan or English as an additional/second language in Australia for linguistic minority students, as well as the teaching of mother tongue. The context of teaching will be made explicit where appropriate. The first half of this discussion will be taken up by a largely descriptive account of the points of contact between sociolinguistics and language teaching.

Sociolinguistics in Communicative Language Teaching

The development of the concept of Communicative Language Teaching (CLT) was generally associated with a break with the grammar-focused approaches to language teaching that dominated practice up to the 1960s and early 1970s. The emerging work with a social orientation in this period, for example Austin (1962), Halliday (1973, 1975), Halliday *et al.* (1964), and Savignon (1983) (among others), was in many ways the vanguard of a paradigm shift in language teaching. At a conceptual level, the work of Hymes (1972b, 1974) on ethnography of communication and communicative competence was particularly influential. His 1972 paper – first presented in 1966 at the Yeshiva Conference on Language Development among Disadvantaged Children – presented an ethnographically oriented formulation of the notion of communicative competence. This paper explicitly addressed language education issues and in part it represented a critique of Chomsky's (1965) highly abstracted notion of linguistic (grammatical) competence. It was designed as a call to language educators to pay attention to '*differential competence* within a *heterogeneous speech community*, both undoubtedly shaped by acculturation' (Hymes, 1972b: 274, original italics).

For Hymes (1972b: 277) a child learning to communicate through language has to acquire 'knowledge of sentences, not only as grammatical, but also as appropriate. He or she acquires competence as to when to speak, when not, and as to what to talk about with whom, when, in what manner'. In other words, there are social rules of use, a dimension of language use 'without which the rules of grammar would be useless' (Hymes, 1972b: 278). This inclusion of the 'social' makes it necessary to raise questions of context of communication and aspects of socio-cultural practice when working towards a theory of language in use. In this connection, Hymes (1972b: 281, original emphasis) suggests that four empirical questions must be raised:

Whether (and to what degree) something is formally **possible**:
Whether (and to what degree) something is **feasible** in virtue of the means of implementation available;
Whether (and to what degree) something is **appropriate** (adequate, happy, successful) in relation to a context in which it is used and evaluated;
Whether (and to what degree) something is in fact done, actually **performed**, and what its doing entails.

The key implications of Hymes' position regarding language teaching, and language education more generally, were quickly taken up by language educators. A notion of competence that appeals to the actual use of language in context is potentially very useful in helping teachers to ground their professional work in concrete terms.

In the move away from grammar-oriented approaches to language teaching, the Hymesian notion of communicative competence offered language educators a dynamic and situated perspective on language and language use. Building on the works of Hymes and others, Canale and

Swain produced a series of seminal papers that can be regarded as the foundation for the formation of the concept of communicative competence in foreign or additional language pedagogy (see Canale, 1983, 1984; Canale & Swain, 1980a, 1980b). These positions were not accepted uncritically, as we will see below with reference to scholars both in the United States (*cf.* Dubin, 1989; Hornberger, 1989) and the United Kingdom (*cf.* Leung, 2005). In these early 1980s, papers by Canale and Swain propose that communicative competence comprises four areas of knowledge and skills:

1. Grammatical competence: This competence is concerned with '... knowledge of lexical items and of rules of morphology, syntax, sentence-grammar semantics, and phonology' (Canale & Swain, 1980b: 29). This type of knowledge and skill will allow the language learner to make use of the basic fabric of a language, so to speak, and to understand and produce the literal or propositional meaning of language expressions.

2. Sociolinguistic competence: This competence, broadly speaking, deals with rules of use, including what Hymes (1972b: 281) means by 'whether (and to what degree) something is in fact done'. In other words, probabilistic rules of occurrence concerning whether something is 'sayable' in a given context.
    [It] addresses the extent to which utterances are produced and understood appropriately in different sociolinguistic contexts depending on contextual factors such as status of participants, purposes of the interaction, and norms or conventions of interaction ... Appropriateness of utterances refers to ... appropriateness of meaning and appropriateness of meaning concerns the extent to which particular communicative functions (e.g. commanding, complaining and inviting), attitudes (including politeness and formality) and ideas are judged to be proper in a given situation. (Canale, 1983: 7)

3. Discourse competence: This competence is concerned with organisational features of spoken and written texts, what Halliday and Hasan (1976) would refer to as cohesion, and what Widdowson (1978) sees as coherence. It deals with the knowledge and skills required to combine lexical and grammatical forms with context- and purpose-relevant meanings to produce different types of unified spoken or written texts, for example, oral and written narratives, business reports and so on.
    Unity of a text is achieved through cohesion in form and coherence in meaning. Cohesion deals with how utterances are linked structurally and facilitates interpretation of a text. For example, the use of cohesion devices such as pronoun, synonyms ... Coherence refers to the relationship among the different meanings in a text, where these meanings may be literal meanings, communicative functions and attitudes (Canale, 1983: 9).

4. Strategic competence: This component of competence refers to addi-
    tional language learners' capacity to achieve communication goals by
    mastery of verbal and non-verbal communication strategies that may
    be called into action for two main reasons: (a) to compensate for
    breakdowns in communication due to limiting conditions in actual
    communication (e.g. momentary inability to recall an idea or gram-
    matical form) or due to insufficient competence in one or more of the
    other areas above; and (b) to enhance the effectiveness of communi-
    cation (e.g. deliberately slow and soft speech for rhetorical effect)
    (Canale, 1983: 11).

Communicative competence, in this formulation, represented a considerable expansion in the conceptual base of additional/second language
curriculum and pedagogy that existed up until that time. It would be fair
to say that the Canale and Swain framework became the bedrock of the
emerging Communicative Language Teaching (CLT) approach in the early
1980s, in which was adopted very quickly by the worldwide enterprise,
indeed industry, of English Language Teaching (ELT). CLT, as a curriculum principle and as a teaching approach, has many manifestations in
teacher education handbooks and manuals, but its popularity among language teachers, curriculum planners and textbook writers has not shown
any sign of decline in the past 25 years or so, as the following statement
from an English language teacher education textbook would demonstrate:

> ... in the early 1970s, a 'sociolinguistic revolution' took place, where
> the emphasis given in linguistics to grammar was replaced by an
> interest in 'language in use' ... The sociolinguistic revolution had a
> great effect on language teaching ... [which led to] a type of syllabus
> which aimed to cater for the teaching of language in use – of commu-
> nicative competence. (Johnson, 2001: 182–183)

The attraction of the emerging CLT approach was initially founded on,
among other things, the principle that curriculum specification should be
context- and participant-sensitive. That is to say, instead of generating
teaching content out of some aspect of the target language system, for
example grammatical structures, CLT would first identify what and how
language is used in the pre-specified domain of use before drawing up a
list of teaching content. This language identification process is meant to be
carried out through a needs analysis (e.g. Brindley, 1989; Yalden, 1983).
However, as Dubin (1989) and Leung (2005) point out, this empirically
oriented approach to curriculum development has been more honoured
in the breach than observance. For example, Brown (2001: 43) offers a set
of characteristics of CLT which includes the following:

- paying attention to 'the components (grammatical, discourse, functional, sociolinguistic, and strategic) of communicative competence';

- use of classroom activities and student tasks that would 'engage learners in the pragmatic, authentic, functional use of language for meaningful purposes';
- use of the teacher as 'a facilitator and guide ... Students are therefore encouraged to construct meaning through genuine linguistic interaction with others'.

This characterisation reflects a widely accepted professional understanding of what passes for 'communicativeness'. However, this rendering of 'communicativeness' departs quite significantly from the early Hymesian aspirations. As Hornberger (1989) points out, Hymes's conceptualisation of communicative competence was intended as a heuristic device for empirical exploration of actual communicative events in specific contexts. This is not the same as saying all individuals involved in any given speech event must have identical competence. Indeed competence 'varies within individuals (from event to event), across individuals, and across speech communities' (Hornberger, 1989: 218). Furthermore, to go back to the four questions raised by Hymes, it is possible for something that is not feasible (from the point of view of an individual participant in a speech event) to occur, for example a person may find himself/herself in a conversation in which there is codeswitching involving a language/s that s/he has little knowledge of. Instead of observing what goes on in actual communication in specific contexts, the emphasis has now been placed on promoting successful language communication in learning activities. Instead of finding out how participants use linguistic (and other semiotic) resources to communicate in specific real-world contexts, the teacher is asked to use their 'expert' knowledge to assist students to achieve meaningful communication (with their peers and teachers) in classroom activities.

Sociolinguistics in classroom ethnography

In this section we will link the work cited above in the area of communicative competence and the meanings attributed to the term, with some examples of actual practice in classroom settings, especially with regard to the uses of literacy. It is undoubtedly the case that the impact of the concept of communicative competence on language teaching has been direct in that it has spawned a teaching approach, CLT. There are, however, other sociolinguistic studies of communication in linguistically diverse settings that have made a contribution to this discussion on language teaching at the level of both theory and pedagogy. At a societal level, answers to questions on patterns of use such as 'who is speaking what to whom in what contexts' can be used for policy making and planning, and resource allocation (e.g. Kaplan & Baldauf, 1997: Chapter 4; Ohannessian & Ansre,

1979; Whitely, 1979). Sociolinguistic surveys, for instance, have been carried out to provide information on students and languages in multilingual communities. As an example, the Linguistic Minority Project (1985) provided insightful information on patterns of language use and language teaching among different groups of Asian and Eastern European minorities in England. That said, this kind of survey work has yet to be carried out systematically and regularly. One such contribution has been Extra (2006), who discusses the urgent need for accurate sociolinguistic data on ethnic and linguistic minorities in the increasingly diverse populations of the European Union for education planning purposes.

A related strand of sociolinguistic work has been ethnographically oriented, examining patterns of language use in specific classroom contexts (as opposed to large-scale societal patterns of use). We will now turn to this line of sociolinguistic study and show some examples of the kinds of contribution it can make to our understanding of the ways language communication is enacted in the classroom. One of the best-known early collections of papers representing this body of work is *Functions of Language in the Classroom* edited by Cazden *et al.* (1972). This is a point made by Hymes in the Introduction to the collection:

> For language in the classroom, what we need to know goes far beyond how the grammar of English is organized ... It has to do with the relationship between a grammar of English and the ways in which English is organized in use by teachers, by children, and by the communities from which they come; with the features of intonation, tone of voice, rhythm ...; with the meanings of all those means of speech to those who use them and those who hear them, not in the narrow sense of ... naming things and stating relationships, but in the fuller sense, as conveying respect ... concern or indifference, intimacy ..., seriousness or play ...; with the appropriateness of one or another means of speech, or way of speaking, to one or another topic, person, situation; in short, with the relation of the structure of language to the structure of speaking. (Hymes, 1972a: xiii)

> The key to understanding language in context is to start, not with language, but with context. (Hymes, 1972a: xix)

The classroom context

A recent volume on the microethnography of the classroom by Bloome *et al.* (2005) provides an apt link between the different traditions under consideration here – the social turn in sociolinguistic work with particular reference to studies of classroom discourse, and the social turn in literacy studies, with particular reference to ethnographic approaches and cross cultural studies (as we will see below).

What the authors mean by a microethnographic perspective and what they hope to accomplish by applying it to classroom events and practices is encapsulated in the claim that 'people are situated, they act in terms of the situation in which they find themselves whilst simultaneously creating that situation' (Bloome *et al.*, 2005: 2). They are critical of approaches that start from too far outside of classroom 'events': rather, they want, to 'hover low' over the immediate data, as Geertz (2000) would have it. The book is full of accounts of classroom events and practices – teachers speaking and gesturing, students responding, students talking irrespective of the teacher, texts weaving through the talk, researchers commenting, what New Literacy Studies would see as the 'literacy events' of small interactions that eventually can be seen as patterned sets of 'literacy practices' (Street, 2000). The authors, then, build upwards and outwards from the participants and the language and literacy events in which they participate. They argue that we can only claim a 'warrant' to draw larger inferences when research is 'grounded in the setting itself' (Bloome *et al.*, 2005: 3). But this does not mean that they are focused only on the 'micro'. However critical they may be of approaches that impose outside ideas and concepts upon the immediate and the local, their larger aim is to help us understand 'macro level contexts' – or rather 'to address the relationship between microlevel contexts (specific events and situations) and macro level contexts' (Bloome *et al.*, 2005: 4).

The tools the authors provide offer a distinctive contribution to the description of both the broader relationships in which people participate and their immediate enactments of meanings. In that sense such studies also contribute to the development of the field of sociolinguistics, especially that sector that is concerned with educational contexts and the learning and teaching of language and literacy. Drawing upon other traditions in sociolinguistics, such as interactional studies (*cf.* Roberts *et al.*, 2001), Bloome and his colleagues invoke and adapt terms, taken from the surrounding disciplines of interactional sociolinguistics, discourse analysis, ethnomethodology, New Literacy Studies and so on, such as 'intertextual', 'contextualisation cues', 'boundary making', 'message units', 'turn taking' and 'literacy events and practices' in order to probe closely the inner workings of these broader features of communication.

The authors, then, link close analysis of linguistic features of social interaction with what Gee (1999) terms the 'social' turn in language study that we noted above. In doing so, they complement other recent studies that have attempted to link issues of power and identity to literacy (Collins & Blot, 2002), to the ethnography of communication (Hornberger, 2003) and to education (Street, 2005).

This book, then, links a number of the traditions in sociolinguistics that we have seen in the debates regarding communicative competence, language learning, etc. Moving beyond traditional microlinguistic approaches, such as Conversation Analysis or narrowly conceived Discourse Analysis, they at the same time reject the outside 'determination' sometimes found in sociological approaches and in some aspects of Critical Discourse Analysis (*cf.* Widdowson's (2004) critique). For Bloome and his colleagues, as for many contemporary sociolinguists, research in language and literacy involves developing theories and tools that take account of both the individual participant and of their social and cultural positionings and responses.

Sociolinguistics in functional grammar

The work of Halliday and his colleagues represents another strand of sociolinguistics that can be seen as part of the move to 'social' rather than autonomous approaches and that has had a significant impact on language teaching. In order to show the contribution of this body of work to language teaching and language education more generally, it is necessary to first give a very brief account of its conceptual and epistemic foundations. The idea of 'function' is understood in terms of the relationship between meaning and linguistic form. In other words, what people mean to say is realised by the specific linguistic means and features they select to manifest their meaning. This functional relationship '... reflects the fact that language has evolved in the service of particular human needs ... what is really significant is that this functional principle is carried over and built into the grammar, so that the internal organization of the grammatical system is also functional in character' (Halliday, 1975: 16). In an account of his son's early language development, Halliday postulated a number of functions, which included instrumental (using language to do things and to satisfy material needs) and regulatory (using language to control the behaviour of other people) and so on. What people choose to mean and say is, in principle, open-ended. Thus there are infinite options in meaning-making and language can be seen as a 'meaning potential' (Halliday, 1975: 16).

The meaning options are categorised in terms of three functional components (often referred to, in the Hallidayan literature, as 'metafunctions'): ideational, interpersonal and textual. With the ideational component 'the speaker expresses his experience of the phenomena of the external world, and of the internal world of his own consciousness' (Halliday, 1975: 17). In other words, language is seen as a means for people to talk about the world from their standpoints. The interpersonal component refers to the 'function of language as a means whereby the speaker participates in ... [a] speech situation' (Halliday, 1975: 17). Through this component, speakers can adopt a role in relation to other participants, express their own judgements and values, and so on. The textual component refers to an 'enabling function ... the function that language has of creating text' (Halliday, 1975: 17). Thus this component is concerned with the deployment and organisation of linguistic resources (in the broadest sense) to form a text (spoken or written) to make meaning in context. These functional components are conceptual and analytical categories. In actual language communication, they are embedded in and realised by instances of speech or writing, the literacy events and practices to which NLS refers. (For a fuller discussion of systemic functional grammar, see, e.g. Halliday & Matthiessen, 2000, 2004.)

Schleppegrell *et al.* (2004) offer an example of how this functional perspective can work to help unpack subject content meaning. Second/additional language students often find the particular ways in which English language wording is used in different academic subjects difficult. This domain- or subject-specific use of language is often referred to as 'register'. Schleppegrell and her colleagues look at ways of helping teachers make subject texts accessible for English as a second/additional language students. In this case, the subject is History in middle school in the United States. Using a functional grammar approach they examine how lexical and grammatical resources are used in school history texts and how explicit discussion on the language of history texts can help students to unpack complex meanings. For instance, one needs to be able to identify events and happenings in history texts (ideational meaning); happenings and events tend to be encoded in action verbs of processes. But history texts comprise more than 'factual' statements on events; they also contain statements of judgement and persuasion (interpersonal meaning). Both ideational meaning and interpersonal meanings are manifested through wording in textbooks and classroom talk (i.e. textual meaning). Therefore it is argued that helping students to understand that there are different types of verbs and that they serve different functions is a useful pedagogic move.

> The verbs used in writing about history can be classified as action verbs such as *fight, defend, build, vote,* and so forth; saying and thinking-feeling verbs such as *said, expressed, supposed, like, resent,* and so forth; and relating verbs such as *is, have, is called,* and so forth. This categorization helps students understand when authors are writing about events (action verbs), when they are giving opinions or telling what others have said (thinking-feeling and saying verbs), and when they are giving background information (relating verbs). (Schleppegrell *et al.,* 2004: 77)

Furthermore, actors and agents (referred to as participants in functional grammatical analysis) are important in history, but they can be difficult to identify sometimes. At a sentence level, for instance, in a statement such as 'Liverpool's slave trade accounted for 15% of Britain's entire overseas trade by the end of the 18th century', it is not clear who the actors were. In fact it is difficult to see what actions and events might be involved in 'overseas trade'. The use of abstract nouns or noun phrases as participants may be conceptually apt as a means of conveying complex historical events and processes, but the language text expressing this kind of meaning can be difficult to decipher. Functional grammatical analysis, with its focus on the relationship between content meaning and language expression, can help to draw attention to abstract and complex expressions that need unpacking.

Another example of the Hallidayan influence can be seen in the teacher development materials produced by the Language In The National Curriculum project (LINC, 1989–1992) in the United Kingdom (Carter, 1990, 1996, 1997; LINC, 1989–1992). This was a government-funded initiative to produce teacher education material that would support the teaching of English (school subject) in the newly introduced statutory National Curriculum in England and Wales in the early 1990s. LINC (1989–1992: 3) took the view that '... pupils' language development can be more effectively supported if teachers know more about the systematic organisation and function of language ... The purpose of the LINC material is to give teachers greater analytic knowledge about language across all areas ... forms and structures of language; relationships between speaker and listener and between writer and reader ...'. This material, covering talk, reading and writing, develops insights from the Hallidayan functional perspective into ideas for classroom pedagogy. For instance, on the theme of teaching 'variations in written language' teachers are invited to consider developing a text-type game for senior secondary students building on the following steps:

Before class, the teacher cuts up the three groups of boxes (printed on card) as shown in Figure 11.1, which are labels of writing purposes, audience and text types, and puts them in three piles.

In class, the teacher shuffles the three piles of cards and puts them face down on a table, then one by one turns up the top card in each pile. Now the random ordering of the cards may turn up in unpredictable combinations such as Complain, Recipe and Unknown Person. The teacher can lead a discussion on questions such as: Is written language appropriate for this purpose and in what situation? What written conventions should the writer be aware of? How would the writer organise the text? Quite clearly this kind of teaching game points to a functional view of language use that relates form to purpose and context in a systematic way. The functional view here pays particular attention to the relationship between language expression as a form of discourse and conventionally established ways of meaning selection for social purposes/action in more or less recognised contexts.

PURPOSES

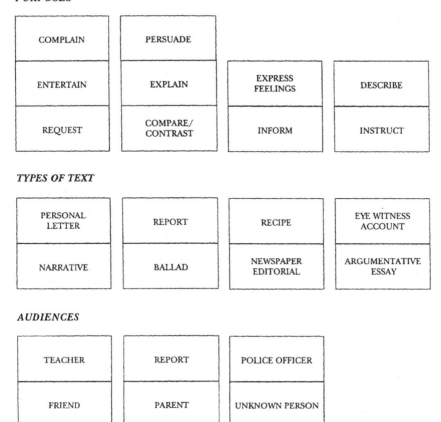

Figure 11.1 The text game (LINC, 1991: 156)

Genre theory in sociolinguistics and literacy studies

This perspective has also informed the development of the genre theory approach to teaching school literacy that emerged in approximately the same period in Australia. The term 'literacy' used in this particular body of work indicated a primary interest in the use of written language for social and institutional purposes but the approach does not exclude talk in its analysis. Cope and Kalantzis (1993: 67), for instance, argue that

> ... writing and speaking have distinctively different linguistic structures; and different ways of using language have different social effect. Literacy, and the types of transformation of oral language that come with literacy, open linguistic doors into certain realms of social action and social power. It follows that literacy teaching, if it is to provide

students with equitable social access, needs to link the different social purposes of language in different contexts to predictable patterns of discourse.

On this view, there are socially and culturally recognised types of text that carry a good deal of power. The socially oriented perspectives adopted by language educators working in this tradition foreground the fact that these powerful text types are situated and purpose-oriented. One can find these powerful texts at different levels of society and in different institutional domains. These texts tend to conform to '[g]enres [which] are conventional structures which have evolved as pragmatic schemes for making certain types of meaning and to achieve distinctive social goals, in specific settings, by particular linguistic means' (Cope & Kalantzis, 1993: 67). By 'linguistic means' is meant language resources at both clause level and whole text level (i.e. discourse). The idea here is that by construing genre in this particular way, it is possible to understand 'how language works; who it works for; why it works' (Cope & Kalantzis, 1993: 84) in a context-sensitive way. Veel (1997), for example, looks at a number of different science texts and relates their linguistic features to the purposes they are designed to serve. The following is an extract of an experimental report in an electronics journal:

> Single-mode fibre lasers (SMFL) possess *a number of advantages* over their bulk counterparts. *By virtue* of their small cores, *very-low* thresholds and high gains can be achieved. Since the typical fibre diameter is about 100 µm, thermal effects which plague glass lasers are *minimal*. The fabrication process is *economical* in dopant ... (Mears *et al.*, 1985: 738, cited in Veel, 1997: 163)

It is argued that this text has not been designed to just report findings but also to be persuasive (the persuasive elements italicised by Veel). The modality of 'can be achieved' signals a sense of 'possibility' and therefore all the 'advantages' are in effect potential new achievements to be acknowledged. In fact, Veel reports that the purpose of the authors of this report was to associate themselves with an innovation and a possible patent. This clearly departs from the widely accepted popular notion of the scientific report being objective, factual and disinterested. By comparison the following extract of a school science text on silicones does not seek to 'sell' the 'facts'; the 'facts' are merely stated as being well-established and timeless (note the prevalence of the declarative statement form in the present tense):

> Silicones are similar to hydrocarbons, but the 'backbones' of the molecules consist of silicon and oxygen atoms, instead of carbon atoms. Attached to the silicon atoms are side-chains of carbon and hydrogen.
>
> Silicones have exceptional resistance to heat. They repel water, and are not affected by most chemicals ... (Messel *et al.*, 1965: 7 – 2, cited in Veel, 1997: 166)

This text, in common with most school science texts, is interested in presenting science as a body of observed, stable and 'true' facts to be learned. In terms of sequencing and staging of information in secondary school science texts, Veel goes on to suggest that there are some clearly identifiable genres. For example, the genre of procedure, which has the social and educational purpose of enabling experiments and observations, has three stages: aim – materials needed – steps; while the genre of causal explanation, which provides an account of why or how an abstract or a not readily observable process takes place, has two stages: identification of phenomena – explanation sequence (comprising a number of phases), and so on. Veel suggests that school science texts tend to follow a knowledge trajectory that starts with the genres related to doing science (e.g. procedures for doing experiments), which is followed by explaining science (e.g. causal explanations), organising scientific information (e.g. descriptive and taxonomic reports), and challenging science (e.g. exposition of argument for or against an issue). This shift from the concrete (doing experiments) to the abstract (arguing against a theory) has also been identified by Coffin (1997) in school history genres where there is a movement from history as story to history as argument. The close attention to how language resources are deployed in the formation of a text in particular subject areas has made writing (and reading) more transparent to teach and at the same time increased awareness of the role played by language in the forming of content meaning.

New Literacy Studies

We now build upon these sociolinguistic accounts of language and literacy with reference to recent approaches that have attempted to take this 'social' dimension further and to consider the issues and meanings of literacy in specific settings, an issue already signalled in the work cited above by Bloome *et al.* in classroom discourse and Cope, Kalantzis and others in Genre Studies. This approach has also challenged assumptions regarding the large consequences, for cognition and for society as a whole, of the acquisition of reading and writing, which are mostly to be found in work by cognitive psychologists but have also affected some sociolinguistic approaches. Psychologists, in particular, studied literacy in terms of the 'problems' of acquisition for individuals and the cognitive changes that can occur when 'successfully' mastered (see Olson & Torrance, 2008, for a comprehensive survey and updating of these approaches). Whilst the concern with cognition and with 'problems' of acquisition continue, a recent shift in perspective has emphasised understanding of literacy practices in their social and cultural contexts. This approach has been particularly influenced by those who have advocated an 'ethnographic' perspective, in contrast with the experimental and often individualistic character of cognitive studies, and the textual, etic perspective of linguistic-based studies of text. The experimental and often individualistic character of previous studies has been challenged by many researchers in the field of literacy studies who now prefer to place the emphasis on understanding literacy practices in context, with greater caution regarding assumptions about the intrinsic nature or consequences of the medium (Gee, 1999; Barton & Hamilton, 1998; Collins, 1995; Heath, 1983; Street, 1993). Much of the work in this approach focuses on the everyday meanings and uses of literacy in specific cultural contexts and, from an educational perspective, links directly to how we understand the work of literacy programmes and pedagogic practices, which themselves then become subject to ethnographic enquiry.

Developments in New Literacy Studies have been usefully summarised in articles by Barton and Hamilton (1998), Besnier and Street (1994), Finnegan (1999), Gee (1999) and Street (1996), whereas books by Barton and Hamilton (1998), Barton *et al.* (2000), Maybin (1993), Street (1995, 2005) and Street and Hornberger (2007) provide fuller accounts of the new approaches (see annotated list at the end). Recent books and articles have also located these approaches to literacy within the broader context of what Gee *et al.* (1996) term 'the new work order' and what Kress and others refer to as 'multi modality' (Kress, 2002; Kress & van Leeuwen, 1996; Kress & Street, 2006; Pahl & Rowsell, 2006).

In trying to characterise these new approaches to understanding and defining literacy, Street has referred to a distinction between an 'autonomous' model and an 'ideological' model of literacy (Street, 1984). The 'autonomous' model of literacy works from the assumption that literacy in itself – autonomously – will have effects on other social and cognitive practices, much as in the early 'cognitive consequences' literature cited above (Goody, 1968, 1986, 1987). The model, he argues, disguises the cultural and ideological assumptions that underpin it and that can then be presented as though they are neutral and universal – a perspective that as we shall see has also been salient in language education more broadly.

Research in the social practice approach challenges this view and suggests that in practice dominant approaches based on the autonomous model are simply imposing Western (or urban, etc.) conceptions of literacy on to other cultures or subgroups within a given society (Street, 2001). The alternative, ideological model of literacy offers a more culturally sensitive view of literacy practices as they vary from one context to another. This model starts from different premises than the autonomous model – it posits instead that literacy is a social practice, not simply a technical and neutral skill; that it is always embedded in socially constructed epistemological principles. The ways in which people address reading and writing are themselves rooted in conceptions of knowledge, identity and being. Literacy, in this sense, is always contested, both its meanings and its practices; hence, particular versions of it are always 'ideological', they are always rooted in a particular world view and a desire for that view of literacy to dominate and to marginalise others (Gee, 1990).

Such an 'ideological' perspective on literacy in the context of power relations demands, according to Street (1995), a recognition of multiple literacies rather than a single unified 'thing' called 'Literacy'. This perspective recognises the ways in which even such definitions of literacy/ ies are themselves part of the 'ideological' work of naming and defining, and entails the recognition that engaging with literacy/ies is always a social act from the outset. In educational contexts, for instance, the ways in which teachers or facilitators and their students interact around learning to read and write are already social practices that affect the nature of the literacy being learned and the ideas about literacy held by the participants, especially the new learners and their position in relations of power. It is not valid to suggest that 'literacy' can be 'given' neutrally and then its 'social' effects only experienced or 'added on' afterwards.

The question this approach raises for those working in this field, including sociolinguists and educators, is, then, not simply that of the 'impact' of literacy – to be measured in terms of a neutral developmental index – but rather of how local people 'take hold' of the new communicative practices being introduced to them, as Kulick and Stroud's (1993) ethnographic description of missionaries bringing literacy to New Guinea villagers makes clear. Literacy, in this sense, is, then, already part of a power relationship and how people 'take hold' of it is contingent on social and cultural practices and not just on pedagogic and cognitive factors. This raises questions that need to be addressed in any literacy programme: What is the power relation between the participants? What are the resources? Where are people going if they take on one literacy rather than another literacy? Who has the power to define and name what counts as literacy? How do recipients challenge the dominant conceptions of literacy?

This approach has implications for both research and practice. Researchers, instead of privileging the particular literacy practices familiar in their own culture, now suspend judgement as to what constitutes literacy among the people they are working with until they are able to understand what it means to the people themselves, and which social contexts reading and writing derive their meaning from. Many people labelled 'illiterate' within the autonomous model of literacy may, from a more culturally sensitive viewpoint, be seen to make significant use of literacy practices for specific purposes and in specific contexts. For instance, studies suggest that even non-literate persons find themselves engaged in literacy activities, as Nabi's (2008) work on the 'hidden literacies' of street sellers and plumbers in Pakistan has demonstrated. In such cases, the boundary between literate/non-literate is less obvious than individual 'measures' of literacy suggest (Doronilla, 1996). Academics have, however, often failed to make explicit the implications of such theory for practical work. In the present conditions of world change, such ivory tower distancing appears no longer legitimate. But likewise, policy makers and practitioners have not always taken on board such 'academic' findings, or have adopted one position (most often that identified with the autonomous model) and not taken account of the many others outlined here. These findings, then, raise important issues both for research into literacy in general and for policy in education in particular. The issue of which literacies are dominant literacies and of the differences between 'standard', informal and vernacular literacies is central to how literacy is defined and situated from the outset.

There has, however, recently, been a critique of this position in turn: Brandt and Clinton (2002) refer to 'the limits of the local' – they and others (*cf.* Collins & Blot, 2002) question the 'situated' approach to literacy as not giving sufficient recognition to the ways in which literacy usually comes from outside of a particular community's 'local' experience. The ethnographic approach associated with New Literacy Studies has emphasised what is actually happening in given groups of people, in small communities or settings, as in Heath's (1983) account of schooled and out-of-school literacies in the Piedmont Carolinas and Street's (1984) account of maktab, commercial and schooled literacies in Iranian villages. The critiques have argued that such accounts are too inward looking and localised and need to take into account the larger influences evident now in the globalised world. Street (2003) summarises a number of these arguments and offers a defence of the 'ethnographic' perspective, noting for instance that the 'local' in the sense of actual uses of literacy in given contexts is always recognised as also infused with influences from outside – such as the larger context of 'maktab' or Quranic literacy in Iranian villages and the employment and political pressures on workers and their families in the Carolinas.

More recently, Maddox (2001) has attempted to bring together the 'situated' approach with that of 'New Literacy Studies', using his own ethnographic field research in Bangladesh to explore the relationship. For instance, he critiques NLS for its 'reluctance ... in examining the role of literacy capabilities and practices in progressive forms of social change and the production of agency'. Like Brandt and Clinton, he wants to recognise the force of 'outside' influences associated with literacy, including the potential for helping people move out of 'local' positions and take account of progressive themes in the wider world. The 'desire to keep records of household income and expenditure' was not just a technical issue but one of authority, gender relations and kinship – literacy (and numeracy) could play a catalytic role in women's breaking free from traditional constraints. He wants, then, to 'shift away from the binary opposition of ideological and autonomous positions that has dominated ... debates in recent years' and develop a 'more inclusive theory that can link the local and the global, structure and agency and resolve some of the theoretical and disciplinary tensions over practice and technology' (Maddox, 2001: 17).

Academic literacies and ELT/EAL

A similar shift from the autonomous model of literacy can be found in the educational literature, where schooled literacy, whether imposed on children or, as in many adult literacy programmes, on adults too, bears little relation to the actual uses and meanings of literacy in people's every-day lives. We will conclude with an example taken from our own teaching and research. We firstly link work in the field of writing support in universities to the theoretical shifts outlined above and then provide a brief example of how these approaches are being worked through in practice in teaching and learning on a 'Widening Participation' programme at King's College London.

The academic literature in both English as an Additional/Second Language (EAL) and 'academic literacies' studies demonstrates that the language and literacy learning issues involved in these activities are also now coming to be understood as meaning-making in social practices (e.g. Boughey, 2000; Gee, 1999; Ivaniĉ & Lea, 2006; Jones *et al.*, 1999; Kress & van Leeuwen, 2001; Lea, 1994, 1998; Lea & Stierer, 1999, 2007; Lea & Street, 1999; Leung & Safford, 2005; Lillis, 1997; Olsen, 1977, 1985, 1994; Ong, 1982; Prior, 1998, 2007; Prior *et al.*, 2006; Russell, 1977, 1993; Schleppegrell & Colombi, 2002; Scribner & Cole, 1981; Thesen & van Pletzen, 2006; Zamel & Spack, 2004) rather than 'technical skills' or 'language deficit'. Earlier work in contrastive rhetoric has established that the expectations of academic writing vary across cultural contexts (Kaplan, 1966; Purves & Purves, 1986). In North America especially, researchers concerned with the history of academic literacy in the academy have addressed questions regarding Writing in the Disciplines (WiD) and academic genres (Bazerman, 1988, 1994, 2004, 2007; Berkenkotter & Huckin, 1995; Donahue, 2008; Russell, 1991; Russell *et al.*, 2009). In the United Kingdom, researchers–practitioners in Queen Mary College London have attempted to take account of these issues by adapting US approaches to Writing in the Disciplines (WiD) to both research and practice regarding the needs of linguistically diverse students in contemporary London (Mitchell & Evison, 2006). At the same time, the adoption of the principles of Communicative Language Teaching (CLT) by ELT professionals has broadened curriculum concerns to include notions of appropriateness and language norms in context (Brown, 2001; Canale & Swain, 1980b; Morrow, 1981; McDonough & Shaw, 2003).

However, despite its conceptual foundations in ethnography of communication (with early references to Hymes), CLT practices, as we saw above, have tended to rely on formal questionnaire and other self-report techniques for student needs identification, and native speaker insider knowledge for curriculum prescription (Dubin, 1989; Leung, 2005). A consequence of this is that, in ELT, pedagogy is culturally tuned to appropriateness in terms of formality of language discourse in general terms (as evidenced by most commercially published ELT textbooks), but it tends not to be able to offer specific guidance for specific domains of contextualised use, such as the variety of academic genres and registers required in higher education (*cf.* Crème & Lea, 1997; Scarcella, 2003). Where genres and registers are taken into account, these are construed as fixed formations into which students can be inducted through explicit instruction. (For a further discussion, see Lillis & Scot, 2007.) This is a fundamental conceptual issue, with major pedagogic implications, that requires further research.

While work in the field of academic literacies has been attuned to the issues of genre, register and student voice (e.g. Ganobcsik-Williams, 2006; Ivaniĉ, 1998, 2004; Lea & Street, 1998, 2006; Lillis, 1999, 2001), it has however tended not to foreground EAL issues. Researchers working in this tradition have sought to explore, in particular, mismatches between student and tutor expectations regarding written discourse and the variation in writing requirements across fields of study in the university context. Research in school-based EAL, on the other hand, has tended to focus on language use, EAL and diversity. The work we describe below attempts to bring these two traditions together and address them in a specific university site. Epistemologically there is a fit between them, at least at the level of conceptualisation of the phenomena to be investigated (Leung, 2005). In both cases, then, the 'problems' commonly associated with students acquiring academic discourse are seen as not simply about language proficiency or language varieties – such as EAL or regional varieties of English – but in the students' deployment of a range of literacy practices, involving registers, modes and genres that are conventionally associated with a particular subject, field or discipline (e.g. Lea & Street, 2006).

The Academic Language and Literacy Development programme at King's College London (KCL) represents a recent attempt to build on the theoretical and applied conceptions summarised above, with respect to both the understanding of academic literacies and the understanding of the social turn in EAL theory and pedagogy. The programme was designed to provide a non-credit bearing English Language Development course for 'Advanced' level (Year 12) students from linguistic minority community backgrounds attending schools in the locality of King's College London, who would like to further their studies at university. This is part of a Widening Participation initiative designed to encourage more people, especially those from communities that have no strong tradition in participating in higher education, to go to university. The programme of work was intended to provide additional opportunities for dedicated 'A' level students from the local areas who were still in the process of learning English as an additional language; it was hoped that participation in the Programme would enhance both their 'A' level performance and their chances of entering higher education.

The team members who taught on the Programme also engaged in ethnographic-style research. They were interested in the relationship between the programme objectives and actual experiences and perceptions of the sessions by the students and the tutors. As one of the tutors who both taught the course and engaged in research with it noted:

> The ALD programme tries to challenge some of the expectations students may have met at school ... about language as narrowly defined ... the course involves issues of discourse, genre, writing as social process ... within a notion of building on what they already had and bring to the programme rather than treating them as a deficit and just fixing that. (Street, personal communication, 2006)

As Scalone and Street (2006) noted in their analysis of the Academic Literacy Development Programme, by expressing personal styles and learning strategies during classroom activities and engaging with their related genres, students participated both in the community of the academy and in the community formed by the students during the course. Furthermore, by engaging with the types of literacy required in higher education in the United Kingdom, they collaboratively constructed an understanding of official requirements and participated in earning-oriented activities, such as discussing in groups how they might write the 'personal; statement' required for university applications and engaging in different forms of argument described by one tutor on the course. Interaction with other students and with tutors was therefore fundamental in making explicit the different types of knowledge that students already used and that they needed to develop and customise to fit Higher Education standards. Linking these findings with the three models of academic literacy proposed by Lea and Street (1998), namely study skills, academic socialisation and academic literacies, the report by Scalone and Street (2006) concludes:

> Treating such students as collaborators in the development of the academic literacies necessary for engagement with HE in the UK, can perhaps offer a different and more supportive route to 'Widening Participation' than the more traditional focus on either study skills or academic socialization. (Scalone & Street, 2006: 133–134)

Concluding Remarks

We conclude by reflecting on some of the ideas and developments discussed above, and then offer a view on the emerging issues that bear on both sociolinguistics and language and literacy teaching. Our comments will be selective to the extent that they are meant to highlight the conceptual and theoretical challenges posed by some of the current debates in the relevant fields including applied linguistics, language education and literacy studies.

The migration of a research perspective from ethnography to language and literacy teaching has, as we have seen, led to noticeable recontextualisation, that is selective interpretation of the concept of communicative competence. It may well be that language teaching (however theorised) demands a relatively stable body of authoritative knowledge as a foundation, whereas a research enterprise such as ethnography would, among other things, encourage the discovery of new findings and a commitment to provisionality. For some language teachers, it may not be all that important to retain a research-oriented perspective in day-to-day classroom work, given the pressures to follow tightly prescribed curricula timelines. Conceptually however, the reduction of the notion of communication to classroom language use and the reliance on teacher expertise to facilitate 'genuine linguistic interaction' have combined to constrict and reify how and what language is used in actual communication practices, leading to an impoverished curriculum base.

The examples given above illustrate the ways in which a research base developed from 'social turn' conceptions of language and literacy can be constructively brought to bear on classroom pedagogy and course design. Key findings and directions for further research and practice that arise from this brief survey include the recognition that learning language and literacy in socially and linguistically diverse educational contexts involves more than learning language as structure and literacy as a set of generic skills. It involves recognition of the constitutive and power dynamics involved in producing and using language and literacy and the interactive nature of the learning environment. We have given some brief indication of how the complexity of what we now know about language and literacy in the 'real' world can be fruitfully engaged with in the classroom but recognise that this movement is at an early stage and, as the authors cited above have advised, the task is immensely rich and difficult and there is still much to do. We hope that this chapter can make a modest contribution to that task.

Suggestions for further reading

Gee, J.P. (1999) The New Literacy Studies: From 'socially situated' to the work of the social. In D. Barton, M. Hamilton and R. Ivaniĉ (eds) *Situated Literacies: Reading and Writing in Context* (pp. 180–196). London: Routledge.
A very helpful overview of the field of New Literacy Studies from one of the main exponents, locating this new field in relation to a series of other perspectives and paradigms.

Heath, S.B., Street, B.V. with Mills, M. (2008) *Ethnography: Approaches to Language and Literacy Research.* New York and London: Teachers College Columbia University.

An insider account of the processes of doing ethnography, drawing upon the authors' own experiences and linking them to key issues that arise, especially those in the fields of language and literacy research.

Hymes, D. (1974) *Foundations in Sociolinguistics: An Ethnographic Approach.* Philadelphia: University of Pennsylvania Press.
A seminal work exploring the contribution of an ethnographic orientation to linguistic description and analysis; an important text for anyone interested in understanding the development of the notion of communicative competence.

Leung, C. (2005) Convivial communication: Recontextualizing communicative competence. *International Journal of Applied Linguistics* 15 (2), 119–144.
A critical review of the renderings of the notion of communicative competence in second/additional language education; the relevance of Hymesian ethnographic sensibilities is discussed against a backdrop of contemporary developments.

Lillis, T. and Scott, M. (2007) Defining academic literacies research: Issues of epistemology, ideology and strategy. *Journal of Applied Linguistics* 4 (1), 5–32.
A recent definitive overview of a new field within which the approach to student writing has been redefined to take account of social practice perspectives on literacy.

Street, B. (ed.) (2005) *Literacies across Educational Contexts: Mediating Learning and Teaching.* Philadelphia: Caslon Publishing.
A theory-conscious collection of papers exploring literacy practices and educational issues in different world locations that include out-of-school learning; formal learning in institutional settings; and learning in early years, higher education and adult education environments.

References

Austin, J.L. (1962) *How to Do Things with Words.* London: Clarendon Press.

Barton, D. and Hamilton, M. (1998) *Local Literacies: Reading and Writing in One Community.* Routledge: London.

Barton, D., Hamilton, M. and Ivaniĉ, R. (eds) (2000) *Situated Literacies: Reading and Writing in Context.* London: Routledge.

Bazerman, C. (1988) *Shaping Written Knowledge: The Genre and Activity of the Experimental Article in Science.* Madison: University of Wisconsin Press.

Bazerman, C. (1994) *Constructing Experience.* Carbondale, IL: Southern Illinois University Press.

Bazerman, C. (2004) Speech acts, genres, and activity systems: How texts organize activity and people. In C. Bazerman and P. Prior (eds) *What Writing Does and How it Does it: An Introduction to Analyzing Texts and Textual Practices* (pp. 309–339). Mawah, NJ: Lawrence Erlbaum Associates.

Bazerman, C. (2007) *Genre and Cognitive Development: Beyond Writing to Learn.* Brazil: Paper presented at the SIGET, Tubarao.

Berkenkotter, C. and Huckin, T. (1995) *Genre Knowledge in Disciplinary Communication.* New York: Lawrence Erlbaum Associates.

Besnier, N. and Street, B. (1994) Aspects of literacy. In T. Ingold (ed.) *Companion Encyclopedia of Anthropology* (pp. 527–562). London and New York: Routledge.

Bloome, D., Carter, S.P., Christian, B.M., Otto, S. and Shuart-Faris, N. (2005) *Discourse Analysis and the Study of Classroom Language and Literacy Events: A Microethnographic Perspective.* Mahwah, NJ: Lawrence Erlbaum Associates.

Boughey, C. (2000) Multiple metaphors in an understanding of academic literacy. *Teachers and Teaching: Theory and Practice* 6 (3), 279–290.

Brandt, D. and Clinton, K. (2002) Limits of the local: Expanding perspectives on literacy as a social practice. *Journal of Literacy Research* 34 (3), 337–356.

Brindley, G. (1989) The role of needs analysis in adult ESL programme design. In R.K. Johnson (ed.) *The Second Language Curriculum* (pp. 63–78). Cambridge: Cambridge University Press.

Brown, H.G. (2001) *Teaching by Principles: An Interactive Approach to Language Pedagogy* (2nd edn). White Plains, NY: Pearson Education.

Canale, M. (1983) From communicative competence to language pedagogy. In J. Richards and J. Schmidt (eds) *Language and Communication* (pp. 2–27). London: Longman.

Canale, M. (1984) A communicative approach to language proficiency assessment in a minority setting. In C. Rivera (ed.) *Communicative Competence Approaches to Language Proficiency Assessment: Research and Application* (pp. 107–122). Clevedon: Multilingual Matters.

Canale, M. and Swain, M. (1980a) *A Domain Description for Core FSL: Communication Skills*. Ontario: Ministry of Education.

Canale, M. and Swain, M. (1980b) Theoretical bases of communicative approaches to second language teaching and testing. *Applied Linguistics* 1 (1), 1–47.

Carter, R. (1990) *Knowledge about Language and the Curriculum: the LINC Reader*. London: Hodder.

Carter, R. (1996) Politics and knowledge about language: The LINC Project. In R. Hasan and G. Williams (eds) *Literacy and Society* (pp. 1–21). London: Longman.

Carter, R. (1997) *Investigating English Discourse: Language, Literacy and Literature*. London: Routledge.

Cazden, B., John, V.P. and Hymes, D. (eds) (1972) *Functions of Language in the Classroom*. New York: Teachers College Press.

Chomsky, N. (1965) *Aspects of the Theory of Syntax*. Cambridge, MA: MIT Press.

Coffin, C. (1997) Constructing and giving value to the past. In F. Christie and J. Martin (eds) *Genres and Institutions: Social Processes in the Workplace and the School* (pp. 196–230). London: Continuum.

Collins, J. (1995) Literacy and literacies. *Annual Review of Anthropology* 24, 75–93.

Collins, J. and Blot, J. (2002) *Texts, Power and Identity*. Routledge: London.

Cope, W. and Kalantzis, M. (1993) *The Powers of Literacy: A Genre Approach to Teaching Writing*. London: Falmer Press.

Crème, P. and Lea, M. (1997) *Writing at University: A Guide for Students*. Buckingham: Open University Press.

Donahue, C. (2008) *Ecrire à l'iniversité: Analyse comparée*. France/Estats-unis. Villeneuve d'Ascq, France: Presses Universitaires du Septentrion.

Doronilla, M.L. (1996) *Landscapes of Literacy: An Ethnographic Study of Functional Literacy in Marginal Philippine Communities*. Hamburg: UIE.

Dubin, F. (1989) Situating literacy within traditions of communicative competence. *Applied Linguistics* 10 (2), 171–181.

Extra, G. (2006) Dealing with multilingualism in multicultural Europe: Immigrant and minority languages at home and school. In C. Leung and J. Jenkins (eds) *Reconfiguring Europe: The Contribution of Applied Linguistics* (pp. 21–40). London: Equinox in association with British Association for Applied Linguistics.

Finnegan, R. (1999) Sociology/anthropology: Theoretical issues in literacy. In D. Wagner, L. Venezky and B. Street (eds) *International Handbook of Literacy*. NJ: Westview Press.

Ganobcsik-Williams, L. (2006) *Teaching Academic Writing in UK Higher Education: Theories, Practice and Models*. London: Palgrave/Macmillan.

Gee, J.P. (1990) Orality and literacy: From the savage mind to ways with words. In *Social Linguistics and Literacy: Ideology in Discourses*. London: Falmer Press.

Gee, J.P. (1999) The New Literacy Studies: From 'socially situated' to the work of the social. In D. Barton, M. Hamilton and R. Ivaniĉ (eds) *Situated Literacies: Reading and Writing in Context* (pp. 180–196). London: Routledge.

Gee, J., Hull, G. and Lankshear, C. (1996) *The New Work Order: Behind the Language of New Capitalism.* Boulder, CO: Westview.

Geertz, C. (2000) *The Interpretation of Cultures.* New York: Basic Books.

Goody, J. (1986) *The Logic of Writing and the Organisation of Society.* Cambridge: Cambridge University Press.

Goody, J. (1987) *The Interface between the Written and the Oral.* Cambridge: Cambridge University Press.

Goody, J. (ed.) (1968) *Literacy in Traditional Societies.* Cambridge: Cambridge University Press.

Halliday, M., MacIntosh, A., and Strevens, P. (1964) *The Linguistic Sciences and Language Teaching.* London: Longman.

Halliday, M.A.K. (1973) *Explorations in the Functions of Language.* London: Edward Arnold.

Halliday, M.A.K. (1975) *Learning How to Mean: Explorations in the Development of Language.* London: Edward Arnold.

Halliday, M.A.K. and (revised by) Matthiessen, C.M.I.M. (2004) *An Introduction to Functional Grammar* (3rd edn). London: Arnold.

Halliday, M.A.K. and Hasan, R. (1976) *Cohesion in English.* London: Longman.

Halliday, M.A.K. and Matthiessen, C.M.I.M. (2000) *Construing Experience Through Meaning: A Language-based Approach to Cognition.* London: Continuum.

Heath, S.B. (1983) *Ways with Words: Language, Life and Work in Communities and Classrooms.* New York: Cambridge University Press.

Heath, S.B., Street, B.V. with Mills, M. (2008) *Ethnography: Approaches to Language and Literacy Research.* New York and London: Teachers College Columbia University.

Hornberger, N. (1989) Tramites and transportes: The acquisition of second language communicative competence for one speech event in Puno, Peru. *Applied Linguistics* 10 (2), 214–230.

Hornberger, N.H. (ed.) (2003) *Continua of Biliteracy: An Ecological Framework for Educational Policy, Research and Practice in Multilingual Settings* (Vol. BEB 41). Clevedon: Multilingual Matters.

Hymes, D. (1972a) Introduction. In C.B. Cazden, V.P. John and D. Hymes (eds) *Functions of Language in the Classroom* (pp. xi–lvii). New York: Teachers College Press.

Hymes, D. (1972b) On communicative competence. In J.B. Pride and J. Holmes (eds) *Sociolinguistics.* London: Penguin.

Hymes, D.H. (1974) *Foundations in Sociolinguistics: An Ethnographic Approach.* Philadelphia: University of Pennsylvania Press.

Ivaniĉ, R. (1998) *Writing and Identity: The Discoursal Construction of Identity in Academic Writing.* Amsterdam: John Benjamins.

Ivaniĉ, R. (2004) Discourses of writing and learning to write. *Language and Education* 18 (3), 220–245.

Ivaniĉ, R. and Lea, M.R. (2006) New contexts, new challenges: The teaching of writing in UK higher education. In L. Ganobcsik-Williams (ed.) *Teaching Academic Writing in UK Higehr Education: Theories, Practice and Models* (pp. 6–15). London: Palgrave/MacMillan.

Johnson, K. (2001) *An Introduction to Foreign Language Learning and Teaching.* Harlow, Essex: Pearson (Longman).

Jones, C., Turner, J. and Street, B. (eds) (1999) *Students Writing in the University: Cultural and Epistemological Issues.* Amsterdam: John Benjamins.

Kaplan, R. (1966) Cultural thought patterns in intercultural education. *Language Learning* 16 (1), 1–20.

Kaplan, R.B. and Baldauf Jr., R.B. (1997) *Language Planning: From Practice to Theory*. Clevedon: Multilingual Matters.

Kress, G. (2002) *Literacy in the New Media Age*. London: Routledge.

Kress, G. and van Leeuwen, T. (1996) *Reading Images: The Grammar of Visual Design* (esp. intro pp. 1–14 and Chapter 1, pp. 15–42). Routledge: London.

Kress, G. and van Leeuwen, T. (2001) *Multimodal Discourse; the Modes and Media of Contemporary Communication*. London: Arnold.

Kress, G. and Street, B. (2006) 'Multi-modality and literacy practices'. Foreword to Travel notes from the New Literacy Studies: Case studies of practice. In K. Pahl and J. Rowsell (eds) *Multilingual Matters* (pp. vii–x). Clevedon: Multilingual Matters.

Kulick, D. and Stroud, C. (1993) Conceptions and uses of literacy in a Papua New Guinean village. In Street, B. (ed.) *Cross Cultural Approaches to Literacy*. Cambridge: Cambridge University Press.

Language in the National Curriculum (1989-1992) LINC material available on CD ROM or DVD. On WWW at http://www.phon.ucl.ac.uk/home/dick/ec/linc.htm. LINC Project. Accessed 12.3.2010.

Lea, M.R. (1994) 'I thought I could write until I cam here': Student writing in higher education. In G. Gibbs (ed.) *Improving Student Learning: Theory and Practice* (pp. 216–226). Oxford: Oxford Centre for Staff Development.

Lea, M.R. (1998) Academic literacies and learning in higher education: Constructing knowledge through texts and experience. *Studies in the Education of Adults* 30 (2), 156–171.

Lea, M. and Street, B. (1998) Student writing in higher education: An academic literacies approach. *Studies in Higher Education* 23 (2), 157–172.

Lea, M. and Street, B. (1999) Writing as academic literacies: Understanding textual practices in higher education. In C. Candlin and K. Hyland (eds) *Writing: Texts, Processes and Practices* (pp. 62–81). London: Longman.

Lea, M.R. and Street, B.V. (2006) The 'Academic Literacies' model: Theory and applications. *Theory into Practice* 45 (4), 368–377.

Lea, M.R. and Stierer, B. (1999) *Student Writing in Higher Education: New Contexts*. Buckingham: Open University Press/SRHE.

Lea, M.R. and Stierer, B. (2007) Writing as professional practice in the university as workplace. Paper presented at the *Society for Research into Higher Education* Annual Conference, Brighton, UK.

Leung, C. (2005) Convivial communication: Recontextualizing communicative competence. *International Journal of Applied Linguistics* 15 (2), 119–144.

Leung, C. and Safford, K. (2005) Non-traditional students in higher education: EAL and literacies. In B. Street (ed.) *Literacies across Educational Contexts* (pp. 303–324). Philadelphia: Caslon Publishers.

Lillis, T. (1997) New voices in academia? The regulative nature of academic writing conventions. *Language and Education* 11 (3), 182–199.

Lillis, T.M. (1999) Whose common sense? Essayist literacy and the institutional practice of mystery. In C. Jones, J. Turner and B. Street (eds) *Student Writing in University: Cultural and Epistemological Issues* (pp. 127–147). Amsterdam: John Benjamins.

Lillis, T.M. (2001) *Student Writing: Access, Regulation, Desire*. London: Routledge.

Lillis, T. and Scott, M. (2007) Defining academic literacies research: Issues of epistemology, ideology and strategy. *Journal of Applied Linguistics* 4 (1), 5–32.

Linguistic Minority Project (1985) *The Other Languages of England*. London: Routledge and Kegan Paul.

Maddox, B. (2001) Literacy and the market: The economic uses of literacy among the peasantry in north-west Bangladesh. In B. Street (ed.) *Literacy and Development* (pp. 137–151). London: Routledge.

Maybin, J. (1993) *Language and Literacy in Social Practice*. Milton Keynes: Open University Press.

McDonough, J. and Shaw, C. (2003) *Materials and Methods in ELT: A Teacher's Guide* (2nd edn). Oxford: Blackwell.

Mears, R.J., Reekie, L., Poole, S. and Payne, D. (1985) Neodymium-doped silica single-mode fibre lasers. *Electronics Letters* 21 (17), 738–740.

Messel, H., Crocker, R. and Barker, E.N. (1965) *Science for High School Students, Book One*. Sydney: The Science Foundation for Physics, University of Sydney.

Mitchell, S. and Evison, A. (2006) Exploiting the potential of writing for educational change at Queen Mary, University of London. In L. Ganobcsik-Williams (ed.) *Teaching Academic Writing in UK Higher Education: Theories, Practice and Models*. London: Palgrave/MacMillan.

Morrow, K. (1981) Principles of communicative methodology. In K. Johnson and K. Morrow (eds) *Communication in the Classroom* (pp. 59–66). Harlow, Essex: Longman.

Nabi, R. (2008) *Hidden Literacies: Ethnographic Case Studies of Literacy and Numeracy from Pakistan*. Uppingham: Uppingham Press.

Ohannessian, S. and Ansre, G. (1979) Some reflections on the educational use of sociolinguistic surveys. In J.B. Pride (ed.) *Sociolinguistic Aspects of Language Learning and Teaching* (pp. 57–70). Oxford: Oxford University Press.

Olsen, D. (1977) From utterance to text: The basis of language in speech and writing. *Harvard Educational Review* 47 (3), 257–281.

Olsen, D. (1994) *The World on Paper*. Cambridge: Cambridge University Press.

Olson, D. (ed.) (1985) *Literacy, Language and Learning*. Cambridge: Cambridge University Press.

Olson, D. and Torrance, N. (eds) (2008) *Cambridge Handbook of Literacy*. Cambridge: Cambridge University Press.

Ong, W. (1982) *Orality and Literacy: The Technologising of the Word*. London: Methuen.

Pahl, K. and Rowsell, J. (eds) (2006) *Travel Notes from the New Literacy Studies: Case Studies in Practice*. Clevedon: Multilingual Matters.

Prior, P. (1998) *Writing/Disciplinarity: A Sociolinguistic Account of Literate Activity in the Academy*. Mahwah, NJ: Lawrence Erlbaum Associates.

Prior, P. (2007) *From Bakhtin to Mediated Multi-Modal Genere Systems*. Brazil: Paper presented at the SIGET, Tubarao.

Prior, P., Hengst, J., Roozen, K. and Shipka, J. (2006) 'I'll be the sun': From reported speech to semiotic remediation practices. *Text and Talk* 26, 733–766.

Purves, A. and Purves, W. (1986) Viewpoints: Culture, text models, and the activity of writing. *Research in the Teaching of English* 20 (2), 174–197.

Roberts, C.M., Byram, A., Barro, S.J. and Street, B. (2001) *Language Learners as Ethnographers*. Clevedon: Multilingual Matters.

Russell, D. (1977) Rethinking genre in school and society: An activity theory analysis. *Written Communication* 14 (4), 504–554.

Russell, D. (1991) *Writing in the Academic Disciplines, 1870–1990: A Curricular History*. Carbondale: South Illinois University Press.

Russell, D., Lea, M.R., Parker, J., Street, B. and Donahue, C. (2009) Exploring notions of genre in 'academic literacies' and 'writing across the curriculum': Approaches across countries and contexts. Paper presented at the *SIGET*, Tubarao, Brazil.

Russell, D.R. (1993) The ethics of teaching ethics in professional communication: The case of engineering publicity at MIT in the 1920s. *Journal of Business and Technical Communication* 7 (1), 84–111.

Savignon, S.J. (1983) *Communicative Competence: Theory and Classroom Practice: Texts and Contexts in Second Language Learning*. Reading, MA: Addison-Wesley.

Scalone, P. and Street, B. (2006) An Academic Language Development Programme (Widening Participation). In C. Leung and J. Jenkins (eds) *Reconfiguring Europe: The Contribution of Applied Linguistics* (pp. 123–137). London: Equinox.

Scarcella, R. (2003) *Academic English: A Conceptual Framework*. Irvine: Linguistic Minority Research Institute, University of California.

Schleppegrell, M.J., Achugar, M. and Orteíza, T. (2004) The grammar of history: Enhancing content-based instruction through a functional focus on language. *TESOL Quarterly* 38 (1), 67–93.

Schleppegrell, M.J. and Colombi, M.C. (eds) (2002) *Developing Advanced Literacy in First and Second Languages: Meaning with Power*. Mahwah, NJ: Lawrence Erlbaum Associates.

Scribner, S. and Cole, M. (1981) *The Psychology of Literacy*. Cambridge, MA: Harvard University Press.

Street, B. (1984) *Literacy in Theory and Practice*. Cambridge: Cambridge University Press.

Street, B. (ed.) (1993) *Cross Cultural Approaches to Literacy*. New York: CUP.

Street, B. (1995) *Social Literacies*. London: Longman.

Street, B. (1996) Academic literacies. In D. Baker, J. Clay and C. Fox (eds) *Alternative Ways of Knowing: Literacies, Numeracies, Sciences* (pp. 101–134). London: Falmer Press.

Street, B. (2000) Literacy events and literacy practices: Theory and practice in the New Literacy Studies. In M. Martin-Jones and K. Jones (eds) *Multilingual Literacies: Reading and Writing Different Worlds* (pp. 17–29). Amsterdam: John Benjamins.

Street, B. (ed.) (2001) *Literacy and Development: Ethnographic Perspectives*. London: Routledge.

Street, B. (2003) What's new in New Literacy Studies? *Current Issues in Comparative Education* 5 (2), 77–91.

Street, B. (2005) (ed.) *Literacies across Educational Contexts: Mediating Learning and Teaching*. Philadelphia: Caslon Publishing.

Street, B. and Hornberger, N. (eds) (2007) *Encyclopedia of Language and Education, Vol. 2: Literacy*. New York: Springer.

Thesen, L. and van Pletzen, E. (eds) (2006) *Academic Literacy and the Languages of Change*. London: Continuum.

Veel, R. (1997) Learning how to mean – scientifically speaking: Apprenticeship into scientific discourse in the secondary school. In F. Christie and J. Martin (eds) *Genre and Institutions: Social Processes in the Workplace and School* (pp. 161–195). London: Continuum.

Whitely, W. (1979) Sociolinguistic survey at the national level. In J.B. Pride (ed.) *Sociolinguistic Aspects of Language Learning and Teaching* (pp. 44–56). Oxford: Oxford University Press.

Widdowson, H. (1978) *Learning Language as Communication*. Oxford: Oxford University Press.

Widdowson, H.G. (2004) *Text, Context, Pretext: Critical Issues in Discourse Analysis*. Oxford: Blackwell.

Yalden, J. (1983) *The Communicative Syllabus: Evolution, Design and Implementation*. Oxford: Pergamon Press.

Zamel, V. and Spack, R. (eds) (2004) *Crossing the Curriculum: Multilingual Learners in College Classrooms*. Mahwah, NJ: Lawrence Erlbaum Associates.

Chapter 12

Multimodal Literacy in Language Classrooms

VINITI VAISH and PHILLIP A. TOWNDROW

Introduction

The exponential rise of computer-mediated communication (CMC) over the last two or three decades has had a tremendous impact on the literacy practices of school going children. In the developed world, for instance in Singapore, children prefer to communicate with their peers through MSN (messenger service network), 'texting' (meaning using short messaging systems or SMS on mobile phones), blogging, Facebook, fanfiction or other such virtual platforms on the computer where like-minded adolescents meet and create communities of practice. In developing countries such as India computer penetration is very low. However, even in this part of the world disadvantaged youth increasingly have access to inexpensive internet cafés and mobile phones through which they 'message' each other.

A comparison of computer penetration in Singapore and India shows a glaring contrast. According to the World Bank, Singapore has one of the highest levels of connectivity in the world: in 2006 for every 100 persons there were 68.2 personal computers and 38.3 internet users (http://siteresources. worldbank.org/DATASTATISTICS/Resources/T5_11_2008pdf). On the other hand, according to data from the United Nations Development Program, for every 100 persons in India, there are only 1.65 internet users and 0.33 subscribers and computer ownership is 0.6 for every 100 persons (http://www.apdip.net/projects/dig-rev/info/in). The implication of this fact is that in Singapore most school going children have access to computers with an internet connection whereas in India most children go through their education without ever having seen a computer.

Equitable access to computers and multimodal literacy is important for the language classroom because the skills involved therein are directly linked with the workplace of the 21st century. According to Jenkins (2006), a key skill in this regard is engaging in 'participatory culture', a term we will explore later in the chapter. Thus, though the national school system in Singapore has the potential for training its students in 21st century skills, the school system in India does not. Having said this about Singapore, this chapter will show that mere access is a necessary but not sufficient condition for teachers to teach multimodal literacy.

One of the key issues regarding new literacy practices is whether or not and how they should be integrated into the language classroom so as to enhance the learning experiences of students. An equally important issue is that of equitable access to technology. Yet another issue relates to what Leander and Lewis (2008) call sociality, which refers to issues of identity and group membership in CMC. Finally there are issues of measuring how literacy has been enhanced or altered, and exactly which aspects of language and literacy acquisition have been enhanced or altered, through the use of technology.

This chapter explores these and related issues through the lens of multimodal literacy. At the outset we would like to situate our subject in the discipline of sociolinguistics. Janks (this volume) writes that a socio-cultural approach to language education refers variously to critical literacy, critical language awareness, critical applied linguistics, New Literacy Studies and multimodal literacies or multiliteracies. She traces the field of 'critical literacy' as theorized practice via four points in time: critical literacy, critical linguistics, multiliteracies, and literacy and space. Finally, she indicates that multiliteracies is an approach to literacy studies, which includes the re-examination of meaning-making in an age where visual modes of representation are in the ascendancy. This chapter is consistent with Janks's overviews of multiliteracies and multimodal literacy as approaches pertinent to the field of critical literacy.

We begin with a section that defines the terminology currently used in our adopted approaches. Thereafter, we look at what might be considered the main goals of multimodal literacy and report research findings in a review of literature on multimodal literacy practices, language classrooms, and teacher education. As part of the research findings, we focus on the Technology in English (TIE) project, which was completed by the Learning Sciences Laboratory at Singapore's National Institute of Education in February 2009. We use preliminary findings from this project to explore links between research and practice in the language classroom. Finally, we conclude the chapter with a look at under-researched topics in this field, which need more attention not only from the international academic community but also from teachers who face challenges posed by technology in their daily teaching and policy makers who want national school systems to be highly wired.

Definition of Key Terms

In this section we describe the way scholars refer to *technology, multimodality* and *multiliteracies* and other related terms.

Technology

The word technology, as it is used herein, generally refers to communication using computers and the internet, though this communication could also be done via mobile phone. Leander and Lewis (2008) use the term 'networked technologies' to separate technologies that facilitate communication between individuals and communities from technology that an individual can practice on his/her own, such as gaming. Regarding early developments of the internet, Leander and Lewis report that Minitel, an online service launched in France in 1982, was a precursor of the world wide web. Customers could use this service to make reservations, chat, check stock prices, etc. much like customers use the internet today. More importantly, Minitel (also called Teletel) affected educational practices at home due to the use of homework help lines, databases with model answers to national examination questions and online registration for university courses.

Castells (2000) in his monumental work on how technology has changed society writes: 'Among information technologies, I include, like everybody else, the converging set of technologies in micro-electronics, computing (machines and software), telecommunications/broadcasting, and opto-electronics' (Castells, 2000: 29). Castells thinks that the information technology revolution is as far reaching as was the 18th century industrial revolution in that it has created a dichotomy between the way people lived, worked and displayed their identity before and after this revolution. According to Castells this fundamental change started with the origin of the internet in the 1960s by the US Defense Department Advanced Research Projects Agency (DARPA) 'to prevent a Soviet takeover or destruction of American communications in the event of nuclear war' (Castells, 2000: 6). Though its origins may be ominous, the internet today is a common household technology that is widely available in most affluent countries at low cost for everyone.

Castells' definition is much broader than the way the word 'technology' is used in the emergent area of language and technology. McGrail (2006, printed from online source, no page) in a study of secondary school language teachers' attitudes toward technology writes:

> The term technology, as it applies in this study, is associated predominantly with computer technology, electronic communication (the Internet, e-mail, chat rooms), and multimedia design tools (digital audio and video). The definition is inclusive in that it embraces the machine-hardware and its peripherals (printers, scanners or servers), software (Inspiration, PowerPoint or Censor [a central monitoring system]) and educational applications (multimedia presentations, online discussions of reading).

We take McGrail's definition as this is very much what language students and teachers think of as technology.

Given these definitions, a key question is: how has technology changed the way we teach and learn literacy? According to the New London Group there are two main changes that we must keep in mind:

> First, we want to extend the idea and scope of literacy pedagogy to account for the context of our culturally and linguistically diverse and increasingly globalized societies, for the multifarious cultures that interrelate and the plurality of texts that circulate. Second, we argue that literacy pedagogy now must account for the burgeoning variety of text forms associated with information and multimedia technologies. (New London Group, 1996: 62–63)

What the New London Group means here is that globalization has fundamentally altered our classrooms by making them more diverse. For instance in a typical classroom in South London it is likely that there are children from Bangladesh, Pakistan and India, and that their dominant home languages are not English. The depth of diversity is increasing in classrooms all over the world as one of the processes in globalization is the flow of large numbers of people through increasingly porous national boundaries. Second, a text or a page of text does not look the way it looked before the technology revolution that happened around the 1960s. A text in today's classroom is likely to be a projected web page. A 'text' of this kind is likely to include some printed text but it might also feature other elements, for example, sounds, images, animations and colors that contribute both singly and collectively to the meanings conveyed.

The use of technology in the classroom gives rise to texts, which often call for 'new literacies' as compared with 'old literacies' (Luke, 2002). The English Language Arts Curriculum for secondary English in Atlantic Canada gives illustrations of what these new literacies look like:

> The use of Hypercard to produce simple interactive multimedia programs, the use of e-mail as a means to co-write a report, the manipulation and incorporation of file transfer documents, the use of pinhole cameras and graphics, and the creation of sound files to be incorporated in student produced communication. (Barrie, 1999: 234)

These literacies are different from those in a literature-based English curriculum where a printed text and its words are the basis of teaching and learning. The tension between old and new literacies for teachers will be taken up again under the heading 'teacher education'.

Multimodality and multimodal literacy

The emergence of new media and the rapidly increasing needs of today's learners are placing unprecedented demands on educational landscapes across disciplines to restructure and transform. In particular, paradigmatic change is sought in the field of literacy pedagogy where the growing presence of digital technologies has produced a vibrant and challenging body of theoretical and practical interest in 'multimodality' – a term which refers to the practice of meaning-making involving the purposeful integration of semiotic resources including, but by no means restricted to, writing, images, speech, gestures, drawing and sound (Emmison & Smith, 2000; Kress, 2003; The New London Group, 1996; van Leeuwen & Jewitt, 2001). In this definition it is important to note the difference between 'medium' and 'mode'. Nelson (2006) points out that these terms often get confused. Medium refers to the way that technology gets disseminated, for instance through a printed book, CD-ROM or computer application, while mode refers to print, gesture, sound, color and other forms of meaning-making.

The notion of meaning-making is central to the examination of multimodality. Lemke (1998) points out that the various modes which interplay with the printed text, like sound, gesture and so on are not merely decorative add-ons to a text in which meaning is derived mainly from the printed word. In a multimodal text, for instance a web-page, all the modes that interplay with each other are integral to meaning 'making the whole far greater than the simple sum of its parts' (Lemke, 1998: 284). Lemke goes on to argue that the major change that technology has made in literacy is a move beyond logocentrism or an overemphasis on the printed word. Though multimodality is not entirely new, and printed texts have always been accompanied by drawings, diagrams, etc. the approach to text has been logocentric which 'has identified language alone as a reliable medium for logical thought, and written language as the primary medium of, first, authoritative knowledge, and lately of all higher cognitive capacities' (Lemke, 1998: 284). However, now that texts are becoming multimodal, it is important to move beyond language and recognize that the printed word is just one of the modes in a set of modes that represent meaning.

With the heterogeneity and hybridity of present-day texts, a central concern in any theory of meaning-making is to understand the implications of multimodality (Cope & Kalantzis, 2000; Kress, 2000, 2003; Kress & van Leeuwen, 2001; Nelson, 2006). As Cope and Kalantzis explain:

> Meaning is made in ways that are increasingly multimodal – in which written-linguistic modes of meaning are part and parcel of visual, audio, and spatial patterns of meaning. Take for instance, the multimodal ways in which meanings are made on the World Wide Web, or in video captioning, or in interactive multimedia, or in desktop publishing, or in the use of written texts in a shopping mall. To find our way around this emerging world of meaning requires a new, multimodal literacy. (Cope & Kalantzis, 2001: para. 4)

Developed primarily on foundational ideas in social semiotics, 'multi-modal literacy' is a term used by Jewitt and Kress (2003) to refer to the different ways in which meanings can be created and communicated in the world today. From this perspective, Kress *et al.* (2001) argue for a new concept of literacy in which all modes and their interactions are to be considered equally and critically interpreted. This stance implies an important shift from the notion of mere competence in literacy to one of literacy as multimodal 'design'. As Baldry and Thibault (2005) expound, the process of designing, representing and interpreting modalities involves the constant interplay between the attributes of semiotic resources as they integrate or combine. In this respect it is important to understand that different semiotic modalities have varying organizational principles for creating meanings. For example, a printed page may feature type-written language and support the logical arrangement of items accompanied by spatial positioning (right, left, top, middle, bottom and so on). Alternatively, a graphical representation is more apt for portraying concepts such as (relative) volume, shape and directional vectors. The identification of the congruency of and discrepancy between modes is a key multimodal literacy capability.

Modes, affordances and knowledge

Modes are the elements of meaning-making that are used in different contexts. Following Kress and van Leeuwen (2001: 22), they are understood to be 'semiotic resources which allow the simultaneous realisation of discourses and types of (inter)action'. That is, modes can be utilised to create links with other times and places, and with other modes (Baldry & Thibault, 2005). From a multimodal perspective, it is essential not only to reflect on content (e.g. what drawings and writings mean) but also on the ways in which different modalities structure what is capable of being communicated.

An illustration of what modes are and how they can be used in the language classroom is available in Jewitt (2002). While observing how students in a year 10 class used a CD-ROM to interpret character in Steinbeck's *Of Mice and Men*, Jewitt found that learning proceeded beyond language when other modes were used. These modes included writing, visual communication (e.g. diagrams, pictures, video), gesture and aural communication (e.g. speech and sound). To this list of modes we can add the mode of color, which, as Kress and van Leeuwen (2006) point out, has potential for meaning-making in different cultural contexts. For instance green and orange in an Indian context are always symbolic of nationalism and patriotism as these are the colors of the Indian flag.

These points lead to a consideration of the affordances of modes. Different modalities of communicative action offer different potentials for meaning-making, and as Jewitt (2008) explains, how a mode is used, what it has been repeatedly used to mean and do, and the social conventions that inform its use in a particular context, all serve to shape its affordance. For example, that which can be drawn may not be done equally, or is done differently, in writing and vice versa. Furthermore, and crucially, the logic and affordances of modes entail users making certain claims about knowledge whether they realize it or not. Substantiating this point, Kress notes in the domain of science:

> If I say, 'a plant cell has a nucleus', I have been forced by the mode to provide a name for the relationship between the cell and the nucleus. I have named it as a relation of possession, 'have'. If I draw the cell, and have been asked to indicate the nucleus, my drawing requires me to place the element that indicates the nucleus somewhere; I cannot avoid that epistemological commitment. (Kress, 2003: 57)

By implication, and generally, multimodal representations of knowledge are realized by the user's design decisions, which are inherently epistemological in nature. Therefore, Kress (2003: 37) points out to educators, in particular, that '[i]t is no longer responsible to let children experience school without ... an understanding of the shift from competent performance to design as the foundational fact of contemporary social and economic life'.

Competent performance with multimodality is further informed by a conceptual distinction made by Lemke (1998: 290) between two matching ways in which meanings are made. First, with 'typological' meaning, language is used to express differences in kind through discrete contrastive categories; for example, up from down or male from female and so on. Second, topological meaning is concerned more with how things appear or sound. The pedagogical importance of understanding the differences between, and the combination of, typological and topological meaning-making is illustrated with the use of electronic slideshow software by teachers. Undoubtedly, the tools and editing functions in popular office suites assist in composition and presentation. The production of slides also forces and foregrounds decision making relating to the amalgamation of words, images and sounds to achieve specific communicative purposes. For example, Figure 12.1 is a prototype of slide designed to assist in the teaching of the comparative adjectives, 'bigger' and 'smaller'. This text exaggerates a contrastive relationship through the purposeful resizing and positioning of photographs and typesetting – the choice of typeface, point size and kerning (the relative spacing between letters and characters). Thus, the dimensions of the photograph of the elephant are greater than those of the field mouse. The elephant is also placed above its counterpart to signify prominence (in the animal kingdom) in terms of stature, weight and strength. Similarly, the words 'bigger' and 'smaller' look markedly different. The word 'bigger' appears in a larger, bold font and is

Figure 12.1 Complementary typological and topological meaning-making strategies using electronic slideshow software

stretched so that it occupies more space on the slide. By contrast, the word 'smaller' is represented in a smaller font with no emphasis and greater compression to convey diminutiveness. For this slide to be successful as a teaching resource, its creator must be aware not only of the work done by images and words but also how these modes can be used distinctively to prompt linguistic production.[1]

Transformation, transduction and resemiotization in multimodal design

Kress (2003: 36) asserts that a theory of multimodal literacy must account for the complementary processes of transformation, which 'operates on the forms and structures within a mode' and transduction, which 'accounts for the shift of semiotic material ... across modes'. Taken together, these processes can account for and motivate new forms of meaning – making through the interaction between modes. Moreover, for Kress (2003: 169), the creative use of semiotic resources is 'normal and unremarkable in every instance of sign-making' because it is considered to be a natural outcome of designing something that is new or innovative.

As far as classroom practice goes this conception of creativity views learners not as little linguists abstracting rules from data but as designers or artists who shape semiotic resources into multimodal texts according to their needs and interests in their particular communicative contexts.

For example, by way of explaining and exemplifying the transition from literacy to multiliteracies, Cummins *et al.* (2007: 128–147) describe a project conducted by teachers and students at an elementary school, 60 miles north of Los Angeles. In project *fresa* ('strawberry' in Spanish) students were engaged in bringing their family lives into the classroom by researching the tough farming histories of their parents and grandparents. The students began by brainstorming their ideas and vocabulary relating to strawberries and then framed their own inquiry questions based on their interests – for example, 'I wonder why the people who pick ... strawberries wear scarves across their noses and faces'? Items like these developed into a jointly constructed questionnaire. Next, the students interviewed their family members and shared their findings in subsequent classroom discussions. The data collected were analyzed and represented in multiple visual forms including drawings, maps and charts. Arguably, these artifacts demonstrated the students' high levels of personal investment, novelty and analytical insight. As a result of the students' knowledge construction, they became concerned about pesticides, low wages and harsh working conditions in the strawberry farming industry. This concern was actualized, socially, by writing an information report that was sent to the state governor who promised to open an investigation based on the students' findings. Finally, the students' work was distributed via the medium of a website dedicated to project *fresa*.

By way of commentary, the pedagogic design of the project *fresa* learning task required students to be the producers of texts rather than mere consumers of printed material. Particularly, the students' work designs featured visual elements (drawings, maps and charts) that both accompanied and extended their messages in ways that could not be expressed as easily, or at all, through linguistic resources alone. The resulting process and production values attained by the project *fresa* students were distinctive in the sense that their multimodal texts were the outcome of personalized learning, local, nonspecialist media production and targeted dissemination. The genius of this project was located in its vital recruitment of digital tools and new media. Arguably, these resources afforded the students hitherto unknown agency and opened up – albeit briefly – a multilingual space where cultural, social and political transactions occurred. Additionally, the students were given unique access to a powerful means of experimentation, information, communication tools (where messages were heard and acted upon) and, perhaps, most importantly a socially oriented purpose for learning that facilitated the expression of their all-too-often minority and marginalized voices.

Finally, resemiotization (Iedema, 2003) emphasizes the transformative dynamics of social meaning-making. In particular, it deals with how meaning-making shifts from one context to the next and attempts to explain why certain semiotics are used to do certain work at particular times. According to Nelson (2006: 63), 'the meaning of a multimodal artefact at any given moment is necessarily shaped by the meanings that are imputed to its component semiotic parts over time, parts that have semiotic histories of their own'.

Multiliteracies

The term 'multiliteracies' has become widely used in the field of language and technology since its conception by the New London Group in 1996. In a seminal paper the New London Group wrote:

> We decided that the outcomes of our discussions could be encapsulated in one word – multiliteracies – a word we chose to describe two important arguments we might have with the emerging cultural, institutional, and global order: the multiplicity of communications channels and media, and the increasing saliency of cultural and linguistic diversity. (New London Group, 1996: 63)

The authors then make a distinction between 'mere literacy', which we take to be traditional literacy, and multiliteracy. They argue that 'mere literacy' privileges language only, what Lemke (1998) in our discussion on modes and multimodality calls logocentrism, and, moreover, a standard nationally accepted form of language which is perceived as correct. Multiliteracy, on the other hand, also focuses on modes of representation other than solely on language and the printed word.

The New London Group authors also propose that there are six design elements in the meaning-making process: Linguistic Meaning, Visual Meaning, Audio Meaning, Gestural Meaning, Spatial Meaning and Multimodal meaning, which refers to the way the first five modes relate to each other. Thus each of these design elements is referred to as a 'mode' by the authors. The authors also emphasize that there are four components of literacy pedagogy: Situated Practice, which draws on lifeworlds of students for meaning-making; Overt Instruction, which is self-explanatory; Critical Framing, which interprets the power relations of the text; and Transformed Practice, in which students redesign the text in question through their interpretation. These concepts will become clearer when we describe the findings of researchers in the area of multimodal literacy as many of them use multiliteracies as a theoretical framework.

It is important that language teachers understand the concept of multiliteracy as this will trigger innovation in the pedagogy and products involved in literacy acquisition. Language teachers need to confront the fact that many of their practices and products, such as working individually on worksheets, are disengaged from new media and authentic texts that children encounter in a technologically rich environment. Innovation in literacy acquisition involves aligning the language classroom with texts we encounter in the real world, which are part of new media in a technologically networked society.

Key Goals for Multimodal Literacy Research

Educational reformers suggest that the emergence of new technologies, new media and new literacy practices will separately and collectively change what, when and how people learn. However, there is, as Ulmer (2003) advises, no consensus in new media education about what skills are needed and what practices are available for citizens to be fully empowered as producers of digital texts. Thus, against this complex and contested backdrop, we provide an overview of what might be reasonably considered the main foci of multimodal literacy given its diverse range of sources and influences. Based largely on Jewitt's (2008) comprehensive review of multimodality and literacy in school classrooms and Warschauer's (2007) critique of the future of digital learning, we identify five education-related objectives that are usefully informed by research on multimodality. These are to: (1) provide rich descriptions of sites of learning; (2) analyze multimodal design work; (3) build theories and articulate concepts concerning meaning-making in multimodal contexts; (4) articulate and develop new pedagogic approaches in response to new media and educational policy initiatives relating to their use; and (5) promote a pluralized notion of literacy and forms of representation and communication.

First, a multimodal perspective on literacy provides a powerful set of tools that can be used to examine sites of learning. For example, in Kress *et al.* (2005), researchers employed video footage and classroom observations to describe in very rich terms the various ways in which teachers and students in nine urban classrooms in London used modes to realize the school subject English. This work is notable for showing how gaze, gestures, body postures, classroom configuration and, of course, speech and writing were used singly and in combination to craft identities and learning outcomes in the classroom context. For example, in one particular case study, a teacher decorated her classroom with posters of film and music stars. Another teacher exhibited extracts from curriculum and examination documents prominently on her walls. Jewitt (2008) contends that these differing actions presented distinct versions of English to the students involved thus situating them, in turn, in different relationships to curriculum content.

Second, the analysis of multimodal design work is founded on the richness provided by strong theoretical descriptions of multimodal texts and classroom interactions. Kress and van Leeuwen (2001), in particular, are highly accomplished at examining the ways in which teachers 'orchestrate' and/or activate modes in their lessons for specific design-based purposes. The case of David, a science teacher, exemplifies the choices made in arranging and sequencing content when explaining the flow of blood in the human body:

> In elaborating the newly complex model in speech, [David] used gestures (mode: gesture) to make signs indicating the pumping action of the heart (rhythmically pushing his semi-raised arms against his body), and in repeating [his] account of the blood's circulation, using [a] diagram, he both used his hands to indicate the motion of the blood (mode: gesture) and at the same time wrote names as labels on parts of the diagram: 'The blood moves around the body, from the heart to the *lungs*, to the small *intestine*, to the *cells*, to the ...' (mode: language as writing). (Kress & van Leeuwen, 2001: 52–53)

Third, the ways in which modes are understood as meaning-making resources and how the relationships between modes are best represented, particularly in prose, require important theory building. By way of illustration, Unsworth (2006) explores how language, image, audio and hypertext can be analyzed to highlight the story-makers' art. Part of this process involves mapping various types of electronic or e-narratives (E-stories for early learners, linear e-narratives, E-narratives and interactive story contexts, hypertext narratives and hypermedia narratives) onto a framework of compositional features expressed as continua (Unsworth, 2006: 89):

- Linear ↔ Hyperlinked
- Monomodal ↔ Multimodal
- Still images ↔ Animation
- Receptive ↔ Interactive
- Fictive ↔ Metafictive

Unsworth contends that the most innovative of his categories of digital fiction are hypermedia narratives, which stimulate 're-creative', interpretive reading; see, for example, *Childhood in Richmond*, accessible from http://wordcircuits.com/gallery/childhood/index.html. However, it is also noted that linear e-narratives can be just as engaging. What is crucial here is developing students' appreciation of the nature of digital storytelling by making explicit how the affordances of modes are used to achieve varying narrative effects. Unsworth's conceptualizations assist greatly in this educative process as they provide a vocabulary for describing and analyzing the compositional features of digital fiction.

Furthermore, once e-literature is described and understood structurally, a basis is provided for its assessment in classrooms. For example, putting aside matters relating to the appropriateness of subject matter, the rubrics used or recommended to generate grades of students' digital storytelling assignments often feature descriptors relating to format (the development of plot and character), image use, point of view, pacing and the coherence of storyline (Ohler, 2007). Arguably, judgments relating to the quality of meaning-making in digital fiction are difficult to make and defend by teachers (working individually or collectively) without knowing, and being able to express, what digital stories are and how they are constructed.

Fourth, the increasing availability of new media and the framing of educational policy initiatives relating to their use raise questions about how to articulate and develop new pedagogic approaches that embrace the multiliteracies pedagogy. For example, in an insightful critical ethnography, Mills (2008) uncovers some of the complexities involved in engaging culturally diverse students in designing multimodal texts. Briefly stated, Mills discovered that students' access to multiliteracies was influenced by a complex intersection of pedagogy, power and discourses in the classroom. For example, students working on the production of animation movies derived different learning experiences depending on their varied lifeworlds outside of the classroom. That is, students from culturally and socioeconomically dominant circumstances were immersed deeply in an environment that required collaborative effort with minimal teacher direction. Conversely, ethnically and socioeconomically marginalized students had a more difficult journey in their learning because of the mismatch between their experiences and the languages of the classroom. Such findings substantiate Warschauer's (2007) view that linguistic ability and basic cultural literacy mediate students' engagement with multimodality. Once acknowledged, it is not so easy to accept the notion that access to digital media is sufficient, alone, to level educational playing fields.

Last, it should be clear by now that the promotion of a pluralized notion of literacy and the use of multiple forms of representation and communication are essential for survival in the digital era. However as Warschauer (2007) explains, while the rationale for multiple literacies might be clear, the critical relationship between new and traditional literacy practices can get lost. Warschauer (2007: 43) contends that 'competence in traditional literacies is often a gateway to successful entry into the world of new literacies'. For example, there can be little exercise of contemporary information literacy in the absence of competent reading ability for any child or adult.

In sum, it would seem that in response to ever-changing social and educational landscapes, scholars of multimodal literacy and multiliteracies seek to identify and implement an educational agenda designed for what some might argue is radical social change. A crucial part of this work involves describing and analyzing in great detail work undertaken by teachers and students in designing, producing and interpreting complex, multimodal texts. As far as pedagogical practices are concerned, contemporary conceptualizations of literacy challenge long-accepted notions of what knowledge is, where it is created and the purposes for which it is used. Arguably, the overriding goal for multimodal literacy as a branch of knowledge and inquiry is to understand how the complexities of communication in the digital era can be dealt with in productive, socially just and equitable ways.

Multimodal Literacy Practices, Language Classrooms and Teacher Education

Research findings in the area of multimodal literacy in language classrooms can be broadly classified into two strands: multimodal literacy practices outside the classroom though with implications for in class literacy, and multimodal literacy practices situated specifically in the language classroom. Both these strands have enormous implications for teacher education, which we have included under a separate heading.

Multimodal literacy practices out of school

Chandler-Olcott and Mahar (2003) and Black (2005) use 'Multiliteracies' as a theoretical framework to explore the way adolescents use literacy outside the classroom. Chandler-Olcott and Mahar (2003) focus on the anime art literacy practices of two adolescent girls. Anime refers to animated films and television series originating in Japan. One of their case-study subjects, Rhiannon, was very involved in writing fanfiction, that is episodic stories using characters and settings from favorite anime cartoons and video games. The authors comment that Rhiannon's teachers in school were not aware that she wrote lengthy fanfiction stories because 'from a multiliteracies perspective, technology integration in her school placed far more emphasis on elements of linguistic design, than on visual, spatial, or audio modes' (Chandler-Olcott & Mahar, 2003: 372). Also, though her teachers perceived Rhiannon as a passive learner, the authors found that she was very pro-active on the computer and actively sought help to improve her skills in web page construction. The other case-study subject in this paper, Eileen, was very skillful in taking any drawing and 'animefying' it. The authors found that Eileen had become an accomplished designer of anime-related multimodal texts by joining a virtual community of people who were also interested in anime art. Along with learning new ways to create texts the two girls in this study were also using online communities to create more satisfying social lives than they had in real time.

Chandler-Olcott and Mahar (2003) conclude that teachers must take note of what their students are doing in terms of literacy practices outside of the classroom for some very important reasons. First some ways in which Eileen and Rhiannon were using literacy are more suited to the workplace than the traditional five-paragraph essay. Taking note of these out-of-class literacy practices will also help teachers create a culture of mentorship in which students can learn from each other. Finally they comment that to do all this, teachers do not need to be trained in technology themselves; however, they must make themselves familiar with the websites their students visit frequently and various online resources that can prove useful in the classroom.

Black's (2005) study is also about fanfiction, though her focus is on female English Language Learners (ELLs). 'Fanfictions are original works of fiction based on forms of popular media such as television, movies, books, music, and video games' (Black, 2005: 118). These fan magazines, also called 'zines', have been part of adolescent culture for a while; however, the change now is that the 'zines' are now in cyberspace and not print based. Black was compelled to explore fanfiction because she was very curious about how her students could spend hours writing such texts on the computer though they were reluctant to write a one-page essay during the English class. Black's study, which is text based, does not use any human subjects and is an exploration of www.fanfiction.net, a popular site amongst school going children and English language learners.

Black uses the idea of 'design' from the New London Group by which they refer to aspects of literacy that extend beyond the decoding and encoding of print. According to the New London Group there are Available Designs, meaning received modes of meaning, which through Designing can become The Redesigned. 'Designing' is the transformation of these modes of meaning in their hybrid and intertextual use. The key difference between Design and writing is that the former is not confined to print and words but is multimodal. This literacy practice is very appealing to language learners because they do not have to depend only on printed words to get their meaning across but can use multiple modes for meaning-making. An illustration of redesigning is the way an author on fanfiction.com combines the plot of the movie, *You've Got Mail*, with well-known anime characters Sakura and Syaoran. The author has written a story about how Sakura and Syaoran meet and fall in love in a chat room unaware that they are roommates in real life.

Black also explores how writers review each other's stories on this site and offer feedback so that they can improve their craft. She finds that in one case a reviewer recasts several paragraphs of a story to model effective uses of conjunctions, subordinate clauses and sentence transition. The reviewers on this site are extremely encouraging with their peers, and though they correct grammar and elements of composition that impede understanding, they also offer positive feedback and ask for more chapters from the author. Black finds that this creates a strong sense of audience for writers who feel that there is someone eagerly waiting to read what they have written. Thus, the emphasis of the reviewers is on the communicative function of language instead of error correction.

How English language learners use literacy practices on the computer to display identity and learn language at the same time have been extensively researched in the case of Chinese Americans (Lam, 2000, 2004). Using a case-study approach to data collection, Lam (2004) shows how Chinese American adolescent girls codeswitch in a bilingual chat room on the computer. The two subjects codeswitched between English and Romanized Cantonese; for instance, they would use Cantonese utterance particles at the end of an English phrase or sentence for rhetorical purposes such as creating humor and role shifting. By using Cantonese in this way the subjects in this study are customizing the global practices of English into their local contexts. At the same time, the subjects are also learning English as a foreign language and socializing themselves into the larger Chinese online community with other adolescents from Hong Kong and Australia.

In a similar study, Lam (2000) explores how Almon, a Chinese American adolescent, constructs textual identity in CMC. There is an in-depth account of the way Almon corresponds with his peers in a virtual community that can be accessed through Almon's home page, which he designed using a Japanese popular idol called Ryoko Hirosue because of his interest in J-pop music. The author concludes that the English Almon is acquiring through CMC is the global English of adolescent pop culture and not the standard English taught in high school classrooms. The classroom excluded Almon because his English was not as good as his peers' and he felt marginalized. However, on the internet, Almon felt a sense of belonging to a community of English language learners.

According to Jenkins *et al.* (2006), today's teens are involved in 'participatory culture' where there are low barriers to artistic and civic engagement, strong peer support and mentorship. Forms of participatory culture include:

- Affiliations: memberships in online communities such as Friendster and Facebook;
- Expressions: new text forms such as zines and fanfiction;
- Collaborative Problem Solving: working in teams to complete tasks; and
- Circulations: shaping the flow of media such as podcasting and blogging.

The implication of participatory culture on literacy is that technology has created learning environments very different from the traditional classroom. Whereas the classroom can be a formal, print-based forum, which valorizes individual achievement, participatory cultures provide for environments that are informal, collaborative and multimodal. Whereas the classroom emphasizes literacies, like the five-paragraph essay, which is a text somewhat removed from the workplace, participatory cultures are about new literacies, which are potentially linked with the workplace.

Multimodal literacy practices in school

One of the results of the widespread use of technology as it impacts schools is the increasing number of one–to-one laptop programs (a program in which each student is given one laptop) in the United States. Education Week reports that about 800 schools in the United States already have laptop programs through the Anytime Anywhere Learning initiative launched by Microsoft Corp. and Toshiba America Information Systems Inc. in 1996. One of these schools is Mott Hall, a school for gifted fourth through eighth graders in New York State. New York's Community School District 6, which includes Mott Hall, now has laptops for 4500 of its 30,000 students (Zehr, 2000). Though there is literature on the effects of these laptop-leasing programs (Sternberg *et al.*, 2007; Zardoya, 2001) we do not review this literature in detail because it is about the use of technology across the curriculum and does not focus specifically on the language classroom.

Multimodal literacy in language classrooms seems to be underresearched and we have had the opportunity to read few small-scale projects in this specific area (Jewitt, 2002; Myers *et al.*, 1998). Jewitt's (2002) study, referred to above, consists of video and observational data from a series of five English literature lessons in a year 10 (Grade 9) class at an inner London secondary school. She explores how modal resources influence the way that children 'read' character in Steinbeck's *Of Mice and Men* with the help of a CD-ROM. She found that though before looking at the CD-ROM most children chose the main characters, George and Lennie, to write about, after using the CD-ROM they chose from a broader range, which included minor characters like Curly, Curly's wife, etc. Because the CD-ROM showed Curly's wife singing a song, music was a key feature of the way that students engaged with this minor character. Though while reading the novel in print form, the students engaged with the characters mainly at the level of narrative, the use of the CD-ROM demanded that they engage with the characters at the level of mode. As a consequence the students noticed that George and Lennie, the main characters in the story, were polarized through differences in their appearance, clothes, voice quality and gestures. Thus, the CD-ROM drew the students into a less logocentric interpretation of character.

Myers *et al.* (1998) explore the way five different groups of English teacher education students and one group of seventh graders authored 'hypermedia'. For the authors the word hypermedia, coined from multi-media and hypertext, means the use of multiple linked windows on the computer screen. In this project, the students used a Macintosh-based software called StorySpace as the hypermedia authoring tool and other software to digitize sound, and image and create original Quicktime videos. The task for the undergraduates was to use hypermedia to explore interpretations of literature whereas for the seventh graders it was learn-ing about poetic devices or reading biographies of famous people.

One example of student work the authors document is that a group of students produced a series of representations of Native American women with the specific goal of challenging the Disney representation of Pocahontas. The authors analyze a series of such results on the basis of 'criticality', which they take to mean a questioning of existing power rela-tions. They conclude that the students, through the juxtaposition of multi-media texts (i.e. music, photos, videos), were better able to deconstruct texts and represent the complexities of power. The authors are convinced that 'As they [the students] selected images, sounds, and print, opposi-tional representations became ideologically framed identities, knowledge came from within the activity of authoring and socially negotiating inter-pretations, personal subjectivity became an act of choosing from various valued possibilities' (Myers *et al.*, 1998: 78).

Teacher education

As is the case with studies on multimodal literacy in language class-rooms, there are also very few studies on the way language teachers deal with multimodal literacy and what they feel about it. McGrail (2006) and Russell and Abrams (2004) focus on just this topic. McGrail presents inter-view data from six secondary school English teachers at a school that had implemented a one-to-one laptop program. The purpose of her study was to find out what secondary school English teachers' attitudes were toward technology in English instruction. McGrail discovered that teachers were ambivalent about the use of technology. First, they resisted the top-down approach to this technology initiative and did not think that their opinions or voice were heard. Second, and this is a point also taken up by Russell and Abrams (2004), the teachers saw a disconnect between writing on the computer and standardized testing, which was always pen-and-paper based. For instance, the teachers pointed out that the Regents' exams (standardized high school exit exams in New York State, USA) were not on the computer. Third, the teachers also felt that using the internet exten-sively resulted in plagiarism and shallow presentations in Powerpoint. Fourth, the English teachers were not sure how to use technology in many of their lessons, which they felt were much better taught or equally well taught without technology. Finally there were problems regarding teacher identity as many of the older teachers were themselves not comfortable with technology.

Russell and Abrams' (2004) large-scale quantitative study was an exploration of how teachers modify their use of computers for writing instruction in response to state testing programs. This study was based on a few items from an 80-item survey in which 5000 teachers from numerous states in the United States with various types of testing programs participated. The authors found that as the stakes associated with testing increase, the percentage of teachers who opt not to use computers for literacy also increases. Similarly teachers who worked in states where there were high stakes testing programs are more likely not to use computers than teachers who work in states where there are moderate stakes testing programs. The rationale of the teachers, as McGrail (2006) also reports, is that since the state mandated tests do not use computers, teachers prefer to prepare students for exams without using computers.

Luke (2002) reviewed literacy education in the state of Queensland, Australia, via a large-scale research project, which included interviews with a sample of teachers out of a total of 30,000. Luke found that the teachers in Queensland viewed students' engagement with new technologies as a sign of print deficit and lacked the training and vocabulary to build bridges between old and new literacies. King and O'Brien (2002: 41) agree with this view stating that 'In schools, print dominates'. At the same time, multimedia is considered 'play' and teachers tell students that they can play on the computers when they have finished their real work. Most importantly, an engagement with multimedia means that teachers need to surrender some control of their classrooms and accept their students as experts. The paradigm shift in the roles of expert and novice is the hardest for teachers.

In a one of a kind large-scale intervention study, Becker and Ravitz (1999) found that the use of technology over a period of about three years changes the pedagogy of teachers from transmissionist to constructivist. Within constructivist pedagogy the teachers:

- Designed activities around teacher/student interests rather than around the curriculum.
- Engaged the students in collaborative group projects.
- Focused on complex ideas rather than definitions and facts.
- Taught students to assess themselves.
- Finally, engaged in learning in front of students rather than presenting themselves as experts.

From among the eight subject teachers that Becker and Ravitz focused on, the teachers of secondary English reported one of the largest number of changes in their pedagogy due to the use of technology.

So far, we have focused on K–12 school systems and teachers therein. There is also some literature, which explores issues of language learning and technology in tertiary education. For instance, Kramsch *et al.* (2000) and Nelson (2006) explore ways that undergraduates learn language in college classrooms. Both papers emphasize the way authorial voice has changed in a multimedia text. In Kramsch *et al.* (2000) the task given to the undergraduates, who were learning Spanish, was to create a CD-ROM for teaching Latin American Culture. In Nelson (2006), the task was digital storytelling about the students themselves. In both studies, the L2 students felt that authoring a multimedia text was a more agentive experience because they had more control over it both as producers and consumers. Though this literature can prove useful it does not deal with many of the issues that concern K–12 school systems such as teacher training, access to computers, task design, which is aligned to school curricula and exams, etc.

Singapore's Technology in English project: A recent study

The 'Technology in English' (TIE) project undertaken by Singapore's National Institute of Education, for which the authors of this chapter are co-principal investigators (Towndrow *et al.*, 2009), was a year-long pilot project conducted in 2008, exploring the impact of a one-to-one laptop program in one of Singapore's secondary schools. This was a prestigious middle-class school where the students are taught English and Mandarin as first languages. The specific research objectives relating to this project concerned how the English language and literature teachers, and their students, used the technology available in their classrooms, an analysis of the multimodal texts produced by students, and a survey of the attitudes of teachers and students toward technology. The study highlighted two main aspects of language teachers' use of new media and digital tools. First, it showed what teachers considered the affordances of wireless digital technology to be and how these might be designed – in the New London Group sense – into their work. Second, the study identified the boundaries and limitations imposed by teachers (again through design decisions) surrounding language presentation and subsequent production in their classrooms, via technology.

Both qualitative and quantitative methods were employed in the study. In the quantitative phase of data collection, we surveyed all of the 350 secondary school students (aged 13–14) in one-year level via an online survey. A modified version of the same survey was administered to the four English language and literature teachers in the school. In the qualitative phase of data collection, we video-recorded one unit of lessons for each of the four English teachers, where a unit was defined as a theme or topic that the teacher covered in approximately one or two weeks. While one researcher was video recording the lesson, another sat at the back of the class and coded the lesson using a coding scheme developed by the research team. At the time of writing this chapter, all the data have been collected and the research team is in the process of data analysis while at the same time embarking on a series of professional development sessions with the four teachers.

Results from the student survey show that the students of this particular secondary school have unlimited access to computers and the internet: 98.9% use a computer at home and 98.3% have access to the internet at home. However, despite a one-to-one laptop program in school they do not use technology in their English classrooms very often. The following tables show the limited use of technology by students in their English language and literature classes:

As can be seen in Table 12.1, nearly 30% of the students reported that they never used interactive digital media in their English language classes. Nearly 40% reported that they never used software. About a quarter of the class has never used a word processor in their English language classes. In Table 12.2, we can see that when asked how often they used the internet and/or the WWW in their literature classes, 43.7% responded: 'never'. The majority of the rest were more or less equally divided between 'once a month' and 'once a week'. Only 9.2% reported that they used the internet and/or the WWW in their literature classes once a day. More than half the students reported that they had never used interactive digital media or software in their literature classes.

In most classes that we observed the teacher used the whiteboard and an overhead projector. In all the classes observed, the students did not use their laptops; and in some cases, they were specifically told to close them. In one exceptional class the teacher showed a movie of the play that the children were reading; however, the teacher did not make a connection for the students between this medium (the movie) and the printed text that they had in their hands. Thus there was no 'transduction' from one medium to another even though the technology was there to support it.

Cindy Lim is an experienced teacher of English language and literature in her late 50s. She is also pursuing a Master's degree at Singapore's National Institute of Education. Cindy hardly uses the MacBook with her secondary 1 boys for various reasons. The first has to do with the inability to give up control. She says: 'OK, MacBook, then what happened was, a boy actually asked can I make notes on my net. The trouble is once you allow, because of the way they are seated, I can't see what they are doing ... I can't see what's on the screen'. Jenkins *et al.* (2006) and Becker and Ravitz (1999) point out that the use of technology challenges traditional pedagogy in a teacher-centered classroom. The use of computers demands a more constructivist pedagogy in which the teacher gives up control and becomes more of a facilitator. It is this new role that Cindy Lim finds challenging.

Table 12.1 Frequency of students' use of ICT resources and digital media in school for English language learning

	Textbook	Textbook + Workbook or Worksheet	Work-sheet only	Electronic Slideshow (PowerPoint, Keynote, etc.)	Word-processor	Internet/World Wide Web	Software (mind-or concept mapping, Comic Book Creator, etc.)	Interactive and digital media (movies, photos, animations, games, virtual-reality, etc.)	Props and/or apparatus	Frequency for other activity
	%	%	%	%	%	%	%	%	%	%
No response	0.0	0.0	0.0	0.0	0.0	0.0	0.0	0.0	0.0	99.7
Never	15.4	11.2	9.5	11.2	26.9	13.7	39.5	30.3	50.4	0.0
Once a month	24.1	17.9	12.3	16.0	16.5	13.7	22.4	27.2	20.7	0.0
Once a week	26.1	32.5	31.7	35.6	30.0	34.5	23.5	24.4	16.2	0.0
Once a day	20.4	24.4	32.8	26.1	17.6	22.1	9.8	10.4	6.4	0.3
More than once a day	14.0	14.0	13.7	11.2	9.0	16.0	4.8	7.8	6.2	0.0

Table 12.2 Frequency of students' use of ICT resources and digital media in school for English literature learning

	Textbook only	Textbook + Workbook or Worksheet	Worksheet only	Electronic Slideshow (PowerPoint, Keynote, etc.)	Word-processor	Internet/ World Wide Web	Software (mind- or concept mapping, Comic Book Creator, etc.)	Interactive and digital media (movies, photos, animations, games, virtual-reality, etc.)	Props and/or appa-ratus	Frequency for other activity
	%	%	%	%	%	%	%	%	%	%
No response	0.0	0.0	0.0	0.0	0.0	0.0	0.0	0.0	0.0	100.0
Never	54.3	44.8	12.6	35.3	46.5	43.7	56.6	47.1	57.7	0.0
Once a month	10.1	13.4	16.0	20.4	21.8	20.2	13.2	21.8	17.1	0.0
Once a week	17.6	22.7	32.5	25.2	16.8	21.8	18.2	18.2	12.6	0.0
Once a day	11.8	12.6	26.6	14.0	10.6	9.2	7.8	8.4	8.7	0.0
More than once a day	6.2	6.4	12.3	5.0	4.2	5.0	4.2	4.5	3.9	0.0

Another of Cindy's concerns has to do with curriculum content and classroom materials.

Cindy: And I was like, you know you can find lots of beautiful things, ah that you can use on the Mac, let's say for other subjects I noticed. But for EL is like it's was something difficult, in the sense of the pedagogy part.

Interviewer: English language is hard.

Cindy: I mean yes, you can do BBC, you can do but it's very different.

In the exchange above Cindy says that though a lot of relevant classroom materials are available on the net for other subjects, English language does not have such materials. It is also difficult for her to align new materials with the pedagogy. Cindy has thought about using the BBC in her English language class but her concern is that BBC English is very different from the way English is spoken in Singapore.

This sliver of data from the TIE project shows that the English language and literature classrooms in this secondary school are not yet sites rich in the use of technology and practice of multimodal literacy. In the course of a presentation we made to all the English teachers of this school on 9 October 2008, we learned that the challenges faced by teachers in incorporating technology were similar to those reported in Russell and Abrams (2004): misalignment between technology and standardized testing. The teachers told the authors that they were reluctant to use computers in the English classroom because this was not the practice in exams, they did know much about technology themselves, and that computers, like phones, could hinder the standard English of their students. As Cindy points out above, some teachers are also concerned about losing control in the classroom due to technology and lack of professional development about how to infuse technology into subjects like the English language. Teacher beliefs about nonstandard English being promoted due to the use of technology were deep rooted in this school. Some of the teachers pointed out that blogs, e-mails, chat rooms, etc. were full of ungrammatical English, which they did not want to encourage in their classrooms. These teachers were apprehensive that technology would encourage 'Singlish', a colloquial variety of English in Singapore.

Conclusions and Directions for Future Research

One of the challenges – and resources – for research in this field is the display and documentation of multimodal student products in a printed journal. Online journals such as *Language Learning & Technology* or journals which also have online platforms like *Teachers College Record* are best positioned to deal with the topic of multimodality. Such journals can provide hyperlinks, which when clicked on, can lead the reader to a visual presentation of the multimedia text under discussion. For instance in both Kramsch *et al.* (2000) and Nelson (2006) there are hyperlinks that connect to specific student products under discussion.

Another challenge in this field is training teachers to socialize children into the ethics of multimedia usage. This includes sensitizing them to inappropriate sites and content that may be harmful to diverse social groups. There is also the issue of ownership of content and plagiarism along with concerns regarding addiction to computer games. Current teacher education programs tend not to emphasize these aspects of cyber-life that are very important for adolescents.

As a field which is barely a few decades old, we find that there is research required in many specific areas. For example, there is a dearth of large-scale quantitative studies with a generalizable sample that can show relationships between gender, race, social class and technology use in the language classrooms. Arguably, there is also a need for studies with an experimental design methodology, which reveal exactly the aspects of language acquisition children learn with technology that those in a control group do not. Finally there is a serious dearth of research on assessing multimodal literacy. How exactly should a teacher grade a multimodal text and how different is this form of assessment from that used with a traditional text? In keeping with this is the issue of the misalignment between use of technology in the classroom and standardized testing. In most countries, standardized testing at the school level still does not use computers extensively; thus teachers are reluctant to spend time incorporating technology in the classroom as this might disenfranchise their students in the exams.

Yet, more positively, a multimodal approach to literacy offers exciting and productive prospects for sociolinguists and language teachers given the affordances of new media and digital technologies, generally. Where available, new media are challenging and changing canonical notions of 'text' and 'reading behaviours'. The works of Jewitt (2002) and Unsworth (2006) indicate that alternative presentations of material – those that go well beyond the written word alone – expand interpretative resources such as 'character' and 'plot' to the point that the construction of meaning from a multimodal text requires the established customized or personalized design-based purposes. Concomitantly, the proliferation of participatory cultures (Jenkins *et al.*, 2006) and purposeful acts of multimodal redesigning (New London Group, 1996) portend even greater shifts of authorial voice and distribution of agency to learners (see the examples of zine and fanfiction authorship above).

Fortunately, the pioneering theoretical work in multimodality and multimodal literacy has assisted researchers and teachers in describing sites of learning and subsequently understanding the genius involved in orchestrating semiotic modes aptly. While it is acknowledged that the introduction of digital technologies into classrooms might not lead to immediate uptake that is reflected in usage statistics or might even perpetuate ethnic and socioeconomic marginalization, productive outcomes are possible – recall the overview of the project *fresa* above – when the foci of classroom-based work are squarely learner-centered. Thus, in our opinion, language teachers would be well advised to know what multimodal literacy is (or could be, in the future) and how multimodal expression can be used in keeping with their learners' needs and interests. It seems to be evident that, where available, digital technologies afford students unprecedented access to new media and publishing outlets where they can demonstrate their expertise.

Note

1. The second author is indebted to Mark Evan Nelson for an extended conversation on the pedagogical implications of typological and topological meanings.

Suggestions for further reading

Cummins, J., Brown, K. and Sayers, D. (2007) *Literacy, Technology and Diversity: Teaching for Success in Changing Times*. Boston: Pearson.
This book, which includes a CD-ROM of templates, monographs and other digital media, presents a highly readable and informative framework for promoting literacy engagement among low-income and minority students. There are many generative ideas here for ICT-based literacy projects with students.

Jenkins, H. (2006) *Convergence Culture: Where Old and New Media Collide*. New York: New York University Press.
The ways media circulates are changing rapidly on a global scale. In this book, MIT professor Henry Jenkins describes through a series of extended case studies – including *American Idol*, 2002 and *The Matrix* 1999) – the technological, industrial, cultural and social changes that occur when content flows currently across multiple media platforms. Chapter 5, Why Heather Can Write, is an intriguing analysis of fanfiction and media literacy activity that illustrates, particularly well, Jenkins' concept of 'participatory culture'.

Kress, G., Jewitt, C., Bourne, J., Franks, A., Hardcastle, J., Jones, K. *et al.* (2005) *English in Urban Classrooms: A Multimodal Perspective on Teaching and Learning*. London: RoutledgeFalmer.
This book describes a study of how English is 'produced' (i.e. shaped by policy, institutions and social relations) in a number of English language classrooms in inner-city London. The authors operationalize concepts in multimodal theory, showing, in particular, how image, gesture, gaze, movement and spatial organization impact on teaching and learning outcomes.

New London Group (1996) A pedagogy of multiliteracies: Designing social futures. *Harvard Educational Review* 66 (1), 60–92.
This seminal paper is essential reading for anyone interested in literacy pedagogy and how this concept might be broadened to include a variety of discourses including multilingualism and multimodality.

Towndrow, P.A. (2007) *Task Design, Implementation and Assessment: Integrating Information and Communication Technology in English Language Teaching and Learning*. Singapore: McGraw-Hill.
If it is accepted that digital technologies can afford students unprecedented access to new media and publishing outlets where they can demonstrate their expertise, then language teachers ought to know how to design classroom interactions to bring about differentiated and multiple outcomes. This short book explains pedagogy and practice with ICT in contemporary language teaching and learning contexts, and illustrates the use of a constructivist framework for describing and analyzing learning tasks involving new media and digital tools in particular contexts.

References

Baldry, A. and Thibault, P. (2005) *Multimodal Transcription and Text Analysis*. London: Equinox.

Barrie, B. (1999) Technology and change in Atlantic Canada's new secondary English language arts curriculum. *English Education* 31 (3), 231–247.

Becker, H.J. and Ravitz, J. (1999) The influence of computer and internet use on teachers' pedagogical practices and perceptions. *Journal of Research on Computing in Education* 31 (4), 356–384.

Black, R.W. (2005) Access and affiliation: The literacy and composition practices of English-language learners in an online fanfiction community. *Journal of Adolescent & Adult Literacy* 49 (2), 118–128.

Castells, M. (2000) *The Rise of the Network Society. The Information Age: Economy, Society and Culture*. Massachusetts: Blackwell Publishers.

Chandler-Olcott, K. and Mahar, D. (2003) 'Tech-savviness' meets multiliteracies: Exploring adolescent girls' technology-mediated literacy practices. *Reading Research Quarterly* 38 (3), 356–385.

Cope, B. and Kalantzis, M. (eds) (2000) *Multiliteracies: Literacy Learning and the Design of Social Futures*. London and New York: Routledge.

Cope, B. and Kalantzis, M. (2001) Putting 'Multiliteracies' to the test. *Newsletter of the Australian Literacies Educators' Association* (February 2001). On WWW at http://www.alea.edu.au/site-content/publications/documents/at/Feature%20article%20Feb%2001.PDF. Accessed 21.7.2009.

Cummins, J., Brown, K. and Sayers, D. (2007) *Literacy, Technology and Diversity: Teaching for Success in Changing Times*. Boston: Pearson.

Emmison, M.J. and Smith, P.D. (2000) *Researching the Visual: Images, Objects, Contexts and Interactions in Social and Cultural Inquiry*. London: Sage.

Iedema, R. (2003) Multimodality, resemiotization: Extending the analysis of discourse as multi-semiotic practice. *Visual Communication* 2 (1), 29–57.

Jenkis, H. (2006) *Convergence Culture: Where Old and New Media Collide*. New York: New York University Press.

Jenkins, H., Clinton, K., Purushotma, R., Robison, A.J. and Weigel, M. (2006) *Confronting the Challenges of Participatory Culture: Media Education for the 21st Century*. Chicago, IL: MacArthur Foundation.

Jewitt, C. (2002) The move from page to screen: The multimodal reshaping of school English. *Visual Communication* 1, 171–195.

Jewitt, C. (2008) Multimodality and literacy in school classrooms. *Review of Research in Education* 32, 241–267.

Jewitt, C. and Kress, G. (eds) (2003) *Multimodal Literacy*. New York: Peter Lang.

King, J. R. and O'Brien, D.G. (2002) Adolescents' multiliteracies and their teachers' needs to know: Toward a digital détente. In D.E. Alvermann (ed.) *Adolescents and Literacies in a Digital World* (pp. 40–51). New York: Peter Lang.

Kramsch, C., A'Ness, F. and Lam, W.S.E. (2000) Authenticity and authorship in the computer-mediated acquisition of L2 literacy. *Language Learning and Technology* 4 (2), 78–104.

Kress, G. (2000) A curriculum for the future. *Cambridge Journal of Education* 30 (1), 133–145.

Kress, G. (2003) *Literacy in the New Media Age*. London: Routledge.

Kress, G., Jewitt, C., Ogborn, J. and Tsatsarelis, C. (2001) *Multimodal Teaching and Learning: The Rhetorics of the Science Classroom*. London: Continuum.

Kress, G., Jewitt, C., Bourne, J., Franks, A., Hardcastle, J., Jones, K. *et al.* (2005) *English in Urban Classrooms: A Multimodal Perspective on Teaching and Learning*. London: RoutledgeFalmer.

Kress, G. and van Leeuwen, T. (2001) *Multimodal DIScourse: The Modes and Media of Contemporary Communication*. London: Arnold.

Kress, G. and van Leeuwen, T. (2006) *Reading Images: The Grammar of Visual Design* (2nd edn). London: Routledge.

Lam, W.S.E. (2000) L2 literacy and the design of the self: A case study of a teenager writing on the internet. *TESOL Quarterly* 34 (3), 457–482.

Lam, W.S.E. (2004) Second language socialization in a bilingual chat room: Global and local considerations. *Language Learning & Technology* 8 (3), 44–65.

Leander, K. M. and Lewis, C. (2008) Literacy and internet technologies. In B. Street and N.H. Hornberger (eds) *Encyclopedia of Language and Education* (Vol. 2: Literacy) (pp. 53–71). New York: Springer.

Lemke, J.L. (1998) Metamedia literacy: Transforming meanings and media. In D. Reinking, M.C. McKenna, L.D. Labbo and R.D. Keiffer (eds) *Handbook of Literacy and Technology: Transformations in a Post-Typographic World* (pp. 283–301). Mahwah: Lawrence Erlbaum Associates.

Luke, A. (2002) What happens to literacies old and new when they're turned into policy. In D.E. Alvermann (ed.) *Adolescents and Literacies in a Digital World* (pp. 186–205). New York: Peter Lang.

McGrail, E. (2006) 'It's a double-edged sword, this technology business': Secondary English teachers' perspectives on a schoolwide laptop technology initiative. In *Teachers College Record* (Vol. 108). On WWW at http://wwwtcrecord.org ID #: 12517. Accessed 23.7.2008.

Mills, K.A. (2008) Transformed practices in a pedagogy of multiliteracies. *Pedagogies: An International Journal* 3 (2), 109–128.

Myers, J., Hammett, R. and McKillop, A.M. (1998) Opportunities for critical literacy and pedagogy in student-authored hypermedia. In D. Reinking M.C. McKenna, L.D. Labbo and R.D. Keiffer (eds) *Handbook of Literacy and Technology: Transformations in a Post-Typographic World* (pp. 63–78). Mahwah, NJ: Lawrence Erlbaum Associates.

Nelson, M.E. (2006) Mode, meaning and synaesthesia in multimedia L2 writing. *Language Learning & Technology* 10 (2), 56–76.

New London Group (1996) A pedagogy of multiliteracies: Designing social futures. *Harvard Educational Review* 66 (1), 60–92.

Ohler, J.B. (2007) *Digital Storytelling in the Classroom: New Media Pathways to Literacy, Learning and Creativity*. Thousand Oaks, CA: Sage Publications.

Russell, M. and Abrams, L. (2004) Instructional uses of computers for writing: The effect of state testing programs. *Teachers College Record* 106 (6), 1332–1357.

Sternberg, B.J., Kaplan, K.A. and Borck, J.E. (2007) Enhancing adolescent literacy achievement through integration of technology in the classroom. *Reading Research Quarterly*. DOI:10.1598/RRQ.42.3.6.

Towndrow, P.A., Vaish, V. and Yusof, W.F.M. (2009) Enhancing criticality: A pilot project with IDM as pedagogical amplifiers in English classes at secondary level. Unpublished report, Learning Sciences Laboratory, National Institute of Education, Nanyang Technological University, Singapore.

Ulmer, G.L. (2003) *Internet Invention: From Literacy to Electracy*. New York: Longman.

Unsworth, L. (2006) *E-Literature for Children: Enhancing Digital Literacy Learning*. London and New York: Routledge/Falmer.

van Leeuwen, T. and Jewitt, C. (eds) (2001) *Handbook of Visual Analysis*. London: Sage.

Warschauer, M. (2007) The paradoxical future of digital learning. *Learning Inquiry* 1, 41–49.

Zardoya, I. (2001) Urban students cross the digital divide through laptop leasing program. *Education* 122 (2), 262–268.

Zehr, M.A. (2000) Laptops for all doesn't mean they're always used. *Education Week* 19 (39), 1–3.

Part 5
Language and Identity

Chapter 13
Language and Identity

BONNY NORTON

Overview: Key Terms and Goals

For the past 10 years, I have taught a graduate course at the University of British Columbia, called 'Language, Discourse, and Identity', which has given me the opportunity to remain connected to the burgeoning literature on language and identity in the field of language education. However, given the immense wealth of this literature, which includes an entire journal devoted to the topic (the *Journal of Language, Identity, and Education*), this chapter, like my course, is selective in orientation. To achieve some balance between depth and breadth, I include some of the classic literature in the area, while making space for new voices and emerging themes. I begin by defining key terms, and then outline what I see as some of the primary goals of this area of research.

As a starting point, and with a view to defining key terms, it is useful to consider why I include the term discourse in the title of my graduate course. In order to understand the relationship between language and identity, as discussed in this chapter, it is important to understand the poststructuralist theory of language, which is defined as discourse. Poststructuralist theories of language achieved much prominence in the late 20th century, and are associated, amongst others, with the work of Bakhtin (1981, 1984), Bourdieu (1977, 1991), Hall (1997) and Weedon (1997). These theories build on, but are distinct from, structuralist theories of language, associated predominantly with the work of Ferdinand de Saussure (1966). For structuralists, the linguistic system guarantees the meaning of signs (the word and its meaning) and each linguistic community has its own set of signifying practices that give value to the signs in a language.

One of the criticisms poststructuralists have levelled at this conception of language is that structuralism cannot account for struggles over the social meanings that can be attributed to signs in a given language. The signs /feminist/, /research/, /sociolinguistics/ for example can have different meanings for different people within the same linguistic community.

While structuralists conceive of signs as having idealized meanings, and linguistic communities as being relatively homogeneous and consensual, poststructuralists take the position that the signifying practices of a society are sites of struggle, and that linguistic communities are heterogeneous arenas characterized by conflicting claims to truth and power. Thus language is not conceived of as a neutral medium of communication, but is understood with reference to its social meaning, in a frequently inequitable world. It is this conception of language that poststructuralists define as 'discourse'.

How does a poststructuralist theory of language as discourse help us to understand the relationship between language and identity? If we take the position that linguistic communities are not homogeneous and consensual, but often heterogeneous and conflicted, we need to understand how power is implicated in relationships between individuals, communities and nations. This is directly relevant to our understanding of the relationship between language and identity. As Bourdieu (1977) notes, the value ascribed to speech cannot be understood apart from the person who speaks, and the person who speaks cannot be understood apart from larger networks of social relationships. Every time we speak, we are negotiating and renegotiating our sense of self in relation to the larger social world, and reorganizing that relationship across time and space. Our gender, race, class, ethnicity, sexual orientation, among other characteristics, are all implicated in this negotiation of identity.

The research of feminist poststructuralists such as Weedon (1997) has been particularly influential in helping language educators to theorize identity, or what feminist poststructuralists call subjectivity, which is derived from the term 'subject'. The use of the term 'subject' is compelling because it serves as a constant reminder that a person's identity must always be understood in relational terms: one is either subject *of* a set of relationships (i.e. in a position of power) or subject *to* a set of relationships (i.e. in a position of reduced power). In this view, the commonsense notion of 'the real me' remains a fiction (see Bhabha, 1987). Three defining characteristics of subjectivity are of particular interest to language educators: the multiple, nonunitary nature of the subject; subjectivity as a site of struggle; and subjectivity as changing over time. From a language educator's perspective, the conceptualization of subjectivity as multiple and changing is consistent with the view that pedagogical practices can be transformative. While some identity positions may limit and constrain opportunities for learners to speak, read or write, other identity positions may offer enhanced sets of possibilities for social interaction and human agency. Indeed, in poststructuralist theory, subjectivity and language are theorized as mutually constitutive. As Weedon (1997) notes, it is through language that a person negotiates a sense of self within and across a range of sites at different points in time, and it is through language that a person gains access to – or is denied access to – powerful social networks that give learners the opportunity to speak. These ideas speak directly to language teachers and learners.

Drawing on these notions of language, discourse, and identity, language educators and researchers have the primary goal of examining the social, historical, and cultural contexts in which language learning and teaching takes place, and how learners and teachers negotiate and sometimes resist the diverse positions those contexts offer them (see monographs by Block, 2007; Clarke, 2008; Day, 2002; Goldstein, 2003; Heller, 2007; Kanno, 2008; May, 2008; Miller, 2003; Nelson, 2009; Norton, 2000; Potowski, 2007; Rampton, 2006; Stein, 2008; Toohey, 2000). These goals represent a shift in the field of language education from a focus on psycholinguistic models of language acquisition to include greater interest in sociological and anthropological dimensions of language learning (Albright & Luke, 2008; Block, 2007; Gao, 2007; Morgan, 2007; Norton & Toohey, 2001; Pavlenko & Blackledge, 2003; Ricento, 2005; Zuengler & Miller, 2006). To better understand these contexts, many language educators are interested in the extent to which relations of power within classrooms and communities promote or constrain the conditions under which learners speak, read or write. We take the position that when learners speak or remain silent; when they write, read or resist, we need to understand the extent to which the learner is valued in a particular classroom, institution or community. At the same time, however, we seek to understand the diverse ways in which learners may challenge both subtle and overt forms of discrimination, and what implications this has for the teaching of language. Language is thus theorized not only as a linguistic system, but as a social practice in which experiences are organized and identities negotiated. More recent developments in notions of 'investment' and 'imagined communities' are discussed under Key Research Findings below.

Common Research Methods and Challenges

Research on the relationship between language and identity tends to be qualitative rather than quantitative, and often draws on critical ethnography, feminist poststructuralist theory, sociolinguistics and linguistic anthropology in seeking to determine both questions and methods. There are a number of common assumptions that many researchers of language and identity bring to our qualitative research projects, three of which are as follows:

First, much identity research rejects the view that any research can claim to be objective or unbiased. In this view, researchers have to understand our own experience and knowledge as well as those of the participants in our studies. This does not suggest that qualitative research is lacking in rigor; on the contrary, all research studies are understood to be 'situated', and the researcher integral to the progress of a research project. In her research in India, Ramanathan (2005: 15) notes for example 'Questions and issues of what are "present" and "absent" clearly underlie what are "visible" and "invisible" in literacy events and practices and are determined, to a large extent, by the researcher's lens'. Second, identity researchers aim to investigate the complex relationship between social structure on the one hand, and human agency on the other, without resorting to deterministic or reductionist analyses. While taking race, class, gender and other structural issues into account in our analysis, we need to ensure that we leave conceptual room for the actions and investments of human agents. Menard-Warwick (2006) makes the case that Bakhtin's theories of language have the potential to resolve some of the contradictions between continuity and change that characterize debates on identity in the fields of second language acquisition and literacy. Third, identity researchers seek to better understand how power operates within society, constraining or enabling human action (Cummins, 2000; Fairclough, 2001; Janks, 2010; Pennycook, 2007). We often draw on Foucault (1980) to understand not only the relationship between knowledge and power, but also the subtle ways in which power operates in society. Foucault notes for example that power is often invisible in that it frequently naturalizes events and practices in ways that come to be seen as 'normal' to members of a community. As Pennycook notes,

> Foucault brings a constant scepticism towards cherished concepts and modes of thought. Taken-for-granted categories such as man, woman, class, race, ethnicity, nation, identity, awareness, emancipation, language or power must be understood as contingent, shifting and produced in the particular, rather than having some prior ontological status. (Pennycook, 2007: 39)

Qualitative research on language and identity is not without its challenges, however, and the following two studies are illustrative of some of its difficulties. Drawing on their research on task-based language learning in urban settings in the United Kingdom, Leung *et al.* (2004) examine the inelegance of qualitative research, arguing that the 'epistemic turbulence' in qualitative research in second language acquisition centres on the question of what constitutes or represents reality. The methodology adopted in their study was to collect naturally occurring data with the use of video and audio recordings, which were supplemented by field notes. They describe the data as 'messy' in that it was difficult to represent and account for data that did not fit neatly into the theoretical construct of task-based language use. Leung *et al.* make the case that researchers need a conceptual framework that acknowledges rather than obscures the messiness of data.

In a very different context, Toohey and Waterstone (2004) describe a research collaboration between teachers and researchers in Vancouver, Canada, with the mutual goal of investigating what practices in classrooms would make a difference to the learning opportunities of minority-language children. While teachers were comfortable discussing and critiquing their educational practices, they expressed ambivalence about translating their practice into publishable academic papers, noting that they felt little ownership over the academic language characteristic of many published journals. To address precisely this type of challenge, Sharkey and Johnson (2003) have initiated a productive and engaging dialogue between researchers and teachers, with the express aim of demystifying research and theory that addresses themes of identity, power and educational change.

Key Research Findings and Future Directions

In this section, I discuss key research findings on language and identity with reference to five areas of research, and then suggest additional directions for the future. The five areas address research on identity and investment, identity and imagined communities, identity categories and educational change, identity and literacy, and identity and resistance.

Identity and investment

In my research with immigrant women in Canada (Norton, 2000; Norton Peirce, 1995), I observed that existing theories of motivation in the field of SLA were not consistent with the findings from my research. Most theories at the time assumed motivation was a character trait of the individual language learner and that learners who failed to learn the target language were not sufficiently committed to the learning process (see e.g. Schumann, 1986). Further, theories of motivation did not pay sufficient attention to unequal relations of power between language learners and target language speakers. My research found that high levels of motivation did not necessarily translate into good language learning, and that unequal relations of power between language learners and target language speakers was a common theme in the data. For this reason, I developed the construct of 'investment' to complement constructs of motivation in the field of SLA. The construct of investment, inspired by the work of Bourdieu (1977, 1991), signals the socially and historically constructed relationship of learners to the target language and their often ambivalent desire to learn and practice it. If learners 'invest' in the target language, they do so with the understanding that they will acquire a wider range of symbolic and material resources, which will in turn increase the value of their cultural capital. Unlike notions of instrumental motivation, which often conceive of the language learner as having a unitary, fixed and ahistorical 'personality', the construct of investment conceives of the language learner as having a complex identity, changing across time and space, and reproduced in social interaction. Thus while motivation can be seen as a primarily psychological construct (Dornyei, 2001), investment must be seen within a sociological framework, and seeks to make a meaningful connection between a learner's desire and commitment to learn a language, and their changing identity.

The construct of investment provides for a different set of questions associated with a learner's commitment to learning the target language. Instead of asking for example 'To what extent is the learner motivated to learn the target language?' the researcher asks, 'What is the learner's investment in the target language practices of this classroom or community?' A learner may be a highly motivated language learner, but may nevertheless have little investment in the language practices of a given classroom or community, which may for example be racist, sexist, elitist or homophobic. Thus despite being highly motivated, a learner could be excluded from the language practices of a classroom, and in time positioned as a 'poor' or unmotivated language learner (see Norton & Toohey, 2001).

By way of illustration, it is instructive to consider a recent classroom-based study conducted by Duff (2002) in a multilingual secondary school. Drawing on macro-level and micro-level contexts of communication in one content-level course, Duff found that the teacher's attempts to foster respect for cultural diversity in the classroom had mixed results. In essence, the English language learners in the class were afraid of being criticized or laughed at because of their limited command of English. As Duff (2002: 312) notes, 'Silence protected them from humiliation'. This silence, however, was perceived by the native English speakers as representing 'a lack of initiative, agency, or desire to improve one's English or to offer interesting material for the sake of the class' (Duff, 2002: 312). It is clear from the classroom data, however, that the English language learners in the class were not 'unmotivated'; rather, it could be argued that they were not 'invested' in the language practices of their classroom, where there were unequal relations of power between the English language learners and native speakers. Their investments were co-constructed in their interactions with their native speaker peers, and their identities a site of struggle.

The construct of investment has sparked considerable interest in the field of applied linguistics and language education (see e.g. Cummins, 2006; Haneda, 2005; McKay & Wong, 1996; Pittaway, 2004; Potowski, 2007; Skilton-Sylvester, 2002), including a special issue on the topic in the *Journal of Asian Pacific Communication* (Arkoudis & Davison, 2008). McKay and Wong (1996) have drawn on this construct to explain the English language development of four Mandarin-speaking students in Grades 7 and 8 in a California school, noting that the needs, desires and negotiations of students are integral to their investment in the target language. Skilton-Sylvester (2002), drawing on her research with four Cambodian women in adult ESL classes in the United States, has argued that traditional views of adult motivation and participation do not adequately address the complex lives of adult learners, and that an understanding of a woman's domestic and professional identities is necessary to explain their investment in particular adult ESL programs. Haneda (2005) has drawn on the construct of investment to understand the engagement of two university students in an advanced Japanese literacy course, concluding that their multimembership in differing communities may have shaped the way they invested in writing in Japanese. Potowski (2007) uses the construct of investment to explain students' use of Spanish in a dual Spanish/English immersion program in the United States, noting that even if a language program is well-run, a learner's investment in the target language must be consistent with the goals of the program if language learning is to meet expectations. Cummins (2006: 59) has drawn on the construct of investment to develop the notion of the identity text, arguing that the construct has emerged as a 'significant explanatory construct' in the second language learning literature.

Identity and imagined communities

An extension of interest in identity and investment concerns the imagined communities that language learners aspire to join when they learn a new language. In Norton (2001), I drew on my research with two adult immigrant language learners to argue that while the learners were initially actively engaged in classroom practices, the realm of their desired community extended beyond the four walls of the classroom. This imagined community was not accessible to their respective teachers, who, unwittingly, alienated the two language learners, who then withdrew from the language classroom. I have drawn on the work of Lave and Wenger (1991), Wenger (1998), and later Anderson (1991) to argue that in many second language classrooms, all of the members of the classroom community, apart from the teacher, are newcomers to the language practices of that community. The question that arises then is what community practices do these learners seek to learn? What, indeed, constitutes 'the community' for them?

In many language classrooms, the community may be, to some extent, a reconstruction of past communities and historically constituted relationships, but also a community of the imagination – a desired community that offers possibilities for an enhanced range of identity options in the future. Such imagined communities can be highly varied, from the imagined community of the more public professional to that of the more local homemaker. Learners have different investments in particular members of the target language community, and the people in whom learners have the greatest investment may be the very people who represent or provide access to the imagined community of a given learner. Of particular interest to the language educator is the extent to which such investments are productive for learner engagement in both the classroom and the wider target language community. In essence, an imagined community assumes an imagined identity, and a learner's investment in the target language must be understood within this context.

Such issues have been taken up more extensively in publications such as Pavlenko and Norton (2007) and in a co-edited special issue of the *Journal of Language, Identity, and Education* on 'Imagined Communities and Educational Possibilities' (Kanno & Norton, 2003) in which a number of scholars have explored the imagined communities of learners in diverse regions of the world; some of whom have subsequently followed up this initial research in more recent publications. In the Japanese context for example, Kanno (2008) examines the relationship between school education and inequality of access to bilingualism in five different Japanese schools promoting bilingual education. She found that while additive bilingualism was promoted for upper-middle-class students, subtractive bilingualism was far more common in schools serving immigrant and refugee children. Kanno argues that in the schools she researched, different visions of children's imagined communities called for different forms of bilingual education, exacerbating existing inequities between students with unequal access to resources.

In Canada, Dagenais *et al.* (2009) have investigated the linguistic landscape in the vicinity of two elementary schools in Vancouver and Montreal, illustrating the ways in which the children imagined the language of their neighbourhoods, and constructed their identities in relation to them. Dagenais *et al.* describe the innovative ways in which researchers and students drew on multimodal resources such as digital photography to document the linguistic landscape of these neighbourhoods, and the way children in both cities were encouraged to exchange letters, posters, photographs and videos. Dagenais *et al.* argue that documenting the imagined communities of neighbourhoods, as depicted and understood by children, can provide much information on the children's understanding of their community, an important consideration for language educators.

In another region of the world, Kendrick and Jones (2008) have drawn on the notion of imagined communities to analyse the drawings and photographs produced by primary and secondary schoolgirls in the Ugandan context. Their research, drawing on multimodal methodologies, sought to investigate the girls' perceptions of participation in local literacy practices, and to promote dialogue on literacy, gender and development. What they found was that the girls' visual images provided insight into their imagined communities, which were associated with command of English and access to education. As they conclude:

> Providing opportunities for girls to explore and consider their worlds through alternative modes of communication and representation has immense potential as a pedagogical approach to cultivate dialogue about the nature of gender inequities, and serve as a catalyst for the positing of imagined communities where those inequities might not exist. (Kendrick & Jones, 2008: 397)

Identity categories and educational change

While much research on language and identity explores the multiple and intersecting dimensions of learners' identities, there is a growing body of research that seeks to investigate the ways in which particular relations of race, gender, class and sexual orientation may impact the language learning process. Innovative research that addresses these issues does not regard such identity categories as 'variables', but rather as sets of relationships that are socially and historically constructed within particular relations of power. Ibrahim's (1999) research with a group of French-speaking continental African students in a Franco-Ontarian High School in Canada explores the impact on language learning of 'becoming black'. He argues that the students' linguistic styles, and in particular their use of Black Stylized English, was a direct outcome of being imagined and constructed as Black by hegemonic discourses and groups. From a slightly different perspective, Taylor's (2004) research in an anti-discrimination camp in Toronto argues for the need to understand language learning through the lens of what she calls 'racialized gender'. The stories of Hue, a Vietnamese girl, and Khatra, a Somali girl, are particularly powerful in this regard, as Hue learns the multiple ways in which she is racialized in her school, and Khatra learns how her body signifies certain ethnic, racial and national identities. Their experiences support the view held by Kubota (2004) that a color-blind conception of multiculturalism does not do justice to the challenges faced by language learners of diverse races and ethnicities.

Similarly, the work of scholars such as Cameron (2006), Pavlenko (2004), Sunderland (2004) and Higgins (this volume) is particularly insightful with regard to intersections of gender and language. Their conception of gender, which extends beyond female–male divides, is understood to be a system of social relationships and discursive practices that may lead to systemic inequality among particular groups of learners, including women, minorities, elderly and disabled. Pavlenko for example argues for the need to understand the intersections between gender and other forms of oppression, noting that both girls and boys who are silenced in the language classroom are more likely those from the working class. A number of these issues are taken up in Norton and Pavlenko (2004), who document research from diverse regions of the world that addresses the relationship between gender and language learning with respect to the dominance of the English language internationally.

In a similar spirit, King (2008), Moffatt and Norton (2008) and Nelson (2009) explore the extent to which sexual orientation might be an important identity category in the language classroom. Of central interest is the way in which a teacher can create a supportive environment for learners who might be gay, lesbian or transgendered. Nelson contrasts a pedagogy of inquiry, which asks how linguistic and cultural practices naturalize certain sexual identities, most notably heterosexuality, with a pedagogy of inclusion which aims to introduce images as well as experiences of gays and lesbians into curriculum materials. Nelson's approach can fruitfully be applied to other issues of marginalization, helping learners to question normative practices in the target culture into which they have entered.

Interest in identity categories and language learning is gaining momentum. Special issues of the *TESOL Quarterly* on 'Gender and Language Education' (Davis & Skilton-Sylvester, 2004) and 'Race and TESOL' (Kubota & Lin, 2006) include insightful debates on gender, race and language learning, while recent monographs by May (2008), Heller (2007) and Rampton (2006) ensure that issues of language, ethnicity and class remain on the radar in the field.

Identity and literacy

Researchers of language and identity have become interested not only in the conditions under which language learners speak, but in the extent to which identities and investments structure their engagement with *texts*, whether these be written, oral or multimodal. There is growing recognition that when a learner engages in textual practices, both the comprehension and construction of the text is mediated by the learner's investment in the activity and the learner's identity. Scholars such as Barton (2007), Blommaert (2008), Hornberger (2003), Kress *et al.* (2004), Martin-Jones and Jones (2000), Prinsloo and Baynham (2008) and Street and Hornberger (2008) have influenced much research on the relationship between literacy and learner identity.

Much emerging research on literacy and learner identity also addresses the impact of literacy practices on relationships beyond the classroom (Kramsch & Thorne, 2002; Lam, 2000; Snyder & Prinsloo, 2007; Warriner, 2007; Warschauer, 2003). Lam (2000) for example who studied the internet correspondence of a Chinese immigrant teenager in the United States who entered into transnational communication with a group of peers, demonstrates how this experience in what she calls 'textual identity' related to the student's developing identity in the use of English. In another context, White (2007) has investigated innovation in distance language teaching in the Australian context, arguing that attention to issues of identity can enhance our understanding of educational innovation. The research of Kramsch and Thorne (2002) indicates, however, that not all transnational internet communication leads to positive identity outcomes. In their study of the synchronous and asynchronous communication between American learners of French in the United States and French learners of English in France, they found that students had little understanding of the larger cultural framework within which each party was operating, leading to problematic digital exchanges.

Identity and resistance

The relationship between language, identity and resistance has become a compelling and fruitful area of research in language education. While larger structural constraints and classroom practices might position learners in undesirable ways, learners, with human agency, can resist these positions in innovative and unexpected ways, as the following three examples illustrate. In exploring what he calls the subversive identities of language learners, Canagarajah (2004a) addresses the intriguing question of how language learners can maintain membership of their vernacular communities and cultures while still learning a second language or dialect. He draws on his research with two very different groups, one in the United States and the other in Sri Lanka, to argue that language learners are sometimes ambivalent about the learning of a second language or dialect, and that they may resort to clandestine literacy practices to create 'pedagogical safe houses' in the language classroom. In both contexts, the clandestine literacy activities of the students are seen to be forms of resistance to unfavourable identities imposed on the learners. At the same time, however, these safe houses serve as sites of identity construction, allowing students to negotiate the often contradictory tensions they encounter as members of diverse communities.

A second example of resistance is found in the work of McKinney and van Pletzen (2004). Working with relatively privileged students at a historically white and Afrikaans university in South Africa, McKinney and van Pletzen introduced critical reading into their first year English studies course using two curriculum units on South African literature. In exploring representations of the apartheid past, McKinney and van Pletzen encountered significant resistance from students to the ways in which they felt uncomfortably positioned by the curriculum materials on offer. McKinney and van Pletzen attempted to create discursive spaces in which both they and the students could explore the many private and political processes through which identities are constructed. In doing so, they re-conceptualized students' resistance more productively as a meaning-making activity that offers powerful teaching moments.

The third example of identity and resistance is drawn from Talmy (2008), who investigated the multiple ways in which English language learners in a Hawai'i high school resisted being positioned as an 'ESL student' in their dedicated-ESL classes. While the school-sanctioned ESL student was expected to bring required materials to class, read assigned fiction, do bookwork, meet assigned dates, follow instructions and work for the full class session, resistant ESL students engaged in a wide variety of oppositional activities, including leaving materials 'at home', talking with friends and playing cards. From a pedagogical point of view, two of Talmy's observations are particularly significant. The first observation is that the ESL teachers began to change their practices in response to the resistance of their students, necessitating a shift in teacher identity; the second is that the students' actions paradoxically turned the ESL program into precisely what the students disliked most, 'an easy, academically inconsequential program that did little to meet their L2 learning or educational needs' (Talmy, 2008: 639).

Future directions

With regard to future directions in the field of language and identity, one area that is receiving increasing attention is that of the language teacher and the language teacher educator (see Clarke, 2008; Hawkins, 2004; Hawkins & Norton, 2009; Morgan, 2004; Pennycook, 2004; Varghese *et al.*, 2005). In a compelling narrative, Pennycook (2004) reflects on his experience of observing a teacher in a TESOL practicum in Sydney, Australia. His experience reminds us that a great deal of language teaching does not take place in well-funded institutes of education, but in community programs, places of worship and immigrant centres, where funds are limited and time at a premium. Of central interest in his narrative is a consideration of the way in which teacher educators can intervene in the process of practicum observation to bring about educational and social change. To this end, Pennycook argues that 'critical moments' in the practicum can be used to raise larger questions of power and authority in the wider society, and provide an opportunity for critical discussion and reflection.

A second area that has much potential for future research on language and identity concerns growing interest in globalization and language learning (see e.g. Block & Cameron, 2002; Garciá *et al.*, 2006; Lin & Martin, 2005; Morgan & Ramanathan, 2005; Pennycook, 2007; Rassool, 2007). Morgan and Ramanathan (2005) argue persuasively that the field of language education needs to consider ways in which English language teaching can be decolonized, proposing that there is a need to decentre the authority that Western interests have in the language teaching industry. In particular, we need to find ways to restore agency to professionals in periphery communities (Kumaravadivelu, 2003; Mutonyi & Norton, 2007; Tembe & Norton, 2008) and to give due recognition to local vernacular modes of learning and teaching (Canagarajah, 2004b). In this regard, special issues of a number of journals are significant, including: special issues of the *TESOL Quarterly* on Language in Development (Markee, 2002) and Language Policies and TESOL (Ramanathan & Morgan, 2007); and two recent issues of the AILA *Review of the International Association of Applied Linguistics* on 'Africa and Applied Linguistics' (Makoni & Meinhof, 2003) and 'World Applied Linguistics' (Gass & Makoni, 2004).

Language, Identity and Classroom Pedagogies

I now turn to the relevance of theories of language and identity for classroom teaching. As Lee's (2008) research in a Canadian post-secondary institution suggests, while many language teachers strive to enhance the range of possibilities available to their students, there is often a disjuncture between the pedagogy as it is conceptualized by the teacher and the practices adopted in the classroom. Despite the best intentions, classroom practices can recreate subordinate student identities, thereby limiting students' access not only to language learning opportunities, but to other more powerful identities.

Lee's findings are consistent with those of Ramanathan (2005) who, in a very different part of the world, found that teachers' language practices can reinforce existing inequities among diverse learners of English. In the Indian context, Ramanathan (2005) investigated how students who had been socialized into either Gujarati or English-medium schools through grades K-12 adjusted to English in English-medium tertiary level institutions. What she found was that students who received English medium instruction through high school were better prepared to succeed in English-medium colleges than those schooled in the vernacular. The English curriculum for the students educated in the English medium tended to focus on the creative analysis of English literature, while the English curriculum for the vernacular students, who were mostly lower-caste Dalit students, made extensive use of grammar and translation. What Ramanathan's research suggests is that pedagogical language practices that are ritualized and allow for little meaning-making on the part of students may limit the learner's language learning progress and access to more powerful identities.

In a recent chapter, Carolyn McKinney and I have argued that responding to diversity in the language classroom requires an imaginative assessment of what is possible as well as a critical assessment of what is desirable (McKinney & Norton, 2008). Clearly, the assessment of what is 'possible' requires ongoing interaction between teachers, administrators and policy-makers, with reference to larger material conditions that can serve to constrain or enable the range of identity positions available to students (see Luke, 2004). The theories of language and identity that I have discussed thus far, I suggest, offer important ways of connecting the possible and the desirable. If we agree that diverse identity positions offer learners a range of positions from which to speak, listen, read or write, the challenge for language educators is to explore which identity positions offer the greatest opportunity for social engagement and interaction. Conversely, if there are identity positions that silence students, then teachers need to investigate and address marginalizing classroom practices.

A number of recent research projects, drawn from diverse regions of the world, are illustrative of the ways in which particular pedagogical practices in language classrooms can offer students opportunities to draw on their multiple identities, promote their investment in learning, and offer possibilities for re-imagining both the present and the future. The projects I examine took place in Mexico, South Africa, Uganda, Canada and the United Kingdom (see also the multiple projects addressed in Norton & Toohey, 2004).

In Mexico, Clemente and Higgins (2008) drew on their longitudinal study of pre-service English teachers in Oaxaca to raise questions about the dominant role that English plays in the globalized political economy, and to illustrate the ways in which the non-native English teachers in their study sought to appropriate and 'perform' English without sacrificing local identities. Defining their research site as a 'contact zone', they describe the way the student teachers confronted the demands of English through various forms of language play in both English and Spanish, making the case that the student teacher groups were safe havens in which participants could play with both languages. Such performances allowed them to explore various identity positions, as a counter-discourse to dominant discourses on the native English teacher. As one student teacher said,

> I have a Mexican accent. English is mine from the very moment I put it into practice and I am able to establish communication. But when I say that the English language is mine, I do not mean to say that I want to take the culture that comes with it. (Clement & Higgins, 2008: 123)

In South Africa, Stein (2008) explored the way in which English language classrooms in under-resourced township schools became transformative sites in which textual, cultural and linguistic forms were re-appropriated and 're-sourced', with a view to validating those practices that had been marginalized and undervalued by the apartheid system. This transformation took place as teachers provided opportunities for English language learners to make use of multimodal resources, including linguistic, bodily and sensory modes, in order to engage in meaning-making. Stein's learners embraced the opportunities they were given to produce multimodal counter-texts that subverted the canon, and to draw on topics sometimes considered taboo.

In a similar spirit, one of the Ugandan projects that our research team at the University of British Columbia has undertaken is to investigate the extent to which multimodal pedagogies that include drawing, photography and drama can be incorporated more systematically into the English curriculum in Uganda (Kendrick *et al.*, 2006; Kendrick & Jones, 2008). Drawing on our research in two regions of the country, we argue that multimodal pedagogies offer teachers innovative ways of validating students' literacies, experiences and cultures, and are highly effective in supporting English language learning in the classroom. In the photography project for example the students' perception of English as being a somewhat restrictive and artificial medium of instruction diminished as English began to be used for communication, expression and ownership of meaning.

Canadian colleagues, most notably Margaret Early and Jim Cummins, have been working on another project that seeks to provide a range of identity options for learners in multilingual schools in Vancouver, Toronto and Montreal. Working with more than 50 teachers, four schoolboards, a teacher's union and non-government literacy organizations, this Multiliteracies Project (www.multiliteracies.ca) seeks to understand the literacy practices of students in and outside of school, to explore innovative classrooms in which teachers engage in multiliterate practices, and to investigate how educational systems influence the multiliteracy practices of schools. The project website provides a workspace for students, teachers and researchers to assemble and organize annotated galleries, construct demonstration classroom projects, and create case studies on what Cummins (2006) has called the 'identity texts' produced by these students.

In the United Kingdom, Wallace (2003) has worked with adult language learners on critical reading courses that address the socially embedded nature of the reading process, exploring text-focussed activities that address how meaning and power is encoded in texts. In doing so, she makes use of a range of popular texts, including newspaper articles, magazine articles, and advertisements. Wallace contrasts her approach with dominant English Foreign Language methodologies such as communicative language teaching and task-based learning, arguing that such approaches can be 'domesticating' for learners, teaching them only how to fit in with dominant cultures rather than to question and reshape powerful discourses.

Wallace's insights provide a useful segue into my concluding thoughts on the relationship between language and identity within the field of language education. In the classroom pedagogies described in this section, and in many transformative classrooms that have been discussed in the literature, the language teachers' conceptions of 'language' and thus 'language teaching' are broad in scope. The teachers conceive of language not only as a linguistic system, but as a social practice in which experiences are organized and identities negotiated. There is recognition that if learners are not invested in the language practices of the classroom, learning outcomes are limited, and educational inequities perpetuated. Further, such teachers take great care to offer learners multiple identity positions from which to engage in the language practices of the classroom, the school and the community. In every region of the world, innovative language teachers are seeking to provide learners with diverse opportunities to take ownership over meaning-making, and to re-imagine an expanded range of identities for the future. In essence, these remarkable teachers are seeking to make the desirable possible.

Suggestions for further reading

Block, D. (2007) *Second Language Identities*. London/New York: Continuum
In this monograph, David Block insightfully traces research interest in second language identities from the 1960s to the present. He draws on a wide range of social theory, and brings a fresh analysis to seminal studies of adult migrants, foreign language learners, and study-abroad students.

Norton, B. (2000) *Identity and Language Learning: Gender, Ethnicity, and Educational Change*. Harlow, England: Longman/Pearson.
Drawing on a longitudinal study of immigrant women in Canada, Bonny Norton draws on poststructuralist theory to argue for a conception of learner identity as multiple, a site of struggle, and subject to change. She also develops the construct of 'investment' to better understand the relationship of language learners to the target language.

Norton, B. & Toohey, K. (eds) (2004) *Critical Pedagogies and Language Learning*. Cambridge: Cambridge University Press.
Identity is a central theme in this collection of articles by leading researchers in language education. Diverse authors address a wide range of contemporary topics on language learning and teaching, including critical multiculturalism, gender, multimodal pedagogies, popular culture and action research.

Pavlenko, A. and Blackledge, A. (eds) (2003) *Negotiation of Identities in Multilingual Contexts*. Clevedon: Multilingual Matters.
The authors in this collection provide insight into the ways in which identities are negotiated in diverse multilingual settings. They analyse the discourses of education, autobiography, politics and youth culture, demonstrating the ways in which languages may be sites of resistance, empowerment or discrimination.

Toohey, K. (2000) *Learning English at School: Identity, Social Relations and Classroom Practice*. Clevedon: Multilingual Matters.
Drawing on a longitudinal ethnography of young English language learners, Kelleen Toohey investigates the ways in which classroom practices are implicated in the range of identity options available to language learners. She draws on sociocultural and poststructural theory to better understand the classroom community as a site of identity negotiation.

References

Albright, J. and Luke, A. (2008) *Pierre Bourdieu and Literacy Education*. Mahwah, NJ: Lawrence Erlbaum Associates.

Anderson, B. (1991) *Imagined Communities: Reflections on the Origin and Spread of Nationalism* (rev. edn). New York: Verso.

Arkoudis, S. and Davison, C. (eds) (2008) Chinese students: Perspectives on their social, cognitive, and linguistic investment in English medium interaction. [Special Issue]. *Journal of Asian Pacific Communication* 18 (1), 1–133.

Bakhtin, M. (1981) *The Dialogic Imagination*. Austin: University of Texas Press.

Bakhtin, M. (1984) *Problems of Dostoevsky's Poetics* (C. Emerson, trans.). Minneapolis: University of Minnesota Press. (Original work published 1963.)

Barton, D. (2007) *Literacy: An Introduction to the Ecology of Written Language* (2nd edn). London: Blackwell.

Bhabha, B. (1987) Interrogating identity: The real me. In L. Appignanesi (ed.) *Identity* (pp. 5–11) London: Institute of Contemporary Arts.

Block, D. (2007) *Second Language Identities*. London: Continuum.

Block, D. and Cameron, D. (eds) (2002) *Globalization and Language Teaching*. New York: Routledge.

Blommaert, J. (2008) *Grassroots Literacy: Writing, Identity, and Voice in Central Africa*. London and New York: Routledge.

Bourdieu, P. (1977) The economics of linguistic exchanges. *Social Science Information* 16 (6), 645–668.

Bourdieu, P. (1991) *Language and Symbolic Power*. In J.B. Thompson (ed.) (G. Raymond & M. Adamson, trans.). Cambridge: Polity Press. (Original work published in 1982.)

Cameron, D (2006) *On Language and Sexual Politics*. New York and London: Routledge.

Canagarajah, S. (2004a) Subversive identities, pedagogical safe houses, and critical learning. In B. Norton and K. Toohey (eds) *Critical Pedagogies and Language Learning* (pp. 116–137). New York: Cambridge University Press.

Canagarajah, S. (ed.) (2004b) *Reclaiming the Local in Language Policy and Practice*. Mahwah, NJ: Lawrence Erlbaum.

Clarke, M. (2008) *Language Teacher Identities: Co-Constructing Discourse and Community*. Clevedon: Multilingual Matters.

Clemente, A. and Higgins, M. (2008) *Performing English with a Postcolonial Accent: Ethnographic Narratives from Mexico*. London: Tufnell Publishing.

Cummins, J. (2000) *Language, Power and Pedagogy: Bilingual Children in the Crossfire*. Clevedon, England: Multilingual Matters.

Cummins, J. (2006) Identity texts: The imaginative construction of self through multiliteracies pedagogy. In O. Garcia, T. Skutnabb-Kangas and M. Torres-Guzman (eds) *Imagining Multilingual Schools: Language in Education and Glocalization* (pp. 51–68). Clevedon: Multilingual Matters.

Dagenais, D., Moore, D., Lamarre, S., Sabatier, C. and Armand, F. (2009) Linguistic landscape and language awareness. In E. Shohamy and D. Gorter (eds) *Linguistic Landscape: Expanding the Scenery* (pp. 253–269). New York: Routledge/Taylor & Francis Group.

Davis, K. and Skilton-Sylvester, E. (eds) (2004) Gender in TESOL [Special issue]. *TESOL Quarterly* 38 (3), 377–544.

Day, E.M. (2002) *Identity and the Young English Language Learner*. Clevedon: Multilingual Matters.

Dornyei, Z. (2001) *Motivational Strategies in the Language Classroom*. Cambridge: Cambridge University Press.

Duff, P. (2002) The discursive co-construction of knowledge, identity, and difference: An ethnography of communication in the high school mainstream. *Applied Linguistics* 23, 289–322.

Fairclough, N. (2001) *Language and Power* (2nd edn). Harlow: Pearson/Longman.

Foucault, M. (1980) *Power/knowledge: Selected Interviews and Other Writings, 1972–1977.* In C. Gordon (ed.) New York: Pantheon Books.

Gao, Y.H. (2007) Legitimacy of foreign language learning and identity research: Structuralist and constructivist perspectives. *Intercultural Communication Studies* XVI (1), 100–112.

Garciá, O., Skutnabb-Kangas, T. and Torres-Guzmán, M.E. (eds) (2006) *Imagining Multilingual Schools: Languages in Education and Glocalization.* Clevedon: Multilingual Matters.

Gass, S.M. and Makoni, S. (eds) (2004) World applied linguistics: A celebration of AILA at 40 [Special Issue]. *AILA Review*, 17, 1–136.

Goldstein, T. (2003) *Teaching and Learning in a Multilingual School: Choices, Risks, and Dilemmas.* Mahwah, NJ: Lawrence Erlbaum Associates.

Hall, S. (1997) *Representation: Cultural Representations and Signifying Practices.* London: Sage.

Haneda, M. (2005) Investing in foreign-language writing: A study of two multicultural learners. *Journal of Language, Identity, and Education* 4 (4), 269–290.

Hawkins, M.R. (ed.) (2004) *Language Learning and Teacher Education: A Sociocultural Approach.* Clevedon: Multilingual Matters.

Hawkins, M. and Norton, B. (2009) Critical language teacher education. In A. Burns and J. Richards (eds) *Cambridge Guide to Second Language Teacher Education* (pp. 30–40). Cambridge: Cambridge University Press.

Heller, M. (2007) *Linguistic Minorities and Modernity: A Sociolinguistic Ethnography* (2nd edn). London: Continuum.

Hornberger, N. (ed.) (2003) *Continua of Biliteracy.* Clevedon: Multilingual Matters.

Ibrahim, A.E.K.M. (1999) Becoming Black: Rap and hip-hop, race, gender, identity, and the politics of ESL learning. *TESOL Quarterly* 33 (3), 349–369.

Janks, H. (2010) *Literacy and Power.* New York and London: Routledge.

Kanno, Y. (2008) *Language and Education in Japan: Unequal Access to Bilingualism.* Basingstoke: Palgrave Macmillan.

Kanno, Y. and Norton, B. (eds) (2003) Imagined communities and educational possibilities [Special issue]. *Journal of Language, Identity, and Education* 2 (4), 1–106.

Kendrick, M. and Jones, S. (2008) Girls' visual representations of literacy in a rural Ugandan community. *Canadian Journal of Education* 31 (3), 372–404.

Kendrick, M., Jones, S., Mutonyi, H. and Norton, B. (2006) Multimodality and English education in Ugandan schools. *English Studies in Africa* 49 (1), 95–114.

King, B. (2008) "Being gay guy, that is the advantage": Queer Korean language learning and identity construction. *Journal of Language, Identity, and Education* 7 (3–4), 230–252.

Kramsch, C. and Thorne, S. (2002) Foreign language learning as global communicative practice. In D. Block and D. Cameron (eds) *Globalization and Language Teaching* (pp. 83–100). London: Routledge.

Kress, G., Jewitt, C., Bourne, J., Franks, A., Hardcastle, J., Jones, K. and Reid, E. (2004) *English in Urban Classrooms: A Multimodal Perspective on Teaching and Learning.* London and New York: Routledge.

Kubota, R. (2004) Critical multiculturalism and second language education. In B. Norton and K. Toohey (eds) *Critical Pedagogies and Language Learning* (pp. 30–52). New York: Cambridge University Press.

Kubota, R. and Lin, A. (2006) Race and TESOL: Introduction to concepts and theories [Special issue]. *TESOL Quarterly* 40 (3), 471–654.

Kumaravadivelu, B. (2003) *Beyond Methods: Macrostrategies for Language Learning*. New Haven, CT: Yale University Press.

Lam, W.S.E. (2000) L2 literacy and the design of the self: A case study of a teenager writing on the internet. *TESOL Quarterly* 34 (3), 457–482.

Lave, J. and Wenger, E. (1991) *Situated Learning: Legitimate Peripheral Participation*. Cambridge: Cambridge University Press.

Lee, E. (2008) The "other(ing)" costs of ESL: A Canadian case study. *Journal of Asian Pacific Communication* 18 (1), 91–108.

Leung, C., Harris, R. and Rampton, B. (2004) Living with inelegance in qualitative research on task-based learning. In B. Norton and K. Toohey (eds) *Critical Pedagogies and Language Learning* (pp. 242–267). New York: Cambridge University Press.

Lin, A. and Martin, P. (2005) *Decolonisation, Globalisation: Language-in-Education Policy and Practice*. Clevedon: Multilingual Matters.

Luke, A. (2004) Two takes on the critical. In B. Norton and K. Toohey (eds) *Critical Pedagogies and Language Learning* (pp. 21–29). New York: Cambridge University Press.

Makoni, S. and Meinhof, U. (eds) (2003) Africa and applied linguistics [Special issue]. *AILA Review* 16, 1–171.

Markee, N. (2002) Language in development. *TESOL Quarterly* 36 (2), 141–247.

Martin-Jones, M. and Jones, K. (2000) *Multilingual Literacies*. Philadelphia/Amsterdam: John Benjamins.

May, S. (2008) *Language and Minority Rights*. London and New York: Routledge.

McKay, S. and Wong, S.C. (1996) Multiple discourses, multiple identities: Investment and agency in second language learning among Chinese adolescent immigrant students. *Harvard Educational Review* 66 (3), 577–608.

McKinney, C. and Norton, B. (2008) Identity in language and literacy education. In B. Spolsky and F. Hult (eds) *The Handbook of Educational Linguistics* (pp. 192–205). London: Blackwell.

McKinney, C. and van Pletzen, E. (2004) "... This apartheid story ... we've finished with it": Student responses to the apartheid past in a South African English studies course. *Teaching in Higher Education* 9 (2), 159–170.

Menard-Warwick, J. (2006) Both a fiction and an existential fact: Theorizing identity in second language acquisition and literacy studies. *Linguistics and Education* 16, 253–274.

Miller, J. (2003) *Audible Difference: ESL and Social Identity in Schools*. Clevedon: Multilingual Matters.

Moffatt, L. and Norton, B. (2008) Reading gender relations and sexuality: Preteens speak out. *Canadian Journal of Education* 31 (31), 102–123.

Morgan, B. (2004) Teacher identity as pedagogy: Towards a field-internal conceptualization in bilingual and second language education. *Bilingual Education and Bilingualism* 7 (2&3), 172–188.

Morgan, B. (2007) Poststructuralism and applied linguistics: Complementary approaches to identity and culture in ELT. In J. Cummins and C. Davison (eds) *International Handbook of English Language Teaching* (pp. 1033–1052). New York: Springer.

Morgan, B. and Ramanathan, V. (2005) Critical literacies and language education: Global and local perspectives. *Annual Review of Applied Linguistics* 25, 151–169.

Mutonyi, H. and Norton, B. (2007) ICT on the margins: Lessons for Ugandan education. Digital literacy in global contexts [Special Issue]. *Language and Education* 21 (3), 264–270.

Nelson, C. (2009) *Sexual Identities in English Language Education: Classroom Conversations*. New York: Routledge.

Norton, B. (2000) *Identity and Language Learning: Gender, Ethnicity and Educational Change*. Harlow: Pearson Education Limited.

Norton, B. (2001) Non-participation, imagined communities, and the language classroom. In M. Breen (ed.) *Learner Contributions to Language Learning: New Directions in Research* (pp. 159–171). London: Pearson Education Limited.

Norton, B. and Pavlenko, A. (eds) (2004) *Gender and English Language Learners*. Alexandria, VA: Teachers of English to Speakers of Other Languages.

Norton, B. and Toohey, K. (2001) Changing perspectives on good language learners. *TESOL Quarterly* 35 (2), 307–322.

Norton, B. and Toohey, K. (eds) (2004) *Critical Pedagogies and Language Learning*. New York: Cambridge University Press.

Norton Peirce, B. (1995) Social identity, investment, and language learning. *TESOL Quarterly* 29 (1), 9–31.

Pavlenko, A. (2004) Gender and sexuality in foreign and second language education: Critical and feminist approaches. In B. Norton and K. Toohey (eds) *Critical Pedagogies and Language Learning* (pp. 53–71). New York: Cambridge University Press.

Pavlenko, A. and Blackledge, A. (eds) (2003) *Negotiation of Identities in Multilingual Contexts*. Clevedon: Multilingual Matters.

Pavlenko, A. and Norton, B. (2007) Imagined communities, identity, and English language teaching. In J. Cummins and C. Davison (eds) *International Handbook of English Language Teaching* (pp. 669–680). New York: Springer.

Pennycook, A. (2004) Critical moments in a TESOL praxicum. In B. Norton and K. Toohey (eds) *Critical Pedagogies and Language Learning* (pp. 327–345). New York: Cambridge University Press.

Pennycook, A. (2007) *Global Englishes and Transcultural Flows*. London and New York: Routledge.

Pittaway, D. (2004) Investment and second language acquisition. *Critical Inquiry in Language Studies* 4 (1), 203–218.

Potowski, K. (2007) *Language and Identity in a Dual Immersion School*. Clevedon: Multilingual Matters.

Prinsloo, M. and Baynham, M. (eds) (2008) *Literacies, Global and Local*. Philadelphia: John Benjamins.

Ramanathan, V. (2005) *The English-Vernacular Divide: Postcolonial Language Politics and Practice*. Clevedon: Multilingual Matters.

Ramanathan, V. and Morgan, B. (eds) (2007) Language policies and TESOL [Special Issue]. *TESOL Quarterly* 41 (3), 447–642.

Rampton, B. (2006) *Language in Late Modernity: Interaction in an Urban School*. Cambridge: Cambridge University Press.

Rassool, N. (2007) *Global Issues in Language, Education and Development: Perspectives from Postcolonial Countries*. Clevedon: Multilingual Matters.

Ricento, T. (2005) Considerations of identity in L2 learning. In E. Hinkel (ed.) *Handbook of Research on Second Language Teaching and Learning* (pp. 895–911). Mahwah, NJ: Lawrence Erlbaum Associates.

Saussure, F.de. (1966) *Course in General Linguistics*. New York: McGraw-Hill.

Schumann, J. (1986) Research on the acculturation model for second language acquisition. *Journal of Multilingual and Multicultural Development* 7 (5), 379–392.

Sharkey, J. and Johnson, K. (eds) (2003) *The TESOL Quarterly Dialogues: Rethinking Issues of Language, Culture, and Power*. Alexandria, VA: Teachers of English to Speakers of Other Languages.

Skilton-Sylvester, E. (2002) Should I stay or should I go? Investigating Cambodian women's participation and investment in adult ESL programs. *Adult Education Quarterly* 53 (1), 9–26.

Snyder, I. and Prinsloo, M. (eds) (2007) The digital literacy practices of young people in marginal contexts. [Special Issue]. *Language and Education: An International Journal* 21 (3), 171–270.

Stein, P. (2008) *Multimodal Pedagogies in Diverse Classrooms: Representation, Rights and Resources.* London and New York: Routledge.

Street, B. and Hornberger, N. (eds) (2008) *Encyclopedia of Language and Education, Vol. 2. Literacy.* Boston: Springer.

Sunderland, J. (2004) *Gendered Discourses.* London: Palgrave Macmillan.

Talmy, S. (2008) The cultural productions of the ESL student at Tradewinds High: Contingency, multidirectionality, and identity in L2 socialization. *Applied Linguistics* 29 (4), 619–644.

Taylor, L. (2004) Creating a community of difference: Understanding gender and race in a high school anti-discrimination camp. In B. Norton and A. Pavlenko (eds) *Gender and English Language Learners* (pp. 95–109). Alexandria, VA: Teachers of English to Speakers of Other Languages.

Tembe, J. and Norton, B. (2008) Promoting local languages in Ugandan primary schools: The community as stakeholder. *Canadian Modern Language Review* 65 (1), 33–60.

Toohey, K. (2000) *Learning English at School: Identity, Social Relations and Classroom Practice.* Clevedon: Multilingual Matters.

Toohey, K. and Waterstone, B. (2004) Negotiating expertise in an action research community. In B. Norton and K. Toohey (eds) *Critical Pedagogies and Language Learning* (pp. 291–310). Cambridge: Cambridge University Press.

Varghese, M., Morgan, B., Johnston, B. and Johnson, K. (2005) Theorizing language teacher identity: Three perspectives and beyond. *Journal of Language, Identity, and Education* 4, 21–44.

Wallace, C. (2003) *Critical Reading in Language Education.* Basingstoke: Palgrave Macmillan.

Warriner, D.S. (ed.) (2007) Transnational literacies: Immigration, language learning, and identity. *Linguistics and Education* 18 (3–4), 201–338.

Warschauer, M. (2003) *Technology and Social Inclusion: Rethinking the Digital Divide.* Boston: MIT Press.

Weedon, C. (1997) *Feminist Practice and Poststructuralist Theory* (2nd edn). Oxford: Blackwell.

Wenger, E. (1998) *Communities of Practice: Learning, Meaning, and Identity.* New York: Cambridge University Press.

White, C. (2007) Innovation and identity in distance language learning and teaching. *Innovation in Language Learning and Teaching* 1 (1), 97–110.

Zuengler, J. and Miller, E. (2006) Cognitive and sociocultural perspectives: Two parallel SLA worlds? *TESOL Quarterly* 40 (1), 35–58.

Chapter 14

Gender Identities in Language Education

CHRISTINA HIGGINS

Introduction

This chapter explores the ways that gendered social relations and ideologies of gender mediate people's experiences in learning and using additional languages. Since readers of this book may be interested in first, second and/or foreign language contexts, attention will be paid to issues surrounding gender that are pertinent to all contexts, but more consideration will be given to the role of gender among second (SL) and foreign language (FL) learners and users. Gender has received a great deal of attention in sociolinguistics since the 1960s, and much of this research has examined the ways that men and women use language to form identities and negotiate their social relationships (*cf.* Coates, 1997; Hall & Bucholtz, 1995; Johnson & Meinhof, 1997; Tannen, 1994). However, there are still relatively few comprehensive treatments of gender which investigate how gender identities are performed in educational contexts, or how gendered identities relate to language learning (though see Norton & Pavlenko, 2004; Pavlenko *et al.*, 2001). Moreover, while studies on sexual orientation have become a key component of gender studies in sociolinguistics and linguistic anthropology over the past decade (e.g. Cameron & Kulick, 2003; Leap, 1995; Livia & Hall, 1997), research on language learners' sexual identities in and around educational contexts remain almost unexplored.

In this chapter, I first examine the concept of gender by discussing the theoretical frameworks guiding past and present research on gender. How we understand gender has a great deal to do with how we do research on gender and how we approach gender issues in educational contexts. The shifts in perspectives have led to changes in research methodologies as well, and so I provide an overview of the methodologies that have become frequently used. Then, I discuss important findings by situating significant research studies into two broad strands. The first strand examines how gender identities of second/foreign learners are shaped by structural constraints and obstacles that learners face when negotiating participation in their communities, including workplaces, schools and home settings. This research generally employs ethnographic methodology to show how learners' access to the target language and culture is mediated by factors including power differentials, race, socioeconomic background, and cultural differences between the first language (L1) and additional language (L2) communities. In the second part, I summarize the goals of researchers who explore how learners respond to gender discourses. The focus of this section is on whether learners develop a new sense of self in their L2 (e.g. Pavlenko, 1998, 2001; Pavlenko & Lantolf, 2000). This area of inquiry shows that many women and girls experience forms of liberation through language learning, particularly in contexts of English language learning (e.g. Gordon, 2004; McMahill, 2001; Pavlenko, 2001; Piller & Takahashi, 2006). On the other hand, similar research also illustrates how learners' negative perceptions of particular L2 gender identities can become an obstacle for their participation in L2 communities (e.g. Kissau & Wierzalis, 2008; Kouritzin, 2003; Ohara, 2001).

After discussing each strand of research, I present suggestions for pedagogical practices that incorporate gendered experiences into learning opportunities. These are not ready-made lesson plans which can be used in any classroom, but rather, are descriptions of pedagogical practices that educators have used in their own classrooms. These practices can act as springboards or points of comparison for educators who are looking for ideas about how to bring gender identities and topics related to gender into their own specific teaching contexts.

From Sex to Gender: A Shift in Terms

While many people think of research on language and gender as the study of men's and women's use of language, the increasingly prevalent use of the term *gender* in contemporary sociolinguistic research is symbolic of a paradigm shift that has taken place over the past several decades (Cameron, 2005; Holmes & Meyerhoff, 2003; Wardhaugh, 1998). Much scholarship until the 1980s was more interested in relating the *sex* of speakers to language variation and describing the features of sex-based language varieties. Most scholars treated sex as a binary category and as a static identity of speakers that could be correlated with speech patterns. Male or female sex was treated as an independent variable and was used to study linguistic variation such as pronunciation or grammar differences. Variationist sociolinguists who have studied English have explored how a speaker's male or female status relates to the use of post-vocalic /r/ (Labov, 1966) and multiple negation in American English (e.g. Wolfram, 1969), and how features such as /ng/ (Trudgill, 1974) and third-person /s/ (Cheshire, 1978) pattern across male and female speakers of British English. The purpose of this research has been to understand how social class structures such as gender, class, and race are related to linguistic forms, and to provide socially based explanations of linguistic variation and change.

Variationist studies have been critiqued for what has been called the 'correlational fallacy' (Cameron, 1997: 59), or the failure to fully *explain* the distribution of socially structured linguistic variation. Much research in the variationist paradigm treats variables such as sex of the speaker as the *cause* of variation rather than investigating *why* it is that men and women (and other sexed identities, often neglected in such research) choose to speak the way they do. Trudgill (1974: 182) has tentatively suggested that women prefer standardized norms because of their powerless positions in society and their need to enhance their social positions through linguistic and other means, but most variationists do not seek explanatory theories in their work on male and female differences.

Researchers who have examined 'men's' and 'women's language' from more hermeneutic perspectives have more frequently sought to situate the features of language that are associated with men and women in explanatory frameworks. In contrast with variationist sociolinguistics, explanations for differential male and female language use are treated as central in this line of inquiry. Lakoff (1975) is well known for her work on 'women's language', which she describes as characterized by features such as greater usage of modals such as *should, could* and *might*, more negative politeness (e.g. *You wouldn't mind, would you?*) and different vocabulary such as more color terms (e.g. *mauve, taupe, ivory*) and a distinct set of adjectives (e.g. *exquisite, lovely, divine*). Taking a feminist perspective, Lakoff argues that women's language is a result of patriarchal social relations and hence is a language that reflects powerlessness and subordination. In contrast to most quantitative variationist approaches, Lakoff takes a theoretical perspective as the starting point in her work, explaining sex-based language differences as the result of men's dominance over women. According to Cameron (2005: 484), Lakoff's ideas draw on concepts in socialization theories that view women as subject to men's power in social, economic, and linguistic spheres of life. Socialization theories also form a foundation for research by Tannen (1990, 1994), who, in contrast, has preferred to describe gendered language as involving male and female 'cultures', rather than including discussions of power difference in her research. Tannen argues that men and women use language differently because they have been exposed to different sociolinguistic subcultures, and hence they employ interactional features such as overlap, eye-contact and topic initiation differently, which sometimes leads to what Tannen calls 'cross-cultural' miscommunication.

While some scholars have argued that Lakoff's work may valorize 'male speech' (e.g. Spender, 1980), and others have critiqued Tannen's work for failing to engage with the politics of language and issues of power (e.g. Crawford, 1995; Freed, 1992), both Lakoff's and Tannen's work is considered seminal since they helped to popularize the view that language is the product of social relations, rather than the cause, as is the case in much variationist work. Hence, their work can be described as *social constructionist* in scope in that both treat men's and women's speech as the result of societal relations and socialization processes. While social constructionist approaches have provided theoretically rich perspectives on gendered language and social relations in society, this kind of research has been seen as limited since it generally treats men and women as relatively homogeneous groups and because it typically examines the language produced by Caucasian, middle-class English speakers, a focus which provides an overly narrow perspective on language and gender. Researchers interested in diversity of gendered and sexual identities have focused their attention on other populations, and on case studies of individuals who break with conventional expectations of gendered identities. Cameron (2005) describes this shift in research since the early 1990s away from social constructionism and toward a post-modern perspective. Research that addresses communication among men and women has increasingly focused on gender as a social and discursive construction in various contexts, rather than as a pre-determined identity or as a fixed trait of individuals (e.g. Bergvall *et al.*, 1996; Bucholtz, 2003; Cameron, 2005; Hall & Bucholtz, 1995; Okamoto & Smith, 2004). This research frequently draws on the ideas of feminist scholar Judith Butler, whose definition of gender is often quoted (1990: 32): 'Gender is the repeated stylization of the body, a set of repeated acts within a highly rigid regulatory frame that congeal over time to produce the appearance of substance, of a "natural" kind of being'. Butler's (1990) discussion of gender as a stylized *performance* is central to much research on gender and sexuality since the concept of *performativity* highlights the constructed and unfixed nature of identities. McElhinny (2003: 24) summarizes how performativity breaks with previous research in gender studies in sociolinguistics. She writes, 'Instead of asking "what are the gender differences?", this approach (an approach which has been called *post-structuralist* or *desconstructive feminist*) leads one to ask "what difference does gender make?" and "how did gender come to make a difference?"' While it may appear that this perspective on gender is an 'evolution' of sorts in academic conceptualizations, Cameron (2005) wisely reminds us that many years before Butler was writing, Simone de Beauvoir ([1949]1972) espoused the view that gender was socially constructed when she wrote how 'womanhood' was not a condition one is born into, but a 'posture' one takes on. The current interest in gender-as-performance should not be seen as an evolution in ways of thinking about gender, then, but rather, as the framework that dominates current scholarship on gender across a number of disciplines.

It should be clear from the discussion of theories reviewed thus far that gender studies on a whole have moved away from analyzing gender as a binary category of male/female and toward investigating how gender is produced in diverse ways in various social practices. From this view, gender is not a characteristic of a person but a performance enacted in daily life that involves an ongoing negotiation between self and society. Through ways of speaking and acting, individuals perform gendered identities that may in turn challenge, comply with or even subvert dominant ideologies of gender. In performing their gendered selves, individuals make choices as to how to *style* themselves, though most scholars would also agree that these choices are not isolated from societal expectations, cultural models and ideologies about gender. For this reason, gender is best understood as 'a complex system of social relations and discursive practices, differentially constructed in local contexts' (Norton & Pavlenko, 2004: 504). Of course, some researchers still treat gender as a dependent variable in research, but this is the result of the researchers' underlying ontological positions that do not distinguish between sex and gender. As Davis and Skilton-Sylvester (2004: 384–385) explain, 'SLA scholars who adhere to a positivist or postpositivist research tradition that values the search for reality (or an approximation of reality) and the belief that findings can be generalized may reject constructivist, critical-feminist, and poststructuralist research paradigms as unscientific'. In contrast, research that examines gender as a complex system of social relations does not seek to make generalizations about gendered experiences, nor does it strive to predict how individuals may experience language learning based on other individuals' experiences.

Methods for Studying Gender

In recent years, the methods used to investigate gendered performances and gendered experience among L1 and L2 language users have mostly employed various approaches to discourse analysis, narrative inquiry and ethnography. Describing mostly L1 contexts, Bucholtz (2003: 43) asserts that discourse-based approaches have become the dominant methodologies in the study of gender, and the same can be said for much sociolinguistic work that investigates the gendered subjectivities of multilingual and L2 speakers. Across L1 and L2 contexts, discourse-based studies also draw on social theories to provide explanatory power to the analyses. For example, Bucholtz and Hall (2004) provide a comprehensive framework for the study of gender and sexuality, drawing on the theoretical concepts of Michel de Certeau to explore how speakers use *tactics of intersubjectivity* to claim gender and sexual identities in discourse. Bucholtz and Hall

(2004: 494) describe these tactics as 'the acts of individuals and groups who do not have access to broader power structures' that position the self and others, and they provide three sets of paired tactics speakers use. Through tactics of *adequation* and *distinction*, speakers construct themselves and others as being sufficiently similar to or different from an object or another speaker(s). Through the tactics of *authentication* and *denaturalization*, speakers can claim how real or false one's identity is. Finally, through *authorization* and *illegitimation*, speakers may endorse or discredit particular social identities, thereby co-legitimating the larger institutional power structures that constrain which identities are culturally sanctioned for a society.

To analyze the relationship between discourse and the politics of knowledge, researchers often make use of various types of *critical discourse analysis* (CDA) to analyze how power relations are encoded in texts and how individuals produce and consume such texts. The bulk of CDA work has focused largely on the analysis of written texts, but it has also been fruitfully applied to other types of data, including interviews, focus-groups and classroom discourse (e.g. Bergvall & Remlinger, 1996; Cahnmann *et al.*, 2005). CDA and critical approaches to representation have also been used to analyze gender representations in textbooks (Martinez-Roldan, 2005; Shardakova & Pavlenko, 2004; Sunderland *et al.*, 2001).

Researchers who focus on the discursive production of identity in talk take a range of microanalytic approaches, including interactional sociolinguistics (IS), ethnomethodology (EM) and conversation analysis (CA) (see chapter by Sidnell, this volume) and narrative inquiry. IS studies often examine misunderstanding in naturally occurring talk by investigating the underlying systems, which produce different inferences among speakers from different backgrounds. Tannen's (1990, 1994) work is an example of IS, for it treats men and women as belonging to separate 'cultures', and it asserts that men and women have different ways of interpreting one another's talk. EM and CA studies also investigate the ways that individuals perform gendered identities (e.g. Edley & Wetherell, 1997; Kitzinger, 2005, 2007; West & Zimmerman, 1987). Unlike poststructuralist or IS work, EM and CA researchers who use these approaches require that gender (and any other social identities) must be shown to be a concern of the interactants in the data, rather than an interest of the analyst.

Also under the umbrella of discourse studies, narrative inquiry is emerging as an insightful methodology in sociolinguistic studies of gender as a way to better understand how men and women think and feel about their experiences interacting with others, and how they discursively construct their perspectives (Bamberg *et al.*, 2006; Pavlenko, 2007). Most narrative inquiry is carried out through interviews with the researcher, but diary studies, autobiographies and web-based technologies also provide sources for narrative data. Researchers who are more interested in understanding the histories, lived experiences and longitudinal experience of individuals take a holistic approach to language and gender by employing ethnography in their work. Ethnography normally involves long-term commitment to a field site so that researchers may develop deep under-standings of the lived experiences of the people they study. Ethnographic methods include observation and field notes, interviews, focus groups, document collection and recording of interaction (Denzin & Lincoln, 2003; Richards, 2003). This work often takes a critical perspective on language and power, and differential access to resources, including language learn-ing opportunities.

In the next section, I review ethnographic and narrative-based research that focuses on how gender identities are shaped by structural constraints and obstacles that learners face when negotiating access to their desired communities of practice. This research shows how learners' access to the target language and culture is mediated by gendered identities and other forces including power differentials, race, socioeconomic background and cultural differences between L1 and L2 communities.

Access to Language Learning Opportunities

Individuals experience differential access to institutionalized and infor-mal language-learning opportunities in gendered ways, particularly in the case of immigrant populations. The issue of access makes Lave and Wenger's (1991) framework of *communities of practice* a particularly useful theoretical model for describing how newcomers to any community find avenues for participation and enculturation into the community. In their model, newcomers gain access through *legitimate peripheral participation*, the term Lave and Wenger (1991: 29) use to 'draw attention to the point that learners inevitably participate in communities of practitioners and that the mastery of knowledge and skill requires newcomers to move toward full participation in the sociocultural practices of a community'. While positive experiences can influence learners' interest in language learning as a pathway toward belonging, negative experiences as well as structural and cultural constraints can be imposing obstacles for many language learners, particularly women. Like newcomers to any commu-nity, language learners often experience a tension at the axis between social structures such as race relations and immigration policies and their own situated participation in society. Some are able to navigate this nexus with success, but many struggle in the process. Eckert and McConnell-Ginet (1992) conceptualize gender as the result of one's engagement in a community of practice, where gender is the product of the interaction between language and other semiotic systems, including dress, free-time activities and peer networks.

Much research on language learners focuses on how they access oppor-tunities to learn and to use their L2 in the face of societal structures such as patriarchy, economic class divisions and poverty, racism, and anti-immigration sentiments. This literature often employs a feminist post-structuralist framework, an approach that seeks to challenge male domination, improve the lives of women, and interrogate the role of dis-course in the (re)production of inequitable gender relations. While post-structuralist research is sometimes found to lack a critical perspective toward oppressed groups, feminist post-structuralism explicitly focuses on structural and coercive power relations that negatively affect women (e.g. Cameron, 1992, 1997; Weedon, 1987). Most studies that explore how indi-viduals negotiate structural and material difficulties as they intersect with gendered relations have been conducted in North America on female immi-grants and refugees, whereas studies that examine how individuals negoti-ate gender discourses have concentrated on a wider range of populations.

Negotiating structural and material constraints

Norton's (2000; Peirce, 1995) research on immigrant women in Canada illustrates very well how learners navigate their experiences between rather fixed social structures and their own capacity as individuals in order to gain a sense of agency in English. Through her longitudinal anal-ysis of the women's diary entries, Norton describes how the women were often silenced due to their marginal positions and their lack of access to opportunities to use English with the people around them. She pays par-ticular attention to the ways in which the women develop varying degrees of investment in English language learning as an avenue for claiming 'the right to speak' (Peirce, 1995: 25). Some women in Norton's study were able to claim legitimacy as English speakers over time. For example, Eva, an immigrant from Poland worked at a fast food restaurant, where all of her coworkers were Anglophone Canadians. However, Eva did not feel she had access to these speakers because of her low-status job. At the beginning of Norton's study, Eva stated, 'I didn't talk to them, and they didn't ask me, maybe they think I'm just like – because I had to do the worst type of work there. It's normal' (Norton, 2000: 62). After several months, however, Eva managed to change her coworkers' perception of her through activities outside the workplace, where she was able to offer symbolic resources such as transportation. She also made a lot of effort to join in conversations with coworkers, and she spent time studying how her coworkers spoke to customers so that she could emulate their ways of interacting. In other words, Eva found ways to overcome her marginal status, and her investment in English provided her with a new sense of legitimacy as an employee at the restaurant.

Not all participants in Norton's study experienced the ability to overcome their marginalized status through their own effort. Another participant, Martina, initially expressed an interest to invest in English as a pathway to improved economic conditions, but she later expressed the view that employers' desire for Canadian experience seemed to be just as important. Martina's low-paying job as a cashier gave her little opportunity to use English, and her social network did not include English speakers. Felicia, another participant who did not experience easy access to English, attributed her experiences to discrimination. Instead of investing her energy in English as a way to enter Canadian networks, Felicia retained a strong connection with other immigrants from her home country, Peru, and described herself as 'a foreigner person who lives here by accident' (Norton, 2000: 56).

Frequently, individuals who do obtain access to language learning opportunities experience gendered constraints in their pursuit of employment. Warriner (2004, 2007) found that community-based adult educational institutions in the United States often linked English with economic opportunity and social mobility, but that such ideologies of English conflicted with many of the narratives she obtained from Sudanese refugee women enrolled in these classes. Though these women were strongly motivated to improve their English so that they could work in order to provide for their families, they often found that the jobs they were guided toward by social service agencies were of the lowest-paying kind. The jobs often did not require much English, despite the fact that they had completed the highest level ESL classes, and in some cases, their GED. Other research on adult education elsewhere in the United States reveals a tendency to position ESL learners in subordinate roles that perpetuate their already disadvantaged socioeconomic status (e.g. Auerbach & Burgess, 1985; Menard-Warwick, 2008; Skilton-Sylvester, 2002).

Finding adequate and affordable childcare is another responsibility that typically falls on women's shoulders. Warriner (2004) reports that refugee women she interviewed often struggled to find employment with reasonable hours which would allow them to look after their children, and that some of them were the sole providers for large families. Though the women were often fairly proficient in English, they frequently struggled to navigate the network of social services that would provide them with information about affordable options. On the other hand, options such as daycare may be deemed inappropriate for some newcomers. Based on her studies on immigrant mothers in Canada, Kouritzin (2000) found that some of the women's opportunities to enroll in English classes were constrained by male-dominated power structures in their families. For example, Deljit, an Indian woman, was not allowed by her husband to put her children in childcare so that she could learn English, for he expressed the view that 'only family should take care of family' (Kouritzin, 2000: 21).

At work, L2 learners may or may not have opportunities to develop their second language. Immigrants with low proficiency in English often work low-paying jobs where they are not afforded further opportunity to develop their English ability, and because they need to keep working in order to support their families, they sometimes feel they cannot take time away from work to take classes. Many Portuguese women in Goldstein's (1997, 2001) studies of workplace interaction in Canada spoke only Portuguese in their factory jobs and had little opportunity to develop their English outside of work. Similarly, Gordon (2004) found that Laotian female refugees in the United States held jobs that only required very low levels of English proficiency; however, many of the women she interviewed reported shifts in their gendered subjectivities as a result of greater access to economic independence. Gordon also found that their roles as mothers often provided them with larger social networks for developing their English than their husbands experienced, and that their higher levels of access to English eventually led to greater proficiency.

In one of the few studies of a male immigrant's experience in the United States, Menard-Warwick (2006a) describes the case of Jorge, a Guatemalan immigrant living in California, whose story reveals another kind of constraint facing many immigrant men: the possibility of physical injury in the workplace. Latino men in the United States are 33% more likely than men of other ethnicities to be injured in the workplace, and immigrants like Jorge experience the highest risk (Menard-Warwick, 2006a: 359). Julio worked in Spanish-medium contexts at a carwash, as a janitor, and then as a sandblaster until a car chassis fell on him in an accident at work. His ensuing loss of physical ability led him to invest in English language classes and computer training as a source of future income.

Other societal structures impact learning opportunities in more subtle ways, such as how individuals have been socialized toward education and whether their families valued school-based forms of literacy. Menard-Warwick (2005) describes how Latina immigrants invest in English education for themselves and for their children in rather different ways, due to their varying experiences with literacy. While most parents strongly value education for their children, studies of immigrant families in the United States such as Valdés (1996) show that many who live in poverty must place greater importance on economic survival. Many parents also become concerned with maintaining their children's linguistic and cultural heritage and may react negatively to seeing their children become majority-language dominant and lose interest in their family's cultural practices (e.g. Kouritzin, 2000; Menard-Warwick, 2005).

Studies on how societal structures intersect with gender in language learning outside of North America are few in number. Research on literacy development in multilingual contexts has yielded much insight regarding the gender inequality girls and women face in gaining access to languages of socioeconomic power. For example, Egbo (2000) describes the historical and contemporary societal constraints facing Nigerian women in their access to education, and hence, their access to literacy development in L1s and L2s, including English. As in many other British-colonized nations, colonial educational authorities in Nigeria established a preference for educating males over females that had long-lasting effects. Nigerian women also face patriarchal structures that promote marriage over schooling and which emphasize domestic roles rather than the development of professional identities. In addition, policy-making bodies are male-dominated in Nigeria, and hence, women tend not to participate in creating policies that affect their own lives. Moreover, tuition-based education required by the structural adjustment policies of the International Monetary Fund has made it nearly impossible for many families to afford school fees for all of their children. In the face of hard economic choices, boys are more likely to be given the opportunity to go to school. Similar findings have been reported in research on Kenya (Kiluva-Ndunda, 2001) and Tanzania (Vavrus, 2002).

Even in resource-rich nations, girls and women face patriarchal obstacles that block their access to opportunities for L2 acquisition and use. Kobayashi (2007a, 2007b) investigates how Japanese corporate structures delimit 'non-elite working women's' opportunities to access English education through overseas programs sponsored by these companies. Many women do not have access to company-sponsored English education in Japan since the almost entirely male elite business and engineering employees who work for large companies are the ones targeted for company-funded English education. Kobayashi (2007a) found that in spite of this circumstance, many such women paid their own way to do study-abroad programs in Canada, often for personal reasons involving expanding their intercultural horizons, rather than for enhancing their job prospects in Japan.

Beyond the structural constraints language learners may encounter outside classroom walls, gender discrimination in classrooms can also act as an obstacle for language learning and development. Though teachers are largely unconscious of it, both male and female teachers frequently give unequal attention to male and female students in classrooms. Many teachers tend to call on male students in classrooms more frequently, and male students often speak up in class without much prompting from the teacher. The result is greater opportunities for male students to participate in question-and-answer routines, which means more opportunities for practice in the target language. Unequal opportunity to verbally participate has been found in studies of students of all ages in the United States. In a study of over 100 classrooms, Sadker and Sadker (1985) found that on average, boys spoke three times as much as girls, and that boys were eight times more likely to respond to the teacher without being called on. Though they are typically unaware of it, male and female teachers tend to give more of their attention to male students in all aspects of classroom talk (AAUW, 1992; Spender, 1980). When teaching boys, greater attention is often given to them for disciplinary reasons, but researchers working in L1 settings have found that both male and female teachers also solicit answers to questions for content-based learning in unequal ways (Croll, 1985; Spender, 1980; Swann, 1998). Boys in L1 settings also produce more words per utterance than do girls, which gives them more of the verbal space in classrooms, and they often tack turns onto other students' responses (Sunderland, 2004; Swann, 1998). In second language settings, these gender discourses in classrooms are often complicit in silencing girls; when these discourses intersect with racial discourses such as the 'model minority', which stereotypes Asian students in western settings as diligent, quiet and rule-abiding (Julé, 2004; McKay & Wong, 1996), these 'quiet' girls are not encouraged to contribute to the classroom dialogue.

Pedagogical practices that engage with structural constraints

Teaching practices that strive to balance male and female students' participation in classrooms can and should be a goal for all teachers, and the first step toward reaching this goal is greater reflection on one's teaching practices. Teachers can develop strategies such as alternating between male and female students when soliciting student responses, or organizing students into groups so that participation is maximized. Swann (1998) found that teachers' eye contact was a crucial determinant in whether boys or girls were selected to answer questions. It was often the case that teachers would finish their question just at the moment when their eyes settled on a male student; moreover, if they finished a question with their gaze on a female student, it was found that the female students would take the opportunity to answer. Finally, in classrooms where oral skill development is not the primary goal, teachers can value other forms of participation, such as written work, equally when considering participation grades for students.

Although structural constraints in society may seem beyond teachers' control, teachers can and should draw on the lived experiences of their students to develop materials and activities (Auerbach & Wallerstein, 1987; Norton & Pavlenko, 2004; Weinstein, 1984). Norton and Pavlenko (2004) describe programs developed for immigrant populations that take problem-posing approaches and which provide learners with the opportunity to conduct research on topics pertinent to them, including housing issues, use of English and their mother tongues and racial prejudice (Frye, 1999; Rivera, 1999). To address students' lived experiences, Menard-Warwick (2004, 2006b) advocates that adult ESL learners be invited to share their life stories orally and in written form, provided they are comfortable sharing their autobiographical details. Her work with adult learners of ESL shows many learners come to invest in English when they make English the language of their lives and of their communities. Menard-Warwick (2006b) documents Latina immigrants' enthusiasm for writing in English and producing short narratives that focus on their personal histories and their families. Similarly, Norton (2000) found that sharing diary entries gave adult learners the opportunity to develop their oral skills and to learn new vocabulary as well. Practical materials for ESL classes are described in Morgan (1998), which provides discussion prompts that encourage learners to talk about issues they face in their own communities, including conflicting perspectives on gender roles. Similarly, Weinstein describes how to draw on learner's lives as curriculum on her website, and she provides links to ESL lessons and handouts, which could easily include gender roles on topics such as health literacy, speaking up to landlords and racial profiling (http://www.gailweinstein.net/).

It is important to note that the purpose of sharing experiences may not always be to seek immediate solutions to challenging problems, but rather, to offer opportunities to develop the target language while engaging in topics that are pertinent to students' lives. Writing in the target language can offer learners the opportunity to make their L2 more personal, particularly if the topics are autobiographical. Though solutions are hard to come by, teachers can develop curricula that relate more directly to the issues that women face in their roles as mothers and wives striving to provide for their families, and which their skills-oriented English classes often do not address. For example, Warriner (2007) suggests that more educators need to reconsider skills-based lessons and to develop pedagogical practices that might enable immigrant and refugee women to navigate their social interactions more successfully and to locate the resources which will help them and their families.

At a very practical level, Kouritzin (2000: 30) reminds us that we need to be more understanding of immigrant and refugee learners' absences, lateness and ambivalence in studying English, based on an understanding of the various difficulties they face, including the contradictory feelings they may have toward the language they are studying. She also asserts that educators ought to find ways in classrooms and beyond to encourage women to create and maintain support systems with other women, 'stressing not so much "survival English" as "integrated survival"' (Kouritzin, 2003: 30). Given the high attrition rate in adult education classes, teachers need to teach English vocabulary and grammar, but they also need to consider what resources their students may need access to, and how they can help them to achieve it.

Negotiating Discourses of Gender

While social structures such as patriarchy and socioeconomic class may seem to be very obvious reasons that explain why women lack access to language education, it is also equally the case that societal expectations and beliefs about men and women circulate in the form of gender discourses, or ways of being 'male' and 'female' in the world that are largely learned unconsciously through socialization processes. Of course, these discourses are the basis of social structures such as patriarchy, which in turn acts as a structural constraint on women's lives and women's access to learning opportunities, as discussed above. However, it is important to highlight that language learning is itself shaped by these discourses, and that both men and women are affected by them. Moreover, as recent explorations of learners' identities show us, it is often the case that language learning becomes a site for challenging and transforming common-sense discourses of gender.

In the following section, I explore how learners experience different gender identities in their L2. Whether learners develop L2 identities has many implications, not only for their success in language learning, but also for their desire to affiliate with target language communities. Learners may find gender identities in the L2 context appealing, and hence their affiliation with these gendered ways of being may afford learners relative ease in learning and using their L2. Alternatively, learners' L1 gendered identities may remain the most strongly valued, potentially leading learners to resist cross-cultural adaptation of any kind.

Discursive assimilation to a new gendered identity

Much research on S/FL gender identities has explored how language learners respond to the new set of subject positions, or identity options, they encounter in their L2. Pavlenko (2001: 133) describes this experience as 'discursive assimilation, (re)positioning, and self-translation' in order to highlight the reinterpretation of the self in a new context. Pavlenko's (1998, 2001, 2005; Pavlenko & Lantolf, 2000) research has eloquently demonstrated how L2 learners in second language contexts discursively reposition themselves in their new environments amidst discourses of gender. Through analyzing language learners' autobiographies, Pavlenko (2001) showed that female immigrants often found the new gendered subject positions more favorable than in their home cultures. Former German citizen Ute Margaret Saine's perspective provides an illustration of this 'self-translation':

> Perhaps not surprisingly, many of my German girlfriends from this and later schools emigrated, like myself, to Italy, England, Brazil, France, and of course, the United States. In order to escape repression, particularly of gender. (Pavlenko, 2001: 146)

Pavlenko (2001) found that the women also experienced ambivalences and tensions because of shifting or multiple gender identities, which often became the most relevant when they discussed their intergenerational relationships. These findings show that many L2 users do not completely abandon the gender identities that they were socialized into in their home culture, but instead, that they often develop the ability to shift between gendered subjectivities, and sometimes they find themselves in between worlds. Pavlenko cites Anna Wierzbicka's narrative about her multiple identities as a Polish immigrant in Australia whose linguistic performances did not always fit in her new environment:

> ... when I was talking on the phone, from Australia, to my mother in Poland (15,000 km away), with my voice loud and excited, carrying much further than is customary in Anglo conversation, my husband would signal to me: 'Don't shout!' (Pavlenko, 2001: 136)

Studies of English language learners have shown that discursive assimilation is often based on a sense of freedom. In foreign language contexts such as Japan, the association of liberation with English is particularly salient, though much of the time it arguably remains largely imagined rather than based on lived experience. McMahill (2001) discusses a feminist class she helped to facilitate for Japanese women who found that English gave them a new 'voice' for expressing themselves without constraint. In English, they felt able to openly discuss their relationships with their mothers, their experiences with gender discrimination at work, and their responses to societal pressures to be married and raise children. Though other women who have lived in English-dominant nations such as the United States report varying degrees of empowerment through English (*cf.* Pavlenko, 2001), the women in McMahill's class treated English as a 'weapon for self-empowerment' as a way to reject patriarchy.

New gender identities among Japanese women learning English have sometimes led these women to invest in cross-cultural relationships with Anglo, English-speaking men as well. More so than providing them with job opportunities or the skills needed to participate in a globalized economy, Japanese women may learn English because of their *akogare* ('desire'), a form of romanticization and eroticization of western people and western ideas (Kelsky, 2001). This desire has been commodified in Japan in women's magazines, expressed through headlines such as '*kaigai seikatsu de mitsukeru atarashii jibun: ryugaku de jinsei wo kaeyoo* in Australia' [Finding a new self overseas: Change your life through *ryugaku* ('studying overseas') in Australia] (Piller & Takahashi, 2006: 64). The changes in life highlight vague notions of 'finding oneself' and also trying new things that cannot be experienced in Japan (Kobayashi, 2007a). However, *akogare* is also often linked to the experience of having romantic relations with white, English-speaking men. Eika, an overseas learner of English in Australia felt that a romantic relationship with an Anglo Australian man was a totally new experience:

> at first, I was surprised ... I thought 'wow, this is the Western world!' in the beginning it was ticklish and felt like it was happening to some-one else. but, I was happy, and it made me feel that I was really with a non-Asian man. the Japanese language does not have the same nuances and so it made me feel like I had been drawn into a different world. what made me happy about it most really was the sound ... the sound of 'honey, darling'. (Piller & Takahashi, 2006: 72, translation theirs)

It is interesting to note that both male and female learners of Japanese find new and appealing identities in their L2. Ohara (forthcoming) reports that many American, Chinese and Korean students at universities in the United States were able to reconstruct their gender identities in Japanese. As a result of their engagement with media, several of the male students were drawn to the Osaka dialect of Japanese, a variety associated with *yakuza* ('gangster') characters and hyper-masculinized ways of speaking. Female students were also drawn to the gender identities depicted in the media, particularly the *burikko* ('cutie') way of speaking, which is charac-terized by a high pitch and hyper-feminized vocabulary and pragmatics such as *yaaadaa*, a way to express one's dislike for something. Of course, both the *yakuza* and *burikko* gender identities are intertwined with what can be called 'youth' identities in Japan, which are by and large a product of the influence of the media. To call them gender identities alone misses the interlinked forces that produce identity options for first and second language speakers.

Resisting L2 gender identities

Another possible outcome of language learning may be that learners will resist particular L2 gender discourses. A clear example is found in Skapoulli's (2004) case study of Nadia, a teen-aged Arabic-speaking Egyptian girl who lived in Cyprus and used Cypriot Greek as her second language. Though Nadia's friends encouraged her to participate in their gendered community of practice comprised of wearing 'sexy' clothes, going to discotheques, and dating boys, she chose not to participate in these practices, and she mostly adhered to her Coptic parents' expecta-tions to be a 'moral' girl. She did not reject all aspects of a Cypriot identity, though, since she used Cypriot Greek, the primary language of young Cypriots. However, Nadia marked herself as different from her youthful peers by making more use of standard Greek than the average teenager.

As Nadia's case illustrates, learners may reject L2 gender identities because they interpret them as threatening to their first language/first cul-ture gendered self. Siegal (1996) provided one of the first illustrations of resistance to L2 gender norms in her study of Mary, a white woman from New Zealand who was learning Japanese in Japan. Mary resisted the use of honorifics and other polite forms of language that she felt violated her identity as an empowered woman. Similarly, female Japanese learners at a US university were found to resist the high pitch, which was treated as a prescriptive norm for Japanese women's language in their foreign language classrooms (Ohara, 2001). While some students felt that using a high pitch was important for fitting in with the culture, others rejected high pitch as a form of feminized performance that is dictated by a patriarchal society. One learner commented on her observations of Japanese women's speech, stating,' [...] they would use those real high voices to try to impress and make themselves look real cute for men. I decided that there was no way I wanted to do that' (Ohara, 2001: 244).

Men may also find particular gender identities threatening to their masculinities. In his memoir about his difficulty learning French, Richard Watson (1995) explains, 'I have a distinct dislike for the sound of spoken French. Many Americans do. Why? Because it is weak. For American men at least, French sounds syrupy and effeminate' (cited in Pavlenko, 2001: 147). Kissau and Wierzalis (2008) found that male secondary students in southwestern Ontario also seemed cautious about expressing their desire to study French due to its associations with gender-specific behaviors. Based on answers to questionnaires from 490 secondary students and follow-up interview data with teachers and students, they discovered that traditional views of what subjects are appropriate for boys and girls proved to be driving students' desire to study French. One of the French teachers explained, 'There's still a lot of sexist thinking that a man doesn't learn languages. A man does math or engineering, or whatever. Sexist behavior still plays a great role. Learning French, it's not perceived as a man's job' (Kissau & Wierzalis, 2008: 408).

In my own research on gender identities in the narratives of western women who use Swahili as an L2 in Tanzania (Higgins, forthcoming), I have found a fair amount of resistance to Tanzanian gender identities as well. Compared to other language learners' stories (e.g. Armour, 2001; Kinginger, 2004, 2008; Miller, 2003; Norton, 2000) in which access to the target language communities of practice were more difficult, the Tanzanian context seems to afford these L2 learners with many opportunities to cross-culturally adapt. Although they have lived in Tanzania for over a decade, the women I have interviewed have by and large not taken these opportunities up. This resistance is shown in their narratives of cross-cultural difference, particularly in how the women establish their stance toward Tanzanian gender expectations. In (1), Tatu, a Tanzanian-born, Canadian-raised Black woman, explains how her behavior in public places is often deemed non-Tanzanian. She intersperses her explanation with evaluative language (indicated in bold) that indicates a gender-based barrier to her own ability to 'become Swahili'. In the excerpt, she is describing her experiences on public transport in Tanzania in which children, who pay a discounted rate, are often prevented from taking a seat so that a full-fare paying adult can sit down.

Excerpt 1: 'A woman would not speak out like that'

T: The fact that I speak out is another thing. People don't do that.
I mean I get on the *daladala* ('bus') and if they don't want the kids to sit down and I tell them [to sit], so then I'm *mzungu* ('foreign') because I'm speaking out, **a woman would not speak out like that**. And so (.) they don't know my background. I think it has nothing to do with that – I think it's just my behavior **my mannerisms are not typical of here**. And so that's what they mean, that I've lived somewhere else foreign.

Tatu's narrative reveals a recognition of cultural difference based on gendered behaviors. She evaluates herself as distinctively non-Tanzanian through her description of what Tanzanian women would and would not do, and she describes her own behavior as atypical. Similarly, Kate, a white US citizen, commented on how gender played a role in her degree of adaptation to conventional Tanzanian living in which women are entirely responsible for domestic concerns. Kate's status as a western woman married to a Tanzanian man prompted me to ask about her gendered behavior at home. She explained that her husband had probably changed more than she had, and she evaluates this circumstance as counter-intuitive through her frame 'even though'. Through framing her husband's transformation as unusual, Kate positions herself as someone who is aware of the local gender expectations but simultaneously as someone who resists them.

(2) 'Half and half' gender roles

C: Do you share those kinds of [domestic] duties, or has it become female, male?

K: We have talked about it. We have a housekeeper now, housegirl now, who does most of that during the day. There was a time when we didn't have, and it was half and half.

C: But it was possible to achieve equal work. It wasn't a cultural barrier?

K: It was something we had to talk about and agree upon. Our lifestyle now is sort of half and half (i.e. half western, half Tanzanian). **Even though** we're living in Tanzania, he's maybe changed his culture like twice more than I have (.) but I think it's mostly the gender things.

It is important to reiterate that gender identity cannot be analyzed without considering the role of other social identities. In the case of the women I interviewed, another identity that became very significant was similar to that of the intercultural couples in Piller's (2002) study, who identified as 'citizens of the world', as well as 'intercultural ambassadors' and even 'intercultural experts'. Hence, rather than having to choose between a North American or a Tanzanian self, the women in my study strongly identified as people who preferred to live and work in the in-between and transnational spaces of international experiences and intercultural relationships. It is interesting to note that Tatu plans to stay in Tanzania for a few years and then move to another country for more work experience as a teacher at international schools. Kate expects to move to a country that is neither her own home, nor the home of her husband. As she explained, 'sometimes it would be good to have a third country where it's not my home and it's not his home, just have a neutral, where we both, neither'.

These studies of resistance to and desire for gender reconstruction are largely on individuals who have a potentially great deal of access to the L2. It is not surprising that the concept of identity reconstruction has been mostly applied to second language settings or study abroad sojourns in which learners have the opportunity to reconstruct their selves in response to cultural differences and new frames of gendered experience. While McMahill's research on Japanese women studying English and Ohara's study of university students in the United States studying Japanese reveals that people in foreign language contexts may also experience identity reconstruction, the opportunities for discursive repositioning of the self are indeed rare in foreign language settings.

The role of gender discourses in classrooms

While direct engagements with the members of the target culture clearly afford opportunities for re-evaluating and reframing one's gender identities, classrooms are common sites for engaging with gender discourses as well. For adult learners, community education classes are often the main source of gender representations in the L2, particularly for adults who work in jobs that do not require use of the majority language. In a study of adult education classes, Menard-Warwick (2008) describes how female learners of English in the United States are positioned in their language classes, noting that much of the time, pre-conceived identities such as 'mother' and 'homemaker' dictate the content of the teaching. While some women contest this positioning, it is often the case that younger learners lack the awareness to do so. Hruska (2004) provides the example of gendered practices in a kindergarten class in New England in the United States in which ESL children's access to English-speaking peers was shaped by gender ideologies. She found Latino male language learners struggled to participate in the social hierarchy that the boys had established through their competitive verbal behavior in the class and in their lively participation in extracurricular sports. Because the ESL students were bussed to the school from some distance, and because sports some-times required a financial investment from their parents, many of the working-class Latino ESL students were not able to become insider mem-bers in their peer groups. These circumstances generally limited English-learning opportunities, unless gendered norms were somehow disrupted. For example, Hruska explains that Francisco, a small, Latino male student with an easy going temperament, appeared to benefit from his positioning as a 'non-competitive' boy since he was not welcomed by other boys in the class; however, he was able to interact extensively with the girls, including the English-speaking girls.

For young L2 learners, subject-matter classrooms are often the key con-texts where they experience gender discourses in the majority language. Appearance, clothing styles, body size and ability in sports can all be criti-cal aspects of gender identity for school-aged boys and girls of all ages. While these factors are shaped by 'structural' constraints in many ways, these ways of being male and female are really enmeshed in the discourses of what is 'cool', what is 'normative' and what is 'acceptable' among ado-lescents. Whether one fits in with particular sub-cultures in schools has tremendous implications for whether one can obtain access to English-speaking peers. McKay and Wong (1996) illustrate how two Chinese boys who had immigrated to California experienced radically different posi-tionings and how they shaped their acquisition of English. While both were interested in sports, it was only the larger and more athletic of the two who developed friendships with non-Chinese students at the school and hence, who developed his oral English proficiency at a much faster pace.

Across an array of schooling contexts, children and adults are exposed to gender discourses, which shape their understandings of who they are. Since adults often have more power to make decisions about their own lives, they likely experience greater agency in their ability to resist certain positionings, as was the case in Menard-Warwick's research on adult immigrants in California. However, for school-aged children, there seems to be very little room for resistance due to peer pressure and the lack of other available subject positions, such as 'developing bilingual' or 'expert Chinese speaker' in many North American schools. Next, I discuss what educators can do to address the role of gender discourses in language learning across a range of contexts.

Pedagogical applications for gender discourses

There is a multitude of ways that teachers from kindergarten through adult education can bring gender discourses explicitly into their class-rooms. First, language teachers in particular need to be familiar with the impact of gender identities and gender discourses on L2 speakers' linguis-tic choices. As was demonstrated above in the discussion of linguistic varieties, learners of languages such as Japanese may value nonstandard-ized dialects over prescribed forms, or they may choose not to raise their pitch to a 'normative' level (Ohara, 2001, forthcoming). These identity choices can be interpreted negatively by teachers, particularly those who only value students' efforts when they come close to the prescriptive norms for the 'standard' version of the target language. However, given the reality of dialect diversity and gender identity diversity (also present among L1 speakers), it is important to allow for a greater range of expres-sive choices in language learning contexts. This may be achieved through providing more materials on language diversity and gender identity to pre-service and in-service language teachers through teacher training. Of course, teachers also need to ensure that their students are making informed choices, and that they are able to consider the ramifications of their choices when interacting with speakers who may or may not appre-ciate how they have chosen to gender identify in their L2.

At the level of curriculum planning, gender discourses can also become a topic of exploration and activities in classrooms. In fact, asking students to make comparisons between L1 and L2 gender identities is compatible with *intercultural pedagogy*, an approach to teaching culture and cultural differences developed by Michael Byram and his colleagues for over a decade (e.g. Byram, 1997; Byram *et al.*, 2001; Byram & Zarate, 1995). Intercultural pedagogy strives to raise intercultural awareness (ICA) among learners with regard to similarities and differences among their first and second cultures. Rather than simply comparing and contrasting, however, which is often how multiculturalism is brought into classrooms, ICA involves reflecting on why one's L1 or home culture is the way it is and trying to make sense of how and why it differs with the L2 or new culture. Through ICA, learners practice their ability to relativize their own value systems, beliefs and behaviors and to develop the ability to see their own cultures from the perspective an outsider might have. While ICA has not focused specifically on gender in an extensive way, it does provide an approach that could easily be applied to gender identities. Through jour-nal entries, role plays, and small-group discussions, gender identity in one's L1 and L2 might be explored as a way for learners to reflect on their lived experiences and to try to obtain outsider perspectives on their own L1 gender identities. Some learners' thoughts about their L1 and L2 gender identities may be quite personal, as was the case with Piller and Takahashi's (2006) study, and so any language learning tasks or activities would need to take into account learners' willingness to speak or write about these topics, and their comfort level with the other members of the class.

Another way that teachers can tackle the important role of gender dis-courses in their own classrooms is to employ critical pedagogy approaches. Though there are many definitions of critical pedagogy, it is generally understood as a teaching approach that helps students to question and critique power relations and which has as its goal a social and educational vision of justice and equality (Freire, 1968/1970; Giroux, 1992; McLaren, 1989). Taking a critical pedagogy approach, teachers can challenge gender stereotypes for all populations by addressing the stereotypes about gender that students may have and making them the subject of discussion and the topic of assignments. These topics can also be addressed in classrooms if and when they emerge as relevant. For example, Hruska (2004) provides examples of how she and a co-teacher worked to draw kindergarten children's attention in sharing time discussions to the gender stereotypes that had become the source of teasing and boundary-drawing between the girls and boys during recreational play. Through asking questions about what boys and girls can do (e.g. climb trees), the teachers attempted to challenge discourses of inequality and exclusion that were held by the boys with regard to what the girls were capable of.

In the context of Japan, Simon-Maeda (2004) encouraged female students at a women's junior college to produce journals about their own experiences and then used them as a way to address the sexism that was often documented in their writing. Saft and Ohara (2004) designed lessons that asked Japanese university students to reflect on gendered words (such as *joi* 'female doctor') and readings on the role of women in society in positions such as *ofisu redii* ('office lady'). Some students resisted critical reflection, and male students tended to be less open to critically reflecting on male privilege and patriarchy than female students. This response is understandable since critical reflection on these topics could be seen as disempowering males. However, if teachers and students can find way to highlight the notions of equality and justice, such resistance might be lessened.

Finally, sexual orientation is another arena that can be addressed using critical pedagogy. Though there is very little research in sociolinguistics that examines links between sexual identities and language education, gay/lesbian/transgender identities are just as relevant to include in activities and assignments that invite students to reflect on who they are and how their sense of self impacts their opportunities to develop their L2s. Examples of such critical pedagogy are few in number, but they include Nelson (2004), who describes how a teacher used lesbian/gay themes to explore cultural perspectives in her ESL class in a community college in the United States. Through activities such as teaching modal verbs by comparing students' interpretations of women walking arm-in-arm, the teacher was able to begin to develop intercultural awareness with the students as they shared their understandings of the scenario. Another example comes from Benesch (1999), who describes how she introduced her ESL students in the United States to the tragic story of Mathew Shepard, a gay college student who was beaten to death in Laramie, Wyoming in 1998. Benesch facilitated a dialogic investigation of students' beliefs about sexualities by using questions to try to encourage learning by drawing on the students' various perspectives, and to probe the underlying reasons for some of the students' homophobia. She explains that a major challenge 'was to ask the students to consider the social origins of their fears as well as alternatives to killing or beating up someone as a way of dealing with those fears' (1999: 578).

Just as the teacher in Nelson's study found a way to encourage her students to critically assess their own inferences about gay and lesbian individuals, Benesch and Byram also advocate for deeper reflection on how we as individuals respond to social behaviors differently, and how our responses are very much shaped by the societies in which we are socialized. To put some distance between students' responses to gender identities, teachers can plan activities which encourage 'dialogic thinking' (Benesch, 1999), a practice which has a lot in common with Byram's intercultural pedagogy approach. Both approaches ask students to consider what presuppositions underlie dominant perspectives, and both ask them to challenge hegemonic views by listening to an array of voices in the analysis of their presuppositions. These practices of decentering and relativizing individuals' interpretations of gendered and sexual identities are productive ways forward in educational contexts.

Suggestions for further reading

Cameron, D. (2005) Language, gender and sexuality: Current issues and new directions. *Applied Linguistics* 26 (4), 482–502.
This state-of-the-art article reviews changes in paradigms, methodologies, and target populations in gender and sexuality studies since 1990. Cameron outlines a shift from a *difference* to a *diversity* approach to gender and sexuality, and she situates this shift within the postmodern turn in discourse and identity studies.

Davis, K.A. and Skilton-Sylvester, E. (guest editors) (2004) *TESOL Quarterly* 38 (3), 377–538.
This special topic issue provides a comprehensive overview of research on gender in contexts of English language learning, followed by research reports in a range of language teaching and learning contexts. The studies include an exploration of gender among university English teachers in Japan, among Laotian adult immigrants in the United States and Laos, and in a kindergarten classroom in the United States that includes Spanish-speaking bilingual children.

Menard-Warwick, J. (2009) *Gendered Identities and Immigrant Language Learning*. Bristol: Multilingual Matters.
This ethnographic study explores the experiences of immigrant adults from Latin America in the context of an adult ESL program in California, in the United States. The author uses case studies and classroom observations to demonstrate how gendered identities constrain opportunities for investing in English for themselves and their children.

Norton, B. and Pavlenko, A. (eds) (2004) *Gender and English Language Learners*. Alexandria, VA: TESOL.
This edited volume explores the fluid nature of gender in multilingual classrooms around the world. Taking a sociocultural perspective, the contributors describe gender inequities in classrooms and ways to address them through innovative pedagogical practices. The majority of chapters focus on North America and

Japan, but the volume also includes chapters on educational contexts in Uganda and Malaysia.

Pavlenko, A., Blackledge, A., Piller, I. and Teutsch-Dwyer, M. (eds) (2001) *Multilingualism, Second Language Learning and Gender*. Berlin: Mouton de Gruyter. This edited volume explores the role of gender in second language learning, teaching, and use within a feminist post-structuralist framework. The contributions examine how gender intersects with power, ideologies, and multilingualism in a range of contexts, including workplace settings, study abroad language learning, and university and community education classrooms.

References

American Association of University Women (1992) *The AAUW Report: How Schools Shortchange Girls*. Washington, DC: Wellesley College Center for Research on Women, AAUW Education Foundation and National Education Association.

Armour, W.S. (2001) 'This guy is Japanese stuck in a white man's body': A discussion of meaning making, identity slippage, and cross-cultural adaptation. *Journal of Multilingual & Multicultural Development* 22, 1–18.

Auerbach, E. and Burgess, D. (1985) The hidden curriculum of survival ESL. *TESOL Quarterly* 19 (3), 475–495.

Auerbach, E. and Wallerstein, N. (1987) *ESL for Action: Problem Posing at Work, a Freire Inspired Teacher's Guide for Workplace and Workplace Health Issues*. Reading, MA: Addison-Wesley.

Bamberg, M., de Fina, A. and Schiffrin, D. (eds) (2006) *Selves and Identities in Narratives and Discourse*. Amsterdam: Benjamins.

Benesch, S. (1999) Thinking critically, thinking dialogically. *TESOL Quarterly* 33 (3), 573–579.

Bergvall, V., Bing, J. and Freed, A. (eds) (1996) *Rethinking Language and Gender Research: Theory and Practice*. London: Longman.

Bergvall, V. and Remlinger, K. (1996) Reproduction, resistance, and gender in educational discourse: The role of critical discourse analysis. *Discourse & Society* 7 (4), 453–579.

Bucholtz, M. (2003) Theories of discourse as theories of gender: Discourse analysis in language and gender studies. In J. Holmes and M. Meyerhoff (eds) *The Handbook of Language and Gender* (pp. 43–68). Malden, MA: Blackwell.

Bucholtz, M. and Hall, K. (2004) Theorizing identity in language and sexuality research. *Language in Society* 33 (4), 501–547.

Butler, J. (1990) *Gender Trouble: Feminism and the Subversion of Identity*. New York: Routledge.

Byram, M. (1997) *Teaching and Assessing Intercultural Communicative Competence*. Clevedon: Multilingual Matters.

Byram, M., Nichols, A. and Stevens, D. (eds) (2001) *Developing Intercultural Competence in Practice*. Clevedon: Multilingual Matters.

Byram, M. and Zarate, G. (1995) *Young People Facing Difference: Some Proposals for Teachers*. Strasbourg: Council of Europe.

Cahnmann, M., Rymes, B. and Souto-Manning, M. (2005) Using Critical Discourse Analysis to understand and facilitate identification processes of bilingual adults becoming teachers. *Critical Inquiry in Language Studies* 2 (4), 195–213.

Cameron, D. (1992) *Feminism and Linguistic Theory*. London: Macmillan.

Cameron, D. (1997) Demythologizing sociolinguistics. In N. Coupland and A. Jaworski (eds) *Sociolinguistics: A Reader and Coursebook* (pp. 55–67). Houndmills: Macmillan.

Cameron, D. (2005) Language, gender and sexuality: Current issues and new directions. *Applied Linguistics* 26 (4), 482–502.

Cameron, D. and Kulick, D. (2003) *Language and Sexuality.* Cambridge: Cambridge University Press.

Cheshire, J. (1978) Present tense verbs in Reading English. In P. Trudgill (ed.) *Sociolinguistic Patterns in British English* (pp. 52–68). London: Edward Arnold.

Coates, J. (1997) *Language and Gender: A Reader.* Oxford: Blackwell.

Crawford, M. (1995) *Talking Difference: On Gender and Language.* Thousand Oaks, CA: Sage.

Croll, P. (1985) Teacher interaction with individual male and female pupils in junior age classrooms. *Educational Research* 27 (3), 220–223.

Davis, K.A. and Skilton-Sylvester, E. (2004) Looking back, taking stock, moving forward: Investigating gender in TESOL. *TESOL Quarterly* 38 (3), 381–404.

de Beauvoir, S. ([1949]1972) *The Second Sex* (H.M. Parshley, trans.). New York: Penguin.

Denzin, N. and Lincoln, Y. (eds) (2003) *The Landscape of Qualitative Research: Theories and Issues.* London: Sage.

Eckert, P. and McConnell-Ginet, S. (1992) Think practically and look locally: Language and gender as community-based practice. *Annual Review of Anthropology* 21, 461–490.

Edley, N. and Wetherell, M. (1997) Jockeying for position: The construction of masculine identities. *Discourse & Society* 8, 203–217.

Egbo, B. (2000) *Gender, Literacy and Life Chances in Sub-Saharan Africa.* Clevedon: Multilingual Matters.

Freed, A. (1992) We understand perfectly: A critique of Tannen's view of cross-sex communication. In K. Hall, M. Bucholtz and B. Moonwomon (eds) *Locating Power: Proceedings of the Second Berkeley Women and Language Conference* (Vol. 1), (pp. 144–152). Berkeley, CA: Berkeley Women and Language Group.

Freire, P. ([1968]1970) *Pedagogy of the Oppressed* (M.B. Ramos, trans.). New York: Continuum.

Frye, D. (1999) Participatory education as a critical framework for an immigrant women's ESL class. *TESOL Quarterly* 33, 501–513.

Giroux, H. (1992) *Border Crossings: Cultural Workers and the Politics of Education.* New York: Routledge.

Goldstein, T. (1997) *Two Languages at Work: Bilingual Life on the Production Floor.* Berlin: Mouton de Gruyter.

Goldstein, T. (2001) Researching women's language practices in multilingual workplaces. In A. Pavlenko, A. Blackledge, I. Piller and M. Teutsch-Dwyer (eds) *Multilingualism, Second Language Learning, and Gender* (pp. 79–98). Berlin: Mouton de Gruyter.

Gordon, D. (2004) "I'm tired. You clean and cook": Shifting gender identities and second language socialization. *TESOL Quarterly* 38 (3), 437–457.

Hall, K. and Bucholtz, M. (eds) (1995) *Gender Articulated: Language and the Socially Constructed Self.* New York: Routledge.

Higgins, C. (forthcoming) "You're such a Swahili!": Western women's resistance to identity slippage in Tanzania. In C. Higgins (ed.) *Negotiating the Self in a Second Language: Identity Formation in a Globalizing World.* Berlin: Mouton de Gruyter.

Holmes, J. and Meyerhoff, M. (eds) (2003) *The Handbook of Language and Gender.* Oxford: Blackwell.

Hruska, B. (2004) Constructing gender in an English dominant kindergarten: Implications for second language learners. *TESOL Quarterly* 38, 459–484.

Johnson, S. and Meinhof, U. (eds) (1997) *Language and Masculinity.* Oxford: Blackwell.

Julé, A. (2004) Speaking in silence: A case study of a Punjabi girl. In B. Norton and A. Pavlenko (eds) *Gender and English Language Learners* (pp. 69–80). Arlington, VA: TESOL.

Kelsky, K. (2001) *Women on the Verge: Japanese Women, Western Dreams*. Durham and London: Duke University Press.

Kiluva-Ndunda, M.M. (2001) *Women's Agency and Educational Policy: The Experiences of the Women of Kilome*. Kenya. Albany, NY: SUNY Press.

Kinginger, C. (2004) Alice doesn't live here any-more: Foreign language learning and identity reconstruction. In A. Pavlenko and A. Blackledge (eds) *Negotiation of Identities in Multilingual Contexts* (pp. 219–242). Clevedon: Multilingual Matters.

Kinginger, C. (2008) *Language Learning in Study Abroad: Case Studies of Americans in France. The Modern Language Journal Monograph Series*. Mahwah, NJ: Erlbaum.

Kissau, S. and Wierzalis, E. (2008) Gender identity and homophobia: The impact on adolescent males studying French. *Modern Language Journal* 92 (3), 402–413.

Kitzinger, C. (2005) Speaking as a heterosexual: (How) does sexuality matter for talk-in-interaction. *Research on Language and Social Interaction* 38 (3), 221–265.

Kitzinger, C. (2007) Is 'woman' always relevantly gendered? *Gender and Language* 1 (1), 39–40.

Kobayashi, Y. (2007a) Japanese working women and English study abroad. *World Englishes* 26 (1), 62–71.

Kobayashi, Y. (2007b) TEFL policy as part of stratified Japan and beyond. *TESOL Quarterly* 41 (3), 566–571.

Kouritzin, S. (2000) Immigrant mothers redefine access to ESL classes: Contradiction and ambivalence. *Journal of Multilingual and Multicultural Development* 21, 14–32.

Labov, W. (1966) *The Social Stratification of English in New York City*. Washington DC: Center for Applied Linguistics.

Lakoff, R. (1975) *Language and Woman's Place*. New York: Harper & Row.

Lave, J. and Wenger, E. (1991) *Situated Learning: Legitimate Peripheral Participation*. Cambridge: Cambridge University Press.

Leap, W. (1995) *Beyond the Lavender Lexicon: Authenticity, Imagination, and Appropriation in Lesbian and Gay Languages*. New York: Taylor & Francis.

Livia, A. and Hall, K. (eds) (1997) *Queerly Phrased: Language, Gender, and Sexuality*. New York: Oxford University Press.

Martinez-Roldan, C. (2005) Examining bilingual children's gender ideologies through critical discourse analysis. *Critical Inquiry in Language Studies* 2 (3), 157–178.

McElhinny, B. (2003) Theorizing gender in sociolinguistics and linguistic anthropology. In J. Holmes and M. Meyerhoff (eds) *The Handbook of Language and Gender* (pp. 21–42). Oxford: Blackwell.

McKay, S. and Wong, S. (1996) Multiple discourses, multiple identities: Investment and agency in second-language learning among Chinese adolescent immigrant students. *Harvard Educational Review* 66, 577–608.

McLaren, P. (1989) *Life in Schools: An Introduction to Critical Pedagogy in the Foundations of Education*. White Plains, NY: Longman.

McMahill, C., Pavlenko, A., Blackledge, A., Piller, I. and Teutsch-Dwyer, M. (2001) Self-expression, gender, and community: A Japanese feminist English class. In A. Pavlenko, A. Blackledge, I. Piller and M. Teutsch-Dwyer (eds) *Multilingualism, Second Language Learning, and Gender* (pp. 307–344). Berlin: Mouton.

Menard-Warwick, J. (2004) "I always had the desire to progress a little": Gendered narratives of immigrant language learners. *Journal of Language, Identity, and Education* 3 (4), 295–311.

Menard-Warwick, J. (2005) Intergenerational trajectories and sociopolitical context: Latina immigrants in adult ESL. *TESOL Quarterly* 39 (2), 165–185.

Menard-Warwick, J. (2006a) "The thing about work": Gendered narratives of a transnational, trilingual Mexicano. *International Journal of Bilingual Education and Bilingualism* 9 (3), 359–415.

Menard-Warwick, J. (2006b) The words become one's own: Immigrant women's perspectives on family literacy activities. *CATESOL Journal* 18 (1), 96–108.

Menard-Warwick, J. (2008) 'Because She Made Beds Every Day'. Social positioning, classroom discourse, and language learning. *Applied Linguistics* 29 (2), 267–289.

Miller, J. (2003) *Audible Difference: ESL and Social Identity in Schools*. Clevedon: Multilingual Matters.

Morgan, B. (1998) *The ESL Classroom: Teaching, Critical Practice, and Community Development*. Toronto: University of Toronto Press.

Nelson, C.D. (2004) Beyond straight grammar: Using lesbian/gay themes to explore cultural meanings. In B. Norton and A. Pavlenko (eds) *Gender and English Language Learners* (pp. 15–28). Alexandria, VA: TESOL.

Norton, B. (2000) *Identity and Language Learning: Gender, Ethnicity and Educational Change*. London: Longman.

Ohara, Y. (2001) Finding one's voice in Japanese: A study of pitch levels of L2 users. In A. Pavlenko, A. Blackledge, I. Piller and M. Teutsch-Dwyer (eds) *Multilingualism, Second Language Learning, and Gender* (pp. 231–256). Berlin: Mouton.

Ohara, Y. (forthcoming) Identity theft or revealing one's true self?: The media and construction of identity in Japanese as a foreign language. In C. Higgins (ed.) *Negotiating the Self in an Another Language: Identity Formation in a Globalizing World*. Berlin: Mouton de Gruyter.

Okamoto, S. and Smith, J.S. (eds) (2004) *Japanese Language, Gender, and Ideology: Cultural Models and Real People*. Oxford: Oxford University Press.

Pavlenko, A. (1998) Second language learning by adults: Testimonies of bilingual writers. *Issues in Applied Linguistics* 9, 3–19.

Pavlenko, A. (2001) "How am I to become a woman in an American vein?": Transformations of gender performance in second language learning. In A. Pavlenko, A. Blackledge, I. Piller and M. Teutsch-Dwyer (eds) *Multilingualism, Second Language Learning and Gender* (pp. 134–174). Berlin: Mouton de Gruyter.

Pavlenko, A. (ed.) (2005) *Bilingual Minds: Emotional Experience, Expression and Representation*. Clevedon: Multilingual Matters.

Pavlenko, A. (2007) Autobiographic narratives as data in applied linguistics. *Applied Linguistics* 28, 289–322.

Pavlenko, A. and Lantolf, J. (2000) Second language learning as participation in the (re)construction of selves. In J. Lantolf (ed.) *Sociocultural Theory and Second Language Learning* (pp. 155–177). Oxford: Oxford University Press.

Peirce, B. (1995) Social identity, investment, and language learning. *TESOL Quarterly* 29, 9–31.

Piller, I. (2002) *Bilingual Couples Talk: The Discursive Construction of Hybridity*. Amsterdam: Benjamins.

Piller, I. and Takahashi, K. (2006) A passion for English: Desire and the language market. In A. Pavlenko (ed.) *Languages and Emotions of Multilingual Speakers* (pp. 59–83). Clevedon: Multilingual Matters.

Richards, K. (2003) *Qualitative Inquiry in TESOL*. New York: Palgrave.

Rivera, K. (1999) Popular research and social transformation: A community-based approach to critical pedagogy. *TESOL Quarterly* 33, 485–500.

Sadker, M. and Sadker, D. (1985) *Promoting Effectiveness in Classroom Instruction*. Educational Research and Information Clearinghouse. Washington, DC: National Institute of Education.

Saft, S. and Ohara, Y. (2004) Promoting critical reflection about gender in EFL classes at a Japanese university. In B. Norton and A. Pavlenko (eds) *Gender and English Language Learners* (pp. 143–154). Alexandria, VA: TESOL.

Shardakova, M. and Pavlenko, A. (2004) Identity options in Russian textbooks. *Journal of Language, Identity and Education* 3 (1), 25–46.

Siegal, M. (1996) The role of learner subjectivity in second language sociolinguistic competency: Western women learning Japanese. *Applied Linguistics* 17, 356–382.

Simon-Maeda, A. (2004) Transforming emerging feminist identities: A course on gender and language issues. In B. Norton and A. Pavlenko (eds) *Gender and English Language Learners* (pp. 127–143). Alexandria, VA: TESOL.

Skapoulli, E. (2004) Gender codes at odds and the linguistic construction of hybridity. *Journal of Language, Identity and Education* 3 (4), 245–260.

Skilton-Sylvester, E. (2002) Should I stay or should I go? Investigating Cambodian women's participation and investment in adult ESL programs. *Adult Education Quarterly* 53 (1), 9–26.

Spender, D. (1980) *Man Made Language*. New York: Routledge.

Sunderland, J. (2004) Classroom interaction, gender, and foreign language learning. In B. Norton and K. Toohey (eds) *Critical Pedagogies and Language Learning* (pp. 222–241). Cambridge: Cambridge University Press.

Sunderland, J., Crowley, M., Abdul Rahim, F., Leontzakou, C. and Shattuck, J. (2001) From bias 'in the text' to 'teacher talk around the text': An exploration of teacher discourse and gendered foreign language textbook texts. *Linguistics and Education* 11 (3), 251–286.

Swann, J. (1998) Talk control: An illustration from the classroom of problems in analysing male dominance of conversation. In J. Coates (ed.) *Language and Gender* (pp. 185–196). Oxford: Blackwell.

Tannen, D. (1990) *You Just Don't Understand*. New York: Morrow.

Tannen, D. (1994) *Gender and Discourse*. Oxford: Oxford University Press.

Trudgill, P. (1974) *The Social Differentiation of English in Norwich*. Cambridge: Cambridge University Press.

Valdés, G. (1996) *Con Respeto, Bridging the Distance between Culturally Diverse Families and Schools*. New York: Teachers College Press.

Vavrus, F. (2002) Postcoloniality and English: Exploring language policy and the politics of development in Tanzania. *TESOL Quarterly* 36 (3), 373–397.

Wardhaugh, R. (1998) *An Introduction to Sociolinguistics* (3rd edn). Oxford: Blackwell.

Warriner, D. (2004) 'The days now is very hard for my family': The negotiation and construction of gendered work identities among newly arrived women refugees. *Journal of Language, Identity and Education* 3, 279–295.

Warriner, D. (2007) "It's just the nature of the beast": Reimagining the literacies of schooling in adult ESL education. *Linguistics and Education* 18 (3–4), 305–324.

Watson, R. (1995) *The Philosopher's Demise: Learning French*. Columbia/London: University of Missouri Press.

Weedon, C. (1987) *Feminist Practice and Poststructuralist Theory*. Oxford: Blackwell.

Weinstein, G. (1984) Literacy and second language acquisition: Issues and perspectives. *TESOL Quarterly* 18 (3), 471–485.

West, C. and Zimmerman, D. (1987) Doing gender. *Gender in Society* 1, 125–151.

Wolfram, W.A. (1969) *A Sociolinguistic Description of Detroit Negro Speech*. Arlington, VA: Center for Applied Linguistics.

Chapter 15
Language and Ethnicity

ANGELA REYES

Language and ethnicity research in education is motivated by several concerns. Some sociolinguists are chiefly interested in ethnic minority achievement in the classroom, exploring the role of language in educational success and failure. Others are primarily concerned with ethnic dialects and ethnic minority languages, examining the role of schools in valuing and supporting linguistic varieties with minimal institutional legitimacy. Still others are mainly fascinated by youth interactional practices, using educational sites to witness the constant doing and undoing of ethnic groups and boundaries through language use. Oftentimes these various concerns overlap, providing complex accounts of how linguistic, ethnic and educational issues are elaborately intertwined. In this chapter, I discuss definitions of ethnicity, sociolinguistic research methods in language and ethnicity, and language and ethnicity research by ethnic group and by educational site. I end with suggestions for future research as well as implications for language educators.

Definitions of Ethnicity

The concept of ethnicity can be quite vexing. What is frustrating about ethnicity and associated concepts (like race and culture) is that they refer to nothing, that is, no *thing*, making these terms essentially – and existentially – indefinable. Unlike words like 'apple' that more straightforwardly index objects, ethnicity is something you just can't grab and bite into. This intangible quality provides much variability in how ethnicity is understood, valued and applied. Even though scientists generally agree that there is no biological evidence to support their importance, ethnicity and race are still commonly perceived as primordial and natural categories. Since it is people – not genetics or nature – that insist on the significance of these categories in the classification of human beings (Le Page & Tabouret-Keller, 1985), several scholars argue that ethnicity and race are *social constructs* with great *political significance*. Because these constructs play a major role in how individuals experience and structure their social worlds, researchers need to pay particular attention to the ways in which ethnicity and race are defined and operationalized in institutional and everyday contexts, especially with regard to linguistic and educational practice.

Since it has been established that ethnicity and race are socially constructed and not biologically determined, what exactly does this 'social construction' involve? How do people understand ethnicity and race, and what do they do with these concepts? According to Waters (1990), people commonly associate ethnicity with distinctions based on national origin, language, religion, food and other cultural markers, and link race to distinctions drawn from physical appearance, such as skin color, hair texture, eye shape and so on. Omi and Winant similarly argue that people construct race in reference to 'different types of human bodies' (Omi & Winant, 1994: 55). This mutual emphasis on perceptions of race as based on phenotypic features, however, has been called into question. Bailey (2002), for example, reveals how Dominican Americans construct identities not on the basis of phenotype but on the basis of language. Although others may perceive them in racial terms (i.e. 'Black'), Dominican Americans construct their identities along ethnolinguistic lines (i.e. 'Spanish'). How mixed-race people are identified and identify themselves also disrupts the phenotype-based approach to racial classification (Bucholtz, 1995). As for ethnicity, the concept is more than 'muddy' (Omi & Winant, 1994: 14), being composed of equally muddy parts, such as culture, language, nation and so on. Understandings of ethnicity fall apart when confronted by groups that accrue complicated transnational identities, such as Puerto Ricans (Zentella, 1997), Japanese returnees (Kanno, 2003), 1.5 generation immigrants who experience part of their formative years in one country and part in another country (Reyes, 2007), and many ethnic minorities who are often positioned as not fully part of either a 'heritage culture' or a 'host country' (Jo, 2001).

It is not enough to say that these groups combine 'multiple' ethnicities or 'two' races, because such statements presuppose that ethnic and racial categories are discrete and pure units to begin with. Even in the most seemingly homogeneous and stable communities, concepts of ethnicity and race do not stand still. Rather, because of past and present mixing, meeting, moving and imagining across national and cultural boundaries, ethnicity and race are more aptly described as ongoing, dynamic processes. Efforts to define ethnicity and race by their content thus ultimately fail, revealing instead how slippery and elusive these categories are.

Hence, several scholars are interested not in the content of ethnic groups but in the construction of ethnic boundaries. Barth (1969), who formulates ethnicity as a function of boundary maintenance, is concerned not with the internal inventories of groups but with how groups create borders between them. Hewitt similarly emphasizes how ethnicity is 'a positional concept, for it has its existence only in relation to other cultures bound within specific political and economic systems' (Hewitt, 1986: 162). Much sociolinguistic research examines the complex ways in which boundaries between ethnic groups are locally constituted, revealing how ethnic identity is not a fixed property of individuals but a social achievement produced through interaction. Rampton (1995), for example, examines how ethnically diverse peer groups problematize the formation and maintenance of ethnicity. He argues that adolescents transgress ethnic boundaries by crossing into languages associated with other ethnic groups, creating 'new ethnicities' (*cf*. Hall, 1988; Gumperz & Cook-Gumperz, 1982), which are produced through emergent communities in contact and thus predicated on difference and diversity, not on primordial bonds. Other studies reveal how different ethnic identities become established within what seems to be a single ethnic group: For example, Mendoza-Denton (1996) shows how Mexican American gang girls identify as either 'Sureñas' (linked to the Spanish-dominant first generation) or 'Norteñas' (linked to the English-dominant second generation), and Kang (2004) reveals how Korean American camp counselors constitute themselves as either 'Korean' (linked to teaching cultural heritage) or 'Korean American'(linked to being a mentor). Studies such as these reveal how ethnicity cannot be defined by what it consists of; rather, ethnic identities shift across interactional contexts in relation to the local ideological divisions that are created between groups.

Ethnicity concerns not just boundaries and mutability, but also power relations, group hierarchies and institutional structures. Who gets defined as 'ethnic', for example, becomes a question with great consequence for how national belonging is conceived and how racial hierarchies are reproduced. Consider what gets included in 'multicultural day' at a school and under 'ethnic restaurants' in a phone book. Oftentimes dominant groups are excluded from these areas because of their unmarked, normative status against which minority groups are unequally positioned (Trechter & Bucholtz, 2001). Such ethnic designations assigned from outside the group are called 'ethnic categories', while designations established from within are called 'ethnic groups' (Jenkins, 1994). Political mobilization may motivate the acceptance of a label from the inside, turning an ethnic category into an ethnic group. For example, 'Asian American', a label that was once imposed and then embraced, became a powerful unifying force for Asian ethnic groups during the Civil Rights Movement in the United States. Such pan-ethnicity, which is the merging of groups of different national origins into new large-scale groupings, was created not on the basis of shared cultural ties but on collective social action against institutionalized inequality (Espiritu, 1992). Ethnicity, thus, achieves extraordinary political importance, not only as it can be deeply rooted in various institutions that may reproduce unequal power relations, but also as it can be creatively appropriated by minority groups as a catalyst for social change.

Finally, I would like to emphasize that ethnicity is not universally understood. The very construction of ethnicity can vary across contexts and can have a multitude of meanings. To be 'black', for example, means something entirely different in the United States than it does in France (Tetreault, 2008), in Brazil (Roth-Gordon, 2007), and so on. Such variation occurs not only across large national scales: ethnicity can be conceptualized in different ways inside national borders as well as within the same community. Moreover, these conceptualizations can change over time or shift in a single interaction. Across and within contexts, ethnicity can also be intertwined with other aspects of identity or have little to no relevance altogether (Heath & McLaughlin, 1993). Researchers must ask why priority should be given to ethnicity, lest they risk a view of 'ethnic absolutism' (Gilroy, 1987), which privileges a fairly static view of ethnicity as more crucial to one's identity than other social categories, such as class, gender, age, and so on.

Methodological Approaches to the Study of Language and Ethnicity

All of the complexity that surrounds the concept of ethnicity may easily overwhelm the researcher. A sociolinguistic approach to the study of ethnicity is ideal for at least three reasons. First, since ethnicity is a social construct, this social construction must involve communication in some way, whether it is language or other semiotic means. Sociolinguists specialize in the collection and analysis of such communication. Second, attending to the role of language in the constitution of ethnic groups and boundaries grounds the researcher in empirical data. Ethnicity becomes observable, allowing researchers to gain a rich understanding of how individuals themselves understand and utilize ethnicity in their daily lives. Third, examining linguistic practices forces researchers to attend to ethnicity as accomplished through situationally bound practices. Sociolinguists can trace the intricacy of ethnic identity as it changes and shifts over time and across contexts, enabling fuller accounts of how ethnicity operates. There are different methodological approaches that sociolinguists employ in the study of ethnicity, and below I outline a few.

Several scholars in the field of sociolinguistics approach the study of language and ethnicity with a distinctiveness-centered model. This model enables the classification of ethnic dialects, allowing researchers to describe in close detail the linguistic features of distinct speech varieties spoken by particular ethnic groups. The distinctiveness-centered model has been adopted by sociolinguists who take a more quantitative approach to the study of language and ethnicity. Much of the early work on African-American English (AAE), for example, falls into this paradigm (e.g. Labov, 1972). Research on Latino English has also relied heavily on quantitative approaches to describe Latino varieties in similar detail (e.g. Fought, 2003). This work has been enormously important in revealing how ethnic varieties are indeed just as grammatical as other speech varieties, including standard varieties. This finding is particularly useful to language educators. Research showing how AAE, for example, is a legitimate variety informs language debates in education, such as the Ebonics controversy (see below). Quantitative work is crucial for understanding how linguistic features are spread across large communities of speakers, and how a particular ethnic dialect is systematic within and across speakers. However, a criticism of quantitative research is that it lacks rich, nuanced accounts of speaker repertoires as they are performed and understood across a wide range of contexts. Moreover, while this work has made an immense impact on how we understand language variation, ethnic groups who do not have a distinctive speech variety are largely ignored within this paradigm.

Other research has shown that issues of language and ethnicity should be concerned not only with the distinctiveness of ethnic varieties, but also with the performance of multiple speech styles in the construction of ethnicity. Taking a more qualitative, ethnographic approach, several sociolinguists explore the ways in which speakers draw on features of ethnic dialects (whether real or imagined) in the production of identity. Much of this research emphasizes improvised aspects of language use, for example, codeswitching (Gumperz, 1982; see also Kamwangamalu, this volume), stylization (Coupland, 2001; see also Jaspers, this volume) and the use of linguistic features associated with an ethnic other, which can be found in studies on language crossing (Rampton, 1995) and mocking (Hill, 1995). Several researchers in this tradition gather data in educational settings since youth interactional practices are particularly rich sites for witnessing this type of language play (e.g. Bailey, 2002). Ethnographic approaches are also enormously important for exploring issues of language and ethnicity among ethnic groups that do not speak a distinct dialect or at least one that is widely recognized (Reyes & Lo, 2009). Some challenges faced by the ethnographic approach include difficulty in describing speech patterns across large numbers of speakers and in producing generalizable findings.

I wish not to present these two approaches as mutually exclusive or in opposition to one another. In fact, many ethnographers must rely on quantitative research when they examine the emergence and significance of linguistic features that get linked to ethnic groups. In addition, there have been many studies that combine both quantitative and qualitative approaches to produce rich, detailed accounts of language and ethnicity in particular communities of practice (e.g. Alim, 2004; Mendoza-Denton, 2008).

Finally, there is a long tradition in sociolinguistic research that concentrates on ethnic minority languages, language shift and maintenance and language planning and policy (e.g. Fishman, 1989; Gal, 1979; Hornberger,

1988). Much of this work is concerned with issues of multilingualism and efforts to revitalize endangered languages. Scholars typically conduct long-term ethnographic studies in an area of the world, document the ways in which two or more language varieties are used and perceived at home, community, institutional and societal levels and situate their research within broader frameworks of educational policy and language politics. Schools and classrooms are often key sites in these studies since issues of language teaching and learning are central to these investigations (e.g. Heller, 1999; Jaffe, 1999).

Language and Ethnicity in the United States

It is impossible to discuss in this chapter all of the ethnic groups that have been the subject of language and ethnicity research. Because of space limitations and because of my own area of expertise, I have thus chosen to focus this section on only a few groups in the United States. This section is also further restricted to issues of language and ethnicity that involve the English language in some way, whether I am discussing ethnic dialects of English, issues of English language contact and shift in ethnic communities or the use of English language varieties in the production of ethnicity.

I would like to emphasize that there is extremely valuable research going on outside of what I explore in this chapter that informs our understanding of language and ethnicity in the United States and in other parts of the world. Some examples of international work that is focused on issues of language and ethnicity and the English language include research in New Zealand (e.g. Holmes, 1997), India (e.g. Kachru, 1983), South Africa (e.g. Mesthrie, 2002), Hong Kong (e.g. Lin, 1996), England (e.g. Hewitt, 1986) and the Philippines (e.g. Bautista, 1997), to name just a mere few. Much – though certainly not all – cross-national research finds that speech varieties spoken by ethnic groups in less powerful positions are often stigmatized while the speech varieties spoken by dominant ethnic groups are not. Dominant group varieties are often institutionalized as the unmarked, normative standard, while subordinate group varieties accrue a litany of negative evaluations, such as 'bad', 'lazy', 'uneducated' and 'corrupt', resulting in a type of iconicity (Gal & Irvine, 1995) that maps such evaluations of speech onto the people who use that speech. But multilingual situations around the world can be quite complex and particular, revealing contexts where bilingualism may be more highly valued than a single language (e.g. Heller, 1999) and languages with limited institutional presence may gain prestige (e.g. Woolard, 1989).

In this section, I will provide brief overviews of language and ethnicity research on African Americans, Latinos, Native Americans, Asian Americans and European Americans. For Native Hawaiians, see Siegel (this volume) on Hawai'i Creole English; for Jewish Americans, see Tannen

(1981); for Alaskan Athabaskans, see Scollon and Scollon (1981). There are, of course, several other ethnic groups in the United States, all of which are worthy of discussion. Due to space limitations and the focus of this chapter, I apologize for the inevitable omissions. Since most research in language and ethnicity has focused on African Americans, I will spend a longer time discussing this work, including the Oakland Ebonics controversy, which has particular relevance to language educators.

African Americans

The speech practices of African slave descendents in the United States have received an enormous amount of attention from sociolinguists over the past half-century. Much of this research is focused on the description and analysis of the distinct ethnic variety that is linked to African American speakers. Over the years, this variety has been referred to by several names: for example, Black English Vernacular, African American Vernacular English, AAE, African American Language and Ebonics. Although each name emphasizes different ideological stances that emerged within particular social climates (e.g. 'black' versus 'African American'; 'English' versus 'language'), many scholars see these terms as more or less synonymous. In this chapter, I follow Green (2002) and use 'African American English' (AAE) to emphasize that AAE is not limited to vernacular forms, but comprises multiple styles that vary according to class, region, gender, age, situation, formality, and so on.

Debates surrounding the origin and future of AAE have preoccupied many sociolinguists. Some researchers argue that AAE originated from a creole (e.g. Dillard, 1972) and they support this claim with evidence from other English-based creoles around the world, including Gullah, which is spoken on the Sea Islands off the coast of Georgia and South Carolina (see Siegel, this volume). Others contend that AAE derives from the dialects of English spoken by early British and other western European settlers in the United States (e.g. Poplack & Tagliamonte, 1989). Scholars have also been concerned with whether AAE is converging with mainstream American English (MAE) and thus becoming more like MAE, or diverging from MAE and thus becoming even more different (e.g. Labov & Harris, 1986).

One of the most important things to know about AAE is that it is a systematic variety with well-defined linguistic rules. Table 15.1 presents just a sample of AAE linguistic features, which have been extensively catalogued in the literature. Some of these features are shared by other English dialects, but many researchers argue that they occur more frequently in AAE (Rickford, 1996). Not all African Americans speak AAE, and not all AAE speakers use AAE all the time. Scholars have found that AAE features occur more frequently in the informal speech of urban, working-class youth (Rickford, 1996). For example, Wolfram (1969) documents such

Table 15.1 Some linguistic features of African American English

Phonology and pronunciation	AAE example	MAE gloss
Simplification of word-final consonant clusters	Lef	Left
	Des	Desk
Realization of final *ng* as *n* in gerunds and participles	Talkin	Talking
Realization of voiceless *th* as *t* or *f*	Tin	Thin
	Baf	Bath
Realization of voiced *th* as *d* or *v*	Den	Then
	Bruvver	Brother
Stress on first rather than second syllable	Pólice	Políce
Syntax and grammar		
Absence of third person present tense -*s*	He walk	He walks
	He don't sing	He doesn't sing
Use of invariant *be* to express habitual aspect	She be late	She is usually late
Absence of copula/auxiliary *is* and *are* for present tense states and actions	She late	She is late (today)
Use of *done* to emphasize the completed nature of an action	She done did it	She has already done it
Use of stressed *BIN* to express remote phase	He BIN married	He has been married for a long time (and still is)
Multiple negation or negative concord	He don't do nothing	He doesn't do anything

Source: Adapted from Rickford (1996: 175–176).

class stratification among AAE speakers in Detroit, and Labov (1972) illustrates how formality of context and familiarity with interlocutor influence the frequency of AAE features in the speech of African American boys in New York City. Females and middle-class speakers have largely been absent from much early work, as noted and corrected by several scholars (e.g. Morgan, 1991).

Oakland Ebonics controversy

It perhaps goes without saying that attitudes toward AAE have not been particularly kind. The general public rarely views AAE as a legitimate, grammatical system; instead, AAE is often negatively evaluated as 'ignorant', 'wrong', 'improper', and so on. These attitudes emerge through institutions, such as schools, where the stakes are high for students who speak AAE. In the 1979 Ann Arbor, Michigan case known as the Black English Trial, 11 African American plaintiffs had been placed in remedial special education classrooms based on evaluations that failed to take into account their linguistic heritage as speakers of AAE (Smitherman, 1981). The judge ruled that the negative attitudes of teachers toward the student vernacular constituted a barrier to equal educational opportunity. Although the judge ruled in favor of the plaintiffs, the main emphasis was on the need for better teacher training, while the practice of using speech pathology to classify AAE speakers as linguistically disabled remained unchallenged (Baugh, 1998).

Less than two decades after the Black English Trial, the Oakland Ebonics resolutions propelled the speech practices of African Americans into the national spotlight. In response to the poor educational performance of its African American students, the school board of Oakland, California, passed a resolution on December 18, 1996, embracing the potential of Ebonics in the teaching of standard English to AAE speakers (Baugh, 2000). This resolution was controversial for several reasons. First, Ebonics (literally: *black sounds*), a term that was unfamiliar to most people, was framed as 'genetically based' and 'not a dialect of English' in the original wording. The resolution was revised less than a month later to remove any reference to genetics and to concede that it was indeed an English dialect. Second, the original wording was ambiguous about the precise role of Ebonics in the classroom. It was not clear whether students would learn standard English through Ebonics, or whether students would be taught in Ebonics or even taught Ebonics. The revised resolution clarified that Ebonics would be used in the classroom to 'move' or 'transition' students from Ebonics to standard English proficiency. Table 15.2 compares two excerpts from the original and amended resolutions, which reveal these changes.

The Oakland Ebonics case has several educational implications for students who speak AAE. Particularly since the resolution legitimized the role of Ebonics in the classroom, it opened up new opportunities for educators to incorporate AAE in the teaching of standard English. One approach, Contrastive Analysis, is considered bidialectal since it focuses on particular points of contrast between the two varieties. Contrasting AAE and standard English in both directions – from AAE to standard English and from standard English to AAE – is crucial, since moving only from AAE to standard English suggests an unequal status between languages (Rickford & Rickford, 2000). While drills can quickly become tedious, scholars point to the effectiveness of other methods that use, for example, literature, which also illustrates how acclaimed authors like Toni Morrison use AAE features in their profession. Delpit (2006) describes

Table 15.2 Excerpts from the Oakland Ebonics resolutions

December 18, 1996	*January 15, 1997*
WHEREAS, these studies have also demonstrated that African Language Systems *are genetically based* and *not a dialect of English*; and	WHEREAS, these studies have also demonstrated that African Language Systems *have origins in West and Niger-Congo languages* and *are not merely dialects of English*; and
WHEREAS, the standardized tests and grade scores of African-American students in reading and language arts skills measuring their application of English skills are substantially below state and national norms and that such deficiencies will be remedied by application of a program featuring African Language Systems principles *in instructing African-American children both in their primary language and in English*; and	WHEREAS, the standardized tests and grade scores of African-American students in reading and language arts skills measuring their application of English skills are substantially below state and national norms and that such deficiencies will be remedied by application of a program featuring African Language Systems principles *to move students from the language patterns they bring to school to English proficiency*; and

Source: Adapted from Rickford and Rickford (2000: 166–169).

several other creative teaching strategies that involve puppet shows, role-playing, theater and the creation of bilingual dictionaries, to name just a few. Rickford (1999) notes that several classroom studies have shown that AAE speakers acquire standard English proficiency more successfully when AAE is integrated in its learning; in fact, some studies have found that if AAE is not incorporated, the presence of AAE features increases in academic tasks where standard English is preferred (Taylor, 1989). Yet if teachers, administrators, students and parents do not recognize and value AAE as a legitimate variety, such negative attitudes may be the main barrier to its efficacy in the classroom. Rickford (1999) urges educators to proceed from the position that AAE speakers come to school having already mastered a linguistic system and are now learning to master another.

Latinos

Although the majority of language and ethnicity research in the United States has focused on African Americans, Latinos have also attracted a great deal of attention from sociolinguists. Much research on Mexican Americans (e.g. Mendoza-Denton, 2008), Puerto Rican Americans (e.g. Urciuoli, 1996), Dominican Americans (e.g. Bailey, 2002) and other Latino groups examines the complexity of ethnicity as it relates to language, race, nation, immigration and other social factors. Issues surrounding the Spanish language are often at the center of this research. Unlike AAE and standard English, which are typically viewed as varieties of the same language, Spanish and English are commonly perceived as separate languages. There are several varieties of Spanish, however, and the tensions and hierarchies created among them can be quite fierce (Zentella, 2004). Because the use of Spanish and English varieties often plays important roles in the construction of ethnicity within Latino communities, research in this area is often centered on issues of bilingualism and codeswitching, which is the alternation between two (or more) language varieties in interaction (see Kamwangamalu, this volume). Certainly not all Latinos speak Spanish: while immigrant and second generation Latinos are often bilingual, it is not uncommon to find monolingual English-speaking Latinos in third and later generations (Fought, 2003). Whether Latinos speak Spanish or not, there are also other available resources for constructing ethnic identity, including Latino English varieties, such as Chicano English, and other ethnic varieties, including AAE.

Attitudes toward Spanish, bilingualism, codeswitching and Latino English varieties can be quite complex among Latino groups. While many Latinos view speaking Spanish as important – if not essential – to Latino ethnicity (Zentella, 1997), there are others who feel conflicted about the role of Spanish in their lives. This is not surprising given the overall negative attitudes toward Spanish and Spanish speakers in the United States. In the face of institutionalized discrimination ranging from mass media discourses that associate Spanish with being poor and uneducated to educational policies like Proposition 227, which essentially dismantled bilingual education in California in 1998, Latinos can hardly be blamed for shifting to English. Codeswitching between Spanish and English (often referred to as 'Spanglish') is still common among bilingual Latinos; and while embraced by Latino youth in particular, there is also a keen awareness that codeswitching is negatively viewed in institutions, such as schools (Urciuoli, 1996). The use of Latino English varieties also becomes important in the construction of ethnic identity for both bilingual and monolingual English-speaking Latinos. Chicano English, the most extensively studied Latino English variety, is spoken primarily by Mexican Americans in the Southwest (Fought, 2003). It initially emerged from language contact between Spanish and English varieties, but is now an ethnic dialect of English since it is learned as a native language (*cf.* pidgins and creoles, Siegel, this volume). Because Chicano English features can sound Spanish, Chicano English speakers are often mistakenly viewed as Spanish speakers who are learning English, even if they are monolingual English speakers (Fought, 2006).

Native Americans

In contrast to Latinos, who are united by a common linguistic heritage through Spanish, Indigenous tribal communities in the United States speak distinct languages, although the numbers of Native American languages and their speakers are rapidly decreasing. Currently, the Native American languages with the most speakers are Navajo (approximately 130,000 speakers in Utah, Arizona, Colorado and New Mexico) followed far behind by Cherokee (approximately 14,000 speakers in North Carolina and Oklahoma) and other languages with around 10,000 speakers, including Lakhota, Apache, Pima and Tohono O'odham (Yamamoto & Zepeda, 2004). Before Europeans arrived on the shores of North America, there were an estimated 400–600 Native American languages that could be grouped into 62 language families (Goddard, 1996). In 1997, there were approximately 175 Native American languages being spoken in the United States; however, only about 20 of these were being learned by children (Krauss, 1998). This means that an alarming 155 of the remaining 175 languages are rapidly vanishing since they have no native speakers in the next generation. Over the past few decades, there have been efforts to revitalize these endangered languages, such as the creation of the Native American Languages Act in the early 1990s, which recognizes the importance of Native American languages and authorizes funds for language revitalization efforts. Several scholars, including Leanne Hinton, Ofelia Zepeda and Teresa McCarty, have also spearheaded community efforts to document languages, train teachers and develop materials. In addition, to meet the educational needs of Native American children, the Indian Education Act of 1972, which is an amendment of the Bilingual Education Act of 1968, provides funds for programs serving Native American communities.

The historical oppression that Native Americans have endured through institutions like boarding schools led to the loss of tribal languages and to the emergence of distinctive linguistic features of Native American English. Leap (1993) explores the contours of this ethnic variety of English and the conditions that produced English fluency among Native Americans. Focusing on the off-reservation boarding schools, which were designed to 'civilize' Native American children away from their families, Leap examines how the sole use of English was highly regulated and brutally enforced. Speaking a Native American language was punishable through mouth-washing with soap, solitary confinement and whippings. Under such severe conditions, it is not surprising that students often acquired English, yet not necessarily at the expense of their tribal languages: students were known to devise covert opportunities to speak Native American languages in school spaces. Analyzing samples of student writing, Leap and others found that the English that Native American children were using shared features that made it distinct from the English they were learning at school. While Leap acknowledges how AAE in the 1600s and Pidgin English (spoken by Chinese American laborers) in the 1800s influenced the development of Native American English, he argues that this dialect cannot be explained simply with reference to pidgin or creole features. Instead, he suggests that students were creating this ethnic variety from a range of linguistic and cultural skills, such as knowledge about language learned from teachers, from peers and from their ancestral languages.

Asian Americans

As with Native Americans, there is no single heritage language shared by Asian Americans, which include groups with origins as diverse as East Asia (e.g. China, Japan), South Asia (e.g. India and Sri Lanka) and Southeast Asia (e.g. Vietnam and Laos). But without a distinct ethnic dialect of English – like those found among African Americans, Latinos and Native Americans – Asian Americans remain one of the least studied ethnic groups in sociolinguistics (Reyes & Lo, 2004). Unlike Native Americans, who are indigenous to the Americas, and African Americans, who were forced into enslavement, Asian Americans – like Latinos – are often perceived as voluntary immigrants to the United States, although their histories are much more complex. From the first major influx of Chinese immigrants during the California gold rush in the mid-1800s to the latest waves of Southeast Asian refugees after the fall of Saigon in 1975, Asian Americans span a wide range of minority experiences even though three prevailing stereotypes suggest otherwise. According to the model minority stereotype (Lee, 1996), Asian Americans are mainstream American English speakers who assimilate smoothly into the white middle class. According to the forever foreigner stereotype (Tuan, 1998), Asian Americans are eternally perceived as newcomers who speak English with foreign accents. According to the problem minority stereotype (Reyes, 2007), Asian Americans – particularly Southeast Asian refugee youth – are seen as poor, urban minorities who participate in delinquent behavior, including the speaking of nonstandard dialects, such as AAE. The perception of Asian Americans as a homogeneous group motivates the willy-nilly application of these contradictory stereotypes, thus denying the complexity of Asian American lived experience and linguistic behavior.

Since efforts to identify an Asian American English have generally been inconclusive (Hanna, 1997; Mendoza-Denton & Iwai, 1993; Spencer, 1950), most sociolinguistic research on Asian Americans focuses on issues of English language learning and heritage language maintenance, although more recent scholarship explores the ways in which English is the main medium through which ethnic identity is produced. In studies on English language learning, researchers explore how Asian immigrants manage the English as a second language (ESL) classroom and ESL identity (e.g. Harklau, 1994). Much scholarship examines these issues in light of Lau v. Nichols, the landmark 1974 US Supreme Court case that ruled in favor of Chinese American students who were denied equal educational opportunities due to the lack of educational services in Chinese. Research on heritage language programs, often called 'Saturday schools', has shown how the learning of a heritage language becomes intimately tied to a sense of ethnic heritage and the creation of hybrid ethnic identities (e.g. He & Xiao, 2008). Finally, research on the production of Asian American ethnicity through the use of English varieties poses an important challenge to the distinctiveness-centered sociolinguistic paradigm in language and ethnicity research. Even though they lack an ethnically distinct variety of English, Asian Americans can establish complex ethnic identities through the use of English, including nonstandard varieties such as AAE (e.g. Chun, 2001).

European Americans

Although the majority of language and ethnicity research is centered on ethnic minorities, sociolinguists are increasingly examining the language practices of European Americans and the linguistic construction of whiteness. As with African Americans, Latinos, Native Americans and Asian Americans, the ethnic identities of European Americans are also socially constructed. Consider, for example, how Italian and Irish immigrants in the early 20th century were once viewed as different racial groups and only over time have they both become perceived as 'white'. While studies have observed European American speech patterns in certain geographic regions and across particular socioeconomic backgrounds (e.g. Eckert, 2000), sociolinguists tend to be less interested in whether European Americans have a distinct dialect and more interested in how whiteness is ideologically constructed. Trechter and Bucholtz (2001) argue that whiteness maintains its power through its absence: it is through its unmarked status that whiteness becomes perceived as normative and other groups become relationally positioned as marginal and inferior. Hill (1999) illustrates this point with Mock Spanish, which is the use of Spanish words and phrases, such as *macho* or *hasta la vista*, by European Americans. She argues that in the construction of white public space, the Spanish spoken by Latinos is highly monitored while the Spanish performed by whites remains invisible as well as ideologically potent: Mock Spanish not only indexes desirable qualities for white users, but also reproduces negative racializing stereotypes of Latinos.

Several studies explore how whiteness becomes unhinged from its unmarked status through the construction of whiteness by both European Americans and non-European Americans. Studies have shown that whiteness becomes linked to linguistic factors, such as speaking standard English, and social factors, such as being middle class, educated and uncool. For example, it is not uncommon for ethnic minorities to be accused of 'acting white' or 'selling out' if they draw on standard features in academic or community contexts (Fordham & Ogbu, 1986). But research on European Americans finds that white identities can be produced regardless of the language variety being spoken. Whether using hyper-standard English in the production of a white 'nerd' identity (Bucholtz, 2001) or AAE in the making of white masculinity (Kiesling, 2001), white-ness in both cases becomes visible as it is constructed in relation to racial ideologies that link standard English to whites and nonstandard English to nonwhites. Research on non-European Americans ranges from elicita-tion studies, such as asking African Americans to imitate whites (Preston, 1992), to more spontaneous enactments, such as Native American 'white-man' jokes (Basso, 1979) or performances of white characters by African-American drag queens (Barrett, 1999) and stand-up comedians (Rahman, 2007). These studies reveal how whiteness is constructed and understood by minority groups, and how racial ideologies and hierarchies can be reproduced and challenged through interaction.

Language and Ethnicity in Education

Now that basic overviews of a few ethnic groups in the United States have been discussed, I will turn to an exploration of issues of language and ethnicity in educational contexts. There are three main models in lan-guage and ethnicity research in education: deficit, difference and emer-gence. Some early work drew on a deficit model, claiming that ethnic minorities experienced chronic school failure because they were cogni-tively deficient and culturally deprived. These claims were completely discredited when studies drawing on a difference model explained how ethnic minorities are not deficient, but socialized into different sets of cul-tural norms that are not recognized or legitimized by mainstream schools. Other work draws on an emergence model, describing how ethnic groups and educational institutions do not possess static characteristics as much as they are in constant negotiation with one another in particular school contexts. This section will focus on classic studies that draw on difference models and more recent research that draws on emergence models. I will not review studies that fall into a deficit model since this work has been invalidated, although it is a model that unfortunately is still found in public discourse.

Difference model

Two pioneering studies on language and ethnicity in the classroom by Susan Philips (1983) and Shirley Brice Heath (1983) argue that minority student failure largely results from a mismatch in speech norms. Using the ethnography of communication (Hymes, 1974), both Philips and Heath carried out multi-year studies that explore how ethnic minorities are socialized into particular speech norms in the home and community that differ from those in the school.

In her ethnography of the Warm Springs Indian reservation in Oregon from 1968 to 1973, Philips finds that verbal participation among Native American and Anglo children varies profoundly in the classroom. She argues that the Native American children have difficulties at school because the 'participant structures' in the classroom are different from those in their community. These participant structures include whole class, small group and one-to-one interactions. In small groups with classmates and in individual interactions with the teacher, the Native American children participate more actively because these two participant structures more closely resemble those in the community. In whole class activities, however, the ways in which Native American children structure attention in terms of eye gaze, turns at talk, and so on, lead to misunderstandings and negative evaluations by the teacher (see also Rymes, this volume).

Drawing from research in the Piedmont Carolinas from 1969 to 1978, Heath provides an ethnographic account of language socialization in Trackton, a black working class community, and Roadville, a white working class community. She finds that children from Trackton and Roadville are socialized into speech norms that are distinct not only from each other, but also from the nearby mainstream community. The mainstream children benefit from having their speech styles valued in the classroom, while the working class children are continually failed by school. For example, the African American children of Trackton are not socialized into answering known-information questions (e.g. 'what color is this?' when asked by someone who can clearly see the color). This interactional routine is a preferred and pervasive one in the classroom as well as in the communities of mainstream children. When Trackton children do not partake in these questioning routines, teachers interpret their nonparticipation as resistance or ignorance.

These two studies illustrate how being socialized into different speech norms can result in the marginalization of ethnic minority children at school. Rather than promoting a view of ethnic minorities as deficient, Philips and Heath argue that the interactional conventions of each community are just as systematic and coherent as those of the dominant group. These studies reveal how ethnic majority groups establish and maintain power by having their speech norms legitimized in institutional settings, such as classrooms. Mainstream practices become accepted as 'normal', 'proper' and 'standard'. Meanwhile, ethnic minority norms become misunderstood or negatively evaluated. Although educational institutions tend not to effectively accommodate ethnic minority groups, some studies have documented school efforts to incorporate community speech norms into classroom practice, such as the Hawaiian 'talk story' in reading lessons (Au, 1980). But oftentimes, mainstream schools insist that competence in dominant speech norms be a prerequisite to full access to American society.

Emergence model

There is educational research that departs from the difference model to embrace a more emergent account of language and ethnicity. This work emphasizes how the link between language and ethnicity is quite dynamic: that speakers are not confined to a set of inherited speech norms, but may draw instead from wide repertoires and various interactional strategies in the performance of ethnic identity (see Kasper & Omori, this volume, on emergent cultural identities). While these studies recognize that socialization greatly influences interactional behavior, they also criticize the difference model for overemphasizing its role and for risking a view of cultural determinism (Erickson & Shultz, 1982; McDermott & Gospodinoff, 1981; Rampton, 1995). Much of this work, in fact, sees difference based on ethnicity as secondary to difference based on political relations between groups. I will discuss some key studies that take an emergent account by focusing on site: mainstream education and language education.

Mainstream education

There are several studies that effectively illustrate how the identities of ethnic minorities are not simply brought to school, but emergent through classroom practice. In her study of Latino primary school children in classroom writing workshops, Orellana (1999) stresses the inventiveness of social identities through written literacy practices. Although all of the students have dark hair and dark eyes, they strongly identify with the blond-haired, blue-eyed characters that they invent in their stories. While the creation of such Anglo images by Latino children may be interpreted as compliant with dominant racial discourses, Orellana argues that these drawings are more likely forms of resistance, allowing students to challenge stereotypes about what Latinos should look like. Drawing from data in a ninth grade classroom in a public high school, Wortham (2006) focuses on the emergent identities of two African American students: Tyisha and Maurice. Considering curricular themes, ideologies of race and gender and the local models of personhood available to students (most notably 'promising girls' and 'unpromising boys'), Wortham closely analyzes classroom interaction across time to trace how student identities develop and shift in unexpected ways. Tyisha, for example, comes to be socially identified in wildly distinct ways despite the fact that she performs a relatively stable identity throughout the academic year: as an outspoken student, expressing and defending her opinions. Tyisha moves from promising to problematic, as more students begin speaking out in class. She then moves from a disruptive outcast to a legitimate dissenter, as curricular themes about individual sacrifice and then reasoned resistance come forth, thus enabling her to inhabit recognizable models of personhood that are introduced in the classroom. Both Orellana and Wortham reveal that students are not confined to fixed models of language and ethnicity. Instead, various identities may become possible in and through the classroom.

There are also several studies that examine the manipulation of ethnically defined speech norms in the strategic display of identity. When ethnic minorities view access to mainstream success through the adoption of mainstream conventions as an illusion, they may maintain even more strict adherence to group-defining norms. For example, Foley (1996) finds that Native American high school students will actively apply the 'silent Indian' stereotype to themselves in order to avoid being bothered by their teachers in the classroom. This enactment of nonparticipation is a result not so much of being socialized into silence in the community, but of knowing that this is a stereotype that circulates and can be inhabited to achieve a particular interactional effect. Fordham (1999) documents two linguistic strategies among African American high school students: 'guerilla warfare' or the strict adherence to the use of AAE in all contexts including the classroom; and 'leasing the standard' in educational contexts while 'retaining ownership of Ebonics' in others. Speaking standard English often elicits accusations of 'acting white', a notion that is tied to hegemony because the students may be seen as agents in their own oppression. Despite these negative evaluations, this style of 'accommodation without assimilation' (Gibson, 1988) becomes a prevalent strategy for the high-achieving African American students in her study.

Finally, work on language crossing in educational contexts is also concerned with the manipulation of multiple ethnic varieties in the production of ethnic identity. This line of research concerns itself with the politics and elasticity of ethnic group boundaries when speakers use language varieties associated with an ethnic other. In his groundbreaking study of multiethnic peer group interaction at an urban middle school in England, Rampton (1995) discusses the out-group use of Panjabi, Creole and Stylized Asian English by Afro-Caribbean, Anglo and Panjabi youth. Language crossing emerges as a multi-vocalic practice with different social meanings depending on the speaker and the language. For example, Panjabi youth cross into Creole, which is spoken primarily by Afro-Caribbean immigrants in England, because it stands for an excitement in youth culture. Rampton argues that Creole crossing is an example of self/voice entanglement. This interlacing of speakers (Panjabi youth) with what they spoke (Creole) signals favorable evaluations of Creole and reflects positively on Panjabi youth. In her ethnographic study of a multiracial urban high school in California, Bucholtz (1999) documents similar types of language crossing in her analysis of stylized performances of AAE by white males. In stories about interracial conflict, Bucholtz finds that the use of AAE positions black masculinity with physical prowess, yet maintains the racial hierarchy that enables white appropriation of African American cultural forms. Both Rampton and Bucholtz consider such political dimensions when youth transgress ethnic boundaries in the construction of identities that defy fixed notions of language and ethnicity.

Language education

Language classrooms are perhaps obvious sites where questions of language and ethnicity become central. Unlike mainstream classrooms in which adherence to mainstream norms is often expected, language classrooms often assume – if not insist – that ethnicity play a role in the teaching and learning of language. Leung *et al.* challenge such assumptions about ethnicity in the field of Teaching English to Speakers of Other Languages (TESOL) through their critique of the 'idealized native speaker'. Particularly in multiethnic urban areas, they question the blanket assumption that ethnic groups simply inherit language traditions:

> a significant number of ethnic minority adolescent pupils demonstrate a weak sense of affiliation to their supposed home/community L1 ... In addition, other ethnic minorities may claim affiliation to linguistic varieties that are supposed to be part of the natural inheritance of other ethnic groups ... At the same time a similar tendency is also visible among ethnic majority pupils ... And there is evidence that some White pupils have a weak affiliation with standard English and use nonstandard forms by choice. (Leung *et al.*, 1997: 557)

Reviewing studies that similarly embrace how ethnicity is produced rather than given, this section covers language and ethnicity research in a variety of language education settings, including second language, foreign language, heritage language, bilingual and dual-language classrooms.

Much research examines the complex emergence of ethnic minority identities in contexts of language education. Drawing from a four-year ethnographic study of a Spanish-English bilingual high school in New York City, Bartlett (2007) examines how the identity of a Dominican immigrant girl, Maria, shifts over time. Bartlett argues that Maria is able to escape the limits of the student with interrupted formal education (SIFE) label and inhabit a 'good student' identity, partly because the local model of success grants high status to Spanish language and literacy. In their two-year ethnographic study of ESL students in a junior high school in California, McKay and Wong (1996) use the concept of investment to explore how four Chinese-speaking immigrant youth invest in the target language as well as in their social identities. McKay and Wong examine how the students adopt various strategies – such as resistance, accommodation and inhabiting the 'quiet Asian' stereotype – to deal with the asymmetrical power relations within which they are unfavorably positioned. In their study of a Spanish-English dual-language program in Arizona, González and Arnot-Hopffer (2003) discuss the relationships between biliteracy development, language ideologies and conceptions of ethnicity among three second grade girls. One girl, Jessica, who comes from a Spanish-dominant home, shifts the ethnic labels she uses to refer to herself: *Blanco* (white), *Mexicana* (Mexican), *Nada* (nothing) and *Mexicana-Americana* (Mexican American). Gonzalez and Arnot-Hopffer discuss these changing terms of ethnic self-reference in light of English language hegemony and shifting language ideologies: in kindergarten, Jessica rejects Spanish, but by second grade, she embraces it as *mi idioma* (my language). Studies on codeswitching in contexts of language education also shed light on emergent identities in response to linguistic hegemony. This work reveals ethnic minority responses to the symbolic domination of a language, such as English (Lin, 1996) or a prestigious variety of French (Heller, 1999).

In heritage language learning contexts where the teacher and students seem to share a common ethnic background, several studies examine how ethnic identities form as language authority in the classroom emerges. In her study of a Korean heritage language program in California, Lo (2004) finds that divisions of ethnic identity among students emerge through shifting epistemic stances of moral evaluation by the teacher. For students who conform to the cultural expectations of a good Korean student, the teacher portrays her access to their thoughts and feelings as more distant and uncertain. For students who do not conform to these expectations, the teacher represents their emotions as self-evident displays of affect. These different authoritative stances produce distinct Korean models of student identification. In a Chinese heritage language classroom, He (2004) examines the emergence of authority around the choice of scripts: *jiantizi*, the simplified official script used in mainland China, and *fantizi*, the traditional script normally used in Taiwan and elsewhere. In teacher–student interaction about which script to use in the classroom, He finds that the expert–novice relationship shifts as teacher authority is not always presupposed to the same degree nor is it always accepted by the students. In her study of Korean American heritage language learners in a university Korean foreign language classroom, Jo (2001) examines the tension between student knowledge of informal Korean and teacher expectations of standard Korean. The informal linguistic variations of students lose their authority once the teacher who represents native authenticity declares that their variations are not standard. While these heritage language learners might be seen as doubly marginalized by both 'native' Korean and English language authorities, Jo argues that students take from both traditions and create new linguistic forms that cross boundaries between different categories of ethnicity and language.

Several studies examine the political consequences when the stigmatization of ethnic groups in language education contexts results in identity divisions. In her ethnography of a French language high school in Toronto, Heller (1999) argues that the politics of identity are shifting from a model rooted in ethnic and linguistic unity to a new model characterized by economic interest and pluralism. Linguistic varieties and language ideologies play important roles in the division of students and in the marginalization of both the 'Quebec students', who are monolingual speakers of the legitimized yet stigmatized Quebec French Vernacular, and the 'Colonized French students', who are monolingual speakers of Standard European French. In a high school ESL class in Hawaii, Talmy (2004) examines how Asian and Pacific Islander ESL students manage the stigmatization of the 'FOB' label (fresh off the boat). He finds that they avoid being positioned as FOB by positioning a newcomer classmate as FOB instead. While the students have successfully escaped the confines of this derogatory label, they have also played a role in the local reproduction of this hierarchical system, which continues to stigmatize students based on ideas of the exoticized cultural and linguistic Other.

Another area of research explores how ethnic varieties can be the target language for immigrant groups. In the field of second language acquisition, there is an assumption that the target variety is the standard variety. Yet deviations from standard forms may not be errors of second language learners; rather, they may reflect learner choices of target varieties and reference groups (Ellis, 1994). In his ethnography of French-speaking Continental African high school students in Ontario, Ibrahim (2003) argues that the racial discourses that construct these immigrant and refugee youth as 'Black' directly influence their identification with Black North Americans and their adoption of Black Stylized English. Choosing AAE as a target variety happens not only among immigrants racialized as black but also among other immigrants of color. Southeast Asian American refugee youth, for example, may identify more with their African American peers, making AAE a more alluring target language (Bucholtz, 2004; Reyes, 2007). As for Latino ESL high school students in New York City, Goldstein (1987) finds a correlation between the amount of reported contact with African Americans and the presence of AAE grammatical features in their speech. These studies reveal how some immigrant groups travel the path of 'segmented assimilation' (Portes & Zhou, 1993), which is the acculturation to a socially and economically marginalized minority community rather than assimilation to the dominant majority. Not unlike African-American students practicing 'guerilla warfare' (Fordham, 1999), second language learners may also be uninspired to incorporate themselves into a mainstream culture that has greeted them with hostility.

Directions for Future Research

There seem to be endless areas to examine in language and ethnicity research. Based on recent scholarly trends that examine how multiple linguistic varieties operate in various learning contexts, I offer three possible directions for building on current educational research: (1) language crossing in language learning contexts; (2) ethnic target varieties for language learners; and (3) media and popular culture in language classrooms. First, more educational research in the productive area of language crossing will continue to inform our understanding of the linguistic construction of ethnicity and ethnic boundaries, particularly with regard to teacher and student identities and classroom practice. As discussed above, most of the educational research on language crossing has so far been conducted in mainstream school settings, but there is much to be explored in language classrooms, including foreign language education (Rampton, 1999). Second, research on ethnic varieties as the target variety of language learners continues to be of pressing concern. Given the increasing global influence of hip-hop culture (Alim, 2006), more exploration in this area will offer important insights into how immigrants of color turn language learning into a symbolic site of political resistance. Finally, another growing area of research explores the role of media and popular culture in language classrooms. Several studies examine how popular cultural references may emerge in the language classroom as meaningful learning resources to students (Rymes, 2003) or as cultural models for inundating immigrants with ideas of national citizenship and consumer capitalism (Zuengler, 2003). More studies that explicitly examine the role of ethnicity are needed in this promising area of research. In all three areas, I would urge researchers to take a multi-sited ethnographic approach, which can provide rich accounts of language and ethnicity across various educational and community contexts.

Relevance to Teachers and Students

Throughout this chapter, I have tried to highlight areas that are of particular relevance to language educators. I will reiterate a few of these points in the closing of this chapter.

I would like to stress again that ethnicity is not a natural category, but a social and political construct. Histories of imbalanced power relations between groups influence the creation of ethnic categories, the formation of ethnic group experiences and the construction of ethnic stereotypes about language and behavior. Ethnic groups and boundaries are not fixed but constantly shifting in response to social and political climates. In fact, it can be quite dangerous for educators to view ethnicity in a static way. Not only can it lead to local misjudgments about student behavior, but also it can contribute to the reproduction of social inequality in education. In reviewing research on mainstream and language classrooms, this chapter revealed how schools are not neutral sites: for example only certain speech norms are assigned legitimate status more easily in the classroom; ethnic groups can be socially and linguistically stigmatized in schools; the manipulation of linguistic features can be a strategy to avoid discrimination in the classroom; and the use of standard English by ethnic minorities can be met with disapproval by classmates. As educators, it is important not to subject students to preconceived notions about the languages, behaviors and abilities that are stereotypically associated with the ethnic groups that students may or may not even identify with.

I would also like to emphasize that there is no one-to-one correspondence between language and ethnicity. Not all members of an ethnic group speak an ethnic variety, and not all ethnic groups have an ethnic variety. For example, an ethnic variety, such as AAE, Chicano English or Native American English, can be used by both members and nonmembers of an ethnic group. Asian Americans, who have no ethnic variety but can be linked to mainstream American English, a foreign accent and nonstandard English, further complicate any natural association between language and ethnicity. In presenting a section that covered language use by ethnic group in this chapter, my goal was not to reify a link between language and ethnicity but to discuss how linguistic issues can be central to the construction of ethnic identities. An important part of this chapter presented the documented systematicity of ethnic varieties, namely AAE. This research reveals that nonstandard varieties are not laden with errors, as popular imagination would have it, but are just as grammatical as standard varieties. This knowledge is absolutely vital for teachers. When deviations from the standard are enacted by students, they may be quickly greeted with confusion, criticism and punishment. Language educators are in powerful positions to correct these judgments. Whether a student is simply complying with his or her own ethnic community norms or strategically deploying an ethnically defined convention for a particular purpose, language educators trained in sociolinguistics are the most prepared to understand the complexity of language and ethnicity in these situations.

Although many educators are already overburdened with meeting the goals of the mandated school curriculum, it would benefit both teachers and students if discussions of language and ethnicity were incorporated into the classroom. Such discussions would help educators learn about the local models of language and ethnicity that students draw on in their understanding of themselves and others. If students speak a distinct ethnic variety, design class activities to uncover the systematicity of the language. For example students could become ethnographers through group projects that document the multiple speech styles heard in the school and community. Have open class discussions and debates about language attitudes, standard English, style shifting and multilingualism. Uncover student understandings of what ethnicity is, what language is and how the two relate. Such activities could become springboards for discussing alternative conceptualizations of language and ethnicity that depart from fixed perspectives.

Suggestions for further reading

Baugh, J. (2000) *Beyond Ebonics: Linguistic Pride and Racial Prejudice*. New York: Oxford University Press.
An immensely readable account of the 1996 Oakland Ebonics case, this book also focuses on how the debates that surrounded this controversial moment in history remain important to current issues in language and education.

Curtis, A. and Romney, A. (eds) (2006) *Color, Race, and English Language Teaching: Shades of Meaning*. Mahwah, NJ: Lawrence Erlbaum.
This book is an edited collection featuring the voices of TESOL professionals of color. Authors offer accounts of their professional experiences in light of their ethnic and racial backgrounds.

Fought, C. (2006) *Language and Ethnicity*. New York: Cambridge University Press.
This is the first monograph on language and ethnicity. There are several sections that focus specifically on educational issues and implications.

Kubota, R. and Lin, A.M.Y. (eds) (2009) *Race, Culture, and Identities in Second Language Education: Exploring Critically Engaged Practice*. New York: Routledge.
This edited collection of studies takes a critical perspective on the role of race and ethnicity in second language teaching and learning.

References

Alim, H.S. (2004) *You Know My Steez: An Ethnographic and Sociolinguistic Study of Styleshifting in a Black American Speech Community*. Durham, NC: Duke University Press.

Alim, H.S. (2006) *Roc the Mic Right: The Language of Hip Hop Culture*. New York: Routledge.

Au, K. (1980) Participation structures in a reading lesson with Hawaiian children: Analysis of a culturally appropriate instructional event. *Anthropology and Education Quarterly* 11 (2), 91–115.

Bailey, B. (2002) *Language, Race, and Negotiation of Identity: A Study of Dominican Americans*. New York: LFB Scholarly Publishing.

Barrett, R. (1999) Indexing polyphonous identity in the speech of African American drag queens. In M. Bucholtz, A.C. Liang and L.A. Sutton (eds) *Reinventing Identities: The Gendered Self in Discourse* (pp. 313–331). New York: Oxford University Press.

Barth, F. (ed.) (1969) *Ethnic Groups and Boundaries: The Social Organization of Culture Difference*. Boston: Little, Brown and Company.

Bartlett, L. (2007) Transnational literacies: Immigration, language learning, and identity. *Linguistics and Education* 18 (3–4), 215–231.

Basso, K.H. (1979) *Portraits of "The Whiteman": Linguistic Play and Cultural Symbols Among the Western Apache*. Cambridge: Cambridge University Press.

Baugh, J. (1998) Linguistics, education, and the law: Educational reform for African-American language minority students. In S.S. Mufwene, J.R. Rickford, G. Bailey and J. Baugh (eds) *African-American English: Structure, History, and Use* (pp. 282–301). New York: Routledge.

Baugh, J. (2000) *Beyond Ebonics: Linguistic Pride and Racial Prejudice*. New York: Oxford University Press.

Bautista, M.L. (ed.) (1997) *English is an Asian Language: The Philippine Context*. Australia: Macquarie Library Pty. Ltd.

Bucholtz, M. (1995) From Mulatta to Mestiza: Passing and the linguistic reshaping of ethnic identity. In K. Hall and M. Bucholtz (eds) *Gender Articulated: Language and the Socially Constructed Self* (pp. 351–374). New York: Routledge.

Bucholtz, M. (1999) You da man: Narrating the racial other in the production of white masculinity. *Journal of Sociolinguistics* 3 (4), 443–460.

Bucholtz, M. (2001) The whiteness of nerds: Superstandard English and racial markedness. *Journal of Linguistic Anthropology* 11 (1), 84–100.

Bucholtz, M. (2004) Styles and stereotypes: The linguistic negotiation of identity among Laotian American youth. *Pragmatics* 14 (2/3), 127–147.

Chun, E. (2001) The Construction of White, Black, and Korean American identities through African American Vernacular English. *Journal of Linguistic Anthropology* 11 (1), 52–64.

Coupland, N. (2001) Dialect stylization in radio talk. *Language in Society* 30, 345–75.

Curtis, A. and Romney, A. (eds) (2006) *Color, Race, and English Language Teaching: Shades of Meaning.* Mahwah, NJ: Lawrence Erlbaum.

Delpit, L. (2006) What should teachers do? Ebonics and culturally responsive instruction. In S.J. Nero (ed.) *Dialects, Englishes, Creoles, and Education* (pp. 93–101). New York: Lawrence Erlbaum.

Dillard, J.L. (1972) *Black English: Its History and Usage in the United States.* New York: Random House.

Eckert, P. (2000) *Linguistic Variation as Social Practice: The Linguistic Construction of Identity in Belten High.* Oxford: Blackwell.

Ellis, R. (1994) *The Study of Second Language Acquisition.* Oxford: Oxford University Press.

Erickson, F. and Shultz, J. (1982) *The Counselor as Gatekeeper: Social Interaction in Interviews.* New York: Academic Press.

Espiritu, Y.L. (1992) *Asian American Panethnicity: Bridging Institutions and Identities.* Philadelphia: Temple University Press.

Fishman, J. (1989) *Language and Ethnicity in Minority Sociolinguistic Perspective.* Clevedon/Philadelphia: Multilingual Matters.

Foley, D.E. (1996) The silent Indian as a cultural production. In B.A. Levinson, D.E. Foley and D.C. Holland (eds) *The Cultural Production of the Educated Person* (pp. 79–81). Albany: State University of New York Press.

Fordham, S. (1999) Dissin' "the Standard": Ebonics as Guerrilla Warfare at Capital High. *Anthropology and Education Quarterly* 30 (3), 272–293.

Fordham, S. and Ogbu, J. (1986) Black students' school success: Coping with the burden of acting white. *Urban Review* 18, 176–206.

Fought, C. (2003) *Chicano English in Context.* New York: Palgrave Macmillan Publishers.

Fought, C. (2006) *Language and Ethnicity.* New York: Cambridge University Press.

Gal, S. (1979) *Language Shift: Social Determinants of Linguistic Change in Bilingual Austria.* New York: Academic Press.

Gal, S. and Irvine, J. (1995) The boundaries of languages and disciplines: How ideologies construct difference. *Social Research* 62 (4), 967–1001.

Gibson, M. (1988) *Accommodation without Assimilation: Sikh Immigrants in an American High School.* Ithaca: Cornell University Press.

Gilroy, P. (1987) *There Ain't No Black in the Union Jack.* London: Hutchinson.

Goddard, I. (ed.) (1996) *Languages (Handbook of North American Indians)* (Vol. 17). Washington, DC: Smithsonian Institution.

Goldstein, L. (1987) Standard English: The only target for nonnative speakers of English? *TESOL Quarterly* 21 (3), 417–436.

González, N. and Arnot-Hopffer, E. (2003) Voices of the children: Language and literacy ideologies in a dual language immersion program. In S. Wortham and B. Rymes (eds) *Linguistic Anthropology of Education* (pp. 213–243). Westport, CT: Praeger.

Green, L. (2002) *African American English: A Linguistic Introduction*. Cambridge: Cambridge University Press.

Gumperz, J.J. (1982) *Discourse Strategies*. New York: Cambridge University Press.

Gumperz, J.J. and Cook-Gumperz, J. (1982) Introduction: Language and the communication of social identity. In J. Gumperz (ed.) *Language and Social Identity* (pp. 22–56). Cambridge: Cambridge University Press.

Hall, S. (1988) New ethnicities. *ICA Documents 7*, 27–31.

Hanna, D.B. (1997) Do I sound 'Asian' to you?: Linguistic markers of Asian American identity. In C. Boberg, M. Meyerhoff and S. Strassel (eds) *University of Pennsylvania Working Papers in Linguistics* (Vol. 4 (2)), (pp. 141–153). Philadelphia: Department of Linguistics, University of Pennsylvania.

Harklau, L. (1994) ESL versus mainstream classes: Contrasting L2 learning environments. *TESOL Quarterly 28*, 241–272.

He, A.W. (2004) Identity construction in Chinese heritage language classes. *Pragmatics 14* (2/3), 199–216.

He, A.W. and Xiao, Y. (eds) (2008) *Chinese as a Heritage Language: Fostering Rooted World Citizenry*. National Foreign Language Resource Center. University of Hawai'i at Manoa. Honolulu: University of Hawai'i Press.

Heath, S.B. (1983) *Ways with Words: Language, Life, and Work in Communities and Classrooms*. Cambridge: Cambridge University Press.

Heath, S.B. and McLaughlin, M.W. (eds) (1993) *Identity and Inner-city Youth: Beyond Ethnicity and Gender*. New York: Teachers College Press.

Heller, M. (1999) *Linguistic Minorities and Modernity: A Sociolinguistic Ethnography*. New York: Longman.

Hewitt, R. (1986) *White Talk Black Talk: Inter-racial Friendship and Communication Amongst Adolescents*. Cambridge: Cambridge University Press.

Hill, J.H. (1995) Mock Spanish: A site for the indexical reproduction of racism in American English. *Language and Culture Online Symposium 2*, October 1995.

Hill, J.H. (1999) Language, race, and white public space. *American Anthropologist 100* (3), 680–689.

Holmes, J. (1997) Maori and Pakeha English: Some New Zealand social dialect data. *Language in Society 26*, 65–101.

Hornberger, N.H. (1988) *Bilingual Education and Language Maintenance*. Dordrecht, The Netherlands: Foris Publications.

Hymes, D. (1974) *Foundations in Sociolinguistics: An Ethnographic Approach*. Philadelphia: University of Pennsylvania Press.

Ibrahim, A.M. (2003) "Whassup, homeboy?" Joining the African Diaspora: Black English as a symbolic site of identification and language learning. In S. Makoni, G. Smitherman, A.F. Ball and A.K. Spears (eds) *Black Linguistics: Language, Society, and Politics in Africa and the Americas* (pp. 169–185). New York: Routledge.

Jaffe, A. (1999) *Ideologies in Action: Language Politics on Corsica*. Berlin: Mouton de Gruyter.

Jenkins, R. (1994) Rethinking ethnicity: Identity, categorization and power. *Ethnic and Racial Studies 17*, 197–223.

Jo, H. (2001) 'Heritage' language learning and ethnic identity: Korean Americans' struggle with language authorities. *Language, Culture and Curriculum 14* (1), 26–41.

Kachru, B.B. (1983) *The Indianization of English: The English Language in India*. Delhi: Oxford University Press.

Kang, M.A. (2004) Constructing ethnic identity through discourse: Self-categorization among Korean American camp counselors. *Pragmatics 14* (2/3), 217–234.

Kanno, Y. (2003) *Negotiating Bilingual and Bicultural Identities: Japanese Returnees Betwixt Two Worlds*. Mahwah, NJ: Lawrence Erlbaum.

Kiesling, S. (2001) Stances of whiteness and hegemony in fraternity men's discourse. *Journal of Linguistic Anthropology* 11 (1), 101–115.

Krauss, M. (1998) The condition of Native North American languages: The need for realistic assessment and action. *International Journal of the Sociology of Language* 132, 9–21.

Kubota, R. and Lin, A.M.Y. (eds) (2009) *Race, Culture, and Identities in Second Language Education: Exploring Critically Engaged Practice*. New York: Routledge.

Labov, W. (1972) *Language in the Inner City: Studies in the Black English Vernacular*. Philadelphia: University of Pennsylvania Press.

Labov, W. and Harris, W.A. (1986) De facto segregation of black and white vernaculars. In D. Sankoff (ed.) *Diversity and Diachrony* (pp. 1–24). Amsterdam: John Benjamins.

Le Page, R.B. and Tabouret-Keller, A. (1985) *Acts of Identity: Creole-based Approaches to Language and Ethnicity*. Cambridge: Cambridge University Press.

Leap, W. (1993) *American Indian English*. Salt Lake City: University of Utah Press.

Lee, S. (1996) *Unraveling the "Model Minority" Stereotype: Listening to Asian American Youth*. New York: Teachers College Press.

Leung, C., Harris, R. and Rampton, B. (1997) The idealised native speaker, reified ethnicities, and classroom realities. *TESOL Quarterly* 31, 543–560.

Lin, A.M.Y. (1996) Bilingualism or linguistic segregation? Symbolic domination, resistance and code-switching in Hong Kong schools. *Linguistics and Education* 8, 49–84.

Lo, A. (2004) Evidentiality and morality in a Korean heritage language school. *Pragmatics* 14 (2/3), 235–256.

McDermott, R. and Gospodinoff, K. (1981) Social contexts for ethnic borders and school failure. In H. Trueba, G. Guthrie and K. Au (eds) *Culture and the Bilingual Classroom* (pp. 212–230). Rowley, MA: Newbury House.

McKay, S. and Wong, S. (1996) Multiple discourses, multiple identities: Investment and agency in second-language learning among Chinese adolescent immigrant students. *Harvard Educational Review* 66, 577–608.

Mendoza-Denton, N. (1996) "Muy Macha": Gender and Ideology in Gang-girls' Discourse about Makeup. *Ethnos* 61 (1–2), 47–63.

Mendoza-Denton, N. (2008) *Homegirls: Language and Cultural Practice Among Latina Youth Gangs*. Hoboken, NJ: Wiley-Blackwell.

Mendoza-Denton, N. and Iwai, M. (1993) "They speak more Caucasian": Generational differences in the speech of Japanese-Americans. In R. Queen and R. Barrett (eds) *SALSA I: Proceedings of the First Annual Symposium About Language and Society – Austin* (pp. 58–67). Austin: Department of Linguistics, University of Texas.

Mesthrie, R. (2002) *Language in South Africa*. Cambridge: Cambridge University Press.

Morgan, M.H. (1991) Indirectness and interpretation in African American women's discourse. *Pragmatics* 1 (4), 421–451.

Omi, M. and Winant, H. (1994) *Racial Formation in the United States: From the 1960s to the 1980s*. New York: Routledge.

Orellana, M. (1999) Good guys and "bad" girls. In M. Bucholtz, A.C. Liang and L.A. Sutton (eds) *Reinventing Identities: The Gendered Self in Discourse* (pp. 64–82). New York: Oxford University Press.

Philips, S.U. (1983) *The Invisible Culture: Communication in Classroom and Community on the Warm Springs Indian Reservation*. New York: Longman.

Poplack, S, and Tagliamonte, S. (1989) There's no tense like the present: Verbal -s inflection in early Black English. *Language Variation and Change* 1, 47–89.

Portes, A. and Zhou, M. (1993) The new second generation: Segmented assimilation and its variants. *The Annals of the American Academy of Political and Social Sciences* 530 (November), 74–96.

Preston, D.R. (1992) Talking black and talking white: A study in variety imitation. In J.H. Hall, N. Doane and D. Ringler (eds) *Old English and New: Studies in Language and Linguistics in Honor of Frederic G. Cassidy* (pp. 327–355). New York: Garland.

Rahman, J. (2007) An ay for an ah: Language of survival in African American narrative comedy. *American Speech* 82 (1), 65–96.

Rampton, B. (1995) *Crossing: Language and Ethnicity Among Adolescents*. London: Longman.

Rampton, B. (1999) Deutsch in Inner London and the animation of an instructed foreign language. *Journal of Sociolinguistics* 3 (4), 480–504.

Reyes, A. (2007) *Language, Identity, and Stereotype Among Southeast Asian American Youth: The Other Asian*. Mahwah, NJ: Lawrence Erlbaum.

Reyes, A. and Lo, A. (2004) Language, identity and relationality in Asian Pacific America: An introduction. *Pragmatics* 14 (2/3), 115–125.

Reyes, A. and Lo, A. (eds) (2009) *Beyond Yellow English: Toward a Linguistic Anthropology of Asian Pacific America*. New York: Oxford University Press.

Rickford, J.R. (1996) Regional and social variation. In S. McKay and N.H. Hornberger (eds) *Sociolinguistics and Language Teaching* (pp. 151–194). New York: Cambridge University Press.

Rickford, J.R. (1999) *African American Vernacular English: Features, Evolution, Educational Implications*. Oxford: Blackwell.

Rickford, J.R. and Rickford, R.J. (2000) *Spoken Soul: The Story of Black English*. New York: Wiley.

Roth-Gordon, J. (2007) Racing and erasing the playboy: Slang, transnational youth subculture, and racial discourse in Brazil. *Journal of Linguistic Anthropology* 17 (2), 246–265.

Rymes, B. (2003) Contrasting zones of comfortable competence: Popular culture in a phonics lesson. *Linguistics and Education* 14 (3–4), 321–335.

Scollon, R. and Scollon, S.B.K. (1981) *Narrative, Literacy and Face in Interethnic Communication*. Norwood, NJ: Ablex.

Smitherman, G. (1981) *Black English and the Education of Black Children and Youth*. Detroit: Wayne State University Center for Black Studies Press.

Spencer, R.F. (1950) Japanese-American language behavior. *American Speech* 25 (4), 241–252.

Talmy, S. (2004) Forever FOB: The cultural production of ESL in a high school. *Pragmatics* 14 (2/3), 149–172.

Tannen, D. (1981) New York Jewish conversational style. *International Journal of the Sociology of Language* 30, 133–149.

Taylor, H. (1989) *Standard English, Black English, and Bidialectalism*. New York: Peter Lang.

Tetreault, C. (2008) *La racaille*: Figuring gender, generation, and stigmatized space in a French *cité*. *Gender and Language* 2 (2), 141–170.

Trechter, S. and Bucholtz, M. (2001) White noise: Bringing language into whiteness studies. *Journal of Linguistic Anthropology* 11 (1), 3–21.

Tuan, M. (1998) *Forever Foreigners or Honorary Whites? The Asian Ethnic Experience Today*. New Brunswick, NJ: Rutgers University Press.

Urciuoli, B. (1996) *Exposing Prejudice: Puerto Rican Experiences of Language, Race, and Class*. Boulder, CO: Westview Press.

Waters, M. (1990) *Ethnic Options: Choosing Identities in America*. Berkeley: University of California Press.

Wolfram, W. (1969) *A Sociolinguistic Description of Detroit Negro Speech*. Washington, DC: Center for Applied Linguistics.

Woolard, K.A. (1989) *Double Talk: Bilingualism and the Politics of Ethnicity in Catalonia*. Stanford, CA: Stanford University Press.

Wortham, S.E.F. (2006) *Learning Identity: The Joint Emergence of Social Identification and Academic Learning*. New York: Cambridge University Press.

Yamamoto, A.Y. and Zepeda, O. (2004) Native American languages. In E. Finegan and J.R. Rickford (eds) *Language in the USA: Themes for the Twenty-first Century* (pp. 153–181). Cambridge: Cambridge University Press.

Zentella, A.C. (1997) *Growing Up Bilingual: Puerto Rican Children in New York*. Malden, MA: Blackwell.

Zentella, A.C. (2004) Spanish in the Northeast. In E. Finegan and J.R. Rickford (eds) *Language in the USA: Themes for the Twenty-first Century* (pp. 182–204). Cambridge: Cambridge University Press.

Zuengler, J. (2003) Jackie Chan drinks Mountain Dew: Constructing cultural models of citizenship. *Linguistics and Education* 14 (3–4), 277–304.

Chapter 16
Language Socialization

PATRICIA A. DUFF

Introduction

Language socialization refers to the acquisition of linguistic, pragmatic and other cultural knowledge through social experience and is often equated with the development of cultural and communicative competence. Research in this area examines these aspects of learning and also how individuals become socialized into particular identities, worldviews or values, and ideologies as they learn language, whether it is their first language or an additional language. Thus, language socialization explores how people learn how to take part in the speech events and activities of everyday life: jokes, greetings, classroom lessons, story-telling or essay or memo writing and also the values underlying those practices. Being able to participate in language practices appropriately, according to local expectations and conventions, allows humans to function well in society.

Various definitions of language socialization exist but one that I have used draws on work by language socialization pioneers Elinor Ochs, Bambi Schieffelin and others: language socialization is 'the lifelong process by which individuals – typically novices – are inducted into specific domains of knowledge, beliefs, affect, roles, identities, and social representations, which they access and construct through language practices and social interaction ...' (Duff, 1995: 508). One of the domains of knowledge is of course language and literacy itself. This 'induction' or socialization[1] of novices such as first- and second-language learners normally occurs through social interaction between those with more proficiency, expertise or experience in language, literacy and culture (often referred to as 'experts' or 'oldtimers'), and those with less proficiency (relative 'novices' or 'newcomers'[2]): older siblings interacting with younger siblings; teachers with students; caregivers with children; and more experienced workers with new employees in a workplace.

By saying that language socialization is a 'lifelong' process (Ochs & Schieffelin, 2008), we mean that children are not the only ones being socialized into appropriate ways of using language ('Say *please, thank*

427

you!'), such as greetings or leave takings (*Hi/Goodbye Grandma! Good night*). As individuals learn to take part in activities at school, or in their faith communities and community centers, or later in higher education or work contexts, they must learn to use oral and written language in increasingly sophisticated ways.

This chapter provides an overview of about three decades of research on language socialization. In the first part, I discuss language socialization theory generally and how it relates to both sociolinguistics and language education in formal and informal contexts. In the second part, I focus on language and literacy socialization in formal educational contexts in particular, such as mainstream subject-area classrooms or language class-rooms in schools, universities or vocational training centers. I then go on to review research methods commonly used in language socialization research, and especially those involving the ethnography of communication and fine-tuned discourse analysis, and present key findings in classroom-oriented language socialization research. Finally, the relevance of research on language socialization for teachers, students and other participants and stakeholders in education is explained and illustrated with concrete examples from recently published research.

Language Socialization: Linguistic and Nonlinguistic Dimensions

Since its inception, language socialization has drawn on a number of disciplines, especially linguistic anthropology, sociology, psychology and (socio)linguistics. It has also been influenced to a great degree by (neo-) Vygotskian sociocultural theory about the highly social, and culturally and historically situated and co-constructed, nature of learning (Duff, 2007a; Ochs & Schieffelin, 2008; Watson-Gegeo, 2004; Watson-Gegeo & Nielsen, 2003). Dell Hymes, one of the 'fathers' of sociolinguistics, was an ardent early champion of language socialization research (Ervin-Tripp, 2009). The focus on mentors' provision of covert or overt assistance to others so they can learn particular uses of language and also the values, subjectivities and affective orientations underlying those language choices points to the core relationship between language socialization and sociolinguistics.

Sociolinguistics often deals with the study of language variation and norms and functions of language use in speech communities according to such variables as gender, social class, region and speech context (e.g. speech event) and provides very detailed accounts of variation across reg-isters, dialects, genres and interlocutors of different status (e.g. McKay & Hornberger, 1996). Language socialization, for its part, examines how people entering new cultures or communities, whether as children or adults, learn what those norms of language use are on the basis of observa-tions and interactions with more experienced members of the culture. For example, language socialization investigates what forms of language use and participation and what kinds of literacy practices might be required for new primary school students or high school students, or law school and medical students in a given culture and how those students learn to accomplish what is expected through social and linguistic experience.

A common focus of classroom studies from a language socialization perspective is how interaction between and among teachers and students typically unfolds in educational contexts and the ideologies and subjectivities associated with the practices. Beginning sequences from elementary classroom lessons in Japan, Brunei (Negara Brunei Darussalam) and Taiwan, respectively, are shown below, adapted from Barnard and Torres-Guzmán (2009). Notice the roles and turn-taking behaviors, both verbal and nonverbal, of the teachers and students, the languages and registers used, and the ways in which the lesson is framed or organized by these openings and, therefore, how the teacher is socializing students, including the class monitors, to comply with local instructional discourse. Words that appear in italics have been translated into English; nonitalicized language was produced in English in the original. Excerpt 1 is from a social studies lesson and Excerpts 2 and 3 are from English lessons.

Excerpt 1 (Japan: T = teacher; Ss = two class monitors)

T: *Okay, let's begin!* ((using Japanese))
Ss: *Sit up straight! We now begin the social studies lesson. Bow!*
Ss: ((All students bow))
T: *Okay. The lesson is called Everybody's Park ...*
    (adapted from Anderson, 2009: 18)

Excerpt 2 (Brunei: T = Teacher; Mo = class monitor)

T: *Where again? Where again?* ((using Bahasa Melayu/Malay
    language)) Ha? Sit down. Okay
Ss: ((Seated in single rows, stand up))
Mo: *Peace be with you,* good morning teacher ((using an Arabic greeting,
    expected by Muslim teachers, followed by English))
Ss: *Peace be with you,* good morning teacher
T: *With you be peace,* good morning, sit down
T: Now, you have your English revision ((writes 'English revision' on
    the blackboard)) Now, what is it today?
Ss: Today is Thursday
T: Again
Ss: Today is Thursday ...
    (adapted from McLellan & Hui, 2009: 57)

Excerpt 3 (Taiwan)

T: *Right, now let's begin with our lesson* ((in Mandarin)). OK, number 2.
    Who is number 2? ((a student raises a hand)) Please stand up.

((student stands)) OK. Can you tell me what this is ((with a flash-card of the picture pepper))

Ss: Pepper.

T: Pepper. Very good. 26. Where is 26? Ok, what is this?

Ss: ((silence))

T: OK, everyone stand up. *Stand up. If you keep quiet, please sit down. That's okay, if you want to stand up, it's all right. I know you want to chat. That's fine. Our rule is that, if you want to talk, you have to stand up.*

T: Ok, it's ok. 26. What is this?

Sa: (xxx)

T: In English. No Chinese.

Ss: Butter ....

(adapted from Tien & Barnard, 2009: 92)

Not surprisingly, in all three contexts, the teacher demonstrates his or her authority and control, from the first sign that the lesson has begun. However, in Excerpts 1 and 2 student monitors also play the role of initiating opening sequences and managing classroom behavior, by telling their peers to sit up straight and bow (Excerpt 1, in Japan), and modeling how the teacher should be formally greeted (using Arabic and English in Excerpt 2 in Brunei, not the Malay vernacular). They are also socializing their peers and mediating communication between the teacher and the class. Excerpt 3 begins more abruptly with students being asked, after just one opening move by the teacher, to stand up and answer questions about the English lesson, even though the responses seem to be part of a chorus of student voices. In the same excerpt, students are referred to by numbers, not by their names, and are expected to speak during the instructional phase in English, not Mandarin Chinese or Taiwanese (local languages the students are bilingual in). We also observe that students are required to comport themselves physically in particular ways, standing when speaking to the teacher in some cases, bowing at the beginning of the lesson (Excerpt 1), putting their hands up to identify themselves as potential speakers, but not speaking unless standing up; and otherwise sitting attentively. Ideologies of respect, the sociolinguistics of polite greetings between teachers and students, and questioning patterns for classroom instruction are all being modeled (see also Howard & Lo, 2009). Students are being socialized in each case into the local norms and practices – and the languages, registers and speech acts – of their school cultures and lessons.

Such opening routines in classroom lessons no doubt vary in some respects across languages and cultures but tend to demonstrate certain commonalities related to focusing students' attention on the day's lesson or on a particular activity, as well as on the teacher's (or a guest speaker's or student presenter's) instruction. The routines also help manage turn-taking.

Beyond these routines, we could look more specifically at the activities or assignments that students must do once instruction has really begun and consider how they are being socialized into those social and linguistic, or discursive, practices. Research might look specifically at the components and criteria for successfully preparing for and then performing an oral presentation, such as a show-and-tell session for young children or a high school science project presentation on the environment. In higher-education contexts, the presentation might be about an important legal case in law school, a particular medical research finding or case history in medical school, or a group presentation on cell phone circuitry in engineering. Thus, language socialization research analyzes how teachers or students lay the foundation for participation in each of those spheres as a presenter, team member, or audience member. The socialization may occur by means of explicit discussion in the course outline, by modeling presentations for students, or by giving instruction and public feedback on presentations that participants can learn from (see Duff, 1995, 2009; Kobayashi, 2004; Morita, 2000; Zappa-Hollman, 2007a). In Excerpt 4, we observe the beginning of a Canadian high school social studies class (Duff, 2009) in which a student is scheduled to make a presentation, and then the feedback (socialization) provided by the teacher afterward. As in the earlier excerpts, students are expected to be quiet and attentive before the instructional phase, the presentation, begins.

Excerpt 4 (Canada)

Teacher:	Sooh, we're **finally** ready for current events so when Dean is paying attention and when Susan
S1:	Yeah.
T:	is a good member of the audience, then we'll start. Yep.
Dean:	((comes up to the front of the class and writes his title on the board)) Uh my article is on ... ((makes his presentation and then is finished))
Ss:	'Applause by class'
T:	Okay. Great. That was a nice uh conversational manner you have when you – it's not like you're reading. That's excellent 'cause you're **not** reading. Nice job there. Uh there may be – What?
S2:	(Nothing?)
T:	There m – no I mean I'm encouraging – that's good public speaking.

(adapted from Duff, 2009: 169)

In this excerpt, then, the teacher again focuses students' attention on the instructional activity performed by Dean, telling students (using Susan as an example) to be good members of the audience, and then praises

Dean after the class applauds for having delivered the presentation in a 'nice conversational manner ... not reading ... that's good public speaking'. The teacher was socializing students into (1) respectful behaviors as audience members in a presentation, including silence and applause at the end, and (2) appropriate presentation behaviors, among other messages.

Thus, one aspect of classroom socialization is teachers' (and students') use of particular linguistic markers to stress the most important components of the content or manner of such presentations, using intensifiers, other adverbs, emphatic speech, imperatives and adjectives describing presentations (e.g. 'wonderful, very interesting, concise, beautiful' versus 'long, ill-prepared, unfocused' (Duff, 1996, 2009); or 'that's excellent, 'cause you're not reading', in the previous excerpt. These terms not only relate to the qualities of presentations but also to the hearer's pleasure or displeasure – their affective stance – with respect to certain kinds of linguistic performance. In addition, their socializing messages are intended not only for the current presenter but for the whole class. The subjectivities being socialized in students might include the identity of a capable, comfortable, and articulate presenter, a bilingual speaker, a good audience member, a budding young scientist, someone who has just been to an interesting tourist destination and has brought back an artifact from the trip, or an experienced and mature language teacher or researcher in graduate school (not just a 'student') who has valuable insights to share (see Garrett, 2007, for a discussion of language socialization into particular subjectivities).

In my research on students' socialization into and through recitation practices in secondary schools in Hungary (Duff, 1995, 1996), I observed how students were being socialized into the identity of educated Hungarians with a thorough knowledge of history and an ability to express themselves well: coherently, fluently, accurately and especially orally. Other recent research has also examined students' socialization into ideologies and identities connected with nationalism that were also linked with language code choice (see Friedman, 2010).

Affective orientations or dispositions and values are commonly learned together with, or through, language. Much early language socialization research with young children, in particular, examined how fear, anger, desire, shame, pride, excitement, or humility are socialized through language and how, for instance, young children in a particular culture might be taught to say certain things to avoid shame or, conversely, might be taught to shame others who have acted unbecomingly. They also learn to express and interpret anger, fear, affection or desire in culturally and linguistically acceptable ways (for a review, see Ochs & Schieffelin, 2008). Shaming or reprimanding has been a common theme in language socialization work with children, both in and out of school, because it is such a pervasive mechanism for ensuring that newcomers comply with local norms rather than risk public or private humiliation by others. People must also learn to express gratitude in culturally and linguistically appropriate ways, or risk being considered rude or self-centered.

Affective stances in formal educational contexts might involve expressing passion or enthusiasm about academic content ('I thought this was a *fascinating* topic' or 'Isn't this piece of lava I found *cool*?'), or conveying one's nervousness about presenting (hedging, stammering, speaking too softly or saying things like 'I'm, um, kind of nervous to be standing up here'). Some of these same behaviors might receive feedback such as, 'Could you speak louder?' or 'Don't say you're nervous; everyone's nervous at first', or laughter and rolling eyes (Duff, 2002). Students might be expected to frame their remarks in the first person: '*I* believe that ...', or they might be asked to present in a somewhat more dispassionate and objective voice '*Scientists* believe that x causes y...'). They might encode their degree of certainty or conviction about a topic (their epistemic stance) in English in ways that they have observed in others, using particular verbs ('I *argue* that ...'), adjectives ('the *best* example') or adverbs (*certainly, obviously*); alternatively, they may be socialized within a particular context to soften or mitigate their opinions with modals auxiliaries (e.g. *may, should, might*) or other markers of less certainty (*possibly, perhaps*, 'I *don't know for sure* but ...'), so as not to seem too arrogant or strident in their claims (see e.g. Morita, 2000; Zappa-Hollman, 2007a). These examples come from English but studies have looked at these sorts of phenomena across a variety of languages and speech events (e.g. Duranti *et al.*, in press).

In addition to examining how people are socialized into the communicative practices of those with more experience in their new discourse communities, studies have looked at how, as languages are learned, so too are other forms of knowledge and other semiotic (meaning-making) systems. Thus, studies have considered how nonlinguistic knowledge is instilled and mediated by language as well as linguistic knowledge. Nonlinguistic knowledge might include understandings and beliefs about the world and of one's place in the world as a high-status person or a low-status person, an insider or an outsider, about prevailing academic, professional or religious epistemologies and values (e.g. Fader, 2006), about gendered or other social identities, or even about knowledge about work and about play (e.g. Kyratzis & Cook-Gumperz, 2008; Paugh, 2008). Thus, language mediates the development of people's identities as individuals with particular traits, roles or subjectivities (as child, girl or boy, student, athlete, teacher, new immigrant, public speaker, Deaf individual; or as a credible lawyer, doctor or engineer). People are also socialized into identities in relation to the groups they are part of or becoming part of (engineers, lawyers) – or they may resist being socialized into particular identities or positioned as such (e.g. as a compliant student), and instead may exert their agency and foreground other identities, as outspoken critic or class clown, for example.

Gendered identities are socialized and co-constructed through language and interaction by parents or teachers and children. When people tell girls or boys to speak or act in a certain way (or, rather, *not* to speak in particular ways that might be at odds with local gendered norms), possibly adding that to *not* comply with those norms would be shameful, inappropriate, immoral, too 'tough' or 'effeminate' or 'weak' and might lead to mockery by others, they are also socializing them into particular values, behaviors and identities. (For recent reviews and examples of gendered language socialization research, see Fader, 2001, 2006; Gordon, 2008; Kyratzis & Cook-Gumperz, 2008; Pavlenko & Piller, 2008.)

People may be socialized, too, into language ideologies that privilege some dialects or varieties or languages (e.g. Excerpts 2 and 3) or historically celebrated speech events (such as recitation activities, Duff, 1996) but not others. Cultural or semiotic content, such as spiritual or moral principles, or ways of engaging with multimedia and digital texts, may also be foregrounded through language and interaction (Baquedano-Lopez & Kattan, 2008; Garrett & Baquedano-Lopez, 2002; Lam, 2008; Ochs & Schieffelin, 2008). Guardado (2009) examined how Hispanic Canadian children in Spanish-language Scouts groups were socialized by leaders (parents) into ideologies of good 'citizenship' (one of the main goals of Scouts); even more importantly, however, they were being socialized into the significance and beauty of Spanish, the value of first-language maintenance and of cultivating a Hispanic identity, and the appropriateness of speaking Spanish with one's peers, even in the face of English hegemony and sometimes contradictory practices by their own leaders and parents with respect to the use of Spanish versus English.

Explicit versus Implicit Language Socialization in Formal and Informal Cross-cultural Educational Contexts

Educational discourse and instruction in each context has its own rules, spoken and unspoken, and its own power dynamics and forms of discursive positioning and socialization (Duff, 2010). Classroom rules or policies are commonly made, broken and contested, although there may not be an official rule book to which participants can turn. Some rules may be explicitly stated in a course outline or explained in the early days of a course or in more general guidelines regarding attendance, punctuality, plagiarism, and academic honesty. For particular kinds of assignments, there may also be clear directions given and precedents or models. Thus, newcomers' socialization may involve explicit or conscious instruction, coaching, or feedback, not only from mentors and policy-makers but also peers, with respect to target norms, conventions and practices.

In classrooms, if students (at all levels of study) shout out answers without raising their hands and thereby being given permission to speak by the teacher, they are likely to be told 'Raise your hands!' or may be 'shshed!'

and they may also be criticized for not complying with classroom rules for participation (as in Excerpt 3). But the socialization process also normally requires extensive experience – being in situations where others are performing the target speech or literacy events or acts according to local conventions. Furthermore, it involves internalization of the rules and self-regulation and then adequate practice and feedback. When the socialization is more implicit than explicit, novices are left to infer and internalize, on their own normative behaviors, norms, and values that they encounter, whether in face-to-face signed or oral interactions, or in virtual interactions in online communities or in various kinds of literacy practices. While implicit socialization in the absence of any explicit modeling or constructive feedback (focus on form) may be effective in some instances, it is risky to assume that it is a generally *adequate* form of socialization, for several reasons: (1) people may not actually *notice* certain important aspects of linguistic form and interaction and will carry on in ways that are not considered appropriate or targetlike and they may be stigmatized by their behaviors (laughed at, criticized, viewed as incompetent) as a result; (2) they may internalize some but not all of the required target practices; and (3) they may never understand the reasons underlying particular practices. In short, implicit learning can be very inefficient learning.

For classroom presentations, for example, the rule may be either explicit or implicit that students should not read a script but should speak to the audience. That message was conveyed indirectly but quite enthusiastically in Excerpt 4. When Dean finished his presentation, the teacher congratulated him for *not* having read his presentation. The teacher had mentioned this principle many times during the year including when the presentations were first assigned and also coached them on the types of topics they should choose. Yet after a series of weekly presentations of this sort, with similar feedback, near the end of the year a relatively new immigrant student from Taiwan, Jean, was asked to make her scheduled presentation, as is shown in Excerpt 5 below. She began by asking 'Do I *have to read* the article?' (emphasis mine). Both a student teacher doing her practice teaching at that time and the regular teacher were present but it was the regular teacher who pointed out that Jean had seen 'lots of current events presentations' during the year and that she shouldn't read the article but should summarize the issue orally. In other words, all of the prior socialization from the year had seemingly not made Jean aware that a presentation should *not* be read, that not just the teacher, but 'we' (the class) 'don't want you just reading your article'. Thus, more scaffolding and practice proved necessary for Jean, who had not yet taken up or internalized that norm.

Excerpt 5 (Canada)

Student T: 'Kay quiet. Let's start.
     T: Shh. Shh. ((to other students)) Jean ((calling her up)).
        Shh. ((to class))

ST:	Okay so uh we'll start the current events and Jean if you want to come up and begin please?
→ Jean:	Do I have to read the article?
ST:	Just write your title on the board
T:	And to answer your question Jean
Jean:	Hmm?
→ T:	To answer your question you've seen lots of current events presentations.
Jean:	Yeah.
→ T:	We don't want you just reading your article right? We want you telling us a summary of the issue right? Right?

(adapted from Duff, 2009: 182)

In the same classroom, the teacher also repeated many times that students were expected to choose topics for their current events presentations that did not simply represent tragedies (such as a plane or car crash) but that were connected with larger social issues and controversies, such as medical ethics (Duff, 2009). However, every time a new 'plane crash' or equivalent presentation was made, he needed to repeat this message.

Not all of language socialization is concerned with codified 'rules' per se, some of it is just conventionalized practice. Mostly it involves local, widely accepted norms of interaction, and of language or literacy use, that must be learned and applied or practiced. Vickers (2007) illustrated how in engineering courses, students working in teams on projects needed to learn, implicitly, to take on certain roles, with the less inexperienced students being socialized into the role – or identity – of *information seekers* or questioners, and the more experienced students *information providers*, explaining relevant principles of computer and electrical engineering to the novices. Gradually, over the course of the year and with experience and growing expertise and confidence, the novices were able to take on greater responsibility for providing explanations. However, these interaction formats and roles were not codified in any way.

Law students must learn to use highly specialized, and often very technical, legal language and a formal register in discussions of legal precedents in law school. This expectation is often made very explicit to new students because knowledge of prior cases and an ability to effectively demonstrate and argue their relevance in new legal situations is a cornerstone of Anglo-American legal practice (Duff, 2008a; Mertz, 1996, 2007). Students must not only know the important past cases relevant to the case they are now dealing with (i.e. they must know law, as a content area), but they must also demonstrate, in rhetorically and legally compelling and accurate ways, the relevance of past cases by recontextualizing or reinterpreting them in the context of the current cases being presented (defended, prosecuted). Yet while some students may be very successful at inferring the appropriate communicative strategies, others may not, for a variety of reasons, without explicit pedagogical intervention or consciousness-raising, a point I will return to.

Language socialization research has always encompassed both *language education* and *language in education* (i.e. socialization/learning *to use language* and socialization/learning *through language*, Ochs & Schieffelin, 2008). However, *education* here should not be equated with formal education. Language socialization research has examined the linguistic and other communicative practices that people are socialized into across a wide range of age groups and geographical, linguistic and social contexts and also how language mediates the acquisition of other kinds of knowledge (about science, law, engineering, about what foods at dinnertime are considered tasty, about the nature of work, or morality; Ochs & Schieffelin, 2008). Informal education contexts range from parent–infant interactions in the home to family dinner table discussions or community center groups (Duff & Hornberger, 2008). The seminal early studies of the socialization of young children (e.g. Schieffelin & Ochs, 1986) examined how people convey expectations to young children regarding norms of communicative competence in their communities, including sociolinguistically or pragmatically appropriate language and literacy use connected with everyday verbal interactions. Studies investigated how children learn, by observation and sometimes prompts, reminders and admonitions to use situationally appropriate greetings, requests and turn-taking behaviors ('Don't interrupt'; 'It's not your turn'; 'Now you can speak') and considered how children learn to take part in other ritualized speech acts, such as teasing, shaming, or insulting one another or engaging in verbal play in the manner that is commonly practiced in their communities (Ochs & Schieffelin, 2008; Schieffelin & Ochs, 1986). The same children may naturally experiment and innovate with language to develop new practices and new codes of language, which create solidarity among their peers but which they were not socialized into by their elders and, indeed, which their elders may dislike or resist (e.g. youth slang or other forms of vernacular language use, graffiti, new instant messaging symbols or codes; Lam, 2008).

Much language socialization research has, nevertheless, and increasingly, been deeply concerned with more *formal* educational processes and issues, such as the accommodation of diverse, often (potentially) disadvantaged, learners within linguistic communities (Duff, 2008b; Heath, 1983). Researchers have sought to discover learners' home and community discourse traditions and any important differences there might be between home and school (or school and work) environments with respect to literacy practices, such as the ways in which children learn to talk about texts. A practical goal has been to help educators and learners negotiate better access to, and participation in, forms of discourse valued in mainstream educational and professional contexts, and also to suggest to educators how they might incorporate familiar home or community interaction practices, such as oral story-telling, to a greater extent to bridge language and literacy traditions. Barnard and Torres-Guzmán's (2009) collection of international case studies of language socialization in elementary and secondary schools from which the above excerpts were drawn reveals the diverse ways in which students are enculturated into the local norms of 'doing school' and being students.

In higher education vocational settings in the United Kingdom, researchers have sought to uncover elements of high-stakes interview discourse that often prevent foreign-born prospective employees from being hired by local companies, with the goal of raising the job seekers' (and in some cases the interviewers') awareness of local interview discourse and features of more successful interviews (e.g. Campbell & Roberts, 2007; Duff, 2008a). Thus, the range of contexts for research on language socialization across the lifespan of individuals as well as at any period in their lives, in which they must learn to participate effectively in multiple discourse communities, is steadily growing.

As language socialization researchers have increasingly situated their research in formal education contexts in schools (both secular and religious), vocational programs, higher education, clinical and professional programs (such as law, medicine, engineering) and other types of programs, as well as in informal settings, the intersection between language socialization and language education has become both more salient and more conflated (e.g. Bayley & Schecter, 2003; Duff & Hornberger, 2008). Increasingly, too, educationally oriented language socialization research has turned its attention to issues in bilingual and multilingual learning communities (or monolingual dominant societies with novices who are, or are becoming, multilingual) in such diverse regions as Japan (Cook, 2008); Hungary (Duff, 1995, 1996), Cameroon (Moore, 1999, 2008), the Solomon Islands (Watson-Gegeo, 1992), and Canada (Bayley & Schecter, 2003; Duff, 2003), as well as in the United States (Baquedano-Lopez & Kattan, 2008; Barnard & Torres-Guzmán, 2009; Bronson & Watson-Gegeo, 2008; He, 2008, to name just a few sources and sites).

Recent studies have, moreover, examined fascinating issues connected with socialization within Deaf communities and educational institutions internationally (Erting & Kuntze, 2008), as well as in communities in which people suffer from various degenerative conditions, such as schizophrenia (Walsh, 2008). In the case of Deaf language socialization, parents in the position of socializing Deaf children into and through language may themselves not be Deaf and may not know sign language and their children may have little or no access to oral language, sign language or lip reading. Their children may eventually attend schools for Deaf children and learn sign language, which they then may try to teach their parents and siblings, in turn: a reversal of directionality from what would normally be expected in language/literacy development in terms of expert–novice relationships. Conversely, Deaf signing parents typically socialize their hearing (and Deaf) children into sign language (e.g. American Sign Language) and Deaf culture, marking the beginning of what usually becomes bilingual socialization into sign language at home and in the local Deaf culture and oral language (e.g. English) which they learn from siblings, peers in the community or at school.

In the case of chronic schizophrenia, participants occasionally have access to expert clinical assistance (or socialization, in other words) to help them regain the communicative competencies they once had, such as being able to engage in ordinary greeting routines and other kinds of small talk, to make requests, and function independently in society. In that sense, the people are seeking to reclaim the expertise they themselves once had through socialization activities with others.

The language socialization research agenda and contexts have thus widened across the decades, often including new population demographics, and situations affected by language contact and language shift, colonialism/postcolonialism, transnationalism and globalization – as well as into new content-area specializations into which people seek membership. This expansion of the purview of language socialization and the linguistic ecology of communities reveals the critical importance of understanding learners' prior experiences of language socialization and how those cumulative socialization experiences affect their present and perhaps future experiences and trajectories as language learners and users, often across multiple communities and timescales (Kramsch, 2002; Wortham, 2005).

In summary, whether for children or for older students or workers seeking successful integration in academic subject areas or professions there has been considerable emphasis on how students learn to engage in sanctioned oral and written discourse practices, how they negotiate the routine oral questions, responses and feedback behaviors of their teachers and peers (or others, such as employers or interviewers), as well as other forms of accepted interaction and literacy practices. The research also has shown how, in the process, many become more sociolinguistically competent participants in, or members of, these local cultures or learning communities (Duff, 2008b). There are also less successful cases resulting in people's withdrawal from the intended communities or not participating with a full mastery of the conventions or practices that are expected. Even people who grow up in the same family or larger community or schooling context may differ considerably in the degree to which they have internalized or are able to use the language and literacy practices they were exposed to earlier, particularly those forms that may be technically or sociolinguistically demanding or sophisticated.

Language socialization involves not only the negotiation and internalization (to some degree) of norms and practices by novices, but also the creation of new, syncretic or hybrid ones (e.g. Duff, 1995), or, for those who are not as successful, the failure to learn expected norms. Another scenario also exists: the conscious rejection or transgression of existing norms, rather than their simple reproduction (Garrett & Baquedano-Lopez, 2002; Kulick & Schieffelin, 2004). For example, Japanese teenage girls may opt to use male first-person pronouns (*boku*, 'I') instead of the unmarked female version (*watashi*) and may use intonation contours, pitch and blunt imperatives with one another in deliberate violation of standard norms of gendered discourse and pronominal use. Such ostensible violations might index a particular stance of toughness or rebellion and anti-feminizing discourse, particularly within female peer groups. Or, to give another example, teenage immigrant students may resist local expectations related to the identity and practices of 'ESL students' that they are expected to display at an American school, whether as 'model minority student' or otherwise compliant and hardworking student keen to learn English and to succeed at school. Instead, they may effect a more apathetic, disdainful stance and identity toward ESL and schooling, and then act out, using verbal and nonverbal behaviors signaling hostility or boredom, to perform that transgressive identity (see Talmy, 2008). Research has therefore noted the agency of learners in their own and others' socialization, including in the socialization of the very 'experts' who are expected to socialize *them* (see e.g. Duff, 1995; Kulick & Schieffelin, 2004; Talmy, 2008) or the outright rejection of those community members' ways of speaking, thinking and being in the world. We will return to this point below, particularly with respect to second language education settings.

Research Methods and Challenges in Language Socialization Studies

Drawing on traditions in linguistic anthropology and classroom research, usually involving various approaches to discourse analysis (e.g. conversation analysis, functional grammatical analysis, intonation analysis), much language socialization research is ethnographic (e.g. Bronson & Watson-Gegeo, 2008; Duff, 1995, 2002, 2008b; Saville-Troike, 2003). Ethnographic research involves understanding the cultural patterns, behaviors and values of groups in their natural local contexts. Since language socialization is related to developmental processes of becoming competent in the linguistic and other communicative ways of the community or culture (terms I use somewhat interchangeably here), a longitudinal perspective is required. Ordinarily, a longitudinal perspective means that the research on particular communities of learners will involve systematic observations by researchers over an extended period and, often, across contexts (Bronson & Watson-Gegeo, 2008; Garrett, 2008; Kulick & Schieffelin, 2004; Watson-Gegeo, 2004). One reason for this prolonged engagement with the community, which is typical of ethnography, is to understand recurring cultural and linguistic patterns of interaction (processes of socialization). Another reason is to observe how learners' abilities, behaviors and orientations to learning and participating in the target practices evolve over time either in the manner anticipated or expected or, rather, in unanticipated ways (i.e. revealing outcomes of socialization). There is generally an attempt to bring together macro and micro-analyses in language socialization research that takes into account the wider context and how the sociocultural context is also constituted in and by micro-level linguistic features.

Even ethnographic language socialization research has, however, paid more attention to the interactional and linguistic *processes* of socialization in real interactional time than to the systematic study of *outcomes*: what people are able to do after significant, cumulative exposure to the language, culture and relevant practices, and not only what they are expected to do and are currently able to do. Indeed, since language socialization is known to be a lifelong and lifewide process, no single study can really be sufficiently longitudinal (or both broad and deep) to capture the ebb and flow of socialization and its many milestones, twists and turns across the lifespan of an individual. In studies more typically limited in duration, the process of language education and enculturation seems to trump detailed analyses and evidence of linguistic, affective and other (e.g. cognitive) outcomes of language socialization in longitudinal perspective.

One strategy often used in narrowing the scope of analysis in language socialization studies is to select a commonplace yet significant activity (speech event) that participants routinely engage in, such as bedtime or mealtime prayers, dinner time conversations, oral academic presentations, guided recitations, or story-telling or story-reading routines, and then to document how they unfold over time and the relevant components, participation structures, and related cultural tools or artifacts. Other studies, however, focus less on the particular activity settings and more on the sociolinguistic dispositions and forms to be mastered, such as those entailed in showing respect to one's elders (Howard, 2008) or politeness and empathy (Cook, 2008).

As in much research in the ethnography of communication or comparable ethnographic research, participants' own perspectives on the socialization process are generally solicited by researchers through interviews if interviewees have the necessary linguistic or metalinguistic skills and maturity to reflect on them or if interpreters are available otherwise. Exceptions or counter-examples and not only typical instances of socialization toward desired goals should be reported by researchers, a common recommendation for interpretive qualitative research (Duff, 2008c).

Some language socialization research does not conform to the method-ological principles outlined earlier in this section. For example, some interview-based studies (such as one I conducted with some colleagues a few years ago, Duff *et al.*, 2000, or other studies reported in Schechter & Bailey, 2003) may have an ethnographic and longitudinal 'perspective' but do not involve the analysis of a large corpus of observed social-interaction data from classrooms or workplaces. Duff *et al.* resorted to interview and document analysis primarily at the request of the participants, who were predominantly immigrant women receiving formal language and voca-tional-skills training in English for the first time in Canada. Although sup-portive of our study, they felt that our (proposed) extended on-site observations might be intrusive and inhibiting. Nonetheless, the many program participants who volunteered to be interviewed multiple times over the course of the year about their experiences of language socializa-tion in the past and present (and those who had completed the program, in their subsequent work experience) shared many very meaningful examples and insights into their own language socialization and their work with elderly or infirm clients, which helped us conceptualize lan-guage socialization in what we felt were productive new ways.

Key Findings in Classroom-oriented Language Socialization Research

Several recent review articles provide thorough summaries of some of the main findings on language socialization in classroom contexts in either first-language or additional-language settings especially (e.g. chapters in Duff & Hornberger, 2008; Zuengler & Cole, 2005). What becomes clear from the research surveyed is that, for many students belonging to the ethnolinguistic majority in their society, language socialization into edu-cational discourse is a relatively smooth and straightforward process that occurs for the duration of one's schooling – and beyond – although it may involve considerable negotiation, trial, error and revision and refinement, all normal aspects of learning. Naturally, as these same learners encounter new forms of discourse and content, they continue to broaden their reper-toire of competencies, their identities, their knowledge of the world and (ideally) their confidence as valued and capable members of the target community. Some will become more adept at the various target practices than others. There is, for most (first language) learners, a kind of (assumed) inevitability to their gaining a certain level of proficiency in most of the everyday pragmatic and other linguistic and literate practices in the target educational culture. The structured support and guided assistance (scaf-folding) appropriate to their level and purposes that they receive at home from parents, older siblings or friends or tutors, combined with their in-class instruction, may be absolutely adequate for their needs.

However, the process may not be as successful or seamless for less established members of communities, ethnolinguistic or socioeconomic minority-group members or others who wield less power, less experience and fewer symbolic and material resources within their new educational and linguistic communities, or may be in postcolonial situations where they do not have sufficient background in the dominant language to enter into educational discourse (Bronson & Watson-Gegeo, 2008; Moore, 1999, 2008; Watson-Gegeo, 1992). Unfortunately, even a short-term lack of success for some of these students may result in such confusion, embarrassment and disappointment that they withdraw from the schooling experience completely.

Several intersecting factors may account for the difficulties these students face. One is that the target language, variety, register or activity (speech event, act) is not familiar to them and they lack the schemata (background cultural knowledge) and scripts (knowledge of routines) to perform as expected. For example, recent study-abroad research has shown areas in which international exchange students' previous home-country, first-language-mediated socialization into academic literacy practices and expectations held by their local teachers may differ substantially from those of their new host institutions and they may flounder as a result (Zappa-Hollman, 2007b).

A second factor is that teachers, mentors and peers may simply assume that new linguistic and cultural practices and the background knowledge associated with them are obvious, comprehensible, transparent, already known or easily acquired and engaged in by newcomers, when in fact they are not. That is, the 'experts' (the primary agents of their academic discourse socialization) may not realize that the practices are alien, even for students who come from the dominant culture, such as middle-class, educated native-English speakers entering undergraduate or graduate school in Anglophone Canada or the United States. These students may have been academically successful enough to enter their university programs but may not have had experience giving particular types of oral presentations (e.g. the summary and critique of a research article), may not have used PowerPoint and other presentation technologies before, or may not have used mixed-mode course tools requiring online bulletin-board postings in response to class discussions and readings (Duff, 2007b; Morita & Kobayashi, 2008; Yim, 2005). They may never have written an academic literature review paper as prescribed in their courses, or a research proposal or an academic curriculum vita (Séror, 2008). Such students may need very explicit instruction and models related to the criteria, components, optimal performance, length restrictions, citation conventions (such as 'APA'), and other attributes of the target activity.

A third factor is that, despite teachers' usually very good intentions, students may be positioned in disadvantageous ways in courses, to the point where the participation structures they are involved in (seating plans, groupwork membership, discussion/presentation groups) or the way they are positioned as 'non-native speakers' or 'shy Japanese females' or masters degree students in a class full of doctoral students, for example, make it very difficult for them to access and participate fully and with the legitimacy they desire in the very practices and social networks they want and need to engage in (Abdi, 2009; Duff, 2002; Morita, 2004; Willett, 1995). They may inadvertently be sidelined by how they are seated, who they are grouped with, the roles they are assigned or roles that are co-constructed for/by them within the class or group. The discourse itself may also marginalize them because it may be impenetrable: too quick, too culturally loaded, too tightly intertextual. The oral language may draw liberally from textual sources and cultural content students are unfamiliar with. My research looking at high school social studies presentations and discussions of current events found that highly intertextual references to pop culture (e.g. reality and game shows on television, movies and popular series such as *The Simpsons*) juxtaposed with discussions of science discoveries and other current social issues were bewildering for many newcomers to the language and culture (Duff, 2004). They were being socialized into a kind of discourse that was clearly valued in the classrooms observed but were not really given the tools to engage with it.

A fourth factor is related to the newcomers' own intentions, learning conditions and trajectories. Educators typically expect newcomers/novices to actively seek membership in their new community. They also normally expect them to strive to attain proficiency in linguistic and pragmatic abilities and other knowledge of their peers and to value the learning opportunities afforded to them both inside and outside of class. Furthermore, educators usually expect that learners will remain invested in their current learning community for a considerable period of time, and that their peers will also facilitate and accommodate their integration within their new groups. However, mitigating circumstances, such as migration, transnationalism, temporary sojourns, cultural conflict and unwelcoming target communities may undermine their learning (Duff, 2003; Norton, this volume). Students may plan to stay in the new community for only a short period; they may reject or resist their status as marginalized participants in the new culture; they may be highly mobile or transnational and may also aspire to quite different future possibilities, including discourse communities and primary languages, than those projected on them by the local educational system (or by their parents) (Duff, 2002, 2003; Talmy, 2008). They may prefer the well established and honored traditions of their prior educational cultures over the current ones. Or they may be blocked entry and access by local members or 'gatekeepers' (Campbell & Roberts, 2007).

One of the most relevant findings for language educators from language socialization research is that explicit consciousness-raising, instruction, scaffolding and feedback may be necessary for newcomers, particularly in diverse learning communities whether for youngsters or advanced graduate students. This in turn has resource implications that need to be budgeted for by responsible educational leaders. Also, for their part, instructors need to better understand different language/literacy learning traditions, the home-language and cultural backgrounds of students and ways of creating effective and inclusive spaces for learning for all in the courses, and not only assume that students must and will, without exception, adapt to the local ways.

Practical Implications of Research on Language Socialization

As indicated in the previous section, language socialization research offers some very practical implications for teachers as well as for students and other stakeholders in education. Bronson and Watson-Gegeo (2008) insist that language socialization work needs to squarely and critically address issues of power, race, class, gender and history that may complicate some students' language socialization opportunities and trajectories. They assert that it should be interventionist in order to engender more equitable discourse practices and greater opportunities for learner agency.

However in Séror's (2008) recent dissertation research examining university instructors' socialization of undergraduate international students' academic writing, he found that teachers' instructions about assignments and their feedback on them was often cryptic, illegible and unspecific, and therefore considered unhelpful by many students. Similarly, in Zappa-Hollman's (2007a) study of oral academic presentations delivered across quite diverse university subject areas (e.g. in medicine, engineering or history), she found that expectations and criteria for good presentations were quite different across program and discipline areas (depending in part on other factors as well, such as point in the course and how many presentations were scheduled per class period). However, there was often very little explicit instruction or modeling for students and little substantive feedback on performances, other than perhaps token remarks such as 'good job' or 'a bit too long'. But in both cases, on written assignments and in oral presentations, students had devoted huge amounts of time in trying to comply with often ill-defined expectations and were perplexed to receive only a phrase or two and a grade at the end of the paper. These situations constitute less than ideal environments for academic discourse socialization into high-stakes oral and literate events.

In research on younger students in public school settings, similarly, greater attention to cultivating a meta-awareness of how language/literacy and certain key speech events work, at the level of grammar or genre/ register, for example, would assist those students who cannot easily induce such content or conventions on their own. Similarly, students coming from other cultures may not understand the basic routines in a classroom, such as how to greet the teacher, how to get turns to speak during class discussions or how to take part in reading circle activities or online discussions.

Finally, in many diaspora and postcolonial contexts, language socialization is a very complicated multilingual, multimodal process that may require competence in more than one cultural, linguistic and discursive system at one time or sequentially, and ultimately in the language of power, the dominant or superordinate language in diglossic situations. Teachers and policy-makers must remember that what is very obvious to them after a lifetime of language and literacy socialization and professional education into the dominant discourses of society may be not at all obvious or even comprehensible to newcomers (e.g. Campbell & Roberts, 2007). Time, careful language planning, modeling, instruction, feedback and guided participation, and bilingual schooling or codeswitching in some contexts, may all prove necessary (Guardado, 2009). Of course, students may not in the end assimilate to the local norms, for various reasons, and perhaps they should not be expected to do so either in every respect (Kramsch, 2002). They may develop innovative hybrid forms of involvement, and hybrid identities and values instead, a cross-fertilization that may ultimately have an impact on the new community and on its other members too.

Siegal's (1994) dissertation reported that the Western women in her study learning Japanese in Japan often eschewed the formal, highly feminized and honorific forms of language that high-proficiency students of Japanese or native speakers would normally be expected to master for professional or public interactions. The women in her study felt that beyond the grammatical or morphological difficulty of such forms, or the complexity of understanding in which contexts and with which interlocutors to use which forms, accepting those speech forms would not be consistent with their personal ideologies and identities as strong, independent Western women. They therefore resisted those forms of socialization and what they stood for.

Students may also learn and relearn languages in sequences that prove highly variable, unpredictable and nonlinear: starting with a heritage (native or ancestral) language spoken in the home; then often shifting to the dominant societal language with public schooling; later adding an additional ('foreign') language at school, and subsequently returning to a study of the heritage language if well disposed to recultivating the latent knowledge and building upon it (e.g. He, 2008). Such sequences, codeswitching, and functional multilingualism are pervasive in much of the world.

Teachers must also have a good understanding of the language/literacy practices students will need when they depart from language programs and enter mainstream academic content classes or move from mainstream classrooms to higher education and workplaces. A growing body of literature identifies mismatches between the practices valued and inculcated in ESL courses, such as the five-part essay, and those subsequently required in freshman composition classes, often more creative and less formulaic structures (Atkinson & Ramanathan, 1995); between low-tier academic tracks at school and more challenging high-tier tracks (Harklau, 1994); and between academic contexts and professional ones (Parks, 2001) (see Duff, 2007b, 2008a).

In addition, teachers need to be more self-aware of their own language and literacy practices and ideologies in classrooms that might prevent students from participating more fully, equitably and competently (Abdi, 2009). Obstacles might result from the way the novices are positioned socially, physically and discursively by others, by question–answer and discussion patterns framed by the teacher, by the validation of some students or by various kinds of discursive and affective alignments between the teacher and some students while other students receive no such validation (Duff, 2002, 2004). Students (or, for that matter, educators) may find themselves excluded from discussion topics by exposure to unfamiliar routines, genres and registers, or because of the incorporation of multiple texts to which they have no access or experience and need some explanation. Further, whereas some cultures may emphasize cultural transmission through oral narratives and may privilege oral assessment in schooling (Duff, 1995, 1996, 2007b), other cultures may be the opposite, privileging and assessing formal written discourse of a particular type instead. Teachers, students and parents must therefore understand the demands and value of each and also the preparation students will need to enter into and participate meaningfully in the new academic culture.

As we have seen and as many others have written, language and literacy socialization is a lifelong process and it is normally a complex combination of social, cultural, linguistic and cognitive factors as well as pedagogical ones. Language educators must remember this principle and appreciate the challenges facing learners in both first- and second-language contexts. In addition, they must themselves continue to adapt to new discourses and to new populations and generations of learners who possess new forms of (e.g. digital) literacies or certain kinds of (socio)linguistic expertise that the teachers may themselves lack (Duff, 1995). Language socialization is, after all, a very dynamic, bidirectional or multidirectional process (Talmy, 2008), one whose normative practices and tools and values are constantly evolving as well.

Notes

1. Other synonyms for socialization are enculturation, initiation and induction.
2. The expert-novice dichotomy is actually a simple rhetorical convention or shorthand, because degree of expertise may shift back and forth between interlocutors or between co-participants depending on their own strengths in

relation to the tasks and topics at hand, especially with older learners, who already have a great deal of experience in different areas.

Suggestions for further reading

Schieffelin, B.B. and Ochs, E.K. (eds) (1986) *Language Socialization across Cultures.* Cambridge: Cambridge University Press.
This book constitutes the seminal first edited volume (12 chapters) dealing with the pragmatic (generally monolingual) socialization of young children across very different languages and cultures; it also lays out the theoretical foundations of language socialization as a new paradigm in language development. It contains the well-known chapter by Heath (1986), 'What no bedtime story means: Narrative skills at home and school', examining the serious implications of disjunctions between home and school literacy practices. NOTE: a fully updated volume by Duranti *et al.* (in press), with chapters by original contributors to this earlier volume and many others, will soon appear in *The Handbook of Language Socialization* (Wiley-Blackwell). When completed, it will be an excellent supplement to this earlier volume.

Garrett, P. and Baquedano-Lopez, P. (2002) Language socialization: Reproduction and continuity, transformation and change. *Annual Review of Anthropology* 31, 339–361.
This comprehensive, well-written review article by former doctoral students of Schieffelin and Ochs, respectively, bridges the gap between the first generation of language socialization research and the burgeoning studies from second-generation researchers and others. It is required reading for anyone working in this area.

Zuengler, J. and Cole, K.M. (2005) Language socialization and L2 learning. In E. Hinkel (ed.) *Handbook of Research in Second Language Teaching and Learning* (pp. 301–316). Mahwah, NJ: Lawrence Erlbaum Associates.
This chapter provides an excellent overview and useful summary of 17 empirical studies conducted on second language socialization, mostly in formal educational contexts in the late 1990s and early 2000s. The chapter is organized chronologically to include language socialization in kindergarten/primary/elementary schools, secondary/high schools, postsecondary institutions, and workplaces.

Bayley, R. and Schecter, S. (eds) (2003) *Language Socialization in Bilingual and Multilingual Societies.* Clevedon: Multilingual Matters.
This edited volume, offers a rich, multi-method and multi-perspectival set of 16 empirical studies dealing with language socialization in Canada, the United States and other countries. Spanning home, school, community and workplace settings, the book's unique contribution is its focus on dynamic socialization processes in bi/multilingual societies approached by authors in different theoretical ways.

Duff, P.A. and Hornberger, N.H. (eds) (2008) *Language Socialization. Encyclopedia of Language and Education* (Vol. 8). New York: Springer.
This new volume in the recently published Springer *Encyclopedia of Language and Education* contains 24 state-of-the art reviews on language socialization within particular age groups, educational contexts, and other discourse communities, in monolingual and multilingual contexts, Western and non-Western, using oral, written, signed or other (visual, graphic) modes of communication. It starts with a 30-year retrospective piece by Ochs and Schieffelin (2008) and moves from more conventional domains of language socialization into areas often overlooked in research: in Deaf communities, in heritage/indigenous-language contexts, in regions attempting linguistic socialization through language-revitalization projects,

in virtual diasporic communities, and in communities of people suffering from mental health disorders, such as chronic schizophrenia.

References

Abdi, K. (2009) Spanish heritage language learners in Canadian high school Spanish classes: Negotiating ethnolinguistic identities and ideologies. Unpublished masters thesis, University of British Columbia, Vancouver, Canada.

Anderson, F.E. (2009) Under the interactional umbrella: Presentation and collaboration in Japanese classroom discourse (Take 1). In R. Barnard and M. Torres-Guzmán (eds) *Creating Classroom Communities of Learning* (pp. 15–35). Bristol: Multilingual Matters.

Atkinson, D. and Ramanathan, V. (1995) "Cultures of writing": An ethnographic comparison of L1 and L2 university writing programs. *TESOL Quarterly* 29, 539–568.

Baquedano-Lopez, P. and Kattan, S. (2008) Language socialization and schooling. In P.A. Duff and N.H. Hornberger (eds) *Language Socialization. Vol. 8, Encyclopedia of Language and Education* (pp. 161–173). New York: Springer.

Barnard, R. and Torres-Guzmán, M. (eds) (2009) *Creating Classroom Communities of Learning.* Bristol: Multilingual Matters.

Bayley, R. and Schecter, S. (eds) (2003) *Language Socialization in Bilingual and Multilingual Societies.* Clevedon: Multilingual Matters.

Bronson, M.C. and Watson-Gegeo, K.A. (2008) The critical moment: Language socialization and the (re)visioning of first and second language learning. In P.A. Duff and N.H. Hornberger (eds) *Language Socialization. Vol. 8, Encyclopedia of Language and Education* (pp. 43–55). New York: Springer.

Campbell, S. and Roberts, C. (2007) Migration, ethnicity and competing discourses in the job interview: Synthesising the institutional and personal. *Discourse and Society* 18, 243–272.

Cook, H.M. (2008) Language socialization in Japanese. In P.A. Duff and N.H. Hornberger (eds) *Language Socialization. Vol. 8, Encyclopedia of Language and Education* (pp. 313–326). New York: Springer.

Duff, P.A. (1995) An ethnography of communication in immersion classrooms in Hungary. *TESOL Quarterly* 29, 505–537.

Duff, P.A. (1996) Different languages, different practices: Socialization of discourse competence in dual-language school classrooms in Hungary. In K. Bailey and D. Nunan (eds) *Voices from the Language Classroom: Qualitative Research in Second Language Education* (pp. 407–433). New York: Cambridge University Press.

Duff, P.A. (2002) The discursive construction of knowledge, identity, and difference: An ethnography of communication in the high school mainstream. *Applied Linguistics* 23, 289–322.

Duff, P.A. (2003) New directions in second language socialization research. *Korean Journal of English Language and Linguistics* 3, 309–339.

Duff, P.A. (2004) Intertextuality and hybrid discourses: The infusion of pop culture in educational discourse. *Linguistics and Education* 14/3–4 (Winter), 231–276.

Duff, P.A. (2007a) Second language socialization as sociocultural theory: Insights and issues. *Language Teaching* 40, 309–319.

Duff, P.A. (2007b) Problematising academic discourse socialisation. In H. Marriott, T. Moore and R. Spence-Brown (eds) *Discourses of Learning and Learning of Discourses* (pp. 1–18). Clayton, Victoria, Australia: Monash University ePress/University of Sydney Press.

Duff, P.A. (2008a) Language socialization, higher education, and work. In P. Duff and N. Hornberger (eds) *Encyclopedia of Language and Education. Volume 8: Language Socialization* (pp. 257–270). New York: Springer.

Duff, P.A. (2008b) Language socialization, participation and identity: Ethnographic approaches. In M. Martin-Jones, M. de Mejia and N. Hornberger (eds) *Encyclopedia of Language and Education* (Vol. 3) (pp. 107–119). *Discourse and Education*. New York: Springer.

Duff, P.A. (2008c) *Case Study Research in Applied Linguistics*. New York: Lawrence Erlbaum Associates/Taylor & Francis.

Duff, P.A. (2009) Language socialization in a Canadian secondary school: Talking about current events (Take 1). In R. Barnard and M. Torres-Guzmán (eds) *Creating Classroom Communities of Learning*. Bristol: Multilingual Matters.

Duff, P.A. (2010) Language socialization into academic discourse communities. *Annual Review of Applied Linguistics* 30.

Duff, P.A. and Hornberger, N.H. (eds) (2008) *Language Socialization. Encyclopedia of Language and Education* (Vol. 8). New York: Springer.

Duff, P.A., Wong, P. and Early, M. (2000) Learning language for work and life: The linguistic socialization of immigrant Canadians seeking careers in healthcare. *Canadian Modern Language Review* 57, 9–57.

Duranti, A., Ochs, E. and Schieffelin, B.B. (2010) *Handbook of Language Socialization*. Malden, MA: Wiley-Blackwell.

Erting, C.J. and Kuntze, M. (2008) Language socialization in deaf communities. In P.A. Duff and N.H. Hornberger (eds) *Language Socialization. Vol. 8, Encyclopedia of Language and Education* (pp. 287–300). New York: Springer.

Ervin-Tripp, S. (2009) Hymes on speech socialization. *Text & Talk* 29, 245–256.

Fader, A. (2001) Literacy, bilingualism, and gender in a Hasidic community. *Linguistics and Education* 12, 261–283.

Fader, A. (2006) Learning faith: Language socialization in a community of Hasidic Jews. *Language in Society* 35, 205–229.

Friedman, D. (2010) Becoming national: Classroom language socialization and political identities in the age of globalization. *Annual Review of Applied Linguistics* 30.

Garrett, P.B. (2007) Language socialization and the (re)production of bilingual subjectivities. In M. Heller (ed.) *Bilingualism: A Social Approach* (pp. 233–256). New York: Palgrave Macmillan.

Garrett, P.B. (2008) Researching language socialization. In K.A. King and N.H. Hornberger (eds) *Research Methods. Encyclopedia of Language and Education* (Vol. 10) (pp. 189–201). New York: Springer.

Garrett, P.B. and Baquedano-López, P. (2002) Language socialization: Reproduction and continuity, transformation and change. *Annual Review of Anthropology* 31, 339–361.

Gordon, D. (2008) Gendered second language socialization. In P.A. Duff and N.H. Hornberger (eds) *Language Socialization. Vol. 8, Encyclopedia of Language and Education* (pp. 231–242). New York: Springer.

Guardado, M. (2009) Speaking Spanish like a Boy Scout: Language socialization, resistance and reproduction in a Spanish language Scout troop. *Canadian Modern Language Review* 66, 101–129.

Harklau, L. (1994) ESL versus mainstream classes: Contrasting L2 learning environments. *TESOL Quarterly* 28, 241–272.

He, A.W. (2008) Heritage language learning and socialization. In P.A. Duff and N.H. Hornberger (eds) *Language Socialization. Vol. 8, Encyclopedia of Language and Education* (pp. 201–213). New York: Springer.

Heath, S.B. (1983) *Ways with Words: Language, Life, and Work in Communities and Classrooms*. New York: Cambridge University Press.

Heath, S.B. (1986) What no bedtime story means: Narrative skills at home and school. In B.B. Schieffelin and E.K. Ochs (eds) *Language Socialization across Cultures* (pp. 97–124). New York: Cambridge University Press. (Reprinted from Heath, S.B. (1982) *Language in Society* 11 (1), 49–76.)

Howard, K.M. (2008) Language socialization and language shift among school-aged children. In P.A. Duff and N.H. Hornberger (eds) *Language Socialization. Vol. 8, Encyclopedia of Language and Education* (pp. 187–199). New York: Springer.

Howard, K.M. and Lo, A. (2009) Mobilizing respect and politeness in classrooms. [Special issue]. *Linguistics and Education* 20 (3).

Kobayashi, M. (2004) A sociocultural study of second language tasks: Activity, agency, and language socialization. Unpublished doctoral dissertation, University of British Columbia, Vancouver, Canada.

Kramsch, C. (ed.) (2002) *Language Acquisition and Language Socialization: Ecological Perspectives*. London: Continuum.

Kulick, D. and Schieffelin, B. (2004) Language socialization. In A. Duranti (ed.) *A Companion to Linguistic Anthropology* (pp. 349–368). Malden, MA: Blackwell.

Kyratzis, A. and Cook-Gumperz, J. (2008) Language socialization and gendered practices in childhood. In P.A. Duff and N.H. Hornberger (eds) *Language Socialization. Vol. 8, Encyclopedia of Language and Education* (pp. 145–157). New York: Springer.

Lam, W.S.E. (2008) Language socialization in online communities. In P.A. Duff and N.H. Hornberger (eds) *Language Socialization. Vol. 8, Encyclopedia of Language and Education* (pp. 301–311). New York: Springer.

McKay, S. and Hornberger, N.H. (eds) (1996) *Sociolinguistics and Language Teaching*. New York: Cambridge University Press.

McLellan, J. and Hui, P.C-W. (2009) Socialisation and 'safetalk' in an upper primary English language classroom in Brunei Darussalam (Take 1). In R. Barnard and M. Torres-Guzmán (eds) *Creating Classroom Communities of Learning* (pp. 53–69). Bristol: Multilingual Matters.

Mertz, E. (1996) Recontextualization as socialization: Text and pragmatics in the law school classroom. In M. Silverstein and G. Urban (eds) *Natural Histories of Discourse* (pp. 229–249). Chicago: The University of Chicago Press.

Mertz, E. (2007) *The Language of Law: Learning to Think Like a Lawyer*. Oxford: Oxford University Press.

Moore, L.C. (1999) Language socialization research and French language education in Africa: A Cameroonian case study. *Canadian Modern Language Review* 56, 329–350.

Moore, L.C. (2008) Language socialization and second/foreign language and multilingual education in non-Western settings. In P.A. Duff and N.H. Hornberger (eds) *Language Socialization. Vol. 8, Encyclopedia of Language and Education* (pp. 175–185). New York: Springer.

Morita, N. (2000) Discourse socialization through oral classroom activities in a TESL graduate program. *TESOL Quarterly* 34, 279–310.

Morita, N. (2004) Negotiating participation and identity in second language academic communities. *TESOL Quarterly* 38, 573–603.

Morita, N. and Kobayashi, M. (2008) Academic discourse socialization in as second language. In P.A. Duff and N.H. Hornberger (eds) *Language Socialization. Vol. 8, Encyclopedia of Language and Education* (pp. 243–255). New York: Springer.

Ochs, E. and Schieffelin, B.B. (2008) Language socialization: An historical overview. In P.A. Duff and N.H. Hornberger (eds) *Language Socialization. Vol. 8, Encyclopedia of Language and Education* (pp. 3–15). New York: Springer.

Parks, S. (2001) Moving from school to the workplace: Disciplinary innovation, border crossings, and the reshaping of a written genre. *Applied Linguistics* 22, 405–438.

Paugh, A. (2008) Language socialization in working families. In P.A. Duff and N.H. Hornberger (eds) *Language Socialization, Vol. 8, Encyclopedia of Language and Education* (pp. 101–113). New York: Springer.

Pavlenko, A. and Piller, I. (2008) Language education and gender. In S. May and N.H. Hornberger (eds) *Language Policy and Political Issues in Education, Vol. 1, Encyclopedia of Language and Education* (pp. 57–69). New York: Springer.

Saville-Troike, M. (2003) *The Ethnography of Communication.* (3rd edn). Malden, MA: Blackwell.

Séror, J. (2008) Socialization in the margins: Second language writers and feedback practices in university content courses. Unpublished doctoral dissertation, University of British Columbia, Vancouver, Canada.

Siegal, M. (1994) Looking East: Learning Japanese as a second language in Japan and the interaction of race, gender and social context. Unpublished doctoral dissertion, University of California, Berkeley.

Talmy, S. (2008) The cultural productions of ESL student at Tradewinds High: Contingency, multidirectionality, and identity in L2 socialization. *Applied Linguistics* 29, 619–644.

Tien, C.-Y. and Barnard, R. (2009) Interaction in a Taiwanese primary school English classroom (Take 1). In R. Barnard and M. Torres-Guzmán (eds) *Creating Classroom Communities of Learning* (pp. 88–107). Bristol: Multilingual Matters.

Vickers, C. (2007) Second language socialization through team interaction among electrical and computer engineering students. *Modern Language Journal* 91, 621–640.

Walsh, I. (2008) Language socialization among people with mental health disorders. In P.A. Duff and N.H. Hornberger (eds) *Language Socialization. Vol. 8, Encyclopedia of Language and Education* (pp. 327–340). New York: Springer.

Watson-Gegeo, K. (1992) Thick explanation in the ethnographic study of child socialization: A longitudinal study of the problem of schooling for Kwara'ae (Soloman Islands) children. In W.A. Corsaro and P.J. Miller (eds) *Interpretive Approaches to Children's Socialization* (pp. 51–66). San Francisco: Jossey-Bass.

Watson-Gegeo, K. and Nielsen, S. (2003) Language socialization in SLA. In C. Doughty and M. Long (eds) *The Handbook of Second Language Acquisition* (pp. 155–177). Malden, MA: Blackwell.

Watson-Gegeo, K. (2004) Mind, language, and epistemology: Toward a language socialization paradigm for SLA. *Modern Language Journal* 88, 331–350.

Willett, J. (1995) Becoming first graders in an L2: An ethnographic study of language socialization. *TESOL Quarterly* 29, 473–503.

Wortham, S. (2005) Socialization beyond the speech event. *Journal of Linguistic Anthropology* 15, 95–112.

Yim, Y.K. (2005) Second language speakers' participation in computer-mediated discussions in graduate seminars. Unpublished doctoral dissertation, University of British Columbia, Vancouver, Canada.

Zappa-Hollman, S. (2007a) Becoming socialized into diverse academic communities through oral presentations. *Canadian Modern Language Review* 63, 455–485.

Zappa-Hollman, S. (2007b) The academic literacy socialization of Mexican exchange students at a Canadian University. Unpublished Doctoral dissertation, The University of British Columbia, Vancouver, Canada.

Zuengler, J. and Cole, K.M. (2005) Language socialization and L2 learning. In E. Hinkel (ed.) *Handbook of Research in Second Language Teaching and Learning* (pp. 301–316). Mahwah, NJ: Lawrence Erlbaum Associates.

Part 6

Language and Interaction

Chapter 17

Language and Culture

GABRIELE KASPER and MAKOTO OMORI

Introduction

. In many ways, the relationship between language and culture plays a key role in education. Classrooms across the world are increasingly populated by students and teachers of diverse language and cultural backgrounds and can therefore be understood as contexts for intercultural communication *par excellence*. On reflection, this is not an entirely new situation, considering that educational settings are meeting places for students and teachers from different regions in a larger society, from different social classes, with different religious and political affiliations, and of traditions and interests that unite and separate people no matter how homogeneous a society believes itself to be. So, instead of seeing the more visibly multilingual and multicultural composition of today's classrooms as an altogether recent phenomenon, it is perhaps better viewed as reinforcing and enriching an entrenched fact of institutional life. Looking at linguistic and cultural diversity in this way raises the question of how language and culture may be understood in relation to each other, and what implications alternative views of this relationship may have for educational practice.

Fundamentally, language and culture play two complementary roles in educational processes. As all human activities are linguistically and culturally mediated, language and culture enable and organize teaching and learning. 'Classroom cultures' are constructed by the students and teachers working together, 'school cultures' are the practices, big and small, more or less functional, through which school life is conducted. Both are shaped, among other factors, by educational policies, curricular priorities and the material conditions of the school. Both are sustained through language and discourse, talk and text, and through hybrid, multimedia forms of communication. But just as language and culture furnish the means for delivering education, they also serve as its object. The role of language and culture as educational goals is most apparent in language teaching, where *language* defines the subject matter. How *culture* figures in language teaching varies greatly in educational theory and practice, ranging from approaches that treat culture as inseparable from language to those for which culture is a nice but dispensable icing on the cake. However, in the teaching and learning of any subject matter, language and culture can be less conspicuous but still present as learning objects even though they are not on the official teaching agenda. For teacher education and development, how to conceptualize the linkage between language and culture, in particular in relation to 'intercultural communication', is a critical question. Answers to it have profound implications for the how's and what's of educational theory and practice.

The chapter starts by discussing various concepts of culture, with a focus on anthropological proposals. It then turns to comparing how intercultural communication is theorized and investigated in different research traditions, grouped together as sociostructural/rationalist and discursive-constructionist approaches. The following sections review how intercultural interaction is treated in prominent sociolinguistic and discourse-analytical frameworks: communication accommodation theory (CAT), cross-cultural speech act pragmatics, interactional sociolinguistics, and conversation analysis (CA) and membership categorization analysis (MCA). The final section extends the discussion to culture in the classroom, pointing out that tying students' identities to their cultures of origin can have serious unwanted ramifications for their participation in classroom activities and educational success in the long term.

Contexts and Concepts

Language and culture across disciplines

Communication between members of different speech communities has been a long-standing research topic across the social sciences (e.g. Kiesling & Bratt Paulston, 2005; Kotthoff & Spencer-Oatey, 2007; Spencer-Oatey, 2008, for recent collections). Within social psychology, cross-cultural communication and intercultural communication are institutionalized as independent disciplines (e.g. Gudykunst, 2005). Cross-cultural and intercultural pragmatics adopts an interdisciplinary approach to examine variable patterns of language-as-action across cultural groups and in intercultural encounters (e.g. Bardovi-Harlig & Hartford, 2005; Blum-Kulka *et al.*, 1989; Gass & Neu, 1996; Kasper & Blum-Kulka, 1993). Interactional (interpretive) sociolinguistics is specifically concerned with interethnic and intercultural interaction (e.g. Bremer *et al.*, 1996; Di Luzio *et al.*, 2001; Gumperz 1982a, 1982b; Rampton, 2006). From sociology, CA and MCA have recently been extended from the study of interaction between members of the same speech community to participants of diverse cultural backgrounds (e.g. Mori, 2003; Nishizaka, 1999). As we will discuss in this chapter, each of these approaches conceptualizes intercultural communication from its own discipline-specific and metatheoretical perspectives, with theories and research strategies ranging from convergent and complementary to incompatible. The social science literature on intercultural discourse furnishes an indispensable resource for pedagogical proposals on how to address 'culture' in diverse educational settings and in second and foreign language education (e.g. Banks & McGee Banks, 2007; Hinkel, 1999; Risager, 2007).

Whatever stance on intercultural communication one may take, language and culture are critically implicated in the topic, and it might therefore seem necessary to define the two concepts and their relationship upfront. Yet this is an extraordinarily difficult and elusive task. Both notions are ubiquitous in ordinary and academic discourse, and they are used with a great variety of meanings in both domains. As research topics, each occupies its own territory, with distinct and complex theoretical, methodological, empirical and institutional histories. The division between linguistics and anthropology as academic disciplines not only reflects but fosters the view of language and culture as independent structures of human life. But their interrelation is recognized and institutionally anchored as well, although to a lesser extent. As one of the traditional branches in anthropology, linguistic anthropology studies linguistic resources and practices from the perspectives of cultural organization, maintenance, reproduction and transformation. For Agar (1994), language and culture are so inextricably intertwined that he coined the hybrid 'languaculture', adapted from Friedrich's (1989) earlier 'linguaculture'. Both terms have gained some currency in language pedagogy (e.g. Risager, 2007) but are less common in linguistic anthropology. As branches of linguistics and anthropology, respectively, sociolinguistics and linguistic anthropology each pursue their own disciplinary agendas, but their perspectives on the linkage between language and culture converge to a significant extent (Hymes, 1964).

Culture in linguistic anthropology

For the purpose of discussing the connection between language and culture as a sociolinguistic topic, it is helpful to consider Duranti's (1997: chap. 2) overview of six perspectives on culture in linguistic anthropology.

- Culture as distinct from nature: Central to this perspective is the nature–nurture debate, in particular the integrity and interrelation of acquisition and socialization of language-as-competence and as social practice.
- Culture as knowledge: Cognitive theories of culture (Goodenough, 1964) range from earlier proposals of category acquisition modeled on grammar to culture as socially distributed knowledge (Hester & Eglin, 1997; Hutchins, 1995).

- Culture as communication: Approaches include structuralist (Lévi-Strauss, 1978) and interpretive semiotics (Geertz, 1973), indexicality and metapragmatics (Silverstein, 1993) and metaphors as folk theories (Lakoff & Johnson, 1980).
- Culture as a system of mediation: Culture comprises sets of physical and symbolic objects that mediate between people and their environment. Language is a critical tool of symbolic mediation (Vygotsky, 1978) and language practices are understood as mediating activity.
- Culture as a system of practices: Replacing generalizing and abstracted concepts of culture as unitary, stable and ahistorical structures of meanings and behavior, poststructuralist practice theories emphasize the constructive role of language and action in concrete social circumstances. Central to Bourdieu's theory of practice (1977) is the notion of habitus, a bundle of socially sanctioned, historically developed, internalized dispositions for institutionalized, routinized socio-discursive practices.
- Culture as a system of participation: Participation centers on the connectivity of language-mediated actions to the local and global world, based on shared cognitive, symbolic and material resources, including inequitable access and obstacles to participation. Influential analytical concepts of participation (Goffman, 1981; H.M. Goodwin, 1990; Philips, 1972) in situated activities shed light on the local construction of engagement in discursive practices.

As this overview suggests, a distinctive difference between theories of culture is whether they conceptualize their object as an abstract, autonomous cognitive system that underlies observable behaviors or as discursively mediated, context-sensitive and context-shaping social actions. In a similar vein, language has been theorized as an abstract, autonomous, conventionalized symbolic system of internal meaning and form relations (Saussure's *langue*), as competence, a cognitive capacity distinct from performance, but also as language *use* in situated socio-communicative actions, as a form of social practice (Bakhtin, 1981; Bourdieu, 1977; Vološinov, 1973). With the view of language as action and use, the *indexical* character of semiotic systems becomes more prominent: whereas a symbolic, representational view understands the relationship between linguistic form and meaning as stable and fixed, indexicality describes the fundamental dependency of meaning on contexts of language use (Levinson, 1983; Silverstein, 2003; Wittgenstein, 1953). As we will see below, indexicality is a key topic in the study of interaction between culturally diverse participants.

Based on the discussion so far, we can suggest that the place where culture and language meet is participants' engagement in discursively mediated social practices. To be sure, such practices include the conceptual and linguistic resources that participants in interaction recruit, including ethnosemantic categories (Eglin, 1980), systems of person reference and address (Braun, 1988; Eglin, 1980) or grammatical forms associated with particular registers and styles (Cook, 2008). But the analytical interest in *practices* directs the researcher's glance away from inferred abstract systems of categories and linguistic forms and toward the ways that participants in social interaction engage linguistic and other semiotic resources to accomplish practical, situated actions (Bilmes, 2008; Enfield & Stivers, 2007; Hester & Eglin, 1997).

The scope, unity, and diversity of culture

Some further conceptual clarification concerning the scope and differentiation of *culture* is in order. In everyday use as well as in much academic discourse, *culture* is commonly understood as *particular* to a given social group and as *shared* within that group. Claims to external (intergroup) distinctiveness and internal (intragroup) homogeneity can serve as powerful ideological tools to implement political agendas, from 19th century nation building in Europe to current restrictions on immigration and equitable social and political rights for residents of different backgrounds in many parts of the world. Yet, against popular belief and research traditions in some social sciences, formulations of culture as exclusively particular are difficult to sustain empirically. As Ochs notes,

> Culture is not only tied to the local and unique, it is also a property of our humanity and as such expected to assume some culturally universal characteristics across communities, codes and users. (...) there are certain commonalties across the world's language communities and communities of practice in the linguistic means to constitute certain situational meanings. (Ochs, 1996: 425)

The range of language-mediated cultural phenomena by which social members anywhere conduct their lives is large, and we will have more to say about some of them in the following sections. They include language-mediated social acts ('speech acts') and activities, narration and reporting the speech of others. Social identities, relationships and epistemic and affective stance are indexed through linguistic and other semiotic resources (e.g. Coupland, 2007; Ochs, 1996). Participation in talk exchanges is made possible through generic interactional procedures, such as turn-taking, sequence organization and repair (Drew, 2005). These fundamental interactional organizations are always configured to the local circumstances and are therefore responsive to, as well as constitutive of, culture-specific social norms and priorities, but such inflections of local culture do not run counter to the overwhelming evidence that the procedural infrastructure of interaction is culturally shared (Moerman, 1988; Schegloff, 2006).

Culture, as the ensemble of discursively mediated practices, has both universal and local dimensions.

Turning to the myth of homogeneity, the practice of referring to particular 'cultures' by the names of nations or ethnic groups (the Finns, the Hawaiians) reinforces the idea that communities that share the same name also share the same practices and belief systems. Throughout its history, anthropology did much to promote views of culture as cohesive ways of being in the world that identify distinct social groups. But the counter positions that came to the fore with poststructuralist critiques in the late 20th century (e.g. Clifford & Marcus, 1986) were foreshadowed much earlier by anthropologists who emphasized the internal diversity of communities, the existence of 'subculture' within the 'generalized culture' (Sapir, 1949: 515). Wallace's succinct formulation of culture as an 'organization of diversity' (Wallace, 1961: 28) and Clifford's portrayal of culture as 'temporal, emergent, and disputed' (Clifford, 1986: 19) sit well with contemporary perspectives on the increasingly multilingual and multicultural communities around the world. Theories and empirical evidence suggest that the cultural fabric of multiethnic neighborhoods, workplaces and educational institutions produces identities marked by fragmentation, hybridity (see Kraidy, 2005, for discussion) and liminality (Rampton, 1999).[1]

Contrasting perspectives on intercultural discourse

How do participants in these and other settings address themselves to intercultural interaction, and what theoretical approaches have been proposed to explicate it? A preliminary answer allows us to distinguish two main perspectives, summarized in Table 17.1 (for a related, in-depth discussion of research paradigms and social theories in sociolinguistics, see Coupland *et al.*, 2001). According to sociostructural theories, social action and language use are determined by macrostructural forces and internalized social norms that powerfully constrain the agency of individuals and social groups. In sociolinguistics, the prototypical example of a sociostructural approach is variationist sociolinguistics in the tradition of William Labov. Rationalist theories, following the sociological tradition of Max Weber, conceptualize social actions as cognitively based, intentional, goal-related means–end calculations. In sociolinguistics, they include such prominent theories as Myers-Scotton's Markedness Model of codeswitching (1993), motivational theories of communicative accommodation (Giles & Coupland, 1991), Grice's theory of meaning (Grice, 1957), Searle's speech act theory (Searle, 1969), relevance theory (Sperber & Wilson, 1986/1995) and Brown and Levinson's politeness theory (Brown & Levinson, 1978/1987). Despite their ontological differences, sociostructural and rationalist perspectives are often merged in research practice, and they

Table 17.1 Contrasting perspectives on intercultural interaction

	Sociostructural/ rationalist	*Discursive-constructionist*
Culture	Unitary, static	Diverse, hybrid, dynamic, resource and construction
Cultural identity		
• Locus	Internal cognitive-affective trait	Co-constructed interactional accomplishment
• Duration & scope	Stable, context-independent, intraculturally shared	Emergent, contingent, contextual, contestable
• Relation to other identities	Dominant	Variably relevant, other identities may be more salient
• Relation to actions and participation	Determines actions and participation	Reflexive, a resource to accomplish actions and organize participation frameworks
Discourse practices and resources	Culturally determined	Construct (cultural) orientations and identities
Cultural diversity	Hazardous, source of miscommunication	Interactional resource
Foregrounded cultural distinctiveness	Disaffiliative	Potentially affiliative, disaffiliative or relationally inconsequential
Research perspective	Etic: relevance of cultural distinctiveness presupposed and conceptualized through exogenous theory	Emic: cultural distinctiveness as a topic for analysis only if visibly relevant to participants

both contrast fundamentally with social-constructionist views of social life. Constructionisms come in many varieties (Holstein & Gubrium, 2008), but they are united in rejecting the view that social phenomena have stable, situation-independent, ahistorical properties (essentialism) and operate on the principles of cause and effect (determinism). Ontological constructionism holds that social reality itself is created through participants' social and, in particular, discursive actions (Harré, 1983), whereas for epistemic constructionism, reality – whether social, psychological or physical – is treated as versions of discursively produced topics (Edwards,

1997). In order to highlight the constitutive role of discourse in the constructionisms relevant to sociolinguistic studies of intercultural interaction, we refer to them collectively as discursive-constructionist.

Consistent with the differences in theories of culture noted earlier in this section, notions of cultural identity come in markedly different versions. In sociostructural/rationalist theories, cultural identity is a stable, intra-psychological, situation-transcendent trait shared by members of the same cultural group. It overdetermines other identities that people may participate in and structures their actions and relations with others.

Discursive-constructionist approaches relocate cultural identity from the privacy of the individual mind to the public sphere of social life. The 'underlying', 'real', 'true' self is dissolved into a relational construct, co-produced by participants in the course of their social activities and reflexively related to them. The critical point is that cultural identities are socially consequential only when they are made *relevant* through publicly observable action in interaction and text. In this sense, identities are something people do rather than something they have (Benwell & Stokoe, 2006). Consequently, orientations to cultural identities are interactionally contingent; they may come and go (and, in fact, never come at all) in the course of an activity.

Sociostructural/rationalist models recognize universal discourse practices and resources, yet research efforts are predominantly directed to identifying cross-cultural differences in communicative style, which in turn are explained as arising from distinctive social-psychological orientations among national groups (individualism–collectivism, masculinity–femininity, etc.; Hofstede, 2001). Discursive-constructionist approaches examine how cultural (and other) identities are produced through interactional arrangements and semiotic resources. While the linguistic resources may be language-specific (examples include address pronouns, interactional and modal particles, discourse markers and honorifics), no a priori assumptions are made about cultural-specific meanings. From sociostructural/rationalist perspectives, cultural diversity is seen as fraught with problems; in fact research on intercultural communication is often motivated by the desire to identify, explain and recommend remedies for miscommunication. Discursive-constructionist studies treat cultural diversity as a resource that participants can exploit to construct social solidarity or antagonism, or that remains without any visible relational consequences.

Finally, the two perspectives take different investigative stances. Sociostructural/rationalist approaches presuppose the omnirelevance of cultural diversity, conceptualized from the vantage point of discourse-external (etic) theory. Under the emic view of discursive-constructionist analysis, no prior assumptions are made about whether cultural diversity plays a role for the participants at all. It becomes a topic for analysis only when the participants show in their interactional conduct that their cultural identities are a concern for them. An emic approach to inter-cultural discourse also implies that problems in the interaction are not invariably attributed to cultural differences. Instead, the policy is to bracket participants' memberships in particular cultural groups as an ana-lytical resource and instead examine how the interactional difficulties arise from the interaction itself.

We will now turn to several prominent approaches to intercultural communication. In the course of our discussion, we will revisit and elabo-rate the concepts and contrasts introduced in Table 17.1.

Communication Accommodation Theory (CAT)

In the tradition of the communication sciences, research on cross-cultural and intercultural communication is predominantly conducted from social-psychological perspectives. The goal of *cross-cultural communication* research is to construct theories that may account for cognitive, behavioral and atti-tudinal differences between cultural groups. *Intercultural communication* aims to explicate the processes of intergroup communication, intergroup and intragroup attitudes and relations and their continuity and change.[2] While there is generally not much intellectual traffic between social-psycho-logical communication research, on the one hand, and sociolinguistics and linguistic anthropology, on the other,[3] one theory that bridges disciplinary divisions is *communication accommodation theory* (CAT).

Originally under the name of speech accommodation theory, CAT was designed as a motivational account for variation in linguistic and temporal features in speech forms, styles and choices of languages and language vari-eties in intergroup communication. On Giles and Coupland's definition,

> accommodation is to be seen as a multiply-organized and contextu-ally complex set of alternatives, regularly available to communicators in face-to-face talk. It can function to index and achieve solidarity with or dissociation from a conversational partner, reciprocally and dynam-ically. (Giles & Coupland, 1991: 60–61)

Specifically, accommodation refers to interlocutors' speech adjustments that may exhibit *behavioral convergence* with or *divergence* from the inter-locutor's (displayed or assumed) speech. Accommodation processes are termed *objective* when a party adjusts their behavior toward the other par-ty's observable communicative conduct and *subjective* when such adjust-ments are grounded in the speaker's beliefs and stereotypical views. For instance, Beebe (1981) reported that bilingual Thai-Chinese children adjusted their vowels to what they believed to be Chinese variants when interviewed by an ethnic Chinese Thai, although the interviewer's vowels did not have the purported phonological properties. The children's subjective convergence produced objective divergence.

CAT also proposes that behavioral convergence and divergence do not necessarily map on corresponding types of psychological accommodation, the ways in which participants' social and personal perceptions of each other align or misalign. White (1989) found in a study of English-medium interactions between Japanese and North American participants that the Japanese participants used significantly more backchannel tokens than the American interlocutors, ostensibly a negative discourse transfer from Japanese. In interlanguage pragmatics, negative pragmatic transfer is typically seen as a cause of intercultural miscommunication (e.g. Kasper & Blum-Kulka, 1993). However, the American participants evaluated Japanese interlocutors who had a distinctly higher rate of backchannels as particularly interested and convivial. In this case, behavioral divergence resulted in psychological convergence. Conversely, Bailey (1997) examined service encounters between the Korean owners and employees of convenience stores and their African-American customers in Los Angeles (USA). In Bailey's analysis, the customers' affiliative strategies (using solidarity-marking address terms, joking, citing common history or disclosing personal information) garnered reserved, non-reciprocating uptake. Here, rather than achieving social solidarity and bridging ethnic boundaries, behavioral convergence had the effect of psychological divergence.[4] The two cases point to the complex relationship between discursive conduct and its psychological conditions and consequences, a challenge that has oriented CAT research on intercultural communication into different directions (Sachdev & Giles, 2006).

In the context of communication science, CAT developed into a general theory of intergroup communication (Gallois *et al.*, 2005). The theory acknowledges that communication is sociohistorically embedded and that interlocutors manage information exchange and identity negotiation by mutually adjusting their interactional conduct on a wide range of discursive, linguistic and temporal features. However, of greater theoretical interest than 'behavioral tactics' are the psychological dispositions and strategies thought to motivate interactional conduct, whereby 'motivation' refers to beliefs and assumptions of intergroup or interpersonal relations rather than goal-related social action. Talk between culturally diverse participants serves as a window to underlying cognitive-affective processes rather than being treated as an object of investigation in its own right. In its dominant current version, proposed by Giles and his associates, CAT is thus two degrees removed from socio-discursive approaches to intercultural communication: first, by privileging interlocutors' perceptions and motivations over their displayed communicative behavior and, second, by emphasizing the roles and interrelations of attitudes, attributions, affect, cognition and intention as causes and effects of intergroup relations over visible social action in intercultural communication. The absence of action-orientation sets social-psychological CAT apart from other sociolinguistic theories in the rationalist paradigm.

CAT has also been taken in a discourse-analytic direction, for instance in studies by Bell (2001) on audience design as a form of discourse accommodation. Bell (2001) investigated the use of the discourse particle *eh* in the same gender and cross-gender interviews between *Pakeha* (white New Zealanders) and Māori (the indigenous people of New Zealand). He found that the Māori male interviewee used *eh* in decreasing rates when being interviewed by a Māori man, a Māori woman, a Pakeha man and a Pakeha woman. All interviewers style-shifted in their use of *eh* in orientation to their interviewee, but the most striking shifts were registered in the speech of the Pakeha male interviewer, who used no *eh*'s at all when speaking with another Pakeha man. Bell argues that *eh* serves as a marker of ingroup identity in Māori–Māori interaction and that demographic similarity is a factor in audience-designed style choices.

In recent appraisals of the theory, proponents of CAT have countered objections contending that CAT endorses essentialist and monolithic views of culture, arguing that CAT is compatible with critical and constructionist reconsiderations of culture and intercultural communication (Meyerhoff, 2001; Ylänne, 2008). To this, it should be added that Giles and Coupland (1991), cited at the beginning of this section, describe accommodation as an ensemble of ubiquitous discourse processes rather than as a phenomenon limited to intercultural interaction. In the context of education, this is a particularly important point because teaching and learning would not be possible without ongoing adjustments of language, interaction and topical content. Just how much and through what discursive methods participants in educational activities accommodate to each others' levels of knowledge, participation and style vary across educational settings. Accommodation, then, not only enables teaching and learning in diverse classroom communities but is itself culturally variable.

Cross-Cultural Speech Act Pragmatics

Few perspectives on language have had such a profound and lasting impact as the insight that using language is doing actions. Against the notion of language as an abstract symbolic system, ordinary language philosophers Ludwig Wittgenstein and John Austin theorized language as a large array of 'language games' – language-mediated actions and activities (Wittgenstein, 1953) – and speech acts, the action (or 'illocutionary force') that an utterance is taken to perform when certain context conditions ('felicity conditions') are satisfied (Austin, 1962). Wittgenstein's and Austin's theories became influential precursors to several schools in the study of discourse, notably ethnomethodology (Heritage, 1984), CA

(Bilmes, 1986) and discursive psychology (Edwards, 1997). In psychology, applied linguistics and speech-act-based cross-cultural pragmatics, it was John Searle's cognitivist version of speech act theory (especially Searle, 1969, 1976) that garnered the most uptake. Building on Grice's (1957) theory of meaning, Searle (1969) defines illocutionary acts, the core object of his theory, as categories of speaker's intentions expressed by means of conventionalized language forms. Whereas for Austin, illocutionary force is complemented by 'perlocution', the effect of the utterance on the hearer, Searle's version eliminates the intrinsically sequential and interactional makeup of speech acts.[5] Via Searle, speech act research acquired a rationalist foundation that had decisive consequences for the theory and methodology of cross-cultural pragmatics.

Searle's approach to speech acts (1969) and his classification of illocutionary acts (1976) have been widely adopted as a framework to study how cross-culturally available speech acts are configured with the resources of different languages. As an empirical extension of Searle's theory, speech act research implicitly combines theories of meaning as speaker intention (e.g. Grice, 1957) and linguistic convention (Bilmes, 1986; Kasper, 2006a). The convention view of meaning (Searle, 1976) underlies the notion that speech acts are normatively performed through particular types of utterances ('conventions of means', Clark, 1979), called semantic formulae (Olshtain & Cohen, 1983) or speech act realization strategies (Blum-Kulka *et al.*, 1989). Semantic formulae are encoded in specialized language-specific resources ('conventions of form', Clark, 1979) and combine to speech act sets, the collection of semantic structures by which a particular speech act can be achieved.[6] For example, the coding scheme developed in the Cross-Cultural Speech Act Realization Project (CCSARP) for the analysis of requests distinguishes three dimensions of request modification (Blum-Kulka *et al.*, 1989): The directness by which requestive meaning is indexed in the form of the 'head act', or request proper (direct, conventionally indirect, nonconventionally indirect); internal modification (intensification and mitigation) of the request through lexical and syntactic forms; and external modification by actions leading up to or following the request (announcements, establishing preconditions, accounts ('grounders') and others). The three dimensions are illustrated in the following extract from an oral proficiency interview.

Dormitory (Kasper, 2006b: 340; IR = interviewer, C = candidate)

IR: I've never been to the dormitories before,
so I don't really have much idea what the
dormitory is like. Can you describe your room
to me perhaps?
C: Oh, my (.) my room (.) my <u>room</u> (.)
my room (.) my room is very <u>d</u>irty now,

The interviewer modifies the upcoming request externally by prefacing it with two consecutively related grounders. The head act has a conventionally indirect form; that is it is composed of an open frame (*can you*) that conventionally signals requestive force. The request proper is internally modified through the explicit dative *to me* and the adverb *perhaps*. Both forms mitigate the request, but in different ways. The explicit mention of the recipient symbolically casts the requested action as being to the requester's benefit, while *perhaps* symbolically lowers the extent to which the candidate is obliged to comply with the request. From the perspective of speech act research, the external and internal modifications make the request more polite. A conversation-analytic reading (see the section on CA below) would note that the pre-posed accounts accomplish reference preparation and project an upcoming question or other directive in the interview (Kasper, 2006b; Taleghani-Nikazm, 2006).

The CCSARP framework has been applied to describe requests in a large number of languages and native and nonnative language varieties, including Australian and US English, Danish, Canadian French, German and Hebrew (Blum-Kulka *et al.*, 1989), several varieties of Spanish (García, 1993; Márquez Reiter, 2000), Greek (Sifianou, 1992), Indonesian (Hassall, 1999), Japanese (Fukushima, 1990), Chinese (Zhang, 1995; Rue & Zhang, 2008) and Korean (Rue & Zhang, 2008). While these studies show that the dimensions of request modification and many of the more specific strategies are cross-culturally shared, they also register differences in categories and instances of linguistic forms and their conventionally associated pragmatic meanings and in the contextual and cross-cultural distribution of request strategies. Although the CCSARP framework has proven itself as a cross-culturally robust etic taxonomy that allows for emic (culture- and language-specific) elaboration, integrating it with systems of honorification and other variations in speech style remains an unresolved challenge.

In order to explicate how alternative action formats may be related to intraculturally and interculturally variable contexts of use, speech act research draws on theories of politeness, predominantly[7] Brown and Levinson's theory (Brown & Levinson, 1987). Based on Grice's Cooperative Principle (Grice, 1975) and Goffman's concept of 'face' (Goffman, 1967), the theory proposes that social actors' reasoning is motivated by the dual purpose of getting an action done in an effective manner while mutually preserving face, defined as the needs for social approval ('positive face') and autonomy ('negative face'). Actors assess how the intended speech act will affect the recipient's and their own face by calculating the added values of three context variables, the power relationship and social distance between speaker and hearer and the magnitude of imposition inherent in the speech act. Choices of speech act strategies depend on the degree to which the intended action poses a threat to their own and their co-participants' face. Just as in the selection of speech act conventions, cross-cultural differences were found in speakers' assessment of context factors as well. For instance, Márquez Reiter *et al.* (2005) established that in the same request contexts, speakers of Peninsular Spanish were more certain that their interlocutors were going to comply with their request than speakers of British English. Fukushima (2000) found significant differences in the assessment of power, social distance and imposition in request contexts between speakers of Japanese and British English. Several studies have noted that associations of directness and politeness vary cross-culturally (Blum-Kulka, 1987, 1997; Lee-Wong, 1999; Márquez Reiter, 2000), an observation that has also been extended to other speech acts (e.g. Félix-Brasdefer, 2008a, on refusals in Mexican Spanish and US English). One important outcome from this research is that politeness is not directly associated with indirectness. Blum-Kulka (1987) reported that in both American English and Hebrew, raters identified conventional indirectness rather than non-conventional indirectness as the most polite request strategy. Furthermore, for members of different speech communities, directness and indirection may index different sets of social values (e.g. Félix-Brasdefer, 2008a, 2008b; Márquez Reiter *et al.*, 2005).

The rationalist stance underwriting speech-act-based cross-cultural pragmatics provides for methods of data collection and analysis that would be difficult to reconcile with interactional theories of action. It is the backdrop to such (typically questionnaire-based) elicitation devices as discourse completion tasks (DCTs), multiple choice and rating scales. DCTs, for instance, purport to plant a prespecified 'pragmatic intention' in the respondent's mind and record how that intention is mapped onto a particular linguistic form (see Kasper, 2000, for different DCT item formats, and Golato, 2005, for a comparison of DCT responses with natural data). Alternatively, in order to overcome the limitations of a one-turn response (usually though not necessarily written) while at the same time maintaining control over the pragmatic purpose of the activity, researchers use role-play to elicit interactional data on the desired speech act. Examples include studies on refusals in American English and Mexican Spanish (Félix-Brasdefer, 2008a), requests and complaints in German and British English (House & Kasper, 1981), requests in Peninsular Spanish and British English (Márquez-Reiter, 2000) and requests in Mandarin Chinese and Korean (Rue & Zhang, 2008). However, even though interactional data permit researchers to examine how participants collaboratively construct speech act sequences, many studies remain firmly within the rationalist paradigm by adopting speaker-centered taxonomies such as the CCSARP coding manual for analysis.

Cross-cultural speech act pragmatics has yielded detailed descriptions of the pragmalinguistic inventories of a range of speech acts and languages and of the general sociopragmatic patterns of their use, both of which are indispensable resources for teaching and testing the pragmatics of a target language (Alcón & Martínez-Flor, 2008). But despite this useful contribution, the approach has a number of shortcomings. One set of problems centers around the inferences drawn from the described pragmatic patterns. The rationale for cross-cultural comparison is to identify contrasts in the speech act usage between speakers of different languages who are assumed to be members of a culture associated with the language. No published study is based on systematic sampling, yet the participants recruited through convenience-and-volunteer sampling are routinely treated as representative of large and empirically diverse social populations. The populations, in turn, are considered homogenous 'cultures', whose putatively defining characteristics ('individualist' versus 'collectivist', 'negative politeness' versus 'positive politeness', e.g. Fukushima, 2000) are understood to determine, or be indexed through, the pragmatic patterns identified in the study. Although it has become a common disclaimer to reject essentializing and homogenizing categorizations, precisely such categorizations are encouraged by the research paradigm itself. A recent development that begins to bring cross-cultural speech act studies on a more sociolinguistically defensible footing is variational pragmatics (Félix-Brasdefer, 2008b; Schneider & Barron, 2008), an effort to examine dialectal pragmatic variation within larger language communities.

A second set of problems derives from the speaker-centered production model. The concern with speaker intention precludes the view of speech acts as actions-in-interaction, jointly produced by at least two participants as sequences within the turn-taking system and larger activities. While different approaches to discourse have demonstrated the important role of linguistic conventions in performing language-mediated action (e.g. Curl & Drew, 2008, for request formats; Heritage & Roth, 1995, for question formats in political interviews), the convention view of meaning gives insufficient recognition to the fundamentally indexical character of language use, and it ignores the temporal, sequential and nonverbal resources and organizations by which participants accomplish action in interaction. Third, the pre-occupation with cultural difference tends to obscure that the structures of social actions and interaction are fundamentally *shared* across human communities, drawing on the same interactional organizations and categories of semiotic resources. A more balanced emphasis on the universal and the local in cross-cultural pragmatics (Kasper & Rose, 2002; Ochs, 1996) has important implications for language pedagogy, as it encourages teachers to acknowledge and build on shared cultural resources in diverse student groups. Cultural sensitivity needs to extend to sameness as well as otherness. Finally, inferences from cross-cultural comparison to intercultural interaction require particular circumspection because the method of comparing and contrasting speech act performance across linguistic and cultural groups cannot address such fundamental interactional processes as accommodation (see the section on CAT) and recipient design (see section on CA).

Interactional Sociolinguistics

We noted that in standard speech act pragmatics, context is treated as a configuration of static, discourse-external social variables. The relationship of discourse-external context to discourse-internal choices of pragmatic strategies is based on a causal or correlational model, where context figures as the independent variable and language use as the dependent variable. On this view, cross-cultural difference can be explained in terms of diverging values of context variables and their impact on the selection of speech act strategies and forms. In interactional sociolinguistics, context is conceptualized in a radically different way.

Proposed by John Gumperz in the 1970s, and inspired by Alfred Schütz's phenomenology, Goffman's microsociology, ethnomethodology and CA, interactional sociolinguistics is an empirically grounded theory of situated interpretation. From these perspectives, the separation of context and behavior collapses as context is seen as emergent, constantly reshaped and reflexively produced through the participants' interactional conduct itself (Auer, 1992; Goodwin & Duranti, 1992). Although all dimensions of behavior bear a reflexive relationship to context (Kasper, 2009), interactional sociolinguistics is particularly interested in non-referential *contextualization cues* or *contextualization conventions*, 'the verbal and non-verbal metalinguistic signs that serve to retrieve the context-bound presuppositions in terms of which component messages are interpreted'. More specifically:

> A contextualization cue is one of a cluster of indexical signs produced in the act of speaking that jointly index, that is invoke, a frame of interpretation for the rest of the linguistic content of the utterance. Such frames are subject to change as the interaction progresses and have different scopes, from individual speech acts to sets of turns and responses, to entire social encounters. (Gumperz, 1996: 379)

Key resources for contextualization are prosody and the temporal organization of speech and nonverbal action, codeswitching between different languages and language varieties, including styles and register and lexical choices such as routine formulae, modal particles and discourse markers (Auer & Di Luzio, 1992; Gumperz, 1982a, 1982b, 1992). Contextualization cues instantiate relevancies in talk and enable inferences to epistemic and affective stance, to claimed, ascribed, and contested identities, actions and activities. These semiotic resources form a critical reservoir of cultural members' interactional competence (Gumperz, 1982a). Although the categories of contextualization are cross-culturally shared, the specific forms and their associations with dimensions of context are often not.

Early interactional sociolinguistic research found that different contextualization practices were a frequent and typically unrecognized source of misunderstanding between members of different speech communities (Gumperz, 1982a, 1982b). Studies of interethnic communication[8] showed that miscommunication and mutual negative attributions become particularly acute when miscues accumulate over the course of an encounter and instantiate diverging frames and activity-level inferences, with potentially serious consequences for participants in high-stake ('gatekeeping') events such as employment interviews (Gumperz *et al.*, 1979), courtroom testimony (Gumperz, 1982a) and a range of activities in educational settings, including undergraduate counseling (Erickson & Shultz, 1982; Fiksdal, 1990), course consultation (Gumperz, 1992, 1996), college-level grade negotiation (Tyler, 1995; Tyler & Davies, 1990) and oral language assessment interviews (Ross, 1998). By showing how miscommunication is interactionally co-produced by the participants through the systematic details of their interaction and displayed conflicting understandings, interactional sociolinguistics furnished a rigorous empirical basis for research on intercultural communication in socially consequential real-life encounters.

Despite this lasting achievement, the early work did not remain without critics. One line of objections concerned the narrow focus on interethnic *mis*communication and its implicit suggestion that intercultural communication is inherently fraught with problems, whereas interaction between members of the same speech community is construed as largely trouble-free. Contrary to this presumption, Coupland *et al.* (1991: 3) describe all language use as 'pervasively and even intrinsically flawed, partial and problematic'. The most compelling support for their contention is the repair apparatus, a small set of generic interactional procedures that interlocutors routinely draw on to address problems in speaking, hearing and understanding (Schegloff *et al.*, 1977). In the main, problems are occasioned through interaction-internal contingencies regardless of interaction-external factors, such as membership in different ethnic groups (Schegloff, 1987). Furthermore, to the extent that interactional difficulties appear to result from conflicting frames[9] (Goffman, 1974), such difficulties may arise out of asymmetries in institutional knowledge and interactionally mediated power relations regardless of participants' ethnicities and cultural backgrounds. Finally, the focus on miscommunication obstructs the view on *successful* intercultural interaction. The interactional competencies and practices that enable participants in intercultural activities to *achieve* understanding require equal analytical scrutiny as communication difficulties and breakdowns (Bremer *et al.*, 1996; Bührig & Thije, 2006).

Critics have also contended that in order to account for miscommunication in intercultural talk, interactional sociolinguistics places too much of the explanatory burden on contextualization cues while neglecting attention to 'pre-text' (Hinnenkamp, 1987), the discourse-external macrostructures, power asymmetries, ideologies and prejudicial attitudes preceding the current interaction (Meeuwis, 1994; Sarangi, 1994; Shea, 1994). As several writers argue, following Giddens (1976), social contexts differ in the extent to which they are 'brought about' – emergent and constructed through the ongoing interaction – and 'brought along' as locally instantiated versions of pre-existing communicative genres and associated frames (Auer, 1992). Lastly, interactional sociolinguistics has been taken to task for assuming an essentialist view of native and nonnative identities and a static, monolithic concept of culture that in turn serves analysts as a resource to explain miscommunication as the result of cultural mismatches and thereby contributes to stereotypical views of intercultural communication (Sarangi, 1994; Shea, 1994).

Many of these problems have been addressed effectively in more recent interactional sociolinguistic research on intercultural discourse. Analytical practices such as bracketing the common-sense notion that cultural diversity is omnirelevant and adopting an emic perspective consistently enable researchers to investigate rather than take as an unexamined given whether cultural diversity is indeed a relevant concern for the participants in an activity. A growing body of literature has examined ordinary conversations and interactions in medical, educational, and legal settings, public and private services, at work places and in other institutional contexts; in a large variety of geographical and socio-historical environments; with participants differing in such 'transportable identities' (Zimmerman, 1998) as social class, race, ethnicity, culture, gender and age; and conducted by means of equally diverse linguistic repertoires. This work converges on the outcome that the most powerful organizing force in social interaction is the activity that participants are engaged in, irrespective of their memberships in transportable social categories. Cultural membership is interrelated in complex ways with the situated identities associated with the current activity and may alternately be backgrounded, foregrounded or neutralized throughout the activity (Bührig & Thije, 2006; Di Luzio *et al.*, 2001; Higgins, 2007). One important methodological implication is that researchers have to tease out whether (successful or problematic) actions in institutional settings are informed by institutional or culture-specific relevancies. In the effort to develop a nonessentialist view on interactions among culturally diverse participants, researchers have argued that intersubjectivity is achieved through aligned *perspectives* rather than shared ethnicity. Reconsidered from this angle, difficulties in intercultural interaction can more productively be seen as resulting from misaligned perspectives than from presumptive cultural mismatches (Shea, 1994; Thije,

2006). With specific reference to interaction in gatekeeping encounters, Sarangi and Roberts (1999: 478) note that 'microethnographic studies have shown what is widely known but rarely admitted, namely that selection and grading and other judgments which will determine outcomes for candidates and clients are based on the interactional accomplishment of solidarity'. Erickson and Shultz's (1982) classic ethnographic microanalysis (Erickson, 1996) showed how in academic advising sessions at a junior college, ethnic and racial differences between adviser and student were inconsequential when the parties were able to establish *situational comembership*, which is shared incumbencies in invested categories (e.g. as athletes, graduates from the same school or practitioners of the same religion) that they made relevant in their talk. Relatedly, Kerekes (2006) found that in employment interviews at a national temporary staffing agency, successful candidates managed to position themselves as 'trustworthy', an assessment that depended on whether the candidate and the staffing supervisor were able to co-construct affiliation rather than the candidates' ethnic background, native or nonnative speaker status or gender. Factors such as discrepancies between information supplied on the application form and in the interview, gaps in employment history, inappropriate references and demands for an inappropriately high salary resulted in distrust and a failed interview when an affiliative relationship had not been established. However, the staffing supervisor set such factors aside when she and the candidate had developed social solidarity through their talk. Lastly, professional competence and domain expertise can be powerful neutralizers of cultural distinctiveness and limited language proficiency. In interactions between a Korean owner of a shop for beauty supplies and his African-American customers, the parties' cultural diversity was for the most part backgrounded against their roles as shopkeeper and customers, and the owner's expertise in hair products for African-Americans rendered his Korean ethnicity irrelevant (Ryoo, 2007).

When ethnic or cultural diversity, or nonnative speaker status for that matter, do become an interactional concern for the participants, the question arises just what such orientations accomplish for them. Aston (1993) identified a number of discourse strategies through which non-acquainted participants in ordinary conversation exploited *non*consociacy and linguistic *in*competence as resources for negotiating comity. In the beauty supply store interactions, Ryoo (2007) noted how a female African-American customer and the shopkeeper collaboratively talked the owner's national and cultural identity as Korean into interactional salience and thereby co-constructed social affiliation. Through such practices, the co-participants achieve the construction of *discursive intercultures* (Koole & Thije, 1994; Thije, 2006), loosely configured sets of emergent and dynamic methods of co-constructing situated talk-in-interaction whose normativity cannot be reduced to that of monocultural and monolingual discourses.

The flipside to cultural distinctiveness as a resource for social solidarity can be seen when participants emphasize their cultural, ethnic or racial distinctiveness as a resource or even as a topic to accomplish non-affiliative agendas. Cutler (2007) analyzed how the competitors in a televised MC battle[10] talked up their racial identities as Black and White through explicit references to Blackness and Whiteness, contextualization cues such as salient phonological features of AAVE and 'White' American English, and asymmetrical uses of address terms. However, these practices were embedded in and contributed to a shared perspective on the culture of hip hop, including the marked status of Whiteness in this culture. In an entirely different context, studies by Eades (e.g. 2003) on cases involving Aboriginal witnesses and defendants in the Australian legal system revealed that legal professionals' knowledge of Aboriginal pragmatic practices can work to opposite effects, both to promote and to obstruct justice. One example of the latter is a case in which defense lawyers misused their understanding of the Aboriginal practices of silence and gratuitous concurrence to harass the adolescent Aboriginal witnesses under cross-examination and manipulate their evidence. As a result, the charges of unlawful deprivation of liberty raised against six police officers who had abducted the boys were dropped. From the discourse analysis of the cross-examination transcripts, the interactional practices through which legal counsel harassed the boys on the witness stand were clearly in evidence. But as Eades argues, the 'power *in* the discourse' does not explain the 'power *behind* the discourse' (Fairclough, 1989). This level of explanation requires connecting the analysis of the micro-politics of courtroom interaction with the macro-politics of race relationships between Aboriginal and Anglo Australians at institutional and socio-historical levels.

Interactional sociolinguistics has proven its effectiveness by continuously sharpening its microanalytic lens while integrating layers of ethnographic context as necessary for profound and innovative analyses of interactions in which cultural distinctiveness may be variably relevant for the participants. Although its disciplinary home in linguistic anthropology and sociolinguistics has furnished theoretical and methodological perspectives that were particularly sensitive to interactions among culturally diverse participants, interactional sociolinguistics has demonstrated its analytical strengths as an approach to intracultural talk as well (e.g. Schiffrin, 1987).

Conversation Analysis and Membership Categorization Analysis

Despite some affinities, the histories and analytical priorities of CA and MCA are distinctly different from those of interactional sociolinguistics. Initiated by the sociologist Harvey Sacks (Sacks, 1992; Sacks *et al.*, 1974;

see also Atkinson & Heritage, 1984; Silverman, 1998), CA and MCA aim to explicate 'the competences that ordinary speakers use and rely on in participating in intelligible, socially organized interaction' (Heritage & Atkinson, 1984: 1). Although usually taken for granted rather than expressly clarified, 'ordinary speakers' are taken to be members of the same speech community (Garfinkel & Sacks, 1970; Schegloff, 1987). With their (implicit) focus on intracultural interaction, CA and MCA pursue a different agenda from that of interactional sociolinguistics. But recent applications of both approaches, separately and jointly, to interactions among culturally diverse participants have proven highly productive in pioneering an ethnomethodological strand of intercultural discourse research.

Through his initial analysis of audio-recorded naturally occurring interactions, Sacks made the revolutionary discovery that talk is organized in a highly systematic fashion – there is 'order at all points' (Sacks, 1984: 22). In a significant move away from traditional sociology, CA and MCA share the premise of ethnomethodology (Garfinkel, 1967; Heritage, 1984) that social members' behavior is not determined by social macrostructures and internalized social norms. Rather, both approaches examine how members orient to and use interactional organizations and semiotic resources (CA) and social categories (MCA) as a matter of their own agency. CA's specific goal is to explicate the 'procedural infrastructure of interaction' (Schegloff, 1992), made up of interlocking interactional organizations: turn-taking, turn design, social actions, sequence organization, preference organization and repair (e.g. Drew, 2005; Sidnell, this volume). This generic apparatus enables all interaction and the concerted ongoing production of a world in common, no matter how torn and contested that world may become at times.

Complementing CA, MCA investigates how participants use categories in the joint accomplishment of their social world. Key questions include how categories are selected in particular contexts, what categorial relations, actions and (more generally) predicates they are associated with, what inferences they enable and what participants locally accomplish through their use (Sacks, e.g. 1984, 1992; Silverman, 1998). Again, this enterprise turns conventional sociology on its head: instead of presupposing that membership in social categories (e.g. being a graduate student, a Korean national, female) determines a person's actions, MCA asks how participants assemble such categories discursively and in what ways category work advances their situated activities. Consequently category incumbents are recognizable through their actions and activities. A category-bound activity is an activity conventionally associated with a membership category, not only empirically but as a normative expectation. Accordingly, participants' use and enactment of categories is a central social process through which 'culture' is locally constituted (Hester &

Eglin, 1997; Silverman, 1998; Watson, 1997). Instead of explaining participants' conduct as a product of culture, MCA elucidates how people talk
culture into being through using social categories.

After Sacks's untimely death in 1975, CA and MCA went their separate
ways, with CA turning into the more influential and elaborated approach
by far. However, researchers in both traditions increasingly argue that the
production and understanding of actions and action sequences are both
categorial and sequential and that the separate analytical strands need to
be brought together (e.g. Edwards, 1998; Hester & Eglin, 1997; Talmy, 2009;
Watson, 1997).

The proposed synthesis is illustrated well in the first studies of intercultural interaction from a combined CA and MCA (M/CA) perspective. In
his seminal analysis of a radio program titled 'My Methods of Learning
Japanese', aired in Japan in the 1990s, Nishizaka (1995, also 1999) argues
that 'interculturality'[11] has to be treated as an interactional accomplishment. In the show, the Japanese host interviews non-Japanese students
about their language learning and related experiences in Japan. Nishizaka's
analysis is animated by Sacks's (1972) observation that through their talk,
participants not only invoke individual categories, but assemble categories into *collections*. By using the paired categories ('standardized relational
pair') 'Japanese person (*nihonjin*)–foreigner (*gaikokujin*)', the host and
guest make the collection 'cultural memberships' relevant. Each of the two
categories is associated with normatively expected and mutually exclusive entitlements. Ownership of the Japanese language, displayed through
claims to understanding, passing judgment and giving advice how to
speak the language, and knowledge about 'Japanese nature', such as locating and identifying by name mountains and rivers in Japan's geography,
are treated by the host as predicates bound to the category 'Japanese
person'.[12] Conversely, the 'foreigner' is normatively expected to display
limited expertise in these matters. The strength of such expectations
becomes especially apparent in their breach. When the host proposes that
technical words pose a particular difficulty for the nonnative speaker, the
guest denies, pointing out that technical terms are typically composed of
Chinese characters and that these are easier for him to understand and
pronounce than (the longer and semantically less transparent) words of
Japanese origin. After a lengthy exchange on the topic, in which the participants make and contest claims to epistemic authority through formulations, interactional particles and change-of-state tokens, the host concludes
by describing the guest as a *henna gaijin* ('strange foreigner'), a category
term implying that the incumbent appropriates entitlements that are not
his – in this case, knowing things about the Japanese language that are
properly known only by native speakers.

A final significant observation from Nishizaka's studies is that participants may contingently re-assemble categories into different collections.

When the host proposes that a guest might sometimes experience under-standing difficulties, the guest shifts away from the categorial relevance of nonnative speakerness by agreeing that the technical terminology used in his company is often troublesome to him. In another episode, after the host has drawn up asymmetrically distributed entitlements to knowledge about Japanese nature, the guest evokes the function of mountains and rivers as regional boundaries and in so doing orients to his professional identity as a student of Japanese history. In both cases, the collection 'membership in a language and cultural community', with its standard relational pairs 'native–nonnative speaker' and 'Japanese person–foreigner', gets replaced by the collection 'professional status' and the contrast pairs 'specialist–layperson'. One important implication from Nishizaka's analysis is that even when participants' cultural and linguistic diversity define the rationale for an entire social activity, as in the case of the radio show, it nonetheless needs to be shown in the participants' con-duct whether such identities are indeed relevant for the participants at any given moment, how such relevancies are interactionally established, and how they may be replaced by other social categories.

In subsequent CA and MCA research, the themes introduced by Nishizaka have been further explored and expanded, together with the range of activities and participant constellations. To start with the latter, multiparty interaction affords participants a wider range of methods to orient themselves to cultural membership than the dyadic interview. Mori (2003) investigated how Japanese and American students initiate topical talk as they get acquainted with each other during the first meet-ing at a 'conversation table', a student-arranged activity for practicing Japanese. In the absence of a shared history, matters associated with cul-tural membership furnish possible topics in first encounters. Similar to the radio host in Nishizaka's studies, the participants categorize each other as 'Japanese' and 'American' by asking questions about Japanese and American cultural objects. For example by asking the American par-ticipants if they have seen any Japanese films, the questioner categorizes the American students as relative novices to Japanese culture. But what is more, specific to the multiparty interaction, the category questions prompt a particular participation structure. In response to the Japanese student's question regarding Japanese movies, the American students respond as a team and thereby categorize the parties in the interaction into 'culturally same' and 'culturally different'. Each party also aligns as a team to repair problems in hearing or understanding in the question-answer sequences.[13] Other methods by which the participants achieve the construction of 'within-group' and 'across-group' relations are speech style and language choice: The Japanese students use addressee-honorifics when talking to the American students while using plain forms to their Japanese peers, and all participants choose the language associated with their team for within-group talk and the language of the other team for talking across groups.

Membership categorization becomes noticeable for participants when the local assembling of a device is somehow obstructed or gets no ratification, for instance when a category incumbent rejects a proposed categorization or acts in a manner treated as 'out of line' with situationally relevant category predicates. Several studies (Day, 1994, 1998, 2006; Fukuda, 2006; Hansen, 2005; Higgins, 2007, 2009; Nishizaka, 1999; Suzuki, 2009; Talmy, 2004, 2008, 2009) show how participants in different kinds of 'intercultural' interaction contest, resist or subvert the ascription of ethnic, national, linguistic, religious or institutional identities. These studies also examine what else gets accomplished through problematic membership categorization. Higgins (2009) analyzes a case in which religious affiliation becomes a matter of contested categorization during pre-topical talk between two Tanzanian journalist colleagues. Asked whether he is Hindu, the respondent repeatedly rejects the ascribed religious identity and various predicates associated with it, while the questioner draws firm boundaries between her own religious identity as a Christian and other religious groups. Subsequently, the questioner treats the separating religious affiliations as a stepping stone toward co-membership in the category of 'helping others not of one's own ethnicity', which in turn serves as a resource to make a request for financial support to her interlocutor. Suzuki (2009) traces how a membership categorization device becomes problematic when some parties to a conversation invoke 'knowing one's blood type' as a tool to partition *nihonjin* (Japanese people) and *gaijin* (white foreigners) into mutually exclusive categories in the collection 'ethnicity'. A participant in the conversation whose identity as *gaijin* is made relevant at some point redraws the boundaries somewhat by accepting her incumbency in the category of *gaijin* while claiming, and subsequently demonstrating, that she does know her blood type. However, rather than treating her own 'deviant case' as occasion for calling into question the entire membership categorization device, the participant confirms that *gaijin* 'generally' do not know their blood type. Through this move she discounts her own case as an 'outlier' that does not challenge the generality of the category-bound predicate. The categorization device thus remains intact and contributes to the local construction of *nihonjinron*, 'theory of Japaneseness'.

Membership categorization and sequential organization, then, are deeply implicated in the production of social relations, affiliations and disaffiliation. M/CA's method of reconstructing membership categorization from the details of participants' interaction affords a rigorously emic lens to the study of culture and identity. Culture, understood as participants' situated production of a shared but not necessarily harmonious social world, can be studied as participants' assembling of membership categorization devices on any particular occasion. As membership categorization involves the organization of social categories into collections, MCA offers an empirical approach to study cultural and other identities as *relational* constructs (Benwell & Stokoe, 2006). Lastly, an incipient literature reveals M/CA's potential for the critical study of intercultural discourse. M/CA's apparatus makes visible how ideologies and inequitable power relations are interactionally produced, reaffirmed and contested in concrete situated engagements. While such analytical outcomes are compatible with several influential poststructuralist theories, M/CA offers a methodology to ground macrosociological propositions in the observable realities of the participants.

Culture in the Classroom

As classrooms around the world are increasingly inhabited by diverse student populations, teachers' charge to offer high quality education for all students poses a significant professional challenge. An extensive educational literature makes recommendations for policies and practices of multicultural education (e.g. Banks & McGee Banks, 2007) and culturally responsive teaching (e.g. Gay, 2000). Culturally responsive pedagogies include practices intended to validate students' cultural identity, encourage active participation and ultimately enhance academic achievement. However, ethnographic and discourse-analytical studies conducted in different North American school settings indicate that teaching to students' assumed cultural identities is a risky undertaking. Pedagogical efforts to foster students' appreciation of cultural diversity are often limited to a 'superficial focus on heroes, holidays, customs and food; a conception of culture as a static corpus of values and beliefs, and a conflation of country, culture, language, nationality and identity' (Talmy, 2004: 157). In keeping with this version of culture is the common practice to position students from immigrant backgrounds as representatives of their culture of origin (Duff, 2002; Harklau, 2000; Talmy, 2004). In the extract from a High School English as a second language (ESL) class in Hawai'i below, the teacher gives instructions about a holiday project.

'Can I do Christmas?' (Talmy, 2004: 158, modified)

1	**Ms Ariel:**	The assignment for – the assignment for everyone
2		in the class is to pick a holiday from their own
3		country or culture (..) and to research it or if
4		you already know about it, fine =
5	**Raven:**	=Yeah, Christmas.
6	**China:**	[New Year!

(lines omitted, Ms Ariel giving further instructions about the assignment)

15	**Raven:**	(talking to China)I'm gonna draw Santa Claus
16		[(inaudible)

17 **Ms Ariel:** [and you'll choose one holiday from where you,
18   you come from [and share it with us.
19 **China:**   [Okay. Miss, I'm not gonna argue,
20   I'm just, can I just do Christmas?
21 **Ms Ariel:** The assignment sheet is right here.
22 **Raven:**   Miss, can I do Christmas? [(inaudible)
23 **Ms Ariel:**   [But the requirement is
24   it's from your country.

The segment shows how cultural membership becomes a contested topic in the micropolitics of the ESL classroom. In her instruction (lines 1–4), Ms Ariel specifies that holidays eligible for the class project must be from the students' 'own country or culture' (treated as equivalent through the alternative conjunction *or*). She thus uses 'holidays' as a category-bound object that partitions students into members of different 'cultures' and as outsiders to US-American culture. Ms Ariel's identity ascription meets instant resistance from Raven and China, who team up to propose to work on non-eligible holidays, Christmas and New Year. Through their coordinated identity-implicative actions, the students resist being positioned by the teacher as members of distant exotic cultures while simultaneously claiming membership in the proximate US culture. The continuation of the excerpt (lines 19–24) shows how ascription, resistance and claims to cultural membership interface with the participants' positions in the institutional hierarchy of the school and their asymmetrically distributed category bound entitlements and obligations. In two consecutive adjacency pairs, China and Raven ask permission to 'do Christmas' for the assignment. In response, Ms Ariel invokes the power of an institutional artifact (the assignment sheet) and the 'requirement' it embodies to prop up her institutional authority and her entitlement to insist that the students do the assignment on her terms.

Similar patterns of cultural identity ascription and resistance have been noticed in other educational settings as well, including mainstream and ESL classes. Duff (2002) describes how in a mainstream high school context in Canada, classroom activities and teachers' categorizations tied students' cultural membership to the pre-immigration stage in their lives, for instance by positioning them as experts in such traditional cultural practices as incense burning for ancestor worship. The observed cycles of institutionally sanctioned essentialism and students' resistance to being persistently exoticized show vividly that the different conceptualizations of culture and cultural identity discussed in this chapter are not only matters of scholarly debate but anchored in conflicting common sense understandings. But beyond recurrent moments of problematic classroom interaction, the contested identity ascriptions have the potential to set educationally undesirable trajectories in motion. A critical outcome from ethnographic classroom research is that rather than encouraging more engagement in classroom activities, the students categorized as cultural others withdrew or minimized their participation, with often detrimental consequences for their academic success in the longer term. Harklau's (2000) longitudinal study observed how three female students' academic performance declined from high school to community college when the long-term residents were locked into novice ESL student status through course assignments appropriate for newcomers. In a series of studies, Talmy documents how multilingual 'generation 1.5' students assigned to ESL class were constructed as 'forever FOB' (fresh off the boat), as permanent new arrivals (Talmy, 2004, 2008, 2009). Harklau's and Talmy's research reveals how the reproduction of students as ESL learners articulates with their construction as cultural outsiders at the macrolevel of institutional organization and at the microlevel of classroom interaction.

In the version of multicultural education in classroom practices discussed above, multiculturalism accrues from the sum of the traditional *mono*cultural identities that teachers ascribe to different students. In another version, the teacher orients to some students' *multi*cultural identities as inherently dilemmatic ('caught between two cultures') regardless of whether the purported dilemma is treated as such by the students themselves (Duff, 2002). The studies cited in this section document how the students resisted either proposal through direct opposition, noncompliance with teacher directives or minimal participation. Through these and other methods, students subvert the teacher's project of constructing multiculturalism on terms that sit uneasily with their own life world.

There is much to be learned from misfired efforts to create multiculturalism in the classroom. Most urgently, they emphasize the continued need for research that puts the construction of cultural identities in educational settings under the microscope. To be sure, in order to scrutinize the multiple interfaces of institutional organization and educational policies at different levels, ethnographic contextualization must be integral to the research. However for analysis and training purposes, it pays off to start by paying close attention to the interaction itself. This strategy makes visible the work of taken-for-granted interactional practices, including the construction of participation and power. When put to work in educational contexts, the approaches to intercultural discourse reviewed in this chapter offer powerful tools for teacher education, professional development and transformative pedagogic practice.

Notes

1. Not all of these characterizations are exclusive to multiethnicity and multilinguality. Bakhtin's (1981) comment on the hybridity of utterances in the modern novel and its affiliated concepts of heteroglossia and dialogicity describe (what Kristeva, 1980, called) *inter*textuality in *intra*lingual variation.

For the anthropologist Victor Turner (1974), liminality is the defining property of transitional life stages such as puberty. The concept has since been extended to any zones of marginality and ambiguity in the lives of persons or groups.

2. The distinction between cross-cultural and intercultural research is not consistently observed in the academic literature.

3. However, Edward T. Hall, the founder of cross-cultural and intercultural communication as an academic discipline, was an anthropologist and his influential books (*The Silent Language*, 1959, *The Hidden Dimension*, 1966) are written from a distinctly anthropological perspective.

4. In another study on Korean–African American service encounter interaction, Ryoo (2007, discussed in the section on interactional sociolinguistics) arrives at quite different conclusions concerning the participants' discursive construction of their social relations.

5. Given certain conditions, an utterance 'achiev[es] the intention to produce a certain illocutionary effect in the hearer. (…) The hearer's understanding the utterance will simply consist of those intentions being achieved' (Searle, 1969: 48).

6. Speech act sets have been proposed for several speech acts, among them apologies (Olshtain & Cohen, 1983), complaints (Olshtain & Weinbach, 1993), compliments and compliment responses (Golato, 2005), and refusals (Félix-Brasdefer, 2008a), although not necessarily under the label of 'speech act set'.

7. On occasion, speech act research draws on other politeness theories, for instance Leech (1983) or Scollon and Scollon (2001). For recent reviews of the major approaches to politeness, see Arundale (2006), Eelen (2001), and Watts (2003).

8. 'Interethnic' and 'intercultural' communication are reference terms used by Gumperz and others. We follow their terminology here, but without assuming that the participants treat their interaction as 'interethnic' or 'intercultural' at all times.

9. For Goffman, frames are 'definitions of a situation (…) built up in accordance with principles of organization which govern events […] and our subjective involvement in them' (Goffman, 1974: 10f).

10. In hip-hop culture, competitions between rappers in front of an audience, with the purpose to ritually insult the opponent and demonstrate superior verbal skill.

11. Nishizaka defines 'interculturality' as 'the fact that people come from different cultures' (1995: 302). Although 'interculturality' in this sense has gained some currency in the recent literature (Higgins, 2007; Mori, 2003, 2007), it is not an entirely felicitous choice of terminology because it merely replaces more transparent terms such as 'cultural difference', 'cultural distinctiveness' or 'membership in a different culture'. In fact, in much of the research reviewed in this section, the participants orient less to *inter*culturality than to firm cultural or ethnic demarcations. The term interculturality might therefore better be reserved for participants' discursive constructions of *intercultures*, as discussed in the section on interactional sociolinguistics.

12. From a sociolinguistic perspective, such categorizing could be as criticized as 'ideological'. After all, languages are not owned by anyone, and language expertise is not tied to cultural or national membership. 'Foreigners' studying Japanese may know more about the language and may use it just as competently as Japanese people. But such sociolinguistically correct arguments would miss MCA's point, which is to explicate how participants construct *their* social world through *their* categorization work, not to assess whether they are right or wrong in the eyes of external observers. For instance, Zimmerman

(2007) shows that participants do not always treat cultural expertise as bound to cultural membership. In talk between Korean speakers of Japanese attending a Japanese university and their Japanese college friends and colleagues at work, the Japanese participants often make claims to expertise in Korean culture. Whether or not speakers treat epistemic authority on cultural and language matters as bound up with membership in a cultural category is evident in their local interactional conduct and may well engender moral judgment from their co-participants but not from the professional ethnomethodologist.

Suggestions for further reading

Alcón Soler, E.S. and Martínez Flor, A. (eds) (2008) *Investigating Pragmatics in Foreign Language Learning, Teaching and Testing.* Bristol: Multilingual Matters.
The book examines how the pragmatics of several foreign languages (English, Indonesian, Japanese, Spanish) is learned, taught and tested in study abroad contexts, language and content classrooms, computer-mediated communication, and translation. Studies are conducted from a range of theoretical perspectives, including sociocultural theory, language socialization, CA and cognitive processing theories. They offer examples of many of the data types commonly used in interlanguage pragmatics, such as authentic interaction, role-play, oral and written discourse completion and verbal report.

Bührig, K. and Thije, J.D. ten (eds) (2006) *Beyond Misunderstanding. Linguistic Analyses of Intercultural Communication.* Amsterdam: Benjamins.
The volume takes issue with the commonsense beliefs that intercultural communication is particularly prone to misunderstanding, and that interaction is 'intercultural' by virtue of participants' diverse cultural backgrounds. The chapters examine interaction in genetic counseling sessions, international team cooperation, telemarketing, workplace settings, and gatekeeping encounters from the theoretical perspectives of functional grammar, systemic functional linguistics, functional pragmatics, CA, linguistic anthropology and critical discourse analysis.

Di Luzio, A., Günthner, S. and Orletti, F. (eds) (2001) *Culture in Communication. Analyses of Intercultural Situations.* Amsterdam: Benjamin.
The book takes an interactional sociolinguistic approach to the study of language and culture. Its main theme is the theoretical nexus among genres, contextualization and ideology in intercultural discourse. The empirical studies analyze interactions among members of cultural subgroups, with particular attention to prosodic, nonverbal, and rhetorical resources, and to institutional asymmetries, identity construction and participation among first and second language speakers.

Higgins, C. (ed.) (2007) Special issue: A closer look at cultural difference: 'Interculturality' in talk-in-interaction. *Pragmatics* 17 (1).
Adopting the perspectives of interactional sociolinguistics and MCA, the research reports in this special issue examine membership in ethnic and national categories as participants' situated, practical achievement. Analyses of diverse interactions bring to the fore how participants' occasioned orientations to cultural diversity are reflexively related to the activity and their situated identities, the interactional resources through which such local relevancies are constructed, and what actions are accomplished through them. The collection concludes with a comparative commentary by Junko Mori.

Nguyen, H.T. and Kasper, G. (eds) (2009) *Talk-in-Interaction: Multilingual Perspectives.* Honolulu: University of Hawai'i, National Foreign Language Resource Center.

The contributions to this volume examine different forms of ordinary conversation and institutional discourse from the perspectives of CA and MCA. Among the focal activities are narrative events, telephone talk among family members, faculty meetings, political television interviews, foreign and second language classrooms, synchronous webchat, and conversations during study abroad. The interactions are conducted in participants' first and second languages, including Chinese, English, Japanese, Kammuang, Korean, Spanish, Swahili, and Vietnamese. Of particular interest for the studies on second and foreign language interaction is the connection between interactional organization, participation and learning.

Spencer-Oatey, H. (ed.) (2008) *Culturally Speaking. Culture, Communication and Politeness Theory* (2nd edn). London: Continuum.
The book approaches cross-cultural and intercultural pragmatics predominantly from social-psychological frameworks, focusing especially on face and politeness. Theoretical accounts include relevance theory, CAT, and spatial concepts of identity. The cross-cultural section features paired comparisons of speech acts and discourse organization, the section on intercultural communication examines interpersonal and workplace interactions between participants from different cultural groups and subgroups. The volume also includes chapters on research methodology.

References

Agar, M. (1994) *Language Shock: Understanding the Culture of Conversation*. New York: Morrow and Co.

Alcón Soler, E. and Martínez-Flor, A. (eds) (2008) *Investigating Pragmatics in Foreign Language Learning, Teaching, and Testing*. Bristol: Multilingual Matters.

Arundale, R. (2006) Face as relational and interactional: A communication framework for research on face, facework, and politeness. *Journal of Politeness Research* 2, 193–216.

Aston, G. (1993) Notes on the interlanguage of comity. In G. Kasper and S. Blum-Kulka (eds) *Interlanguage pragmatics* (pp. 224–250). New York: Oxford University Press.

Atkinson, J.M. and Heritage, J. (eds) (1984) *Structures of Social Action: Studies in Conversation Analysis*. Cambridge: Cambridge University Press.

Auer, P. (1992) Introduction: John Gumperz' approach to contextualization. In P. Auer and A. Di Luzio (eds) *The Contextualization of Language* (pp. 1–38). Amsterdam: Benjamin.

Auer, P. and Di Luzio, A. (eds) (1992) *The Contextualization of Language*. Amsterdam: Benjamin.

Austin, J. (1962) *How to do Things with Words*. Oxford: Oxford University Press.

Bailey, B.H. (1997) Communication of respect in interethnic service encounters. *Language in Society* 26, 327–356.

Bakhtin, M.M. (1981) In M. Holquist (ed.) *The Dialogic Imagination: Four Essays* (C. Emerson and M. Holquist, transl.). Austin, TX: University of Texas Press.

Banks, J.A. and McGee Banks, C.A. (eds) (2007) *Multicultural Education: Issues and Perspectives* (6th edn). New York & Chichester: Wiley.

Bardovi-Harlig, K. and Hartford, B. (eds) (2005) *Interlanguage Pragmatics*. Mahwah, NJ: Erlbaum.

Beebe, L. (1981) Social and situational factors affecting the communicative strategy of dialect code-switching. *International Journal of the Sociology of Language* 32, 139–149.

Bell, A. (2001) Back in style: Reworking audience design. In P. Eckert and J.R. Rickford (eds) *Style and Sociolinguistic Variation* (pp. 139–169). New York: Cambridge University Press.

Benwell, B. and Stokoe, E. (2006) *Discourse and Identity*. Edinburgh: Edinburgh University Press.

Bilmes, J. (1986) *Discourse and Behavior*. New York: Plenum.

Bilmes, J. (2008) Generally speaking: Formulating an argument in the US Federal Trade Commission. *Text & Talk* 28, 193–217.

Blum-Kulka, S. (1987) Indirectness and politeness in requests: Same or different? *Journal of Pragmatics* 11, 131–146.

Blum-Kulka, S. (1997) *Dinner Talk: Patterns of Sociability and Socialization in Family Discourse*. Mahwah, NJ: Lawrence Erlbaum.

Blum-Kulka, S., House, J. and Kasper, G. (1989) *Cross-cultural Pragmatics: Requests and Apologies*. Norwood, NJ: Ablex.

Bourdieu, P. (1977) *Outline of a Theory of Practice*. Cambridge: Cambridge University Press.

Braun, F. (1988) *Terms of Address: Problems of Patterns and Usage in Various Languages and Cultures*. Berlin: Mouton de Gruyter.

Bremer, K., Roberts, C., Vasseur, M-T., Simonot, M. and Broeder, P. (1996) *Achieving Understanding: Discourse in Intercultural Encounters*. London: Longman.

Brown, P. and Levinson, S. (1978/1987) *Politeness: Some Universals in Language Use*. Cambridge: Cambridge University Press. (Original version 1978.)

Bührig, K. and Thije, J.D. ten (eds) (2006) *Beyond Misunderstanding. Linguistic Analyses of Intercultural Communication*. Amsterdam: Benjamins.

Clark, H.H. (1979) Responding to indirect speech acts. *Cognitive Psychology* 11, 430–477.

Clifford, J. (1986) Introduction: Partial truths. In J. Clifford and G.E. Marcus (eds) *Writing Culture: The Poetics and Politics of Ethnography* (pp. 1–26). Berkeley, CA: University of California Press.

Clifford, J. and Marcus, G.E. (eds) (1986) *Writing Culture: The Poetics and Politics of Ethnography*. Berkeley, CA: University of California Press.

Cook, H.M. (2008) *Socializing Identities Though Speech Style*. Bristol: Multilingual Matters.

Coupland, N. (2007) *Style. Language Variation and Identity*. Cambridge: Cambridge University Press.

Coupland, N., Sarangi, S. and Candlin, C.N. (eds) (2001) *Sociolinguistics and Social Theory*. Harlow, England: Longman/Pearson Education.

Coupland, N., Wiemann, J.M. and Giles, H. (1991) Talk as "problem" and communication as "miscommunication": An integrative analysis. In N. Coupland, H. Giles and J.M. Wiemann (eds) *"Miscommunication" and Problematic Talk* (pp. 1–17). London: Sage.

Curl, T.S. and Drew, P. (2008) Contingency and action: A comparison of two forms of requesting. *Research on Language and Social Interaction* 41, 129–153.

Cutler, C. (2007) The co-construction of Whiteness in an MC battle. *Pragmatics* 17, 9–22.

Day, D. (1994) Tang's dilemma and other problems: Ethnification processes at some multilingual workplaces. *Pragmatics* 4, 315–336.

Day, D. (1998) Being ascribed, and resisting, membership of an ethnic group. In C. Antaki and S. Widdicombe (eds) *Identities in Talk* (pp. 151–170). London: Sage.

Day, D. (2006) Ethnic and social groups and their linguistic categorization. In K. Bührig and J. ten Thije (eds) *Beyond Misunderstanding. Linguistic Analyses of Intercultural Discourse* (pp. 217–244). The Hague, Netherlands: Benjamins.

Di Luzio, A., Günthner, S. and Orletti, F. (eds) (2001) *Culture in Communication. Analyses of Intercultural Situations*. Amsterdam: Benjamin.

Drew, P. (2005) Conversation analysis. In K.L. Fitch and R.E. Sanders (eds) *Language and Social Interaction* (pp. 71–102). Mahwah, NJ: Erlbaum.

Duff, P.A. (2002) The discursive co-construction of knowledge, identity, and difference: An ethnography of communication in the high school mainstream. *Applied Linguistics* 23, 289–322.

Duranti, A. (1997) *Linguistic Anthropology*. Cambridge: Cambridge University Press.

Eades, D. (2003) The politics of misunderstanding in the legal system: Aboriginal English speakers in Queensland. In J. House, G. Kasper and S. Ross (eds) *Misunderstanding in Spoken Discourse* (pp. 199–226). London: Longman.

Edwards, D. (1997) *Discourse and Cognition*. London: Sage.

Edwards, D. (1998) The relevant thing about her: Social identity categories in use. In C. Antaki and S. Widdicombe (eds) *Identities in Talk* (pp. 15–33). Thousand Oaks, CA: Sage.

Eelen, G. (2001) *A Critique of Politeness Theories*. Manchester: St. Jerome.

Eglin, P. (1980) *Talk and Taxonomy: a Methodological Comparison of Ethnosemantics and Ethnomethodology with Reference to Terms for Canadian Doctors*. Amsterdam: Benjamins.

Enfield, N.J. and Stivers, T. (eds) (2007) *Person Reference in Interaction*. Cambridge: Cambridge University Press.

Erickson, F. (1996) Ethnographic microanalysis. In S.L. McKay and N.H. Hornberger (eds) *Sociolinguistics and Language Teaching* (pp. 283–306). Cambridge: Cambridge University Press.

Erickson, F. and Shultz, J. (1982) *The Counselor as Gatekeeper: Social Interaction in Interviews*. New York: Academic Press.

Fairclough, N. (1989) *Language and Power*. London: Longman.

Félix-Brasdefer, C. (2008a) *Politeness in Mexico and the United States*. Amsterdam: Benjamins.

Félix-Brasdefer, J.C. (2008b) Sociopragmatic variation: Dispreferred responses in Mexican and Dominican Spanish. *Journal of Politeness Research* 4, 81–110.

Fiksdal, S. (1990) *The Right Time and Pace: A Microanalysis of Cross-Cultural Gatekeeping Interviews*. Norwood, NJ: Ablex.

Friedrich, P. (1989) Language, ideology, and political economy. *American Anthropologist* 91, 295–312.

Fukuda, C. (2006) Resistance against being formulated as cultural other: The case of a Chinese student in Japan. *Pragmatics* 16, 429–456.

Fukushima, S. (1990) Offers and requests: Performance by Japanese learners of English. *World Englishes* 9, 317–325.

Fukushima, S. (2000) *Requests and Culture*. Bern: Peter Lang.

Gallois, C., Ogay, T. and Giles, H. (2005) Communication accommodation theory: A look back and a look ahead. In W.B. Gudykunst (ed.) *Theorizing About Intercultural Communication* (pp. 121–148). Thousand Oaks, CA: Sage.

García, C. (1993) Making a request and responding to it: A case study of Peruvian Spanish speakers. *Journal of Pragmatics* 19, 127–152.

Garfinkel, H. (1967) *Studies in Ethnomethodology*. Cambridge: Polity Press.

Garfinkel, H. and Sacks, H. (1970) On formal structures of practical action. In J.C. McKinney and E.A. Tiryakian (eds) *Theoretical Sociology: Perspectives and Developments* (pp. 338–366). New York: Appleton-Century-Crofts.

Gass, S.M. and Neu, J. (eds) (1996) *Speech Acts Across Cultures*. Berlin: Mouton de Gruyter.

Gay, G. (2000) *Culturally Responsive Teaching: Theory, Research, and Practice*. New York: Teachers College Press.

Geertz, C. (1973) *The Interpretation of Cultures*. New York: BasicBooks.

Giddens, A. (1976) *New Rules of Sociological Method*. London: Hutchinson.

Giles, H. and Coupland, N. (1991) *Language: Context and Consequences*. Milton Keynes: Open University Press.

Goffman, E. (1967) *Interaction Ritual*. New York: Doubleday.

Goffman, E. (1974) *Frame Analysis*. Harmondsworth: Penguin.

Goffman, E. (1981) *Forms of Talk*. Oxford: Blackwell.

Golato, A. (2005) *Compliments and Compliment Responses*. Amsterdam: Benjamins.

Goodenough, W. (1964) Cultural anthropology and linguistics. In D. Hymes (ed.) *Language in Culture and Society* (pp. 36–39). New York: Harper & Row.

Goodwin, C. and Duranti, A. (1992) Rethinking context: an introduction. In A. Duranti and C. Goodwin (eds) *Rethinking Context* (pp. 1–42). Cambridge: Cambridge University Press.

Goodwin, H.M. (1990) *He-said-she-said: Talk as Social Organization Among Black Children*. Bloomington, IN: Indiana University Press.

Grice, H.P. (1957) Meaning. *Philosophical Review* 66, 377–388.

Grice, H.P. (1975) Logic and conversation. In P. Cole and J.L. Morgan (eds) *Syntax and Semantics vol. 3: Speech Acts* (pp. 41–58). New York: Academic Press. (Original 1967).

Gudykunst, W.B. (ed.) (2005) *Theorizing about Intercultural Communication*. Thousand Oaks, CA: Sage.

Gumperz, J.J. (1982a) *Discourse Strategies*. Cambridge: Cambridge University Press.

Gumperz, J.J. (1982b) *Language and Social Identity*. Cambridge: Cambridge University Press.

Gumperz, J.J. (1992) Contextualization and understanding. In A. Duranti and C. Goodwin (eds) *Rethinking Context* (pp. 229–252). Cambridge: Cambridge University Press.

Gumperz, J. (1996) The linguistic and cultural relativity of conversational inference. In J.J. Gumperz and S.L. Levinson (eds) *Rethinking Linguistic Relativity* (pp. 374–406). Cambridge: Cambridge University Press.

Gumperz, J., Judd, T. and Roberts, C. (1979) *Crosstalk. A Study of Cross-cultural Communication. Background Materials and Notes to Accompany the B.B.C. Film*. Southall: National Centre for Industrial Language Training.

Hall, E.T. (1959) *The Silent Language*. New York: Doubleday.

Hall, E.T. (1966) *The Hidden Dimension*. New York: Doubleday.

Hansen, A.D. (2005) A practical task: Ethnicity as a resource in social interaction. *Research on Language and Social Interaction* 38, 63–104.

Harklau, L. (2000) From the "good" kids to the "worst": Representations of English language learners across educational settings. *TESOL Quarterly* 34, 35–68.

Harré, R. (1983) *Personal Being*. Oxford: Blackwell.

Hassall, T. (1999) Request strategies in Indonesian. *Pragmatics* 9, 585–606.

Heritage, J. (1984) *Garfinkel and Ethnomethodology*. Cambridge: Polity Press.

Heritage, J. and Atkinson, J.M. (1984) Introduction. In J.M. Atkinson and J. Heritage (eds) *Structures of Social Action: Studies in Conversation Analysis* (pp. 1–15). Cambridge: Cambridge University Press.

Heritage, J. and Roth, A. (1995) Grammar and institution: Questions and questioning in the broadcast news interview. *Research on Language and Social Interaction* 28, 1–60.

Hester, S. and Eglin, P. (1997) Membership categorization analysis: An introduction. In S. Hester and P. Eglin (eds) *Culture in Action* (pp. 1–23). Washington D.C.: International Institute for Ethnomethodology and Conversation Analysis & University Press of America.

Higgins, C. (2007) Constructing membership in the in-group: Affiliation and resistance among urban Tanzanians. *Pragmatics* 17, 49–70.

Higgins, C. (2009) "Are you Hindu?:" Resisting membership categorization through language alternation. In H.T. Nguyen and G. Kasper (eds) *Talk-in-Interaction: Multilingual Perspectives* (pp. 111–136). Honolulu: University of Hawai'i, National Foreign Language Resource Center.

Hinkel, E. (ed.) (1999) *Culture in Second Language Teaching and Learning*. Cambridge: Cambridge University Press.

Hinnenkamp, V. (1987) Foreigner talk, code switching and the concept of trouble. In K. Knapp, W. Enninger and A. Knapp-Potthof (eds) *Analyzing Intercultural Communication* (pp. 137–180). Amsterdam: Mouton.

Hofstede, G. (2001) *Culture's Consequences* (2nd edn). Thousand Oaks, CA: Sage.

Holstein, J.A. and Gubrium, J.F. (eds) (2008) *Handbook of Constructionist Research*. New York: Guilford Press.

House, J. and Kasper, G. (1981) Politeness markers in English and German. In F. Coulmas (ed.) *Conversational Routine* (pp. 157–185). The Hague: Mouton.

Hutchins, E. (1995) *Cognition in the Wild*. Cambridge, MA: MIT Press.

Hymes, D. (ed.) (1964) *Language in Culture and Society*. New York: Harper & Row.

Kasper, G. (2000) Data collection in pragmatics. In H. Spencer-Oatey (ed.) *Culturally Speaking* (pp. 316–341). London & New York: Continuum.

Kasper, G. (2006a) Speech acts in interaction: Towards discursive pragmatics. In K. Bardovi-Harlig, C. Félix-Brasdefer and A. Omar (eds) *Pragmatics and Language Learning* (Vol. 11), (pp. 281–314). Honolulu: National Foreign Language Resource Center.

Kasper, G. (2006b) When once is not enough: Politeness in multiple requests. *Multilingua* 25, 323–349.

Kasper, G. (2009) Categories, context and comparison in conversation analysis. In H.T. Nguyen and G. Kasper (eds) *Talk-in-Interaction: Multilingual Perspectives* (pp. 1–28). Honolulu: University of Hawai'i, National Foreign Language Resource Center.

Kasper, G. and Blum-Kulka, S. (eds) (1993) *Interlanguage Pragmatics*. New York: Oxford University Press.

Kasper, G. and Rose, K.R. (2002) *Pragmatic Development in a Second Language*. Oxford: Blackwell.

Kerekes, J. (2006) Winning an interviewer's trust in a gatekeeping encounter. *Language in Society* 35, 27–57.

Kiesling, F.S. and Bratt Paulston, C. (eds) (2005) *Intercultural Discourse and Communication*. Malden, MA: Blackwell.

Koole, T. and Thije, J.D. ten (1994) *The Construction of Intercultural Discourse*. Amsterdam: Rodopi.

Kotthoff, H. and Spencer-Oatey, H. (eds) (2007) *Handbook of Intercultural Communication*. Berlin: Mouton de Gruyter.

Kraidy, M.M. (2005) *Hybridity, or the Cultural Logic of Globalization*. Philadelphia: Temple University Press.

Kristeva, J. (1980) *Desire in Language: A Semiotic Approach to Literature and Art*. New York: Columbia University Press. (French original 1966.)

Lakoff, G. and Johnson, M. (1980) *Metaphors We Live By*. Chicago: University of Chicago Press.

Lee-Wong, S.M. (1999) *Politeness and Face in Chinese Culture*. Frankfurt: Peter Lang.

Leech, G. (1983) *Principles of Pragmatics*. London: Longman.

Levinson, S. (1983) *Pragmatics*. New York: Cambridge University Press.

Lévi-Strauss, C. (1978) *Myth and Meaning*. New York: Schocken Books.

Márquez Reiter, R. (2000) *Linguistic Politeness in Britain and Uruguay: A Contrastive Study of Requests and Apologies*. Amsterdam: Benjamins.

Márquez Reiter, R., Rainey, I. and Fulcher, G. (2005) A comparative study of certainty and conventional indirectness: Evidence from British English and Peninsular Spanish. *Applied Linguistics* 26, 1–31.

Meeuwis, M. (1994) Leniency and testiness in intercultural communication: Remarks on ideology and context in interactional sociolinguistics. *Pragmatics* 4, 391–408.

Meyerhoff, M. (2001) Dynamics of differentiation: On social psychology and cases of variation. In N. Coupland, C. Candlin and S. Sarangi (eds) *Sociolinguistics and Social Theory* (pp. 61–87). London: Longman.

Moerman, M. (1988) *Talking Culture: Ethnography and Conversation Analysis*. Philadelphia: University of Philadelphia Press.

Mori, J. (2003) The construction of interculturality: A study of initial encounters between Japanese and American students. *Research on Language and Social Interaction* 36, 143–184.

Mori, J. (2007) Reconstructing the participants' treatments of 'interculturality': Variations in data and methodologies. *Pragmatics* 17, 71–94.

Myers-Scotton, C. (1993) *Social Motivations for Codeswitching*. Oxford: Clarendon.

Nishizaka, A. (1995) The interactive constitution of interculturality: How to be a Japanese with words. *Human Studies* 18, 301–326.

Nishizaka, A. (1999) Doing interpreting within interaction: The interactive accomplishments of a "Henna Gaijin" or "Strange Foreigner". *Human Studies* 22, 235–251.

Ochs, E. (1996) Linguistic resources for socializing humanity. In J.J. Gumperz and S. Levinson (eds) *Rethinking Linguistic Relativity* (pp. 407–437). Cambridge: Cambridge University Press.

Olshtain, S. and Cohen, A.D. (1983) Apology: A speech act set. In N. Wolfson and E. Judd (eds) *Sociolinguistics and Language Acquisition* (pp. 18–35). Rowley, MA: Newbury House.

Olshtain, E. and Weinbach, L. (1993) Interlanguage features of the speech act of complaining. In G. Kasper and S. Blum-Kulka (eds) *Interlanguage Pragmatics* (pp. 108–122). Oxford: Oxford University Press.

Philips, S.U. (1972) Participant structures and communicative competence: Warm Springs children in community and classroom. In C.B. Cazden, V.P. John and D. Hymes (eds) *Functions of Language in the Classroom* (pp. 370–394). New York: Teachers College Press.

Rampton, B. (1999) Sociolinguistics and cultural studies: New ethnicities, liminality and interaction. *Social Semiotics* 9, 355–374.

Rampton, B. (2006) *Language in Late Modernity: Interaction in an Urban School*. Cambridge: Cambridge University Press.

Risager, K. (2007) *Language and Culture Pedagogy: From a National to a Transnational Paradigm*. Clevedon: Multilingual Matters.

Ross, S. (1998) Divergent frame interpretations in Oral Proficiency Interview interaction. In R. Young and A.W. He (eds) *Talking and Testing. Discourse Approaches to the Assessment of Oral Proficiency* (pp. 333–353). Amsterdam: John Benjamins.

Rue, Y-J. and Zhang, G.Q. (2008) Request strategies: A comparative study in Mandarin Chinese and Korean. Amsterdam: John Benjamins.

Ryoo, H. (2007) Interculturality serving multiple interactional goals in African American and Korean service encounters. *Pragmatics* 17, 71–94.

Sachdev, I. and Giles, H. (2006) Bilingual accommodation. In T.K. Bhatia and W.C. Ritchie (eds) *The Handbook of Bilingualism* (pp. 353–378). Oxford: Blackwell.

Sacks, H. (1972) An initial investigation of the usability of conversational data for doing sociology. In D. Sudnow (ed.) *Studies in Social Interaction* (pp. 31–74). New York: Free Press.

Sacks, H. (1984) Notes on methodology. In J.M. Atkinson and J. Heritage (eds) *Structures of Social Action: Studies in Conversation Analysis* (pp. 21–27). Cambridge: CUP.

Sacks, H. (1992) In G. Jefferson (ed.) *Lectures on Conversation* (2 Vols). Oxford: Blackwell.

Sacks, H., Schegloff, E.A. and Jefferson, G. (1974) A simplest systematics for the organization of turn taking for conversation. *Language* 50, 696–735.

Sapir, E. (1949) Cultural anthropology and psychiatry. In D.G. Mandelbaum (ed.) *Selected Writings of Edward Sapir in Language, Culture and Personality* (pp. 509–521). Berkeley & Los Angeles: University of California Press.

Sarangi, S. (1994) Intercultural or not? Beyond celebration of cultural differences in miscommunication analysis. *Pragmatics* 4, 409–427.

Sarangi, S. and Roberts, C. (1999) Hybridity in gatekeeping discourse. In S. Sarangi and C. Roberts (eds) *Talk, Work and Institutional Order* (pp. 473–503). Berlin: Mouton de Gruyter.

Schegloff, E.A. (1987) Some sources of misunderstanding in talk-in-interaction. *Linguistics* 25, 201–218.

Schegloff, E.A. (1992) Repair after next turn: The last structurally provided defense of intersubjectivity in conversation. *American Journal of Sociology* 98, 1295–1345.

Schegloff, E.A. (2006) Interaction: The infrastructure for social institutions, the natural ecological niche for language, and the arena in which culture is enacted. In N.J. Enfield and S.C. Levinson (eds) *Roots of Human Society* (pp. 70–96). Oxford: Berg.

Schegloff, E.A., Jefferson, G. and Sacks, H. (1977) The preference for self-correction in the organization of repair in conversation. *Language* 53, 361–382.

Schiffrin, D. (1987) *Approaches to Discourse*. Oxford: Blackwell.

Schneider, K.P. and Barron, A. (eds) (2008) *Variational Pragmatics: A Focus on Regional Varieties in Pluricentric Languages*. Amsterdam/Philadelphia: John Benjamins.

Scollon, R. and Scollon, S.B.K. (2001) *Intercultural communication* (2nd edn). Oxford: Blackwell.

Searle, J.R. (1969) *Speech Acts: An Essay in the Philosophy of Language*. Cambridge: Cambridge University Press.

Searle, J.R. (1976) A classification of illocutionary acts. *Language in Society* 5, 1–23.

Shea, D.P. (1994) Perspective and production: Structuring conversational participation across cultural borders. *Pragmatics* 4, 357–390.

Sifianou, M. (1992) *Politeness Phenomena in England and Greece: a Cross-cultural Perspective*. Oxford: Clarendon.

Silverman, D. (1998) *Harvey Sacks: Social Science and Conversation Analysis*. New York: Oxford University Press.

Silverstein, M. (1993) Metapragmatic discourse and metapragmatic function. In J. Lucy (ed.) *Reflexive Language* (pp. 33–58). New York: Cambridge University Press.

Silverstein, M. (2003) Indexical order and the dialectics of sociolinguistic life. *Language and Communication* 23 (3–4), 193–229.

Spencer-Oatey, H. (ed.) (2008) *Culturally Speaking* (2nd edn). London & New York: Continuum.

Sperber, D. and Wilson, D. (1986/1995) *Relevance: Communication and Cognition.* Oxford: Blackwell.

Suzuki, A. (2009) When gaijin matters: Theory-building activities in Japanese multiparty interaction. In H.T. Nguyen and G. Kasper (eds) *Talk-in-Interaction: Multilingual Perspectives* (pp. 89–109). Honolulu: University of Hawai'i, National Foreign Language Resource Center.

Taleghani-Nikazm, C. (2006) *Request Sequences: The Intersection of Grammar, Interaction and Social Context.* Amsterdam: John Benjamins.

Talmy, S. (2004) Forever FOB: The cultural production of ESL in a high school. *Pragmatics* 14, 149–172.

Talmy, S. (2008) The cultural productions of the ESL student at Tradewinds High: Contingency, multidirectionality, and identity in L2 socialization. *Applied Linguistics* 29, 619–644.

Talmy, S. (2009) Resisting ESL: Categories and sequence in a critically "motivated" analysis of classroom interaction. In H.T. Nguyen and G. Kasper (eds) *Talk-in-Interaction: Multilingual Perspectives* (pp. 181–213). Honolulu: University of Hawai'i, National Foreign Language Resource Center.

Thije, J.D. ten (2006) The notions of perspective and perspectivising in intercultural communication research. In K. Bührig and J.D. ten Thije (eds) *Beyond Misunderstanding. Linguistic Analyses of Intercultural Communication* (pp. 97–151). Amsterdam: John Benjamins.

Turner, V. (1974) *Dramas, Fields, and Metaphors: Symbolic Action in Human Society.* Ithaca: Cornell University Press.

Tyler, A. (1995) The coconstruction of cross-cultural miscommunication. *Studies in Second Language Acquisition* 17, 129–152.

Tyler, A. and Davies, C. (1990) Cross-linguistic communication missteps. *Text* 10, 385–411.

Vološinov, V.I. (1973) *Marxism and the Philosophy of Language.* New York: Seminar Press.

Vygotsky, L.S. (1978) *Mind in Society: The Development of Higher Psychological Processes.* Cambridge, MA: Harvard University Press.

Wallace, A.F.C. (1961) *Culture and Personality.* New York: Random House.

Watson, D.R. (1997) Some general reflections of 'categorization' and 'sequence' in the analysis of conversation. In S. Hester and P. Eglin (eds) *Culture in action* (pp. 49–75). Washington DC: International Institute for Ethnomethodology and Conversation Analysis & University Press of America.

Watts, R.J. (2003) *Politeness.* Cambridge: Cambridge University Press.

White, S. (1989) Backchannels across cultures: A study of Americans and Japanese *Language in Society*, 18, 59–76.

Wittgenstein, L. (1953) *Philosophical Investigations.* Oxford: Blackwell.

Ylänne, V. (2008) Communication accommodation theory. In H. Spencer-Oatey (ed.) *Culturally Speaking* (2nd edn), (pp. 164–186). London: Continuum.

Zhang, Y. (1995) Indirectness in Chinese requesting. In G. Kasper (ed.) *Pragmatics of Chinese as a Native and Target Language* (pp. 69–118). Honolulu: University of Hawai'i, Second Language Teaching and Curriculum Center.

Zimmerman, D.H. (1998) Identity, context and interaction. In C. Antaki and S. Widdicombe (eds) *Identities in Talk* (pp. 87–106). London: Sage.

Zimmerman, E. (2007) Constructing Korean and Japanese interculturality in talk: Ethnic membership categorization among users of Japanese. *Pragmatics* 17, 71–94.

Chapter 18
Conversation Analysis

JACK SIDNELL

Introduction

Conversation analysis (hereafter CA) is an approach to language and social interaction that emerged in the mid- to late 1960s through the collaboration of the sociologists Harvey Sacks and Emmanuel Schegloff as well as a number of their students, most importantly, Gail Jefferson (see Lerner, 2004). Although it originated in the United States within sociology, today working conversation analysts are to be found not only in the United States but also in England, France, Germany, the Netherlands, Japan, Korea, Canada, Australia, Finland and elsewhere, in departments of anthropology, communication studies, education, linguistics and others in addition to sociology. In their earliest studies, Sacks, Schegloff and Jefferson worked out a rigorous method for the empirical study of talk-in-interaction and, as a result, their findings have proven robust and cumulative. Indeed, these pioneering studies (e.g. Sacks, 1974; Sacks *et al.*, 1974; Schegloff, 1968; Schegloff & Sacks, 1973; Schegloff *et al.*, 1977 among others) from the 1960s and 1970s have provided the foundation for subsequent research so that we now have a large body of strongly interlocking findings about fundamental domains of human social interaction such as turn-taking, action sequencing and repair (see below). In this brief overview of CA, I begin by outlining the main goals and principles of the field. I discuss how CA emerged out of a convergence of ethnomethodology, Goffman's work on social interaction and a number of other research frameworks of the late 1960s suggesting that a pivotal and transformative moment came when Sacks, Schegloff and Jefferson realized that analysts could use the same methods in *studying* conversation that conversationalists used in *producing* and *understanding* it. I then turn to consider a single fragment of conversation in some detail, suggesting that it, as any other such fragment, can be seen as the product of multiple, intersecting 'machineries' or 'organizations of practice'. In the next section of the chapter I consider the methods of CA focusing in particular on the use of collections to isolate and define a focal practice or phenomenon that is the object of study. I show that it is within the context of a collection that one can begin to describe the practice or phenomenon as a set of normative practices and orientations revealed in the participants' own conduct. Finally, I discuss the relevance of CA for research on classroom interaction and language learning.

Conversation Analysis: A Brief History and Some Key Terms

The standard history of CA begins with the sociologists Erving Goffman and Harold Garfinkel.[1] Goffman's highly original and innovative move was to direct attention to the fundamentally social character of co-present interaction – the ordinary and extraordinary ways in which people interact with one another (see especially Goffman, 1964, 1981). Goffman insisted that this – what he later described as the 'interaction order' (Goffman, 1983) – constituted a social institution that both formed the foundation of society at large and exhibited special properties specific to it. Very early in his career (e.g. Goffman, 1957), Goffman showed that interaction was its own system – a special kind of social institution with its own specific properties quite irreducible to anything else, be it language, individual psychology, culture or 'external characteristics' such as race, class and gender.

In a more or less independent but parallel movement, in the late 1950s and early 1960s, Harold Garfinkel (1967) was developing a critique of mainstream sociological thinking that was to develop into ethnomethodology. Garfinkel studied with Talcott Parsons in the social relations program at Harvard but was heavily influenced by the phenomenology of Alfred Schutz and Edmond Husserl. Parsons was concerned with what he described, in a monumental study, as the 'structure of social action', and developed a model in which, to put it very crudely, actors employed means to achieve ends within particular circumstances. For Parsons, social order is a product of socialization and the internalization of norms – this internalization in fact creates society from the mass of individuals. Garfinkel challenged this conventional wisdom by arguing that, to the extent that social life is regulated by norms, this rests upon a foundation of practical reasoning. People, Garfinkel suggested, must determine what norms, precedents, traditions and so on apply to any given situation. As such, an explanation of human conduct that involves citing the rules or norms being followed is obviously inadequate since the question remains as to how it was decided that these were the relevant rules or norms to follow! Moreover, how did the people involved decide how decisions were to be made in the first place? Followed through to its logical conclusion, practical reasoning always seems to result in infinite regress. Language presents a special case of just this kind of thing. If people frequently mean more than they say which of course they do (e.g. 'I'm not happy', 'Well! that was interesting'), how are we able to determine what in fact they mean in any given case? Garfinkel noted that in fact, in the course of their everyday activities, members of society do not seem bothered by the kind of radical indeterminacy this would seem to imply. Rather, they adopt an attitude to everyday life that seems to largely circumvent these potential problems. For instance Garfinkel noted that unless given reason not to, people generally assume that things are as they seem – they trust, that is, in ordinary appearances. By the early to mid-1960s, Harvey Sacks was deeply immersed in themes that Garfinkel and Goffman had developed, and it is common and not entirely inaccurate to say that CA emerged as a synthesis of these two currents – it was the study of practical reasoning (Garfinkel) applied to the special and particular topic of social interaction (Goffman).

The sequential organization of understanding in conversation

One of the key insights of early CA was that conversationalists' *methods* of practical reasoning are founded upon the unique properties of conversation as a system. For instance, conversationalists inspect next turns to see if and how their own talk has been understood. That is, they exploit the systematic properties of conversation in reasoning about it. As analysts we can exploit the same resource. Consider the following fragment from one of Sacks' recordings of the Group Therapy Sessions.[2]

(1) (Sacks, 1995a: vol. I: 281).[3]

```
1    Roger:      On Hollywood Boulevard the other night they were
2                giving tickets for dirty windshields ((door opens))
3    Jim:        hh
4    Therapist:  Hi, Jim [c'mon in.
5    Jim:                [H'warya
6    Therapist:  Jim, this is uh Al,
7    Jim:        Hi
8    Therapist:  Ken,
9    Jim:        Hi
10   Ken:        Hi
11   Therapist:  Roger.
12   Roger:    → Hi
13   Jim:        Hi
14   Therapist:  Jim Reed.
```

Sacks (1995a [1966]) draws attention to 'the *prima facie* evidence afforded by a subsequent speaker's talk' in his analysis of the therapist's turns at lines 8 and 11 as recognizable introductions. Thus, when, at line 12, Roger responds to the

> utterance with his name (...) not with 'What' (as in an answer to a summons), indeed not with an utterance to the therapist at all, but with a greeting to the newly arrived Jim, he shows himself (to the others there assembled as well as to us, the analytic overhearers) to have attended and analyzed the earlier talk, to have understood that an introduction sequence was being launched, and to be prepared to participate by initiating a greeting exchange in the slot in which it is he who is being introduced. (Schegloff, 1995: xliii)

Thus a response displays a hearing or analysis of the utterance to which it responds. Such a hearing or analysis is 'publicly available as the means by which previous speakers can determine how they were understood' (Heritage, 1984a, 1984b). The third position in a sequence is then a place to accept the recipients' displayed understanding or, alternatively, to repair it (see Schegloff, 1992; Sidnell, 2006). Heritage writes:

> By means of this framework, speakers are released from what would otherwise be an endless task of confirming and reconfirming their understandings of each other's actions ... a context of publicly displayed and continuously updated intersubjective understandings is systematically sustained ... Mutual understanding is thus displayed ... 'incarnately' in the sequentially organized details of conversational interaction. (Heritage, 1984a: 259)

The empirical basis of conversation analysis

As has already been suggested in the preceding paragraph, CA is deeply committed to a rigorously empirical method. In his lectures, Sacks made a series of penetrating arguments about the importance of basing a study of conversation on recorded examples (see Sacks, 1984a; Heritage, 1984a; Jefferson, 1985, for discussion of this issue). This is not simply a matter of finding examples that will illustrate the point one is trying to make but rather of *beginning* with the stubborn, recalcitrant, complex details of actual conversation and using them to locate and define whatever argument one ends up with. Recordings provided Sacks with a terra firma on which to base a rigorously empirical discipline in which any analysis was accountable to the details of actual occurrences in the world. Sacks writes:

> I started to work with tape-recorded conversations. Such materials had a single virtue, that I could replay them. I could transcribe them somewhat and study them extendedly – however long it might take. The tape-recorded materials constituted a 'good-enough' record of

what happened. Other things, to be sure, happened, but at least what was on the tape had happened. It was not from any large interest in language or from some theoretical formulation of what should be studied that I started with tape-recorded conversations, but simply because I could get my hands on it and I could study it again and again, and also consequentially, because others could look at what I had studied and make of it what they could, if, for example, they wanted to be able to disagree with me. (Sacks, 1984a)

As Sacks goes on to note, we don't have very good intuitions about conversation (as we seem to for syntax, which is apparently the contrast he was making) nor are we capable of remembering or imagining the details of what happens in conversation. Consider that, as Heritage (1984a, 1984b) notes, the following example is not unusual in its level of complexity:

(2) NB VII: 2

```
01   Edn:   =Oh honey that was a lovely luncheon I shoulda ca:lled you
02          s:soo[:ner but I:]l:[lo:ved it.Ih wz just deli:ghtful[: l.] =
03   Mar:        [((f))  Oh:::] [°(    )                         [Well] =
04   Mar:   =I wz gla[d  y o u] (came).]
05   Edn:            ['nd yer f:] friends] 'r so da:rli:ng, =
06   Mar:   = Oh :::[: it wz:]
07   Edn:           [e-that P]a :t isn'she a do:[:ll?]
08   Mar:                                       [iY e]h isn't she pretty,
09          (.)
10   Edn:   Oh: she's a beautiful girl. =
11   Mar:   = Yeh I think she's a pretty gir[l.
12   Edn:                                   [En that Reinam'n::
13          (.)
14   Edn:   She SCA:RES me. =
```

So there are some rather obvious reasons why conversation analysts insist on working from actual recordings of conversation rather than imagined, remembered or experimentally produced examples. There is also at least one rather less obvious but absolutely critical reason that goes to the very heart of CA as a practice. Sacks explains:

I want to argue that, however rich our imaginations are, if we use hypothetical, or hypothetical-typical versions of the world we are constrained by reference to what an audience, an audience of professionals, can accept as reasonable. That might not appear to be a terrible constraint until we come to look at the kinds of things that actually occur. Were I to say about many of the objects we work with 'Let us suppose that this happened; now I am going to consider it', then an audience might feel hesitant about what I would make of it by reference to whether such things happen. That is to say, under such a constraint many things that actually occur are debarred from use as a basis for theorizing about conversation. I take it that this debarring affects the character of social sciences very strongly. (Sacks, 1984a)

Here, then, Sacks notes that if one works with invented examples (or even recollected examples) one is constrained 'by reference to what an audience, an audience of professionals, can accept as reasonable'. The problem is that we know from studying the recordings of conversations that many apparently counter-intuitive and quite unexpected things actually do happen. If invented instances of such occurrences were presented to 'an audience of professionals' they might respond with, 'but people don't say such things', 'People don't talk like that' and so on. As Sacks notes, then, the use of recordings can open up a whole range of phenomena that no one would have ever suspected even existed.

> We will be using observation as a basis for theorizing. Thus we start with things that are not currently imaginable, by showing that they happened. We can then come to see that a base for using close looking at the world for theorizing about it is that from close looking at the world we can find things that we could not, by imagination, assert were there. (Sacks, 1984a, 1984b: 25)

Intersecting machineries

So, given these considerations we should now turn to some actual bit of recorded conversation and attempt to analyze it even if, given the constraints imposed by an overview chapter, we can only give it some cursory attention. The following is the transcript of the first few seconds of a telephone conversation between Deb, a woman in her fifties, and her boyfriend, Dick. The call comes the morning after Deb had hosted a party with some guests attending from out of town.

(3) Deb and Dick

```
                    (ring)
                    (r[
01  Deb:      [Hello:?hh
02  Dick:    Good morning. =
03  Deb:     = Hi:, howareya.
04  Dick:    Not too ba:d. Howareyou?
05  Deb:     I'm fi::ne
06  Dick:    Howdit g[o?
07  Deb:              [.h Oh: just grea:t, <everybody:st- still here.
08  Dick:    Oh really(h) =
09  Deb:     = Yeah
10  Dick:    Oh they stayed. Okay.
11  Deb:     Yea:h
```

I'm going to suggest that this fragment of conversation – indeed, any fragment of conversation, can be usefully understood as the product of multiple intersecting 'machineries' or 'organizations of practice' (Schegloff, 2006). I realize that a term like 'machineries' or a phrase such as 'organizations of practice' may seem a bit obscure, but what I mean is actually fairly straightforward. Basically there is an organized set of practices involved in, first, getting and, second, constructing a turn, another such organized set of practices involved in producing a sequence of actions, another set of practices involved in the initiation and execution of repair and so on. Sacks sometimes used the metaphor of machines or machinery to describe this.

> In a way, our aim is ... to get into a position to transform, in what I figure is almost a literal, physical sense, our view of what happened here as some interaction that could be treated as the thing we're study-ing, to interactions being spewed out by machinery, the machinery being what we're trying to find; where, in order to find it we've got to get a whole bunch of its products. (Sacks, 1995b: 169)

The machinery metaphor is quite revealing. Clearly, this is a highly 'decentralized' or 'distributed' view of human action that places the emphasis not on the internal cognitive representations of individuals or on their 'external' attributes (doctor, woman, etc.) but on the structures of activity within which they are embedded.

If we think about this little fragment in these terms – that is, as the prod-uct of multiple, simultaneously operative and relevant organizations of practice or 'machineries' for short – we can get some good analytic lever-age on what may at first seem quite opaque.

Let us start by noting that there is an organization relating to occasions or encounters taken as wholes – this is what we refer to as 'overall struc-tural organization' or, simply, 'overall organization'. For a given occasion there are specific places within it that particular actions are relevantly done. An obvious example is that greetings are properly done at the begin-ning of an encounter rather than at its conclusion. Similarly, introductions between participants who do not know one another are relevant at the outset of an exchange. At the conclusion of an event – a job interview, an exam, a dinner party, etc. – a discussion or report of 'how it went' may become relevant. And, of course, this is precisely what Deb understands Dick to be inviting at line 06 with 'Howdit go'.

There is another sense in which the overall organization of talk is rele-vant to what happens here. Think then about where this question 'Howdit go' comes not in relation to these people's lives (after Dick supposes the party is over) but rather in relation to this call. Specifically, the talk that immediately precedes this question is devoted to a series of tasks – getting the attention of the recipient via the ringing of the telephone and sub-sequently displaying that attention via 'hello' (i.e. summons-answer, see

Schegloff, 1968), identifying, recognizing and aligning the participants (Schegloff, 1979), so-called 'personal state inquiries' (Jefferson, 1980; Sacks, 1975; Schegloff, 1986). Taken together, we can see that the talk up to and including line 05 constitutes an 'opening'. So, what does that mean for the utterance we are now concerned with? Where can this 'Howdit go' be said to occur? Briefly, this is what Schegloff calls 'anchor position' – precisely because whatever is said here is vulnerable to being heard as 'why I'm calling', as 'the reason for the call' and thus as something its speaker accords some importance (see also Sacks, 1984b). Now we can not go into a detailed analysis of this here but let us note that where participants reach this position (and there are many calls in which they never do for one reason or another) and the caller does *not* indicate what they are calling about, that may be oriented to as an absence. Consider then the following opening from a conversation between two close friends:

(4) Hyla & Nancy

```
01                      ((ring))
02   Nancy:             H'llo:?
03   Hyla:              Hi:,
04   Nancy:             ↑HI::.
05   Hyla:              Hwaryuhh =
06   Nancy:             =↓Fi:ne how'r you,
07   Hyla:              Oka:[y,
08   Nancy:                 [Goo:d,
09                          (0.4)
10   Hyla:              ·mkhhh[hhh
11   Nancy:    →              [What's doin,
12                            (·)
13   Hyla:     →    aAh:, noth[i : n :,  ]
14   Nancy:    →               [Y'didn't g]  o meet Grahame? =
```

In this fragment, Hyla has called Nancy. A reciprocal exchange of personal state inquiries ends with Nancy's assessment 'good' at line 08. Here then the participants have reached 'anchor position' but instead of the caller raising a first topic there is silence and some audible breathing from Hyla at lines 09–10. This occasions Nancy's 'What's doin', at line 11. With 'What's doin', Nancy invites Hyla (the caller) to raise a first topic and thereby displays an orientation to this as a place to do just that. And notice that when Hyla responds with 'Ah nothin' Nancy pursues a specific topic by asking 'Y'didn't go meet Grahame?'.

And still another sense in which we can talk about the overall organization of the call has to do with where in the course of a day a call occurs (see Sacks, 1984b). Consider the following in which, in the course of a radio documentary, a woman reports knowing 'something was wrong' and 'something wasn't right' by virtue of the time she received a phone call ('early on Easter Monday probably around seven or eight').

> The day that I found out about Dave's death, was early on Easter Monday probably around seven or eight and it was my mother call-ing me on my cell phone and I knew that for her to call me early on a holiday you know something was wrong, something wasn't right. The first thing she asked me was- was if I was watching the news… (CBC's The Current, 'Sunday Morning Mission', November 11th, 2008)

So, those are three ways in which this little fragment of conversation or some part of it (e.g. the utterance 'Howdit go') is organized by reference to its place in a larger overall structure. Now let us consider the same bit of talk in terms of turn-taking and turn construction. Let us just make some very basic observations in this respect about the construction of Dick's question. Begin by noting that although it is made up of four words, in a basic respect, this is produced as a single unit. Of course it is a single sen-tence but, more relevant for current purposes, it is a single turn. In their classic paper on turn-taking, Sacks *et al.* (1974) argued that turns at talk are made up of turn constructional units (TCUs) and that, in English at least, there is a sharply delimited set of possible unit-types. In English, TCUs are single words, phrases, clauses and sentences. Consider the following example.

(5) Debbie and Shelley 5: 35–40

```
35                    whatever: an [.hhh
36   Shelley:                      [you were at the halloween thing.
37   Debbie:    huh?
38   Shelley:   the halloween p[arty
39   Debbie:                   [ri:ght.
```

Shelley's talk at line 36 exemplifies the use of a sentential TCU. Debbie's turns at lines 37 and 39 are both composed of single lexical items. Shelley's turn at 38 illustrates the use of a single phrase to construct a turn. And going back to our example: 'Howdit go'? is similarly a sentential TCU.

Sacks *et al.* (1974: 702) suggested that TCUs have a feature of 'project-ability'. They write that these unit-types 'allow a projection of the unit-type under way, and what, roughly, it will take for an instance of that unit-type to be completed'. This means, of course, that a recipient (and potential next speakers) need not *wait* for a current speaker to come to the actual completion of her talk before starting her own turn. Rather, because TCUs have a feature of projectability, the next speaker/recipient can anticipate – or project – *possible* points of completion within the emerging course of talk and target those points as places to start up her own contribution. We can see this very clearly in an example such as the following:

(6) Parky (Cited in Sacks *et al.*, 1974)

```
01  Tourist:      Has the park cha:nged much,
02  Parky:        Oh:: ye:s,
03                (1.0)
04  Old man:      Th'Funfair changed it'n [ahful lot [didn'it.
05  Parky:  →                             [Th-      [That-
06  Parky:  →     That changed it,
```

In this example, at lines 05–06, Parky begins an incipient next turn at the first point of possible completion in Old Man's turn. Parky starts up here and again at the next point of possible completion not by virtue of any silence (by the time he starts there is no hearable silence) but by virtue of the projected possible completion of the TCU, which constitutes a potential transition relevance place. Evidence such as this leads to the conclusion that 'transfer of speakership is coordinated by reference to such transition relevance places' (Sacks *et al.*, 1974: 703).

Returning to the fragment from the conversation between Deb and Dick, notice that the transitions between speakers are managed in such a way as to minimize both gap and overlap. We now have a partial account of how participants are able to achieve this. Co-participants monitor the syntactic, prosodic and broadly speaking pragmatic features of the current turn to find that it is about to begin, now beginning, continuing, now coming to completion – they anticipate, that is, points at which it is possibly complete. A point of possible unit completion is a place for possible speaker transition – what Sacks *et al.* (1974) define as a 'transition relevance place'. There is of course much more that could relevantly be said about this fragment along these lines but since this is merely meant to introduce different 'organizations of practice' that go into a single fragment we now move on to consider the organization of talk into sequences. Before we are done I will return to consider issues of turn-taking briefly.

It is obvious enough that in conversation, actions often come in pairs and that a first action such as a complaint, a request or an invitation makes relevant a next, responsive action (or a delimited range of actions). If that action is not produced, it can be found, by the participants, to be missing where any number of things did not happen but are nevertheless not missing in the same sense. Schegloff (1968) described this relationship between a first and second action as one of 'conditional relevance' and the unit itself as an 'adjacency pair' (see Schegloff & Sacks, 1973).

What kind of organization is the adjacency pair? It is not a statistical probability and clearly not a categorical imperative. Rather, the organization described is a norm to which conversationalists hold one another accountable. The normative character of the adjacency pair is displayed in participants' own conduct in interaction. For example, as the principle of conditional relevance implies, when a question does not receive an answer, questioners treat the answer as 'noticeably' absent. The questioner asker's orientation to a missing answer can be seen in three commonly produced types of subsequent conduct: pursuit, inference and report. In the following example (from Drew, 1981) the mother asks the child, Roger, what time it is.

(7) Drew, 1981: 249

```
1   M:   What's the time- by the clock?
2   R:   Uh
3   M:   What's the time?
4        (3.0)
5   M:   (Now) what number's that?
6   R:   Number two
7   M:   No it's not
8        What is it?
9   R:   It's a one and a nought
```

After Roger produces something other than an answer at line 2, the mother repeats the question at line 3. Here then a failure to answer prompts the pursuit of a response (see Pomerantz, 1984). When this second question is met with three seconds of silence, the mother transforms the question, now asking, 'What number's that'? Notice that the first question, 'What's the time?', poses a complex, multi-faceted task for the child – He must first identify the numbers to which the hands are pointing and subsequently use those numbers to calculate the time. In response to a failure to answer this question, the mother takes this complex task and breaks it down into components. Thus, in her subsequent conduct the mother displays an inference that the child did not answer because he was not able to do so.

Although it does not happen here, questioners may also report an absent answer saying such things as 'You are not answering my question', 'He didn't answer the question', or 'She didn't reply'. In public inquiries, for instance, lawyers commonly suggest that the witness is not answering the question that has been asked of them (see Ehrlich & Sidnell, 2006; Sidnell, 2004; Sidnell, 2010b).

An infinite number of things can be accurately described as absent after the occurrence of a first pair part. The next speaker did not blow his nose, scratch his head, jump up and down, sing 'O' Canada', etc. The point here is that the first pair part of an adjacency pair has the capacity to make some particular types of conduct noticeably or relevantly absent such that their non-occurrence is just as much an event as their occurrence.

Hence, of course, we can see that 'Howdit go' is a sequence initiating first action – the first part of an adjacency pair that makes relevant a second, here an answer. Before turning to consider the response that is produced we need to first consider in some more detail the design of this turn. Consider specifically that Dick employs the past tense – 'How *did* it go?' he asks. Clearly, with this Dick locates the party in time – specifically, a time prior to the point at which this conversation is taking place. Although we cannot, here, deal with exactly how it does this, past tense in this context conveys that the thing being talked about (the 'it'/the party) is over and complete.

So, there is a problem with the way in which Dick has formulated his question since, as it turns out, it is not quite right to say that the party is over (the guests have stayed and thereby continued the event). But at the same time the question *is* answerable as it stands – Dick has asked how it went and the party proper is over. In asking this question Dick creates a position for Deb to produce an answer. Thus there are two different actions relevant next:

1. Answer the question.
2. Address the problem with how the question has been formulated.

By virtue of the conditional relevance established by the question, anything that occurs in this slot ('they're still here' for instance) may be inspected for how IT answers the question. If it cannot be heard as answering the question it may be inspected by the recipient for how it accounts for not answering the question. In short, anything that occurs here can be inspected for its relevance to the question asked and can thus serve as the basis for further inference. Imagine this pair of utterances without the 'just great' such that 'everybody's still here' comes as a response to 'Howdit go?'. Simplifying things somewhat, the problem with this is that 'everybody's still here' could easily be heard by a recipient as 'it didn't go well' or 'it went too long' or 'I'm trying to get them out'. There is then a built in reason for answering this question in a straightforward way simply because any *other* way of responding might suggest a negative assessment and invite further inquiries.

At the same time, if she chooses simply to answer Dick's question and respond with 'just great' alone, Deb has allowed a mistaken assumption go unchallenged and uncorrected. This too is something to be avoided. As we have already noted there are certain things that become relevant at the completion of an event – a report to interested parties, an assessment, the reporting of news and so on. Dick's question, by locating the event in the past, proposes the relevance of those activities; indeed, it invites them. But to the extent that the event is not, in fact, over, these activities are not the relevant ones to do. There are then a number of intersecting reasons why Deb would like to do this assessment, 'just great' first as a response to Dick's question but, at the same time, to not allow the misunderstanding contained in Dick's question to pass to without being corrected.

So what in fact happens? Deb produces the correction, 'everybody:st-still here.', without releasing the turn after 'just great'. Sounds like the last consonant in 'great' can be produced either with or without a release of air. Here, rather than produce this last sound (aspiration) of the last segment ('t') of the last word ('great') of this turn unit, Deb moves immediately into the first sound of 'everybody'. So, one resource for talking through a possible completion is to withhold the production of the actual completion of the TCU and instead move directly into the next component of the turn. In this way a speaker can talk in such a way that a projectable point of completion never actually occurs. Here is another example that I noted in passing. This happened in a faculty meeting and the person was talking about the administration of a large university:

(8) They always try to do tha- it's- it's just the way that they work.

Here the speaker is clearly coming to a point of possible completion with 'that' but manages to avoid this by never actually producing the last sound of the word, substituting instead the first sound of the next turn unit. Returning to the example with Deb and Dick, we can see that Deb uses this practice to get two relevant tasks done in a single turn-at-talk without risking the possibility of Dick self-selecting at the first possible completion. We thus have some interactional motivation for this compressed transition space. Moreover, we can see that the organization of action into sequences, the organization of talk into turns (and into TCUs) and the organization of talk into an overall structure do not operate independently of one another. Although we can think of these heuristically as semi-autonomous organizations, in practice they are thoroughly interdigitated. This is what I mean when I say the utterance (or the turn-at-talk) is a product of multiple, intersecting, concurrently operative organizations of practice or machineries.

CA necessarily begins with the detailed analysis of a single instance of interaction – this is what we refer to as 'case-by-case' analysis and it means taking each instance on its own terms, trying to get a handle on its singularity and what the participants were doing in that case and what practices they were using to accomplish those outcomes. This is a fundamental and irreducible aspect of the conversation analytic method but, in order to develop a formal account of some particular practice or phenomenon, it must be complemented by a view across instances based on a collection.

Research Methods in Conversation Analysis

In this section, I will discuss the use of collections in CA. After the detailed analysis of some particular instance has generated a set of promising observations about a possibly researchable phenomenon, the conversation analyst must set about building a collection of cases since it is within the context of a collection that one can begin to describe the phenomenon as a set of normative practices and orientations revealed in the participants' own conduct. In this section, I am going to focus on a collection of what I describe as 'next turn repeats'.[4]

Question-intoned repeats

When making a collection, it is best to *initially* cast the net as widely as possible and gather *all* instances that are potentially relevant (You can always throw them out later). For 'next turn repeats' this procedure will quickly result in a large and heterogeneous collection. For example it would include cases such as the following in which some part of the prior turn is repeated with 'questioning' intonation (see Jefferson, 1972; Schegloff *et al.*, 1977; Sidnell, 2010a):

(9) Mary the tax Lady_ XTR1

```
01              ((click))
02    Anita:    Hello: ¿
03    Ben:      hHello, Ma:ry?
04    Anita:    (0.2)    ((kids speaking)) No:
05              (0.3)
06    Ben:      No, not Ma:ry? hh
07    Anita:    No, it's not Ma:ry = there's no Mary he:re (.) I don' think: hh
08              (3.0)
09    Ben:      Th' tax lady:
10              (0.2)
11    Anita:→   The ^tax lad(h)y::?
12    Ben:      Ya hhh =
13    Anita:    =Nop-. Wha number were you callin'.
```

(10) Boil an egg – YYZ

```
00              ((Telephone rings))
01    Amy:      What do you want me to pick up?
02    Betty:    Nothi:ng but I want to know how you boil an egg.
03              (1.0)
04              (h)hard boil.
05    Amy:      Oh oka::y and I just read this you know
06              because I always let the water boil but
07              you're not supposed to (.hh) put it in and
08              you (.hh) bring it to a boil (.) but then
09              turn it down 'cause you're really not
10              supposed to boil the e::gg
11              (0.4)
12              you let it (.) uh simmer or you know on me:dium,
```

13	**Betty:**	R<u>i</u>:ght
14	**Amy:**	fo:r· [t w] elve minutes.
15	**Betty:**	[((sniff))]
16	**Betty:** →	Twelve minutes?
17	**Amy:**	Well I always do it faster than th(h)at (hh)
18	**Betty:**	okay =
19	**Amy:**	=I just boil the shit out of it [but]
20	**Betty:**	[How]
21		do you know when it's done?

We could make a range of observations about these examples. First, notice that in (9), Anita repeats the whole of Ben's prior turn, whereas in (10) Betty repeats only the final phrase of what Amy has just said. Second, notice the different sequential positions in which the repeats occur. In (9) Ben has called looking for 'Mary'. When Anita cannot recognize anybody by that name, Ben offers 'The tax lady' as an alternative. It is this that Anita repeats. In (10), Amy is giving her daughter Betty advice on how to boil an egg. When she concludes this with 'you let it (.) uh simmer or you know on Me:dium, fo:r twelve minutes'. Betty repeats 'twelve minutes' with questioning intonation. And notice that in the first case, a repeat of 'the tax lady' occasions confirmation with 'yeah', whereas in the second a repeat of 'twelve minutes' encourages Amy to significantly modify her advice. This suggests that there is an element of challenge to the repeat in (10) not present in (9). This, it seems, is a product of the sequential position in which the repeat occurs – in (9) the repeat is responsive to an unfamiliar name, whereas in (10) it is responsive to advice or instructions on how to boil an egg. This element of challenge is especially visible in an example such as (11). This fragment comes from a video recording of three four-year-old children playing. It begins with Matty challenging a prior claim, which was unfortunately not recorded. When Matty asserts that there are 'no ponies inside farms', Tina replies 'Ye:s. so:me'. After a short pause she continues by grounding her claim in prior experience by saying 'I went to a real farm before'. At line 05, Grace begins a turn in which she proposes 'an' once (.) I: rode on a pony'. When this receives no uptake from the other children, Grace turns to the adult in the room saying 'I really did'. The adult produces a minimal acknowledgment token and Grace continues by providing the name of the place where she rode on the pony – Centre Island. Tina picks up on this mention of Centre Island saying something partially inaudible, which is confirmed by Grace with 'yes' at line 15. Matty then produces a questioning repeat of 'Centre Island'? and Grace responds with a confirmation. This 'I've been there' appears to be particularly oriented to the challenge that Matty's questioning repeat is heard to embody. It is clear that part of Grace's claim involves her having been to Centre Island – if this is where she rode on a pony, then she surely must have been there. Thus, in responding to Matty's questioning repeat with 'Yes. I've been there', Grace seems oriented to a possible challenge to the veracity of her claim.

(11) ICS_02_16_06(1of2)JKT6.mov 00: 17

```
01  M:       There's no ponies inside fa:r:ms. =
02  T:       Ye:s. so:me.
03           (0.2)
04           I went to a real farm bef[ore
05  G:                             [an' once (.)
06           I: rode on a pony.
07           (0.2)
08           I really did. ((looks to adult))
09  L:       (mhm)
10  G:→      At centre island I rode on a pony.
11           (0.8)
12  M:       (how [        )
13  T:            [(       ) centre island?
14           (0.4)
15  G:       yes.
16           (0.6)
17  M:→      centre island?
18  G:       yes. I've been there. (.) On: a ferry.
19           (0.8)
20           a ferry boat.
```

While they differ in a number of respects then, these cases (lines 9–11) are fundamentally similar in comparison to the other instances we are about to examine. Specifically, in these cases a question intoned repeat establishes the relevance of confirmation in next turn. Depending on the sequential location in which this occurs, the repeat may be hearable as challenging the accuracy or truthfulness of the talk that is repeated.

Repeats with (falling) final intonation

In the next set of examples the repeat is produced with final intonation indicated by a period.

(12) YYZ

```
27  Clare:   Just we've got- Michael and I did the resourcing for next
28          → week and it's just- it's = just ughu(h)h(hh) .hh and it's a
29           short wee:k so
30           (.)
31  Alice:→  Yeah:- Oh: yeah it is a short week.=
32  Clare:   Ye[ah
33  Alice:     [.hh[hh
34  Clare:         [so (.) I'm rilly rilly sorry,
```

(13) [G1:T3 6:41]

```
01  Gina:    I'm gonna see if this will work.
02           (1.0)
03           Okay it does_
04           (0.2)
05        →  W[ell almost.
06  Tina:     [No it doesn't.
07  Jim:   ⇒ Well almost yea:h.
```

Again these examples differ in many respects but let us start by noting the ways they are alike and contrast with the previous cases. We have already noted that the intonation of the repeat differs – in these cases the repeat is produced with final, downward intonation as opposed to the questioning or rising intonation of 9–11.[5] Notice also the position in which these repeats occur. In (12), Clare has been telling Alice (her boss) that she does not have time to 'do the budget next week'. In accounting for this bit of bad news she reports that she 'did the resourcing for next week' and goes on to note that 'it's a short wee:k'. Notice then that Alice's 'oh: yeah it *is* a short week' not only confirms what Clare is saying it also shows, by virtue of the 'Oh:' (see Heritage, 1984a, 1984b), that Alice had forgotten this. Notice also that the repeat involves some modification of what was originally said – specifically 'it's a short week' becomes 'it *is* a short week' (see Stivers, 2005). In (13), three children are playing with blocks, and in line 1, Gina announces 'I'm gonna see if this will work'. She then places the marble in the maze of blocks and, when it comes out the other end, announces 'okay it does'. However, the marble then begins to roll back into the maze occasioning Gina's modification with 'well almost' and Tina's 'No it doesn't'. Jim then confirms what Gina has said by repeating her words and appending 'yeah'. In both these cases the repeat speaker is not initiating repair of the repeated portion of talk (as in 9–11) but rather confirming what a prior speaker has just said.

Next turn repeats and topical expansion

Another 'type' of next turn repeat is illustrated by the example below. Here Ann is reporting to Bev on the behavior of a mutual acquaintance who is pregnant. When she mentions 'gravol' in line 04, Bev repeats this word, emphasizing with increased volume and heightened intonation the first syllable.

(14) YYZ_T1A_A&D_1_Oct_09_06.mp3 2.03

```
01  Bev:   anyway [.hhhh
02  Ann:          [I know.
03         (0.2)
```

04 **Ann:** an' i- (.) gra:<u>v</u>ol an all these (s[   )
05 **Bev:** →   [gr↑<u>a</u>:vo:l
06 **Ann:** She takes gravol al- everyda:y.

The response Ann produces in line 06 suggests that she does not hear the repeat as indicating a problem of hearing or understanding as is common for the question intoned repeats we discussed earlier. Nor does she hear this as confirming what she has just said. Rather such penultimate-stress repeats appear to mark something that someone has just said as newsworthy and invite elaboration.[6] Notice that in (14), Bev's repeat of gravol prompts Ann to elaborate on this aspect of the telling. In the following case it is the repeat speaker who elaborates on the repeated item – characterizing it as 'ridiculous':

(15) Virginia 4: 1–8

01 **Pru:** I[t's so frustrating havin'a mothuh]
02 **Mom:**   [If you saved yer- if you saved yeral]lowan[ce,
03 **Pru:**   [hhh ·hhh
04 **Mom:** [(if you) save yer allowance, an:' um: you could get =
05 **Pru:** [w(h)ith a °sho°°(p)
06 **Mom:** =these little extr[a things.
07 **Vir:** →   [A(h)llo::wan(h)ce? I o(h)nly g(h)et
08   fi(h)ve d(h)ollars a week.That's rid(h)i(h)c(h)ul(h)ous.

Here Virginia has been asking her mother to let her have a dress, which her mother apparently has in her shop. The request has been turned down and Virginia has expressed her disappointment. At line 01 of the fragment, Prudence, Virginia's brother's girlfriend, says, somewhat ambiguously, that 'it's so frustrating having a mother with a shop' (The ambiguous character of this utterance is discussed in Schegloff, 2005). In lines 02–06 Mom suggests that if she saved her allowance Virginia could get 'these little extra things' (e.g. the dress). This sets the stage for Virginia's turn at lines 07–08. Virginia first repeats part of Mom's earlier turn-at-talk with clear stress on the penultimate syllable, thereby locating in it something problematic – 'allowance'. She then rejects this as a remedy to her problem on the grounds that the amount is too little. And, finally, assesses the remedy by characterizing it as 'ridiculous' (This example from Virginia involves a convergence of two 'types' of repeats: those with penultimate stress and those inflected by laughter. Of course, as Jefferson (1972) has noted, there is nothing which prevents laughter from infecting any kind of next turn repeat and such cases of convergence are quite common.)

'Laugh-token' repeats

Consider now what Gail Jefferson (1972) describes as a 'laugh token' repeat 'whereby one demonstrates "appreciation", "enjoyment", etc. of the product-item; where laugh tokens alternate with syllables of the repeat' (1972: 299). The following case is taken from talk among four-year-old children:

(16) ICS_02_09_06(1of2)JKT4.mov 32: 47

```
01  Nora:      My dad is a doctor and my mom is a professor
02  Cathy:     A professor(h) ha ha ha ha ha
03  Nora:      heh hah hah
```

Here when Nora announces that her dad is a doctor and her mom a professor, Cathy repeats 'a professor' in next turn position. By virtue of the laughter that infiltrates the repeat, Cathy takes up a stance towards what Nora has just said, appreciating it as something funny (see also Goodwin & Goodwin, 1987). Notice that such laugh token repeats, like laughter in general, are typically treated as invitations to laugh by their recipients and may thus initiate sustained bouts of joint laughter. Jefferson suggests that:

> the 'laugh token' repeat differs from the 'questioning' repeat not only in that they do not 'mean' the same thing (for example, that the former demonstrates some sort of approval and the latter demonstrates some sort of disapproval), but in that they do not do the same work. Laugh tokens in general are regularly associated with termination of talk and it can be proposed that the laugh token repeat is regularly associated with termination of talk with reference to its product-item. (Jefferson, 1972: 300)

The proper way for a recipient to handle a laugh token repeat then according to Jefferson is to 'ignore it, since, if it is heard as an object signaling appreciation via laughter, then it is a terminator' (Jefferson, 1972: 301). However, Jefferson also notes that a laugh token repeat can 'converge' with a questioning repeat 'if it is found to be possibly non-appreciative; that is, it may then call for some remedial work'. Consider the following fragment in this light – here Shelagh Rogers is interviewing interim President of the University of Toronto Frank Iacobucci. At the time of the interview, Iacobucci was a Supreme Court justice in Ottawa. Prior to this he had been Dean of the University of Toronto law school. The interviewer's first question here invokes this previous history with the University.

(17) Sounds like Canada – Iacobucci 20/4/05

```
01  SR:       [(it- di-) an this is a retur:n to you fer
02            the- to the University of Toronto.
03  FI:       That's right I: ah I was uh u-in the university
04            fer nearly twenty years then went to Ottawa,
05            (.)
06      →     °h to do things there: an' [(    turn )
07  SR:                                  [hhh hah heh
08      →     to do thi(h)ngs there. =
```

```
09  FI:      = right.
10  SR:      ri[ght.
11  FI:        [(uh huh) =
12  SR: →    to do ↑big things the[re.
13  FI:                           [we:ll I- uhm I- I was:
14          Look. = I've been very fortunate. I: been very
15          very fortunate to have had the opportunities
16          to serve.
```

At line 03 Iacobucci confirms that this is a 'return' saying that he was 'in the university for nearly twenty years' before going to Ottawa. He then adds an increment to his turn 'to do things there'. This elicits a loud segment of laughter from the interviewer and a repeat of 'to do things there'. Although it is not produced with rising intonation, Iacobucci appears to treat this repeat as initiating repair and confirms, in line 09, that this is indeed what he said. The interviewer then repeats this confirmation (right) before going on to provide a reformulation and correction of what Iacobucci has said. Here then the interviewer's repeat works to isolate a piece of the prior talk, making it available for further operations to be performed upon it. Those further operations – such as inserting 'big' at line 12 – mark what Iacobucci has said as 'modest'. What we want to see here then is a contrast between, on the one hand, repeats that highlight *something that someone has said* and, on the other, repeats that highlight *the way something was put*. So in (10) it is not *the expression* twelve minutes that is brought into focus but the advice to boil an egg for this long (similarly for (12) it is not the expression 'short week'). In these last few examples, however, the repeat appears to pick up on the way that something was put, not so much what has been said but the *way* it was said, the word or words themselves. This is particularly obvious perhaps for laugh token repeats such as 'a professor' but is also true for repeats that locate, highlight and comment upon 'modesty'. Indeed, in some cases this focus on the way something was put is made explicit in the subsequent talk. For instance in the following example when, talking about the train business, Hunter Harrison describes himself as having 'some knack for it', the interviewer repeats this characterization and subsequently suggests that it is an 'understatement'. Because 'having some knack for it' was said about the speaker, describing this as an understatement implicates a compliment. Evidence for this analysis is to be found in line 16 where that implied compliment is accepted and appreciated with 'Thank you'.

(18) Hunter Harrison – The Current 2: 23

```
01  I:     So when didja fall in love with it.
02         (0.4)
03  HH:    Early on. uh once I learned thet uh oil
04         'n bearings wondn't the thing I wantid
```

```
05         tuh do (.) .hhhh as I started lookin'
06         'round an' seein' other opportunities
07         I:: uh (.) uh all o' sudden fell in love
08         with the business .hh I'm not (above for
09         a foamer) as I call'em bu' I have enjoyed
10      → this business an' I developed some knack
11         for it. and uh .h I've stayed with it fer
12         a long time.
13   I:  → Some knack for it. I think some would say
14         that's an understatement.
15         (0.2)
16   HH:  Well thank you.
17   I:   heh . . .
```

I have tried to illustrate the method of collecting through a focus on next turn repeats. We have seen that although a collection of this sort is deeply heterogeneous, it is nevertheless possible to identify commonalities across instances. These commonalities reveal, of course, the underlying norms to which conversationalists orient in producing and understanding talk-in-interaction. Even in this very brief consideration then we begin to see that, by drawing on the basic techniques and concepts of CA, we can develop descriptions of conversation as a massive and intricate web of practices.

At this point I need to sound a cautionary note: I have talked here about *types* of 'next turn repeat' but this should not be taken too literally. There are many dangers involved of thinking in terms of types. The greatest concern is that once you construct a typology, it is all too easy to slip into a kind of coding procedure in which the actual details of the talk are ignored in favor of sorting instances into the categories you assume they belong to. Moreover, 'type' implies a contrast with 'tokens' – almost as if there could be a 'true' abstract (Platonic) type that secured the identity of all the tokens of next turn repeats. While this may be a reasonable way of thinking about certain kinds of linguistic phenomena, it does not work well for conversation as Sacks warned in his lectures cited above. After all, we have seen even in this very brief consideration the 'types' are not necessarily discrete – laughter can inflect question intoned repeats, penultimate stress repeats as well as those that locate modesty.

A central point I have tried to illustrate here is that a given practice need not, and in fact rarely does, map to a single action – a question-intoned repeat *can* initiate repair, but it can *also* forward a telling, challenge a previous speaker's account or confirm that what was heard was heard correctly (and this need not involve repair). The relationship between practice and action in conversation is a wholly contingent one [see

Schegloff (1997), for an illuminating analysis of 'boundary cases' in a study of other-initiated repair for more on this issue].

Before leaving this topic, let us just note the obvious but nevertheless crucial point that for some bit of talk to come off as a repeat of what someone has just said requires something in addition to using the same words. In the following case from the last moments of a phone call the speakers use exactly the same words one after the other but this is clearly *not* repetition.

(19) John and George – Source (unknown)

```
12  G:    Okay
13  J:    Okay [bye
14  G:         [Bye
```

And in (20) the participants are again four-year-old children here discussing a specific kind of camel.

(20) ICS_02_02_06(2of2)JKT2.mov 1: 55 (Detail)

```
19  M:    Yeah are they scary for you?
20  W:    no. (0.4) they're scar:y- all of-
21        every people are scared of these ones.
22  M:  → an- no but not me::
23  W:  → not me::
```

Here, in line 23, Walt uses precisely the same words as Michael has just used – indeed, as the transcription suggests he says 'not me::' with much the same prosody as well. However, Walt does not say this *as a repeat* of what Michael has said but rather on his own behalf – he, like Michael, is claiming – in a magnificent reversal of what he has claimed earlier – that he is also not afraid of these camels. A repeat then, at least as it is understood here, is not defined on the basis of form alone – rather this is a practice and is constituted in part by the sequential context in which it is embedded.

CA, Classroom Interaction and Language Learning

Classroom interaction has long been a focus of conversation analytic work. Pioneering studies by Mehan (1979a, 1979b) and McHoul (1978) described some of the basic structures of interaction in classrooms of various kinds including the kinds of sequences associated with asking 'known answer' or 'exam' questions (see also Heritage, 1984a, 1984b; Mehan, 1985). More recently, a number of books have appeared that examine instruction in the language teaching classroom as well as native–non-native speaker talk within a CA framework (see Gardner & Wagner, 2004; Markee, 2000; Seedhouse, 2004; see also Richards & Seedhouse, 2005). As these studies are especially relevant to the themes of the current volume; I review a selection of them below.

Interactional organization in the language classroom

Seedhouse (2004) provides a useful overview of what he describes as the 'interactional architecture' of the language classroom. Drawing on the framework for the analysis of institutional talk developed by Drew and Heritage (1992), Seedhouse argues that the language classroom consists of a set of normatively organized activities to which participants can be seen to orient. The idea here is that 'classroom talk in fact subsumes a network of inter-related speech exchange systems' (Markee, 2002) and that these vary with the 'pedagogical focus'. So, for instance in 'form-and-accuracy' contexts, the teacher typically maintains tight control of turn-taking by modeling forms that students are expected to repeat as in the following case:

(21) Seedhouse, 2004: 102–103,

```
1    T:    now I want everybody (.) to listen to me.
2          (1.8)
3          and when I say you are going to say after me,
4          (.) you are going to say what I say. (.) we can try.
5          I've got a lamp. a lamp. <say after me> I've got a lamp.
6    LL:   I've got a lamp.
7    T:    (.) I've got a glass, a glass, <say after me>
8          I've got a glass
9    LL:   I've got a glass
10   T:    I've got a vase, a vase <say after me> I've got a vase
11   LL:   I've got a vase.
```

Or by posing questions the answers of which involve the use of a standard frame as in the following:

(22) Seedhouse, 2004: 102–103

```
1    T:    I have. fine. I've got a trumpet.
2          >have you got a trumpet Anna?<
3    L15:  ah er erm yes I have
4    T:    I've got a radio. have you got a radio e:r (.) e:r Alvin?
5    L16:  yes I have.
```

This contrasts with what Seedhouse (2004: 111) describes as 'meaning and fluency' contexts in which there is an emphasis on 'maximizing the opportunities for interaction' and, as such, a turn-taking organization that is markedly more like conversation. Rather than being tightly controlled by the teacher, turn-taking is locally organized as in conversation with each possible completion presenting an opportunity for speaker transition.

(23) Seedhouse, 2004: 112

```
1    L1:   OK. as you see this is a music box,
2          (.) .hh and my mother made it. it's=
3    L2:   =oh, your mother made it?=
4    L1:   =yes, my mother made it. .hh the thing is that when:
5          (.) this is the first thing she did (.) like this,
6          with .hh painting and everything, .hh so nobody.
7          nobody thought that it was going to come out like this.
8          [h a hh] that's the point. that's why
9    LL:   [heehee]
10   L1:   this is special because it took her about three weeks
11         to: to make it, .hh and erm she put erm a really special
12         interest in that and tried to, to make it the best that,
13         er she could. so, (.) so, that's all. (1.5)
```

Seedhouse then shows the way the basic structures of interaction are adapted to the specific tasks of the language classroom. Although we have just briefly touched on the organization of turn-taking in two differently focused pedagogical activities, Seedhouse reviews many other aspects of interaction including repair and action sequencing.

Features and Practices of the Language Classroom and Second Language Conversations

I now turn to consider some apparently distinctive features and practices of the language classroom and of talk between native and non-native speakers. Many of these apparently distinctive features have their roots in an orientation to 'language' that is, broadly speaking, pedagogic. That is, teachers and learners (again broadly defined) display persistent concern with notions of 'correctness' or of 'getting it right' (pronunciation, grammar, lexical selection) that goes beyond what is typical of conversation between native speakers. We know in fact that in talk between native and even fluent speakers of a language, many errors of speaking pass by without any orientation to them *as* errors. So, for instance in the following radio interview, the interviewee's answer includes at lines 08–11 the clearly problematic construction 'it's not sure whe:ther: you know journalists are comfortable sorta turning in each other' in which the speaker seems to have blended together 'it's not clear …' and 'I'm not sure …'

(24) As it happens. Feb 11.05.mov. QT: 7.56

```
02   Q:   °hh but- uh wha- [so what has the
03   A:                    [crazy
04   Q:   rest of the press gallery:
05        (.)
```

```
06            thought about this.uh done about this.
07   A:       °hh I think for a number of reasons
08            they didn't speak up I- uh-uh one it's
09            not sure whe:ther: you know journalists
10            are comfortable sorta turning in each
11            other.
12            (.)
13            I don't know to what degree that's sort
14            of a:: you know written pact maybe they
15            don't do it
```

Although she has opportunity to do so at line 12, the interviewer does not correct or in any other way orient to this grammatical stumble. In their paper on the organization of repair, Schegloff *et al.* accounted for the paucity of such corrections by noting:

> When the hearing/understanding of a turn is adequate to the production of a correction by 'other', it is adequate to allow production of a sequentially appropriate next turn. Under that circumstance, the turn's recipient ('other') should produce the next turn, not the correction (and, overwhelmingly, that is what is done). Therein lies another basis for the empirical paucity of other-corrections: those who could do them do a sequentially appropriate next turn instead. (Schegloff *et al.*, 1977: 380)

In the contexts Schegloff *et al.* (1977) analyze then, the production of sequentially appropriate next turns (one manifestation of the principle of progressivity; see Schegloff, 2007: 14–15) is typically prioritized relative to correcting otherwise adequate prior turns-at-talk.

However, in the context of language learning, 'correctness' takes on a pedagogical importance and these priorities may be reversed. That is, a standard of 'correct' replaces a standard of 'good-enough', which is typical of ordinary conversation. Kurhila (2005) shows that the repair of grammatical forms is overwhelmingly initiated by the non-native speakers in NS–NNS interaction. An example from her research is included as (25) below:

(25) Kurhila

In data from NS–NNS of Finnish, NNS has been telling a story about two babies who were mixed up in a birth clinic

```
001 NNS:   .hhhh Sitte he   (0.2)   huomaa huomu- huom-huoma =
                  then they          notice + PRS + 3
           .hhhh Then they           notice notid- noti- notic =
002 NS:    =Jo [o houmas ]
              ye [s notice + PST +3
           =Ye [s noticed]
```

```
003 NNS:      [huomat    ]  °huomas°
              [          ]  notice + PST + 3
              [notic     ]  °noticed°
004 NS:    °Jo°
           °Yes°
005        (0.4)
006 NS:    Mitas siina tapahtu sitte
           What        happened then
```

Kurhila explains:

> While describing an event to the NS, the NNS uses the verb huomata
> 'notice' in line 001, and begins to search for the correct form. He first
> produces the third person present tense form (huomaa) after which he
> repeats modified versions of the beginning of the word. The NS com-
> pletes the already begun word (line 002) after the NNS's third modifi-
> cation. The completion is the past tense form of the verb, which can be
> assumed to be the target form, since the NNS has mostly used the past
> tense in his narrative. The NNS accepts the completion by repeating it
> (line 003). (Kurhila, 2005: 146)

Brouwer (2004) shows a similar orientation by NNS to the relevance of
correct pronunciation. Here also it is common for the NNS to initiate repair
either by pauses, 'uhs' and sound stretches, by producing the item with
rising intonation or by repeating the item. Consider the following case in
which B is a Dutch speaker of Danish and S is Danish.

(26) Brouwer Rucksack
Carry around a rucksack or a special brand. B then says that she finds
that strange, and continues:

```
1    B:    ja det har vi ikke i Hol↓land at vi –alle ha:r (.)
           yeah we do not have that in Holland that we all have
2          d samme:: (0.4)
           the same
3→         oh ↑rygsa:k
           {rucksack}
4          (0.2)
5→         ryg↑sak
6          (0.2)
7→   S:    ↑ryg↓sæk
8→   B:    rygsæk
9          (0.3)
10         ↓så (1.0)
           so
```

Here then, in the course of producing his turn-at-talk, B encounters trouble with the item *rygsaek*. He marks the item as a source of trouble by pausing before its initial saying (lines 002–003), by producing this initial saying with rising intonation (line 003) and, further, by repeating the item (line 005). S, the native speaker in this exchange, offers a correction (producing the item with standard pronunciation) and B subsequently accepts this by repeating it in line 008 (Word clarification repairs as studied by Mazeland and Zaman-Zadeh (2004) present another interesting case in which NNS can be seen to orient to properties of the target language code).

Lerner (1995) has described the instructor/teacher's use of incomplete utterances in inviting student participation. Koshik (2002) focuses on teachers' use of such 'designedly incomplete utterances' in one-on-one, second-language writing conferences as a practice for eliciting students' self-correction of their written language errors. Koshik's aim is to show how such 'practices of ordinary conversation can be adapted for specialized institutional tasks' (Koshik, 2002: 278). The following example illustrates the practice:

(27) Koshik (2002: 287)

```
181  TJ:      .h: ((reading)) >he died not from injuries.<
182           (0.5) ((TJ and SH gaze silently at text))
183           but drowned
184           (1.2) ((TJ and SH gaze silently at text))
185      →    <after he>
186           (4.5) ((TJ and SH gaze silently at text))
187  SH:→    had been?
188  TJ:      there ya go.
189           (4.0) ((TJ writes on text))
190           had been left there for thirteen hours
191           °without any aid.°
192  SH:      um hum.
```

Here the teacher is reading a portion of the student's text. He produces this as a series of verb phrase segments the completion of each of which is marked by final intonation or by a pause (or by both). The last segment (at line 185) is what Koshik describes as designedly incomplete – it locates an error in the written text. Recognizing this, the student produces the correction, which is subsequently accepted by the instructor.

In this brief review of some of the literature we have seen that participants in these language learning contexts often display an orientation to notions of 'correctness' unlike that typical of ordinary conversation. We have also seen both student/NNS and teacher/NS adapting the practices and organizations of conversation to the tasks and activities of the language classroom. These studies then illustrate some of what makes the language classroom context the context that it is. Carroll's (2004) study of restarts among Japanese novice speakers of English provides an interesting counterpoint. As Carroll notes, whether they occur in the speech of native or non-native speakers, it is rather easy to think of restarts, such as the following, as 'disfluencies', as 'speech production errors', as 'false starts' – in short as 'failures'.

(28) Carroll – 205

S: dyu: did you: (0.7) did you watch?

Carroll notes that this appears to be a clear case of NNS disfluency with the speaker starting the turn three times. Moreover, the inter-turn pause of seven-tenths of a second appears to provide further evidence of production difficulties. However, through a detailed analysis of this and other similar examples, Carroll shows that an alternative, 'non-deficient' analysis is possible. We know from previous studies of ordinary conversation that turn-restarts are often used (1) to repair possibly impaired talk produced in overlap (Schegloff, 1987) and (2) to solicit the gaze of a recipient (Goodwin, 1979). Carroll shows convincingly that many instances of turn-restarting in NNS talk can be accounted for in exactly the same way. For instance in the example above:

(29) Carroll – 205

```
1   A:   yes yes .hh [mm:]
2   S:               [dyu]:  did you: (0.7)   did you watch?
```

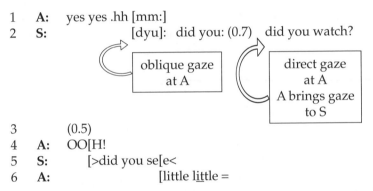

```
3        (0.5)
4   A:   OO[H!
5   S:     [>did you se[e<
6   A:                 [little little =
```

What initially looks like a case of NNS disfluency actually turns out to be an altogether typical deployment of a generic practice of talk-in-interaction in no way specific to NNS talk (see also Rymes, this volume, on correctness as secondary to communicative goal). While Carroll's particular concern is to characterize these as 'skilled interactional achievements' and to challenge an understanding of them as disfluencies, to my mind this study provides evidence for an even more fundamental point. When analyzing speakers *as* NNS (or *as* women, or *as* African-Americans, or *as* members of the working class) it is dangerously easy to attribute any and all peculiarity as a feature of NNS talk (or as a feature of the talk or women, African-Americans, the working class, etc.). And, to the casual observer at least, 'NNSness' seems to present a particularly clear case in which features of the talk are unavoidably linked to the speakers' categorical identity. Carroll's important study shows that such assumptions are not necessarily warranted even for those phenomena that, on the face of it, seem most obviously associated with non-native speaker talk.

Conclusion

In this brief review, I hope to have introduced some of the main principles and concerns of CA and also to have shown how the basic methods and analytic tools of CA can provide significant insight into the organization of classroom interaction and language learning. Several key points can be summarized and repeated here.

First, CA developed within sociology and has inherited from that tradition a strongly empirical orientation. Analysis involves tacking back and forth between the details of particular instances and patterns that occur across a collection of cases.

Second, any given fragment of conversation can be seen as the unique product of several different, interlocking 'organizations of practice' or 'machineries'. An analysis of some particular fragment that aims to be comprehensive must consider, at a minimum, organizations of turn-construction and turn-taking, action sequencing, repair and overall structure. CA is a fundamentally qualitative approach, and a collection-based analysis of some recurrent and relatively stable phenomenon (next turn repeats that initiate repair, compressed transition spaces, 'oh'-prefaced responses to inquiry) necessarily involves a detailed case-by-case analysis of each instance on its own terms as a first step.

Third, a basic finding is that, in conversation and other forms of talk-in-interaction, intersubjectivity is accomplished and maintained through publicly displayed understandings conveyed by responses to prior talk. A first speaker may find that a response betrays a partial, incorrect or otherwise problematic understanding of her talk and can attempt to repair this in a subsequent turn. Because this 'architecture of intersubjectivity', as Heritage (1984a, 1984b) described it, is, by its very nature, public, analysts can use it to empirically ground their own analyses. Indeed, a key point is that analysts can employ the same methods in studying conversation that participants used in producing it.

Of course, a review like this one can only scratch the surface of what is an extremely diverse area of research. The reader who wants to go further should return to some of the pioneering studies mentioned at the beginning of this chapter (Sacks *et al.*, 1974; Schegloff, 1968; Schegloff *et al.*, 1977). These early papers sketched whole domains of interactional organization (action sequencing, turn-taking, and repair) and continue to provide

conversation analysts with basic resources and analytical tools for conducting their own research.

Appendix: Transcription Conventions

I.   Temporal and sequential relationships

    Overlapping or simultaneous talk is indicated in a variety of ways.

[Separate left square brackets, one above the other on two successive
[lines with utterances by different speakers, indicates a point of over-
    lap onset, whether at the start of an utterance or later.

]   Separate right square brackets, one above the other on two successive
]   lines with utterances by different speakers indicates a point at
    which two overlapping utterances both end, where one ends while
    the other continues, or simultaneous moments in overlaps which
    continue.

=   Equal signs ordinarily come in pairs – one at the end of a line, and
    another at the start of the next line or one shortly thereafter. They are
    used to indicate two things:
    (1) If the two lines connected by the equal signs are by the same
    speaker, then there was a single, continuous utterance with no break
    or pause, which was broken up in order to accommodate the place-
    ment of overlapping talk.
    (2) If the lines connected by two equal signs are by different speak-
    ers, then the second followed the first with no discernable silence
    between them, or was 'latched' to it.

(0.5) Numbers in parentheses indicate silence, represented in tenths of a
    second; what is given here in the left margin indicates 0.5 seconds of
    silence. Silences may be marked either within an utterance or
    between utterances.

(.)   A dot in parentheses indicates a 'micropause', hearable but not read-
    ily measurable without instrumentation; ordinarily less than 0.2 of a
    second.

II.   Aspects of speech delivery, including aspects of intonation

    The punctuation marks are not used grammatically, but to indicate
.   intonation. The period indicates a falling, or final, intonation contour,
?   not necessarily the end of a sentence. Similarly, a question mark
,   indicates rising intonation, not necessarily a question, and a comma
¿   indicates 'continuing' intonation, not necessarily a clause boundary.
(¿)   The inverted question mark is used to indicate a rise stronger than
    a comma but weaker than a question mark.

: :	Colons are used to indicate the prolongation or stretching of the sound just preceding them. The more the colons, the longer the stretching. On the other hand, graphically stretching a word on the page by inserting blank spaces between the letters does not necessarily indicate how it was pronounced; it is used to allow alignment with overlapping talk.
-	A hyphen after a word or part of a word indicates a cut-off or self-interruption, often done with a glottal or dental stop.
<u>w</u>ord	Underlining is used to indicate some form of stress or emphasis, either by increased loudness or higher pitch. The more the under-lining, the greater the emphasis.
<u>wo</u>rd	Therefore, underlining sometimes is placed under the first letter or two of a word, rather than under the letters which are actually raised in pitch or volume.
WOrd	Especially loud talk may be indicated by upper case; again, the louder, the more letters in upper case. And in extreme cases, upper case may be underlined.
°	The degree sign indicates that the talk following it was markedly quiet or soft.
°word°	When there are two degree signs, the talk between them is mark-edly softer than the talk around it.

Combinations of underlining and colons are used to indicate intonation contours:

_:	If the letter(s) preceding a colon is (are) underlined, then there is an 'inflected' falling intonation contour on the vowel (You can hear the pitch turn downward).
:	If a colon is itself underlined, then there is an inflected rising intonation contour on the vowel (i.e. you can hear the pitch turn upward).
↑ or ^ ↓	The up and down arrows mark sharper rises or falls in pitch than would be indicated by combinations of colons and underlining, or they may mark a whole shift, or resetting, of the pitch register at which the talk is being produced.
> < < >	The combination of 'more than' and 'less than' symbols indicates that the talk between them is compressed or rushed. Used in the reverse order, they can indicate that a stretch of talk is markedly slowed or drawn out. The 'less than' symbol by itself indicates that the immediately following talk is 'jump-started' (i.e. sounds like it starts with a rush).
hhh	Hearable aspiration is shown where it occurs in the talk by the letter *h* – the more *h*'s, the more aspiration. The aspiration may represent breathing, laughter, etc. If

(hh)	it occurs inside the boundaries of a word, it may be enclosed in parentheses in order to set it apart from the sounds of the word
°hh	(as in the utterance below). If the aspiration is an inhalation, it is shown with a dot before it (usually a raised dot).

III. Other markings

(( ))	Double parentheses are used to mark the transcriber's descriptions of events, rather than representations of them: ((cough)), ((sniff)), ((telephone rings)), ((footsteps)), ((whispered)), ((pause)), and the like.
(word)	When all or part of an utterance is in parentheses, or the speaker identification is, this indicates uncertainty on the transcriber's part, but represents a likely possibility.
( )	Empty parentheses indicate that something is being said, but no hearing (or, in some cases, speaker identification) can be achieved.

IV. Multi-linear transcription conventions

In two-line transcripts (examples (25) and (26)) the first line is a broad phonetic representation of the talk in the original language. The second line presents an English gloss.

Notes

1. It is a bit problematic to call Goffman a sociologist plain and simple, since although he clearly was one, he was other things as well. Goffman was trained in large part by anthropologists (Hart at Toronto and Warner at Chicago), he conducted fieldwork in a society different from his own (the Shetland Islands), his intellectual heroes were Durkheim (equal parts sociologist and anthropologist) and Radcliffe-Brown and his influence was perhaps greatest among linguistic anthropologists and sociolinguists (with whom he affiliated in the last ten years of his life at Penn).
2. 'The Group Therapy Sessions' (or GTS) refers to a series of recording that Sacks made in the early 1960s and upon which he based many of his early analyses of conversation. These typically consist of three or four 'teenage' boys and a therapist (Dan) although in some of the recordings there is also a 'teenage' girl present (Louise).
3. Examples are presented using the transcription conventions developed by Gail Jefferson (see the appendix for a guide to their use). The data come from a variety of sources. The heading gives some indication of the provenance of the data (e.g. NB = 'Newport Beach', a series of recordings made in the late 1960s by Harvey Sacks).
4. For more on repeating in next turn and making collections, see Schegloff (1997). Notice that the example 'Oh: just grea:t, < everybody:st- still here' suggests other collectible phenomena, for example compressed transition spaces (see Local & Walker, 2004, 2005), answers that correct a question's presuppositions (see Ehrlich & Sidnell, 2006), and 'oh'-prefaced responses to inquiry (see Heritage, 1998).

5. It is not hard to see the relevance of questioning or rising intonation. A question establishes a next position for a response of some kind: an answer or a confirmation. While downwardly intoned, assertive repeats may elicit responses, they do not seem to invite responses in the same way.
6. I call these 'penultimate stress repeats' because this is where the stress occurs in multi-syllabic words – see, for instance, Virginia's 'allowance' in example 15. And notice that speakers can insert syllables so as to make such repeats possible for words composed of a single syllable – so, for example, 'green' can become '*gree*-een'.

Suggestions for further reading

Gardner, R. and Wagner, J. (eds) (2004) *Second Language Conversations*. London, New York: Continuum.
An interesting collection of studies focused on conversations involving non-native speakers of various languages.

Sacks, H. (1995a) *Lectures on Conversation* (vol. I & II). Malden: Blackwell.
Sacks' lectures from 1964 to 1972 given to undergradutae classes at the University of California, Los Angeles and Irvine. Illustrates Sacks' unique approach, which involved addressing fundamental questions of sociology and anthropology through attention to the details of ordinary conversation. Essential reading.

Sacks, H., Schegloff, E.A. and Jefferson, G. (1974) A simplest systematics for the organization of turn-taking for conversation. *Language* 50, 696–735.
This classic study of turn-taking in ordinary conversation exhibits the more technical approach to CA. The account of turn-taking provides a key resource for all subsequent CA studies. The article also discusses a number of important ideas (e.g. adjacency pairs, recipient design) whose relevance extends beyond turn-taking to other domains of interactional organization.

Schegloff, E.A. (1997b) Practices and actions: Boundary cases of other-initiated repair. *Discourse Processes* 23, 499–545.
A exceptionally clear discussion of other-initiated repair and the conversation analytic use of collections.

Sidnell, J. (2010) *Conversation Analysis: An Introduction*. Malden: Blackwell.
An overview of the methods and key findings on CA focusing on the foundational studies of Sacks, Schegloff and Jefferson. Individual chapters cover 'Turn-taking', 'Action and understanding', 'Repair', 'Topic', and so on.

References

Brouwer, C. (2004) Doing pronunciation: A specific type of repair sequence. In R. Gardner and J. Wagner (eds) *Second Language Conversations* (pp. 93–113). London and New York: Continuum.

Carroll, D. (2004) Restarts in novice turn beginnings: Disfluencies or interactional achievements. In R. Gardner and J. Wagner (eds) *Second Language Conversations* (pp. 201–220). London and New York: Continuum.

Drew, P. (1981) Adults' corrections of children's mistakes. In P. French and M. MacLure (eds) *Adult-Child Conversations* (pp. 244–267). London: Croom Helm.

Drew, P. and Heritage, J. (1992) Analyzing talk at work: An introduction. In P. Drew and J. Heritage (eds) *Talk at Work: Interaction in Institutional Settings* (pp. 3–65). Cambridge: Cambridge University Press.

Ehrlich, S. and Sidnell, J. (2006) 'I think that's not an assumption you ought to make': Challenging presuppositions in inquiry testimony. *Language in Society* 35 (5), 655–676.

Gardner, R. and Wagner, J. (eds) (2004) *Second Language Conversations*. London and New York: Continuum.

Garfinkel, H. (1967) *Studies in Ethnomethodology*. Englewood Cliffs, NJ: Prentice-Hall.

Goffman, E. (1957) Alienation from interaction. *Human Relations* 10 (1), 47–60.

Goffman, E. (1964) The neglected situation. *American Anthropologist* 66 (6), 133–136.

Goffman, E. (1981) *Forms of Talk*. Philadelphia: University of Pennsylvania Press.

Goffman, E. (1983) The interaction order. *American Sociological Review* 48, 1–17.

Goodwin, C. (1979) The interactive construction of a sentence in natural conversation. In G. Psathas (ed.) *Everyday Language: Studies in Ethnomethodology* (pp. 97–121). New York: Irvington Publishers.

Goodwin, C. and Goodwin, M. (1987) Concurrent operations on talk: Notes on the interactive organization of assessments. *IPrA Papers in Pragmatics* 1 (1), 1–55.

Heritage, J. (1984a) *Garfinkel and Ethnomethodology*. Cambridge: Polity Press.

Heritage, J. (1984b) A change-of-state token and aspects of its sequential placement. In J.M. Atkinson and J. Heritage (eds) *Structures of Social Action: Studies in Conversation Analysis* (pp. 299–345). Cambridge: Cambridge University Press.

Heritage, J. (1998) Oh-prefaced responses to inquiry. *Language in Society* 27 (3), 291–334.

Jefferson, G. (1972) Side sequences. In D. Sudnow (ed.) *Studies in Social Interaction* (pp. 294–338). New York: Free Press.

Jefferson, G. (1980) On "trouble-premonitory" response to inquiry. *Sociological Inquiry* 50, 153–185.

Jefferson, G. (1985) An exercise in the transcription and analysis of laughter. In T. Van Dijk (ed.) *Handbook of Discourse Analysis Volume 3* (pp. 25–34). New York: Academic Press.

Koshik, I. (2002) Designedly incomplete utterances: A pedagogical practice for eliciting knowledge displays in error correction sequences. *Research on Language & Social Interaction* 35 (3), 277–309.

Kurhila, S. (2005) Different orientations to grammatical correctness. In K. Richards and P. Seedhouse (eds) *Applying Conversation Analysis* (pp. 143–158). Basingstoke: Palgrave Macmillan.

Lerner, G.H. (1995) Turn design and the organization of participation in instructional activities. *Discourse Processes* 19 (1), 111–131.

Lerner, G.H. (ed.) (2004) *Conversation Analysis: Studies From the First Generation*. Amsterdam: John Benjamins.

Local, J. and Walker, G. (2004) Abrupt-joins as a resource for the production of multi-unit, multi-action turns. *Journal of Pragmatics* 36 (8), 1375–1403.

Local, J. and Walker, G. (2005) 'Mind the gap': further resources in the production of multi-unit, multi-action turns. *York Papers in Linguistics (Second Series)* 3, 133–143.

Markee, N. (2000) *Conversation Analysis*. Mahwah, NJ: Lawrence Erlbaum Associates.

Markee, N. (2002) Language in development: Questions of theory, questions of practice. *TESOL Quarterly* 36 (3), 265–274.

Mazeland, H. and Zaman-Zadeh, M. (2004) The logic of clarification. Some observations about word-clarification repairs in Finnish-as-a-lingua-franca interactions. In R. Gardner and J. Wagner (eds) *Second Language Conversations* (pp. 132–156). London and New York: Continuum.

McHoul, A. (1978) The organization of turns at formal talk in the classroom. *Language in Society* 7, 183–213.

Mehan, H. (1979a) 'What Time Is It, Denise?': Asking known information questions in classroom discourse. *Theory into Practice* 18 (4), 285–294.

Mehan, H. (1979b) *Learning Lessons*. Cambridge, MA: Harvard University Press.

Mehan, H. (1985) The structure of classroom discourse. In T. Van Dijk (ed.) *Handbook of Discourse Analysis Volume 3* (pp. 120–131). New York: Academic Press.

Pomerantz, A. (1984) Pursuing a response. In J.M. Atkinson and J. Heritage (eds) *Structures of Social Action: Studies in Conversation Analysis* (pp. 152–163). Cambridge: Cambridge University Press.

Richards, K. and Seedhouse, P. (eds) (2005) *Applying Conversation Analysis*. Basingstoke: Palgrave Macmillan.

Sacks, H. (1974) An analysis of the course of a joke's telling in conversation. In R. Bauman and J. Sherzer (eds) *Explorations in the Ethnography of Speaking* (pp. 337–353). Cambridge: Cambridge University Press.

Sacks, H. (1975) Everyone has to lie. In M. Sanches and B.G. Blount (eds) *Sociocultural Dimensions of Language Use* (pp. 57–80). New York: Academic Press.

Sacks, H. (1984a) Notes on methodology. In J.M. Atkinson and J. Heritage (eds) *Structures of Social Action: Studies in Conversation Analysis* (pp. 21–27). Cambridge: Cambridge University Press.

Sacks, H. (1984b) On doing 'Being Ordinary'. In J.M. Atkinson and J. Heritage (eds) *Structures of Social Action: Studies in Conversation Analysis* (pp. 413–429). Cambridge: Cambridge University Press.

Sacks, H. (1995a) *Lectures on Conversation* (Vol. I). Malden: Blackwell.

Sacks, H. (1995b). *Lectures on Conversation* (Vol II). Malden: Blackwell.

Sacks, H., Schegloff, E.A. and Jefferson, G. (1974) A simplest systematics for the organization of turn-taking for conversation. *Language* 50, 696–735.

Schegloff, E.A. (1968) Sequencing in conversational openings. *American Anthropologist* 70, 1075–1095.

Schegloff, E.A. (1979) Identification and recognition in telephone openings. In G. Psathas (ed.) *Everyday Language: Studies in Ethnomethodology* (pp. 23–78). New York: Irvington Publishers.

Schegloff, E.A. (1986) The routine as achievement. *Human Studies* 9 (2–3), 111–151.

Schegloff, E.A. (1987) Recycled turn beginnings: A precise repair mechanism in conversation's turn-taking organisation. In G. Button and J.R.E. Lee (eds) *Talk and Social Organisation* (pp. 70–85). Clevedon: Multilingual Matters.

Schegloff, E.A. (1992) Repair after next turn: The last structurally provided defense of intersubjectivity in conversation. *American Journal of Sociology* 97 (5), 1295–1345.

Schegloff, E.A. (1995) Introduction. In H. Sacks and G. Jefferson (eds) *Lectures on Conversation* (Vol. 1), (pp. ix–lxii). Oxford: Basil Blackwell.

Schegloff, E.A. (1997) Practices and actions: Boundary cases of other-initiated repair. *Discourse Processes* 23, 499–545.

Schegloff, E.A. (2005) On Integrity in Inquiry ... of the investigated, not the investigator. *Discourse Studies* 7 (4–5), 455–480.

Schegloff, E.A. (2006) Interaction: The infrastructure for social institutions, the natural ecological niche for language, and the arena in which culture is enacted. In N.J. Enfield and S.C. Levinson (eds) *Roots of Human Sociality. Culture, Cognition and Interaction* (pp. 70–96). Oxford: Berg.

Schegloff, E.A. (2007) *Sequence Organization in Interaction: A Primer in Conversation Analysis I*. Cambridge: Cambridge University Press.

Schegloff, E.A., Jefferson, G. and Sacks, H. (1977) The preference for self-correction in the organization of repair in conversation. *Language* 53, 361–382.

Schegloff, E.A. and Sacks, H. (1973) Opening up closings. *Semiotica* 8, 289–327.

Seedhouse, P. (2004) *The Interactional Architecture of the Language Classroom: A Conversation Analysis Perspective.* Oxford: Blackwell.

Sidnell, J. (2004) There's risks in everything: Extreme case formulations and accountability in inquiry testimony. *Discourse and Society* 15 (6), 745–766.

Sidnell, J. (2006) Repair. In J. Verschueren and J-O. Ostman (eds) *Handbook of Pragmatics.* Amsterdam: John Benjamins.

Sidnell, J. (2010a) Questioning repeats in the talk of four-year old children. In H. Gardner and M. Forrester (eds) *Analysing Interactions in Childhood: Methods and Applications* (pp. 103–127). Wiley.

Sidnell, J. (2010b) The design and positioning of questions in inquiry testimony. In S. Ehrlich and A. Freed (eds) *'Why Do You Ask?': The Function of Questions in Institutional Discourse* (pp. 20–41). New York: Oxford University Press.

Stivers, T. (2005) Modified repeats: One method for asserting primary rights from second position. *Research on Language and Social Interaction* 38 (2), 131–158.

Chapter 19

Classroom Discourse Analysis: A Focus on Communicative Repertoires

BETSY RYMES

Classroom discourse analysis is probably the most direct application of sociolinguistic insights to teachers' daily practice. This chapter illustrates this point by showing how researchers and teachers may use the concept of 'communicative repertoire' as a lens for understanding and analyzing interaction in classrooms. I also demonstrate why an understanding of how students develop and become aware of their own communicative repertoire – rather than correctness in any homogeneous standard target language – is a relevant goal and application of the analysis of classroom discourse.

Communicative Repertoire

A **communicative repertoire** is the collection of ways individuals use language and literacy and other means of communication (gestures, dress, posture, or accessories) to function effectively in the multiple communities in which they participate. This concept grows out of John Gumperz's initial observations of the complex ways multilingualism was deployed across social groups in India. Here, he found, switching languages functioned in many of the same ways stylistic switching functions in monolingual communities. Gumperz was fascinated with the social effects of switching and mixing languages among bilinguals. Even the verbs 'switching' and 'mixing' seemed inadequate to describe the systematic ways parts of different, linguistically demarcated 'languages', were being used. To reflect the nexus of grammatical distinctions between languages and the social effects of linguistic choices, he coined the term *verbal repertoire*. (Gumperz, 1964, 1965). For Gumperz, a verbal repertoire is potentially more extensive than a 'language', including 'the totality of linguistic forms regularly employed in the community in the course of socially significant interaction' (Gumperz, 1971: 184).

Gumperz initially coined the term 'verbal repertoire' to address the massive variety of languages deployed in multilingual communities within India. By doing so, he reconceptualized the object of linguistic study, illustrating that the term linguists traditionally used to demarcate communities of speakers, 'language', was descriptively inadequate in a setting of *societal multilingualism* (*cf.* Sridhar, 1996). His insights have since been generalized to monolingual communities as well. This conceptualization makes it clear that all communities have a range of varieties that are functionally distinct and appropriate in different kinds of social events. Individuals' communicative repertoires may include multiple languages, or may consist primarily of a range of varieties within a language.

In this chapter, I want, like Gumperz, to emphasize the significant contributions of social situation and communicative goals to an individual's language use – whether that speaker is described as multilingual or monolingual. I also try to capture the centrality of an individual's communicative goals by using the slightly modified phrase, 'communicative repertoire'. This term differs slightly from 'verbal repertoire' in that it focuses on the resources deployed by individuals, rather than attempting to generalize about the 'verbal repertoire' of 'the community' of speakers.

An individual's communicative repertoires are inevitably more developed in one social realm and more limited in another. Like a pianist who may have an expansive 'classical repertoire', but a limited repertoire of 'folk songs' or 'jazz', an individual speaker may have a well-developed 'academic' repertoire, but a very limited 'football fan' or 'blind date' repertoire. A two-year-old may have a vast repertoire that is functionally communicative with her mother, but she may not be considered a viable communication partner in many other contexts – a university seminar for example. Nevertheless, even a two-year-old is developing distinct repertoires for different social contexts and will have a different repertoire for speaking with her mother than she uses at day care or with her older brothers.

Human development across the life span consists in large part of the growing awareness and accumulation of such communicative repertoires and the effects they have (Bruner, 1983). This is true for babies, as they take increasingly active roles in the various communicative realms in which they participate; it is also true for every living being who moves in and out of different social settings with varying communicative expectations. Wolfe (2004) entertainingly captures this in his novel of collegiate life, *I am Charlotte Simmons*. In this fictional world, all characters struggle to find their voice in the prestigious environs of 'Dupont University'. In the following passage, Charlotte, a scholarship girl from Southern

Appalachia, wrestles with how to write home to her parents about her initial experiences as a freshman:

> Dear Momma and Daddy,
>
> I'll admit my eyes blurred with mist when I saw you drive off in the old pickup.
>
> *The old pickup? ... my eyes blurred with mist? ...* What on earth did she think she was writing? ... She rocked forward with another trill of low-grade guilt to confront her letter home ... *the old pickup.* Daddy is totally dependent on the poor, miserable old truck, and I'm treating it like it's something quaint. *Eyes blurred with mist ...* Yuk! She could just imagine Momma and Daddy reading *that.* The 'pretty writing'. (Wolfe, 2004: 158)

Charlotte labels her academic/literary repertoire 'pretty writing' and recognizes that this part of her repertoire has very different functionality in her home community than it does in a community of academics. Indeed her own 'coming of age' is a process of coming to terms with her rapidly expanding communicative repertoires and their effective uses. For her, the journey through 'Dupont University' is one that exposes her to a vast range of new communicative repertoires. Her challenge is to understand them and to be able to use them to her advantage – and to transcend the loneliness that she initially feels, trapped in a communicative repertoire that she shares neither with her new acquaintances at Dupont nor with her family back home.

Charlotte Simmons' interior monologue about 'pretty writing' encapsulates a struggle that countless students have about the way they speak and the language choices they make across academic, family and other social contexts. Charlotte Simmons' fictional insights resonate with the experiences of non-fictional personalities who have come from humble origins, but gone on to excel in the most elite institutions of higher learning. For example, *The New York Times* describes Supreme Court Justice Clarence Thomas, and a current nominee to the Supreme Court, Sonia Sotomayor, as questioning the adequacy of their own repertoires when they began to attend prestigious universities: both were worried 'what others would think when they opened their mouth (p. 1)':

> Ms. Sotomayor had grown up in the Bronx speaking Spanish; Mr Thomas's relatives in Pin Point, Ga., mixed English with Gullah, a language of the coastal South. Both attended Catholic school, where they were drilled by nuns in grammar and other subjects. But at college, they realized they still sounded unpolished. (Kantor & Gonzalez, 2009: 1, 21)

As this narrative of these highly successful people indicates, Thomas and Sotomayor were aware that part of their success would depend on the way they managed their own ways of speaking.

This awareness of communicative repertoire and its effects is also echoed in the ways everyday high-school students talk about their feelings about their own language habits. Speakers of multiple languages in particular encounter this tussle among repertoires. Consider, for example, the words of Seba, a ninth grade girl, originally from Morocco, now attending a Philadelphia area high school, musing about what her multiple languages mean to her.

> I definitely I think Arabic is the most popular language that I speak 'cause everybody – every person loves to speak Arabic because they think is- everyone speaks Arabic. They say – like, any kind of person likes to speak Arabic because it's popular. Anywhere you go, people say, 'oh hey' in Arabic. I'm like, everybody knows that. So, I think Arabic is the one language I love to keep going on.

> And I used to take Spanish when I was in my home country. And, I used to take a lot of classes. I used to learn a lot of languages, but I didn't keep going on them. So when I came here. My mom, she does speak Spanish, she tried to push me, but I'm like no I have to learn English, so I forgot about Spanish. I forgot a little about French. But I'm holding on Arabic. Yeah. It's the only language that I can talk with my mom.

> All the words we say in home are like half Arabic, half English, half French, half – all the languages they're like mixed together.

Seba, like the fictional Charlotte Simmons, seems to be trying to account for the ways of speaking that attach her to home. In United States, she says, 'I have to learn English, so I forgot about Spanish'. Still she is clearly part of a social milieu, even in the United States, in which 'every person loves to speak Arabic'. Arabic, she says, is 'the most popular language'. As a ninth grader in a Philadelphia area high school, English is clearly important, but other languages continue to play an important role in her life: Arabic is, she says, 'the only language that I can talk with my mom'. She also describes her language at home, with her mother, as a mixture of many languages. Her repertoires cannot simply be demarcated by the standard names or linguistic distinctions between standard 'English' or 'Arabic'. She recognizes that 'the words we say at home' are not simply textbook versions of language, but a more complicated repertoire of 'half Arabic, half English, half French, half – all the languages they're like mixed together'.

These three, wide-ranging examples illustrate critical issues in the analysis of communicative repertoires:

(1) *'Correctness' is a construction that functions secondarily to communicative goals*. Charlotte Simmons is not worrying how 'correct' her language is in her letter home. She is attempting to modulate it to be *appropriate* (*cf.* Hornberger, 1989; Hymes, 1972) to the community of speakers

she is addressing (her small-town parents back home). Similarly, Seba does not care about linguistic purity at home, but rather calls on 'all the languages ... mixed together'. In many situations speaking text-book-like English would be communicatively disastrous (see also Sidnell, this volume, on orientations to correctness in the second language classroom).

(2) *One's repertoires emerge and/or recede according to use and context.* Charlotte Simmons rekindles her 'home' register in the letter to her parents, but finds it a struggle to use this language while steeped in her new academic context. Seba similarly describes how she 'used to learn a lot of languages' but finds that now she is mainly just 'holding on to Arabic' (and English) in the United States.

(3) *Accommodation to the communicative repertoires of one's interlocutors is inevitable, although the directionality of accommodation – or, who accommodates to whom – varies.* Charlotte Simmons, out of respect and deference to her parents, accommodates to their expectations and communicative habits (rather than expecting them to accommodate to her 'pretty writing'). The Supreme Court justices accommodate to the higher education repertoire in which they want to fully participate (rather than asserting the validity of their own Spanish- or Gullah-influenced speech in that context). In radical contrast, Seba sees all of her languages as allowing her to accommodate to the communicative needs of her mother (rather than accommodating to an ideology of linguistic purity or a sense of English as an official language).

(4) *What has come to be labeled 'language' is just one aspect of a much broader and communicatively relevant category, 'communicative repertoire'.* All language users deploy different ways of speaking to different types of people or in different social situations. While Charlotte Simmons is discussing different ways of using the 'same language', ('English'), Seba is discussing different languages that she labels 'Arabic', 'Spanish', 'French' and 'English'.
What's useful in each of these cases is not the labeling of distinct 'languages', but the recognition that in varied contexts, different communicative repertoires account for communicative success.

(5) Building metalinguistic awareness of communicative repertoires is a life-long process, facilitated by travel across social boundaries. Charlotte Simmons seems to be painfully aware of the contrast between her 'pretty language' and the expectations her parents have of a letter from her. Clarence Thomas and Sonia Sotomayor recognize the effects their varied repertoires had in shaping their impressions at elite colleges. Seba displays awareness that her multiple languages function differently in the United States than they did in Morocco. Each of these examples illustrates how traversing social boundaries can create metalinguistic awareness, illuminating the different functionality of their repertoires.

Gaining this kind of metalinguistic awareness of multiple repertoires and the role one's own repertoire plays in communicative success (or failure) is a primary goal of pursuing classroom discourse analysis. In the following sections, I discuss, in order, how each of these features of 'communicative repertoire' is illuminated through the analysis of classroom communication.

Communicative Repertoires in Classroom Discourse

Rethinking correctness

Spend a few minutes in any classroom discussion and it becomes clear that being 'correct' and speaking in a 'polished' manner is, for many students, not top priority. In fact, sometimes, students – even when they know 'correct' answers or 'polished' ways of speaking – find it socially problematic to use that repertoire. To return briefly to Tom Wolfe's fictional 'Dupont University' for example, a 'giant' basketball player, 'JoJo', who covertly wants to be an intellectual, finds himself trapped into performing ignorance when he starts to give a thoughtful response to a question about *Madame Bovary*. When the professor asks the class why Madame Bovary's husband performed a risky, but potentially heroic, operation, JoJo begins:

> 'He did it', said the Giant, 'because his wife had all these ambitions...'
> (p. 108)

Immediately, JoJo's teammates in the class sense that this answer may be (horror!) accurate, and they begin to sarcastically give each other fist bumps and exclaim, 'Hey, JoJo read the book', and '... we got us another *scholar*...'. After the professor settles the commotion and encourages JoJo to continue, with a 'Mr Johanssen? As you were saying', Mr Johannsen (*ne* JoJo) faces a choice. Which of his repertoires will he use here? The 'Mr Johanssen' repertoire or the 'JoJo' repertoire? He responds:

> Oh yeah. He did the operation because ... his wife wanted some money to buy some stuff. (pp. 108–109)

Clearly, he has chosen his 'JoJo' repertoire, affiliated with his basketball peers, and disaffiliated from his aspiring scholarly self. Being 'correct' in this classroom was not the difficult job for 'JoJo'; rather the difficult part about giving the right answer was that it called on a repertoire that would lead him to be completely cut off from (and humiliated by) his basketball peers.

In real classrooms, just as in Tom Wolfe's fictional university, finding voice in ways that are recognized by the teacher as 'correct' while still maintaining face among peers can be a complicated negotiation. Often, students draw on an entirely different repertoire in their peer-to-peer communication, while a teacher attempts to continue with his own lesson, as in the following High-School discussion of 'current events' (Gutiérrez *et al.*, 1995).

Teacher: What did the Supreme Court decision in *Brown versus the Board of Education*, have to do with?
Student: James Brown?
Student: Richard Brown?
Student: Shut-up
Student: You shut up
Student: James Brown?
Student: Al Green
Teacher: ((attempting to call on someone))Ye:::s?

Here, clearly, James Brown and Al Green are elements of a communicative repertoire that some of these high-school students revel in, but to which their teacher is not attuned (or is, perhaps, deliberately ignoring). But even this brief example illustrates that some students are more fluent in the 'James Brown' repertoire than others. When another student attempts to join in the banter with 'Richard Brown' (certainly not recognizable as a musical icon like James Brown or Al Green) that student receives a swift 'shut up', which is countered with an inelegant 'you shut up'. Clearly, this student is lacking facility in a newly emergent repertoire. When another student comes up with 'Al Green', he steers the repartee back into the 'James Brown' repertoire. Now, the teacher tries to resuscitate the teacher repertoire with a characteristic, long-drawn-out 'ye::::s' in an attempt to call on a student and bolster the teacher-fronted turn-taking pattern that characterizes a traditional school-talk repertoire, but with little response. As the teacher-centered discussion proceeds, the students continue their banter about James Brown, building a student-centered, classroom 'underlife' (Goffman, 1974).

The 'James Brown' repertoire emerges above largely because students share a common, mass-mediated inventory of references that can swiftly establish a new repertoire as common communicative currency between students. Just as the high-school students use a reference to popular culture to create their own communicative realm tangential to the teacher's, the elementary school children in the example below, use the reference to a Pokemon character, 'Chansey', to accomplish the same interactional function. While the teacher is drawing on a teacher repertoire to draw students into sounding out, then pronouncing, a word on a card in the Phonics Game™, the students make another connection. I have indented their side-play about 'Chansey the Pokemon' to make the foray into the students' Pokemon-repertoire visible in the transcript (Rymes, 2001):

Teacher: -C- -H- says?
David: Can
Rene: an- chan-

Teacher:	Chan- -C- -Y-
	(2.0)
Rene:	Chances.
Teacher:	Cha:n:c:y
Rene:	Chancy.
Rene:	Ohp ((looking at David and
	smiling)) Pokémon.
David:	It's a Pokémon.
Teacher:	And you have to tell me why the
	–a- is short.

In this example, at least two clear communicative repertoires are in play. One is the teacher–student academic display repertoire in which she patiently coaxes correct answers out of Rene. But as soon as the word 'Chancy' is articulated fully, Rene and David launch another repertoire, that of Pokémon fans. Just as the name 'Brown' prompted student repertoires involving 'James Brown', here 'Chancy' gets taken up as 'Chansey', a Pokemon™, another mass-media icon that provides common ground among the students and, simultaneously, a departure from the teacher's repertoire.

As these examples illustrate, 'correctness' on the teacher's terms is not always what students are working to achieve. A more useful way of describing the action in the above examples is a careful negotiation of repertoires. In JoJo's case, his performance of being *not* correct covered for his 'knowing'. In the cases of the James Brown and Chansey examples, being correct was redefined on student terms as awareness of mass-media icons. But in all these cases, are students learning any more in the teacher repertoire than they are in their own? In the Chansey example, these students are English Language Learners in a pullout program. And, over the course of the semester, their digressions from the phonics game, while technically 'off-task', produced far more extended talk in English than their careful sounding out of game cards with the teacher. So, departures from the classroom repertoire, and the expectations of correctness within it, need not be departures from language learning.

Inversely, *a performance* of correctness can function as a cover for *not* knowing. This phenomenon has been described variably as 'passing' (Goffman, 1959); 'studenting' (Knobel, 1999) or 'procedural display' (Bloome *et al.*, 1989). Learning the repertoire for 'passing' as correct has been noted particularly among English Language Learners who learn to use contextualization cues (Gumperz, 1982), rather than a literal understanding of the content of what is being said, to hone in on 'right answers' (Rymes & Pash, 2001) or to pass as fluent in English (Monzó & Rueda, 2009).

For example, in the excerpt below, taken from a small book discussion among second graders, in which Rene is the only English Language

Learner, Rene quickly chimes in with the 'right' answer, on the heels of his classmates. This is representative of Rene's tendency to deftly use his peers' responses to formulate his own identity as competent (Here, the square brackets indicate overlapping talk):

Teacher: What do all the men have on their heads?
Tiffany: Ha[ts
Rene: [Hats

In other cases, Rene reads a teacher's intonation or phrasing of a question, to arrive at the 'correct' answer. As in conversation, sometimes one just needs to know what one's interlocutor wants to hear:

Teacher: What is ↑wrong with ↓that. Is there anything wrong with that?
Sara: No.
David: No.
Rene: No.

As Monzó and Rueda (2009) point out, this kind of 'passing' as fluent in English can become especially common in English-Only contexts, in which alternative communicative repertoires are quashed. Such passing practices, like the more overtly disruptive practices of playing dumb or building a student-centered underlife, may keep students from direct engagement with what is deemed correct in the teacher's mind. Monzó and Rueda insightfully add, however, that even in cases of passing, deft use of this seemingly superficial repertoire may be a way to preserve one's social identity as competent while more privately learning what needs to be learned. Whether students are using their range of repertoires to affiliate with peers, to distance themselves from the teacher or to hide certain gaps in other repertoires, a close look at all these interactional phenomena highlights delicate maneuvers students deploy each day to both preserve their dignity and negotiate their status in widely varying communities – including the academic community.

Emerging and receding repertoires

Instead of focusing on 'correctness', looking at 'communicative repertoires' entails a new approach to pedagogy. We can begin to understand this shift in pedagogical strategy, by noticing how communicative repertoires emerge and recede in classroom talk, and monitoring the results. For example, I noticed many years ago, while doing research at an alternative school in Los Angeles, in which many students had been in jail and were currently on parole, that the topic of 'jail' occasionally emerged in discussions between teachers and students. Sometimes these discussions went smoothly, sometimes they led to conflict, sometimes they led to a dead end – even when the same teacher was involved. Upon closer look at the communicative repertoires involved, it seemed that when the teacher's repertoire emerged as dominant, discussions faltered. In one such case, after students had begun a discussion of their own jail time, the teacher, Tim, had begun to tell about his own experience being arrested and put in jail for 'driving while black'. This attempt at empathy led to an abrupt end to student sharing when he uttered something apparently unique to his own repertoire as a moral summing up of his own experience:

Tim:	They put me in jail for five days.
Felipe:	For what?
Grace:	((coughs twice))
Joe:	Five days that ain't nothing five days.
Grace:	Oh yeah
Joe:	I was locked up for two [months.
Felipe:	((to Tim)) Where at?
Tim:	[It was a long time for me::
	I decided that that was not proper.

After Tim used 'not proper' to assess his own experience with jail, students' questions about his experiences slowed and then stopped. It seems clear that students would never describe their own experiences as 'not proper'. Indeed, they had been using very different terms to describe their experiences. While Tim says, 'they put me in Jail', Felipe was 'locked up'. What Tim admits was a 'long time' for him, the students claim, 'ain't nothing'. Still, even this exchange of repertoires ceases after the teacher's talk takes on what seems to be a naïve, moralizing tone. When he goes on to coax a lesson-learned out of the group, the pace of the discussion comes to a halt, and after a long pause, students simply seem to be trying to give him what he wants to hear.

Tim:	What wh- wh what do people hope to gain by putting you in jail?
	((One second pause))
Felipe:	((sigh)) Teach him a lesson or something.
Tim:	Okay. Teach him a lesson.

In this conversation, student and teacher repertoires emerged as distinct, and dialogue faltered. However, in another jail discussion, this teacher seemed to assimilate to his students' repertoire. In this discussion, several girls had been talking about how many good-looking men there are in jail, when suddenly Keneisha, who has just returned from a brief jail visit, makes a statement about her own experience there:

Keneisha:	I ain't never wanna go back.
	((0.8 second pause))
Tim:	I hear ya.

In this conversation at the same school, but with different students, several weeks later, instead of reacting to a student story about jail with moralizing adult lexicon, Tim leaned back in his chair and uttered the casually empathic, 'I hear ya'. After this emergent matching of repertoires, the discussion flowed. Ultimately, the students in the second group ended up agreeing with the teacher's perspective that going to jail is 'not proper', although they never used that diction to express it. In this way, the teacher, by modulating his repertoire, earned 'rights to advise' these students (for further analysis of these contrasting examples, see Rymes, 1997).

In the first jail discussion, Tim's repertoire emerged as a stark contrast to the students'. But in the second, when he spoke, his repertoire modulated as he voiced empathy with Keneisha. This opportunity for the expression of like-mindedness seemed to emerge as a matter of chance. But awareness of circulating repertoires and their effects can build once it is acknowledged as a valuable activity. Recognizing the ebb and flow of teacher and student repertoires across contexts makes it possible to do more than simply focus on a correct 'standard', or the 'proper' thing to do, and to focus instead, on moving across discourse boundaries so that human connection and relevant learning can occur.

Accommodating repertoires different from our own

Recognizing new repertoires need not mean that we conform to student repertoires or expect them to learn our own. Just as a fulfilling conversation involves much more than giving ones' interlocutor pat answers or what we think they want, classroom talk need not involve students giving the teacher what they think she wants to hear – or for that matter, a teacher trying to sound just like her students! In any sustained dialog, however, conversationalists begin to take on characteristics of each other's communicative repertoire. Similarly, over the course of a year, participants in a classroom community will probably begin to take on aspects of one another's repertoires. Sometimes, this involves 'giving the teacher what she wants' (as when students try to 'pass' as English fluent); at other times, it may involve giving in to 'peer pressure' (as when JoJo plays 'dumb'). As Tim, the teacher above illustrates, in the best cases, an individual carefully modulates his or her repertoire to achieve dialogue with others. No one is 'giving in' but both are gaining by occupying a third position in which collaboration across repertoires is possible.

As Sonia Nieto (1999) writes, 'accommodation' must be bidirectional. Students accommodate to school routines and repertoires, but teachers accommodate to students' repertoires as well. Not surprisingly, schools that do well show evidence of both kinds of accommodation: Students are learning repertoires of school success; teachers are learning that students' native repertoires are valuable (e.g. Lucas *et al.*, 1990; Sheets, 1995). When students' native communicative repertoires are recognized, they begin to see themselves as academically capable (i.e. capable of expanding their repertoire). These studies also illustrate that for schools to be successful, they do not necessarily need new curriculum or radical restructuring, but a change in culture and attitude – a change that recognizes that with teaching comes a commitment to build knowledge *of* our students as much as to build knowledge *in* our students.

'Communicative repertoire' rather than 'language': Analyzing classroom discourse

Just as Gumperz (1971) found linguistic distinctions alone inadequate to account for verbal behavior, Makoni and Pennycook (2007) point out that the term 'language' itself is a construction, one that has become historically reified, but that rarely is something of use to actual speakers. However, speaking analytically, if we are not analyzing 'language' in classrooms, where do we start? With 'communicative repertoire'. But how do we recognize distinct repertoires without demarking boundaries linguistically? We use locally defined boundaries as discerned in classroom talk. This can involve different kinds of words (Chancy versus Chansey; 'ambitions' versus 'stuff') or names (JoJo versus Mr Johansen), different ways of speaking ('that was not proper' versus 'I hear ya'; 'put me in jail' versus 'got locked up'), gestures (fist bumps versus a pleased nod; sitting up straight versus slouching), and turn-taking habits (hands raised versus massively overlapping talk), and sometimes, these repertoires will include multiple 'languages' as well (cf. Fassler, 2003; Martin-Jones & Saxena, 2003).

Work in sociolinguistics and classroom discourse over the last 30 years has illuminated more refined tools to define and recognize communicative repertoires. We know about different narrative styles (Au, 1980; Michaels, 1981), turn-taking patterns (Erickson, 1996; Mehan, 1985), participation frameworks (Goffman, 1974; Philips, 1984) and the role of passing and underlife in institutions (Goffman, 1959). But now that research has given us exemplary descriptions of finite structural distinctions (like turn-taking patterns or narrative styles) and generalized institutional epiphenomena (like the production of 'underlife' or patterns of 'passing'), language teachers (and their students) must learn to recognize how these features coalesce to form distinct communicative repertoires in our classrooms. The goal of classroom discourse analysis should be *everyone's* heightened awareness of the communicative repertoires in play and how they can be deployed with facility and elegance – and to useful ends. A starting point in working to this awareness, I would argue, is to have students document the characteristics of their own repertoires. Students could start with the categories and questions suggested in Figure 19.1. Add more as they emerge (and new categories inevitably will).

Use these categories to begin investigating your own and your peers language use in the classroom:

Names/Nicknames What different names do you and your peers use for students and teachers?

Popular Culture References What pop cultural icons do students and teachers allude to?

Gestures What are some characteristic gestures students and teachers use?

Turn-taking habits Is highly overlapping speech common and expected? Are long pauses more

the norm?

Ways of telling stories What characteristic ways of telling stories do you and your peers have?

Languages in play What languages are in use? By whom?

Pronunciation of certain words Are different languages pronounced differently by different

people? Which are used/not used?

Figure 19.1 Categories for classroom communicative repertoire comparison

Gaining metalinguistic awareness

A critical goal of classroom discourse analysis then is to develop communicative repertoires of our students and their awareness of their functionality across contexts. As Canagarajah has emphasized, 'We have to develop the sensitivity to decode differences in dialects as students engage with a range of speakers and communities. What would help in this venture is the focus on developing a metalinguistic awareness' (2007: 238). To achieve the goal of increased metalinguistic awareness, I want to emphasize the new critical territory opened up by the everyday practice of classroom discourse analysis. When the goal is the achievement of greater metalinguistic awareness, the *process* of doing classroom discourse analysis can be as important as the findings. Doing classroom discourse analysis potentially develops new habits of meta-discursive reflection in teachers and students, habits that are critical in contemporary multilingual, ever-globalizing educational contexts.

What would this look like in practice? Teachers and students, by analyzing discourse in their classroom and school, can begin to notice the range of repertoires and their functional value. 'Discourse Notebooks', in which teachers and students record and discuss language variation as they hear it, can be a good starting place. Each page in the discourse notebook can use the same kinds of categories illustrated in Figure 19.1, above, with additional local categories being added as needed. Discussions of the discourse notebooks are likely to lead to important metalinguistic insights and directions for further investigation. Recording and transcribing key events and then analyzing them as a class can add further detail and direction to this project.

Research Methods

Classroom discourse analysis

To gain more finely grained metalinguistic awareness, teacher/researchers also can supplement informal discourse notebooks with more systematic classroom discourse analysis. Classroom discourse analysis is an ideal way to understand the range of repertoires circulating in a classroom and how they are distributed across different classroom events. So, just as Gumperz (1964, 1971) began to explore verbal repertoire by noticing how individuals used multiple languages differently and deliberately on different social occasions, a classroom discourse analyst studies the relationship between classroom events and language use within them.

An X-ray view of classroom discourse studies might reveal the following basic skeletal steps:

(1) Identify distinct classroom events.
(2) Characterize the language within those events.
(3) Identify variations in the language within those events.

Initially, classic classroom discourse studies focused primarily on steps 1 and 2 mentioned above, describing normative expectations for classroom talk. For example, Hugh Mehan's (1985) study identified teacher-fronted classroom events (step 1) and the ubiquitous 'Initiation-Response-Evaluation' turn taking pattern within them (step 2). This research also characterized the typical kind of questions (known-answer) and answers (brief and swiftly offered) that are most functional within this event.

Other early studies, however, also were intent on identifying individual variations within distinct classroom speech events (step 3). Sarah Michaels, for example, identified the 'sharing time' classroom event (step 1), and characterized typical, successful storytelling turns within that event (step 2). She found that successful stories were topic centered on a single topic (e.g. making sand candles) and that the teacher was able to ask follow-up questions with facility. But Michaels also identified unsuccessful storytelling turns and began to investigate why those stories were not working (Step 3). She found that the African–American children in the class were bringing a distinctly different communicative repertoire to sharing time, in which sharing involved chaining together a series of personal events that included many family members, memories and details.

Other studies, rather than comparing individuals within a speech event, have compared language across speech events and how the language expectations within those events affect student verbal behavior. Susan Philips (1984), for example, documented distinct participation frameworks within classrooms on the Warm Springs Indian reservation and characterized the different turn-taking patterns within each of those events. Then she investigated participation patterns within each of those distinct events.

She found that Indian students remained silent during teacher-fronted events, but were highly involved in collaborative group work. By raising awareness of how students participated differently in different events, she illuminated elements of the Indian students' communicative repertoire that were unrecognized by many educators and thus not available as resources on which to build further learning activities. Philips's study suggested that simple shifts in classroom arrangements for speech events could have radical effects on the educational experiences of Indians on the Warm Springs Reservation (see also Reyes, this volume).

Doing Classroom Discourse Analysis

These days, teachers inspired by these studies have begun to conduct similar studies on their own classrooms. Teacher-researchers have been especially drawn to the comparative framework exemplified by Michael's work, comparing student repertoires within a single event. Steve Griffin (2004), for example, used Michael's methods to study sharing time in his elementary school classroom, investigating the troubling non-normative and increasingly disruptive participation of one student. Eventually, his own transcript analysis led him to change his sharing time procedures, largely because he was able to describe the type of radical new story his one troubling student was contributing. Soon after, all the students wanted to experiment with this storytelling style and sharing time took on a lively new quality, with everyone in the classroom expanding their communicative repertoire.

While teachers-doing-discourse-analysis like Steve Griffin are more and more common these days, when classroom discourse analysis emerged as a methodology, it was mainly the work of university researchers, who schlepped around with mountains of recording equipment and spent hours back at the laboratory transcribing and analyzing. Hugh Mehan and his colleagues even referred to themselves as the 'schleppers' back in the 1980s. Fortunately, recording equipment is now light, compact and relatively inexpensive. There is nothing to stop teachers from clicking the 'record' button and seeing what they discover. As a result, the initial methodological challenge for a teacher-researcher is largely conceptual: to identify those events worthy of recording and then carefully investigated that language once it is recorded. Following the tried and true steps taken in discourse analyses can be an initial jumping off point for a novice classroom discourse analyst:

(1)   Spend some time identifying the different speech events in the classroom. Identify either a focal event or relevant comparative events.
(2)   Record the focal event and begin to characterize the language in that event. To do so, you will not need to fully transcribe the talk. Start by

listening to the tape and, using the categories listed in Figure 19.1 as an initial guide, identify instances of talk that make this event distinctive. For example, listen for multilingualism and its effects; listen for the use of names and nicknames; listen for greetings, brand names, praise or politeness tokens. Begin to characterize this event's normative language patterns. Transcribe those instances of talk that are most relevant to this characterization.

(3) Look for variation in language use within that event or across comparison events. You may want to investigate the participation of one 'disruptive' student, as Griffin did. Alternatively, like Philips, you may want to investigate how certain students participate differently across different events.

Once you have recorded an event, transcribed it, and begun to see the repertoires in play, you will be hooked. And, as you begin to see how language use differs across events, you discover a vast range of communicative repertoires. This can be empowering for a teacher and for students. As you become more metalinguistically facile, you will be able to more clearly identify the kinds of language use in your classroom, and to more clearly articulate for students the kinds of language you hope they will be able to produce in different situations.

Conclusion: Understanding Communicative Repertoires as a Postmethods Pedagogy

Walk into any United States public school in a major metropolitan area. Look around. Listen. Stroll down the hall. Step into a classroom. What do you see? What do you hear? Chances are you see and hear dozens of communicative repertoires in play, many of which are only minimally understood by you. Imagine you are a language teacher in this context. What are your responsibilities here? How could you possibly be the 'expert'? I am suggesting that by developing understandings of communicative repertoires in their teaching context, teachers can become experts in helping students navigate this complex communicative terrain.

Classroom discourse analysis, then, can be a way of implementing what Kumaravadivelu (2001) has called 'postmethods' pedagogy. Why postmethods? Teaching methods, especially in the language classroom, presuppose a 'language' that must somehow be transmitted into students' heads. Even a method like the 'communicative approach' sees communication as a means to a different end: correct, native-like language use. What I am proposing is awareness of communicative repertoires as an end in itself. This would not be achieved by role-playing or by invoking imaginary repertoires of 'native speakers', but through a collective empirical investigation of circulating repertoires and their everyday uses and misuses.

Through this kind of work, we can help students learn how they can use their repertoires to, as Canagarajah puts it, 'shuttle between communities, and not to think of only joining *a* community' Canagarajah (2007: 238). Such a goal is absolutely essential to become 'culturally relevant teachers' (Ladson-Billings, 2004), to 'create pride in cultural and linguistic differences' (Monzó & Rueda, 2009: 38), and for teachers and students, more generally, to develop as culturally effective human beings.

Suggestions for further reading

Griffin, S. (2004) I need people: Storytelling in a second-grade classroom. In C. Ballenger (ed.) *Regarding Children's Words: Teacher Research on Language and Literacy.* New York: Teachers College Press.

This chapter, a modern-day follow up to Sarah Michael's classic on narrative style (see below), illustrates how a teacher puts discourse analysis to use in his own classroom to understand different narrative styles during sharing time. Through descriptions and transcripts of one student's non-normative storytelling turns, Griffin illustrates how his own acceptance of initially disturbing and potentially disruptive storytelling positively transformed 'sharing time' in his classroom. Griffin's research as a classroom teacher illustrates how classroom discourse analysis can promote metalinguistic awareness of communicative repertoires, and, in turn, expand the communicative repertoires of all children in a classroom.

Makoni, S. and Pennycook, A. (eds) (2007) *Disinventing and Reconstituting Languages.* Clevedon: Multilingual Matters.

This collection presents a new theoretical framework for applied linguistics and individual chapters illustrate what this new framework might look like in practice in a number of contexts. The framework outlines how language teaching could benefit by shifting the focus from linguistic distinctions invented by that discipline to the complex communicative concerns of speakers themselves. The applications of this framework then illustrate, in practical terms, how this approach can improve practice by refocusing language education on the communicative resources needed to traverse social boundaries and thrive in mulilingual/multicultural contexts.

Martin-Jones, M. and Saxena, M. (2003) Bilingual resources and 'funds of knowledge' for teaching and learning in multi-ethnic classrooms in Britain. In A. Creese and P. Martin (eds) *Multilingual Classroom Ecologies* (pp. 61–76). Clevedon: Multilingual Matters.

This chapter describes an ethnographic study of a classroom in Britain in which multilingual classroom aides facilitate the use of multiple languages as resources for learning. Focusing on three classroom assistants who use Panjabi and Urdu with children, transcripts of classroom talk illustrate how both language and non-verbal cues afford home school connections for multilingual primary school children.

Mehan, H. (1985) *The Structure of Classroom Discourse. Handbook of Discourse Analysis, Vol. 3: Discourse and Dialogue* (pp. 119–131). London: Academic Press.

This chapter introduced the notion of 'Initiation-Response-Evaluation' as a routine essential to competent classroom participation. Through transcripts of an elementary school discussion, Mehan illustrates this pattern's control over how talk unfolds. Most radically, his analysis provides empirical evidence that becoming successful as a learner in a classroom involves not only the mastery of content, but also competence in socially normative verbal behavior.

Michaels, S. (1981) Sharing time: Children's narrative styles and differential access to literacy. *Language in Society* 10, 423–442.
This article has become a classic in the field and illustrates how the genre of storytelling during primary school 'sharing time' varies considerably across white children and black children in one classroom. Michaels identifies two distinct styles of narration and argues that, while the teacher initially misunderstands the black narrative style as digressive and incoherent, these children's narratives are not 'incorrect' but, instead, highly communicative and functional narrative genres in a different social milieu. This research illustrates clearly how metalinguistic awareness of narrative style could provide greater access to literacy to all children.

References

Au, K.H. (1980) On participation structures in reading lessons. *Anthropology and Education Quarterly* 11, 91–115.

Bloome, D., Puro, P. and Theodorou, E. (1989) Procedural display and classroom lessons. *Curriculum Inquiry* 19 (3), 265–291.

Bruner, J. (1983) *Child's Talk: Learning to Use Language*. New York: W.W. Norton.

Canagarajah, S. (2007) After disinvention: Possibilities for communication, community, and competence. In S. Makoni and A. Pennycook (eds) *Disinventing and Reconstituting Languages* (pp. 233–239). Clevedon: Multilingual Matters.

Erickson, F. (1996) Going for the zone: The social and cognitive ecology of teacher–student interaction in classroom conversations. In D. Hicks (ed.) *Discourse, Learning, and Schooling* (pp. 29–62). Cambridge: Cambridge University Press.

Fassler, R. (2003) *Room for Talk: Teaching and Learning in a Multilingual Kindergarten*. New York: Teachers College Press.

Goffman, E. (1959) *The Presentation of Self in Everyday Life*. New York: Anchor Books.

Goffman, E. (1974) *Frame Analysis: An Essay on the Organization of Experience*. Boston: Northeastern University Press.

Griffin, S. (2004) I need people: Storytelling in a second-grade classroom. In C. Ballenger (ed.) *Regarding Children's Words: Teacher Research on Language and Literacy* (pp. 22–30). New York: Teachers College Press.

Gumperz, J. (1964) Linguistic and social interaction in two communities. *American Anthropologist* 66, 6 (part 2), 137–154.

Gumperz, J. (1965) Language. *Biennial Review of Anthropology* 4, 84–120.

Gumperz, J. (with A. Dil). (1971) *Language in Social Groups*. Palo Alto: Stanford University Press.

Gumperz, J. (1982) *Discourse Strategies*. Cambridge: Cambridge University Press.

Gutiérrez, K., Rymes, B. and Larson, J. (1995) James Brown vs. Brown v. The Board of Education: Script, counterscript, and underlife in the classroom. *Harvard Educational Review* 65 (3), 445–471.

Hornberger, N.H. (1989) Trámites and transportes: The acquisition of second language communicative competence for one speech event in Puno, Peru. *Applied Linguistics* 10 (2), 214–230.

Hymes, D.H. (1972) On communicative competence. In J.B. Pride and J. Holmes (eds) *Sociolinguistics: Selected Readings* (pp. 269–293). Harmondsworth: Penguin Books.

Knobel, M. (1999) *Everyday Literacies: Students, Discourse and Social Practice*. New York: Peter Lang Publishing.

Kumaravadivelu, B. (2001) Toward a postmethod pedagogy. *TESOL Quarterly* 35, 537–560.

Ladson-Billings, G. (2004) *Crossing Over to Canaan: The Journey of New Teachers in Diverse Classrooms.* San Francisco: Jossey-Bass.

Lucas, T., Henze, R. and Donato, R. (1990) Promoting the success of Lation language minority students: An exploratory study of six high schools. *Harvard Educational Review* 60 (3), 315–340.

Makoni, S. and Pennycook, A. (eds) (2007) *Disinventing and Reconstituting Languages.* Clevedon: Multilingual Matters.

Martin-Jones, M. and Saxena, M. (2003) Bilingual resources and 'funds of knowledge' for teaching and learning in multi-ethnic classrooms in Britain. In A. Creese and P. Martin (eds) *Multilingual Classroom Ecologies* (pp. 61–76). Clevedon: Multilingual Matters.

Mehan, H. (1985) The structure of classroom discourse. *Handbook of Discourse Analysis, Vol. 3: Discourse and Dialogue* (pp. 119–131). London: Academic Press.

Michaels, S. (1981) Sharing time: Children's narrative styles and differential access to literacy. *Language in Society* 10, 423–442.

Monzó, L. and Rueda, R. (2009) Passing for English fluent: Latino immigrant children masking language proficiency. *Anthropology & Education Quarterly* 40 (1), 20–40.

Nieto, S. (1999) *The Light in Their Eyes: Creating Multicultural Learning Communities.* New York: Teachers College Press.

Philips, S.U. (1984) *The Invisible Culture.* New York: Longman.

Rymes, B. (1997) Rights to advise: Advice as an emergent phenomenon in student-teacher talk. *Linguistics in Education* 8 (4), 409–337.

Rymes, B. and Pash, D. (2001) Questioning identity: The case of one second language learner. *Anthropology and Education Quarterly* 32 (3), 276–300.

Sheets, R.H. (1995) From remedial to gifted: Effects of culturally centered pedagogy. *Theory into Practice* 34 (3), 186–193.

Sridhar, K.K. (1996) Societal multilingualism. In N. Hornberger and S. McKay (eds) *Sociolinguistics and Language Teaching* (pp. 47–70). Cambridge and New York: Cambridge University Press.

Wolfe, T. (2004) *I am Charlotte Simmons.* New York: Picador.

Part 7

Language and Education

Chapter 20

Language and Education: A Limpopo Lens

NANCY H. HORNBERGER

Not long ago, I sat in class at the University of Limpopo with Sepedi-speaking students enrolled in their final year of a three-year undergraduate bachelor of arts programme, taught through the medium of both English and Sepedi (SeSotho sa Leboa), one of nine African languages officially recognized in South Africa's Constitution of 1993. This innovative program in Contemporary English and Multilingual Studies (CEMS) was founded in 2003 by Professors Esther Ramani and Michael Joseph in direct and creative response to the openings afforded by South Africa's multilingual language policy (Granville *et al.*, 1998; Joseph & Ramani, 2004, 2006; Ramani *et al.*, 2007). CEMS is to date South Africa's only bilingual university-level program in English and an African language. My fieldnote from that day reads:

> Toward the end of today's Contemporary English Language Studies (CELS) 302 Language and Thought class, professor Michael and I step outside to warm ourselves in the sun while the three students present (Delinah, Elizabeth, Sibongile) confer among themselves, freely codeswitching in Sepedi and English, as to which of six child language development paradigms introduced in class last week best corresponds to a short text excerpt by K.C. Fuson 1979 describing a caretaker's interaction with a child. Earlier in today's class we engaged intensively in activities designed by Michael to deepen our understanding of Vygotskyan private speech and prepare the students to engage in their third-year research project exploring Sepedi-speaking children's private speech: today's activities included writing silently and then discussing our own uses of private speech, gauging various data sources such as diaries, interviews, and questionnaires along a likert scale of soft to hard data, and now consideration of this case in terms of Vygotskyan, Piagetian, Hallidayan, Behaviorist, and Chomskyan paradigms, among others. For their research project,

they will over the course of the semester each observe, videotape, and analyze the private speech of a 4-to-6-year-old child in their own community.

As Michael and I step outside, we are immediately approached by a broadly smiling young woman who turns out to be one of the first CEMS graduates, Mapelo Tlowane, who has caught sight of her professor and comes over to greet him warmly. She reports she's doing well, her language consulting business started jointly with fellow CEMS-graduate Thabo is picking up, and she's recently had two job interviews in the translation and communication field. She glowingly states she feels well-prepared and ready for whatever challenges this work might bring, exuding a contagious enthusiasm and confidence that visibly light up the faces of the current CEMS students when Michael invites her in to the class to greet them. After her brief visit of a few minutes, the three students return to their academic task with renewed energy and focus, and perhaps a strengthened conviction of the value of language-oriented research and study. (Limpopo, August 5, 2008)

A postscript from Michael Joseph, a year later:

Mapelo (Tlowane) has joined us as a junior staff at the beginning of 2009. She is the first teacher (within this first ever bilingual degree) who is a student from the Degree, and she has all the brimming enthusiasm, confidence and bilingual competence that such a course needs.

CELS 302 has started with Finkie and Abram (whom you interviewed) and 4 others presenting introspective data on egocentric speech (just today). As with all the previous 4 batches no one doubts the universality of such speech or its cognitive function. They just find it strange that no one pointed out that such speech should have any special value and could therefore be researched. Their journey into the readings of Vygotsky, Piaget, Chomsky, Skinner is matched by their even more unpredictable search for their research subject – a child between 4 and 6 years. It's quite exciting for me as well, as their experiential knowledge drawn from within their communities and language are just not there in any of the great books, and I am always thrown into the deep end of being a learner once more discovering their culture and the great ideas in the literature, one unlocking the other. (Personal communication, 28 July, 2009)[1]

This classroom scene and postscript recapitulate the core themes of the present volume. They bespeak a multilingual context in which policy, ideology and relations of power are key. There is a fluid and flexible (Blackledge & Creese, 2009; Creese & Blackledge, 2008) use of languages as media of instruction in the classroom, in keeping with local multilingual practices. The curricular content draws not only on academic scholarship but also on students' lived experiences and identities. Finally, and perhaps most importantly, the teacher's classroom practices create a space of awareness and acceptance of, and access to, a wide communicative – and academic – repertoire for the students.

The Limpopo class and program are – in my way of thinking and the founders' and participants' as well – instances of biliteracy 'in which communication occurs in two (or more) languages in and around writing' (Hornberger, 1990: 213; see also Hornberger, 1989, 2003; Hornberger & Skilton-Sylvester, 2000). The multilingual language contact (Kamwangamalu[2]), fluid language use (Pennycook), locally grounded multimodal pedagogies (Janks) and socially sensitive pedagogy (McKay) that infuse and inform the CEMS program instantiate the multiple and complex interrelationships between language and literacy that the continua of biliteracy framework represents – as to context, media, content and development of biliteracy, respectively.

The work of the program offers confirmation of the principle that the more their learning contexts allow learners to draw on all points of the continua, the greater are the chances for their full biliterate development (Hornberger, 1989: 289). An analysis of the teaching and learning there, through the lens of the continua of biliteracy, suggests that, for these bilingual learners, the *development* of biliteracy indeed occurs 'along intersecting first language–second language, receptive–productive, and oral–written language skills continua; through the *medium* of two (or more) languages and literacies whose linguistic structures vary from similar to dissimilar, whose scripts range from convergent to divergent, and to which the developing biliterate individual's exposure varies from simultaneous to successive; in *contexts* that encompass micro to macro levels and are characterized by varying mixes along the monolingual–bilingual and oral–literate continua; and … with *content* that ranges from majority to minority perspectives and experiences, literary to vernacular styles and genres, and decontextualized to contextualized language texts' (Hornberger & Skilton-Sylvester, 2000: 96). Crucially, the program's founders have taken care to contest the traditional power weighting of the continua toward decontextualized monolingual English-only instruction by paying attention to what have traditionally been the less powerful ends of the continua, emphasizing contextualized multilingual instruction grounded in the students' local experience and thereby empowering them in their academic studies.

The present volume recounts many such instances of critically aware and empowering language education and language use in education, alongside theoretical and empirical explorations of the rationale and outcomes of such instances. Herein, we use the terms *language, language variety* and *communicative repertoire* in their widest sense, including different language varieties in bilingual or multilingual settings, different dialects, creole varieties, styles, registers or other differentiated language use in monolingual settings, as well as multimodal and literate varieties; in Rymes' apt phrase 'the collection of ways individuals use language and literacy and other means of communication (gestures, dress, posture, accessories) to function effectively in the multiple communities in which they participate'. Likewise, biliteracy, as I use the term here and elsewhere, encompasses not only *bi*lingual, but also *tri*lingual and *multi*lingual repertoires, and indeed any differentiated communicative repertoire. Instances of biliteracy may include biliterate classrooms and programs, and also events, actors, interactions, practices, activities, sites, situations, societies and worlds.

All teachers are language planners in the classroom (Lo Bianco) and the decisions and actions educators take around language have profound implications for learners' futures (Kasper & Omori, McGroarty, Norton). This is as true for Indigenous, immigrant and other language minority learners (Kamwangamalu, Rymes), as it is for second and foreign language learners (Higgins, Kubota, McKay, Sidnell), for heritage language learners (Duff, Reyes), for dialect, creole, or pidgin speakers within so-called monolingual settings (Siegel), for Deaf learners (Duff), as well as for differentiated language use along the lines of gender and sexuality (Higgins), ethnicity (Reyes), class and race (Alim), style and styling variation (Jaspers), literate and multimodal practices (Janks, Street & Leung, Vaish & Towndrow), and other fluid and complex communicative practices (Pennycook). Here, drawing from all the foregoing chapters, and using the Limpopo instance and the four themes above as frame, I will highlight some of the ways in which language and language use shape and mediate young peoples' participation in educational opportunities and, ultimately, their contributions, real and potential, to their communities, societies and the world.

Power, Ideology and Equity: Contexts of Biliteracy

Limpopo's CEMS program emerged in the ideological and implementational space opened up at the end of apartheid and the establishment of South Africa's new Constitution in 1993, recognizing 11 official languages (Hornberger, 2002). In the years immediately following the birth of the New South Africa, Ramani and Joseph joined colleagues in advocating that universities develop multilingual language policies, require the teaching/learning of African languages as subject and introduce their use as medium of instruction (Granville *et al.*, 1998; Joseph & Ramani, 1997). They went on to match their words with deeds, in founding CEMS. Drawing on their experience with CEMS, they argue that acquisition language planning (LP) can drive corpus LP – importantly, that there is a site of resource building for African languages within pedagogic use of the languages as media of instruction (Ramani *et al.*, 2007).

To grasp the significance and achievements of this university-level bilingual program in English and Sepedi (Sotho), it is necessary to understand the multilingual context in which it arose – a context of vast inequity and asymmetry of power. South African scholars Bloch and Alexander describe the postapartheid language situation of South Africa in terms of the context continua of biliteracy, thus:

> English is the dominant and hegemonic language because of its global status as the language of business, the internet, etc., but also because it has served in the course of many decades of struggle as the, to some extent mythical, language of national unity and language of liberation. There is no doubt at all that it has been, and continues to be, the language of wider communication for all middle-class South Africans, including the current political class.

> Situated along the micro–macro context continuum, between English and the indigenous African languages, is Afrikaans ... [which] came to be associated with the struggle of the Afrikaner people against British imperialism ... and with the racist policies and practices of the Afrikaner nationalist movement. ... As a result black South Africans ... regard it as 'the language of the oppressor.' ... However, the real power of Afrikaans as the lingua franca of the commercial farming zone and of the formerly white-dominated rural towns makes it a language that it is still necessary to learn for purely economic reasons.

> Close to the micro end of the continuum lie clustered together the nine indigenous African languages which were accorded official status in 1993–4. The hierarchy even among these languages is of major significance in the South African context since the allocation of the meagre resources that are available ... depends on where in terms of power/ status along the continua they are officially deemed to be located. Roughly, we could say that Zulu, Xhosa, Tswana, Pedi, Sotho, Tsonga, Swati, Ndebele, and Venda in that order constitute a segment of the steep gradient of South Africa's official languages. They all have very few high-status functions and the attitude of most of their speakers could be described by the term 'static maintenance syndrome' (pace Baker, 1996), that is, they are prepared to keep their languages alive for community and family uses but see no point in trying to develop and modernise them for higher economic, political and cultural functions. (Bloch & Alexander, 2003: 91–92)

In this context, CEMS is a project which, similar to Bloch and Alexander's own efforts through the Project for the Study of Alternative Education in

South Africa, is 'demonstrating as well as reclaiming the power of the powerless' (Bloch & Alexander, 2003: 93), an active participant in the multiplying effort to 'shift the balance of power in favour of those for whom ostensibly the democratic transition was initiated' (Bloch & Alexander, 2003: 117).

The pervasiveness of unequal power relations, and the role of policy and ideology in furthering or transforming them, is a consistent theme across the chapters in this volume, beginning from McGroarty's introductory overview and call for educators to take up the challenge of deconstructing and reconstructing the language ideologies surrounding our efforts. She emphasizes how language ideologies frame and influence our language use in not always directly observable ways, and (following Blommaert, 1999) how the more a linguistic ideology is reproduced across time and institutions, the more likely it is to become normalized, that is taken unquestioningly as normal and common sense, even while it may, and invariably does, reinforce unequal power relationships across individuals and groups. From Freirean-inspired critical literacy and critical language awareness approaches (Janks, Pennycook, Alim), to concerns around inequitable access to and investment in languages/literacies/modalities (Higgins, McKay, Norton, Street & Leung, Vaish & Towndrow), to matters of unequal power relationships and linguistic capital in situations of language contact and shift (Kamwangamalu, Reyes, Siegel), or hierarchical perceptions and evaluations of different styles, registers and varieties of language (Jaspers, Kubota, LoBianco, Rymes) or asymmetrical positionings of speakers (Duff, Kasper & Omori), there is a reiterated call for educators to challenge – through word and deed, discourse and practice – these power inequities and the language ideologies that uphold them, wherever we encounter them.

'Flow, Fixity and Fluidity': Media of Biliteracy

CEMS is a dual-language program, offering instruction through the medium of English in the Contemporary English Language Studies (CELS) modules taught by Professors Ramani and Joseph and through the medium of Sepedi in Multilingual Studies (MUST) modules taught now by CEMS alumna Mapelo Tlowane and formerly by PhD student Mamphago Modiba, herself recently appointed to a permanent position in the University's Department of Education. Students from other majors may opt to take the CELS sequence as a minor, but students enrolled in the CEMS degree follow a course of study consisting of six modules each taught through the medium of English and of Sepedi. Further, as shown in the classroom scene above, students make frequent, flexible and fluid use of Sepedi in their English-medium classes (and vice versa).

Not shown in this excerpt, but evident in the classes and activities of the program, the communicative repertoire on tap includes not only South

African English, Afrikaans and local varieties of Sepedi (e.g. Kilobedu variety discussed in CELS 202 class, 6 August, 2008), but also other South African languages spoken locally – especially Venda and Tsonga, foreign languages accessible through the internet and other technologies, as well as Indian English and occasional words and phrases of Hindi, Tamil, Kannada and colloquial Hindustani spoken by Ramani and Joseph, who transplanted themselves from their native India to South Africa in the early 1990s to teach at the Universities of Witwatersrand and Natal, respectively. In terms of the media continua of biliteracy, then, these learners and their teachers are making simultaneous use of structures and scripts ranged along continua from similar to dissimilar and convergent to divergent, as well as of a rich repertoire of styles, registers, modes and modalities, all comprising what Hymes, in the ethnography of communication, referred to as the instrumentalities of communication. The flow and fluidity of languages in the classroom reflect but also expand local multilingual communicative practices.

In myriad and marvelous ways, the authors herein call into question the notion of separate and enumerable languages (Pennycook), adopting instead a view of language – and literacy – as social practice, both in and out of school (Norton, Kasper & Omori, Street & Leung). Although the undeniable existence and imposition of standards (McKay), norms for literacy (McGroarty), prescriptive rhetorical patterns (Kubota), correctness in language teaching (Sidnell), and even the privileging of certain academic literacies (Street & Leung) are premised on notions of language as bounded entity, of 'fixity' as Pennycook puts it, actual language use continually leaks around the edges, indeed flows (Pennycook) and overflows, as shown in the rich array of communicative hybridity and creativity portrayed within these chapters. The recognition of classroom codeswitching as a communicative resource (Kamwangamalu, McGroarty, Reyes), of pidgins/creoles (Siegel) and Ebonics (Alim, Reyes) as rule-governed varieties along a continuum of similarity/dissimilarity with standard varieties, of styles, styling and stylizations (Jaspers, Reyes) as social actions and performances, of correctness as secondary to communicative goals whether in one's first (Rymes) or second (Sidnell) language are all ways of acknowledging the fluidity and flexibility of language in use.

Vaish and Towndrow discuss transformation, transduction and resemiotization in multimodal design, referring to the shifting meaning of semiotic signs within modes, across modes and across contexts, respectively. Janks provides numerous illustrative examples of multilingual and multimodal critical literacy pedagogies in South Africa and elsewhere that draw students' attention to and capitalize on the fluidity of language and of 'meaning-making in an age of the visual sign', from activities on multilingualism in her own *Critical Language Awareness Series* that seek to 'destabilize both a unitary and a normative view of English', to multilingual, multimodal story-telling projects with South African township children who, in performing their stories, draw on semiotic 'resources of spoken language, space, gesture, narrative, and vocalization ... ways of saying, doing, and being ... learnt in [the] community' (Stein, 2008: 58). Arguing similarly for the inevitability of multimodality in popular culture, and for the transformative possibilities in choices of language, genre and style in language performance, Pennycook suggests that the mixing, borrowing, shifting and sampling of music, languages, lyrics and ideas characteristic of hip hop culture present new possibilities not only for imagined languages, but also for imagined traditions and imagined identities as well. We turn next to those possibilities.

Community, Culture and Identity: Content of Biliteracy

Michael's postscript – about the Limpopo students' journey into the readings of Vygotsky, Piaget, Chomsky, Skinner, matched by their 'even more unpredictable search' for their research subject – a 4-to-6-year-old child in their own community – recapitulates the intertwining of academic and experiential knowledge that has stood out to me as a striking characteristic of the CEMS program ever since my first visit in 2004 as plenary speaker for a conference convened by Ramani and Joseph. It was the South African Applied Linguistics Association's annual conference, whose theme 'Ten years of multilingualism in South Africa: fact or fantasy?', called for a critical evaluation of South Africa's groundbreaking multilingual policy on the occasion of its 10th anniversary. At that time, two first year, first cohort CEMS students interviewed me about both my scholarship and my personal history, in an informative exchange of views on the value of multilingualism and Indigenous languages in South Africa and other parts of the world. The students were well prepared and the interview was conducted professionally; at the same time, they displayed a winning personal enthusiasm and engagement with the topic, clearly grounded in their own multilingual experience and identities, in turn enhanced by their academic reflections and explorations on these issues.

If learning is meaning-making, it is about the tasks and materials (McGroarty), texts (LoBianco) and genres (Kubota), science and math, law and medicine (Duff), etc. that are the stuff of meaning-making. Yet, it is not only about the construction of academic knowledge but also about the construction of identities (Kamwangamalu, Jaspers, Alim, Siegel, Norton, Higgins, Reyes, Kasper & Omori). It is discourses and performances, as well as texts (Lo Bianco), it is interpersonal as well as ideational and textual meaning options (Street & Leung, citing Halliday), it is as much about the architecture of intersubjectivity as about the sequential organization of talk (Sidnell). In content continua of biliteracy terms, it is about minority/oppressed/marginalized identities, communities and cultures as well as majority/dominant ones, about vernacular as well as literary genres and styles, and about contextualized meanings and texts as much as decontextualized ones.

If we are to welcome the cultures, communities and identities of our students in our classrooms, we must begin by understanding that they are socially constructed and ever-changing categories, rather than intrinsic and immutable ones. Identities are multiple, nonunitary, changing over time, and importantly, sites of struggle (Norton); cultural identities are something people do rather than something they have (Kasper & Omori); gendered identities are discursively negotiated, assimilated or resisted (Higgins); ethnic identities are not simply brought to school, but emergent through classroom practice and sometimes strategically displayed, perhaps by enacting a stereotype or by crossing into language varieties associated with an ethnic other (Reyes); language users employ styles and styling nonstop 'to (re)build their social surroundings as well as the self- and other-identities that are part of it' (Jaspers); communities may be imagined (Norton, McKay) or constructed through practice (Higgins, Kubota, Pennycook, Street & Leung). These recognitions of culture, identity and community as emergent and mutable have/do not necessarily come easily in the language teaching disciplines: research and practice in contrastive rhetoric has been criticized for its prescriptive pedagogy and essentialist characterization of the Other (Kubota), while a tendency toward Othering discourses regarding approaches to knowledge and learning styles has also been evident in the implementation of communicative English language teaching in Outer and Expanding Circle countries (McKay), and even culturally responsive pedagogy and multicultural education are susceptible to a conception of culture as a static corpus of values and beliefs, and a conflation of country, culture, language, nationality and identity, accompanied by a tendency to position students from immigrant backgrounds as representatives of their culture and community of origin (Kasper & Omori).

On the other hand, when teachers stretch their classroom practices to allow for students' emergent identity negotiation, language styling and mixing, and mediation between popular culture and official curriculum, that is, when they 'play along, this stretching could be mutually enjoyable and lead to high amounts of on-task activity' (Jaspers). Jaspers describes such a case in a working class secondary school in Antwerp, Belgium, where both Moroccan ethnic minority students and working class Dutch-speaking students regularly engaged in a practice which they called 'doing ridiculous', slowing down the lesson in not entirely unruly ways, sometimes stylizing Standard Dutch or Antwerp dialect to evoke varying identities for varying effects. Some teachers managed to play along, enabling the lesson to move forward in productive ways, though perhaps not as originally planned. Rymes points out that accommodation to the communicative repertoires of one's interlocutors is inevitable, but that it can and should be bidirectional; it is not just that students are expected to accommodate to school routines and repertoires, but that teachers must accommodate as well: 'when students' native repertoires are recognized, they begin to see themselves as academically capable – that is as capable of expanding their repertoire' (Rymes). Alim outlines a powerful set of sociolinguistic and ethnographic pedagogical activities – including 'Real Talk', 'Language in My Life' and 'Hiphopography' – that build on 'linguistically profiled and marginalized' students' communicative repertoires, knowledge of popular culture and engagement with the Black community to develop their critical awareness of sociolinguistic variation and the systematicity of Black language, reflexive awareness and validation of their own speech behavior, exploration of localized lexical usage in peer culture and critical interrogation of linguistic profiling and discrimination. He argues that critical language awareness 'has the potential to help students and teachers abandon old, restrictive and repressive ways of thinking about language and to resocialize them into new, expansive and emancipatory ways of thinking about language and power' – and from there, to move from studying the relationships between language, society and power – to changing them. What he describes is an approach where 'sociolinguistics, research, and pedagogy come together, a crucial relationship that is about teaching towards a better world' (Pennycook).

Awareness, Acceptance and Access: Development of Biliteracy

'The overall aim of the [CEMS] degree is to produce bilingual specialists, who will play a key role in promoting the official multilingual policy of South Africa'. So reads the program description, setting forth an aim that is reiterated in program posters and on a regular basis in classes as well. One eye-catching poster, for example, poses and answers the question:

> What can I do with a BA CEMS degree? You can be – a Researcher, a Media presenter, a Bilingual Teacher, a Language Consultant, a Journalist, a Translator, an Interpreter, a Cultural Activist or Join any Profession in Health, Education, Welfare, Tourism, that needs a BILINGUAL EXPERT! (see Figure 20.1)

This aim is an expression of the social justice agenda that Ramani and Joseph explicitly and eloquently articulate in their published writings, in curricula and materials of the program, and in their daily discourse with CEMS students. Situated in South Africa's poorest province, in a historically Black university where English has been the only language of instruction and African languages and ways of knowing traditionally excluded,

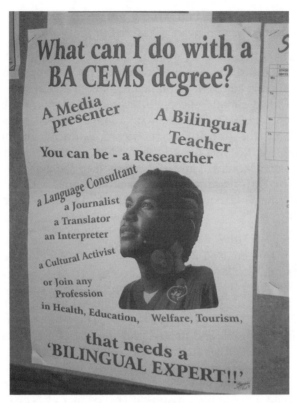

Figure 20.1 University of Limpopo: What can I do with a BA CEMS degree?

the very existence of an academic program that incorporates African language and knowledge as resources constitutes a transformation of relationships between language, society and power. The program's preparation of Black African undergraduates for careers in journalism, translation, language consulting, education and other professions is a further step toward social transformation. It was this sense of transformative power and possibility that rippled through the CELS 302 class when Mapelo visited that day and shared her exuberant confidence with the students.

Social justice is pursued only with considerable struggle, and CEMS is no exception. From its beginnings and before, Ramani and Joseph have fought for recognition and status for the program and their students within the University. As each hurdle is passed, new ones arise; and program staff and students are vigilant to confront them when they do. So, for example, in CELS 302 class one day, Michael expressed his dismay and anger over a protest announcement posted around campus that day by the Pan-African student movement, PASMA, including among its list of complaints the 'useless' CELS/MUST program, which moreover they claimed was not even a properly registered program.

> Michael asks the students: did you see the poster? How did you feel? Shocked? Disturbed? Angry? Confused? He goes on to assure them CELS/MUST (aka CEMS) is in fact registered and approved and that students have already successfully graduated from the program in 2005, 2006, and 2007. This opens up a longer discussion with the students about the principles and accomplishments of the program, including a critical reading of the PASMA poster. Delinah asks, 'why do they say it's useless?' and Michael replies: 'We don't know. PASMA stands for Pan-Africanism and Black consciousness; how can you advocate that and not support African languages?' (fieldnotes, July 31, 2008)

The socially sensitive pedagogy (McKay), or humanizing pedagogy (Kamwangamalu), enacted daily in CEMS classes encompasses not only critical metalinguistic awareness and acceptance of the communicative repertoires students bring to the class, but also a concern for students' access to the academic literacies and professional identities they need in order to become empowered social actors – locally in Limpopo, nationally in South African society and indeed globally as citizens of the world. In terms of the continua of biliterate development, it is a pedagogy that seeks to build students' oral and written, receptive and productive language and literacy skills in their L1, L2 and indeed all the language varieties, modes and modalities at their disposal. This pedagogy is evident in practices we have already identified in the Limpopo CEMS program, illuminated by insights from this volume's chapters – fluid and flexible use of languages, curricular content drawing on students' lived experiences and identities as well as academic scholarship, and 'regular chances to hear and interact with successful program graduates who [return to] share accounts of the successes and difficulties they [continue] to face, helping younger participants realize that the demands for persistence and hard work [are] relevant' (McGroarty, citing Abi-Nader's 1990 study of a model program for Spanish-speaking high schoolers in the United States).

CEMS' pedagogy of awareness, acceptance and access recapitulates themes that have cropped up again and again in the pages of this volume. In addition to calls for critical language awareness (Alim, Janks, Pennycook) and intercultural awareness (Kubota), Siegel highlights the awareness approach as the most promising of the ways pidgins and creoles have been incorporated into schooling; and Duff points out that 'meta-awareness of how ... key speech events work, at the level of grammar and genre/register, ... [assists] students who cannot easily induce such content or conventions on their own', or who have access to fewer symbolic and material resources within their new educational and linguistic communities, even while they may be highly competent in other cultural, linguistic, and discursive systems.

Practices of acceptance of students' communicative repertoires, highlighted and recommended in this volume's chapters and instantiated in CEMS, include peer teaching, where teachers do not share a first language with the students, as a strategy for encouraging learners to switch to the language they know as springboard for acquiring a target language (Kamwangamalu); offering learners a range of identity positions with the greatest opportunity for social engagement and interaction through speaking, listening, reading and writing (Norton); engaging with structural constraints on male and female participation and with the gendered discourses that mediate students' learning (Higgins); helping students learn how they can use their repertoires to 'shuttle between communities and not to think of only joining *a* community' (Rymes, citing Canagarajah, 2007: 238).

Indeed, there is a profound concern in this volume for equitable access to communicative repertoires and the identities and communities they represent. Specifically and recurringly, authors highlight the compelling necessity of equality of access to target language and culture (Higgins), to institutionalized and informal language learning opportunities (Higgins), to legitimate language in Bourdieu's sense (Janks), to dominant languages (Janks), to the standard language (Lo Bianco, McGroarty), to new discourses (Janks), to particular styles (Jaspers), to multiple forms of language inside and outside school settings (McGroarty), to language learning opportunities (Norton) and through and beyond language, to education in the dominant language (Siegel), to literacy (Rymes), to computers and multimodal literacies (Vaish & Towndrow), to more powerful identities and powerful social networks (Norton), to social goods (Janks), to resources (Alim), to imagined communities (McKay, Norton) and communities of practice (Higgins).

The Saturday-morning Academic Language and Literacy Development (ALLD) program at King's College London (KCL) is designed with the goal of providing access to university studies for aspiring youth of linguistic minority backgrounds in the immediate KCL neighborhood, by means of a noncredit bearing English Language Development course during their final year of secondary school (Street & Leung). Taking up Cope and Kalantzis' (1993: 67) admonition that 'literacy teaching, if it is to provide students with equitable social access, needs to link the different social purposes of language in different contexts to predictable patterns of discourse', ALLD combines a social practices view of literacy (Street, 1984, 1995), a dynamic and situated notion of communicative competence (Hymes, 1972, 1974) and a functional view of linguistic form in relation to meaning-making (Halliday, 1975), to engage students in collaborative development of the types of academic literacies required in UK higher education, such as the personal statement required for university applications. Street, who teaches in the program and also documents it ethnographically, reflects on the intent of the programme to 'challenge some of the expectations students may have met at school ... about language as narrowly defined ... The course involves issues of discourse, genre, writing as social process ... within a notion of building on what they already had and bring to the programme rather than treating them as a deficit and just fixing that'. Like CEMS in Limpopo, ALLD enacts a pedagogy of awareness, acceptance and access.

Lo Bianco (this volume) argues persuasively for an activity-centered approach to LP, with teachers as central actors. 'Public texts of policy are the solidified and already-decided form of language planning. Public debate is the ongoing, discursive consideration of future LP. In their performance role teachers enact past policy and make continuing LP in activities of language development and socialisation'. Lo Bianco's claim that teachers bring authenticity, experience and immediacy to enacted LP takes us full circle back to the Limpopo classroom scene which opened this chapter.

We have seen that CEMS was created in the ideological and implementational space opened up in the New South Africa, an initiative in the context of a nationwide effort to turn language ideologies and relations of power toward social justice and equity. We have observed that, in pursuit of this goal, CEMS classroom practices make fluid and flexible use of languages as media of instruction, draw on both academic and identity resources for texts, materials and curriculum, and foster critical awareness and acceptance of students' communicative repertoires, identities and imagined communities. CEMS founders Ramani and Joseph, and their colleagues, Modiba and now Tlowane, are indeed central actors in LP from the bottom up (Hornberger, 1996), in the complete sense of Lo Bianco's activity-centered approach: interrogating and working in the spaces opened up by public texts of South African policy, engaged in ongoing debate and discursive consideration of LP with their students and with colleagues at Limpopo, nationally, and internationally, and enacting LP activities of language development and socialization on a daily basis with their students.

The classroom scene which opened this chapter took place in 'The Book Club', a long room lined with books and occupied at one end by a seminar-style table covered with batik cloth. This is a space carved out and created by Ramani and Joseph in the years before CEMS, to foster in first year University students a love and practice of reading (Joseph & Ramani, 2002), and which they and CEMS students have jealously guarded since then. It is quite literally a space for cultivating multilingualism and language learning, critical language awareness and multimodalities, critical and academic literacies, empowered social identities and transformative ideologies. Yet one more way in which these sociolinguistically informed educators, like those depicted and exhorted in this volume, open up ideological and implementational space for multilingualism and social justice, from the bottom-up.

Notes

1. I am grateful to Esther Ramani and Michael Joseph for inviting me to sojourn with them, and for their unstinting generosity and collegial collaborations throughout the visit and since. My thanks also to the Fulbright Senior Specialist program for sponsoring my visit.
2. Throughout this chapter, I will refer to other chapters within the volume by author's last name only.

References

Abi-Nader, J. (1990) 'A house for my mother': Motivating Hispanic high school students. *Anthropology and Education Quarterly*, 21, 41–58.

Blackledge, A. and Creese, A. (2009) *Multilingualism*. London: Continuum.

Bloch, C. and Alexander, N. (2003) A luta continua!: The relevance of the continua of biliteracy to South African multilingual schools. In N.H. Hornberger (ed.) *Continua of Biliteracy: An Ecological Framework for Educational Policy, Research, and Practice in Multilingual Settings* (pp. 91–121). Clevedon: Multilingual Matters.

Blommaert, J. (1999) The debate is open. In J. Blommaert (ed.) *Language Ideological Debates* (pp. 1–38). Berlin: Mouton.

Canagarajah, S. (2007) After disinvention: Possibilities for communication, community, and competence. In S. Makoni and A. Pennycook (eds) *Disinventing and Reconstituting Languages* (pp. 233–239). Clevedon: Multilingual Matters.

Cope, W. and Kalantzis, M. (1993) *The Powers of Literacy: A Genre Approach to Teaching Writing*. London: Falmer Press.

Creese, A. and Blackledge, A. (2008) Flexible bilingualism in heritage language schools. Unpublished manuscript.

Granville, S., Janks, H., Mphahlele, M., Reed, Y., Watson, P., Joseph, M. and Ramani, E. (1998) English with or without g(u)ilt: A position paper on language in education policy for South Africa. *Language and Education* 12 (4), 254–272.

Halliday, M.A.K. (1975) *Learning How to Mean: Explorations in the Development of Language*. London: Edward Arnold.

Hornberger, N.H. (1989) Continua of biliteracy. *Review of Educational Research* 59 (3), 271–296.

Hornberger, N.H. (1990) Creating successful learning contexts for bilingual literacy. *Teachers College Record* 92 (2), 212–229.

Hornberger, N.H. (ed.) (1996) *Indigenous Literacies in the Americas: Language Planning from the Bottom Up*. Berlin: Mouton.

Hornberger, N.H. (2002) Multilingual language policies and the continua of biliteracy: An ecological approach. *Language Policy* 1 (1), 27–51.

Hornberger, N.H. (ed.) (2003) *Continua of Biliteracy: An Ecological Framework for Educational Policy, Research and Practice in Multilingual Settings*. Clevedon: Multilingual Matters.

Hornberger, N.H. and Skilton-Sylvester, E. (2000) Revisiting the continua of biliteracy: International and critical perspectives. *Language and Education: An International Journal* 14 (2), 96–122.

Hymes, D.H. (1972) On communicative competence. In J.B. Pride and J. Holmes (eds) *Sociolinguistics: Selected Readings* (pp. 269–293). Harmondsworth: Penguin Books.

Hymes, D.H. (1974) *Foundations in Sociolinguistics: An Ethnographic Approach.* Philadelphia: University of Pennsylvania Press.

Joseph, M. and Ramani, E. (1997) Making monolinguals multilingual: A psycholinguistic research project in the teaching and learning of Zulu. *AD Issues (University of Western Cape: Academic Development Centre)* 5 (1), 15–17.

Joseph, M. and Ramani, E. (2002) Discovering and developing book lovers through a Foundation-Year module. In L.A. Kasanga and T.J. Lebakeng (eds) *Paradigm Shift in South African Higher Education* (pp. 53–63). South Africa.

Joseph, M. and Ramani, E. (2004) Academic excellence through language equity: A new bilingual degree (in English and Sesotho sa Leboa). In H. Griesel (ed.) *Curriculum Responsiveness: Case Studies in Higher Education* (pp. 237–261). Pretoria: South African Universities Vice-Chancellors Association.

Joseph, M. and Ramani, E. (2006) English in the World does not mean English Everywhere: The Case for Multilingualism in the ELT/ESL profession. In R. Rubdy and M. Saraceni (eds) *English in the World: Global Rules, Global Roles* (pp. 186–199). London: Continuum.

Ramani, E., Kekana, T., Modiba, M. and Joseph, M. (2007) Terminology development versus concept development: Insights from a dual-medium BA degree. *Southern African Linguistics and Applied Language Studies* 25 (2), 207–233.

Stein, P. (2008) *Multimodal Pedagogies in Diverse Classrooms: Representation, Rights, and Resources.* London and New York: Routledge.

Street, B. (1984) *Literacy in Theory and Practice.* New York: Cambridge University Press.

Street, B.V. (1995) *Social Literacies: Critical Approaches to Literacy in Development, Ethnography, and Education.* London: Longman.

Index